INSECTS

BY DAVID SHARP

in two volumes

VOL

2

INSECTS, PART II

DOVER PUBLICATIONS, INC.
NEW YORK

International Standard Book Number: 0-486-22646-8
Library of Congress Catalog Card Number: 70-116820

Manufactured in the United States of America
Dover Publications, Inc.
180 Varick Street
New York, N.Y. 10014

CONTENTS

CHAPTER VII

CHAPTER VIII

"Men are poor things; I don't know why the world thinks so much of them."—*Mrs. Bee*, by L. & M. Wintle.

SCHEME OF THE CLASSIFICATION ADOPTED
IN THIS BOOK

Order.	Sub-order, Division, or Series.	Family.	Sub-Family or Tribe.	Group.
HYMENOPTERA (*continued from Vol. V*).	**Petiolata.** (*continued from Vol. V*).			

HYMENOPTERA (*continued*)   Aculeata (p. 4)

Tubulifera (p. 1)   CHRYSIDIDAE (p. 1).

ANTHOPHILA (p. 10)
APIDAE (p. 10)
- Archiapides (p. 21).
- Obtusilingues (p. 22).
- Andrenides (p. 23).
- Denudatae (p. 29).
- Scopulipedes (p. 32).
- Dasygastres (p. 35).
- Sociales (p. 53).

DIPLOPTERA (p. 71)
- EUMENIDAE (p. 72).
- VESPIDAE (p. 78).
- MASARIDAE (p. 88).

FOSSORES (p. 90)
SCOLIIDAE (p. 94)
- Mutillides (p. 94).
- Thynnides (p. 96).
- Scoliides (p. 97).
- Sapygides (p. 99).
- Rhopalosomides (p. 100).

POMPILIDAE (p. 101).

SPHEGIDAE (p. 107)
- Sphegides (p. 107).
- Ampulicides (p. 114).
- Larrides (p. 116).
- Trypoxylonides (p. 118).
- Astatides (p. 119).
- Bembecides (p. 119).
- Nyssonides (p. 123).
- Philanthides (p. 124).
- Mimesides (p. 127).
- Crabronides (p. 128).

HETEROGYNA (p. 131)
FORMICIDAE (p. 131)
- Camponotides (p. 144).
- Dolichoderides (p. 157).
- Myrmicides (p. 158)
  - Myrmicini (p. 159).
  - Attini (p. 165).
  - Pseudomyrmini (p. 168).
  - Cryptocerini (p. 169).
- Ponerides (p. 170).
- Dorylides (p. 174)
  - Ecitonini (p. 175).
  - Dorylini (p. 177).
- Amblyoponides (p. 180).

Order.	Sub-Order, Division, or Series.	Family.	Sub-Family or Tribe.
COLEOPTERA (p. 184)	**Lamelli-cornia** (p. 190)	PASSALIDAE (p. 192).	
		LUCANIDAE p. 193).	
		SCARABAEIDAE (p. 194)	Coprides (p. 195).
			Melolonthides (p. 198).
			Rutelides (p. 198).
			Dynastides (p. 199).
			Cetoniides (p. 199).
	Adephaga or **Caraboidea** (p. 200)	CICINDELIDAE (p. 201).	
		CARABIDAE (p. 204)	Carabides (p. 206).
			Harpalides (p. 206).
			Pseudomorphides (p. 206).
			Mormolycides (p. 206).
		AMPHIZOIDAE (p. 207).	
		PELOBIIDAE (p. 207).	
		HALIPLIDAE (p. 209).	
		DYTISCIDAE (p. 210).	
	Polymorpha (p. 213)	PAUSSIDAE (p. 213).	
		GYRINIDAE (p. 215).	
		HYDROPHILIDAE (p. 216).	
		PLATYPSYLLIDAE (p. 219).	
		LEPTINIDAE (p. 220).	
		SILPHIDAE (p. 221).	
		SCYDMAENIDAE (p. 223).	
		GNOSTIDAE (p. 223).	
		PSELAPHIDAE (p. 223).	
		STAPHYLINIDAE (p. 224).	
		SPHAERIIDAE (p. 227).	
		TRICHOPTERYGIDAE (p. 227).	
		HYDROSCAPHIDAE (p. 228).	
		CORYLOPHIDAE (p. 228).	
		SCAPHIDIIDAE (p. 229).	
		SYNTELIIDAE (p. 229).	
		HISTERIDAE (p. 230).	
		PHALACRIDAE (p. 231).	
		NITIDULIDAE (p. 231).	
		TROGOSITIDAE (p. 232).	
		COLYDIIDAE (p. 233).	
		RHYSODIDAE (p. 234).	
		CUCUJIDAE (p. 234).	
		CRYPTOPHAGIDAE (p. 235).	
		HELOTIDAE (p. 235).	
		THORICTIDAE (p. 236).	
		EROTYLIDAE (p. 236).	
		MYCETOPHAGIDAE (p. 237).	
		COCCINELLIDAE (p. 237).	
		ENDOMYCHIDAE (p. 239).	
		MYCETAEIDAE (p. 239).	
		LATRIDIIDAE (p. 240).	
		ADIMERIDAE (p. 240).	
		DERMESTIDAE (p. 241).	
		BYRRHIDAE (p. 242).	
		CYATHOCERIDAE (p. 243).	
		GEORYSSIDAE (p. 243).	
		HETEROCERIDAE (p. 243).	
		PARNIDAE (p. 243).	
		DERODONTIDAE (p. 244).	

(Continued on the next page.)

Order.	Sub Order, Division, or Series.	Family.	Sub-Family or Tribe.
COLEOPTERA (*continued*)	**Polymorpha** (*continued*)	CIOIDAE (p. 245).	
		SPHINDIDAE (p. 245).	
		BOSTRICHIDAE (p. 246).	
		PTINIDAE (p. 246)	Ptinides (p. 246). Anobiides (p. 246).
		MALACODER-MIDAE (p. 248)	Lycides (p. 248). Drilides (p. 248). Lampyrides (p. 248). Telephorides (p. 248).
		MELYRIDAE (p. 252).	
		CLERIDAE (p. 253)	
		LYMEXYLONIDAE (p. 254).	
		DASCILLIDAE (p. 255).	
		RHIPICERIDAE (p. 256).	
		ELATERIDAE (p. 256).	Throscides (p. 260). Eucnemides (p. 260). Elaterides (p. 260). Cebrionides (p. 260). Perothopides (p. 260). Cerophytides (p. 260).
		BUPRESTIDAE (p. 261).	
	Heteromera (p. 262)	TENEBRIONIDAE (p. 263).	
		CISTELIDAE (p. 264).	
		LAGRIIDAE (p. 264).	
		OTHNIIDAE (p. 265).	
		AEGIALITIDAE (p. 265).	
		MONOMMIDAE (p. 265).	
		NILIONIDAE (p. 265).	
		MELANDRYIDAE (p. 265).	
		PYTHIDAE (p. 265).	
		PYROCHROIDAE (p. 266).	
		ANTHICIDAE (p. 266).	
		OEDEMERIDAE (p. 266).	
		MORDELLIDAE (p. 267).	
		CANTHARIDAE (p. 269).	
		TRICTENOTOMIDAE (p. 275).	
	Phytophaga (p. 276)	BRUCHIDAE (p. 276)	
		CHRYSOMEL-IDAE (p. 278)	Eupoda (p. 280). Camptosomes (p. 281). Cyclica (p. 282). Cryptostomes (p. 282).
		CERAMBYCIDAE (p. 285)	Prionides (p. 287). Cerambycides (p. 287). Lamiides (p. 287).
	Rhyncho-phora (p. 288)	ANTHRIBIDAE (p. 290).	
		CURCULIONIDAE (p. 290).	
		SCOLYTIDAE (p. 294).	
		BRENTHIDAE (p. 295).	
		AGLYCYDERIDAE (p. 297).	
		PROTERHINIDAE (p. 298).	
	Strepsiptera (p. 298)	STYLOPIDAE (p. 298).	

Order.	Sub-Order, Division, or Series.	Family.	Sub-Family or Tribe.
LEPIDOPTERA (p. 304)	**Rhopalocera** (p. 341)	NYMPHALIDAE (p. 343)	Danaides (p. 344). Ithomiides (p. 346). Satyrides (p. 347). Morphides (p. 348). Brassolides (p. 349). Acraeides (p. 350). Heliconiides (p. 351. Nymphalides (p. 352).
		ERYCINIDAE (p. 354)	Erycinides (p. 355). Libytheides (p. 355).
		LYCAENIDAE (p. 356).	
		PIERIDAE (p. 357).	
		PAPILIONIDAE (p. 359).	
		HESPERIIDAE (p. 363.	
	Heterocera (p. 366)	CASTNIIDAE (p. 371).	
		NEOCASTNIIDAE (p. 372).	
		SATURNIIDAE (p. 372).	
		BRAHMAEIDAE (p. 374).	
		CERATOCAMPIDAE (p. 375).	
		BOMBYCIDAE (p. 375).	
		EUPTEROTIDAE (p. 376).	
		PEROPHORIDAE (p. 377).	
		SPHINGIDAE (p. 380).	
		COCYTIIDAE (p. 382).	
		NOTODONTIDAE (p. 383).	
		CYMATOPHORIDAE (p. 386).	
		SESIIDAE (p. 386).	
		TINAEGERIIDAE (p. 387).	
		SYNTOMIDAE (p. 388).	
		ZYGAENIDAE (p. 390).	
		HIMANTOPTERIDAE (p. 392).	
		HETEROGYNIDAE (p. 392).	
		PSYCHIDAE (p. 392).	
		COSSIDAE (p. 395).	
		ARBELIDAE (p. 396).	
		CHRYSOPOLOMIDAE (p. 396).	
		HEPIALIDAE (p. 396).	
		CALLIDULIDAE (p. 400).	
		DREPANIDAE (p. 400).	
		LIMACODIDAE (p. 401).	
		MEGALOPYGIDAE (p. 404).	
		THYRIDIDAE (p. 404).	
		LASIOCAMPIDAE (p. 405).	
		ENDROMIDAE (p. 406).	
		PTEROTHYSANIDAE (p. 406).	
		LYMANTRIIDAE (p. 406).	
		HYPSIDAE (p. 408).	
		ARCTIIDAE (p. 408).	
		AGARISTIDAE (p. 410).	
		GEOMETRIDAE (p. 411).	
		NOCTUIDAE (p. 414).	
		EPICOPEIIDAE (p. 418).	
		URANIIDAE (p. 419).	
		EPIPLEMIDAE (p. 420).	
		PYRALIDAE (p. 420).	
		PTEROPHORIDAE (p. 426).	
		ALUCITIDAE (p. 426).	
		TORTRICIDAE (p. 427).	
		TINEIDAE (p. 428).	
		ERIOCEPHALIDAE (p. 433).	
		MICROPTERYGIDAE (p. 435).	

Order.	Sub-Order, Division, or Series.	Family.	Sub-Family or Tribe.
DIPTERA (p. 438)	**Orthorrha-pha Nemo-cera** (p. 455)	CECIDOMYIIDAE (p. 458). MYCETOPHILIDAE (p. 462). BLEPHAROCERIDAE (p. 464). CULICIDAE (p. 466). CHIRONOMIDAE (p. 468). ORPHNEPHILIDAE (p. 470). PSYCHODIDAE (p. 470). DIXIDAE (p. 471). TIPULIDAE (p. 471) BIBIONIDAE (p. 475). SIMULIIDAE (p. 477). RHYPHIDAE (p. 478).	Ptychopterinae (p. 472). Limnobiinae (p. 473). Tipulinae (p. 475).
	Orthorrha-pha Bra-chycera (pp. 455, 478)	STRATIOMYIDAE (p. 478). LEPTIDAE (p. 479). TABANIDAE (p. 481). ACANTHOMERIDAE (p. 483). THEREVIDAE (p. 484). SCENOPINIDAE (p. 484). NEMESTRINIDAE (p. 484). BOMBYLIIDAE (p. 485). ACROCERIDAE (p. 489). LONCHOPTERIDAE (p. 490). MYDAIDAE (p. 491). ASILIDAE (p. 491). APIOCERIDAE (p. 492). EMPIDAE (p. 492). DOLICHOPIDAE (p. 493).	
	Cyclorrha-pha As-chiza (pp. 455, 494)	PHORIDAE (p. 494). PLATYPEZIDAE (p. 496). PIPUNCULIDAE (p. 496). CONOPIDAE (p. 497). SYRPHIDAE (p. 498).	
	Cyclorrha-pha Schi-zophora (pp. 456, 503)	MUSCIDAE ACALYPTRATAE (p. 503). ANTHOMYIIDAE (p. 506). TACHINIDAE (p. 507). DEXIIDAE (p. 510). SARCOPHAGIDAE (p. 510). MUSCIDAE (p. 511). OESTRIDAE (p. 514).	
	Pupipara (pp. 456, 517)	HIPPOBOSCIDAE (p. 518). BRAULIDAE (p. 520). STREBLIDAE (p. 521). NYCTERIBIIDAE (p. 521).	
APHANIPTERA (pp. 456, 522)		PULICIDAE (p. 522).	
THYSANO-PTERA (p. 526)		**Terebrantia** (p. 531). **Tubulifera** (p. 531).	

Order.	Sub-Order.	Series.	Family.
HEMIPTERA (p. 532)	**Heteroptera** (pp. 543, 544)	GYMNOCER-ATA (p. 544)	PENTATOMIDAE (p. 545). COREIDAE (p. 546). BERYTIDAE (p. 548). LYGAEIDAE (p. 548). PYRRHOCORIDAE (p. 549). TINGIDAE (p. 549). ARADIDAE (p. 550). HEBRIDAE (p. 551). HYDROMETRIDAE (p. 551). HENICOCEPHALIDAE (p. 554). PHYMATIDAE (p. 554). REDUVIIDAE (p. 555). AËPOPHILIDAE (p. 559). CERATOCOMBIDAE (p. 559). CIMICIDAE (p. 559). ANTHOCORIDAE (p. 560). POLYCTENIDAE (p. 560). CAPSIDAE (p. 561). SALDIDAE (p. 562).
		CRYPTOCER-ATA (p. 562)	GALGULIDAE (p. 562). NEPIDAE (p. 563). NAUCORIDAE (p. 565). BELOSTOMIDAE (p. 565). NOTONECTIDAE (p. 567). CORIXIDAE (p. 567).
	Homoptera (pp. 543, 568)	TRIMERA (p. 544)	CICADIDAE (p. 568). FULGORIDAE (p. 574). MEMBRACIDAE (p. 576). CERCOPIDAE (p. 577). JASSIDAE (p. 578).
		DIMERA (p. 544)	PSYLLIDAE (p. 578). APHIDAE (p. 581). ALEURODIDAE (p. 591).
		MONOMERA (p. 544).	COCCIDAE (p. 592).
	Anoplura (p. 599.)		PEDICULIDAE (p. 599).

CHAPTER I

SERIES 2. TUBULIFERA OR CHRYSIDIDAE——SERIES 3. ACULEATA——
GENERAL——CLASSIFICATION——DIVISION I. ANTHOPHILA OR BEES

THE First Series——Parasitica——of the Sub-Order Hymenoptera
Petiolata was discussed in the previous volume. We now pass
to the Second Series.

Series 2. Hymenoptera Tubulifera.

*Trochanters undivided; the hind-body consisting of from three
to five visible segments; the female with an ovipositor,
usually retracted, transversely segmented, enveloping a fine,
pointed style. The larvae usually live in the cells of other
Hymenoptera.*

The Tubulifera form but a small group in comparison with
Parasitica and Aculeata, the other two Series of the Sub-Order.
Though of parasitic habits, they do not appear to be closely allied
to any of the families of Hymenoptera Parasitica, though M. du
Buysson suggests that they have some affinity with Proctotrypidae ;
their morphology and classification have been, however, but little
discussed, and have not been the subject of any profound investigation. At present it is only necessary to recognise one family,
viz. Chrysididae or Ruby-wasps.[1] These Insects are usually of
glowing, metallic colours, with a very hard, coarsely-sculptured
integument. Their antennae are abruptly elbowed, the joints
not being numerous, usually about thirteen, and frequently so

---

[1] Systematic monograph, Mocsáry, Budapest, 1889. Account of the European
Chrysididae, R. du Buysson in André, *Spec. gen. Hym.* vol. vi. 1896.

connected that it is not easy to count them. The abdomen is, in the great majority, of very peculiar construction, and allows the Insect to curl it completely under the anterior parts, so as to roll up into a little ball; the dorsal plates are very strongly arched, and seen from beneath form a free edge, while the ventral plates are of less hard consistence, and are connected with the dorsal plates at some distance from the free edge, so that the abdomen appears concave beneath. In the anomalous genus

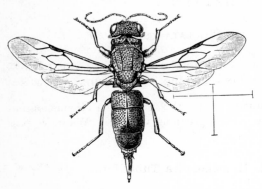

Cleptes the abdomen is, however, similar in form to that of the Aculeate Hymenoptera, and has four or five visible segments, instead of the three or four that are all that can be seen in the normal Chrysididae. The larvae of the Ruby-flies have the same number of segments

F:G. 1.—*Chrysis ignita*, ♀.   England.

as other Hymenoptera Petiolata. The difference in this respect of the perfect Chrysididae from other Petiolata is due to a greater number of the terminal segments being indrawn so as to form the tube, or telescope-like structure from which the series obtains its name. This tube is shown partially extruded in Fig. 1; when fully thrust out it is seen to be segmented, and three or four segments may be distinguished. The ovipositor proper is concealed within this tube; it appears to be of the nature of an imperfect sting; there being a very sharply pointed style, and a pair of enveloping sheaths; the style really consists of a trough-like plate and two fine rods or spiculae. There are no poison glands, except in *Cleptes*, which form appears to come very near to the Aculeate series. Some of the Chrysididae on occasions use the ovipositor as a sting, though it is only capable of inflicting a very minute and almost innocuous wound.

Although none of the Ruby-flies attain a large size, they are usually very conspicuous on account of their gaudy or brilliant colours. They are amongst the most restless and rapid of Insects;

they love the hot sunshine, and are difficult of capture. Though not anywhere numerous in species, they are found in most parts of the world. In Britain we have about twenty species. They usually frequent old wood or masonry, in which the nests of Aculeate Hymenoptera exist, or fly rapidly to and fro about the banks of earth where bees nest. Dr. Chapman has observed the habits of some of our British species.[1] He noticed *Chrysis ignita* flying about the cell of *Odynerus parietum*, a solitary wasp that provisions its nest with caterpillars; in this cell the *Chrysis* deposited an egg, and in less than an hour the wasp had sealed the cell. Two days afterwards this was opened and was found to contain a larva of *Chrysis* a quarter of an inch long, as well as the Lepidopterous larvae stored up by the wasp, but there was no trace of egg or young of the wasp. Six days after the egg was laid the *Chrysis* had eaten all the food and was full-grown, having moulted three or four times. Afterwards it formed a cocoon in which to complete its metamorphosis. It is, however, more usual for the species of *Chrysis* to live on the larva of the wasp and not on the food; indeed, it has recently been positively stated that *Chrysis* never eats the food in the wasp's cell, but there is no ground whatever for rejecting the evidence of so careful an observer as Dr. Chapman. According to M. du Buysson the larva of *Chrysis* will not eat the lepidopterous larvae, but will die in their midst if the *Odynerus* larva does not develop; but this observation probably relates only to such species as habitually live on *Odynerus* itself. The mother-wasp of *Chrysis bidentata* searches for a cell of *Odynerus spinipes* that has not been properly closed, and that contains a full-grown larva of that wasp enclosed in its cocoon. Having succeeded in its search the *Chrysis* deposits several eggs—from six to ten; for some reason that is not apparent all but one of these eggs fail to produce young; in two or three days this one hatches, the others shrivelling up. The young *Chrysis* larva seizes with its mouth a fold of the skin of the helpless larva of the *Odynerus*, and sucks it without inflicting any visible wound. In about eleven days the *Chrysis* has changed its skin four times, has consumed all the larva and is full-fed; it spins its own cocoon inside that of its victim, and remains therein till the following spring, when it changes to a pupa, and in less than three weeks there-

[1] *Ent. Mag.* vi. 1869, p. 153.

after emerges a perfect *Chrysis* of the most brilliant colour, and if it be a female indefatigable in activity. It is remarkable that the larva of *Chrysis* is so much like that of *Odynerus* that the two can only be distinguished externally by the colour, the *Odynerus* being yellow and the *Chrysis* white; but this is only one of the many cases in which host and parasite are extremely similar to the eye. *Chrysis shanghaiensis* has been reared from the cocoons of a Lepidopterous Insect—*Monema flavescens*, family Limacodidae—and it has been presumed that it eats the larva therein contained. All other Chrysids, so far as known, live at the expense of Hymenoptera (usually, as we have seen, actually consuming their bodies), and it is not impossible that *C. shanghaiensis* really lives on a Hymenopterous parasite in the cocoon of the Lepidopteron.

Parnopes carnea frequents the nests of *Bembex rostrata*, a solitary wasp that has the unusual habit of bringing from time to time a supply of food to its young larva; for this purpose it has to open the nest in which its young is enclosed, and the *Parnopes* takes advantage of this habit by entering the cell and depositing there an egg which produces a larva that devours that of the *Bembex*. The species of the anomalous genus *Cleptes* live, it is believed, at the expense of Tenthredinidae, and in all probability oviposit in their cocoons which are placed in the earth.

Series 3. Hymenoptera Aculeata.

The females (whether workers or true females) provided with a sting: trochanters usually undivided (monotrochous). Usually the antennae of the males with thirteen, of the females with twelve, joints (exceptions in ants numerous).

These characters only define this series in a very unsatisfactory manner, as no means of distinguishing the "sting" from the homologous structures found in Tubulifera, and in the Proctotrypid division of Hymenoptera Parasitica, have been pointed out. As the structure of the trochanters is subject to numerous exceptions, the classification at present existing is an arbitrary one. It would probably be more satisfactory to separate the Proctotrypidae (or a considerable part thereof) from the Parasitica, and unite them with the Tubulifera and Aculeata in a great series, characterised by the fact that the ovipositor is withdrawn into the body in a direct manner so as to be entirely internal, whereas in the Parasitica it is not withdrawn in this manner, but remains truly an external organ, though in numerous cases concealed by a process of torsion of the terminal segments. If this were done it might be found possible to divide the great group thus formed into two divisions characterised by the fact that the ovipositor in one retains its function, the egg

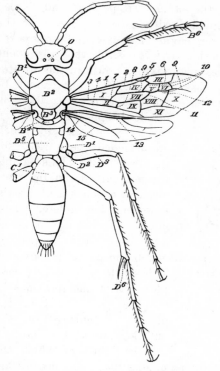

Fig. 2.—Diagram of upper surface of *Priocnemis affinis* ♀, Pompilidae. *o*, ocelli; B^1, pronotum; B^2, mesonotum; B^3, scutellum of mesonotum; B^4, post-scutellum or middle part of metanotum; B^5, propodeum or median segment (see vol. v. p. 491); B^6, combing hairs, pecten, of front foot: C^1, first segment of abdomen, here not forming a pedicel or stalk: D^1, coxa; D^2, trochanter; D^3, femur; D^6, calcaria or spurs of hind leg: 1 to 15, nervures of wings, viz. 1, costal; 2, post-costal; 3, median; 4, posterior; 5, stigma; 6, marginal; 7, upper basal; 8, lower basal; 9, 9, cubital; 10, the three sub-marginal; 11, first recurrent; 12, second recurrent; 13, anterior of hind wing; 14, median; 15, posterior: I to XI, the cells, viz. I, upper basal; II, lower basal; III, marginal; IV, V, VI, first, second and third sub-marginal; VII, first discoidal; VIII, third discoidal; IX, second discoidal; X, first apical; XI, second apical.

passing through it (Proctotrypidae and Tubulifera), while in the other the organ in question serves as a weapon of offence and defence, and does not act as a true ovipositor, the egg escaping at its base. It would, however, be premature to adopt so revolutionary a course until the comparative anatomy of the organs concerned shall have received a much greater share of attention.[1]

We have dealt with the external anatomy of Hymenoptera in

[1] For new views on this subject see note on p. 602.

Vol. V. ; so that here it is only necessary to give a diagram to explain the terms used in the descriptions of the families and sub-families of Aculeata, and to discuss briefly their characteristic structures.

The Sting of the bee has been described in detail by Kraepelin, Sollmann, Carlet [1] and others. It is an extremely perfect mechanical arrangement. The sting itself — independent of the sheaths and adjuncts—consists of three elongate pieces, one of them a gouge-like director, the other two pointed and barbed needles ; the director is provided with a bead for each of the needles to run on, these latter having a corresponding groove ; the entrance to the groove is narrower than its subsequent diameter, so that the needles play up and down on the director with facility, but cannot be dragged away from it ; each needle is provided with an arm at the base to which are attached the muscles for its movement. This simple manner of describing the mechanical arrangement is, however, incomplete, inasmuch as it includes no account of the means by which the poison is conveyed. This is done by a very complex set of modifications of all the parts ; firstly, the director is enlarged at the anterior part to form a chamber, through which the needles play ; the needles are each provided with a projecting piece, which, as the needle moves, plays in the chamber of the director, and forces downwards any liquid that may be therein ; the poison-glands open into the chamber, and the projections on the needles, acting after the manner of a piston, carry the poison before them. The needles are so arranged on

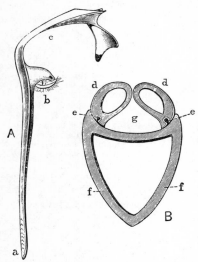

FIG. 3.—Sting of bee. **A**, One of the needles separated ; *a*, the barbed point ; *b*, piston ; *c*, arm. **B**, Transverse section of the sting : *dd*, the two needles ; *e*, bead for guiding the needles ; *f*, director ; *g*, channel of poison. (After Carlet.)

[1] *Ann. Sci. Nat.* (7) ix. 1890, p. 1.

the director that they enclose between themselves and it a space that forms the channel along which the poison flows, as it is carried forwards by the movement of the pistons attached to the needles. If the needles be thrust into an object quite as far as, or beyond, the point of the director much poison may be introduced into a wound, as the barbs are provided with small orifices placed one above the other, while if this be not the case much of the liquid will flow on the outside of the object.

According to Carlet the poison of the bee is formed by the mixture of the secretions of two glands, one of which is acid and the other alkaline; it is very deadly in its effects on other Insects. We shall see, however, that the Fossorial Hymenoptera, which catch and sting living prey for their young, frequently do not kill but only stupefy it, and Carlet states that in this group the alkaline gland is absent or atrophied, so that the poison consists only of the acid; it is thus, he thinks, deprived of its lethal power. Moreover, in the Fossoria the needles are destitute of barbs, so that the sting does not remain in the wound. Bordas, however, states [1] that in all the numerous Hymenoptera he has examined, both acid and alkaline glands exist, but exhibit considerable differences of form in the various groups. He gives no explanation of the variety of effects of the poison of different Aculeata.

The larvae (for figure of larva of *Bombus*, see Vol. V. p. 488) are, without known exception, legless grubs, of soft consistence, living entirely under cover, being protected either in cells, or, in the case of social Hymenoptera, in the abodes of the parents. The larvae of Ants and fossorial Hymenoptera have the anterior parts of the body long and narrow and abruptly flexed, so that their heads hang down in a helpless manner. All the larvae of Aculeates, so far as known, are remarkable from the fact that the posterior part of the alimentary canal does not connect with the stomach till the larval instar is more or less advanced; hence the food amongst which they live cannot be sullied by faecal matter. The pupa is invariably soft, and assumes gradually the colour of the perfect Insect. Almost nothing is known as to the intimate details of the metamorphosis, and very little as to the changes of external form. According to Packard a period intervenes between the stadium of the full-grown larva and that of the pupa, in which a series of changes he speaks of as semi-pupal

[1] *C. R. Ac. Paris*, cxviii. 1894, p. 873.

are passed through ; these, however, have not been followed out in the case of any individual, and it is not possible to form any final idea about them, but it seems probable that they are largely changes of external shape, in conformity with the great changes going on in the internal organs. Owing to the fragmentary nature of observations, much obscurity and difference of opinion have existed as to the metamorphosis of Aculeate Hymenoptera. Sir S. Saunders gives the following statement as to the larva of a wasp of the genus *Psiliglossa*,[1] just before it assumes the pupal form : " The respective segments, which are very distinctly indi-cated, may be defined as follows :—The five anterior, including the head, are compactly welded together, and incapable of separate action in the pseudo-pupa state ; the third, fourth, and fifth bearing a spiracle on either side. The thoracical region termi-nating here, the two anterior segments are assignable to the development of the imago head, as pointed out by Ratzeburg." This inference is not, however, correct. We have seen that in the perfect Insect of Petiolate Hymenoptera the first abdominal segment is fixed to the thorax, and Saunders' statement is in-teresting as showing that this assignment of parts already exists in the larva, but it in no way proves that the head of the imago is formed from the thorax of the larva. It has been stated that the larvae of the Aculeata have a different number of seg-ments according to the sex, but this also is incorrect. The difference that exists in the perfect Insects in this respect is due to the withdrawal of the terminal three segments to the interior in the female, and of two only in the male. The larva consists of fourteen segments, and we find this number distributed in the female perfect Insect as follows : one constitutes the head, four segments the thorax and propodeum, followed by six external seg-ments of the restricted abdomen, and three for the internal structures of the abdomen. This agrees with Forel's statement that in the ants the sting is placed in a chamber formed by three segments.

The development of the sting of the common bee has been studied by Dewitz.[2] It takes place in the last larval stage. Although nothing of the organ is visible externally in the adult larva, yet if such a larva be placed in spirit, there can be seen within the skin certain small appendages on the ventral surface of the penultimate and antepenultimate abdominal segments

---

[1] *Trans. ent. Soc. London*, 1873, p. 408.   [2] *Zeitschr. wiss. Zool.* xxv. 1875, p. 184.

(Fig. 4, A) placed two on the one, four on the other ; these are the rudiments of the sting. In the course of development the terminal three segments are taken into the body, and the external pair of the appendages of the twelfth body segment (the ninth abdominal) become the sheaths of the sting, and the middle pair become the director ; the pair of appendages on the eleventh segment give rise to the needles or spiculae. The sting-rudiments at an earlier stage (Fig. 4, C) are masses of hypodermis connected with tracheae ; there is then but one pair on the twelfth segment, and this pair coalesce to form a single mass ; the rudiments of the pair that form the director are differentiated secondarily from the primary pair of these masses of hypodermis. A good deal of discussion has taken place as to whether the component parts of the sting — gonapophyses — are to be considered as modifications of abdominal extremities (*i.e.* abdominal legs such as exist in Myriapods). Heymons is of opinion that this is not the case, but that the leg-rudiments and gonapophysal rudiments are quite distinct.[1] The origin

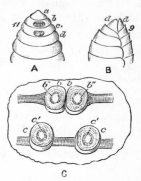

Fig. 4.—Development of sting of the bee : **A** and **C**, ventral ; **B**, side view. **A**, End of abdomen of adult larva : *a, b, c, d*, the last four segments, *c* being the eleventh body segment, 11 ; *b* bearing two pairs, and *c* one pair, of rudiments. **B**, Tip of abdomen of adult bee : 9, the ninth, *d*, the tenth body segment. **C**, Rudiments in the early condition as seen within the body : *c*, first pair ; *b*, the second pair not yet divided into two pairs ; *b″, c′*, commencement of external growths from the internal projections. (After Dewitz.)

of the sting of Hymenoptera (and of the ovipositor of parasitic Hymenoptera) is very similar to that of the ovipositor of *Locusta* (Vol. V. p. 315 of this work), but there is much difference in the history of the development of the rudiments.

Dewitz has also traced the development of the thoracic appendages in Hymenoptera.[2] Although no legs are visible in the adult larva, they really arise very early in the larval life from masses of hypodermis, and grow in the interior of the body, so that when the larva is adult the legs exist in a segmented though rudimentary condition in the interior of the body. Dewitz's study of the wing-development is less complete.

[1] *Morph. Jahrb.* xxiv. 1896, p. 192.   [2] *Zeitschr. wiss. Zool.* xxx. 1878, p. 78.

Four primary divisions of Aculeates are generally recognised, viz. Anthophila (Bees), Diploptera (Wasps), Fossores (Solitary Wasps), Heterogyna (Ants). Though apparently they are natural, it is impossible to define them by characters that are without some exceptions, especially in the case of the males. Ashmead has recently proposed [1] to divide the Fossores ; thus making five divisions as follows :—

Body with more or less of the hairs on it plumose .   1. Anthophila.
Hairs of body not plumose.
    Pronotum not reaching back to tegulae   .   2. Entomophila
                                      [= Fossores part]
    Pronotum reaching back to tegulae.
        Petiole (articulating segment of abdomen) simple without scales or nodes.
            Front wings in repose with a fold making them narrow
                                        3. Diploptera.
            Front wings not folded   .   .   .   4. Fossores [part].
        Petiole with a scale or node (an irregular elevation on the upper side)
                                        5. Heterogyna.

We shall here follow the usual method of treating all the fossorial wasps as forming a single group, uniting Ashmead's Entomophila and Fossores, as we think their separation is only valid for the purposes of a table ; the Pompilidae placed by the American savant in Fossores being as much allied to Entomophila as they are to the other Fossores with which Ashmead associates them.

Division I. Anthophila or Apidae—Bees.

Some of the hairs of the body plumose ; parts of the mouth elongated, sometimes to a great extent, so as to form a protrusible apparatus, usually tubular with a very flexible tip. Basal joint of hind foot elongate. No wingless adult forms ; in some cases societies are formed, and then barren females called workers exist in great numbers, and carry on the industrial operations of the community. Food always derived from the vegetable kingdom, or from other Bees.

There are about 150 genera and 1500 species of bees at present known. Some call the division Mellifera instead of Anthophila. The term Apidae is used by some authorities to denote all the bees, while others limit this term to one of the families

[1] *Proc. ent. Soc. Washington,* iii. 1896, p. 334.

or sub-divisions. The bees are, as a rule, distinguished from other Hymenoptera by the hairs, by the great development of the mouth parts to form a proboscis (usually, but not correctly, called tongue), and by the modification of the hind-legs; but these distinctive characters are in some of the species exhibited in so minor a degree of perfection that it is not easy to recognise these primitive forms as Anthophila. A few general remarks on the three points mentioned will enable the student to better appreciate the importance of certain points we shall subsequently deal with.

The bees are, as a rule, much more covered with hair than any other of the Hymenoptera. Saunders[1] states that he has examined the structure of the hairs in all the genera of British Aculeata, and that in none but the Anthophila do branched and plumose hairs occur. The function of this kind of hairs is unknown; Saunders suggests[1] that they may be instrumental in the gathering of pollen, but they occur in the parasitic bees as well as in the males, neither of which gather pollen. The variety of the positions they occupy on the body seems to offer but little support to the suggestion. Not all the hairs of the bee's body are plumose, some are simple, as shown in Fig. 5, A, and this is specially the case with the hairs that are placed at the edges of the dilated plates for carrying

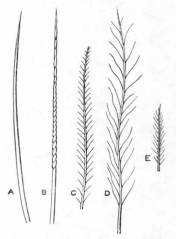

Fig. 5.—Hairs of Bees : **A**, simple hair from abdomen of *Osmia* ; **B**, spiral hair from abdomen of *Megachile* ; **C**, plumose hair from thorax of *Megachile* ; **D**, from thorax of *Andrena dorsata* ; **E**, from thorax of *Prosopis*.

pollen. In some forms there is an extensive system of simple hairs all over the body, and the " feathers " are distributed between these; and we do not see any reason for assuming that the feathered are superior to the simple hairs for gathering and carrying pollen. Some bees, *e.g. Prosopis, Ceratina*, have very little hair on the body, but nevertheless some plumose hairs are always present even though they be very short.

[1] *Trans. ent. Soc.* 1878, p. 169.

The hind-legs of bees are very largely used in the industrial occupations of these indefatigable creatures; one of their chief functions in the female being to act as receptacles for carrying pollen to the nest: they exhibit, however, considerable diversity. The parts most modified are the tibia and the first joint of the hind-foot. Pollen is carried by other parts of the body in many bees, and even the hind-leg itself is used in different ways for the

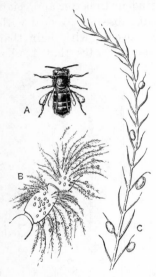

FIG. 6.—**A**, Worker of the honey-bee (*Apis mellifica*), with pollen plates laden ; **B**, basal portions of a middle-leg (trochanter with part of coxa and of femur) with plumose hairs and grains of pollen ; **C**, one hair bearing pollen-grains.

purpose : sometimes the outer face of the tibia is highly polished and its margins surrounded by hair, in which case pollen plates are said to exist (Fig. 6, A); sometimes the first joint of the tarsus is analogous to the tibia both in structure and function ; in other cases the hind-legs are thick and densely covered with hair that retains the pollen between the separate hairs. In this case the pollen is carried home in a dry state, while, in the species with pollen plates, the pollen is made into a mass of a clay-like consistence.[1] The legs also assist in arranging the pollen on the other parts of the body. The males do not carry pollen, and though their hind-legs are also highly modified, yet the modifications do not agree with those of the female, and their functions are in all probability sexual.

The parasitic bees also do not carry pollen, and exhibit another series of structures. The most interesting case in this series of modifications is that found in the genus *Apis*, where the hind-leg of male, female, and worker are all different (Fig. 25); the limb in the worker being highly modified for industrial purposes. This case has been frequently referred to, in consequence of the difficulty that exists in connection with its heredity, for the

---

[1] The mode of wetting the pollen is not clear. Wolff says it is done by an exudation from the tibia ; H. Müller by admixture of nectar from the bee's mouth. The latter view is more probably correct.

structure exists in neither of the parents. It is, in fact, a case of a very special adaptation appearing in the majority of the individuals of each generation, though nothing of the sort occurs in either parent.

The proboscis of the bee [1] is a very complex organ, and in its extremely developed forms exhibits a complication of details and a delicacy of structure that elicit the admiration of all who study it. In the lower bees, however, especially in *Prosopis*, it exists in a comparatively simple form (Fig. 9, B, C), that differs but little from what is seen in some Vespidae or Fossores. The upper lip and the mandibles do not take any part in the formation of the bee's proboscis, which is consequently entirely made up from the lower lip and the maxillae, the former of these two organs exhibiting the greatest modifications. The proboscis is situate on the lower part of the head, and in repose is not visible ; a portion, and that by no means an inconsiderable one, of its modifications being for the purpose of its withdrawal and protection when not in use. For this object the under side of the head is provided with a very deep groove, in which the whole organ is, in bees with a short proboscis, withdrawn ; in the Apidae with a long proboscis this groove also exists, and the basal part of the proboscis is buried in it during repose, while the other parts of the elongate organ are doubled on the basal part, so that they extend backwards under the body, and the front end or tip of the tongue is, when in repose, its most posterior part.

For the extrusion of the proboscis there exists a special apparatus that comes into play after the mandibles are unlocked and the labrum lifted. This extensive apparatus cannot be satisfactorily illustrated by a drawing, as the parts composing it are placed in different planes ; but it may be described by saying that the cardo, or basal hinge of the maxilla, changes from an oblique to a vertical position, and thrusts the base of the proboscis out of the groove. The maxillae form the outer sheath of the proboscis, the lower lip its medial part (see Figs. 7 and 9) ; the base of the lower lip is attached to the submentum, which rises with the cardo so that labium and maxillae are lifted together ; the co-operation of these two parts is effected by an angular piece called the lorum, in which the base of the submentum rests ; the

---

[1] In studying the proboscis the student will do well to take a *Bombus* as an example ; its anatomy being more easily deciphered than that of the honey-bee.

submentum is articulated with the mentum in such a manner that the two can either be placed in planes at a right angle to one another, or can be brought into one continuous plane, and by this change of plane the basal part of the tongue can also be thrust forwards. There is considerable variety in the lengths of these parts in different genera, and the lorum varies in shape in accordance with the length of the submentum. The lorum is a peculiar piece, and its mechanical adaptations are very remarkable; usually the base of the submentum rests in the angle formed by the junction of the two sides of the lorum, but in *Xylocopa*, where the submentum is unusually short, this part reposes

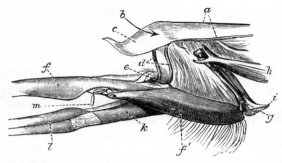

Fig. 7.—Side view of basal portions of proboscis of *Bombus*. *a*, Epipharyngeal sclerites ; *b*, arrow indicating the position of the entrance to pharynx, which is concealed by the epipharynx, *c* ; *d*, hypopharyngeal sclerites ; *e*, vacant space between the scales of the maxillae through which the nectar comes : *f*, lobe ; *f'*, stipes ; *g*, cardo of maxilla : *h*, encephalic pillar on which the cardo swings ; *i*, angle of junction of lores and submentum lorum ; *k*, mentum ; *l*, base of labial palp ; *m*, maxillary palp.

in a groove on the back of the lorum, this latter having a very broad truncated apex instead of an angular one; in the condition of repose the apex of the lorum rests in a notch on the middle of the back of the oral groove, and in some of the forms with elongate submentum, this depression is transformed into a deep hole, or even a sort of tunnel, so as to permit the complete stowing away of the base of the tongue, which would otherwise be prevented by the long submentum; another function of the lorum appears to be that, as it extends, its arms have an outward thrust, and so separate the maxillae from the labium. In addition to these parts there are also four elongate, slender sclerites that are only brought into view on dissection, and that no doubt assist in correlating the movements of the parts of the mouth and hypopharynx; one pair of these strap-like pieces extends backwards from the two sides of the base of the epipharynx; Huxley called them sclerites of the oesophagus; a better name would be epipharyngeal sclerites (Fig. 7, a): the other pair pass from the terminations of the epipharyngeal sclerites, along the front face of the hypopharynx, down to the mentum, their lower parts being concealed by the stipites of the maxillae; these are the hypopharyngeal sclerites, and we believe it will prove that they play a highly important part in deglutition.   When the labrum of a bee is raised and the proboscis depressed, the epipharynx is seen hanging like a curtain from the roof of the head; this structure plays an important part in the act of deglutition.   The entrance to the pharynx, or commencement of the alimentary canal, is placed below the base of the epipharynx.   As we are not aware of any good delineations of the basal parts of the proboscis we give a figure thereof (Fig. 7).   The maxillae in the higher bees are extremely modified so as to form a sheath, and their palpi are minute; in the lower bees the palpi have the structure usual in mandibulate Insects.

Returning to the consideration of the lower lip, we find that there is attached to the mentum a pair of elongate organs that extend forwards and form a tube or sheath, enclosed by the maxillary sheath we have previously mentioned; these are the greatly modified labial palpi, their distal parts still retaining the palpar form; and in the lower bees the labial palpi are, like the maxillary, of the form usual in mandibulate Insects.   Between the labial palps and the central organ of the lip there is attached a pair of delicate organs, the paraglossae.

There remains for consideration the most remarkable part of the proboscis, the long, delicate, hairy organ which the bee thrusts out from the tip of the shining tube formed by the labial palps and the maxillae, described above, and which looks like a prolongation of the mentum.   This organ is variously called ligula, lingua, or tongue.[1]   We prefer the first of these names.

According to Breithaupt and Cheshire the structure of the ligula is highly remarkable; it is a tube (filled with fluid from the body cavity), and with a groove underneath caused by a large part of the circumference of the tube being invaginated; the

---

[1] Leuckart proposed the term lingula; but the word gives rise to the impression that it is a mistake for either lingua or ligula.   Packard calls the part "hypopharynx."

invaginated part can be thrust out by increase of the pressure of the fluid in the tube. A portion of the wall of the invaginate part is thickened so as to form a chitinous rod.

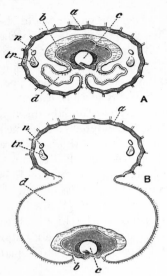

FIG. 8.—Transverse section of ligula of honey-bee, diagramatic. **A**, With the long sac invaginate. **B**, evaginate: *a*, chitinous envelope with the bases of the hairs; *b*, rod; *c*, groove of rod; *d*, lumen due in **A** to invagination of the rod, in **B** to its evagination; *n*, nerve; *tr*, trachea.

This description will suffice for present purposes, as the other parts of the mouth will be readily recognised by the aid of figure 9, A, B, C. In the exquisitely endowed South American genus *Euglossa* (Fig. 18), the proboscis is somewhat longer than the whole of the body, so that its tip in repose projects behind the body like a sting.

The correct nomenclature of the parts connected with the lower lip is not definitely settled, authorities not being agreed on several points. The whole of the proboscis is usually called the tongue; this, however, is admittedly an erroneous application of this term. The terminal delicate, elongate, flexible organ is by some called the tongue; but this again is wrong: the lingua in Insects is the hypopharynx; this part is developed in a peculiar manner in bees, but as it is not tongue-like in shape, the term lingua is not suitable for it, and should be dismissed altogether from the nomenclature of the bee's trophi; it is used at present in two different senses, both of which are erroneous. We see no objection to describing the flexible apical portion of the proboscis as the ligula. The lorum is probably a special part peculiar to the higher bees; according to Saunders it is not present as a specialised part in some of the primitive forms.[1] The application of the terms mentum, submentum and hypoglottis is open to the same doubts that exist with regard to them in so many other

---

[1] For figures and descriptions of the proboscides of British bees, refer to E. Saunders, *Jour. Linn. Soc.* xxiii. 1890, pp. 410-432, plates III.-X.: and for details of the minute structure and function to Cheshire, *Bees and Bee-keeping*, vol. i.

Insects, and we have omitted the term hypoglottis altogether, though some may think the mentum entitled to that name.

The way in which the proboscis of the bee acts has been very largely discussed, with special reference to the question as to whether it is a sucking or a licking action. It is impossible to consider either of these terms as applicable. The foundation of the action is capillary attraction, by which, and by slight movements of increase and contraction of the capacity of various parts, the fluid travels to the cavity in front of the hypopharynx: here the scales of the maxillae leave a vacant space, (Fig. 7, *e*) so that a cup or cavity is formed, the fluid in which is within reach of the tip of the dependent epipharynx (*c*), which hangs down over the front of the hypopharynx (and is so shaped that its tip covers the cup); it is between these two parts that the fluid passes to reach the pharynx. It is no doubt to slight movements of the membranous parts of the hypopharynx and of the

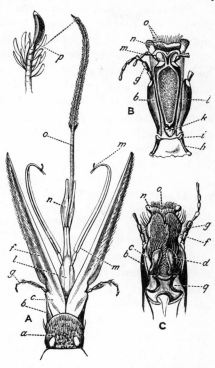

FIG. 9.—**A**, Proboscis of a "long-tongued" bee, *Anthophora pilipes ;* **B**, lower, **C**, upper view of proboscis of an "obtuse-tongued" bee, *Prosopis pubescens. a*, Labrum ; *b*, stipes ; *c*, palpiger ; *d*, scale : *f*, lobe ; *g*, palpus ; *h*, cardo, of maxilla : *i*, lorum ; *k*, submentum ; *l*, mentum ; *m*, labial palp ; *n*, paraglossa ; *o*, ligula ; *p*, tip of ligula (with "spoon" at tip and some of the hairs more magnified) ; *q*, hypopharyngeal sclerites.

epipharynx that the further progress of the nectar is due, aided by contraction and expansion of the pharynx, induced by muscles attached to it. It should be recollected that in addition to the movements of the head itself, the hypopharynx is constantly changing its dimensions slightly by the impulses of the fluid of the general body cavity; also that the head changes its position, and that the proboscis is directed downwards as well as forwards. Those who wish to pursue this subject should refer to the works of Breithaupt [1] and Cheshire.

The other external characters of the Bees call for little remark. The pronotum is never very large or much prolonged in front, and its hind angles never repose on the tegulae as they do in the wasps,[2] but extend backwards below the tegulae. The hind body is never narrowed at the base into an elongate pedicel, as it so frequently is in the Wasps and in the Fossors; and the propodeum (the posterior part of the thorax) is more perpendicular and rarely so largely developed as it is in the Fossors; this last character will as a rule permit a bee to be recognised at a glance from the fossorial Hymenoptera.

Bees, as every one knows, frequent flowers, and it is usually incorrectly said that they extract honey. They really gather nectar, swallow it, so that it goes as far as the crop of their alimentary canal, called in English the honey-sac, and is regurgitated as honey. Bertrand states that the nectar when gathered is almost entirely pure saccharose, and that when regurgitated it is found to consist of dextrose and levulose:[3] this change appears to be practically the conversion of cane- into grape-sugar. A small quantity of the products of the salivary glands is added, and this probably causes the change alluded to; so that honey and nectar are by no means synonymous. According to Cheshire the glandular matter is added while the nectar is being sucked, and is passing over the middle parts of the lower lip, so that the nectar may be honey when swallowed by the bee. In addition to gathering nectar the female bees are largely occupied in collecting pollen, which, mixed with honey, is to serve as food for the colony. Many, if not all, bees eat pollen while collecting it. The mode in which they accumulate the pollen, and the mechanism of its conveyance from hair to hair till it reaches the part of the body it must attain in order to be removed for packing in the cells, is not fully understood, but it appears to be accomplished by complex correlative actions of various parts; the head and the front legs scratch up the pollen, the legs move with great rapidity, and the pollen ultimately reaches its destination. The workers of the genus *Apis,* and of some other social

[1] Breithaupt, *Arch. Naturges.* lii. Bd. i. 1886, p. 47.
[2] See Fig. 26, p. 71.   [3] *Bull. Mus. Paris,* i. 1895, p. 38.

bees, have the basal joint of the hind foot specially adapted to deal with pollen (Fig. 25, 2). We have already mentioned the modifications of the legs used for its conveyance, and need here only add that numerous bees—the Dasygastres—carry the pollen by aid of a special and dense clothing of hairs on the underside of the abdomen.

The buzzing of bees (and other Insects) has been for long a subject of controversy: some having maintained that it is partially or wholly due to the vibration of parts connected with the spiracles, while others have found its cause in the vibrations of the wings. According to the observations of Pérez and Bellesme,[1] two distinct sounds are to be distinguished. One, a deep noise, is due to the vibration of the wings, and is produced whenever a certain rapidity is attained; the other is an acute sound, and is said to be produced by the vibrations of the walls of the thorax, to which muscles are attached; this sound is specially evident in Diptera and Hymenoptera, because the integument is of the right consistence for vibration. Both of these observers agree that the spiracles are not concerned in the matter.

The young of bees are invariably reared in cells. These (except in the case of the parasitical bees) are constructed by the mothers, or by the transformed females called workers. The solitary bees store the cells with food, and close up each cell after having laid an egg in it, so that in these cases each larva consumes a special store previously provided for it. The social bees do not close the cells in which the larvae are placed, and the workers act as foster-mothers, feeding the young larvae after the same fashion as birds feed their nestling young. The food is a mixture of honey and pollen, the mixing being effected in various ways and proportions according to the species; the honey seems to be particularly suitable to the digestive organs of the young larvae, and those bees that make closed cells, place on the outside of the mass of food a layer more thickly saturated with honey, and this layer the young grub consumes before attacking the drier parts of the provisions. The active life of the larva is quite short, but after the larva is full-grown it usually passes a more or less prolonged period in a state of quiescence before assuming the pupal form. The pupa shows the limbs and other parts of the perfect Insect in a very distinct manner, and the

[1] *C.R. Ac. Paris*, lxxxvii. 1878, pp. 378 and 535.

development of the imago takes place gradually though quickly. Some larvae spin cocoons, others do not.

A very large number of bees are parasitic in their habits, laying an egg, or sometimes more than one, in the cell of a working bee of some species other than their own; in such cases the resulting larvae eat and grow more quickly than the progeny of the host bee, and so cause it to die of starvation. It has been observed that some of these parasitic larvae, after eating all the store of food, then devour the larva they have robbed. In other cases it is possible that the first care of the parasitic larva, after hatching, is to eat the rival egg.

The taxonomy of bees is in a very unsatisfactory state. The earlier Hymenopterists were divided into two schools, one of which proposed to classify the bees according to their habits, while the other adopted an arrangement depending on the length of the parts of the mouth, the development of the palpi, and the form and positions of the organs for carrying pollen. Neither of these arrangements was at all satisfactory, and some entomologists endeavoured to combine them, the result being a classification founded partly on habits and partly on certain minor structural characters. This course has also proved unsatisfactory; this is especially the case with exotic bees, which have been placed in groups that are defined by habits, although very little observation has actually been made on this point. Efforts have recently been made to establish an improved classification, but as they relate solely to the European bees they are insufficient for general purposes.

The more important of the groups that have been recognised are—(1) the Obtusilingues, short-tongued bees, with the tip of the lingua bifid or broad; (2) Acutilingues, short-tongued bees, with acute tip to the tongue; these two groups being frequently treated of as forming the Andrenidae. Coming to the Apidae, or the bees with long and folded tongues, there have been distinguished (3) Scopulipedes, bees carrying pollen with their feet, and (4) Dasygastres, those that carry it under the abdomen; some of the parasitic and other forms have been separated as (5) Denudatae (or Cuculinae); the Bombi and the more perfectly social bees forming another group, viz. (6) Sociales. A group Andrenoides, or Panurgides, was also proposed for certain bees considered to belong to the Apidae though exhibiting many points of resemblance with the Andrenidae. This arrangement is by no means satisfactory, but as the tropical bees have been but little collected, and are only very imperfectly known, it is clear that we cannot hope for a better classification till collections have been very much increased and improved. The arrangement adopted in Dalla Torre's recent valuable catalogue of bees [1] recognises no less than fourteen primary divisions, but is far from satisfactory.

The two genera *Prosopis* and *Sphecodes* have been recently formed into a special family, ARCHIAPIDAE, by Friese,[2] who, however, admits that the association is not a natural one. The term should be limited to *Prosopis* and the genera into which it has been, or shortly will be, divided. The primitive nature of the members of this genus is exhibited in all the external

characters that are most distinctive of bees; the proboscis (Fig. 9, B, C), is quite short, its ligula being very short, and instead of being pointed having a concave front margin. The body is almost bare, though there is some very short feathered plumage. The hind legs are destitute of modifications for industrial purposes. Owing to these peculiarities it was for long assumed that the species of *Prosopis* must be parasites. This is, however, known not to be the

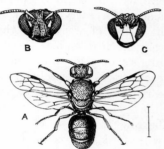

FIG. 10. — *Prosopis signata.* Cambridge. **A**, Female ; **B**, front of head of female ; **C**, of male.

case so far as many of the species are concerned. They form cells lined with a silken membrane in the stems of brambles and other plants that are suitable, or in burrows in the earth, or in the mortar of walls ; individuals of the same species varying much as to the nidus they select. The food they store in these cells is much more liquid than usual, and has been supposed to be entirely honey, since they have no apparatus for carrying pollen. Mr. R. C. L. Perkins has, however, observed that they swallow both pollen and nectar, brushing the first-named substance to the mouth by aid of the front legs. He

---

[1] *Catalogus Hymenopterorum*, Leipzig, 10 vols. 1892-96 ; *Bees*, vol. x.
[2] *Zool. Jahrb. Syst.* iv. 1891, p. 779. This paper is a most valuable summary of what is known as to the habits of European solitary bees, but is less satisfactory from a systematic point of view.

has ascertained that a few of the very numerous Hawaiian species of the genus are really parasitic on their congeners : these parasites are destitute of a peculiar arrangement of hairs on the front legs of the female, the possession of which, by some of the non-parasitic forms, enables the bee to sweep the pollen towards its mouth.   These observations show that the structural peculiarities of *Prosopis* are correlative with the habits of forming a peculiar lining to the cell, and of gathering pollen by the mouth and conveying it by the alimentary canal instead of by external parts of the body.   *Prosopis* is a very widely distributed genus, and very numerous in species.   We have ten in Britain ; several of them occur in the grounds of our Museum at Cambridge.

The species of the genus *Colletes* are hairy bees of moderate size, with a good development of hair on the middle and posterior femora for carrying pollen.   They have a short, bilobed ligula like that of wasps, and therein differ from the Andrenae, which they much resemble.   With *Prosopis* they form the group Obtusi-lingues of some taxonomists.   They have a manner of nesting peculiar to themselves ; they dig cylindrical burrows in the earth, line them with a sort of slime, that dries to a substance like gold-beater's skin, and then by partitions arrange the burrow as six to ten separate cells, each of which is filled with food that is more liquid than usual in bees.   Except in regard to the ligula and the nature of the cell-lining, *Colletes* has but little resemblance to *Prosopis ;* but the term Obtusilingues may be applied to *Colletes* if *Prosopis* be separated as Archiapidae. We have six species of *Colletes* in Britain.

Sphecodes is a genus that has been the subject of prolonged difference of opinion.   The species are rather small shining bees, with a red, or red and black, abdomen, almost without pollen-collecting apparatus, and with a short but pointed ligula.   These characters led to the belief that the Insects are parasitic, or, as they are sometimes called, cuckoo-bees.   But evidence could not be obtained of the fact, and as they were seen to make burrows it was decided that we have in *Sphecodes* examples of industrial bees extremely ill endowed for their work. Recent observations tend, however, to prove that *Sphecodes* are to a large extent parasitic at the expense of bees of the genera *Halictus* and *Andrena*.   Breitenbach has taken *S. rubicundus* out of the brood-cells of *Halictus quadricinctus* ; and on one of the few

occasions on which this bee has been found in Britain it was in circumstances that left little doubt as to its being a parasite of *Andrena nigroaenea.*   Marchal[1] has seen *S. subquadratus* fight with *Halictus malachurus,*
and kill it previous to taking possession of its burrows; and similar observations have been made by Ferton. As the older observations of Smith, Sichel, and Friese leave little doubt that *Sphecodes* are sometimes industrial bees, it is highly probable that we have in this genus the interesting con-

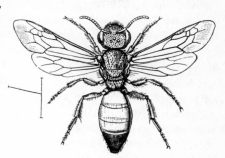

FIG. 11.—*Sphecodes gibbus* ♀.   Britain.

dition of bees that are sometimes parasitic, at other times not; but so much obscurity still prevails as to the habits of *Sphecodes* that we should do well to delay accepting the theories that have been already based on this strange state of matters.[2] Friese states that in *Sphecodes* the first traces of collecting apparatus exist; and, accepting the condition of affairs as being that mentioned above, it is by no means clear whether we have in *Sphecodes* bees that are abandoning the parasitic habit or commencing it; or, indeed, whether the condition of uncertainty may not be a permanent one.   It is difficult to decide as to what forms are species in *Sphecodes* owing to the great variation. The Hymenopterist Forster considered that 600 specimens submitted to him by Sichel represented no less than 140 species, though Sichel was convinced that nearly the whole of them were one species, *S. gibbus.*   It has recently been found that the male sexual organs afford a satisfactory criterion.   The position of *Sphecodes* in classification is doubtful.

The great majority of the species of short-tongued bees found in Britain belong to the genera *Andrena* and *Halictus,* and with some others constitute the ANDRENIDES of many writers.   *Halictus* includes our smallest British bees.   Their economy escaped the earlier observers, but has recently been to some extent unravelled by Smith, Fabre, Nicolas, Verhoeff, and others, and proves to be

[1] *Bull. Soc. ent. France,* 1894, p. cxv.
[2] Marchal, *Rev. Sci.* 15th February 1890, and Ferton, *t.c.* 19th April.

of great interest and variety.   Fabre observed *H. lineolatus* and
H. sexcinctus[1] under circumstances that enabled him to give them
continuous attention, whenever requisite, throughout a whole year.
These bees are to a certain extent social ; they are gregarious ; each
bee works for its own progeny, but there is collaboration between
members of a colony, inasmuch as a piece of general work is
undertaken from which more families than one derive benefit.
This common work is a gallery, that, ramifying in the earth,
gives access to various groups of cells, each group the production
of a single *Halictus ;* in this way one entrance and one corridor
serve for several distinct dwellings.   The work of excavation is
carried on at night.   The cells are oval, and are covered on the
interior with a delicate waterproof varnish ; Fabre considers this
to be a product of the salivary glands, like the membrane we
noticed when speaking of *Colletes.*   In the south of France both
sexes of these species are produced from the nests in September,
and then the males are much more numerous than the females ;
when the cold weather sets in the males die, but the females
continue to live on in the cells underground.   In the following
spring the females come out and recommence working at the
burrows, and also provision the cells for the young ; the new
generation, consisting entirely of females, appears in July, and
from these there proceeds a parthenogenetic generation, which
assumes the perfect form in September, and consists, as we have
above remarked, in greater part of males.   Pérez,[2] however,
considers that Fabre's observations as to the parthenogenetic
generation were incomplete, and that males might have been
found a little earlier, and he consequently rejects altogether
the occurrence of parthenogenesis in *Halictus.*   Nicolas confirms Fabre's observations, so far as the interesting point of the
work done for common benefit is concerned ; and adds that the
common corridor being too narrow to permit of two bees passing,
there is a dilatation or vestibule near the entrance that facilitates
passage, and also that a sentinel is stationed at this point.

Smith's observations on *Halictus morio* in England lead one
to infer that there is but one generation, the appearance of which
extends over a very long period.   He says, " Early in April the
females appeared, and continued in numbers up to the end of

[1] *C.R. Ac. Paris,* lxxxix. 1879, p. 1079, and *Ann. Sci. Nat.* (6), ix. 1879, No. 4.
[2] *Act. Soc. Bordeaux,* xlviii. 1895, p. 145.

June "; then there was an interval, and in the middle of August males began to appear, followed in ten or twelve days by females. Hence it is probable that in different countries the times of appearance and the number of generations of the same species may vary. Verhoeff has described the burrows of *Halictus quadricinctus* with some detail. The cells, instead of being distributed as usual throughout the length of the burrow one by one, are accumulated into a mass placed in a vault communicating with the shaft. This shaft is continued downwards to a depth of 10 cm., and forms a retreat for the bees when engaged in construction. Several advantages are secured by this method, especially better ventilation, and protection from any water that may enter the shaft. The larvae that are present in the brood-chambers at any one moment differ much in their ages, a fact that throws some doubt on the supposed parthenogenetic generation. No cocoons are formed by these *Halictus*,

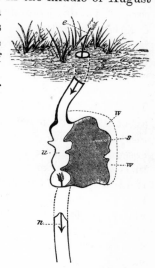

Fig. 12.—Nesting of *Halictus quadricinctus*. *u*, Original burrow, with entrance *e* thereto; *n*, retreat or continuation of the burrow; *w*, the vaults; *s*, the accumulation of cells. (After Verhoeff, *Verh. Ver. Rheinl.* xlviii. 1891; scale not mentioned.)

the polished interior of the cell being a sufficiently refined resting place for metamorphosis. Verhoeff states that many of the larvae are destroyed by mouldiness; this indeed, he considers to be the most deadly of the enemies of Aculeate Hymenoptera. The nest of *Halictus maculatus* has also been briefly described by Verhoeff, and is a very poor construction in comparison with that of *H. quadricinctus*.

The genus *Andrena* includes a great number of species, Britain possessing about fifty. They may be described in a general manner as Insects much resembling the honey-bee— for which, indeed, they are frequently mistaken—but usually a little smaller in size. Many of the bees we see in spring, in March or April, are of this genus. They live in burrows in the ground, preferring sandy places, but frequently selecting a gravel path as the locality for their operations; they nearly always live in colonies. Great difficulties attend their study on account of several points in their economy, such as, that the sexes are different, and frequently not found together; also that there may be two generations of a species in one year, these being more or less different from one another. Another considerable difficulty arises from the fact that these bees are subject to the attacks of the parasite *Stylops*, by which their form is more or less altered. These Insects feed in the body of the bee in such a way as to affect its nutrition without destroying its life; hence they offer a means of making experiments that may throw valuable light on obscure physiological questions. Among the effects they produce in the condition of the imago bee we may mention the enfeeblement of the sexual distinction, so that a stylopised male bee becomes less different than it usually is from the female, and a stylopised female may be ill developed and less different than usual from the male. The colours and hair are sometimes altered, and distortion of portions of the abdominal region of the bee are very common. Further particulars as to these parasites will be found at the end of our account of Coleoptera (p. 298). We may here remark that these *Stylops* are not the only parasitic Insects that live in the bodies of Andrenidae without killing their hosts, or even interrupting their metamorphoses. Mr. R. C. L. Perkins recently captured a specimen of *Halictus rubicundus*, from which he, judging from the appearance of the example, anticipated that a *Stylops* would emerge; but instead of this a Dipterous Insect of the family Chloropidae appeared. Dufour in 1837 called attention to a remarkable relation existing between *Andrena aterrima* and a parasitic Dipterous larva. The larva takes up a position in the interior of the bee's body so as to be partly included in one of the great tracheal vesicles at the base of the abdomen; and the bee then maintains the parasite in its position, and at the same time supplies it with air by causing two tracheae to grow

Fig. 13.—Parasitic Dipterous larva in connection with tracheal system of *Andrena aterrima*. (After Dufour.)

into its body. Dufour states that he demonstrated the continuity of the tracheae of the two organisms, but it is by no means clear that the continuity was initially due to the bee's organisation.

Dasypoda hirtipes appears to be the most highly endowed of the European Andrenides. The Insects of the genus *Dasypoda* are very like *Andrena,* but have only two in place of three submarginal cells (just beneath the stigma) on the front wing. The female of *D. hirtipes* has a very dense and elongate pubescence on the posterior legs, and carries loads of pollen, each about half its own weight, to its nest.

FIG. 14.—*D. hirtipes* ♀.   Britain.

The habits of this insect have been described by Hermann Müller.[1] It forms burrows in the ground after the fashion of *Andrena;* this task is accomplished by excavating with the mandibles ; when it has detached a certain quantity of the earth it brings this to the surface by moving backwards, and then distributes the loose soil over a considerable area.   It accomplishes this in a most beautiful manner by means of the combined action of all the legs, each pair of these limbs performing its share of the function in a different manner ; the front legs acting with great rapidity—making four movements in a second—push the sand backwards under the body, the bee moving itself at the same time in this direction by means of the middle pair of legs ; simultaneously, but with a much slower movement, the hind legs are stretched and moved outwards, in oar-like fashion, from the body, and thus sweep away the earth and distribute it towards each side.   This being done the bee returns quickly into the hole, excavates some more earth, brings it up and distributes it.   Each operation of excavation takes a minute or two, the distribution on the surface only about fifteen seconds.   The burrow extends to the length of one or two feet, so that a considerable amount of earth has to be brought up ; and when the Insect has covered one part of the circumference of the mouth of the hole with loose earth, it makes another patch, or walk, by the side of the first. The main burrow being completed, the Insect then commences the formation of brood-chambers in connection with it.   Three to six such chambers are formed in connection with a burrow ; the lower one is first made and is provisioned by the bee : for this

[1] *Verh. Ver. Rheinland,* xli. 1884, p. 1.

purpose five or six loads of pollen are brought to the cell, each load being, as we have already remarked, about half the weight of the Insect. This material is then formed into a ball and made damp with honey ; then another load of pollen is brought, is mixed with honey and added as an outer layer to the ball, which is now remodelled and provided on one side with three short feet, after which an egg is placed on the top of the mass ; the bee then sets to work to make a second chamber, and uses the material resulting from the excavation of this to close completely the first chamber. The other chambers are subsequently formed in a similar manner, and then the burrow itself is filled up. While engaged in ascertaining these facts, Müller also made some observations on the way the bee acts when disturbed in its operations, and his observations on this point show a very similar instinct to that displayed by *Chalicodoma*, referred to on a subsequent page. If interrupted while storing a chamber the Insect will not attempt to make a fresh one, but will carry its stock of provisions to the nest of some other individual. The result of this proceeding is a struggle between the two bees, from which it is satisfactory to learn that the rightful proprietor always comes out victorious. The egg placed on the pollen-ball in the chamber hatches in a few days, giving birth to a delicate white larva of curved form. This creature embraces the pollen-ball so far as its small size will enable it to do so, and eats the food layer by layer so as to preserve its circular form. The larva when hatched has no anal orifice and voids no excrement, so that its food is not polluted ; a proper moulting apparently does not take place, for though a new delicate skin may be found beneath the old one this latter is not definitely cast off. When the food, which was at first 100 to 140 times larger than the egg or young larva, is all consumed the creature then for the first time voids its refuse. During its growth the larva becomes red and increases in weight from ·0025 grains to ·26 or ·35 grains, but during the subsequent period of excretion it diminishes to ·09 or ·15 grains, and in the course of doing so becomes a grub without power of movement, and of a white instead of a red colour. After this the larva reposes motionless for many months—in fact, until the next summer, when it throws off the larval skin and appears as a pupa. The larval skin thus cast off contrasts greatly with the previous delicate condition of the integument, for this last exuvium is thick and rigid. Although it voids no excrement till much later the union of the stomach and hind-intestine is accomplished when the larva is half-grown. A larva, from which Müller took away a portion of its unconsumed food-store, began directly afterwards to emit excrement. The pupa has greater power of movement than the resting larva; when it has completed its metamorphosis and become a perfect Insect, it, if it be a female, commences almost immediately after its emergence to form burrows by the complex and perfect series of actions we have described.

Parasitic Bees (DENUDATAE).—This group of parasitic bees includes fourteen European genera, of which six are British. They form a group taxonomically most unsatisfactory, the members having little in common except the negative characters of the absence of pollen-carrying apparatus. Although there is a great dearth of information as to the life-histories of parasitic bees, yet some highly interesting facts and generalisations about their relations with their hosts have already been obtained. Verhoeff has recently given the following account of the relations between the parasitic bee *Stelis minuta* and its host *Osmia leucomelana:*—The *Osmia* forms cells in blackberry stems, provisions them in the usual manner, and deposits an egg in each. But the *Stelis* lays an egg in the store of provisions before the *Osmia* does, and thus its egg is placed lower down in the mass of food than that of the legitimate owner, which is in fact at the top. The *Stelis* larva emerges from the egg somewhat earlier than the *Osmia* larva does. For a considerable time the two larvae so disclosed consume together the stock of provisions, the *Osmia* at the upper, the *Stelis* at the lower, end thereof. By the consumption of the provisions the two larvae are brought into proximity, and by this time the *Stelis* larva, being about twice the size of the *Osmia* larva, kills and eats it. Verhoeff witnessed the struggle between the two larvae, and states further that the operation of eating the *Osmia* larva after it has been killed lasts one or two days. He adds that parasitic larvae are less numerous than the host larvae, it being well known that parasitic bees produce fewer offspring than host bees. Verhoeff further states that he has observed similar relations to obtain between the larvae of other parasitic bees and their hosts, but warns us against concluding that the facts are analogous in all cases.

Fabre has made us acquainted with some points in the history of another species of the same genus, viz. *Stelis nasuta*, that show a decided departure from the habits of *S. minuta*. The first-named Insect accomplishes the very difficult task of breaking open the cells of the mason-bee, *Chalicodoma muraria*, after they have been sealed up, and then, being an Insect of much smaller size than the *Chalicodoma*, places several eggs in one cell of that bee. Friese informs us that parasitic bees and their hosts, in a great number of cases, not only have in the perfect state the tongue similarly formed,

FIG. 15.—*Nomada sex-fasciata* ♀.
Britain.

but also frequent the same species of flower; thus *Colletes daviesanus* and its parasite *Epeolus variegatus* both specially affect the flowers of *Tanacetum vulgare*. Some of the parasitic bees have a great resemblance to their hosts; *Stelis signata*, for instance, is said to be so like *Anthidium strigatum* that for many years it was considered to be a species of the genus *Anthidium*.

In other cases not the least resemblance exists between the parasites and hosts. Thus the species of *Nomada* that live at the expense of species of the genus *Andrena* have no resemblance thereto. Friese further tells us that the *Andrena* and *Nomada* are on the most friendly terms. *Andrena*, as is well known, forms populous colonies in banks, paths, etc., and in these colonies the destroying *Nomada* flies about unmolested; indeed, according to Friese, it is treated as a welcome guest. He says he has often seen, and in several localities, *Nomada lathburiana* and *Andrena ovina* flying peacefully together. The *Nomada* would enter a burrow, and if it found the *Andrena* therein, would come out and try another burrow; if when a marauding *Nomada* was in a burrow, and the rightful owner, returning laden with pollen, found on entering its home that an uninvited guest was therein, the *Andrena* would go out in order to permit the exit of the *Nomada*, and then would again enter and add the pollen to the store. Strange as this may seem at first sight, it is really not so, for, as we have before had occasion to observe, there is not the slightest reason for believing that host Insects have any idea whatever that the parasites or inquilines are injurious to their

race.   Why then should they attack the creatures ?   Provided the
parasites do not interfere in any unmannerly way with the hosts
and their work, there is no reason why the latter should resent
their presence.   The wild bee that seals up its cell when it has
laid an egg therein, and then leaves it for ever, has no conception
of the form of its progeny ; never in the history of the race of the
Andrena has a larva seen a perfect insect and survived thereafter,
never has a perfect Insect seen a larva.   There is no reason whatever for believing that these Insects have the least conception of
their own metamorphosis, and how then should they have any
idea of the metamorphosis of the parasite ?   If the *Andrena* found
in the pollen the egg of a parasitic *Nomada*, it could of course
easily remove the egg; but the *Andrena* has no conception
that the presence of the egg ensures the death of its own
offspring and though the egg be that of an enemy to its race,
why should it resent the fact ?   Is it not clear that the race has
always maintained itself notwithstanding the enemy ?   Nature has
brought about that both host and parasite should successfully
co-exist ; and each individual of each species lives, not for itself,
but for the continuance of the species ; that continuance is provided for by the relative fecundities of host and guest.   Why
then should the *Andrena* feel
alarm ?   If the species of *Nomada*
attack the species of *Andrena* too
much it brings about the destruction of its own species
more certainly than that of the
Andrena.

Such extremely friendly relations do not, however, exist between all the parasitic bees and
their hosts.   Friese says that, so

FIG. 16.—*Melecta luctuosa* ♀.   Britain.

far as he has been able to observe, the relations between the two
are not in general friendly.   He states that marauders of the
genera *Melecta* and *Coelioxys* seek to get out of the way when
they see the pollen-laden host coming home.   But he does not
appear to have noted any other evidence of mistrust between the
two, and it is somewhat doubtful whether this act can properly
be interpreted as indicating fear, for bees, as well as other
animals, when engaged in work find it annoying to be interfered

with ; it is the interest of the parasite to avoid annoyance and to be well-mannered in its approaches. Shuckard, however, says that battles ensue between the parasite *Melecta* and its host *Anthophora*, when the two bees meet in the burrows of the *Anthophora*.[1]

We shall have occasion to remark on some of the habits of *Dioxys cincta* when considering the history of the mason-bee (*Chalicodoma*), but one very curious point in its economy must here be noticed. The *Dioxys*, which is a much smaller bee than the *Chalicodoma*, lays an egg in a cell of the latter, and the resulting larva frequently has more food in the cell than it can consume ; there is, however, another bee, *Osmia cyanoxantha*, that frequently takes advantage of an unoccupied cell in the nest of the *Chalicodoma*, and establishes its own offspring therein. The *Dioxys*, it seems, cannot, or at any rate does not, distinguish whether a cell is occupied by *Chalicodoma* or by *Osmia*, and sometimes lays its egg in the nest of the *Osmia*, though this bee is small, and therefore provides very little food for its young. It might be supposed that under these conditions the *Dioxys* larva would be starved to death ; but this is not so ; it has the power of accommodating its appetite, or its capacity for metamorphosis, to the quantity of food it finds at its disposal, and the egg laid in the *Osmia* cell actually produces a tiny specimen of *Dioxys*, only about half the natural size. Both sexes of these dwarf *Dioxys* are produced, offering another example of the fact that the quantity of food ingested during the lifetime of the larva does not influence the sex of the resulting imago.

The highly endowed bees that remain to be considered are by some writers united in a group called Apidae, in distinction from Andrenidae. For the purposes of this work we shall adopt three divisions, Scopulipedes, Dasygastres, Sociales.

The group SCOPULIPEDES includes such long-tongued, solitary bees as are not parasitic, and do not belong to the Dasygastres. It is not, however, a natural group, for the carpenter-bees (*Xylocopa*) are very different from *Anthophora*. It has recently been merged by Friese with Andrenides into a single group called Podilegidae. Four British genera, *Ceratina*, *Anthophora*, *Eucera* and *Saropoda* (including, however, only seven

---

[1] It is impossible for us here to deal with the question of the origin of the parasitic habit in bees. The reader wishing for information as to this may refer to Prof. Pérez's paper, *Act. Soc. Bordeaux*, xlvii. 1895. p. 300.

species), are referred to the Scopulipedes; in some forms a considerable resemblance to the Bombi is exhibited, indeed the female of one of our species of *Anthophora* is so very like the worker of *Bombus hortorum* var. *harrisellus*, that it would puzzle any one to distinguish them by a superficial inspection, the colour of the hair on the hind legs being the only obvious difference. *Anthophora* is one of the most extensive and widely distributed of the genera of bees. Some of the species make burrows in cliffs and form large colonies which are continued for many years in the same locality. Friese has published many details of the industry and metamorphoses of some of the species of this genus; the most remarkable point he has discovered being that *A. personata* at Strasburg takes two years to accomplish the life-cycle of one generation. Some of the European species of the genus have been found to be very subject to the attacks of parasites. An anomalous beetle, *Sitaris*, has been found in the nests of *A. pilipes;* and this same *Anthophora* is also parasitised by another beetle, *Meloe*, as well as by a bee of the genus *Melecta*.

The genus *Xylocopa* [1] contains many of the largest and most powerful of the bees, and is very widely distributed over the earth. In Europe only four or five species have been found, and none of them extend far northwards, *X. violacea* being the only one that comes so far as Paris. They are usually black or blue-black in colour, of broad, robust build, with shining integuments more or less covered with hair. *X. violacea* is known as the carpenter-bee from its habit of working in dry wood; it does not touch living timber, but will form its nest in all sorts of dried wood. It makes a cylindrical hole, and this gives access to three or four parallel galleries in which the broad cells are placed; the cells are always isolated by a partition; the bee forms this by cementing together with the products of its salivary glands the fragments of wood it cuts out. Its habits have been described at length by Réaumur, who alludes to it under the name of " abeille perce-bois." This bee hibernates in the imago condition, both sexes reappearing in the spring. Possibly there is more than one generation in the year, as Réaumur states that specimens that were tiny larvae on the 12th of June had by the 2nd of July consumed all their stock of provisions; they then fasted for a few days, and on the 7th or 8th of July became pupae, and in the first

---

[1] Refer to p. 70 *postea*, note, as to a recent discovery about *Xylocopa*.

days of August were ready to emerge as perfect Insects. Thus
the whole cycle of metamorphoses is passed through in about
eight weeks.   This species, though very clever in drilling holes,
does not hesitate to appropriate old burrows should they be at
hand.   Fabre observed that it was also quite willing to save
itself labour by forming its cells in hollow reeds of sufficient
calibre.   We have figured the larva and pupa of this species in
the previous volume (p. 170).

Xylocopa chloroptera in E. India selects a hollow bamboo for
its nidus; it cements together the pieces obtained in clearing

FIG. 17.—Xylocopa (Koptorthosoma), sp. near flavonigrescens, ♂. Sarawak.

out the bamboo, and uses them as horizontal partitions to separate
the tube into cells.   The species is much infested with a small
Chalcid of the genus Encyrtus: 300 specimens of the parasite
have been reared from a single larva of the bee; two-thirds of
the larvae of this bee that Horne endeavoured to rear were
destroyed by the little Chalcid.

The most beautiful and remarkable of all the bees are
the species of Euglossa.   This genus is peculiar to Tropical
America, and derives its name from the great length of the
proboscis, which in some species surpasses that of the body.   The
colours in Euglossa proper are violet, purple, golden, and metallic
green, and two of these are frequently combined in the most har-
monious manner; the hind tibia is greatly developed and forms
a plate, the outer surface of which is highly polished, while the
margins are furnished with rigid hairs.   Very little is known as
to the habits of these bees; they were formerly supposed to be

social; but this is doubtful, Bates having recorded that *E. surinamensis* forms a " solitary nest." Lucas concluded that *E. cordata* is social, on the authority of a nest containing " a dozen individuals." No workers are known. The species of *Eulema* have a shorter tongue than *Euglossa*, and in form and colour a good deal resemble our species of *Bombus* and *Apathus*.

The group DASYGASTRES includes seven European genera, four being British (*Chelostoma* being included in *Heriades*). The ventral surface of the hind body is densely set in the females with regularly arranged hairs, by means of which the pollen is carried. In many of the Dasygastres (*Megachile*, *e.g.*) the labrum is very large, and in repose is inflected on to the lower side of the head, and closely applied to the doubled-in tongue, which it serves to protect; the mandibles then lock together out-

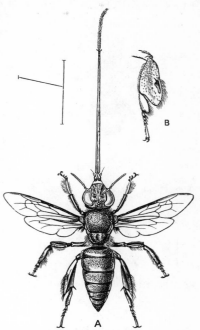

Fig. 18. — *Euglossa cordata*, ♂. Amazons. **A,** The Insect with extended proboscis; **B,** outer face of hind tibia and tarsus.

side the labrum, which is thus completely concealed. This group includes some of the most interesting of the solitary bees.

The genus *Chalicodoma* is not found in our own country, but in the South of France there exist three or four species. Their habits have given rise to much discussion, having been described by various naturalists, among whom are included Réaumur and Fabre. These Insects are called mason-bees, and construct nests of very solid masonry. *C. muraria* is in appearance somewhat intermediate between a honey-bee and a *Bombus;* it is densely hairy, and the sexes are very different in colour. It is solitary in its habits, and usually chooses a large stone as a solid basis for its habitation. On this a cell is formed, the material used being a kind of cement made by the Insect from the mixture of a suitable sort of earth with the material secreted by its own salivary glands; the amount of cement used is reduced by the artifice of building small stones into the walls of the cell; the stones are selected with great care. When a cell about an inch in depth has been formed in this manner, the bee commences to fill it with food, consisting of honey and pollen; a little honey is brought and is discharged into the cell, then some pollen is added. This bee, like other Dasygastres, carries the pollen by means of hairs on the under surface of the body; to place this pollen in the cell the Insect therefore enters backwards, and then with the pair of hind legs brushes and scrapes the under surface of the body so as to make the pollen fall off into the cell; it then starts for a fresh cargo; after a few loads have been placed in the receptacle, the Insect mixes the honey and pollen into a paste with the mandibles, and again continues its foraging until it has about half filled the cell; then an egg is laid, and the apartment is at once closed with cement. This work is all accomplished, if the weather be favourable, in about two days, after which the Insect commences the formation of a second cell, joined to the first, and so on till eight or nine of these receptacles have been constructed; then comes the final operation of adding an additional protection in the shape of a thick layer of mortar placed over the whole; the construction, when thus completed, forms a sort of dome of cement about the size of half an orange. In this receptacle the larvae pass many months, exposed to the extreme heat of summer as well as to the cold of winter. The larvae, however, are exposed to numerous other perils; and we have already related (vol. v. p. 540) how *Leucospis gigas* succeeds in perforating the masonry and depositing therein an egg, so that a *Leucospis* is reared in the cell instead of a *Chalicodoma*.

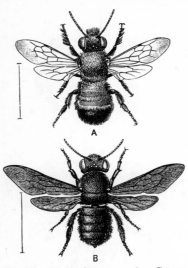

Fig. 19.—*Chalicodoma muraria.*   Greece.
A, Male ; B, female.

This Insect has been the object of some of J. H. Fabre's most instructive studies on instinct.[1]   Although it is impossible for us here to consider in a thorough manner the various points he has discussed, yet some of them are of such interest and importance as to demand something more than a passing allusion.

We have mentioned that the nest of *Chalicodoma* is roofed with a layer of solid cement in addition to the first covering with which the bee seals up each cell.   When the metamorphoses of the imprisoned larva have been passed through, and the moment for its emergence as a perfect Insect has arrived, the prisoner has to make its way through the solid wall by which it is encompassed.   Usually it finds no difficulty in accomplishing the task of breaking through the roof, so that the powers of its mandibles must be very great.   Réaumur has, however, recorded that a nest of this mason-bee was placed under a glass funnel, the orifice of which was covered with gauze, and that the Insects when they emerged from the nest were unable to make their way through the gauze, and consequently perished under the glass cover ; and he concluded that such insects are only able to accomplish the tasks that naturally fall to their lot.   By some fresh experiments Fabre, however, has put the facts in a different light.   He remarks that when the Insects have, in the ordinary course of emergence, perforated the walls of their dark prison,´they find themselves in the daylight, and at liberty to walk away ; when they have made their escape from a nest placed under a glass cover, they, having no knowledge of glass, find themselves in daylight and imprisoned by the glass, which, to their inexperience, does not appear to be an obstacle, and they therefore, he thought, might perhaps exhaust themselves in vain efforts to pass through this invisible obstacle.   He therefore took some cocoons containing pupae from a nest, placed each one of them in a tube of reed, and stopped the ends of the reeds with various substances, in one case earth, in another pith, in a third brown paper ; the reeds were then so arranged that the Insects in them were in a natural position ; in due course all the Insects emerged, none of them apparently having found the novel nature of the obstacle a serious impediment.   Some complete nests were then taken with their inmates, and to the exterior of one of them a sheet of opaque paper was closely fastened, while to another the same

[1] *Souvenirs entomologiques.* 4 vols. Paris, 1879 to 1891.

sort of paper was applied in the form of a dome, leaving thus a considerable space between the true cover of the nest and the covering of paper. From the first nest the Insects made their escape in the usual manner, thus again proving that paper can be easily pierced by them. From the second nest they also liberated themselves, but failed to make their way out through the dome of paper, and perished beneath it; thus showing that paper added to the natural wall caused them no difficulty, but that paper separated therefrom by a space was an insuperable obstacle. Professor Pérez has pointed out that this is no doubt due to the large space offered to the bee, which consequently moves about, and does not concentrate its efforts on a single spot, as it of course is compelled to do when confined in its natural cell.

The power of the mason-bee to find its nest again when removed to a distance from it is another point that was tested by Du Hamel and recounted by Réaumur. As regards this Fabre has also made some very valuable observations. He marked some specimens of the bee, and under cover removed them to a distance of four kilometres, and then liberated them; the result proved that the bees easily found their way back again, and indeed were so little discomposed by the removal that they reached their nests laden with pollen as if they had merely been out on an ordinary journey. On one of these occasions he observed that a *Chalicodoma*, on returning, found that another bee had during her absence taken possession of her partially completed cell, and was unwilling to relinquish it; whereupon a battle between the two took place. The account of this is specially interesting, because it would appear that the two combatants did not seek to injure one another, but were merely engaged in testing, as it were, which was the more serious in its claims to the proprietorship of the cell in dispute. The matter ended by the original constructor regaining and retaining possession. Fabre says that in the case of *Chalicodoma* it is quite a common thing for an uncompleted cell to be thus appropriated by a stranger during the absence of the rightful owner, and that after a scene of the kind described above, the latter of the two claimants always regains possession, thus leading one to suppose that some sense of rightful ownership exists in these bees; the usurper expressing, as it were, by its actions the idea—Before I resign my claims I must require you to go through the exertions that will prove you to be really the lawful owner.

Another experiment was made with forty specimens of *Chalicodoma pyrenaica*, which were removed to a distance of four kilometres and then liberated. About twenty of the individuals had been somewhat injured by the processes of capturing, marking, and transferring, and proved unable to make a proper start. The others went off well when released, and in forty minutes the arrivals at the nest had already commenced. The next morning he was able to ascertain that fifteen at least had found their way back, and that it was probable that most of the uninjured bees had reached home ; and this although, as Fabre believed, they had never before seen the spot where he liberated them.

These observations on the power of *Chalicodoma* to regain its nest attracted the attention of Charles Darwin, who wrote to M. Fabre, and suggested that further observations should be made with the view of ascertaining by means of what sense these bees were able to accomplish their return. For it must be borne in mind that this bee is very different from the domestic bee, inasmuch as it enjoys but a brief life in the winged state, and it is therefore to be presumed that an individual has no knowledge of such comparatively distant localities as those to which Fabre transported it. Further observations made by the Frenchman have unfortunately failed to throw any light on this point. Darwin thought it might possibly be some sensitiveness to magnetic conditions that enabled the bees to return home, and suggested that they should be tested as to this. Fabre accordingly made some minute magnets, and fixed one to each bee previous to letting them loose for a return journey. This had the effect of completely deranging the bees ; and it was therefore at first thought that the requisite clue was obtained. It occurred to the experimenter, however, to try the plan of affixing small pieces of straw to the bees instead of magnets, and on this being done it was found that the little creatures were just as much deranged by the straws as they were by the magnets : thus it became evident that no good grounds exist for considering that the bees are guided by magnetic influences.

One of the species [1] of *Chalicodoma* observed by Fabre fixes

---

[1] The "*Chalicodome des galets*" or *C.* "*des murailles*" of the French writer ; in some places he speaks of the species as being *C. muraria*, in others as *C. parietina*.

its nests to the small boulders brought down and left by the Rhone on the waste places of its banks. This habit afforded Fabre an opportunity of removing the nests during the process of construction, and of observing the effect this produced on the architects. While a bee that had a nest partially constructed was absent, he removed the stone and the nest attached to it from one situation to another near at hand and visible from the original site. In a few minutes the bee returned and went straight to the spot where the nest had been; finding its home absent it hovered for a little while around the place, and then alighted on the vacated position, and walked about thereon in search of the nest; being after some time convinced that this was no longer there, it took wing, but speedily returned again to the place and went through the same operations. This series of manoeuvres was several times repeated, the return always being made to the exact spot where the nest had been originally located; and although the bee in the course of its journeys would pass over the nest at a distance of perhaps only a few inches, it did not recognise the object it was in search of. If the nest were placed very near to the spot it had been removed from— say at a distance of about a yard—it might happen that the bee would actually come to the stone to which the nest was fixed, would visit the nest, would even enter into the cell it had left partially completed, would examine circumspectly the boulder, but would always leave it, and again return to the spot where the nest was originally situated, and, on finding that the nest was not there, would take its departure altogether from the locality. The home must be, for the bee, in the proper situation, or it is not recognised as the desired object. Thus we are confronted with the strange fact that the very bee that is able to return to its nest from a distance of four kilometres can no longer recognise it when removed only a yard from the original position. This extraordinary condition of the memory of the Insect is almost inconceivable by us. That the bee should accurately recognise the spot, but that it should not recognise the cell it had itself just formed and half-filled with honey-paste, seems to us almost incredible; nevertheless, the fact is quite consistent with what we shall subsequently relate in the case of the solitary wasp *Bembex*. A cross experiment was made by taking away the stone with the attached nest of the bee while the latter

was absent, and putting in its place the nest of another individual in about the same stage of construction ; this nest was
at once adopted by the bee, which indeed was apparently in no
way deranged by the fact that the edifice was the work of another.
A further experiment was made by transposing the positions of
two nests that were very near together, so that each bee when
returning might be supposed to have a free choice as to which
nest it would go to. Unhesitatingly each bee selected the nest
that, though not its own, was in the position where its own had
been. This series of experiments seems to prove that the *Chalci-
doma* has very little sense as to what is its own property, but, on
the other hand, has a most keen appreciation of locality. As,
however, it might be supposed that the bees were deceived by the
similarity between the substituted nests, Fabre transposed two
nests that were extremely different, one consisting of many cells,
the other of a single incomplete cell ; it was, of course, a necessary
condition of this experiment that each of the two nests, however
different in other respects, should possess one cell each in similar
stages of construction ; and when that was the case each bee
cheerfully adopted the nest that, though very different to its
own, was in the right place. This transposition of nests can be
rapidly repeated, and thus the same bee may be made to go on
working at two different nests.

Suppose, however, that another sort of change be made. Let
a nest, consisting of a cell that is in an early stage of construction, be taken away, and let there be substituted for it a cell
built and partially stored with food. It might be supposed that
the bee would gladly welcome this change, for the adoption of
the substituted cell would save it a great deal of work. Not so,
however ; the bee in such a case will take to the substituted cell,
but will go on building at it although it is already of the full
height, and will continue building at it until the cell is made as
much as a third more than the regulation height. In fact the
bee, being in the building stage of its operations, goes on building, although in so doing it is carrying on a useless, if not an
injurious, work. A similar state ensues when the Insect ceases
to build and begins to bring provisions to the nest ; although a
substituted cell may contain a sufficient store of food, the bee goes
on adding to this, though it is wasting its labours in so doing.
It should be noted that though the bee must go through the

appropriate stages of its labours whether the result of so doing be beneficial or injurious, yet it is nevertheless to some extent controlled by the circumstances, for it does not in such cases complete what should have been the full measure of its own individual work; it does not, for instance, raise the cell to twice the natural height, but stops building when the cell is about one-third larger than usual, as if at that stage the absurdity of the situation became manifest to it.

Fabre's experiments with the *Chalicodoma* are so extremely instructive as regards the nature of instinct in some of the highest Insects, that we must briefly allude to some other of his observations even at the risk of wearying the reader who feels but little interest in the subject of Insect intelligence.

Having discovered that a mason-bee that was engaged in the process of construction would go on building to an useless or even injurious extent, Fabre tried another experiment to ascertain whether a bee that was engaged in the process of provisioning the nest, would do so in conditions that rendered its work futile. Taking away a nest with completely built cell that a bee was storing with food, he substituted for it one in which the cell was only commenced, and therefore incapable of containing food; when the bee with its store of provisions reached this should-be receptacle it appeared to be very perplexed, tested the imperfect cell with its antennae, left the spot and returned again; repeating this several times it finally went to the cell of some stranger to deposit its treasure. In other cases the bee broke open a completed cell, and having done so went on bringing provisions to it, although it was already fully provisioned and an egg laid therein: finally, the little creature having completed the bringing of this superfluous tale of provisions, deposited a second egg, and again sealed up the cell. But in no case does the bee go back from the provisioning stage to the building stage until the cycle for one cell of building, provisioning, and egg-laying is completed: but when this is the case, the building of a fresh cell may be again undertaken. This is a good example of the kind of consecutive necessity that seems to be one of the chief features of the instinct of these industrious little animals. Another equally striking illustration of these peculiarities of instinct is offered by interfering with the act of putting the provisions into the cell. It will be recollected that when the bee brings provisions to add to the stock, it carries both honey and pollen; in order to deliver these it begins by entering head first into the cell and disgorging the honey, then emerging it turns round, enters backwards and scrapes off the pollen from its body. If after the honey has been discharged, the bee be interfered with and gently removed to a slight distance with a straw, it returns to complete its task, but instead of going on with the actions at the point at which the interruption took place, it begins the series over again, going in——at any rate partially——head first, although it has no honey to discharge, and having performed this useless ceremony it then emerges, turns round and adds the pollen. This illustration is in some respects the reverse of what might have been expected, for the Insect here does not continue the act at the interrupted point, but begins the series of actions afresh.

It would be reasonable to suppose that an Insect that takes the pains to provide for the safety of its progeny by constructing a complex edifice of cement, secures thereby the advantage of protection for its young. But this is far from being the case. Notwithstanding the cement and the thick dome of mortar, the *Chalicodoma* is extremely subject to the attacks of parasites. The work performed by the creature in constructing its mass of masonry is truly astounding; Fabre calculated from measurements he made that for the construction and provisioning of a single cell, the goings and comings of the bee amounted to 15 kilometres, and it makes for each nest sometimes as many as fifteen cells. Notwithstanding all this labour, it would appear that no real safety for the larvae is obtained by the work. Some sixteen——possibly more——other species of Insects get their living off this industrious creature. Another bee, *Stelis nasuta*, breaks open the cells after they have been completely closed and places its own eggs in them, and then again closes the cells with mortar. The larvae of this *Stelis* develop more rapidly than do those of the *Chalicodoma*, so that the result of this shameless proceeding is that the young one of the legitimate proprietor—— as we human beings think it——is starved to death, or is possibly eaten up as a dessert by the *Stelis* larvae, after they have appropriated all the pudding.

Another bee, *Dioxys cincta*, is even more audacious; it flies about in a careless manner among the *Chalicodoma* at their work, and they do not seem to object to its presence unless it interferes with them in too unmannerly a fashion, when they brush it aside. The *Dioxys*, when the proprietor leaves the cell, will enter it and taste the contents; after having taken a few mouthfuls the impudent creature then deposits an egg in the cell, and, it is pretty certain, places it at or near the bottom of the mass of pollen, so that it is not conspicuously evident to the *Chalicodoma* when the bee again returns to add to or complete the stock of provisions. Afterwards the constructor deposits its own egg in the cell and closes it. The final result is much the same as in the case of the *Stelis*, that is to say, the *Chalicodoma* has provided food for an usurper; but it appears probable that the consummation is reached in a somewhat different manner, namely, by the *Dioxys* larva eating the egg of the *Chalicodoma,* instead of slaughtering the larva. Two of the Hymenoptera Parasitica are very destructive to the *Chalicodoma,* viz. *Leucospis gigas* and *Monodontomerus nitidus ;* the habits of which ·ve have already discussed (vol. v. p. 543) under Chalcididae. Lampert has given a list of the Insects attacking the mason-bee or found in its nests; altogether it would appear that about sixteen species have been recognised, most of which destroy the bee larva, though some possibly destroy the bee's destroyers, and two or three perhaps merely devour dead examples of the bee, or take the food from cells, the inhabitants of which have been destroyed by some untoward event. This author thinks that one half of the bees' progeny are made away with by these destroyers, while Fabre places the destruction in the South of France at a still higher ratio, telling us that in one nest of nine cells, the inhabitants of three were destroyed by the Dipterous Insect, *Anthrax trifasciata,* of two by *Leucospis,* of two by *Stelis,* and of one by the smaller Chalcid; there being thus only a single example of the bee that had not succumbed to one or other of the enemies. He has sometimes examined a large number of nests without finding a single one that had not been attacked by one or other of the parasites, and more often than not several of the marauders had attacked the nest.

It is said by Lampert and others that there is a passage in Pliny relating to one of the mason-bees, that the Roman author had noticed in the act of carrying off stones to build into its nest; being unacquainted with the special habits of the bee, he seems to have supposed that the insect was carrying the stone as ballast to keep itself from being blown away.

The bees of the genus *Anthidium* are known to possess the habit of making nests of wool or cotton, that they obtain from plants growing at hand. We have one species of this genus of bees in Britain; it sometimes may be seen at work in the grounds of our Museum at Cambridge: it is referred to by Gilbert White, who says of it, in his *History of Selborne:* " There is a sort of wild bee frequenting the garden-campion for the sake of its tomentum, which probably it turns to some purpose in the business of nidification. It is very pleasant to see with what address it strips off the pubes, running from the top to the bottom of a branch, and shaving it bare with the dexterity of a hoop-shaver. When it has got a bundle, almost as large as itself, it flies

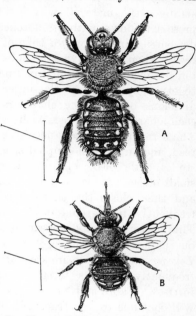

Fig. 20.—*Anthidium manicatum,* Carder-bee. **A,** Male ; **B,** female.

away, holding it secure between its chin and its fore legs." The species of this genus are remarkable as forming a conspicuous exception to the rule that in bees the female is larger than the male. The species of *Anthidium* do not form burrows for themselves, but either take advantage of suitable cavities formed by other Insects in wood, or take possession of deserted nests of other bees or even empty snail-shells. The workers in cotton, of which our British species *A. manicatum* is one, line the selected receptacle with a beautiful network of cotton or wool, and inside this place a finer layer of the material, to which is added some sort of cement that prevents the honied mass stored by the bees in this receptacle from passing out of it. *A. diadema,* one of the species that form nests in hollow stems, has been specially observed by Fabre ; it will take the cotton for its work from any suitable plant growing near its nest, and does not confine itself to any particular natural order of plants, or even to those that are indigenous to the South of France. When it has brought a ball of cotton to the nest, the bee spreads out and arranges the material with its front legs and mandibles, and presses it down with its forehead on to the cotton previously deposited; in this way a tube of cotton is constructed inside the reed; when withdrawn, the tube proved to be composed of about ten distinct cells arranged in linear fashion, and connected firmly together by means of the outer layer of cotton; the transverse divisions between the chambers are also formed of cotton, and each chamber is stored with a mixture of honey and pollen. The series of chambers does not extend quite to the end of the reed, and in the unoccupied space the Insect accumulates small stones, little pieces of earth, fragments of wood or other similar small objects, so as to form a sort of barricade in the vestibule, and then closes the tube by a barrier of coarser cotton taken frequently from some other plant, the mullein by preference. This barricade would appear to be an ingenious attempt to keep out parasites, but if so, it is a failure, at any rate as against *Leucospis*, which insinuates its eggs through the sides, and frequently destroys to the last one the inhabitants of the fortress. Fabre states that these *Anthidium*, as well as *Megachile*, will continue to construct cells when they have no eggs to place in them; in such a case it would appear from his remarks that the cells are made in due form and the extremity of the reed closed, but no provisions are stored in the chambers.

The larva of the *Anthidium* forms a most singular cocoon. We have already noticed the difficulty that arises, in the case of these Hymenopterous larvae shut up in small chambers, as to the disposal of the matters resulting from the incomplete assimilation of the aliment ingested. To allow the once-used food to mingle with that still remaining unconsumed would be not only disagreeable but possibly fatal to the life of the larva. Hence some species retain the whole of the excrement until the food is entirely consumed, it being, according to Adlerz, stored in a special pouch at the end of the stomach; other Hymenoptera, amongst which we may mention the species of *Osmia*, place the excreta in a vacant space. The *Anthidium* adopts, however, a most remarkable system: about the middle of its larval life it commences the expulsion of "frass" in the shape of small pellets, which it fastens together with silk, as they are voided, and suspends round the walls of the chamber. This curious arrangement not only results in keeping the embarrassing material from contact with the food and with the larva itself, but serves, when the growth of the latter is accomplished, as the outline or foundations of the cocoon in which the metamorphosis is completed. This cocoon is of a very elaborate character ; it has, so says Fabre, a beautiful appearance, and is provided with a very peculiar structure in the form of a small conical protuberance at one extremity pierced by a canal. This canal is formed with great care by the larva, which from time to time places its head in the orifice in process of construction, and stretches the calibre by opening the mandibles. The object of this peculiarity in the fabrication of the elaborate cocoon is not clear, but Fabre inclines to the opinion that it is for respiratory purposes.

Other species of this genus use resin in place of cotton as their working material. Among these are *Anthidium septemdentatum* and *A. bellicosum*. The former species chooses an old snail-shell as its nidus, and constructs in it near the top a barrier of resin, so as to shut off the part where the whorl is too small ; then beneath the shelter of this barrier it accumulates a store of honey-pollen, deposits an egg, and completes the cell by another transverse barrier of resin ; two such cells are usually constructed in one snail-shell, and below them is placed a barricade of small miscellaneous articles, similar to what we have described in speaking of the cotton-working species of the genus. This bee completes its metamorphosis, and is ready to leave the cell in early spring. Its congener, *A. bellicosum*, has the same habits, with the exception that it works later in the year, and is thus exposed to a great danger, that very frequently proves fatal to it. This bee does not completely occupy the snail-shell with its cells, but leaves the lower and larger portion of the shell vacant. Now, there is another bee, a species of *Osmia*, that is also fond of snail-shells as a nesting-place, and that affects the same localities as the *A. septemdentatum ;* very often the *Osmia* selects for its nest the vacant part of a shell, the other part of which is occupied by the *Anthidium ;* the result of this is that when the metamorphoses are completed, the latter bee is unable to effect its escape, and

thus perishes in the cell.   Fabre further states with regard to
these interesting bees, that no structural differences of the feet
or mandibles can be detected between the workers in cotton and
the workers in resin ; and he also says that in the case where
two cells are constructed in one snail-shell, a male individual is
produced from the cell of the greater capacity, and a female from
the other.

Osmia is one of the most important of the genera of bees
found in Europe, and is remarkable for the diversity of instinct
displayed in the formation of the nests of the various species.
As a rule they avail themselves for nidification of hollow
places already existing ; choosing excavations in wood, in the

mortar of walls, and even in
sandbanks ; in several cases
the same species is found to
be able to adapt itself to
more than one kind of these
very different substances. This
variety of habit will render
it impossible for us to do
justice to this interesting
genus within the space at
our disposal, and we must
content ourselves with a con-

FIG. 21.—*Osmia tricornis,* ♀.   Algeria.

sideration of one or two of the more instructive of the traits
of *Osmia* life.   *O. tridentata* forms its nest in the stems of
brambles, of which it excavates the pith ; its mode of working
and some other details of its life have been well depicted by
Fabre.   The Insect having selected a suitable bramble-stalk with
a cut extremity, forms a cylindrical burrow in the pith thereof,
extending the tunnel as far as will be required to allow the
construction of ten or more cells placed one after the other in
the axis of the cylinder ; the bee does not at first clear out quite
all the pith, but merely forms a tunnel through it, and then
commences the construction of the first cell, which is placed at
the end of the tunnel that is most remote from the entrance.
This cavity is to be of oval form, and the Insect therefore cuts
away more of the pith so as to make an oval space, but somewhat
truncate, as it were, at each end, the plane of truncation at the
proximal extremity being of course an orifice.   The first cell

thus made is stored with pollen and honey, and an egg is deposited. Then a barrier has to be constructed to close this chamber; the material used for the barrier is the pith of the stem, and the Insect cuts the material required for the purpose from the walls of the second chamber; the excavation of the second chamber is, in fact, made to furnish the material for closing up the first cell. In this way a chain of cells is constructed, their number being sometimes as many as fifteen. The mode in which the bees, when the transformations of the larvae and pupae have been completed, escape from the chain of cells, has been the subject of much discussion, and errors have arisen from inference being allowed to take the place of observation. Thus Dufour, who noted this same mode of construction and arrangement in another Hymenopteron (*Odynerus nidulator*), perceived that there was only one orifice of exit, and also that the Insect that was placed at the greatest distance from this was the one that, being the oldest of the series, might be expected to be the first ready to emerge ; and as the other cocoons would necessarily be in the way of its getting out, he concluded that the egg that was last laid produced the first Insect ready for emergence. Fabre tested this by some ingenious experiments, and found that this was not the case, but that the Insects became ready to leave their place of imprisonment without any reference to the order in which the eggs were laid, and he further noticed some very curious facts with reference to the mode of emergence of *Osmia tridentata*. Each Insect, when it desires to leave the bramble stem, tears open the cocoon in which it is enclosed, and also bites through the barrier placed by the mother between it and the Insect that is next it, and that separates it from the orifice of exit. Of course, if it happen to be the outside one of the series it can then escape at once ; but if it should be one farther down in the Indian file it will not touch the cocoon beyond, but waits patiently, possibly for days ; if it then still find itself confined it endeavours to escape by squeezing past the cocoon that intervenes between it and liberty, and by biting away the material at the sides so as to enlarge the passage ; it may succeed in doing this, and so get out, but if it fail to make a side passage it will not touch the cocoons that are in its way. In the ordinary course of events, supposing all to go well with the family, all the cocoons produce their inmates in a state for emergence within a week or two, and so all get out. Frequently, however, the emergence is prevented by something having gone wrong with one of the outer Insects, in which case all beyond it perish unless they are strong enough to bite a hole through the sides of the bramble-stem. Thus it appears that whether a particular *Osmia* shall be able to emerge or not depends on two things—(1) whether all goes well with all the other Insects between it and the orifice, and (2) whether the Insect can bite a lateral hole or not ; this latter point also largely depends on the thickness of the outer part of the stem of the bramble. Fabre's experiments on these points have been repeated, and his results confirmed by Nicolas.

The fact that an *Osmia* would itself perish rather than attack the cocoon of its brother or sister is certainly very remarkable, and it induced Fabre to make some further experiments. He took some cocoons containing dead specimens of *Osmia*, and placed them in the road of an *Osmia* ready for exit, and found that in such case the bee made its way out by demolishing without any scruple the cocoons and dead larvae that intervened between it and liberty. He then took some other reeds, and blocked the way of exit with cocoons containing living larvae, but of another species of Hymenoptera. *Solenius vagus* and *Osmia detrita* were the species experimented on in this case, and he found that the *Osmia* destroyed the cocoon and living larvae of the *Solenius*, and so made its way out. Thus it appears that *Osmia* will respect the life of its own species, and die rather than destroy it, but has no similar respect for the life of another species.

Some of Fabre's most instructive chapters are devoted to the habits and instincts of various species of the genus *Osmia*. It is impossible here to find space even to summarise them, still more impossible to do them justice; but we have selected the history just recounted, because it is rare to find in the insect world instances of such self-sacrifice by an individual for one of the same generation. It would be quite improper to generalise from this case, however, and conclude that such respect for its own species is common even amongst the Osmia. Fabre, indeed, relates a case that offers a sad contrast to the scene of self-sacrifice and respect for the rights of others that we have roughly portrayed. He was able to induce a colony of *Osmia tricornis* (another species of the genus, be it noted) to establish itself and work in a series of glass tubes that he placed on a table in his laboratory.   He marked various individuals, so that he was able to recognise them and note the progress of their industrial works. Quite a large number of specimens thus established themselves and concluded their work before his very eyes.   Some individuals, however, when they had completed the formation of a series of cells in a glass tube or in a reed, had still not entirely completed their tale of work.   It would be supposed that in such a case the individual would commence the formation of another series of cells in an unoccupied tube.   This was not, however, the case. The bee preferred tearing open one or more cells already completed —in some cases, even by itself—scattering the contents, and de- vouring the egg ; then again provisioning the cell, it would deposit a fresh egg, and close the chamber.   These brief remarks will perhaps suffice to give some idea of the variety of instinct and habit that prevails in this very interesting genus.   Friese observes that the variety of habits in this genus is accompanied as a rule by paucity of individuals of a species, so that in central Europe a collector must be prepared to give some twenty years or so of attention to the genus before he can consider he has obtained all the species of *Osmia* that inhabit his district.

As a prelude to the remarks we are about to make on the leaf-cutting bees of the genus *Megachile* it is well to state that the bee, the habits of which were described by Réaumur under the name of " l'abeille tapissière," and that uses portions of the leaves of the scarlet poppy to line its nest, is now assigned to the genus *Osmia*, although Latreille, in the interval that has elapsed since the publication of Réaumur's work, founded the genus *Anthocopa* for the bee in question.   *Megachile* is one of the most important of the genera of the Dasygastres, being found in most parts of the world, even in the Sandwich Islands ;   it consists of bees averaging about the size of the honey-bee (though some are considerably larger, others smaller), and having the labrum largely developed ; this organ is capable of complete inflection to the under side of the head, and when in the condition of repose it is thus infolded, it underlaps and protects the larger part of the lower lip ; the mandibles close over the infolded labrum, so that, when the Insect is at rest, this appears to be altogether absent.   These bees are called leaf-cutters, from their habit of forming the cells for their nest out of pieces of the leaves of plants. We have several species in Britain; they are very like the common honey-bee in general appearance, though rather more robustly formed. These Insects, like the Osmiae, avail themselves of existing hollow places as receptacles in which to place their nests. *M. albocincta* frequently takes possession of a deserted worm-burrow in the ground. The burrow being longer than necessary the bee commences by cutting off the more distant part by means of a barricade of foliage; this being done, it proceeds to form a series of cells, each shaped like a thimble with a lid at the open end (Fig. 22, A). The body of the thimble is formed of large oval pieces of leaf, the lid of smaller round pieces; the fragments are cut with great skill from the leaves of growing plants by the Insect, which seems to have an idea of the form and size of the piece of foliage necessary for each particular stage of its work.

Horne has given particulars as to the nest of *Megachile anthracina* (*fasciculata*), an East Indian species.[1] The material employed

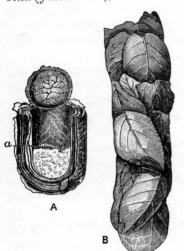

FIG. 22.—Nidification of leaf-cutting bee, *Megachile anthracina*. **A**, one cell separated, with lid open; the larva (*a*) reposing on the food; **B**, part of a string of the cells. (After Horne.)

was either the leaves of the Indian pulse or of the rose. Long pieces are cut by the Insect from the leaf, and with these a cell is formed; a circular piece is next cut, and with this a lid is made for the receptacle. The cells are about the size and shape of a common thimble; in one specimen that Horne examined no less than thirty-two pieces of leaf disposed in seven layers were used for one cell, in addition to three pieces for the round top. The cells are carefully prepared, and some kind of matter of a gummy nature is believed to be used to keep in place the pieces forming the interior layers. The cells are placed end to end, as shown in Fig. 22, B; five to seven cells form a series, and four or six series are believed to be constructed by one pair

[1] *Trans. Zool. Soc. London*, vii. 1870, p. 178.

of this bee, the mass being located in a hollow in masonry or some similar position.   Each cell when completed is half filled with pollen in the usual manner, and an egg is then laid in it. This bee is much infested by parasites, and is eaten by the Grey Hornbill (*Meniceros bicornis*).

Megachile lanata is one of the Hymenoptera that in East India enter houses to build their own habitations.   According to Horne both sexes take part in the work of construction, and the spots chosen are frequently of a very odd nature.   The material used is some kind of clay, and the natural situation may be considered to be the interior of a hollow tube, such as the stem of a bamboo ; but the barrel of a gun, and the hollow in the back of a book that has been left lying open, have been occasionally selected by the Insect as suitable.   Smith states that the individuals developed in the lower part of a tubular series of this species were females, " which sex takes longer to develop, and thus an exit is not required for them so soon as for the occupants of the upper cells which are males."   *M. proxima*, a species almost exactly similar in appearance to *M. lanata,* makes its cells of leaf-cuttings, however, and places them in soft soil.

Fabre states that *M. albocincta,* which commences the formation of its nest in a worm-burrow by means of a barricade, frequently makes the barricade, but no nest ; sometimes it will indeed make the barricade more than twice the proper size, and thus completely fill up the worm burrow.   Fabre considers that these eccentric proceedings are due to individuals that have already formed proper nests elsewhere, and that after completing these have still some strength remaining, which they use up in this fruitless manner.

The **Social bees** (SOCIALES) include, so far as is yet known, only a very small number of genera, and are so diverse, both in habits and structure, that the propriety of associating them in one group is more than doubtful; the genera are *Bombus* (Fig. 331, vol. v.), with its commensal genus or section, *Psithyrus* (Fig. 23); *Melipona* (Fig. 24), in which *Trigona* and *Tetragona* may at present be included, and *Apis* (Fig. 6); this latter genus comprising the various honey-bees that are more or less completely domesticated in different parts of the world.

In the genus *Bombus* the phenomena connected with the social life are more similar to what we find among wasps

than to what they are in the genus *Apis*.   The societies come to
an end at the close of the season, a few females live through the
winter, and each of these starts a new colony in the following
spring.   Males, females and workers exist, but the latter are
not distinguished by any good characters from the females, and
are, in fact, nothing but more or less imperfect forms thereof;
whereas in *Apis* the workers are distinguished by structural
characters not found in either of the true sexes.

Hoffer has given a description of the commencement of a
society of *Bombus lapidarius*.[1]   A large female, at the end of May,
collected together a small mass of moss, then made an expedition
and returned laden with pollen; under cover of the moss a cell
was formed of wax taken from the hind-body and mixed with
the pollen the bee had brought in; this cell was fastened to a
piece of wood; when completed it formed a subspherical receptacle, the outer wall of which consisted of wax, and whose interior
was lined with honey-saturated pollen; then several eggs were
laid in this receptacle, and it was entirely closed.   Hoffer took
the completed cell away to use it for museum purposes, and the
following day the poor bee that had formed it died.   From
observations made on *Bombus agrorum* he was able to describe
the subsequent operations; these are somewhat as follows:—The
first cell being constructed, stored, and closed, the industrious
architect, clinging to the cell, takes a few days' rest, and after
this interval commences the formation of a second cell; this is
placed by the side of the first, to which it is connected by a
mixture of wax and pollen; the second cell being completed a
third may be formed; but the labours of the constructor about
this time are augmented by the hatching of the eggs deposited
a few days previously; for the young larvae, having soon disposed
of the small quantity of food in the interior of the waxen cell,
require feeding.   This operation is carried on by forming a small
opening in the upper part of the cell, through which the bee
conveys food to the interior by ejecting it from her mouth
through the hole; whether the food is conveyed directly to
the mouths of the larvae or not, Hoffer was unable to observe;
it being much more difficult to approach this royal founder
without disturbing her than it is the worker-bees that carry on
similar occupations at a subsequent period in the history of the

[1] *Mt. Ver. Steiermark*, xxxi. 1882, p. 69.

society. The larvae in the first cell, as they increase in size, apparently distend the cell in an irregular manner, so that it becomes a knobbed and rugged, truffle-like mass. The same thing happens with the other cells formed by the queen. Each of these larval masses contains, it should be noticed, sister-larvae all of one age; when full grown they pupate in the mass, and it is worthy of remark that although all the eggs in one larval mass were laid at the same time, yet the larvae do not all pupate simultaneously, neither do all the perfect Insects appear at once, even if all are of one sex. The pupation takes place in a cocoon that each larva forms for itself of excessively fine silk. The first broods hatched are formed chiefly, if not entirely, of workers, but small females may be produced before the end of the season. Huber and Schmiedeknecht state that though the queen provides the worker-cells with food before the eggs are placed therein, yet no food is put in the cells in which males and females are produced. The queen, at the time of pupation of the larvae, scrapes away the wax by which the cocoons are covered, thus facilitating the escape of the perfect Insect, and, it may also be, aiding the access of air to the pupa. The colony at first grows very slowly, as the queen can, unaided, feed only a small number of larvae. But after she receives the assistance of the first batch of workers much more rapid progress is made, the queen greatly restricting her labours, and occupying herself with the laying of eggs; a process that now proceeds more and more rapidly, the queen in some cases scarcely ever leaving the nest, and in others even becoming incapable of flight. The females produced during the inter-mediate period of the colony are smaller than the mother, but supplement her in the process of egg-laying, as also do the workers to a greater or less extent. The conditions that deter-mine the egg-laying powers of these small females and workers are apparently unknown, but it is ascertained that these powers vary greatly in different cases, so that if the true queen die the continuation of the colony is sometimes effectively carried on by these her former subordinates. In other cases, however, the reverse happens, and none of the inhabitants may be capable of producing eggs: in this event two conditions may be present; either larvae may exist in the nest, or they may be absent. In the former case the workers provide them with food, and the colony may thus still be continued; but in the latter case, there being no profitable occupation for the bees to follow, they spend the greater part of the time sitting at home in the nest.

Supposing all to go well with the colony it increases very greatly, but its prosperity is checked in the autumn; at this period large numbers of males are produced as well as new queens, and thereafter the colony comes to an end, only a few fertilised females surviving the winter, each one to commence for herself a new colony in the ensuing spring.

The interior of the nest of a bumble-bee (*Bombus*) frequently presents a very irregular appearance; this is largely owing to the fact that these bees do not use the cells as cradles twice, but form others as they may be required, on the old remains. The cells, moreover, are of different sizes, those that produce workers being the smallest, those that cradle females being the largest, while those in which males are reared are intermediate in size. Although the old cells are not used a second time for rearing brood they are nevertheless frequently adapted to the purposes of receptacles for pollen and for honey, and for these objects they may be increased in size and altered in form.

It may be gathered from various records that the period required to complete the development of the individual *Bombus* about midsummer is four weeks from the deposition of the egg to the emergence of the perfect Insect, but exact details and information as to whether this period varies with the sex of the Insect developed are not to be found. The records do not afford any reason for supposing that such distinction will be found to exist: the size of the cells appears the only correlation, suggested by the facts yet known, between the sex of the individual and the circumstances of development.

The colonies of *Bombus* vary greatly in prosperity, if we take as the test of this the number of individuals produced in a colony. They never, however, attain anything at all approaching to the vast number of individuals that compose a large colony of wasps, or that exist in the crowded societies of the more perfectly social bees. A populous colony of a subterranean *Bombus* may attain the number of 300 or 400 individuals. Those that dwell on the surface are as a rule much less populous, as they are less protected, so that changes of weather are more prejudicial to them. According to Smith, the average number of a colony of *B. muscorum* in the autumn in this country is about 120—viz. 25 females, 36 males, 59 workers. No mode of increasing the nests in a systematic manner exists in this genus; they do not place the cells in stories as the wasps do; and this is the case notwithstanding the fact that a cell is not twice used for the rearing of young. When the ground-space available for cell-building is filled the *Bombus* begins another series of cells on the ruins of the first one. From this reason old nests have a very irregular appearance, and this condition of seeming disorder is greatly increased by the very different sizes of the cells themselves. We have already alluded to some of these cells, more particularly to those of different capacities to suit the sexes of the individuals to be reared in them. In addition to these there are honey-tubs, pollen-tubs, and the cells of the *Psithyrus* (Fig. 23), the parasitic but friendly inmates of the *Bombus*-nests. A nest of *Bombus*, exhibiting the various pots projecting from the remains of empty and partially destroyed cells, presents, as may well be imagined, a very curious appearance. Some of the old cells apparently are partly destroyed for the sake of the material they are composed of. Others are formed into honey-tubs, of a make-shift nature. It must be recollected that, as a colony increases, stores of provisions become absolutely necessary, otherwise in bad weather the larvae could not be fed. In good weather, and when flowers abound, these bees collect and store honey in abundance; in addition to placing it in the empty pupa-cells, they also form for it special receptacles; these are delicate cells made entirely of wax filled with honey, and are always left open for the benefit of the community. The existence of these honey-tubs in bumble-bees' nests has become known to our country urchins, whose love for honey and for the sport of bee-baiting leads to wholesale destruction of the nests. According to Hoffer, special tubs for the storing of pollen are sometimes formed; these are much taller than the other cells. The *Psithyrus* that live in the nests with the *Bombus* are generally somewhat larger than the latter, and consequently their cells may be distinguished in the nests by their larger size. A bumble-bees' nest, composed of all these heterogenous chambers rising out of the ruins of former layers of cells, presents a scene of such apparent disorder that many have declared that the bumble-bees do not know how to build.

Although the species of *Bombus* are not comparable with the hive-bee in respect of the perfection and intelligent nature of their work, yet they are very industrious Insects, and the construction of the dwelling-places of the subterranean species is said to be carried out in some cases with considerable skill, a dome of wax being formed as a sort of roof over the brood cells. Some work even at night. Fea has recorded the capture of a species in Upper Burmah working by moonlight, and the same industry may be observed in this country if there be sufficient heat as well as light. Godart, about 200 years ago, stated that a trumpeter-bee is kept in some nests to rouse the denizens to work in the morning : this has been treated as a fable by subsequent writers, but is confirmed in a circumstantial manner by Hoffer, who observed the performance in a nest of *B. ruderatus* in his laboratory. On the trumpeter being taken away its office was the following morning filled by another individual. The trumpeting was done as early as three or four o'clock in the morning, and it is by no means impossible that the earliness of the hour may have had something to do with the fact that for 200 years no one confirmed the old naturalist's observation.

One of the most curious facts in connection with *Bombus* is the excessive variation that many of the species display in the colour of the beautiful hair with which they are so abundantly provided. There is not only usually a difference between the sexes in this respect, but also extreme variation within the limits of the same sex, more especially in the case of the males and workers ; there is also an astonishing difference in the size of individuals. These variations are carried to such an extent that it is almost impossible to discriminate all the varieties of a species by inspection of the superficial characters. The structures peculiar to the male, as well as the sting of the female, enable the species to be determined with tolerable certainty. Cholodkovsky,[1] on whose authority this statement as to the sting is made, has not examined it in the workers, so that we do not know whether it is as invariable in them as he states it to be in queens of the same species. According to Handlirsch,[2] each

---

[1] *Zool. Anz.* vii. 1884, p. 312.
[2] *SB. Ges. Wien.* xxxviii. 1888, p. 34.

species of *Bombus* has the capacity of variation, and many of the varieties are found in one nest, that is, among the offspring of a single pair of the species, but many of the variations are restricted to certain localities. Some of the forms can be considered as actual (" fertige ") species, intermediate forms not being found, and even the characters by which species are recognised being some-what modified. As examples of this he mentions *Bombus silvarum* and *B. arenicola, B. pratorum* and *B. scrimshiranus.* In other cases, however, the varieties are not so discontinuous, intermediate forms being numerous; this condition is more common than the one we have previously described; *B. terrestris, B. hortorum, B. lapidarius* and *B. pomorum* are examples of these variable species. The variation runs to a considerable extent in parallel lines in the different species, there being a dark and a light form of each; also each species that has a white termination to the body appears in a form with a red termination, and *vice versâ.* In the Caucasus many species that have everywhere else yellow bands possess them white; and in Corsica there are species that are entirely black, with a red termination to the body, though in continental Europe the same species exhibit yellow bands and a white ter-mination to the body. With so much variation it will be readily believed that much remains to be done in the study of this fascinating genus. It is rich in species in the Northern hemi-sphere, but poor in the Southern one, and in both the Ethiopian and Australian regions it is thought to be entirely wanting.

The species of the genus *Psithyrus* (*Apathus* of many authors) inhabit the nests of *Bombus;* although less numerous than the species of the latter genus, they also are widely distributed. They are so like *Bombus* in appearance that they were not distinguished from them by the earlier entomologists; and what is still more remarkable, each species of *Psithyrus* resembles the *Bombus* with which it usually lives. There appear, however, to be occasional exceptions to this rule, Smith having seen one of the yellow-banded *Psithyrus* in the nest of a red-tailed *Bombus.* *Psithyrus* is chiefly distinguished from *Bombus* by the absence of certain characters that fit the latter Insects for their industrial life; the hind tibiae have no smooth space for the conveyance of pollen, and, so far as is known, there are only two sexes, males and per-fect females. The *Bombus* and *Psithyrus* live together on the best terms, and it appears probable that the latter do the former no harm beyond appropriating a portion of their food supplies. Schmiedeknecht says they are commensals, not parasites; but it must be admitted that singularly few descriptions of the habits and life-histories of these interesting Insects have been recorded.

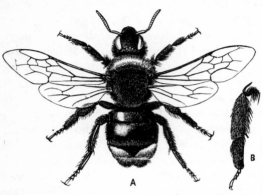

FIG. 23.—*Psithyrus vestalis*, Britain. **A**, Female, × ¾; **B**, outer side of hind leg.

Hoffer has, however, made a few direct observations which confirm, and at the same time make more definite, the vague ideas that have been generally prevalent among entomologists. He found and took home a nest of *Bombus variabilis*, which contained also a female of *Psithyrus campestris*, so that he was able to make observations on the two. The *Psithyrus* was much less industrious than the *Bombus*, and only left the nest somewhat before noon, returning home again towards evening; after about a month this specimen became still more inactive, and passed entire days in the nest, occupying itself in consuming the stores of honey of its hosts, of which very large quantities were absorbed, the *Psithyrus* being much larger than the host-bee. The cells in which the young of the *Psithyrus* are hatched are very much larger than those of the *Bombus*, and, it may therefore be presumed, are formed by the *Psithyrus* itself, for it can scarcely be supposed that the *Bombus* carries its complaisance so far as to construct a cell specially adapted to the superior stature of its uninvited boarder. When a *Psithyrus* has been for some time a regular inhabitant of a nest, the *Bombus* take its return home from time to time as a matter of course, displaying no emotion whatever at its entry. Occasionally Hoffer tried the introduction of a *Psithyrus* to a nest that had not previously had one as an inmate. The new arrival caused a great hubbub among the *Bombus*, which rushed to it as if to attack it, but did not do so, and the alarm soon subsided, the *Psithyrus* taking up the position in the nest usually affected by the individuals of the species. On introducing a female *Psithyrus* to a nest of *Bombus* in which a *Psithyrus* was already present as an established guest, the latter asserted its rights and drove away the new comer. Hoffer also tried the experiment of placing a *Psithyrus campestris* in the nest of *Bombus lapidarius*—a species to which it was a stranger; notwithstanding its haste to fly away, it was at once attacked by the *Bombus*, who pulled it about but did not attempt to sting it.

When *Psithyrus* is present in a nest of *Bombus* it apparently affects the inhabitants only by diminishing their stores of food to so great an extent that the colony remains small instead of largely increasing in numbers. Although *Bombus variabilis*, when left to itself, increases the number of individuals in a colony to 200 or more, Hoffer found in a nest in which *Psithyrus* was present, that on the 1st of September the assemblage consisted only of a queen *Bombus* and fifteen workers, together with eighteen specimens of the *Psithyrus*, eight of these being females.

The nests of *Bombus* are destroyed by several animals, probably for the sake of the honey contained in the pots; various kinds of small mammals, such as mice, the weasel, and even the fox, are known to destroy them; and quite a fauna of Insects may be found in them; the relations of these to their hosts are very little known, but some undoubtedly destroy the bees' larvae, as in the case of *Meloe, Mutilla* and *Conops*. Birds do not as a rule attack these bees, though the bee-eater, *Merops apiaster*, has been known to feed on them very heavily.

The genera of social bees known as *Melipona, Trigona* or *Tetragona*, may, according to recent authorities, be all included in one genus, *Melipona*. Some of these Insects are amongst the smallest of bees, so that one, or more, species go by the name of "Mosquitobees." The species appear to be numerous, and occur in most of the tropical parts of the continents of the world, but unfortunately very little is known as to their life-histories or economics; they are said to form communities consisting at times of a countless number of individuals; but it has not been thoroughly ascertained whether these are the produce of a single queen, as in the case of the hive-bee, or whether there may be more than one egg-producer in each community. The late F. Smith thought the former of these alternatives would prove to be correct. These mosquito-bees are frequently spoken of as stingless bees, but this is not quite correct, for although they do not sting,

von Ihering[1] says that all the essential elements of the sting
are present, the pointed or penetrating part of the apparatus
being stunted.

It would serve no useful purpose to attempt to construct the
social history of these stingless bees from the numerous brief
scattered accounts in entomological literature, for they refer to
different species; it is, however, positively stated by Smith on the
authority of Peckolt[2] that *Trigona mosquito* sends off swarms after
the manner of the hive-bee in this country, and that after search-
ing six hives only one royal female could be found in each.

The nests of many of these little bees are rich in honey, and
they have a host of enemies from man and monkeys downwards;

FIG. 24.—*Melipona* sp. ♀.   Amazons.

and as they do not defend
themselves by stinging, it might
be supposed they would have
but a poor time of it. From
the accounts that have been
published we may, however,
gather that they are rich in
devices for the protection of
their nests, and for the exclusion of intruders. Bates has
given some particulars as to
Melipona interrupta (*fasciculata*); it is about one-third
shorter than the hive-bee, and its colonies are composed of an immense number of individuals. The workers are usually occupied
in gathering pollen; but they also collect clay in a similar manner,
and convey it to the nest, where it is used for building a wall to
complete the fortification of the nest, which is placed either in a
suitable bank, or in a trunk of a tree; in either situation it is
completely built in with clay. A nest which Bates saw opened
contained about two quarts of pleasantly-tasted liquid honey.
Forty-five species of these little bees were found in different
parts of the Amazons Valley, the largest kind being half an inch
in length, the smallest very minute, not more than one-twelfth
of an inch. These little creatures are thus masons as well
as workers in wax and resin, and they are also gatherers of
nectar, pollen, and resin.

[1] *Ent. Nachr.* xii. 1886, p. 177.   [2] *Tr. ent. Soc. London*, 1868, p. 133.

According to Gosse, one of these bees is well known in Jamaica, where they are called " Angelitos," in consquence of their not stinging people. He observed a nest of this bee in a tree, and found it to be much infested by black ants anxious to obtain entrance to it ; three bees, however, stood sentinel in the entrance, so as to completely block it and keep out intruders, but the middle bee moved on one side out of the way directly one of its fellows wished to come in or out of the nest. The honey accumulated by this species is kept in clusters of cups about the size of a pigeon's egg, at the bottom of the hive and away from the brood-cells. The queen or mother-bee is lighter in colour than the others, and has the hind body twice the length of theirs.

Hockings [1] has given us some details as to the natural history of two of these bees that inhabit Australia, where they are called " Karbi " and " Kootchar," the first being, it is supposed, *Trigona carbonaria*, Smith : it is usually about three-sixteenths of an inch in length, the queen, when fully developed, being nearly twice that length. The comb is built in a most peculiar form, being, it is said, in the shape of a spiral staircase, and tapering towards the ends : honey-pots and pollen are constructed for the storage of food. The comb is encased in wax, and outside it a labyrinth of waxen passages is formed. The entrance to the colony is guarded by a line of bees who inspect every one that arrives, and it is surprising to see how soon a stranger is discovered and pounced upon before it has time even to alight ; the intruder, when caught, is held by several bees, who put it on the rack by holding and stretching out its limbs to their full extent, retaining it in this position for as long as an hour, by which time the unfortunate prisoner is usually dead. These bees, as well as many other allied species, fight desperately with their mandibles, and are apparently of a very fierce disposition. The other species, called " Kootchar," is said to produce a very large number of drones, and the habits and dispositions of the bees differ considerably from those of the " Karbi " : the entrance to their hive is guarded by a pipe of propolis (a sort of resinous wax) about an inch in length, having an exceedingly sticky outer edge, and it is by this pipe alone that access to the interior can be gained. At night the entrance is closed by numerous minute globules of semi-fluid gum placed against it, thus forming a thin wall full of air-holes.

[1] *Tr. ent. Soc. London*, 1884, p. 149.

The colonies of " Kootchar " can be united by taking away a queen and then packing her brood-nest, bees and all, against that of the colony it is to be joined to. This cannot be done with the " Karbi." The account given by Mr. Hockings contains a great many other interesting details, and there can be no doubt that a full account of the natural history of these Insects would be very instructive.

Fritz Müller has recorded a singular case bearing on the instinct of these social Insects: he says that a nest of a small *Trigona* was built in a hollow tree, and that as a consequence of the irregularity of the hole the bees were obliged to give a very irregular shape to their combs of honey. These bees were captured and put in a spacious box (presumably together with the irregular comb, but this he unfortunately does not mention): after a year, " when perhaps not a single bee survived of those which had come from the canella tree," they still continued to build irregular combs, though quite regular combs were built by several other communities of the same species that he had kept. These bees, he also tells us, do not use pure wax for the construction of their combs, but mix it with resin or gum that gives it a peculiar odour and appearance. He captured two communities of a common *Melipona*, one of which had the combs made of dark reddish brown, the other of pale yellowish brown, wax, and in captivity in a distant locality each of the two communities continued to form its comb in the same way, thus showing the continuity that prevails in these cases as long as circumstances permit. Müller thinks this due to imitation, but it seems at least as probable that it is due to perception of the properties of the nest. The nest has a certain colour that the worker-bee matches.

Several species of the *Melipona* and *Trigona* were imported from Brazil to France, and kept there for some time in captivity by M. Drory. Girard has published [1] some details as to these colonies, and is of opinion that some of them indicate an intelligence or instinct superior to that of the honey-bee. The queen-bee of *M. scutellaris* seems to display more intelligence than the corresponding sex of *A. mellifica*. The mode of feeding the larvae apparently differs from that of *A. mellifica*, a provision of pollen being first placed in the cell, then some honey; when

---

[1] *Ann. Soc. ent. France* (5), iv. 1874, p. 567.

sufficient food for the whole consumption of a larva is accumulated the queen deposits an egg in the cell, which is at once completely closed by the worker. The interior of the abode of these bees is quite dark, only a very small orifice being left, and in this a sentinel is constantly on the alert. The same writer states that *Trigona crassipes* has the very peculiar habit of always locating its brood-comb in the nest of a species of *Termes*.

The honey-bee, *Apis mellifica* (Fig. 6), is considered the highest form attained by the Anthophilous division of the Hymenoptera. The differentiation of the three forms, male, female, and worker, is here carried to a greater degree of perfection than in the other bees. The drones are the males ; the individuals we see gathering honey are always workers, neither the male nor the female in this species taking any part in procuring food for themselves or for the colony. In addition to this the colonies formed may be described as permanent : they do not come to an end at the close of one season, and provision is made for the formation of a new colony while the old one still persists, by means of a peculiar process called swarming. The life-history of *Apis mellifica* and its anatomy and physiology have been discussed in a whole library of works, and we need only notice the chief features. When a swarm of bees leaves a hive it consists of the queen-bee or female, and a number of workers, these latter being, in fact, the surplus population that has been produced in the hive. The swarm is not a nuptial flight, as is often supposed, but an act of emigration. When this swarm has been housed, the bees commence operations in their new quarters, by secreting wax ; they are enabled to do this by having consumed much saccharine food ; the wax is produced by means of glands in the hind-body over the inner faces of the ventral plates of the abdominal rings, and it makes its appearance there, after passing from the interior of the body through some peculiar membranes on the ventral segments, in the form of thin projecting plates. These the bee takes off with an apparatus on the hind pair of legs and applies, after working up with the mandibles, to form the cells in which young ones are to be reared and food stored. A large number of bees working in common thus produce the regular and beautiful structure known as the comb ; the queen afterwards lays an egg in each cell, and as these soon hatch, great labour is thrown on the workers, which have then to feed the young ; this they do by eating honey and pollen, which, being formed into a sort of pap by a portion of their digestive organs, is then regurgitated and given to the young, a quantity of it being placed in the cell, so that the larva is bathed by it, and possibly may absorb the food by the skin as well as the mouth. When the colony is in good progress and young bees emerge, these act as nurses, the older ones cease to prepare food and act as foragers, bringing in honey and pollen which are each stored in separate cells. The larva in the cell increases its size and sheds a very delicate skin several times; when the larva has reached its full size no more food is supplied, but the worker-bees seal up the cell by means of a cover formed of pollen and wax, in such a manner as to be pervious to air: sealed up in the cell the larva spins a cocoon for itself, remains therein for a little time as a larva, then changes to a pupa, and thereafter bites its way out through the cover of the cell, and appears for the first time as a new being in the form of a worker-bee; the whole process of development from the egg-state to the perfect condition of the worker-bee occupies about three weeks.

When the denizens of a hive are about to produce another queen, one or more royal cells are formed; these are much larger than the ordinary worker-cells, and of a quite different form. In this cell is placed an egg, not differing in any respect from the egg that, if placed in an ordinary cell, produces a worker; when the egg has produced a larva this is tended with great care and fed throughout its life with royal jelly. This food appears to be the same as that supplied to an ordinary worker-larva when it is first hatched; but there is this difference, that whereas the worker-larva is weaned, and supplied, after the first period of its existence, with food consisting largely of honey, pollen and water, the queen-larva is supplied with the pap or royal jelly until it is full grown. Some difference of opinion exists as to this royal jelly, some thinking that it is a different substance from what the workers are fed with; and it is by no means improbable that there may be some difference in the secretion of the glands that furnish a part of the material composing the pap. The queen is produced more rapidly than workers are, about sixteen days being occupied in the process of her development. Only one queen is allowed in a hive at a time; so that when several queen-cells are formed, and queen-larvae nurtured in them, the first one that is developed into a perfect queen goes round and stings the royal nymphs to death while they are still in their cells. The production of drones is supposed to depend chiefly on the nature of the egg laid by the queen; it being considered that an unfertilised egg is deposited for this purpose. There is still some doubt on this point, however. Though there is no doubt that drones are produced in great numbers from unfertilised eggs, yet there is not evidence that they cannot also be produced from fertilised eggs.[1] The drone-cells are somewhat larger than the ordinary worker-cells, but this is probably not of much import, and it is said that the larvae intended to produce drones receive a greater proportion of pap than worker-larvae do: about twenty-four days are required to produce a drone from the egg.

From this sketch it will be seen that the production of the worker (or third sex, as it is improperly called, the workers being really females atrophied in some points and specially developed in others) is dependent on the social life, in so far at any rate as the special feeding is concerned. There is good reason for supposing that *A. mellifica* has been kept in a state of domestication or captivity for an enormous period of time; and this condition has probably led to an increase of its natural peculiarities, or perhaps we should say to a change in them to suit a life of confinement. This is certainly the case in regard to swarming, for this process takes place with comparative irregularity in *Apis mellifica* in a wild condition. The killing of superfluous queens is also probably a phenomenon of captivity, for it varies even now in accordance with the numbers of the colony. It is interesting to notice that in confinement when a swarm goes from the hive it is the old queen that accompanies it, and this swarm as a rule settles down near the old hive, so that the queen-bee being already fertilised, the new swarm and its subsequent increase are nothing but a division of the old hive, the total products of the two having but a single father and mother. When a second swarm goes off from a hive it is accompanied by a young queen, who frequently, perhaps, in the majority of cases, is unfertilised; this swarm is apt to fly for long distances, so that the probability of cross-fertilisation is

[1] See Pérez, *Act. Soc. Bordeaux*, xxxiii. 1880, p. lxv.; and Cameron, *Tr. Soc. Glasgow*, n. s. ii. 1889, p. 194.

greatly increased, as the fertilisation of the young new queen is effected during a solitary flight she makes after the colony has settled down.   But in a state of nature the colonies do not send off swarms every year or once a year, but increase to an enormous extent, going for years without swarming, and then when their home is really filled up send off, it may be presumed, a number of swarms in one year.   Thus the phenomena of bee-life in a wild condition differ considerably from those we see in artificial confinement.   And this difference is probably greatly accentuated by the action of parasites, the proportions of which to their guests are in a state of nature liable to become very great; as we have seen to be the case in *Bombus*.

Under these circumstances it is not a matter for surprise when we find that the honey-bee has formed distinct races analogous to those that exist in the case of the domesticated vertebrate animals.   The knowledge of these races is, however, at present very little advanced, and is complicated by the fact that only imperfect information exists as to the true species of the genus *Apis*.   There is a bee very like our common honey-bee found in southern Europe called *A. ligustica;* this is certainly a variety of *A. mellifica*, and the same remark applies to a bee found in Egypt, and called *A. fasciata*.   This gives the honey-bee a very wide distribution, extending possibly over the whole of the palaearctic region : besides this, the species has been introduced into various other parts of the world.

According to Karsch the honey-bee shows in Germany several varieties, all of which belong to the northern form, which may be spoken of as the *A. domestica* of Ray ; the *A. ligustica* and *A. fasciata* form as we have said distinct races, and it is a remarkable fact that these races remain distinct even when imported into other climates ; though for how long a period of time this remains true there is very little evidence to show.   The northern form, *A. domestica*, is now found in very widely separated parts of the world, in some of which it is wild ; Smith mentions it as occurring in the West India islands, throughout the North American continent as far south as Mexico, even in Central and Southern Africa, and in Australia and New Zealand.   The var. *ligustica* has been found also at the Cape of Good Hope.   The other species known of the genus *Apis* all belong to the Old World, so that there is very little doubt that *A. mellifica* is also a true native of the eastern hemisphere, and its original home may possibly have been not far from the shores of the eastern portion of the Mediterranean sea.   Seven or eight other species of *Apis* are known, all but one of which occur in Asia, extending as far as Timor and Celebes.   The exceptional one, *A. adansonii,* occurs in tropical Africa and in Madagascar.   Gerstaecker thought these species might be reduced to four, but Smith's statement that the males and even the workers show good distinctive characters seems to be correct. Very little is known as to the honey-bees of China and Japan.

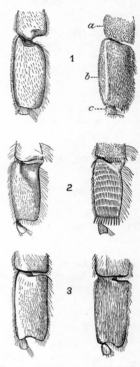

The queen-bee greatly resembles the worker, but has the hind body more elongated; she can, however, always be distinguished from the worker by the absence of the beautiful transverse, comb-like series of hairs on the inner side of the first joint of the hind foot, the planta, as it is called by the bee-keeper: she has also no wax plates and differs in important anatomical peculiarities.   The male bee or drone is very different, being of much broader, more robust build, and with very large eyes that quite meet in the middle of the upper part of the head: he also has the hind leg differently shaped.   The form of this limb enables the male of *A. mellifica* to be distinguished from the corresponding sex of allied species of the genus.

FIG. 25.—Portions of hind-feet, 1, of male, 2, of worker, 3, of queen, of the honey-bee; series on the left, outer faces; on the right, inner faces.   *a,* Tip of tibia: *b,* first joint; *c,* second joint of tarsus.

We are indebted to Horne for some particulars as to the habits of *A. dorsata,* an allied East Indian species.   He informs us that these bees greatly disfigure buildings, such as the Taj Mahal at Agra, by attaching their pendent combs to the marble arches, and are so pertinacious that it is almost useless to destroy the nests.   This bee is said to be so savage in its disposition that it cannot be domesticated; it attacks the sparingly clad Hindoos with great ferocity when they disturb its nest. Notwithstanding its inclination and power to defend its societies this Insect appears to be destroyed wholesale. Colonel Ramsay failed to establish hives of it, because the Insects were eaten up by lizards. The crested honey-buzzard carries off large portions of the comb, and devours it on a branch of some tree near by, quite regardless of the stings of the bees; while the fondness of bears for the honey of the " Dingar," as this species is called, is well known.

NOTE TO P. 33 : It has just been discovered that a most remarkable symbiosis, with structural modification of the bee, exists between the females of *Xylocopa*, of the Oriental sub-genus *Koptorthosoma*, and certain Acarids. A special chamber, with a small orifice for entry, exists in the abdomen of the bee, and in this the Acari are lodged.—See Perkins, *Ent. Mag.* xxxv. 1899, p. 37.

NOTE TO P. 80 : referring to the habits of social wasps in warm countries. The anticipation we ventured to indulge in is shown to be correct by the recent observations of Von Ihering.[1] He states that social wasps in Brazil may be divided into two great groups by their habits, viz. 1. Summer communities, lasting for one year, and founded annually by fertilised females that have hibernated—example, *Polistes ;* 2. Perennial communities, founded by swarms after the fashion of bee colonies—examples, *Polybia, Chartergus.*

[1] *Ann. Nat. Hist.* (6), xix. 1897, p. 136.

NOTE TO VOL. V. PP. 545, 546 : The development of *Encyrtus fuscicollis* has now been studied by Marchal, who has discovered the existence of embryonic dissociation. The chain of embryos and the epithelial tube in which they are placed, are formed as follows : the *Encyrtus* deposits an egg in the interior of the egg of the *Hyponomeuta*. This does not kill the egg of the Lepidopteron, but becomes included in the resulting caterpillar. The amnion of the Chalcid egg lengthens, and forms the epithelial tube ; while the cells within it become dissociated in such a way as to give rise to a chain of embryos, instead of a single embryo.—*C.R. Ac. Paris*, cxxvi. 1898, p. 662, and translation in *Ann. Nat. Hist.* (7), ii. 1898, p. 28.

CHAPTER II

Division II. Diploptera—Wasps.

Anterior wings longitudinally plicate in repose; the pronotum extending back, so as to form on each side an angle reposing on the tegula; the basal segments of the hind body not bearing nodes or scales; the hind tarsi formed for simple walking. The species either solitary or social in their habits; some existing in three forms, males, females, and workers.

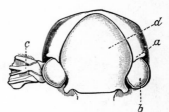

FIG. 26.—Upper aspect of pronotum and mesonotum of a wasp, *Eumenes coarctata*. *a*, Angle of pronotum ; *b*, tegula ; *c*, base of wing ; *d*, mesonotum.

THIS division of Hymenoptera includes the true wasps, but not the fossorial wasps. The name applied to it has been suggested by the fact that the front wings become doubled in the long direction when at rest, so as to make them appear narrower than in most other Aculeata (Fig. 27). This character is unimportant in function so far as we know,[1] and it is not quite constant in the division, since some of the Masaridae do not exhibit it. The character reappears outside the Diploptera in the genus *Leucospis* —a member of the Chalcididae in the parasitic series of Hymenoptera—the species of which greatly resemble wasps in coloration. A better character is that furnished by the well-marked angle,

[1] Janet has suggested that the folding is done to keep the delicate hind-margins of the wings from being frayed.

formed by the pronotum on the dorsal part (Fig. 26). By a glance at this part a Diplopterous Insect can always be readily distinguished.

Three families are at present distinguished in the Diploptera, viz. Eumenidae, Vespidae and Masaridae. We anticipate that Eumenidae and Vespidae will ultimately be found to constitute but one family.

Fam. 1. Eumenidae—Solitary True Wasps.

Claws of the feet toothed or bifid; middle tibiae with only one spur at tip. Social assemblages are not formed, and there is no worker-caste, the duties of nest-construction, etc., being performed solely by the female.

The Eumenidae, or solitary wasps, are very little noticed by the ordinary observer, but they are nevertheless more numerous than the social Vespidae, about 800 species being known. In Britain we have sixteen species of the solitary, as against seven of the social wasps. The Eumenidae exhibit a considerable diversity in form and structure; some of them have the pedicel at the base of the abdomen very elongate, while in others this is so short as to be imperceptible in the ordinary position of the body. A repetition of similar differences of form occurs in the social wasps, so that notwithstanding the difference in habits there seems to be no satisfactory way of distinguishing the members of the two families except by the structure of the claws and tibial spurs.

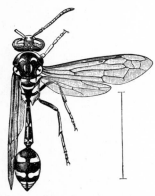

Fig. 27.—*Eumenes flavopicta* ♀. Burma. The wings on the left in the position of repose, to show folding.

Fabre has sketched the habits of a species of *Eumenes*, probably *E. pomiformis*. This *Eumenes* constructs with clay a small vase-like earthenware vessel, in the walls of which small stones are embedded (like Fig. 28, B). This it fills with food for the young. The food consists of caterpillars to the number of fourteen or sixteen for each nest. These caterpillars are believed to be stung by the parent-wasp (as is the case in the fossorial Hymenoptera), but complete evidence of this does not seem to be extant, and if it be so, the stinging does not completely deprive the caterpillars of the capacity of movement, for they possess the power of using their mandibles and of making strokes, or kicking with the posterior part of the body. It is clear that if the delicate egg of the *Eumenes* or the delicate larva that issues from it were placed in the midst of a mass of this kind, it would probably suffer destruction ; therefore, to prevent this, the egg is not placed among the caterpillars, but is suspended from the dome covering the nest by a delicate thread rivalling in fineness the web of the spider, and being above the mass of food it is safe. When the young larva leaves the egg it still makes use of the shell as its habitation, and eats its first meals from the vantage-point of this suspension ; although the mass of the food grows less by consumption, the little larva is still enabled to reach it by the fact that the eggshell splits up to a sort of ribbon,

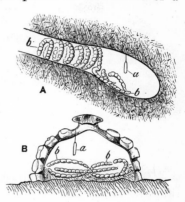

FIG. 28.—Nidification of solitary wasps : section through nest, **A**, of *Odynerus reniformis ;* **B**, of *Eumenes arbustorum*. *a*, The suspended egg of the wasp ; *b*, the stored caterpillars. (After André.)

and thus adds to the length of the suspensory thread, of which it is the terminal portion. Finally the heap of caterpillars shrinks so much that it cannot be reached by the larva even with the aid of the augmented length of the suspensory thread ; by this time, however, the little creature has so much increased in size and strength that it is able to take its place amongst the food without danger of being crushed by the mass, and it afterwards completes its metamorphosis in the usual manner.

It is known that other species of *Eumenes* construct vase-like nests ; *E. unguiculata*, however, according to an imperfect account given by Perris, makes with earth a closed nest of irregular shape, containing three cells in one mass. The saliva of these builders has the power of acting as a cement, and of forming with the clay a very impenetrable material. One species, *E. coarctata*, L. of this genus occurs in Britain. The clay nests (Fig. 29) of this Insect are often attached to the twigs of shrubs, while those of the two species previously mentioned are

usually placed on objects that offer a large surface for fixing the foundations to, such as walls. According to Goureau the larva of this species forms in one corner of its little abode, separated by a partition, a sort of dust-heap in which it accumulates the various débris resulting from the consumption of its stores.

FIG. 29. — Nest of *Eumenes coarctata :* **A**, the nest attached to wood : **B**, detached, showing the larva. *a*, the larva ; *b*, the partition of the cell. (After André.)

Eumenes conica, according to Horne, constructs in Hindostan clay-nests with very delicate walls. This species provisions its nest with ten or twelve green caterpillars ; on cne occasion this observer took from one cell eight green caterpillars and one black. It is much attacked by parasites owing, it is thought, to the delicacy of the walls of the cells, which are easily pierced ; from one group of five cells two specimens only of the *Eumenes* were reared.

Odynerus, with numerous sub-genera, the names of which are often used as those of distinct genera, includes the larger part of the solitary wasps ; it is very widely distributed over the earth, and is represented by many peculiar species even in the isolated Archipelago of Hawaii ; in Britain we have about fifteen species of the genus. The *Odynerus* are less accomplished architects than the species of *Eumenes,* and usually play the more humble parts of adapters and repairers ; they live either in holes in walls, or in posts or other woodwork, or in burrows in the earth, or in stems of plants. Several species of the sub-genus *Hoplopus* have the remarkable habit of constructing burrows in sandy ground, and forming at their entry a curvate, freely projecting tube placed at right angles to the main burrow, and formed of the grains of sand brought out by the Insect during excavation and cemented together. The habits of one such species were described by Réaumur, of another by Dufour ; and recently Fabre has added to the accounts of these naturalists some important information drawn from his own

observations on *O. reniformis*. This Insect provisions its cell
with small caterpillars to the number of twenty or upwards (Fig.
28, A.) The egg is deposited before the nest is stocked with food;
it is suspended in such a manner that the suspensory thread
allows the egg to reach well down towards the bottom of the
cell. The caterpillars placed as food in the nest are all curled
up, each forming a ring approximately adapted to the calibre of
the cell. Fabre believes these caterpillars to be partly stupefied
by stinging, but the act has not been observed either by himself,
Réaumur, or Dufour. The first caterpillar is eaten by the wasp-
larva from its point of suspension ; after this first meal has been
made the larva is supposed to undergo a change of skin ; it then

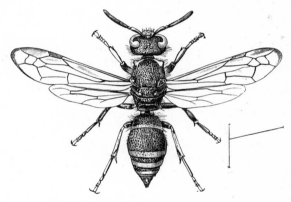

Fig. 30.—*Odynerus antilope* ♀. Britain.

abandons the assistance of the suspensory thread, taking up a
position in the vacant chamber at the end of the cell and drawing the caterpillars to itself one by one. This arrangement
permits the caterpillars to be consumed in the order in which
they were placed in the cell, so that the one that is weakest on
account of its longer period of starvation is first devoured.
Fabre thinks all the above points are essential to the successful
development of this wasp-larva, the suspension protecting the egg
and the young larva from destruction by pressure or movement
of the caterpillars, while the position of the larva when it leaves
the thread and takes its place on the floor of the cell ensures its
consuming the food in the order of introduction ; besides this the
caterpillars used are of a proper size and of a species the

individuals of which have the habit of rolling themselves up in a ring ; while, as the calibre of the tube is but small, they are unable to straighten themselves and move about, so that their consumption in proper order is assured. Some interesting points in the habits of an allied species, *O. (Pterocheilus) spinipes* have been observed by Verhoeff ; the facts as regards the construction and provisioning of the cell are almost the same as in *O. reniformis.* The species of *Odynerus* are very subject to the attacks of parasites, and are, it is well known, destroyed to an enormous extent by Chrysididae. Verhoeff says that the wasp in question supplied food much infested by entoparasites ; further, that a fly, *Argyromoeba sinuata,* takes advantage of the habit of the *Odynerus* of leaving its nest open during the process of provisioning, and deposits also an egg in the nest ; the *Odynerus* seems, however, to have no power of discovering the fact, or more probably has no knowledge of its meaning, and so concludes the work of closing the cell in the usual way ; the egg of the *Argyromoeba* hatches, and the maggot produced feeds on the caterpillars the wasp intended for its own offspring. Verhoeff observed that the egg of the wasp-larva is destroyed, but he does not know whether this was done by the mother *Argyromoeba* or by the larva hatched from her egg. Fabre's observations on allied species of Diptera render it, however, highly probable that the destruction is effected by the young fly-larva and not by the mother-fly.

Mr. R. C. L. Perkins once observed several individuals of our British *O. callosus* forming their nests in a clay bank, and provisioning them with larvae, nearly all of which were parasitised, and that to such an extent as to be evident both to the eye and the touch. In a few days after the wasps' eggs were laid, swarms of the minute parasites emerged and left no food for the *Odynerus.* Curiously, as it would seem, certain of the parasitised and stored-up larvae attempted (as parasitised larvae not infrequently do), to pupate. From which, as Mr. Perkins remarks, we may infer that (owing to distortion) the act of paralysing by the wasp had been ineffectual. Mr. Perkins has also observed that some of the numerous species of Hawaiian *Odynerus* make a single mud-cell, very like the pot of an *Eumenes,* but cylindrical instead of spherical. This little vessel is often placed in a leaf that a spider curls up ; young molluscs of the genus *Achatinella* also avail themselves of this shelter, so that a curious colony is formed, consisting of the *Odynerus* in its pot, of masses of the young spiders, and of the little molluscs.

Horne has recorded that the East Indian *O. punctum* is fond of availing itself of holes in door-posts where large screws have been; after the hole has been filled with provisions, the orifice is covered over level with the surface of the wood so that it eludes human observation. It is nevertheless discovered by an Ichneumon-fly which pierces the covering with its ovipositor and deposits an egg within.

The genus *Abispa* is peculiar to Australia and includes some very fine solitary wasps, having somewhat the appearance of very large *Odynerus:* these Insects construct a beautiful nest with a projecting funnel-shaped entrance, and of so large a size that it might pass for the habitation of a colony of social wasps; it appears, however, that this large nest is really formed by a single female.

The species of the genus *Rhygchium* are also of insecticide habits, and appear to prefer the stems of pithy plants as the nidus for the development of the generation that is to follow them. Lichtenstein says that a female of the European *R. oculatum* forms fifteen to twenty cells in such a situation, and destroys 150 to 200 caterpillars, and he suggests that, as it is easy to encourage these wasps to nest in a suitable spot, we should utilise them to free our gardens from caterpillars, as we do cats to clear the mice from our apartments.

The East Indian *R. carnaticum* seems to have very similar habits to its European congener, adapting for its use the hollow stems of bamboos. Horne has recorded a case in which a female of this species took possession of a stem in which a bee, *Megachile lanata*, had already constructed two cells; it first formed a partition of mud over the spot occupied by the bee, this partition being similar to that which it makes use of for separating the spaces intended for its own young. This species stores caterpillars for the benefit of its larvae, and this is also the case with another Eastern species, *R. nitidulum*. This latter Insect, however, does not nidificate in the stems of plants, but constructs clay cells similar to those of *Eumenes*, and fixes them firmly to wood. *Rhygchium brunneum* is said by Sir Richard Owen to obliterate hieroglyphic inscriptions in Egypt by its habit of building mud nests amongst them. An individual of this wasp was found by Dr. Birch when unrolling a mummy—"There being every reason to believe that the Insect had remained in the position in which it was found ever since the last rites were paid to the ancient Egyptian."

Fam. 2. Vespidae—Social Wasps.

Claws of the feet simple, neither toothed nor bifid, middle tibiae with two spurs at the tip. Insects living in societies, forming a common dwelling of a papery or card-like material ; each generation consists of males and females and of workers —imperfect females—that assist the reproductive female by carrying on the industrial occupations.

The anterior wing possesses four submarginal cells, as in the Eumenidae. The attention of entomologists has been more directed to the habits and architecture than to the taxonomy of these Insects, so that the external structure of the Insects themselves has not been so minutely or extensively scrutinised as is desirable ; de Saussure, the most important authority, bases his classification of the Insects themselves on the nature of the nests they form. These habitations consist of an envelope, protecting cells similar in form to the comb of the honey-bee, but there is this important difference between the two, that while the bee forms its comb of wax that it secretes, the wasps make use of paper or card that they form from fragments of vegetable tissue, —more particularly woody fibre—amalgamated by means of cement secreted by glands ; the vegetable fragments are obtained by means of the mandibles, the front legs playing a much less important part in the economy of the Vespidæ than they do in that of the bees and fossorial Hymenoptera.

In most of the nests of Vespidæ the comb is placed in stages or stories one above the other, and separated by an intervening space, but in many cases there is only one mass of comb. It is the rule that, when the cells of the comb are only partially formed, eggs are deposited in them, and that the larva resulting from the egg is fed and tended by the mother, or by her assistants, the workers ; as the larvae grow, the cells are increased in correspondence with the size of the larva; the subsequent metamorphosis to pupa and imago taking place in the cells after they have been entirely

closed.   The food supplied is of a varied nature according to
the species, being either animal or vegetable, or both.

Although the nests of the social wasps are very elaborate constructions, yet they serve the purposes of the Insects for only a
single season.   This is certainly the case in our own country.
Here each nest is commenced by a single female or queen; she
at first performs unaided all the duties for the inauguration of

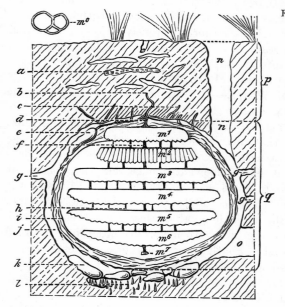

FIG. 31.—Section of the subterranean nest of the common wasp, *Vespa germanica*, in position. (After Janet.) *a*, One of the chambers of an ant's nest, *Lasius flavus*, placed above the wasps' nest; *b*, root to which the first attachment of the nest was made; *c*, secondary attachments; *d*, the first-made attachment; *e*, a flint within the envelopes of the nest; *f*, the chief suspensory pillar of the second layer of comb; *g*, lateral galleries; *h*, one of the secondary pillars of suspension between two layers of comb; *i*, the layers of wasp-paper forming the envelope of nest; *j*, vacant space round the nest; *k*, flints that fell to the bottom during the work of excavation; *l*, numerous larvae of a fly, *Pegomyia inanis* (?) placed vertically in ground beneath the nest; m^1 to m^7, the layers of comb, in m^2 the cells are indicated, in m^8 (above the main figure) the arrangement of the three cells forming the commencement of the new layer of comb, m^7, is shown; *n*, gallery of access from surface; *o*, burrow of a mole; *p*, interval of 90 mm. between top of nest and surface; *q*, height of the nest, 163 mm.

the colony; she lays the foundation of the cells, deposits the
eggs in them, feeds the young, and thus rears a brood of workers
that at once assist her, and for the future relieve her of a considerable portion of her former occupations; the nest is by them
added to and increased, till the cold weather of the autumn is at
hand; at this time many males and females are produced; the
cold weather either destroys the inhabitants of the nest, or reduces their vitality so that it is impossible for them to pursue
successfully the avocations necessary for their subsistence, and

they succumb to adversity.   The young females, however, hibernate, and each one that lives through the winter is the potential
founder of a new nest in the way we have already described.   It
might be supposed that in tropical countries where no cold
season occurs the phenomena would be different, that the colonies
would be permanent, and that the nests would be inhabited until
they were worn out.   De Saussure, however, informs us that this
is not the case, but that in the tropics also the colonies die off
annually.   " The nests are abandoned," he says, " without it being
possible to discover the reason, for apparently neither diminution
of temperature nor scarcity of food cause them (the Insects) to
suffer.   One is tempted to suppose that the death of the Insects
is the result of a physiological necessity."

Nests of Social Wasps.—In Europe wasps' nests disappear
very soon after they are deserted.   As it would appear from de
Saussure's conclusions that in the tropics as well as in the temperate
regions the rule is that the colonies endure only a portion of one
year, and that a new nest is commenced by a single founder once
in twelve months, it is a somewhat remarkable fact that some
tropical wasp-nests are much more durable than the lives of the
inhabitants require, so that solidly constructed nests are often
found hanging to the trees long after they have been deserted,
and are sometimes overgrown with moss.   Cuming has recorded
the fact that he found in South America an old wasp-nest that had
been taken possession of by swallows.   We do not assign, however, much importance to the views of de Saussure, because we
may anticipate that enquiry will reveal much variety in the
habits of tropical and sub-tropical wasps.   It is known that
species exist that store up honey, after the fashion of bees, and
von Ihering has recently shown [1] that in Brazil, species of several
genera form new colonies by swarming, after the manner of bees.
So that it is possible that certain colonies may remain for a long
period in the same nest.

Much more variety exists in wasps' nests than would be supposed probable ; those formed by some of the tropical species of
Vespidae are enveloped in so solid and beautifully constructed an
envelope of papier-maché, that they resist with complete success
the torrential rains of the tropics ; while some of those found in
our own country are made of extremely soft and delicate paper,

[1] *Zool. Anz.* xix. 1896, p. 449.   See also note, *antea,* p. 70.

which is probably chiefly glandular products. Our British Vespidae number only eight species, all belonging to the one genus *Vespa,* and yet they exhibit three different modes of nidification. *Vespa vulgaris, V. germanica* and *V. rufa* form subterranean nests, while *V. arborea, V. sylvestris* and *V. norvegica* suspend their habitations from the branches of trees, bushes, or strong annual plants. *Vespa crabro,* the hornet, usually adopts an intermediate course, forming its nest above ground, but in a spot where it is protected and concealed. The favourite habitat of this formidable Insect is the interior of an old tree, but the hornet will sometimes avail itself of the protection of a thatched roof. Both it and other arboreal species are said, however, to occasionally make subterranean nests. It is ascertained that *V. austriaca,* the eighth species, is an inquiline.

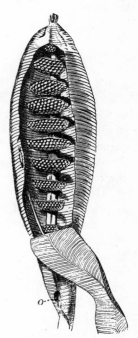

FIG. 32.—Nest of (?) *Polybia* sp. The envelope partly cut open ; *o,* entrance. (After de Saussure.)

De Saussure,[1] the monographer of the social wasps, classifies them according to the architecture of their nests. He establishes three groups : (1) Stelocyttares, in which the layers of comb are not connected with the envelope, but are supported by pillars made by the wasps (Fig. 31) ; (2) Poecilocyttares, an unsatisfactory group of which the chief characteristics appear to be that the nest is always covered by an envelope, and the comb is supported by an object such as the branch of a tree, round, or on, which the envelope is placed (Fig. 32) ; (3) Phragmocyttares, in which the layers of comb are supported, in part or entirely, by the envelope of the nest, communication being effected by a hole in each layer of the comb (Fig. 33). de Saussure's classification is far from satisfactory. There are many social wasps that construct nests destitute of any proper envelope ; as an example of this, we may mention the species of

[1] *Monographie des guêpes sociales,* Geneva, 1853-1858, pp. cc. and 356, plates i.-xxxvii.

the abundant genus *Polistes ;* these Insects make hexagonal cells, of paper-like material, forming an irregular comb, or mass, attached to bushes by a stalk near its centre; these nests are placed so that the mouths of the open cells look downwards. The species of *Ischnogaster* (Fig. 34) make layers of comb, connected by a pedicel, but without any envelope; these Insects form a section of Stelocyttares called Gymnodomes.

Most of the nests of the Poecilocyttares have only a single layer of comb. The wasps of the genera *Synoeca* and *Polybia* have the habit of spreading a layer of cells on a leaf, or on the bark of a tree, and of covering this with an envelope that is pierced by a single orifice only, but that does not rest on the cells, and so allows circulation of the Insects between the cells and the envelope. This appears to be the arrangement in a nest of *Synoeca cyanea* preserved in the British Museum; in this construction a large layer of cells is moulded on the branch of a tree, whose contour, for a length of two or three feet, it consequently follows; while outside the mass there is placed a continuous envelope, leaving a considerable distance between it and the cells.

It would be impossible in the space at our disposal to give a satisfactory account of all the forms of wasp-nests, and we must therefore refer the student to de Saussure's work, confining ourselves to a brief notice of some specially interesting forms. The habitation of the Brazilian *Polybia* (*Myrapetra*) *scutellaris* is a very solid, closed structure, covered externally with rough knobs or angular projections. Although of very large size— it may be upwards of two feet in length—it is suspended from a branch, and has but one orifice; the arrangement of the combs in the interior is that of the Phragmocyttares, they being firmly attached to the outer envelope, and so placed as to form a curved surface, the convexity of which is downwards : the number of wasps in a well-developed nest of this kind must be very great. This species is said to be a honey-gathering wasp.

One of the best known of the South American wasps' nests is the construction (Fig. 33) of *Chartergus chartarius ;* these nests are so regularly shaped, and formed of papier-maché so compact and solid, as to look like stone : this edifice is attached in a very firm manner to the branch of a tree, and has a single portal of entry beneath ; its interior arrangement is much like that of *Myrapetra scutellaris.*

A very remarkable wasp's nest is preserved in the British Museum of Natural History; it is considered to be the work of *Montezumia dimidiata* Sauss. an Eumenid wasp; it is a large mass of cells encircling the branch of a tree, which therefore projects somewhat after the manner of an axle through the middle: the cells are very numerous, and are quite as regular as those of the most perfect of the combs of bees: the mass is covered with a very thick layer of paper, the nest having somewhat the external appearance of half a cocoa-nut of twice the usual size.

FIG. 33.—Section of nest of *Chartergus chartarius.* South America. *o*, Entrance. (After de Saussure.)

Apoica pallida, a South American Insect, forms a nest in a somewhat similar manner to *Polistes*, but it is covered on its outer aspect by a beautiful paper skin, so that the nest looks somewhat like a toadstool of large size attached to the branch of a tree.

The nests of the Insects of the genus *Polybia*—which we have already mentioned as located by de Saussure in his unsatisfactory group Poecilocyttares—usually have somewhat the form and size of pears or apples suspended to twigs of trees or bushes; these little habitations consist of masses of cells, wrapped in wasp-paper, in which there are one or more orifices for ingress and egress. Smith says that the combs in the nest of *P. pygmaea* are of the most exquisite construction, and that it is by no means an uncommon circumstance to find the outer envelope of the nest ornamented with patches of delicate hexagonal tracery. This nest is about the size of an orange.

We have already noticed the variety of nests formed by our British species of the genus *Vespa;* in other parts of the world the edifices formed by species of *Vespa* attain a very large size. *V. crabroniformis* in China, and *V. velutina* in India, make nests several feet or even yards in length, inhabited by an enormous number of individuals; they are apparently constructed of a material like brittle paper, and are arranged much like the nests of our British hornet, *V. crabro.* *Vespa orientalis* mixes a considerable quantity of earth with the paper it uses for its constructive efforts.   In the British Museum collection there is a nest said to be that of the Japanese hornet, *V. japonica.*   This is completely covered by a paper envelope, and has apparently only a single small orifice for ingress and egress.   In the same collection there is a nest from Bahia (believed to be that of a social wasp, though of what species is unknown), the outer wall of which is apparently formed entirely of earth, and is a quarter or half an inch thick : the comb inside appears also to be formed of clay, the whole forming an elaborate construction in pottery.   One is tempted to believe it may prove to be the production of a social Eumenid.

Habits of Social Wasps.——We have already briefly noticed the way in which a colony of wasps is founded, but some further particulars as to the mode in which the society is increased and developed may be mentioned.   The queen-wasp makes at first only a very small group of three or four incomplete cells ; each cell is at first circular, or nearly so, and moreover is of smaller diameter than it will afterwards be.   In each of the first three or four incomplete cells an egg is laid, and more cells are commenced ; but as the eggs soon hatch and produce larvae that grow rapidly, the labours of the queen-wasp are chiefly directed to feeding the young.   At first she supplies them with saccharine matter, which she procures from flowers or fruits, but soon gives them a stronger diet of insect meat.   This is procured by chasing living Insects of various kinds.   Some species of wasps prefer particular kinds of Insects, and the hornet is said to be very fond of the honey-bee, but as a rule Diptera are the prey selected.   When an Insect has been secured, the hard and innutritious parts are bitten off, and the succulent parts, more especially the thorax which contains chiefly muscular tissue, are reduced to a pulp by means of the mandibles; this is offered to the larvae, which are said to stretch out their heads to the mother to receive the food, after the manner of nestling birds.   When a larva is full grown it spins a cocoon in the cell and changes to a pupa.   It is said by some entomologists that the queen-wasp closes the cell for the purpose of the larval metamorphosis; but this is contradicted by others, and is probably erroneous.   In about a month, or a little less, from the time of deposition of the egg, the perfect Insect is ready for issue, and almost immediately after leaving its cell it assists in the work that is going on for the development of the society.   The

Insects produced at this early period of the colony are exclusively workers, *i.e.* imperfect females. They relieve the queen of the task of supplying the larvae with food, and she henceforth remains within the nest, being, it is said, herself fed by her workers; the society now rapidly increases in numbers, and fresh combs are formed, the upper layer being always the oldest. About the month of August, cells of larger size than those that have previously been constructed are formed, and in these males and perfect females are produced; in a few weeks after this the colony languishes and becomes extinct. When it is no longer possible for the enfeebled wasps to carry out their tasks of feeding the brood, they drag the larvae out of the cells and destroy them. An uncertain number of queen-wasps seek protected nooks in which to pass the winter, and each of these queens may be the founder of a nest in the ensuing spring. It should be remarked that de Saussure states that all the intermediate grades between perfect and imperfect females exist, and Marchal's recent observations confirm this. There is in fact no line of demarcation between worker and queen in the wasps as there is in the honey-bee. Von Siebold long since drew attention to the existence of parthenogenesis in certain species of wasps, and it appears probable that it is of common occurrence.

Our knowledge of the social life of European wasps has recently been much increased by the observations of two French naturalists, P. Marchal and C. Janet. The latter has given an elaborate history of a nest of the hornet, showing the rate and variations of increase in numbers. His observations on this and other species indicate that warmth is of the utmost importance to wasps; the Insects themselves create a considerable amount of heat, so that the temperature of their abodes is much greater than that of the air. He considers that in Europe an elevated temperature is essential for the development of the individual,[1] and that the chief object of the various wrappers of paper with which the Insects surround their nests is to keep up this high temperature. These envelopes give a great deal of trouble to the Insects, for they have to be repeatedly

---

[1] Hence probably the great difference in the abundance of wasps in different years: if a period of cold weather occur during the early stages of formation of a wasp family, operations are suspended and growth delayed; or death may even put an end to the nascent colony.

destroyed and reformed, as the combs they contain increase in size. Marchal's observations [1] relate chiefly to the production of the sexes and worker-forms, in the subterranean species, *Vespa germanica* and *V. vulgaris*. The layers of comb include cells of two sizes. The upper layers, which are the first formed, consist of small cells only : the lower combs are constructed (at Paris) early in August, and consist of larger cells from which males and large females are reared. The males are, however, reared also in large numbers in the small cells. If the queen be removed, the workers become fertile, and produce parthenogenetically many eggs, but all of the male sex. He entertains no doubt that even when the queen is in full vigour the workers produce males if there is an abundant food supply.

The social wasps at present known number 500 or 600 species. *Polistes* is a very extensive genus, and it has also a very wide geographical distribution ; some of the species—and those found in widely-distant parts of the world—are remarkable on account of their excessive variation in colour, and it is worthy of note that the extreme forms have been more than once taken from the same nest.

Next to *Polistes*, *Vespa* is the most numerous in species, about 150 being known, and it is to this genus that all our British social wasps belong. No Insects are better known in our islands than these wasps, owing to the great numbers of individuals that occur in certain seasons, as well as to their frequently entering our habitations and partaking of our food, and to the terror that is occasioned by their supposed ferocity and desire to sting. This last feature is a complete mistake ; wasps never sting unless they are roused to do so by attacks, or by considerable interference with their work. The only real danger arises from the fact that a wasp may be occasionally taken into the mouth with fruit, or may be handled unawares. When they are flying about they are perfectly harmless unless attacked or irritated, and even if they settle on the person no danger of their stinging exists unless movement is made. Sichel correctly states that a person may station himself close to a wasp's nest and remain there without any risk at all, provided that he makes no movement ; indeed, it is more than probable that if no movement, or if only gentle

[1] *CR. Ac. Paris*, cxvii. 1893, p. 584 ; *op. cit.* cxxi. 1895, p. 731 ; *Arch. Zool. exper.* (3) iv. 1896, pp. 1-100.

movement, be made, the wasps are unaware of the presence of an intruder.   It is, however, well ascertained that if they are molested at their work, more especially when they are actually engaged in the duties of the nest, they are then extremely vin- dictive, and follow for a considerable distance those who have irritated them.   The East Indian *V. velutina* is specially fierce when aroused, and is said by Horne to have followed a party

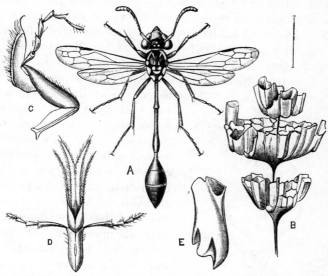

Fig. 34.—*Ischnogaster mellyi.* Java. **A**, Female imago (the line at the side shows its length) ; **B**, nest, **C**, maxilla ; **D**, labium ; **E**, mandible (tip downwards).   The nest is probably upside down, although shown here as by de Saussure.

through dense jungle for miles, and on some occasions to have stung animals, and even human beings, to death.

This vindictiveness is, however, only an exceptional mood due to some interference with the colony.   Even the hornet, not- withstanding its threatening appearance, is harmless unless unduly provoked ; its nests and their inhabitants can be kept in domesticity, exhibited to strangers, even moved from place to place, yet the hornets will not take offence if due gentleness be observed.   It is said that wasps will rear the progeny of a neigh- bour in circumstances where this assistance is necessary.   Hess has related a case in which a queen-hornet had commenced a nest, and was killed by an accident, leaving young brood in the comb

unprovided for : as a result many of the helpless grubs died, and
others were in a state of starvation, when a strange queen-hornet
appeared, associated itself with the comb, and, adopting the orphan
brood, nourished them and brought them to their full size.

We have already alluded to the fact that, so far as external
structure is concerned, there is no great difference between the
social and the solitary wasps. Both, too, run through analogous
series of forms and colours, and the genus *Ischnogaster* (Fig. 34)
seems to connect the two groups by both its structure and mode
of life. The social habits are in many species only inferred, and
with greater knowledge will probably prove fallacious as a guide
to classification ; indeed we have already said that in the genus
Vespa—perhaps the most perfectly social of all the wasps—there

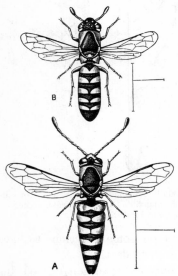

is one species that has no worker,
and that lives, it is supposed, as
a parasite, in the nests of its
congeners. For this species, *V.
austriaca*, it has been proposed to
create a separate genus, *Pseudo-
vespa*, on account of this peculiarity
of habit, although no structural
character has been detected that
could distinguish it. De Saussure
has stated his conviction that
workers do not exist in some of
the exotic genera, so that it appears
highly probable that with the progress of knowledge the present division between social and solitary
wasps will prove untenable.

Remains of Insects referred to
the genera *Polistes* and *Vespa*
have been found in tertiary strata

Fig. 35.--*Masaris vespiformis*. **A,** male ;
B, female. Egypt. (After Schaum.)

in various parts of Europe and in North America.

Fam. 3. Masaridae.

*Anterior wing with two complete sub-marginal cells. Antennae
usually incrassate or clubbed at the extremity. Claws distinctly or obsoletely dentate.*

This is a group of fifty or sixty species with but few genera, and most of its components appear to be Insects of the greatest rarity.   In their appearance the Insects of this Family differ considerably from the other Diploptera, and as the wings are only imperfectly, or not at all, plicate, it must be admitted that the systematic affinities of the group require reconsideration.   The pronotal structure is, however, completely that of Diploptera. The typical form of the Family, *Masaris vespiformis*, though described a hundred years since, is a species of such extreme rarity, and its sexes are so different, that entomologists have only recently been able to agree about it.   It has been found in Egypt and Algeria.   The genera *Ceramius, Jugurthia, Quartenia* and *Coelonites* are also members of the Mediterranean fauna, while *Paragia* is Australian, and *Trimeria* South American. Several species of the genus *Masaris* inhabit North America, and Cresson has recently described another Masarid genus from the same country, under the name of *Euparagia.*

The little that is known of their natural history is almost limited to an account given by Giraud of the habits of *Ceramius lusitanicus*, of which species he found a colony near Briançon.   The Insect makes nests in the earth ; they are entered by means of a chimney - like passage analogous to what is formed by certain *Odynerus ;* the gallery when completed is about six centimetres long, and at its extremity is an earthen cell in which the larva lives ; this is fed by the mother, who brings to it from time to time a supply of a paste, described as being somewhat like dried honey.   The growth of the larva is believed to be rapid.

FIG. 36. — Cells constructed by *Coelonites abbreviatus.* (After André.)

Some fragmentary observations made by Lichtenstein on *Coelonites abbreviatus* have also been recorded. This species, near Montpellier, constructs earthen cells ; they are not, however, subterranean, but are placed side by side on the dry stems of plants (Fig. 36) : these cells are stored with a material similar to that supplied by *Ceramius lusitanicus* to its young.

CHAPTER III

Division III. Fossores.

Aculeate Hymenoptera, in which the abdomen, though very diverse in form, does not bear prominences on the upper aspect of the basal segments ; front wing without longitudinal fold along the middle ; hairs of body not plumose. Only two forms (male and female) of each species.

FOSSORIAL Hymenoptera are distinguished from other Aculeates at present only by negative characters, *i.e.* they are Aculeates, but are not ants, bees or wasps. According to their habits they fall into four, by no means sharply distinguished, groups—(1) those that form no special receptacles for their young, but are either of parasitic or sub-parasitic habits, or take advantage of the abodes of other Insects, holes, etc. ; (2) constructors of cells of clay formed into pottery by the saliva of the Insect, and by drying ; (3) excavators of burrows in the ground ; (4) makers of tunnels in wood or stems of plants. Several species make use of both of the last two methods. The habits are carnivorous ; the structures formed are not for the benefit of the makers, but are constructed and stored with food for the next generation. Their remarkable habits attracted some attention even 2000 years or more ago, and were to some extent observed by Aristotle. The great variety in the habits of the species, the extreme industry, skill, and self-denial they display in carrying out their voluntary labours, render them one of the most instructive groups of the animal kingdom. There are no social or gregarious forms, they are true individualists, and their lives and instincts offer many subjects for reflection.   Unlike the social Insects they can learn nothing whatever from either example or precept. The skill of each individual is prompted by no imitation.   The life is short, the later stages of the individual life are totally different from the earlier : the individuals of one generation only in rare cases see even the commencement of the life of the next ; the progeny, for the benefit of which they labour with

Fig. 37.—*Sceliphron nigripes* ♀ (Sub-Fam. Sphegides).   Amazons.   × $\frac{3}{2}$.

unsurpassable skill and industry, being unknown to them.   Were such a solicitude displayed by ourselves we should connect it with a high sense of duty, and poets and moralists would vie in its laudation.   But having dubbed ourselves the higher animals, we ascribe the eagerness of the solitary wasp to impulse or instinct, and we exterminate their numerous species from the face of the earth for ever, without even seeking to make a prior acquaintance with them.   Meanwhile our economists and moralists devote their volumes to admiration of the progress of the civilisation that effects this destruction and tolerates this negligence.

It should be noted that in the solitary as in the social Insects the males take no part whatever in these industrial occupations, and apparently are even unaware of them. It is remarkable that, notwithstanding this, the sexual differences are in the majority less than is usual in Insects. It is true that the various forms of Scoliidae exhibit sexual distinctions which, in the case of Thynnides and Mutillides are carried to an extreme degree, but these are precisely the forms in which skill and ingenuity are comparatively absent, the habits being rather of the parasitic than of the industrial kind, while the structure is what is usually called degraded (*i.e.* wingless). The great difference between the habits of the sexes, coupled with the fact that there is little or no difference in their appearance, has given rise to a curious Chinese tradition with regard to these Insects, dating back to Confucius at least.[1] The habit of stinging and storing caterpillars in a cell, from which a fly similar to itself afterwards proceeds having been noticed, it was supposed to be the male that performed these operations; and that when burying the caterpillars he addressed to them a spell, the burden of which is "mimic me." In obedience the caterpillars produce the wasp, which is called to this day "Jiga," that is in English "mimic me." The idea was probably to the effect that the male, not being able to produce eggs, used charmed caterpillars to continue the species.

Summary of the Prey of Fossores.

Group of Fossores.	Food or Occurrence.
Fam. Scoliidae.	
Sub-Fam. Mutillides . .	As parasites on Hymenoptera Aculeata.
,, Thynnides . .	(?) Parasites on Lepidopterous pupae.
,, Scoliides . . .	Larvae of Coleoptera [(?) spiders in the case of *Elis 4-notata*].
,, Rhopalosomides.	Unknown.
,, Sapygides . .	The provisions stored by bees. Caterpillars (teste Smith).
Fam. Pompilidae	Spiders. Rarely Orthoptera (Gryllidae and Blattidae, teste Bingham) or Coleoptera.
Fam. Sphegidae. Sub-Fam. Sphegides . .	Orthoptera (especially Locustidae), larvae of Lepidoptera, Spiders [(?) same species (*Sceliphron madraspatanum* and *Sphex coeruleus*), both spiders and caterpillars].

---

[1] Kumagusu Minakata, in *Nature*, l. 1894, p. 30.

Group of Fossores.	Food or Occurrence.
Fam. Sphegidae.	
Sub-Fam. Ampulicides.	Orthoptera (Blattidae only).
,, Larrides	Orthoptera of various divisions. Aculeate Hymenoptera, in the case of *Palarus*. [Spiders stolen from nests of *Pelopaeus* by *Larrada*.]
,, Trypoxylonides.	Spiders, caterpillars, Aphidae.
,, Astatides	*Astata boops* uses Pentatomid bugs, cockroaches, and even Aculeate Hymenoptera (*Oxybelus*, teste Smith).
,, Bembecides	Diptera and *Cicada*.
,, Nyssonides	Diptera, Homoptera (*Gorytes mystaceus* takes *Aphrophora* out of its "cuckoo-spit").
,, Philanthides.	Aculeate Hymenoptera (*Philanthus*). Hard beetles, viz. Curculionidae, Buprestidae, Chrysomelidae (*Cerceris*).
,, Mimesides	Small Homoptera, even Aphidae. Diptera (Tipulidae) in Hawaii.
,, Crabronides	Diptera, Aphidae [? the same species of wasps both of these]. Other small Homoptera. Ants (in the case of *Fertonius*). Parasitic optera (in the case of *Lindenius*).

Great diversity of opinion exists as to the classification of the Fossores. This arises chiefly from the incomplete state of the collections studied, and from the fact that the larger part of the works published are limited to local faunae. Opinions as to the families vary; some admitting only three or four, others upwards of twenty. After consideration of the various views, the writer thinks it best to admit at present only three families, which speaking broadly, correspond with habits, viz. (1) Scoliidae, subterranean stingers; (2) Pompilidae, runners; (3) Sphegidae, stingers above ground.

1. Scoliidae. Pronotum and tegulae in contact. Abdomen with the plane of the ventral surface interrupted by a chink between the first and second segments. Numerous wingless forms.
2. Pompilidae. Pronotum and tegulae in contact. Abdomen with the plane of the ventral surface not interrupted -by a chink. Legs very long. No wingless forms.
3. Sphegidae. Pronotum and tegulae not in contact. No wingless forms.

We shall treat as sub-families those divisions of Scoliidae and Sphegidae considered by many as families.

Fam. 1. Scoliidae.

The members of this family, so far as is known, display less perfect instincts than the Sphegidae and Pompilidae, and do not construct cells or form burrows.   Information as to the habits is almost confined to European forms.   We adopt five sub-families.

Sub-Fam. 1. Mutillides.—*The sides of the pronotum reach the tegulae : the female is destitute of wings and ocelli, frequently having the parts of the thorax so closely soldered that the divisions between them are obliterated : the males are winged, furnished with ocelli, and having the thoracic divisions distinct ; intermediate tibiae with two apical spurs.   Front wing with two or three sub-marginal cells.   The larvae live parasitically at the expense of other Hymenoptera Aculeata.*

The Mutillides have some resemblance to ants, though, as they are usually covered with hair, and there is never any node at the base of the abdomen, they are readily distinguished from the Formicidae.   The great difference between the sexes is their most striking character.   Their system of coloration is often very remarkable, the velvet-like pubescence clothing their bodies being variegated with patches of sharply contrasted vivid colour ; in other cases the contrast of colour is due to bare, ivory-like spaces.   They have the faculty of stridulating, the position and nature of the organ for the purpose being the same as in ants.

Very little exact information exists as to the habits and life-histories of the species.   Christ and Drewsen, forty or fifty years ago, recorded that *M. europaea* lives in the nests of bees of the genus *Bombus,* and Hoffer has since made some observations on the natural history of the same species in South East Europe, where this *Mutilla* is found in the nests of ten or eleven species of *Bombus,* being most abundant in those of *B. agrorum,* and *B. variabilis ;* occasionally more individuals of *Mutilla* than of bees may be found in a nest.   He supposes that the egg of the *Mutilla* is placed in the young larva of the *Bombus,* and hatches in about three days ; the larva feeds inside the bee-larva, and when growth is completed a cocoon is spun in the interior of the pupa-case of the bee.   When the perfect Insects emerge, the males leave the nest very speedily, but the females remain for some time feeding on the bees' honey.   Females are usually produced in greater numbers than males.   This account leaves

much to be desired.   From the observations of Radoszkowsky
it is clear that other species of Mutillides are by no means
confined to the nests of *Bombus* but live at the expense of
Aculeate Hymenoptera of various groups.   This naturalist asserts
that the basal abdominal segment of the parasite resembles in
form that of the species on which it preys.

The apterous condition of the females of Mutillides and
Thynnides is very anomalous in the Fossors ; this sex being in
the other families distinguished for activity and intelligence.
The difference between the sexes is also highly remarkable.   The
males differ from the females by the possession of wings and by the
structural characters we have mentioned, and also in a most striking

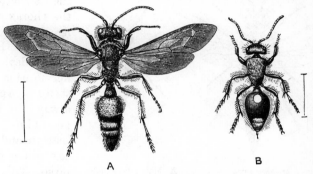

Fig. 38.—*Mutilla stridula*.   Europe.   **A**, Male ; **B**, female.

manner in both colour and form ; Burmeister, indeed, says that in
South America—the metropolis of Mutillides—there is not a single
species in which the males and females are alike in appearance ; this
difference becomes in some cases so extreme that the two sexes of
one species have been described as Insects of different families.

Upwards of one thousand species are assigned to the genus
Mutilla, which is distributed over the larger part of the world ;
there is so much difference in these species as to the nervuration
of the wings in the males, that several genera would be formed
for them were it not that no corresponding distinctions can be
detected in the females.   Three or four species of *Mutilla* are
described as being apterous in the male as well as in the
female sex ; they are very rare, and little is known about them.
Only three species of Mutillides occur in Britain, and they are
but rarely seen, except by those who are acquainted with their

habits. The African and East Indian genus, *Apterogyna*, includes some extremely peculiar Hymenoptera; the males have the wing nervuration very much reduced, and the females are very ant-like owing to the deep constriction behind the first abdominal ring.

Sub-Fam. 2. Thynnides.—*Males and females very different in form; the male winged, the front wing with three, or only two, sub-marginal cells; the female wingless and with the thorax divided into three sub-equal parts.*

The Thynnides are by some entomologists not separated from the Mutillides; but the distinction in the structure of the thorax of the females is very striking. In the Thynnides the nervuration of the wing appears always to extend to the outer margin, and in the Mutillides not to do so. This family is represented in

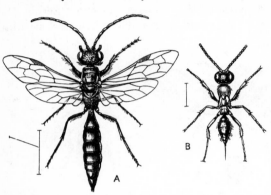

FIG. 39.—*Methoca ichneumonides.* **A**, Male; **B**, female. Britain.

Britain by a single very rare Insect, *Methoca ichneumonides*: to the unskilled observer the female would appear to be without doubt an ant. This Insect is by some considered as the type of a family distinct from the Thynnides proper. Thynnides are numerous in Australia. Very little is really known as to their habits, though it has been stated that they are parasitic on Lepidoptera, Bakewell having obtained specimens from sub-terranean cocoons of that Order. Those who are interested in differences between the sexes of one species should examine the extraordinary examples of that phenomenon presented by the Thynnides; the dissimilarity throughout the group—which is now of considerable extent—being so extreme that no ento-mologist would from simple inspection believe the two sexes to have any connection; but the fact that they are so con-nected has been demonstrated beyond doubt. In very few cases, however, have the sexes been matched, so that at present males are no doubt standing in the lists of Hymenoptera as one species and their females as other species.

Sub-Fam. 3. Scoliides.—*Pronotum reaching back to the tegulae; legs stout; intermediate tibiae with one apical spur; both sexes winged; the nervures not extending to the posterior (i.e. distal) margin.*

This group includes some of the largest and most powerful of the Aculeate Hymenoptera. Its members are usually hairy Insects with thick legs, the colour being black, more or less variegated with bands or spots of red or yellow; the hind body is elongate, has only a very short pedicel, and in the male is usually terminated by three projecting spines. The pronotum is of variable dimensions, but its front angles are always co-

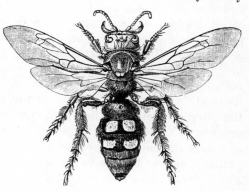

Fig. 40.—*Scolia haemorohoidalis* ♀. Europe.

adapted with the points of insertion of the front wings. The nervuration of the front wings is confined to the basal part, the extensive apical or outer area possessing no nervures. There is frequently a great difference in the size of the two sexes of the same species, the female being very much larger than the other sex. The larvae, so far as is known, devour those of Lamellicorn Coleoptera.

Fabre has investigated the habits of some of the species of Scoliides found in France, and has informed us that their means of subsistence consists of larvae of the larger Lamellicorn beetles, *Cetonia, Oryctes, Anoxia,* and *Euchlora;* these beetles belong to very different divisions of the Lamellicornia, but they have in common the fact that their larvae are of subterranean habits, living in the earth or in accumulations of débris in which there is a large proportion of vegetable matter or roots. The female *Scolia* penetrates into the ground in order to find the Lamellicorn larvae necessary as food for its progeny. *Scolia bifasciata* attacks the larvae of several species of *Cetonia,* and *S. (Colpa)* *interrupta* chooses the larvae of the chafers *Anoxia villosa* and *A. matutinalis.* The mother *Scolia* enters the ground in August or September, and having found a suitable larva stings it and deposits an egg on the ventral surface of the prey ; the paralysed larva is left where it was found, no attempt being made to place it in a special receptacle. The egg is placed on the ventral surface, well behind the feet, under a mass of matter in the alimentary canal. Shortly after being hatched the. young destroyer penetrates with its head the skin of the victim, and in this position commences to feed ; it is necessary that it should obtain its food without killing the *Cetonia* larva, for it cannot prosper on decaying food, so that if the *Cetonia* larva die the *Scolia* larva likewise perishes ; the latter, accordingly, does not withdraw its head from the interior of the victim, but remains always in the same position, as it grows larger extending its head forwards into the front part of the interior of its victim ; the internal organs of the latter are consumed in a systematic order so as to delay bringing about its death till the last moment, and thus all the interior of the *Cetonia* larva is appropriated till nothing remains but an empty skin. By a series of experiments, Fabre showed how essential it is that this apparently revolting operation should be carried on with all details strictly *en règle.* If the head of the *Scolia* larva be taken out from the victim and applied to another part of the body of the *Cetonia,* the result is that it cannot eat ; even if it be replaced in the original situation, after being taken away, it frequently happens that the *Cetonia* larva dies, its death involving also that of the destroyer. It is necessary, too, that the victim should be paralysed, for if an intact *Cetonia* larva be taken and bound down in such a position that it cannot move, and if a small orifice in its skin be made in the proper spot and a young *Scolia* larva be placed on it, the little parasite will avail itself of the opportunity and commence to feed on the larva provided for it, but the latter will speedily die, and the *Scolia* necessarily perishes with it. Thus both the paralysis of the victim and the special mode of eating are essential to the life of the *Scolia.* The operation of stinging the larva so as to produce the necessary paralysis, or rather insensibility, is a difficult one, and requires great skill and patience. The *Cetonia* larva is of large size, and must be pierced in one particular spot ;

in order to reach this the *Scolia* mounts on its victim, and is frequently dislodged by its struggles; sooner or later, however, the proper position is obtained by the wasp, and the larva is then stung in the exact spot necessary to allow the sting (and the poison introduced by it) to reach the most important of the nervous ganglia that control the movements of the body, this spot being, in the case of the *Cetonia*, the line of demarcation between the pro- and meso-thorax, on the middle line of the ventral surface of the body. The *Scolia* gives but one sting to the victim, and this it will not administer until it can do so exactly in the proper place. This practice of devouring the victim slowly, without killing it till all is eaten, is very widely spread in the Hymenoptera, and it is satisfactory to find that we may infer from Fabre's observations that it is not so horrible as it would at first appear; for it is probable that the stinging prevents decomposition of the victim, not by reason, as some have supposed, of the poison injected by the wasp having an antiseptic effect, but rather by means of destroying sensibility, so that the creature does not die from the pain, as it is believed it did in certain cases where Fabre induced the young *Scolia* larva to feed on a victim that had not been stung. We may here remark that very little exact information exists as to the operation of stinging. Fabre attaches great importance to the sting being inflicted on a nerve-ganglion. Whether a sting that did not reach this part might not have a sufficient effect appears, how- ever, doubtful.[1]

A remarkable form of Scoliides, with wings of smaller size than usual and deeply divided, has been described by Saunders under the name *Pseudomeria graeca*. Still more remarkable is *Komarovia victoriosa* found in Central Asia; in this Insect the male retains the appearance of a slender, pallid *Scolia*, but the female differs totally in form, and has the peculiar wings so re- duced in size as to be useless for flight.

Sub-Fam. 4. Sapygides.—*Closely allied to the Scoliides, but pos- sessing slender legs and antennae; also the first abdominal segment is less disconnected from the second, so that the outline*

---

[1] As this work is passing through the press we receive a book by Mr. and Mrs. Peckham on *The Instincts and Habits of the Solitary Wasps*, Madison, 1898. They are of opinion that, in the case of some species, it does not matter much whether the victim is or is not killed by the stinging.

is less interrupted ; the eyes are deeply emarginate ; the hind body is not spinose at the apex.

The economy of *Sapyga*, the only genus, has been the subject of difference of opinion.   The views of Latreille and others that these species are parasitic upon bees is confirmed by the observations of Fabre, from which it appears that *S. 5-punctata* lives in the burrows of species of the bee-genus *Osmia*, consuming the store of provisions, consisting of honey-paste, that the bee has laid up for its young.   According to the same distinguished observer, the *Sapyga* larva exhibits hypermetamorphosis (*i.e.* two consecutive forms), and in its young state destroys the egg of the bee ; but his observations on this point

Fig. 41.—*Sapyga 5-punctata* ♀, Britain.

are incomplete and need repetition. We have two species of *Sapyga* in Britain ; they differ in colour, and the sexes of *S. 5-punctata* also differ in this respect ; the abdomen, spotted with white in both sexes, is in the female variegate with red.   Smith found our British *Sapyga 5-punctata* carrying caterpillars.

Sub-Fam. 5. Rhopalo-somides. — *Antennae elongate, spinigerous ; ocelli very prominent ; tarsi of peculiar structure, their claws bifid.*

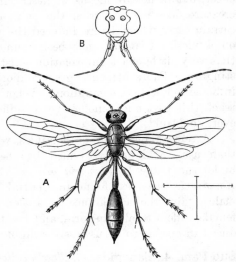

Fig. 42.—*Rhopalosoma poeyi.* **A**, female imago ; **B**, front of head.   Cuba.   (After Westwood.)

This sub-family has recently been proposed by Ashmead[1] for

¹ *P. ent. Soc. Washington*, iii. 1896, p. 303.

an extremely rare American Insect that had previously been placed by Cresson among parasitic Hymenoptera. Westwood classed *Rhopalosoma* among Diploptera, saying of it " animal quoad affinitates excrucians." We reproduce Westwood's figure, but not being acquainted with the Insect we can express no opinion as to whether it is allied to the Scoliidae or to the Sphegidae. The habits are, we believe, quite unknown.

Fam. 2. Pompilidae.

Pronotum at the sides reaching the tegulae; hind body never definitely pedicellate, though the first segment is sometimes elongate and conical; hind legs long; eyes elliptic in form, not emarginate.

The Pompilidae are perhaps the most extensive and important of the groups of Fossores, and are distributed over all the lands of the globe, with the exception of some islands and of the inclement arctic regions. The sting of the Pompilidae, unlike that of most of the Fossores, inflicts a burning and painful wound; the creatures sometimes attain a length of two or three inches, and a sting from one of these giants may have serious results. Although there is considerable variety in the external form of the members of the group, the characters given above will enable a Pompilid to be recognised with approximate certainty. The elongation of the hind legs includes all the parts, so that while the femur extends nearly as far back as the extremity of the body—in dried examples at any rate—the tibiae and the long tarsi extend far beyond it ; thus these Insects have great powers of running ; they are indeed remarkable for extreme activity and vivacity. They may frequently be seen running rapidly on the surface of the ground, with quivering wings and vibrating antennae, and are probably then employed in the search for prey, or some other of the operations connected with providing a store of food for their young. Spiders appear to be their special, if not their only, prey. Several authors have recorded details as to the various ways in which the prey is attacked. Fabre has observed the habits of several species, and we select his account of the *modus operandi* of species of the genera *Pompilus* and *Calicurgus*, in their attacks on poisonous spiders that inhabit holes in the ground or in walls. The wasp goes to the mouth of the spider's burrow, and the latter then dashes to the entry, apparently enraged at the audacity of its persecutor. The *Calicurgus* will not actually enter a burrow when there is a spider in it, because if it did so the spider would speedily dispose of the aggressor by the aid of its poisonous fangs. The *Calicurgus*, therefore, has recourse to strategy with the object of getting the spider out of its nest; the wasp seizes its redoubtable foe by one foot and pulls; probably it fails to extract the spider, and in that case rapidly passes to another burrow to repeat its tactics; sooner or later a spider is in some moment of inattention or incapacity dragged from its stronghold, and, being then comparatively helpless, feels itself at a disadvantage and offers but a feeble resistance to the wasp, which now pounces on its body and immediately inflicts a sting between the fangs of the foe, and thus

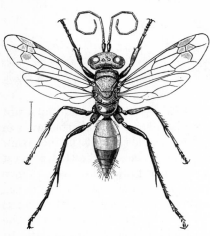

Fig. 43.—*Calicurgus hyalinatus* ♀.   Britain.

at once paralyses these dangerous weapons; thereafter it stings the body of the spider near to the junction of the abdomen and cephalothorax, and so produces complete inactivity. Having secured its prey, the wasp then seeks a suitable hole in which to deposit it; probably an empty burrow of a spider is selected for the purpose, and it may be at a height of several feet in a wall; the Hymenopteron, walking backwards, drags its heavy prey up the wall to bring it to the den. When this is accomplished an egg is deposited on the spider, and the wasp goes in search of a fragment or two of mortar, with which the mouth of the burrow is finally blocked. Fabre's accounts refer to the habits of several species, and give a good insight into some points of the instincts of both the spider and the wasp. It seems that a sense of superiority is produced in one or other of the foes, according as it feels itself in suitable conditions; so that though a spider out of its burrow and on the ground is speedily vanquished by the Pompilid, yet if the two be confined together in a vase, both are shy and inclined to adopt defensive or even evasive tactics, the result probably being that the wasp will be killed by the spider during the night, that being the period in which the attacking powers of the spider are more usually brought into play.

It seems to be the habit of some *Pompilus* to procure a victim before they have secured a place for its reception ; and Fabre took advantage of this fact, and made very interesting observations on some points of the instinct of these wasps. Having found a *Pompilus* that, after having caught a spider and paralysed it, was engaged in making a retreat for its reception, he abstracted the booty, which was deposited at the top of a small tuft of vegetation near to where the *Pompilus* was at work. In this case the burrow in course of preparation was subterranean, and was formed by the *Pompilus* itself, which therefore could not, while it was engaged underground, see what took place near it. It is the habit of the wasp to leave its work of excavation from time to time, and to visit the prey as if to assure itself of the safety of this object, and to enjoy the satisfaction of touching it with the mouth and palping it. Desirous of testing the wasp's memory of locality, Fabre took the opportunity, while the Insect was working at the formation of its burrow, of removing, as we have said, the booty from the place where it had been deposited, and putting it in another spot some half-yard off. In a short time the *Pompilus* suspended work and went straight to the spot where it had deposited its property, and finding this absent, entered on a series of marches, counter-marches, and circles round the spot where it had left the prey, as if quite sure that this was really the place where the desired object ought to be. At last convinced that the paralysed prey was no longer where it had been placed, the *Pompilus* made investigations at a greater distance and soon discovered the spider. Fabre recounts that its movements then appeared to indicate astonishment at the change of position that it thus ascertained to have occurred. The wasp, however, soon satisfied itself that this was really the very object it was seeking, and seizing the spider by the leg slightly altered its position by placing it on the summit of a small tuft of vegetation ; this latter proceeding being apparently always carried out by this species of *Pompilus*. Then it returned to its excavation, and Fabre again removed the spider to a third spot ; the wasp when it next rested from its work made its way immediately to the second spot, where it had last left the spider, thus showing that it possessed an accurate memory for locality; the wasp was very much surprised at the absence of the valued prize and persisted in seeking it in the immediate vicinity without once returning to the place where it had been first located. Fabre repeated this manoeuvre five times, and the *Pompilus* invariably returned at once to the spot where it had last left its prey. The acute memory for localities displayed by this Insect seems to be more or less general throughout the Aculeate Hymenoptera, and is of very great importance to them. The power of finding the object appears to depend on sight, for when Fabre, after removing the spider to a fresh spot, made a slight depression in the ground, placed the spider in it and covered it over with a leaf, the wasp did not find it. At the same time, the Insect's sight must be a very different sense from our own, for the wasp, when seeking its lost booty, frequently passed within a couple of inches of it without perceiving it, though it was not concealed.

Belt gives an example of the habits of the Mexican *Pompilus polistoides*. He noticed it, when hunting for spiders, make a dart at a web in the centre of which a spider was stationed; by this movement the creature was frightened and fell to the ground, where it was seized by the wasp and stung. The *Pompilus* then dragged its prisoner up a tree and afterwards flew off with it, the burden being probably too heavy for conveyance to the nest without the vantage of an elevation to start from.

Several modifications adopted by Pompilidae in their mode of stinging their spider-victims have been recorded by Ferton; these we cannot allude to in detail, but will nevertheless mention that one species stings the body of its spider-prey at random, and that in other cases it would appear that the paralysis of the spider is evanescent. In short, there are various degrees of perfection in the details of the art of stinging.

The most remarkable of the forms of Pompilidae are the numerous species of *Pepsis*, a genus peculiar to America, whence upwards of 200 species are already known.[1] Some of them attain a length of two inches or more, and are able to conquer the largest spiders; even the formidable *Mygale avicularis* succumbs to their agility and skill. Some of these *Pepsis* have beautifully coloured wings; according to Cameron, this may be

---

[1] Monograph by Lucas, *Berlin ent. Zeitschr.* xxxix. 1894.

due to scales. *P. formosus,* Say, is called in Texas the tarantula-killer; according to Buckley, its mode of attack on the huge spider is different from that made use of by its European ally. When it discovers a tarantula it flies " in circles in the air, around its victim. The spider, as if knowing its fate, stands up and makes a show of fighting, but the resistance is very feeble and of no avail. The spider's foe soon discovers a favourable moment and darts upon the tarantula, whom it wounds with its sting, and again commences flying in circles." The natural retreat of this huge spider, *Mygale hentzii,* is in holes in the ground, and this account does not inform us whether the spider allows itself to be overcome when in its nest, or is only attacked when out of its retreat.

The genus *Mygnimia* includes a very large number of species, and has a wider geographical distribution than *Pepsis,* being found in the tropical regions of both the Old and New Worlds, some of them rivalling in size and ferocity the larger specimens of the genus *Pepsis.* In the Insects of this genus there is usually a more or less distinct small space of more pallid colour on the middle of each front wing. *Parapompilus* is a curious genus consisting of Insects of a great variety of peculiar coloration, and having the wings short, so as to be of little use for flight. *P. gravesii* is an inhabitant of Chili.

Agenia carbonaria and *A. hyalipennis* are small and feeble Insects inhabiting the south of Europe. *A. carbonaria* extends to the south of England. They construct, as nests for their offspring, small earthenware vessels, differing in form according to the species, those of *A. hyalipennis* being vase-like in shape, while those of *A. carbonaria* are contracted near the mouth, something after the fashion of a wide-mouthed bottle. The Insect is able by some means—Fabre thinks by the use of saliva—to varnish the interior of the vessel so that it will not absorb water; the outside of the cells is, however, not so protected, and speedily crumbles away when exposed to the action of water; hence the vessel is placed in a protected situation, such as in a tree-stump, or a hole in a wall, or even in an empty snail-shell under a heap of stones. The cells are stored with spiders that have been paralysed by stinging and that serve as food for the larva of the *Agenia.* The larva of *A. carbonaria* has been described, and some particulars as to its habits have been given by Verhoeff.

It has been stated that this wasp does not paralyse its prey by stinging, but substitutes a process of biting to prevent the spider from hurting the larva that is to feed on it; and Verhoeff's observations seem to show that the legs of the spider are broken by some proceeding of the kind. The *Agenia* larva is of peculiar shape, the head not being inflexed, while the pleurae of each segment, from the second onwards, are prominent, so as to give the outline of the body a scalloped appearance. This larva is much infested by an Ichneumon that devours, it appears, not only the larva itself, but also the spider that was destined to be food for the larva. Verhoeff seems to have found some evidence that *Pompilus sericeus* may also be a parasite on the *Agenia*.

The construction of earthenware cells, instead of the burrows usual in Pompilidae, by the species of this genus is one of the cases alluded to in our introductory remarks as to allied Fossores exhibiting different habits. Mr. Pride has recently sent us from Brazil similar earthen vessels constructed by some Pompilid.

The habits of Pompilids of the genus *Ceropales* are analogous to those of the parasitic bees. Pérez has recently given us information as to a very curious form of parasitism in this genus; he says that when a *Pompilus* has obtained a spider as provision for its young, it is pursued by a *Ceropales*, which lays an egg on the spider, thus as it were substituting in advance its own young for that of the *Pompilus*. Information as to the subsequent course of events in this case is not at present forthcoming. In another case a *Ceropales* was observed to oviposit on the spider, not while this is being carried in, but subsequently by entering the nest for the purpose; a habit quite similar to that of some parasitic bees. Ferton has recently made the unexpected discovery that some *Pompilus* act as robbers; one individual taking away by force the spider that another has captured and is carrying off.

Lichtenstein described a Pompilid larva, that he afterwards ascertained to be *Calicurgus hyalinatus*, as possessing the extra-ordinary habit of feeding as an external parasite fixed to the dorsal surface of a spider; thus repeating, it would appear, the habits of some of the Ichnemonidae, though the perfect Insect (Fig. 143) does not differ in structure from its congeners. Emery has given an account of some Pompilids that do not bury their prey, but after stinging it and depositing an egg, simply leave the spider on the spot.

Buller has described the habits of a Pompilid in New Zealand ; his account is interesting because it shows a remarkable similarity in the proceedings of this antipodean wasp to those of its congeners on our own side of the world. The species is not scientifically named, but it appears that it is known in New Zealand as "the Mason-bee." It forms a nest of yellow clay consisting apparently of about eight cells, each of which is filled with one or more spiders in a paralysed condition. The figure given of the larva of this Insect by Buller shows it to possess a peculiarly formed head.

It is pleasing to find that Pompilidae do not make use of cruel methods when others will serve their purpose. We are informed that a large Australian Pompilid—*Priocnemis bicolor*—may find a *Cicada* sucking sap from a hole it has pierced in a tree. The *Priocnemis* has not the art of making the puncture necessary to procure sap, so the wasp seizes the *Cicada*, and shakes it till it leaves its hold and flies away, when the *Priocnemis* takes its place and sips the sap. It is added that the wasp never hurts the *Cicada*.

Fam. 3. Sphegidae.

Pronotum free from the tegulae ; when the stigmatic lobes extend as far back as the wing-insertion, they are placed below it and separated by a space from it.

This large assemblage of Fossores is the one about which the greatest difference of opinion prevails. It is based entirely on the prothoracic characters mentioned above, and cannot be looked on as natural. We shall, however, follow Kohl[1] in treating for the present as only one family the divisions considered by many as distinct families. They are ten in number.

Sub-Fam. 1. Sphegides.—*Hind body with a slender pedicel of variable length ; two spurs on the middle tibia. The propodeum usually horizontally elongate.*[2]

This group includes a great number of species, about 200 of which are referred to the genus *Sphex*.

[1] "Die Gattungen der Sphegiden," *Ann. Hofmus. Wien.* xi. 1896, pp. 233-596. Seven plates.

[2] We will take this opportunity of correcting an error in the explanation of Fig. 333 of the preceding volume, showing the propodeum, etc. of *Sphex chrysis. f* points to a division of the mesonotum, not of the metanotum, as there stated.

The habits of one species of this genus have been fully described by Fabre; he assigns to the species the name of *S. flavipennis*, but Kohl considers that it is more probably *S. maxillosus*. This Insect forms its nests, in the South of France, in the ground, excavating a main shaft with which are connected cells intended for the reception of the provisions for the young. The entrance to the burrow is formed by piercing a hole in the side of a very slight elevation of the soil. Thus the entrance to the construction consists of a horizontal gallery, playing the part of a vestibule, and this is used by the *Sphex* as a place of retreat and shelter for itself; at the end of the vestibule, which may be two or three inches long, the excavation takes an abrupt turn downwards, extending in this manner another two or three inches, and terminating in an oval cell the larger diameter of which is situate in a horizontal plane. When this first cell has been completed, stored with food, and an egg laid in it, the entrance to it is blocked up, and another similar cell is formed on one side; a third and sometimes a fourth are afterwards made and provisioned, then the Insect commences anew, and a fresh tunnel is formed; ten such constructions being the number usually prepared by each wasp. The Insect works with extreme energy, and as the period of its constructive activity endures only about a month, it can give but two or three days to the construction and provisioning of each of its ten subterranean works. The provisions, according to Fabre, consist of a large species of field-cricket, of which three or four individuals are placed in each cell. Kohl states, however, that in Eastern Europe an Insect that he considers to be the same species as Fabre's *Sphex*, makes use of locusts as provisions, and he thinks that the habit may vary according to the locality or to the species of Orthoptera that may be available in the neighbourhood. However that may be, it is clear from Fabre's account that this part of the *Sphex's* duties do not give rise to much difficulty. The cricket, having been caught, is paralysed so that it may not by its movements destroy the young larva for whose benefit it is destined. The *Sphex* then carries it to the burrow to store it in one of the cells; before entering the cell the Insect is in the habit of depositing its prey on the ground, then of turning round, entering the burrow backwards, seizing as it does so the cricket by the antennae, and so dragging it into the cell, itself going back-

wards.   The habit of depositing its prey on the ground enabled
Fabre to observe the process of stinging; this he did by himself
capturing a cricket, and when the wasp had momentarily quitted
its prey, substituting the sound cricket for the paralysed one.
The *Sphex*, on finding this new and lively victim, proceeds at
once to sting it, and pounces on the cricket, which, after a brief
struggle, is overcome by the wasp; this holds it supine, and then
administers three stings, one in the neck, one in the joint between
the pro- and meso-thorax, and a third at the base of the abdomen,
these three spots corresponding with the situation of the three
chief nervous centres governing the movements of the body.
The cricket is thus completely paralysed, without, however, being
killed.   Fabre proved that an Insect so treated would survive for
several weeks, though deprived of all power of movement.
Three or four crickets are placed by the wasp in each cell, 100
individuals or upwards being thus destroyed by a single wasp.
Although the sting has such an immediate and powerful effect
on the cricket, it occasions but a slight and evanescent pain to a
human being; the sting is not barbed, as it is in many bees and
true wasps, and appears to be rarely used by the Insect for any
other purpose than that of paralysing its victims.   The egg is
laid by the *Sphex* on the ventral surface of the victim between
the second and third pairs of legs.   In three or four days the
young larva makes its appearance in the form of a feeble little
worm, as transparent as crystal; this larva does not change its
place, but there, where it was hatched, pierces the skin of the
cricket with its tiny head, and thus begins the process of feeding; it does not leave the spot where it first commenced to feed,
but gradually enters by the orifice it has made, into the interior
of the cricket.   This is completely emptied in the course of
six or seven days, nothing but its integument remaining; the
wasp-larva has by this time attained a length of about 12 millimetres, and makes its exit through the orifice it entered by, changing its skin as it does so.   Another cricket is then attacked and
rapidly consumed, the whole stock being devoured in ten or twelve
days from the commencement of the feeding operations; the consumption of the later-eaten crickets is not performed in so delicate
a manner as is the eating of the first victim.   When full-grown,
the process of forming a cocoon commences: this is a very elaborate operation, for the encasement consists of three layers, in

addition to the rough silk that serves as a sort of scaffolding on the exterior : the internal coat is polished and is of a dark colour, owing to its being coloured with a matter from the alimentary canal : the other layers of the cocoon are white or pale yellow. Fabre considers that the outer layers of the cocoon are formed by matter from the silk-glands, while the interior dark coat is furnished by the alimentary canal and applied by the mouth of the larva : the object of this varnish is believed to be the exclusion of moisture from the interior of the cocoon, the subterranean tunnels being insufficient for keeping their contents dry throughout the long months of winter. During the whole of the process of devouring the four crickets, nothing is ejected from the alimentary canal of the larva, but after the cocoon is formed the larva ejects in it, once for all, the surplus contents of the intestine. Nine months are passed by the Insect in the cocoon, the pupal state being assumed only towards the close of this period. The pupa is at first quite colourless, but gradually assumes the black and red colour characteristic of the perfect wasp. Fabre exposed some specimens of the pupa to the light in glass tubes, and found that they went through the pupal metamorphosis in just the same manner as the pupae that remained in the darkness natural to them during this stage of their existence.

Sphex coeruleus is frequently stated to have the habit of provisioning its nests with both Orthoptera and Spiders ; but Kohl considers with reason that this record is, as regards spiders, a mistake, arising probably from a confusion with some other Insect of similar appearance, such as *Pelopaeus (Sceliphron) coeruleus*. *S. coeruleus* is no doubt the same as *S. (Chlorion) lobatus,* which Rothney observed in East India, provisioning its nests with Orthoptera. He discovered a nest in process of construction, and during the absence of the mother-wasp abstracted from the burrow a large field-cricket that she had placed in it ; he then deposited the Orthopteron near the cell ; the parent *Sphex* on returning to work entered the tunnel and found the provision placed therein had disappeared ; she came out in a state of excitement, looked for the missing cricket, soon discovered it, submitted it to the process of malaxation or kneading, and again placed it in the nest, after having cleared it from some ants that had commenced to infest it. She then disappeared, and Rothney repeated the experiment ; in due course the same series of operations was performed, and were repeated many times, the *Sphex* evidently acting in each case as if either the cricket had disappeared owing to its being incompletely stunned, or to its having been stolen by ants. Finally, the observer placed the cricket at a greater distance from the nest, when it recovered from the ill-treatment it had received sufficiently to make its escape. The points of interest in this account are the fact that the cricket was only temporarily paralysed, and that the wasp was quite able to cope with the two special difficulties that must frequently occur to the species in its usual round of occupations.

The genus *Ammophila* is of wide distribution, and its species make vertical tunnels in the ground. The habits of some of the species found in France have been described by Fabre. The Insect does not inhabit the burrow while it is in process of formation, but quits it; and some of the species temporarily close the entry to the incomplete nest with a stone. The tunnel is a simple shaft with a single cell at its termination; this is stored with caterpillars, the different species of *Ammophila* selecting different grubs for the purpose. *A. hirsuta* hibernates in the perfect state, and carries on its work in the spring; it chooses a single larva of considerable size belonging to one of the nocturnal Lepidoptera, and this it paralyses by a series of about nine stings, of which one is implanted in each segment from the first thoracic ring backwards; it forms the burrow only after the food to be placed therein has been obtained. The caterpillar used is subterranean in habit, and the *Ammophila* detects the larva by some sense, the nature of which appears at present quite uncertain. *A. holosericea* chooses smaller larvae of the family Geometridae, and uses only one or two stingings to paralyse each larva; several caterpillars are used to provision a single cell, and they are often selected of different colours.

Marchal has also published an important account of the proceedings of *A. affinis;* he confirms Fabre's observations, and even adds to their interest by suggesting that the *Ammophila* administers special stings for the purpose of paralysing the mandibles of the caterpillar and depriving it of any power of afterwards injuring the larva that will feed on it. He thinks the mother-*Ammophila* herself profits by appropriating an exudation from the victim.

Some species of Sphegides have the curious habit of choosing the interiors of human habitations as the spots most suitable for the formation of their own domestic establishments. Fabre has given a charming account of the habits of *Pelopaeus* (*Sceliphron*) *spirifex*, a species that inhabits the South of Europe, and that forms its nests in the cottages of the peasants. The spot usually selected is a nook in the broad, open fireplace, out of reach of the flames, though not of the smoke; here the *Pelopaeus* forms a nest of earth, consisting of ten to fifty cells, the material being mud or clay brought in little balls by the aid of the Insect's mandibles; about twenty visits are required in order to complete one cell, so that for the construction of a large nest of fifty cells, about one thousand visits must be made by the Insect. It flies in and out of the house apparently not at all incommoded by the human habitants, or by the fact that the peasant's potage may be simmering on the fire quite close to where the fearless little creature is carrying on its architectural operations. The cells are stored with spiders, of which the wasp has to bring a plentiful supply, so that its operations extend over a considerable period. The prey is captured by the *Pelopaeus* whilst on the wing, and carried off at once, being probably stung by the wasp during the process of transit; apparently it is killed by the operation, not merely paralysed. Only small spiders are taken by this species, and the larva of the *Pelopaeus* consumes them in a short time, one by one, before the process of decomposition sets in; the egg, too, is laid on the first spider introduced, and this is of course at the bottom of the cell, so that the spiders are eaten by the wasp's larva in the order in which they were brought to the cell. The cell is sealed up when full, the number of spiders placed in it being on the average about eight. The larva completes its task of consuming the store in about ten days, and then forms a cocoon for its metamorphosis. Two or three generations are produced in a single year, the autumnal one passing eight or nine months in the clay cells, which are lodged in a nook of the peasant's hearth, and exposed to the smoke of his fire during all the months of winter. *Pelopaeus* (*Sceliphron*) is a genus including many species;[1] several of them are known

---

[1] *Pelopaeus* disappears from the new catalogue of Hymenoptera as the name of a valid genus; its species being assigned to *Sceliphron* and various other genera. We have endeavoured, as regards this name, to reconcile the nomenclature of previous authors with that used in the new catalogue by placing the generic name adopted in the latter in brackets.

to be specially attached to the habitations of human beings. Roth has given an account of the habits of *P. (Sceliphron) laetus* in Australia; he says that in some parts it is very difficult to keep these wasps out of the houses; the nest is formed of mud, and constructed on the furniture or in any part of a room that suits the fancy of the Insect. This it must be admitted is, according to human ideas, liable to the charge of being very capricious. Roth timed a wasp building its nest, and found that it brought a fresh load of mud every two or three minutes. If the wasp be allowed to complete the nest undisturbed, she does so by adding to the exterior diagonal streaks of mud, so giving to the nest the look of a small piece of the bark of a common acacia. The construction consists of from ten to twenty cells, and when completed is provisioned with spiders for the use of the young. This wasp is much pestered by parasites, some of which prevent the development of the larvae by consuming the spiders intended by the mother-wasp for its young. A fly, of the Order Diptera, is said to follow the wasp when carrying a spider, and to deposit also an egg on the food; as the Dipterous larvae have more rapid powers of assimilation, the *Pelopaeus* larvae are starved to death; and their mildewed remains may be found in the cell, after their enemies have become fully developed and have flown away. Another parasite is said to eat the wasp-larva, and attains this end by introducing an egg through the mud wall and the cocoon of the wasp—a habit that seems to indicate a *Leucospid* parasite. *Tachytes australis*, a wasp of the sub-family Larrides also dis-possesses this *Pelopaeus* in a manner we shall subsequently describe. This fragment of natural history from Australia has a special interest, for we find repeated there similar complex biological relations to those existing in the case of the European congeners.

P. (Sceliphron) madraspatanus is common in the north-west provinces of Hindostan, and is called the "mud-dauber" by the European residents. According to Horne it constructs its cells in the oddest places, but chiefly about the inhabited apartments in houses. It is perfectly fearless when engaged in building : the cells are four to six in number, and are usually provisioned with spiders to the number of about twenty. On one occasion it was observed that green caterpillars were stored instead of spiders. The species is said to be protected by a peculiar odour as well as by its sting; it is also stated that it disguises its edifice when completed by making it look like a dab of mud, and on one occasion " rays of mud were observed round the nest, even more exactly imitating a lump of mud thrown with some force." *P. (Sceliphron) bilineatus,* formerly thought to be a variety of *P. madraspatanus,* builds its nests in hedges and trees.

Sub-Fam. 2. Ampulicides.—*Prothorax long and narrow, forming a neck in front; clypeus beak-like; four submarginal cells, the outer one being complete; metathorax elongate, the posterior part of the metasternum deeply divided to allow a perfect inflection of the abdomen.*

This is one of the smallest of the divisions of the Sphegidae, but has a very wide distribution, being represented in both the Eastern and Western Hemispheres. It is allied to the Sphegides, but differs by the prolongation of the neck and of the head, and by the articulation between the petiole and thorax being placed on the under surface of the body; the wing-nervures are said to be of inferior importance owing to their frequently differing in individuals of the same species. These Insects appear to be rare in individuals, as well as few in species, and but little has been recorded as to their habits; but it is known that they live on cockroaches. Perkins has given a brief sketch of the habits of *Ampulex sibirica* that is of great interest, but requires confirmation. He says that this Insect, in West Africa, enters apartments where cockroaches abound, and attacking one, that may probably be four times its own size, succeeds, after a struggle, in sting-ing it; the cockroach instantly becomes quiet and submissive, and suffers itself to be led away and placed in confinement in some

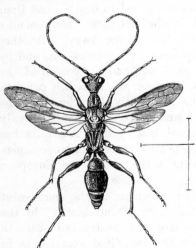

Fig. 44.—*Ampulex compressa.* Male. East India.

spot such as a keyhole, and in one case was apparently prevented from afterwards escaping, by the wasp carrying some
heavy nails into the keyhole.   The larva of the *Ampulex* may
be presumed to live on the Blattid, as it is added that dead
bodies of the cockroaches are frequently found with the empty
cocoon protruding from them.   This account, if correct, points to
some features in the habits of this Insect that are unique.   A
remark made by Rothney in reference to the habits of *A. (Rhinopsis) ruficornis* seems to indicate some similar instinct on the
part of that species ; he says, " I also saw two or three of these
wasps collar a peculiar cockroach by the antennae and lead it off
into a crack in the bark, but as the cockroach reappeared smiling
each time, I don't know what was up."   The same observer records
that this species associates with *Sima rufonigra,* an ant it greatly resembles in appearance, as well as with a spider that is also of similar
appearance (Fig. 72).   Schurr has given a brief account of the
proceedings of *Ampulex compressa,* and his statements also tend
to confirm the correctness of Perkins' report.   The habits of a
species of *Ampulex* were partially known to Réaumur, who
described them on the authority of M. Cossigni.   The species is
believed to be *A. compressa,* which occurs not only in East India,
but also in the island of Bourbon, the locality where M. Cossigni
made his observation : his account is, like the others, a mere
sketch of certain points observed, the most important of which
is that when *Ampulex* cannot introduce the cockroach into a
hole that it has selected as suitable, it bites off some portions
of the body in order to reduce the poor Insect to the necessary
extent.

From these fragmentary observations it would appear that
the sting of the *Ampulex* has not so powerful a paralysing effect
as that of most other Fossores ; and that the *Ampulex* does
not form any nest, but takes advantage of suitable holes and
crevices to store the victim in ; also that it displays considerable ingenuity in the selection of materials with which to block
up the cavity in which it has placed the partially incapacitated
creature.

The genus *Dolichurus* is by some entomologists considered
the type of a sub-family allied to the Ampulicides ; it long
consisted of a small and rare European Insect, but some exotic
species have recently been added to it.   It will probably prove not

sufficiently distinct from Ampulicides, although the pronotum is much shorter, but Handlirsch has recently observed that the European species attacks Blattidae as do the normal Ampulicides; and Ferton has recorded that *D. haemorrhous* lives at the expense of *Loboptera decipiens*, the wasp depositing its egg on the left intermediate femur of the prey. This is placed in a solitary cell, and is entirely consumed by the larva, life being preserved till within a few hours of the end of the repast, which occupies altogether eight days.

Sub-Fam. 3. Larrides.—*Hind body not pedicellate, or with only a short pedicel ; one spur on the middle tibia ; labrum inconspicuous. Marginal cell of the front wings appendiculate,*[1] *or mandibles excised externally, or both.*

This group is by some writers called Tachytides instead of Larrides, as owing to a change of nomenclature *Tachytes* may now be considered its principal genus. It is in connection with this and the neighbouring sub-families of Sphegidae that some of the greatest taxonomical difficulties exist. We include in Larrides the " *Miscophus* group " of Kohl.

The species of the genus *Tachytes* seem to have habits very similar to those of the genus *Sphex ;* they form shafts in the earth and provision them with Orthoptera ; like the *Sphex* and other Fossores, they have the habit, when they fly to their tunnel with a victim, of depositing it for a short time on the ground close to the mouth of the burrow while they turn round and enter backwards ; and, after doing this they again seize their prey and drag it into the burrow. Fabre availed himself of an opportunity to remove the prey while the Hymenopteron was entering the hole alone ; as a result it had to come out again to seek the object ; this it soon found, and carried to the hole, relinquishing it again as usual while it turned round ; Fabre repeated the operation several times, and always with the same result ; the wasp, though it might have kept hold of the victim while it turned, and thus have saved itself from losing the precious object, never did so.

---

[1] When a second cell is more or less perfectly marked out, the cell with which it is connected is said to be appendiculate. The nervures frequently extend beyond the complete cells towards the outer margin, forming "incomplete" cells ; only complete cells are counted, except when "incomplete" is mentioned.

One species of *Tachytes* in the south of France selects as its prey Orthoptera of the family Mantidae, Insects of a highly ferocious disposition, and provided with most powerful front legs, capable of cutting in two by a single act the body of an aggressor like the *Tachytes;* the latter is, however, by no means dismayed by the arms of its future victim, but hovering above the latter for some time, as if to confuse it, and causing it repeatedly to turn its very mobile head, the *Tachytes* at last pounces down

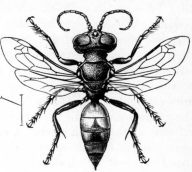

FIG. 45.—*Tachytes pectinipes* ♀. Britain.

and instantaneously stings the *Mantis* in the nerve centre between the formidable arms, which at once are reduced to incapacity ; subsequently the *Tachytes* paralyses each of the other pairs of legs, and then carries off its victim.

Larra anathema chooses mole-crickets as the viand for its young, and *Tachysphex panzeri* selects grasshoppers of the family Acridiidae. *Larra pompiliformis* (= *Tachytes niger,* Fabre) sometimes associates itself with *Sphex flavipennis* (? *S. maxillosus,* according to Kohl), forming its burrow amidst the works of a colony of that species, and making use, like the *Sphex,* of crickets for provender. This led Fabre to believe that the *Larra* stole its prey from the *Sphex,* but he has since withdrawn this indictment, and declares that the *Larra* obtains its crickets by the more honourable, if not more humane, process of catching and stinging them itself. Smith has informed us, on the faith of his own observation, that *L. pompiliformis* uses both Lepidopterous larvae and grasshoppers for its stores.

T. (Larrada) australis, according to Whittell, plays the part of a burglar, breaking open the cells of *Pelopaeus (Sceliphron) laetus* after they have been completed and stored with spiders ; it then takes possession of the cell, and curiously enough the *Pelopaeus* permits this, although the cell contains its egg and the store of food that is intended for the use of its own young. To us this seems very strange, but it is probable that the *Pelopaeus* has no idea of the consequences of the intruder's operations ;

it being one of the strange facts of nature that these highly endowed creatures never even see the offspring for whose welfare they labour with such extraordinary ingenuity and perseverance. Neither can we suppose that they have a conception of it derived from a knowledge of their own individual history; for their very complete metamorphosis is scarcely reconcilable with any such recollection on their part. It may possibly therefore be the case that, having no idea whatever of the offspring, they are equally destitute of any conception that it will be destroyed by the operations of the *Larrada*. However this may be, Whittell informs us that both wasps skirmish about for a little as if each were mistrustful and somewhat afraid of the other; this ends by the *Pelopaeus* withdrawing its opposition and by the *Larrada* taking possession of the cell, which it then proceeds to divide into two, using for the purpose of the partition portions of the material of the nest itself; possibly it is only a contraction of the size of the cell, not a true division, that is effected; however this may be, after it is accomplished the *Larrada* deposits its own egg in the cell, having, it is believed by Whittell, previously destroyed that of the *Pelopaeus*. Judging from what occurs in other species it is, however, more probable that the destruction of the egg or young of the *Pelopaeus* is carried out by the larva of the *Larrada* and not by the parent-wasp. From a remark made by Maindron as to the proceedings of *Larrada modesta*, in Ternate, it seems probable that its habits may prove to be similar to those of *L. australis*, for it frequents the nests of *Pelopaeus* after they have been completed.

Sub-Fam. 4. Trypoxylonides.—*Differ from Larrides by the inner margin of the eyes being concave, and the marginal cell not appendiculate. (In* Trypoxylon *there is only one distinct submarginal and one distinct discoidal cell, a second of each being indicated faintly.)*

The nervuration of *Trypoxylon* is very peculiar, and differs from that of the widely-distributed genus *Pison*, though according to Kohl's views the two may be correctly associated to form this sub-family. The species of *Trypoxylon* are apparently rather fond of human propinquity, and build clay- or mud-nests in or near houses. *T. albitarse* has this habit, and is well known in Southern Brazil under the name of "*Marimbouda da casa*";

this Insect, like *Pelopaeus*, stores its nest with spiders, and Peckholt has remarked that however great may be the number of spiders placed by the mother-wasp in a cell, they are all consumed by the larva, none ever being found in the cell after the perfect Insect escapes therefrom.   The European *T. figulus* forms a nest either in bramble-stems or in sandy soil or walls; it makes use of spiders as provisions.

Sub-Fam. 5. Astatides.—*Eyes very large in the male, meeting broadly on the vertex ; two spurs on the middle tibia.*

We have two species of the genus *Astata* in Britain : one of them—*A. boops*—is known to form burrows in the ground, each of which contains only a single cell; this, it appears, is usually provisioned with bugs of the genus *Pentatoma*, Insects remarkable for their strong and offensive odour.   St. Fargeau records that this species also makes use of a small cockroach for forming the food - store : thus exhibiting an unique catholicity in the toleration of the disagreeable ; almost the only point of connection between bugs and cockroaches being their disagreeable character.

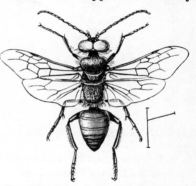

FIG. 46.—*Astata boops*, male.   Britain.

acter.   According to Smith, *Oxybelus*, another genus of Fossores, is also used.   Authorities are far from agreement as to the validity and relations of the sub-family Astatides.   It consists only of the widely-distributed genus *Astata*, with which the North American *Diploplectron* (with one species) is doubtfully associated.

Sub - Fam. 6. Bembecides. — *Labrum frequently elongate ; wing - nervures extending very near to the outer margin ; marginal cell of front wing not appendiculate ; mandibles not emarginate externally ; hind body stout, not pedicellate.*

The elongation of the labrum, though one of the most trustworthy of the characters of the Bembecides, cannot be altogether relied on owing to the variation it presents both in this and the allied sub-families. The Bembecides carry their prey to their young tucked underneath their own bodies and hugged to the breast; they affect loose, sandy soils for nidification; make use, in the great majority of the cases where the habits are known, of Diptera for provisions, and give these dead to the young; making repeated visits to supply fresh food to the progeny, which notwithstanding this fact, are distributed in isolated burrows.

One of the most interesting of Fabre's studies of the instincts of Hymenoptera is devoted to *Bembex rostrata*. The Bembecides have the habit of forming their nests in the ground in wide expanses of sand, and of cover-ing them up, they leave them so that there appears to be absolutely nothing by which the exact position of the nest can be traced; nevertheless the *Bembex* flies direct to it with-out any hesitation. How neces-sary it is to these Insects to possess this faculty of finding their nests will be understood when we recall that the *Bembex*

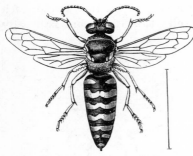

Fig. 47.—*Bembex rostrata* ♂. Europe.

does not provision its nest once and for all, but supplies the young at first with only insufficient food, and has therefore to return at daily, or other intervals, with a fresh store of provisions. The burrow is made in the sand by means of the fore-legs; these work with such rapidity and skill that a constant stream of sand flows out behind the Insect while it is engaged in the act of excavation. The nest or cell in which the larva is to live, is formed by this process of digging; but no fastening together of the material occurs, nor does any expedient seem to be resorted to, other than that of making a way through the sand by clearing out all the pieces of stick or stone that might diminish facility of access. The cell being formed, the *Bembex* leaves the spot in search of prey, and when it has secured a victim in the shape of a two-winged fly, it returns therewith to the burrow, and the booty is placed therein, an egg being deposited on it. The wasp then leaves the burrow, disguising, however, the spot where it is situate, and flies away; to proceed possibly with the formation of other burrows.[1] In the course of twenty-four hours the egg hatches, and the larva in two or three days completely devours the stock provided for it.   The mother-wasp then returns with another fly—this time probably a larger one—penetrates rapidly to the bottom of the burrow, and again retreats, leaving the second stock of provisions for the benefit of the greedy larva. These visits of supply are repeated with increased frequency, as the appetite of the larva for the benefit of which they are made increases with its growth.   During the fourteen or fifteen days that form this portion of the life-cycle, the single larva is supplied with no less than fifty to eighty flies for food. To furnish this quantum, numerous visits are made to each burrow, and as the mother *Bembex* has several burrows—though how many does not appear to be known—her industry at this time must be very great.   All the while, too, a great danger has to be avoided, for there is an enemy that sees in the booty brought by the *Bembex* to its young, a rich store for its own progeny.   This enemy is a feeble, two-winged fly of the family Tachinidae and the genus *Miltogramma;* it hangs about the neighbourhood of the nests, and sooner or later finds its opportunity of descending on the prey the *Bembex* is carrying, choosing for its purpose a moment when the *Bembex* makes a brief delay just at the mouth of the burrow; then down comes the *Miltogramma* and lays one, two, or three eggs on some portion of the booty that may be projecting from beneath the body of the wasp.   This latter carries in the food for its own young, but thus introduces to the latter the source of its destruction, for the *Miltogramma* larvae eat up the supply of food intended for the *Bembex* larvae, and if there be not enough of this provender they satisfy their voracity by eating the *Bembex* larva itself.   It is a remarkable fact that notwithstanding the presence of these strange larvae in the nest the mother *Bembex* continues to bring food at proper intervals, and, what is stranger still, makes no effort to rid the nest of the intruders : returning to the burrow with a supply of food she finds therein not only her legitimate offspring, a single tenant, but several others, strangers, it may be to the number of twelve ; although she would have no difficulty in freeing the nest from this band of little brigands, she makes no attempt to do so, but continues to bring the

[1] See on this point the note on p. 130.

supplies. In doing so she is fulfilling her duty; what matters it that she is nourishing the enemies of her race? Both race and enemies have existed for long, perhaps for untold periods of time, why then should she disturb herself, or deviate from her accustomed range of duties? Some of us will see in such proceedings only gross stupidity, while others may look on them as sublime toleration.

The peculiar habits of *Bembex rostrata* are evidently closely connected with the fact that it actually kills, instead of merely paralysing, its prey; hence the frequent visits of supply are necessary that the larvae may have fresh, not putrefying, food; it may also be because of this that the burrow is made in a place of loose sand, so that rapid ingress may be possible to the *Bembex* itself, while the contents of the burrow are at the same time protected from the inroads of other creatures by the burrow being filled up with the light sand. Fabre informs us that the *Bembex* larva constructs a very remarkable cocoon in connection with the peculiar nature of the soil. The unprotected creature has to pass a long period in its cocoon, and the sandy, shifting soil renders it necessary that the protecting case shall be solid and capable of keeping its contents dry and sound. The larva, however, appears to have but a scanty supply of silk available for the purpose of constructing the cocoon, and therefore adopts the device of selecting grains of sand, and using the silk as a sort of cement to connect them together. For a full account of the ingenious way in which this difficult task is accomplished the reader should refer to the pages of Fabre himself. Bembecides appear to be specially fond of members of the Tabanidae (or Gad-fly family) as provender for their young. These flies infest mammals for the purpose of feasting on the blood they can draw by their bites, and the Bembecides do not hesitate to capture them while engaged in gratifying their blood-thirsty propensities. In North America a large species of Bembecid sometimes accompanies horsemen, and catches the flies that come to attack the horses; and Bates relates that on the Amazons a Bembecid as large as a hornet swooped down and captured one of the large blood-sucking Motuca flies that had settled on his neck. This naturalist has given an account of some of the Bembecides of the Amazons Valley, showing that the habits there are similar to those of their European congeners.

Sphecius speciosus is a member of the Stizinae, a group recognised by some as a distinct sub-family. It makes use, in North America, of Insects of the genus *Cicada* as food for its young. Burrows in the ground are made by the parent Insect; the egg is deposited on the *Cicada*, and the duration of the feeding-time of the larva is believed to be not more than a week; the pupa is contained in a silken cocoon, with which much earth is incorporated. Riley states that dry earth is essential to the well-being of this Insect, as the *Cicada* become mouldy if the earth is at all damp. As the *Cicada* is about twice as heavy as the *Sphecius* itself, this latter, when about to take the captured burden to the nest, adopts the plan of climbing with it to the top of a tree, or some similar point of vantage, so that during its flight it has to descend with its heavy burden instead of having to rise with it, as would be necessary if the start were made from the ground.

Sub-Fam. 7. Nyssonides.—*Labrum short; mandibles entire on the outer edge; hind body usually not pedicellate; wing with the marginal cell not appendiculate.*

This group has been but little studied, and there is not much knowledge as to the habits of the species. It is admitted to be impossible to define it accurately. It is by some entomologists considered to include *Mellinus*, in which the abdomen is pedicellate (Fig. 48), while others treat that genus as forming a distinct sub-family, Mellinides. Kohl leaves *Mellinus* unclassified. Gerstaecker has called attention to the fact that many of the Insects in this group have the trochanters of the hind and middle legs divided: the division is, as a rule, not so complete as it usually is in Hymenoptera Parasitica; but it is even more marked in some of these Nyssonides than it is in certain of the parasitic groups.

Mellinus arvensis is one of our commonest British Fossores, and we are indebted to the late F. Smith for the following account of its habits: " It preys upon flies, and may be commonly observed resorting to the droppings of cows in search of its prey; it is one of the most wary and talented of all its fraternity; were it at once to attempt, by a sudden leap, to dart upon its victim, ten to one it would fail to secure it; no, it does no such thing, it wanders about in a sort of innocent, unconcerned way, amongst the deluded flies, until a safe opportunity presents itself, when

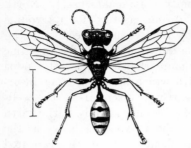

FIG. 48.—*Mellinus arvensis* ♀. Britain.

its prey is taken without any chance of failure ; such is its ordinary mode of proceeding. At Bournemouth the flies are more active, more difficult to capture, or have they unmasked the treacherous *Mellinus?* and is it found necessary to adopt some fresh contrivance in order to accomplish its ends ? if so, it is not deficient in devices. I noticed once or twice, what I took to be a dead specimen of *Mellinus*, lying on patches of cow-dung ; but on attempting to pick them up off they flew ; I at once suspected the creature, and had not long to wait before my suspicions were confirmed. Another, apparently dead fellow, was observed ; and there, neither moving head or foot, the treacherous creature lay, until a fine specimen of a Bluebottle ventured within its grasp, when, active as any puss, the *Mellinus* started into life, and pounced upon its victim."

Lucas states that in the north of France *Mellinus sabulosus* provisions its nest with Diptera, which it searches for on the flowers of Umbelliferae, and then carries to its nest. This is a burrow in the earth, and when it is reached the Hymenopteron deposits its Insect burden for a moment on the ground while it turns round in order to enter the burrow backwards. The same writer states that two varieties of this Insect live together—or rather in the same colonies—and make use of different species of Diptera, even of different genera, as food for their young. These Diptera are stung before being placed in the nest. The stinging does not kill the Insect, however, for Lucas was able to keep one specimen alive for six weeks after it had passed this trying ordeal.

Sub-Fam. 8. Philanthides.—*Labrum small ; anterior wings with three complete submarginal cells ; hind body constricted at the base but not so as to form a slender pedicel.*

This sub-family contains Insects resembling wasps or Cra-bronides in appearance, and is, as regards the pronotal structure, intermediate between the two great divisions of the Fossores, for the pronotal lobe extends nearly or quite as far back as the tegulae, and in *Philanthus* the two come into almost actual contiguity.

The species of the genus *Cerceris* are numerous in Europe, and several of them are known to make burrows in the ground, and store them with beetles for the benefit of the future larvae. The beetles chosen differ in family according to the species of *Cerceris ;* but it appears from the observations of Fabre and Dufour that one kind of *Cerceris* never in its selection goes out of the limits of a particular family of beetles, but, curiously enough, will take Insects most dissimilar in form and colour provided they belong to the proper family. This choice, so wide in one direction and so limited in another, seems to point to the existence of some sense,

Fig. 49.—*Philanthus triangulum* ♂.   Britain.

of the nature of which we are unaware, that determines the selection made by the Insect.   In the case of our British species of *Cerceris,* Smith observed *C. arenaria* carrying to its nest Curculionidae of very diverse forms; while *C. labiata* used a beetle —*Haltica tabida*—of the family Chrysomelidae.

The beetles, after being caught, are stung in the chief articulation of the body, that, namely, between the pro- and mesothorax.   *Cerceris bupresticida* confines itself exclusively to beetles of the family Buprestidae.   It was by observations on this Insect that Dufour first discovered the fact that the Insects stored up do not decay : he thought, however, that this was due to the liquid injected by the wasp exercising some antiseptic power; but the observations of Fabre have shown that the preservation in a fresh state is due to life not being extinguished ; the stillness, almost as if of death, being due to the destruction of the functional activity of the nerve centres that govern the movements of the limbs.

It has long been known that some species of *Cerceris* prey on bees of the genus *Halictus*, and Marchal has recently described in detail the proceedings of *C. ornata*. This Insect catches a *Halictus* on the wing, and, holding its neck with the mandibles, bends her body beneath it, and paralyses it by a sting administered at the front articulation of the neck. The *Halictus* is subsequently more completely stunned or bruised by a process of kneading by means of the mandibles of the *Cerceris*. Marchal attaches great importance to this " malaxation "; indeed, he is of opinion that it takes as great a part in producing or prolonging the paralysis as the stinging does. Whether the malaxation would be sufficient of itself to produce the paralysis he could not decide, for it appears to be impossible to induce the *Cerceris* to undertake the kneading until after it has reduced the *Halictus* to quietude by stinging.

Fabre made some very interesting observations on *Cerceris tuberculata*, their object being to obtain some definite facts as to the power of these Insects to find their way home when removed to a distance. He captured twelve examples of the female, marked each individual on the thorax with a spot of white paint, placed it in a paper roll, and then put all the rolls, with their prisoners, in a box ; in this they were removed to a distance of two kilometres from the home and then released. He visited the home five hours afterwards, and was speedily able to assure himself that at any rate four out of the twelve had returned to the spot from whence they had been transported, and he entertained no doubt that others he did not wait to capture had been equally successful in home-finding. He then commenced a second experiment by capturing nine examples, marking each with two spots on the thorax, and confining them in a dark box. They were then transported to the town of Carpentras, a distance of three kilometres, and released in the public street, " in the centre of a populous quarter," from their dark prison. Each *Cerceris* on being released rose vertically between the houses to a sufficient height, and then at once passed over the roofs in a southerly direction—the direction of home. After some hours he went back to the homes of the little wasps, but could not find that any of them had then returned; the next day he went again, and found that at any rate five of the *Cerceris* liberated the previous day were then at home. This record is of considerable interest owing to two facts, viz. that it is not considered that the *Cerceris* as a rule extends its range far from home, and that the specimens were liberated in a public street, and took the direction of home at once.

Philanthus apivorus is one of the best known of the members of this sub-family owing to its habit of using the domestic honey-bee as the food for its offspring. In many respects its habits resemble those of *Cerceris ornata*, except that the *Philanthus* apparently kills the bee at once, while in the case of the *Cerceris*, the *Halictus* it entombs does not perish for several days. The honey-bee, when attacked by the *Philanthus*, seems to be almost incapable of defending itself, for it appears to have no power of finding with its sting the weak places in the armour of its assailant. According to Fabre, it has no idea of the *Philanthus* being the enemy of its race, and associates with its destroyer on amicable terms previous to the attack being made on it. The *Philanthus* stings the bee on the under-surface of the mentum ; afterwards the poor bee is subjected to a violent process of kneading, by which the honey is forced from it, and this the destroyer greedily imbibes. The bee is then carried to the nest of the *Philanthus*. This is a burrow in the ground; it is of unusual depth—about a yard according to Fabre—and at its termination are placed the cells for the reception of the young; in one of these cells the bee is placed, and an egg laid on it : as the food in this case is really dead, not merely in a state of anæsthesia, the *Philanthus* does not complete the store of food for its larvae all at once, but waits until the latter has consumed its first stock, and then the mother-wasp supplies a fresh store of food. In this case, therefore, as in *Bembex*, the mother really tends the offspring.

Sub-Fam. 9. Mimesides. — *Small Insects with pedicellate hind body, the pedicel not cylindric ; mandibles not excised externally ; inner margin of eyes not concave ; middle tibia with one spur ; wings with two, or three, submarginal cells.*

Mimesides is here considered to include the Pemphredonides of some authors. Mimesides proper comprises but few forms, and those known are small Insects. *Psen concolor* and *P. atratus* form their nests in hollow stems, and the former provisions its nest with Homopterous Insects of the family Psyllidae. Little information exists as to their habits; but Verhoeff states that

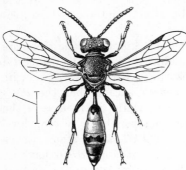

the species of *Psen*—like members of the Pemphredoninae—do not form cocoons.

The Pemphredonine subdivision includes numerous small and obscure Insects found chiefly in Europe and North America (Fig. 51, *P. lugubris*); they resemble the smaller black species of Crabronides, and are distinguished from them chiefly by the existence of at least two complete, submarginal cells on the anterior wing instead of one.

Fig. 50.—*Mimesa bicolor* ♂ .
Britain.

The species of *Passaloecus* live in the burrows that they form in the stems of plants; *Pemphredon lugubris* frequents the decayed wood of the beech.   The larva and pupa of the latter have been described by Verhoeff; no cocoon is formed for the metamorphosis.   Both these genera provision their nests with Aphidae.   This is also the case with *Stigmus pendulus*, but the burrows of this species form a complex system of diverticula proceeding from an irregular main channel formed in the pithy stems of bushes.

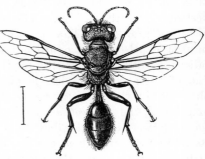

Fig. 51.—*Pemphredon lugubris* ♀ .   Britain.

Cemonus unicolor, according to Giraud, forms its burrows in bramble-stems, but it also takes advantage, for the purposes of nidification, of the abandoned galls of *Cynips*, and also of a peculiar swelling formed by a fly—*Lipara lucens*—on the common reed, *Arundo phragmites*.   This species also makes use of Aphidae, and Verhoeff states that it has only an imperfect instinct as to the amount of food it stores.

Sub-Fam. 10. Crabronides —*Pronotum short, front wing with one complete submarginal and two discoidal cells: hind body*

*variable in form, pedicellate in some abnormal forms, but more
usually not stalked.*

The Crabronides (*Vespa crabro*, the hornet, is not of this sub-
family) are wasp-like little Insects, with unusually robust and
quadrangular head.   They frequently have the hind tibiae more
or less thickened, and the clypeus covered with metallic hair.
It appears at present
that they are specially
attached to the tem-
perate regions of the
northern hemisphere,
but this may possibly be
in part due to their
having escaped attention
elsewhere.   In Britain
they form the most im-
portant part of the
fossorial Hymenoptera,
the genus *Crabro*
(with numerous sub-

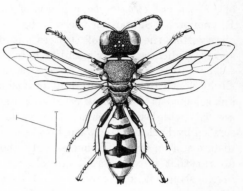

FIG. 52.—*Crabro cephalotes* ♀.   Britain.

genera) itself comprising thirty species.   The males of some of
the forms have the front tibiae and tarsi of most extraordinary
shapes.   They form burrows in dead wood, or in pithy stems,
(occasionally in the earth of cliffs), and usually store them with
Diptera as food for the larvae : the wings and dried portions of
the bodies of the flies consumed by Crabronides are often exposed
to view when portions of old wood are broken from trees.

The genus *Oxybelus* is included by some systematists, but
with doubt, in this sub-family ; if not placed here, it must form a
distinct sub-family.   It has the metathorax spinose, and the sub-
marginal and first discoidal cells are not, or are scarcely, separated.

Crabro leucostomus has been observed by Fletcher to form
cells for its larvae in the soft wood of broken willows : the food
stored therein consists of two-winged flies of the family Dolicho-
podidae.   This *Crabro* is parasitised by an Ichneumonid of the
genus *Tryphon*, and by a two-winged fly of uncertain genus, but
belonging to the family Tachinidae.   The metamorphoses of
Crabro chrysostomus have been briefly described by Verhoeff :
the food stored consists of Diptera, usually of the family Syr-

phidae; the larva spins an orange-red cocoon, passes the winter therein, and assumes the pupal form in the spring; there is, he says, a segment more in the female pupa than there is in the male.

The species of the sub-genus *Crossocerus* provision their nests with Aphididae, but *C. wesmaeli* makes use, for the purpose, according to Ferton, of an elegant little fly of the family Tipulidae; according to Pissot this same wasp also makes use of a species of *Typhlocyba,* a genus of the Homopterous division of Rhynchota. Supposing there to be no mistake as to this latter observation, the choice of Diptera and of Homoptera by the same species indicates a very peculiar habit.

Fertonius (Crossocerus) luteicollis in Algeria forms cells at a slight depth in sandy soil, and provisions them with ants. The ant selected is *Tapinoma erraticum,* and the individuals captured are the wingless workers. The mode of hunting has been described by Ferton; the wasp hovers over one of the ant-paths at a distance of a few millimetres only above the surface, and when an ant that is considered suitable passes, the *Fertonius* pounces on it, stings it, and carries it off to the burrow; forty or fifty ants are accumulated in a cell, the egg is laid in the heap of victims about one-third of the depth from the bottom; the resulting larva sucks the ants one by one, by attaching itself to the thorax behind the first pair of legs. There is a very interesting point in connection with the habits of this species, viz. that the ants are not only alive, but lively; they have, however, lost the power of co-ordinating the movements of the limbs, and are thus unable to direct any attack against the feeble larva. Ferton thinks there are three generations of this species in a single year.

NOTE.—In a note on p. 99 we have mentioned the new publication of Mr. and Mrs. Peckham on the habits of Fossores. We may here add that it contains much fresh information on these Insects, together with criticisms of the views of Fabre and others. One of the points most noteworthy is that they have observed *Crabro stirpicola* working night and day for a period of forty-two consecutive hours. They made experiments on *Bembex spinolae* with a view of ascertaining whether the female provisions two nests simultaneously; as the result they think this improbable. If the female Bembecid make nests only consecutively, it is clear it must have but a small fecundity. The larval life extends over about fifteen days; and if we allow three months as the duration of life of a female, it is evident that only about six young can be produced in a season.

CHAPTER IV

HYMENOPTERA ACULEATA *CONTINUED*——DIVISION IV. FORMICIDAE OR ANTS

Division IV. Heterogyna or Formicidae—Ants.

The segment, or the two segments, behind the propodeum, either small or of irregular form, so that if not throughout of small diameter, the articulation with the segment behind is slender, and there is great mobility. The trochanters undivided. The individuals of each species are usually of three kinds, males, females and workers; the latter have no wings, but the males and females are usually winged, though the females soon lose the flying organs. They live in communities of various numbers, the majority being workers. The larvae are helpless maggots fed and tended by the workers or by the female.

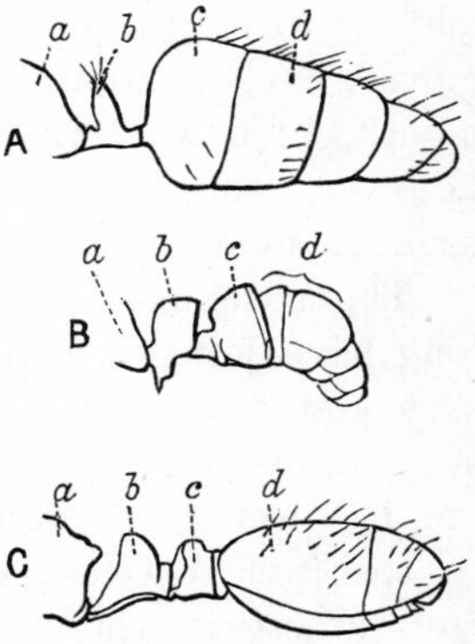

FIG. 53 —Abdomens of ants. **A**, Of *Camponotus rubripes* (Formicides); **B**, of *Ectatomma auratum* (Ponerides); **C**, of *Aphaenogaster barbara* (Myrmicides). *a*, Propodeum; *b*, first abdominal segment forming a scale or node; *c*, second; *d*, third abdominal segment.

In ants the distinction between the three great regions of the body is very marked. The abdomen is connected with the propodeum in a peculiar manner, one or two segments being detached from the main mass to form a very mobile articulation. This is the most distinctive of the characters of ants. The structure and form of these parts varies greatly in the family: and the Amblyoponides do not differ in a marked manner from the Scoliidae in fossorial Hymenoptera.

The arrangement of the parts of the mouth is remarkable, and results in leaving the mandibles quite free and unconnected with the other trophi; the mouth itself is, except during feeding, closed completely by the lower lip and maxilla assuming an ascending vertical direction, while the upper lip hangs down and overlaps the lower lip, being closely applied to it; so that in Ponerides

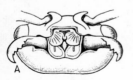 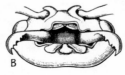

FIG. 54.—Front of head of *Dinoponera grandis*.
A, Mouth closed; B, open.

the palpi, except the apices of the maxillary pair, are enclosed between the upper and lower lips (Fig. 54, A). In Cryptocerini the palpi are not covered by the closed lips, but are protected by being placed in chinks at the outsides of the parts closing the mouth. The mandibles of ants can thus be used in the freest manner without the other parts of the mouth being opened or even moved. The mandibles close transversely over the rest of the mouth, and when shut are very firmly locked. There are, however, some ants in which the lips remain in the position usual in mandibulate Insects.

The antennae, except in the males of some species, have a long basal joint and are abruptly elbowed at its extremity. The eyes and ocelli vary excessively, and may be totally absent or very highly developed in the same species. The winged forms are, however, never blind. The size of the head varies extremely in the same species; it is frequently very small in the males, and largest in the workers. In some ants the worker-caste consists of large-headed and small-headed individuals; the former are called soldiers, and it has been supposed that some of them may act the part of superior officers to the others. It should be clearly understood that there is no definite distinction between soldiers and workers; so that in this respect they are widely different from Termites.

The complex mass forming the thorax is subject to great change of structure in the same species, according as the individuals are winged or wingless. The sutures between the dorsal

(notal) pieces are frequently obliterated in the workers, while
they are distinct in the males and females, and the pieces themselves are also much larger in size in these sexed individuals.
The pro-mesothoracic stigma is
apparently always distinct; the
meso-metathoracic one is distinct
in the male *Dorylus,* but can scarcely
be detected in the winged forms of
other ants, owing to its being enclosed within, and covered by, the
suture between the two segments:
in the workers, however, it is usually
quite conspicuous. The posterior
part of the thoracic mass, the propodeum or median segment, is of
considerable size; no transverse
suture between the component pieces
of this part can be seen, but its
stigma is always very distinct. The
peduncle, or pedicel, formed by the
extremely mobile segment or seg-

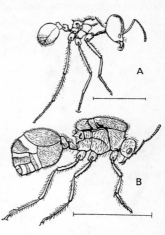

Fig. 55.—*Oecodoma cephalotes.* South
America. **A,** Worker major; **B,**
female after casting the wings.

ments at the base of the abdomen (already noticed as forming the most conspicuous character of the family), exhibits much

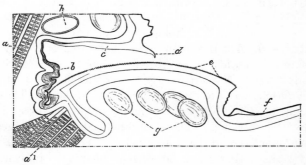

Fig. 56.—Stridulating organ of an ant, *Myrmica rubra,* var. *laevinodis.* Sagittal section
of part of the 6th and 7th post-cephalic segments. (After Janet.) *a, a[1],* muscles;
b, connecting membrane (corrugated) between 6th and 7th segments: *c,* 6th segment; *d,* its edge or scraper; *e,* striate area, or file on 7th segment; *f,* posterior
part of 7th segment; *g,* cells, inside body; *h,* trachea.

variety. Sometimes the first segment bears a plate or shield
called a scale (Fig. 53, A, *b*); at other times there are two

small segments (Fig. 53, B, C, *b*, *c*) forming nodes or knots, of almost any shape. The articulations between these segments are of the most perfect description. In many ants these parts bear highly developed stridulating organs, and the delicacy and perfection

FIG. 57.—Combs and brushes on front leg of an ant, *Dinoponera grandis* (tip of tibia, bearing the comb-like spur, and the base of the first joint of the tarsus; cf. fig. 75). A, Inner, B, outer aspect.

of the articulations allow the parts to be moved either with or without producing stridulation. In the male sex the peduncle and its nodes are much less perfect, and possess comparatively little capacity for movement; in the male of *Dorylus* (Figs. 79, A, and 80, *f*) the single node is only imperfectly formed. The eyes and ocelli of the males are usually more largely developed than they are in the female, though the head is much smaller.

The legs of ants are elongate, except in a few forms; the Cryptocerini and the males of Dorylides being the most conspicuous exceptions. The tarsi are five-jointed, the basal joint being disproportionately elongate, so that in use it acts in many species as if it were a portion of the tibia, the other four joints forming the functional foot. The front tibiae are furnished with a beautiful combing apparatus (Fig. 57).

Features of Ant-life.—In order that the reader may realise the nature of ant-life we may briefly recount its more usual and general features. Numerous eggs are produced in a nest by one or more queens, and are taken care of by workers. These eggs hatch and produce helpless maggots, of which great care is taken by the workers. These nurses feed their charges from their own mouths, and keep the helpless creatures in a fitting state by transporting them to various chambers in conformity with changes of temperature, humidity, and so on. When full grown the maggots change to pupae. In some species the maggots form cocoons for themselves, but in others this is not the case, and the pupae are naked.[1] After a brief period of

[1] The pupae and cocoons of ants are usually called by the uninstructed, "ants' eggs." In this country they are used as food for pheasants.

pupal life a metamorphosis into the perfect Insect occurs. The creatures then disclosed may be either winged or wingless; the wingless are the workers and soldiers—imperfect females—the winged are males or females fully developed. The workers remain in or near the nest they were produced in, but the winged individuals rise into the air for a nuptial flight, often in great numbers, and couple. When this is accomplished the male speedily dies, but the females cast their wings and are ready to enter on a long life devoted to the production of eggs. From this account it will be gathered that males are only found in the nests for a very short time; the great communities consisting at other periods entirely of the two kinds of females and of young. The imperfect females are themselves in some species of various kinds; each kind being restricted, more or less completely, to a distinct kind of duty.

No Insects are more familiar to us than ants; in warm countries some of them even invade the habitations of man, or establish their communities in immediate proximity to his dwellings. Their industry and pertinacity have, even in remote ages, attracted the attention and admiration of serious men; some of whom—we need scarcely mention Solomon as amongst them— have not hesitated to point out these little creatures as worthy of imitation by that most self-complacent of all the species of animals, *Homo sapiens*.

Observation has revealed most remarkable phenomena in the lives of these Insects. Indeed, we can scarcely avoid the conclusion that they have acquired in many respects the art of living together in societies more perfectly than our own species has, and that they have anticipated us in the acquisition of some of the industries and arts that greatly facilitate social life. The lives of individual ants extend over a considerable number of years—in the case of certain species at any rate—so that the competence of the individual may be developed to a considerable extent by exercise; and one generation may communicate to a younger one by example the arts of living by which it has itself profited. The prolonged life of ants, their existence in the perfect state at all seasons, and the highly social life they lead are facts of the greatest biological importance, and are those that we should expect to be accompanied by greater and wider competence than is usually exhibited by Insects. There can indeed be little doubt that ants are really not only the " highest " structurally or mechanically of all Insects, but also the most efficient. There is an American saying to the effect that the ant is the ruler of Brazil. We must add a word of qualification; the competence of the ant is not like that of man. It is devoted to the welfare of the species rather than to that of the individual, which is, as it were, sacrificed or specialised for the benefit of the community. The distinctions between the sexes in their powers or capacities are astonishing, and those between the various forms of one sex are also great. The difference between different species is extreme ; we have, in fact, the most imperfect forms of social evolution coexisting, even locally, with the most evolute.

These facts render it extremely difficult for us to appreciate the ant ; the limitations of efficiency displayed by the individual being in some cases extreme, while observation seems to elicit contradictory facts. About two thousand species are already known, and it is pretty certain that the number will reach at least five thousand. Before passing to the consideration of a selection from what has been ascertained as to the varieties of form and of habits of ants we will deal briefly with their habitations and polymorphism, reserving some remarks as to their associations with other Insects to the conclusion of this chapter.

Nests.—Ants differ greatly from the other Social Hymenoptera in the nature of their habitations. The social bees construct cells of wax crowded together in large numbers, and the wasps do the like with paper ; the eggs and young being placed, each one in a separate cell, the combinations of which form a comb. Ants have, however, a totally different system ; no comb is constructed, and the larvae are not placed in cells, but are kept in masses and are moved about from place to place as the necessities of temperature, air, humidity and other requirements prompt. The habitations of ants are in all cases irregular chambers, of which there is often a multiplicity connected by galleries, and they sometimes form a large system extending over a considerable area. Thus the habitations of ants are more like those of the Termites than those of their own allies among the Hymenoptera. They are chiefly remarkable for their great variety, and for the skilful manner in which they are adapted by their little artificers to particular conditions. The most usual form in Europe, is a number of subterranean chambers, often under the shelter of a stone, and connected by galleries. It is of course very difficult to trace exactly the details of such a work, because when excavations are made for the purposes of examination, the construction becomes destroyed; it is known, however, that some of these systems extend to a considerable depth in the earth, it is said to as much as nine feet, and it is thought the object of this is to have access to sufficiently moist earth, for ants are most sensitive to variations in the amount of moisture; a quite dry atmosphere is in the case of many species very speedily fatal. This system of underground labyrinths is sometimes accompanied by above-ground buildings consisting of earth more or less firmly cemented together by the ants; this sort of dwelling is most frequently adopted when the soil in which the nests are placed is sandy; it is probable that the earth is in such cases fastened together by means of a cement produced by the salivary glands of the ants, but this has not been determined with certainty; vaulted galleries or tunnels of this kind are constructed by many species of ants in order to enable them to approach desired objects.

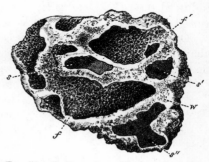

FIG. 58.—Portion of combined nest of *Formica fusca* and *Solenopsis fugax*. (After Forel.) × ⅔. *f, f'*, Chambers of *Formica*, recognisable by the coarser shading; *s, s'*, chambers of the *Solenopsis* (with finer shading); *s''*, opening in one of the chambers, the entrance to one of the galleries that connects the chambers of the *Solenopsis; w*, walls forming the foundations of the nest and the limits of the chambers.

In South America *Camponotus rufipes* and other species that habitually dwell in stumps, in certain districts where they are liable to inundations, build also nests of a different nature on trees for refuge during the floods. In Europe, a little robber-ant, *Solenopsis fugax*, constructs its dwelling in combination with that of *Formica fusca* (Fig. 58), in such a manner that its chambers cannot, on account of the small size of the orifices, be entered by the much larger *Formica*. Hence the robber obtains an easy living at the expense of the larger species. The Sauba or Sauva ants of South America (the genus *Atta* of some, *Oecodoma* of other authors) appear to be most proficient in the art of subterranean mining. Their systems of tunnels and nests are known to extend through many square yards of earth, and it is said on the authority of Hamlet Clark that one species tunnelled under the bed of the river Parahyba at a spot where it was as broad as the Thames at London Bridge.

A considerable number of ants, instead of mining in the ground, form chambers in wood; these are usually very close to one another, because, the space being limited, galleries cannot be indulged in. *Camponotus ligniperdus* in Europe, and *C. pennsylvanicus* in North America, work in this way.

Our British *Lasius fuliginosus* lives in decayed wood. Its chambers are said by Forel to consist of a paper-like substance made from small fragments of wood. *Cryptocerus* burrows in branches. *Colobopsis* lives in a similar manner, and Forel informs us that a worker with a large head is kept stationed within the entrance, its great head acting as a stopper; when it sees a nest-fellow desirous of entering the nest, this animated and intelligent front-door then retreats a little so as to make room for ingress of the friend. Forel has observed that in the tropics of America a large number of species of ants live in the stems of grass. There is also quite a fauna of ants dwelling in hollow thorns, in spines, on trees or bushes, or in dried parts of pithy plants; and the tropics also furnish a number of species that make nests of delicate paper, or that spin together by means of silk the leaves of trees. One eastern

Fig. 59.—Ant-plant, *Hydnophytum montanum*. Java. (After Forel.)

species—*Polyrhachis spinigera*—fabricates a gauze-like web of silk, with which it lines a subterranean chamber after the manner of a trap-door spider.

Some species of ants appear to find both food and shelter

entirely on the tree they inhabit, the food being usually sweet stuff secreted by glands of the plant. It is thought that the ants in return are of considerable benefit to the plant by defending it from various small enemies, and this kind of symbiosis has received much attention from naturalists. A very curious condition exists in the epiphytic plants of the genera *Myrmecodia* and *Hydnophytum;* these plants form large bulb-like (Fig. 59) excrescences which, when cut into, are found to be divided into chambers quite similar to those frequently made by ants. Though these structures are usually actually inhabited by ants, it appears that they are really produced by the plant independent of the Insects.

Variability and Polymorphism of Ants.—Throughout the Hymenoptera there are scattered cases in which one of the sexes appears in dimorphic form. In the social kinds of bees and wasps the female sex exists in two conditions, a reproductive one called queen, and an infertile one called worker, the limits between the two forms seeming in some cases (honey-bee) to be absolute as regards certain structures. This sharp distinction in structure is rare; while as regards fertility intermediate conditions are numerous, and may indeed be induced by changing the social state of a community.[1] In ants the phenomena of the kind we are alluding to are very much more complex. There are no solitary ants; associations are the rule (we shall see there are one or two cases in which the association is with individuals of other species). In correlation with great proclivity to socialism we find an extraordinary increase in the variety of the forms of which species are made up. In addition to the male and female individuals of which the species of Insects usually consist, there are in ants workers of various kinds, and soldiers, all of which are modified infertile females. But in addition to the existence of these castes of infertile females, we find also numerous cases of variability or of dimorphism of the sexual individuals; and this in both sexes, though more usually in the female. Thus there exists in ants an extraordinary variety in the polymorphism of forms, as shown by the table on p. 141, where several very peculiar conditions are recorded.

The complex nature of these phenomena has only recently

---

[1] The parthenogenetic young produced by worker females are invariably of the male sex.

become known, and as yet has been but little inquired into.   The
difference between the thoracic structure in the case of the winged
and wingless females of certain species (Fig. 55, and in vol. v.
fig. 339) is enormous, but in other species this difference appears
to be much less.   The ordinary distinctions between the queen-
female and worker-females appear to be of two kinds; firstly,
that the former is winged, the latter wingless;[1] and secondly, that
the former possesses a *receptaculum seminis*, the latter does not.
In a few cases it would seem that the dimorphism of winged
and wingless forms is not complete, but that variability exists.
Intermediate conditions between the winged and wingless forms
are necessarily rare ; nevertheless a certain number have already
been detected, and specimens of *Lasius alienus* have been found
with short wings.   In rather numerous species some or all of
the fertile females depart from the usual state and have no wings ;
(a similar condition is seen, it will be recollected, in Mutillides
and Thynnides of the neighbouring family Scoliidae).   A dimorphism as regards wings also exists in the male sex, though it is
only extremely rarely in ants that the males are wingless.   Never-
less a few species exist of which only wingless males have been
found, and a few others in which both winged and wingless
individuals of this sex are known to occur.   The wingless males of
course approach the ordinary workers (= infertile wingless females)
in appearance, but there is not at present any reason for
supposing that they show any diminution in their male sexual
characters.   The distinction between workers and females as
based on the existence or non-existence of a *receptaculum seminis*
has only recently become known, and its importance cannot yet
be estimated.   The adult, sexually capable, though wingless forms,
are called ergatoid, because they are similar to workers ('Εργατης,
a worker).[2]

[1] The student must recollect that the winged female ants cast their wings
previously to assuming the social life.   The winglessness of these females is a
totally different phenomenon from that we here allude to.
[2] See Forel, *Verh. Ges. deutsch. Naturf.* lxvi. 1894, 2, pp. 142-147 ; and Emery
Biol. Centralbl. xiv. 1894, p. 53.   The term ergatoid applies to both sexes ; a species
with worker-like female is ergatogynous ; with a worker-like male ergatandrous.

Table of the Chief Forms of Polymorphism in Ants.

Name of Ants.	Ordinary Winged Male.	Ergatoid Male.	Ordinary Winged Female.	Ergatoid Fertile Female.	Intermediate between Female and Worker.	Soldier.	Worker Major.	One or more kinds of Worker Minor.
Myrmica, Polyrhachis, etc.	+		+				+	
Camponotus, Atta, Pheidologeton, etc.	+		+				+	+
Pheidole, subg. Colobopsis	+		+			+		+
Eciton hamatum, E. quadriglume, E. foreli, etc.	+			+		+	+	+
Cryptocerus discocephalus, etc.	+		+			+	+	+
Strongylognathus	+		+			+		
Carebara and Solenopsis (except S. geminata)	+		+					+
Solenopsis geminata	+		+				+	+
Formica rufa	+		+		{ + exceptionally			
Ponera punctatissima	+	+	+				+	
Ponera ergatandria	?	+	+				+	
Cardiocondyla emeryi	+		+	+			+	
C. wroughtonii and C. stambuloffi		+	+				+	
Formicoxenus nitidulus		+	+				+	
Tomognathus	+			+			+	
Odontomachus haematodes	+		+		{ + exceptionally			
Polyergus	+		+	+				
Dorylus, Anomma, Eciton part.	+			+			+	+
Aenictus	+							+
Leptogenys, Diacamma	+			+	+		+	
Myrmecocystus melliger, M. mexicanus	+		+				{ + and honeypots	+
Ponera eduardi	+		+				{ + eyes large	{ + eyes obsolete
Anergates		+	+					

In addition to the above there are apparently cases of females with post-metamorphic growth in Dorylides, but these have not yet been the subject of investigation.

Much has been written about the mode in which the variety of forms of a single species of ant is produced. As to this there exists but little actual observation or experiment, and the subject has been much complicated by the anxiety of the writers to display the facts in a manner that will support some general theory. Dewitz was of opinion that workers and queens of ants were produced from different kinds of eggs. This view finds but little support among recent writers. Hart in recording the results of his observations on the parasol ant (of the genus *Atta*) —one of the species in which polymorphism is greatest—says [1] that these observations prove that " ants can manufacture at will, male, female, soldier, worker or nurse," but he has not determined the method of production, and he doubts it being " the character of the food." There is, however, a considerable body of evidence suggesting that the quality or quantity of the food, or both combined, are important factors in the treatment by which the differences are produced. The fact that the social Insects in which the phenomena of caste or polymorphism occur, though belonging to very diverse groups, all feed their young, is of itself very suggestive. When we add to this the fact that in ants, where the phenomena of polymorphism reach their highest complexity, the food is elaborated in their own organs by the feeders that administer it, it appears probable that the means of producing the diversity may be found herein. Wasmann has pointed out that the ants'-nest beetle, *Lomechusa,* takes much food from the ants, and itself destroys their young, and that in nests where *Lomechusa* is abundant a large percentage of ergatogynous forms of the ants are produced. He attributes this to the fact that the destruction of the larvae of the ant by the beetle brings into play the instinct of the ants, which seek to atone for the destruction by endeavouring to produce an increased number of fertile forms ; many ergatogynous individuals being the result. This may or may not be the case, but it is clear that the ants' instinct cannot operate without some material means, and his observation adds to the probability that this means is the food supply, modified either qualitatively or quantitatively.

The existence of these polymorphic forms led Herbert Spencer to argue that the form of an animal is not absolutely

[1] *Nature* li. 1894, p. 125.

determined by those "Anlagen" or rudiments that Weismann and his school consider to be all important in determining the nature or form of the individual, for if this were the case, how can it be, he asked, that one egg may produce either a worker, nurse, soldier or female ant ?   To this Wasmann (who continued the discussion) replied by postulating the existence of double, triple or numerous rudiments in each egg, the treatment the egg receives merely determining which of these rudiments shall undergo development.[1]   Forel seems to have adopted this explanation as being the most simple.   The probability of Weismann's hypothesis being correct is much diminished by the fact that the limit between the castes is by no means absolute.   In many species intermediate forms are common, and even in those in which the castes are believed to be quite distinct, intermediate forms occur as very rare exceptions.[2]   Emery accounts [3] for the polymorphism, without the assistance of the Weismannian hypothetical compound rudiments, by another set of assumptions ; viz. that the phenomenon has been gradually acquired by numerous species, and that we see it in various stages of development ; also that variation in nutrition does not affect all the parts of the body equally, but may be such as to carry on the development of certain portions of the organisation while that of other parts is arrested.   Speaking broadly we may accept this view as consistent with what we know to be the case in other Insects, and with the phenomena of post-embryonic development in the class.   But it must be admitted that our knowledge is at present quite inadequate to justify the formulation of any final conclusions.

The geological record of Formicidae is not quite what we should have expected.   They are amongst the earliest Hymenoptera ; remains referred to the family have been found in the Lias of Switzerland and in the English Purbecks.   In Tertiary times Formicidae appear to have been about the most abundant of all Insects.   At Florissant they occur in thousands and form in individuals about one-fourth of all the Insects found there. They have also been met with numerously in the European Tertiaries, and Mayr studied no less than 1500 specimens found

[1] *Biol. Centralbl.* xv. 1895, p. 640.
[2] Prof. Forel has favoured the writer by informing him of several cases of these rare intermediate forms he has himself detected.
[3] *Biol. Centralbl.* xiv. 1894, p. 53.

in amber. Formicides and Myrmicides are more abundant than Ponerides, but this latter group has the larger proportion of extinct genera; conditions but little dissimilar to those existing at present.

Classification of Ants.—Ants are considered by many entomologists to form a series called Heterogyna. They can, however, be scarcely considered as more than a single family, Formicidae, so that the serial name is superfluous. Their nearest approach to other Aculeates is apparently made, by *Amblyopone*, to certain Mutillides (*e.g. Apterogyna*) and to the Thynnides, two divisions of Scoliidae. Emery considers Dorylides rather than Amblyoponides to be the most primitive form of ants, but we are disposed to consider Forel's view to the effect we have above mentioned as more probably correct. The point is, however, very doubtful. The condition of the peduncle is in both the sub-families we have mentioned very imperfect compared with that of other ants. Both these sub-families are of very small extent and very imperfectly known. We shall also follow Forel in adopting six sub-families, Camponotides, Dolichoderides, Myrmicides, Ponerides, Dorylides, and Amblyoponides. Emery rejects the Amblyoponides as being merely a division of the Ponerides. This latter group displays the widest relations of all the sub-families, and may be looked on as a sort of central form. The Camponotides and Dolichoderides are closely allied, and represent the highest differentiation of the families in one direction. The Myrmicides are also highly differentiated, but are not allied to the Camponotides and Dolichoderides.[1]

Sub-Fam. 1. Camponotides.—*Hind body furnished with but one constriction, so that only a single scale or node exists on the pedicel. Poison-sac forming a cushion of convolutions, on which is situate the modified sting, which forms merely an ejaculatory orifice for the poison.*

The members of this very extensive division of ants can be readily distinguished from all others, except the Dolichoderides, by the absence of a true sting, and by the peculiar form of the hind body; this possesses only a single scale at the base, and has no

---

[1] Forel's latest views on this subject will be found in the *Ann. Soc. ent. Belgique* xxxvii. 1893, p. 161; the very valuable paper by Emery, in *Zool. Jahrb. Syst.* viii. 1896, p. 760.

constriction at all on the oval, convex and compact mass of the abdomen behind this. The cloacal orifice is circular, not, as in other ants, transverse. These characters are accompanied by a difference in habits. The Camponotides, though they do not sting, produce poison in large quantity, and eject it to some distance. Hence, if two specimens are confined in a tube they are apt to kill one another by the random discharges they make. Janet suggests that in order to neutralise the effect of this very acid poison, they may have some means of using, when they are in their natural abodes, the alkaline contents of a second gland with which they are provided. We shall mention the characters by which the Camponotides are distinguished from the small sub-family Dolichoderides when we deal with the latter.

The sub-family includes 800 or more species. *Camponotus* itself is one of the most numerous in species of all the genera of Formicidae, and is distributed over most parts of the earth. We have no species of it in Britain, but in the south of Europe the *Camponotus* become very conspicuous, and may be seen almost everywhere stalking about, after the fashion of our British wood-ant, *Formica rufa*, which in general appearance *Camponotus* much resembles.

Until recently, the manner in which fresh nests of ants were founded was unknown. In established nests the queen-ant is fed and tended by the workers, and the care of the helpless larvae and pupae also devolves entirely on the workers, so that the queens are relieved of all functions except that of producing eggs. It seemed therefore impossible that a fresh nest could be established by a single female ant unless she were assisted by workers. The mode in which nests are founded has, however, been recently demonstrated by the observations of Lubbock, M'Cook, Adlerz, and more particularly by those of Blochmann, who was successful in observing the formation of new nests by *Camponotus ligniperdus* at Heidelberg. He found under stones in the spring many examples of females, either solitary or accompanied only by a few eggs, larvae or pupae. Further, he was successful in getting isolated females to commence nesting in confinement, and observed that the ant that afterwards becomes the queen, at first carries out by herself all the duties of the nest : beginning by making a small burrow, she lays some eggs, and when these hatch, feeds and tends the larvae and pupae ; the first specimens of these latter that become perfect Insects are workers of all sizes, and at once undertake the duties of tending the young and feeding the mother, who, being thus freed from the duties of nursing and of providing food while she is herself tended and fed, becomes a true queen-ant. Thus it seems established that in the case of this species the division of labour found in the complex community, does not at first exist, but is correlative with increasing numbers of the society. Further observations as to the growth of one of these nascent communities, and the times and conditions under which the various forms of individuals composing a complete society first appear, would be of considerable interest.

An American species of the same genus, *C. pennsylvanicus*, the carpenter-ant, establishes its nests in the stumps of trees. Leidy observed that solitary females constructed for themselves cells in the wood and closed the entrances, and that each one in its solitary confinement reared a small brood of larvae. The first young produced in this case are said to be of the dwarf caste, and it was thought by the observer that the ant remained not only without assistance but also without food during a period of some weeks, and this although she was herself giving food to the larvae she was rearing.

Adlerz states that the females or young queens take no food while engaged in doing their early work, and that the large quantity of fat-body they possess enables them to undergo several months of hunger. In order to feed the young larvae they use their own eggs or even the younger larvae. It is to the small quantity of food rather than to its nature that he attributes the small size of the first brood of perfect workers. M. Janet [1] has recently designed an ingenious and simple apparatus for keeping ants in captivity. In one of these he placed a solitary female of *Lasius alienus*, unaccompanied by any workers or other assistants. and he found at the end of 98 days that she was taking care of a progeny consisting of 50 eggs, 2 larvae, 5 pupae in cocoons, 5 without cocoons. On the 102nd day workers began to emerge from the cocoons.[2] From these observations it is evident that the queen-ant, when she begins her nest, lives under conditions extremely different from those of the royal state she afterwards reaches.

[1] *Ann. Soct. ent. France*, 1893, p. 467.
[2] *Ann. Soc. ent. France*, 1893, *Bull.* p. cclxiv.

In many kinds of ants the full-grown individuals are known to feed not only the larvae by disgorging food from their own mouths into those of the little grubs, but also to feed one another. This has been repeatedly observed, and Forel made the fact the subject of experiment in the case of *Camponotus ligniperdus*. He took some specimens and shut them up without food for several days, and thereafter supplied some of them with honey, stained with Prussian blue; being very hungry, they fed so greedily on this that in a few hours their hind bodies were distended to three times their previous size. He then took one of these gorged individuals and placed it amongst those that had not been fed. The replete ant was at once explored by the touches of the other ants and surrounded, and food was begged from it. It responded to the demands by feeding copiously a small specimen from its mouth : when this little one had received a good supply, it in turn communicated some thereof to other specimens, while the original well-fed one also supplied others, and thus the food was speedily distributed. This habit of receiving and giving food is of the greatest importance in the life-history of ants, and appears to be the basis of some of the associations that, as we shall subsequently see, are formed with ants by numerous other Insects.

Oecophylla smaragdina, a common ant in Eastern Asia, forms shelters on the leaves of trees by curling the edges of leaves and joining them together. In doing this it makes use of an expedient that would not be believed had it not been testified by several competent and independent witnesses. The perfect ant has no material with which to fasten together the edges it curls ; its larva, however, possesses glands that secrete a supply of material for it to form a cocoon with, and the ants utilise the larvae to effect their purpose. Several of them

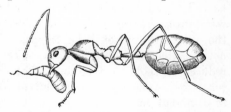

Fig. 60.—*Oecophylla smaragdina*. Worker using a larva for spinning.

combine to hold the foliage in the desired position, and while they do so, other ants come up, each one of which carries a larva in its jaws, applies the mouth of the larva to the parts where the cement is required, and makes it disgorge the sticky

material. Our figure is taken from a specimen (for which we
are indebted to Mr. E. E. Green) that was captured in the act
of bearing a larva.

Formica rufa, the Red-ant, Wood-ant, or Hill-ant, is in this
country one of the best-known members of the Formicidae. It
frequents woods, especially such as are composed, in whole or
part, of conifers, where it forms large mounds of small sticks,
straws, portions of leaves, and similar material. Although at
first sight such a nest may appear to be a chaotic agglomeration,
yet examination reveals that it is arranged so as to leave many
spaces, and is penetrated by galleries ramifying throughout its
structure. These mound-nests attain a considerable size when the
operations of the industrious creatures are not interfered with, or
their work destroyed, as it too often is, by ignorant or mischievous
persons. They may reach a height of three feet or near it, and
a diameter of twice that extent. The galleries by which the
heaps are penetrated lead down to the earth below. From the
mounds extend in various directions paths constantly traversed
by the indefatigable ants. M'Cook observed such paths in the
Trossachs ; they proceed towards the objects aimed at in lines
so straight that he considers they must be the result of some
sense of direction possessed by the ants ; as it is impossible to
suppose they could perceive by the sense of sight the distant
objects towards which the paths were directed : these objects in
the case M'Cook describes were oak-trees up which the ants
ascended in search of Aphides.

M'Cook further observed that one of the oak-trees was reached
by individuals from another nest, and that each of the two parties
was limited to its own side of the tree, sentinels being placed on
the limits to prevent the trespassing of an intruder ; he also
noticed that the ants saw an object when the distance became
reduced to about an inch and a half from them. This species is
considered to be wanting in individual courage ; but when acting
in combination of vast numbers it does so with intelligence and
success. It does not make slaves, but it has been observed by
Bignell and others that it sometimes recruits its numbers by
kidnapping individuals from other colonies of its own species.
Its nests are inhabited by forty or fifty species of guests of various
kinds, but chiefly Insects. Another ant, *Myrmica laevinodis*,
sometimes lives with it in perfect harmony, and *Formicoxenus*

nitidulus lives only with *F. rufa*.   Amongst the most peculiar of its dependants we may mention large beetles of the genera *Cetonia* and *Clythra,* which in their larval state live in the hills of the wood-ant.   It is probable that they subsist on some of the vegetable matter of which the mounds are formed.   Adlerz has given some attention to the division of labour amongst the different forms of the workers of ants, and says that in *F. rufa* it is only the bigger workers that carry building and other materials, the smaller individuals being specially occupied in the discovery of honey-dew and other Aphid products.   In *Camponotus* it would appear, on the other hand, that the big individuals leave the heavy work to be performed by their smaller fellows.

The wood-ant and its near allies have been, and indeed still are, a source of great difficulty to systematists on account of the variation that occurs in the same species, and because this differs according to locality.   Our European *F. rufa* has been supposed to inhabit North America, and the interesting accounts pub- lished by M'Cook of the mound-making ant of the Alleghanies were considered to refer to it.   This Insect, however, is not *F. rufa,* as was supposed by M'Cook, but *F. exsectoides,* Forel.   It forms colonies of enormous extent, and including an almost in- credible number of individuals.   In one district of about fifty acres there was an Ant City containing no less than 1700 of these large ant-hills, each one teeming with life.   It was found by transferring ants from one hill to another that no hostility whatever existed between the denizens of different hills ; the specimens placed on a strange hill entered it without the least hesitation.   Its habits differ in some particulars from those of its European congener ; the North American Insect does not close the formicary at night, and the inquilines found in its nest are very different from those that live with *F. rufa* in Europe. Whether the typical wood-ant occurs in North America is doubtful, but there are races there that doubtless belong to the species.

F. sanguinea is very similar in appearance to its commoner congener *F. rufa,* and is the only slave-making ant we possess in Britain.   This species constructs its galleries in banks, and is of very courageous character, carrying out its military operations with much tactical ability.   It is perfectly able to live without the assistance of slaves, and very frequently does so ; indeed it has been asserted that it is in our own islands (where, however, it is comparatively rare) less of a slave-owner than it is in Southern Europe, but this conclusion is very doubtful. It appears when fighting to be rather desirous of conquering its opponents by inspiring terror and making them aware of its superiority than by killing them; having gained a victory it will carry off the pupae from the nest it has conquered to its own abode, and the ants of the stranger-species that develop from these pupae serve the conquerors faithfully, and relieve them of much of their domestic duties. The species that *F. sanguinea* utilises in this way in England are *F. fusca, F. cunicularia,* and possibly *Lasius flavus.* Huber and Forel have given graphic accounts of the expeditions of this soldier-ant. In the mixed colonies of *F. sanguinea* and *F. fusca* the slaves do most of the house-work, and are more skilful at it than their masters. Adlerz says that one of the slaves will accomplish twice as much work of excavation in the same time as the slave-owner; these latter being lazy and fond of enjoyment, while the slaves are very industrious.

Polyergus rufescens, an European ant allied to *Formica,* is renowned since the time of Huber (1810) as the slave-making or Amazon ant. This creature is absolutely dependent on its auxiliaries for its existence, and will starve, it is said, in the midst of food unless its servitors are there to feed it. Wasmann, however, states that *Polyergus* does possess the power of feeding itself to a certain extent. Be this as it may, the qualities of this ant as warrior are superb. When an individual is fighting alone its audacity is splendid, and it will yield to no superiority of numbers; when the creatures are acting as part of an army the individual boldness gives place to courage of a more suitable sort, the ants then exhibiting the act of retreating or making flank movements when necessary. If a *Polyergus*

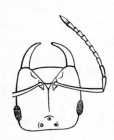

Fig. 61.—Head of *Polyergus rufescens.* (After André.)

that is acting as a member of a troop finds itself isolated, and in danger of being overpowered, it has then no hesitation in seeking safety even by flight. This species is provided with mandibles of a peculiar nature; they are not armed with teeth, but are pointed and curved; they are therefore used after the manner of poignards, and when the ant attacks a foe it seizes the head between the points of these curved mandibles, and driving them with great force into the brain instantly paralyses the victim.

Mandibles of this shape are evidently unfitted for the purposes of general work, they can neither cut, crush, nor saw, and it is not impossible that in their peculiar shape is to be found the origin of the peculiar life of *Polyergus*: we find similar mandibles reappearing amongst the aberrant Dorylides, and attaining a maximum of development in the ferocious *Eciton*; they also occur, or something like them, in a few aberrant Myrmicides; and in the male sex of many other ants, which sex exercises no industrial arts, this sort of mandible is present.

The ants that *Polyergus* usually attacks in order to procure slaves are *Formica fusca* and *F. fusca*, race *auricularia*; after it has routed a colony of one of these species, *P. rufescens* pillages the nest and carries off pupae and some of the larger larvae to its own abode. When the captives thus deported assume the imago state, they are said to commence working just as if they were in their own houses among their brothers and sisters, and they tend their captors as faithfully as if these were their own relatives: possibly they do not recognise that they are in unnatural conditions, and may be quite as happy as if they had never been enslaved. The servitors are by no means deficient in courage, and if the place of their enforced abode should be attacked by other ant-enemies they defend it bravely. The fact that *P. rufescens* does not feed its larvae has been considered evidence of moral degeneration, but it is quite possible that the Insect may be unable to do so on account of some deficiency in the mouth-parts, or other similar cause. The larvae of ants are fed by nutriment regurgitated from the crop of a worker (or female), and applied to the excessively minute mouth of the helpless grub: for so delicate a process to be successfully accomplished, it is evident that a highly elaborated and specialised arrangement of the mouthparts must exist, and it is by no means improbable that the capacity of feeding its young in true ant-fashion is absent in *Polyergus* for purely mechanical reasons.

M'Cook states that the North American ant, *Polyergus lucidus*, which some entomologists consider to be merely a variety of the European species, makes slaves of *Formica schaufussi*, itself does no work, and partakes of food only when fed by its servitors. He did not, however, actually witness the process of feeding. When a migration takes place the servitors deport both the males and females of *P. lucidus*. M'Cook adds that the servitors appear to be really mistresses of the situation, though they avail themselves of their power only by working for the advantage of the other species.

The honey-ant of the United States and Mexico has been investigated by M'Cook and others; the chief peculiarity of the

species is that certain individuals are charged with a sort of honey till they become enormously distended, and in fact serve as leather bottles for the storage of the fluid. The species *Myrmecocystus hortideorum* and *M. melliger*, are moderate-sized Insects of subterranean habits, the entrance to the nest of *M. hortideorum* being placed in a small raised mound. The honey is the product of a small gall found on oak leaves, and is obtained by the worker-ants during nocturnal expeditions, from which they return much distended; they feed such workers left at home as may be hungry, and then apparently communicate the

Fig. 62.—*Myrmecocystus mexicanus.* Honey-pot ant, dorsal view.

remainder of the sweet stuff they have brought back to already partly charged "honey-bearers" left in the nest. The details of the process have not been observed, but the result is that the abdomens of the bearers become distended to an enormous extent (Figs. 62, 63), and the creatures move but little, and remain suspended to the roof of a special chamber. It is considered by M'Cook that these living honey-tubs preserve the food till a time when it is required for the purposes of feeding the community. The distension is produced entirely by the overcharging of the honey-crop, the other contents of the abdomen being

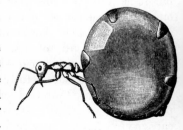

Fig. 63.—*Myrmecocystus mexicanus.* Lateral view.

forced by the distention to the posterior part of the body.
Lubbock has since described an Australian ant, *Melophorus
inflatus,* having a similar peculiar habit, but belonging to the
allied tribe Plagiolepisii.   Quite recently a South African honey-
tub ant belonging to the distinct genus *Plagiolepis* (*Ptrimeni*
For.) has been discovered, affording a proof that an extremely
specialised habit may arise independently of relation between the
Insects, and in very different parts of the world.

Species of the genus *Lasius* are amongst the most abundant
of the ant-tribe in Britain.   They are remarkable for their constructive powers.   *L. niger,* the common little black garden-ant,
forms extensive subterranean galleries, and is extremely successful
in the cultivation of various forms of Aphidae, from the products
of which the species derives a large part of its subsistence.   The
ants even transport the Aphidae to suitable situations, and thus
increase their stock of this sugary kind of cattle, and are said to
take the eggs into their own dwellings in the autumn so that
these minute and fragile objects may be kept safe from the
storms and rigours of winter.   These little creatures are brave,
but when attacked by other ants they defend themselves chiefly
by staying in their extensive subterranean galleries, and blocking
up and securing these against their assailants.

L. fuliginosus, another of our British species, has very different
habits, preferring old trees and stumps for its habitation ; in the
hollows of these it forms dwellings of a sort of card ; this it
makes from the mixture of the secretions of its salivary glands
with comminuted fragments of wood, after the fashion of wasps.
It is a moderate-sized ant, much larger than the little *L. niger,*
and is of a black colour and remarkably shining ; it gives off
a very strong but by no means disagreeable odour, and may be
seen on the hollow trees it frequents, stalking about in large
numbers in a slow and aimless manner that contrasts strikingly
with the active, bustling movements of so many of its congeners.
When this species finds suitable trees near one another, a colony
is established in each ; the number of individuals thus associated
becomes very large, and as the different colonies keep up intercommunication, this habit is very useful for purposes of defence.
Forel relates that he once brought a very large number of
Formica pratensis and liberated them at the base of a tree in
which was a nest of *L. fuliginosus ;* these latter, finding them-

selves thus assaulted and besieged, communicated in some way, information of the fact to the neighbouring colonies, and Forel soon saw large columns of the black creatures issuing from the trees near by and coming with their measured paces to the assistance of their *confrères*, so that the invaders were soon discomfited and destroyed.   Although the European and North American representatives of the sub-family Camponotides live together in assemblies comprising as a rule a great number of individuals, and although the separate nests or formicaries which have their origin from the natural increase of a single original nest keep up by some means a connection between the members, and so form a colony of nests whose inhabitants live together on amicable terms, yet there is no definite information as to how long such association lasts, as to what is the nature of the ties that connect the members of the different nests, nor as to the means by which the colonies become dissociated.   It is known that individual nests last a long time.   Charles Darwin has mentioned in a letter to Forel that an old man of eighty told him he had noticed one very large nest of *Formica rufa* in the same place ever since he was a boy.   But what period they usually endure is not known, and all these points probably vary greatly according to the species concerned.   It has been well ascertained that when some ants find their nests, for some unknown reason, to be unsuitable the inhabitants leave their abodes, carrying with them their young and immature forms, and being accompanied or followed by the various parasites or commensals that are living with them. Wasmann and other entomologists have observed that the ants carry bodily some of their favourite beetle-companions, as well as members of their own species.   Forel observed that after a nest of *Formica pratensis* had been separated into two nests placed at a considerable distance from one another so as to have no intercommunication, the members yet recognised one another as parts of the same family after the lapse of more than a month ; but another observation showed that after some years of separation they were no longer so recognised.

    Although it is now well ascertained that ants are able to distinguish the individuals belonging to their own nests and colonies from those that, though of their own species, are not so related to them, yet it is not known by what means the recognition is effected ; there is, however, some reason to suppose that it

is by something of the nature of odour.   One observer has noticed
that if an ant fall into water it is on emerging at first treated as
if it were a stranger by its own friends ; but other naturalists have
found this not to be the case in other species.   Contact with
corrosive sublimate deprives ants for a time of this power of
recognising friends, and under its influence they attack one
another in the most ferocious manner.

   The nests and colonies of the species of Camponotides we
have considered are all constructed by societies comprising a
great number of indi-
viduals ;   there   are,
however, in the tropics
numerous species that
form their nests on
foliage, and some of
these contain only a
few individuals.   The
leaf-nests (Fig. 64) of
certain species of *Poly-*
rhachis are said to be
formed of a paper-like
material, and to con-
tain each a female and
about 8 or 10 worker
ants.   Forel [1] has examined nests of several

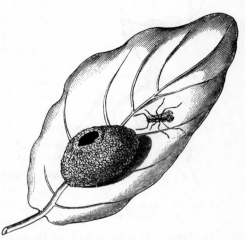

FIG. 64.—Nest of *Polyrhachis* sp.   (After Smith.)

Indian species, and finds they differ from those of other ants in
consisting of a single cavity, lined with silk like that of a spider.
These nests are further said to be constructed so as to render
them either inconspicuous or like other objects on the leaves ;
P. argentea covers its small dwelling with little bits of vegetable
matter, and a nest of *P. rastella* was placed between two leaves
in such a manner as to be entirely hidden.   All the species of
the genus do not, however, share these habits, *P. mayri* making
a card-nest, like *Dolichoderus* and some other ants.   The species
of the genus *Polyrhachis* are numerous in the tropics of the Old
World.

   Forbes noticed that a species of this genus, that makes its
paper-like nest on the underside of bamboo-leaves produces a noise

[1] Forel, *J. Bombay Soc.* viii. 1893, p. 36.

by striking the leaf with its head in a series of spasmodic taps. The same observer has recorded a still more interesting fact in the case of another species of this genus—a large brown ant—found in Sumatra. The individuals were " spread over a space, perhaps a couple of yards in diameter, on the stem, leaves, and branches of a great tree which had fallen, and not within sight

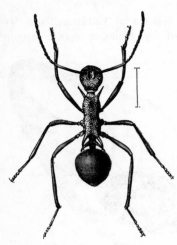

of each other ; yet the tapping was set up at the same moment, continued exactly the same space of time, and stopped at the same instant ; after the lapse of a few seconds all recommenced at the same instant. The interval was always of about the same duration, though I did not time it ; each ant did not, however, beat synchronously with every other in the congeries nearest to me ; there were independent tappings, so that a sort of tune was played, each congeries dotting out its own music, yet the beginnings and endings of the musical parties were strictly synchronous."

Fig. 65.—*Polyrhachis pandurus*, worker. Singapore.

Mr. Peal has also recorded that an ant—the name is not mentioned, but it may be presumed to be an Assamese species— makes a concerted noise loud enough to be heard by a human being at twenty or thirty feet distance, the sound being produced by each ant scraping the horny apex of the abdomen three times in rapid succession on the dry, crisp leaves of which the nest is usually composed. These records suggest that these foliage-ants keep up a connection between the members of different nests somewhat after the same fashion as do so many of the terrestrial Camponotides. Although the species of Camponotides have no special organ for the production of sound in the position in which one is found in Myrmicides and Ponerides, yet it is probable that they are able to produce a sound by rubbing together other parts of the abdomen.

Sub-Fam. 2. Dolichoderides.—*Hind body furnished with but one constriction so that only a single scale or node is formed ; Sting rudimentary ; the poison-sac without cushion.*

The Dolichoderides are similar to Camponotides in appearance, and are distinguished chiefly by the structure of the sting and the poison apparatus. To this we may add that Forel also considers the gizzard to be different in the two sub-families, there being no visible calyx in the Dolichoderides, while this part is largely developed in the Camponotides. This is one of the least extensive of the sub-families of ants, not more than 150 species being yet discovered. Comparatively little is known of the natural history of its members, only a very small number of species of Dolichoderides being found in Europe. The best known of these (and the only British Dolichoderid) is *Tapinoma erraticum,* a little ant of about the size of *Lasius niger,* and somewhat similar in appearance, but very different in its habits. *T. erraticum* does not cultivate or appreciate Aphides, but is chiefly carnivorous in its tastes. Our knowledge of it is due to Forel, who has noticed that it is very fond of attending the fights between other ants. Here it plays the part of an interested spectator, and watching its opportunity drags off the dead body of one of the combatants in order to use it as food. Although desti-tute of all power of stinging, this Insect has a very useful means of defence in the anal glands with which it is provided ; these secrete a fluid having a strong characteristic odour, and possessing apparently very noxious qualities when applied to óther ants. The *Tapi-noma* has no power of ejecting the fluid to a distance, but is very skilful in placing this odorous matter on the body of an opponent by touching the latter with the tip of the abdomen ; on this being done its adversary is usually discomfited. This

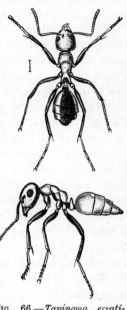

Fig. 66.—*Tapinoma errati-cum,* worker. Britain. Upper side and profile.

Insect is subterranean in its habits, and is said to change its abode very frequently. *T. erraticum* occurs somewhat rarely in Britain. Forel has also noted the habits of *Liometopum micro-cephalum*, another small European species of Dolichoderides. It is a tree-ant, and by preference adopts, and adapts for its use, the burrows made by wood-boring beetles. It forms extremely populous colonies which may extend over several large trees, the inhabitants keeping up intercommunication by means of numerous workers. No less than twelve mighty oaks were found to be thus united into a colony of this ant in one of the Bulgarian forests. The species is very warlike, and compensates for the extreme minute-ness of its individuals by the skilful and rapid rushes made by combined numbers on their ant-foes of larger size.

Fritz Müller has given a brief account, under the name of the Imbauba ant, of a Brazilian arboreal ant, that forms small nests in the interior of plants. The species referred to is no doubt an *Azteca*, and either *A. instabilis*, or *A. mulleri*. The nests are founded by fertilised females which may frequently be found in the cells on young *Cecropia* plants. Each internode, he says, has on the outside, near its upper part, a small pit where the wall is much thinner, and in this the female makes a hole by which she enters. Soon afterwards the hole is completely closed by a luxuriant excrescence from its margins, and it remains thus closed until about a dozen workers have developed from the eggs of the female, when the hole is opened anew from within by the workers. It is said that many of the larvae of these ants are devoured by the grubs of a parasite of the family Chalcididae. This Insect is thought to protect the plant from the attacks of leaf-cutting ants of the genus *Atta*.

We may here briefly remark that much has been written about the benefits conferred on plants by the protection given to them in various ways by ants : but there is reason to suppose that a critical view of the subject will not support the idea of the association being of supreme importance to the trees.[1]

Sub-Fam. 2. Myrmicides.—*Pedicel of abdomen formed of two well-marked nodes (knot-like segments). Sting present (absent in the Cryptocerini and Attini). (It should be noted that the*

[1] See von Ihering, *Berlin. ent. Zeitschr.* xxxix. 1894, p. 364 ; and Forel, *Ann. Soc. ent. Belgique*, xl. 1896, p. 170.

workers of the genera Eciton *and* Aenictus *of the sub-family*
Dorylides have, like the Myrmicides, two nodes in the pedicel.)

This sub-family consists of about 1000 species, and includes
a great variety of forms, but, as they are
most of them of small size, they are less
known than the Camponotides, and much
less attention has been paid to their
habits and intelligence. Forel, until recently, adopted four groups: Myrmicini,
Attini, Pseudomyrmini and Cryptocerini;
but he is now disposed to increase this
number to eight.[1] They are distinguished
by differences in the clypeus, and in the
form of the head; but it must be noted
that the characters by which the groups
are defined are not in all cases fully
applicable to the males. The Crypto-
cerini are in external structure the most highly modified of
Hymenoptera, if not of all the tribes of Insecta.

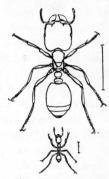

FIG. 67.—*Pheidologeton labo-*
riosus, large and small
workers. East India.

i. The MYRMICINI proper are defined by Forel as having the
antennae inserted near the middle, a little behind the front, of
the head, which has carinae on the inner
sides, but none on the outer sides, of the
insertions of the antennae; the clypeus extends between the antennae.

Certain genera of small European ants of
the group Myrmicini display some most
anomalous phenomena. This is especially
the case in *Formicoxenus, Anergates* and
Tomognathus. The facts known have, however, been most of them only recently discovered, and some obscurity still exists as to
many of even the more important points
in these extraordinary life-histories.

It has long been known that the little
Formicoxenus nitidulus lives as a guest
in the nests of *Formica rufa,* the wood-ant; and another
similar ant, *Stenamma westwoodi,* which shares the same life,

FIG. 68.—*Formicoxenus*
nitidulus, male. (After
Adlerz.)

---

[1] *Ann. Soc. ent. Belgique,* xxxvii. 1893, p. 163.

was declared by Nylander and Smith to be its male; it was however shown some years ago by André that this is a mistake, and that *S. westwoodi* is really the male of another ant that had till then been called *Asemorhoptrum lippulum*. This correction left the workers and females of *Formicoxenus nitidulus* destitute of a male, but Adlerz has recently discovered that the male of this species is wingless and similar to the worker, the female being a winged Insect as usual. It is very curious that the characters by which the male is distinguished from the worker should vary in this species; but according to Adlerz this is the case, individuals intermediate in several points between the males and workers having been discovered. This phenomenon of quite wingless males in species where the female is winged is most exceptional, and is extremely rare in Insects; but it occurs, as we shall see, in one or two other Myrmicides. Charles

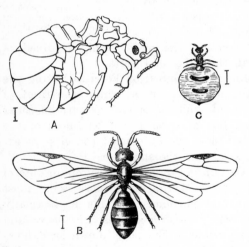

Darwin made the very reasonable suggestion that winged males may be developed occasionally as an exceptional phenomenon, and it is very probable that this may be the case, though it has not yet been demonstrated. *Formicoxenus nitidulus* occurs in England in the nests of *Formica rufa* and of *F. congerens*, but we are not aware that the male has ever been found in this country. The genus *Anergates* is allied to *Formicoxenus*,

FIG. 69.—*Anergates atratulus.* Europe. **A**. male, with part of hind leg broken off; **B**, female, with wings: **C**, female, after casting the wings and becoming a queen.

and occurs in Central Europe, but has not been found in Britain; the female, as in *Formicoxenus*, is winged and the male wingless, but there is no worker-caste; the male is a rather helpless creature, and incapable of leaving the nest. The species lives in company with *Tetramorium caespitum*, a little ant very like *Myrmica*, and not uncommon in South-East England. The female *Anergates* is at first an active little creature with wings, but after these are lost the body of the Insect becomes extremely distended as shown in Fig. 69, C; the creature is in this state entirely helpless, and as there are no workers, the *Anergates* is completely dependent, for the existence of itself and its larvae, on the friendly offices of the *Tetramorium* that lives with it. The mode of the association of these two Insects is at present both unparalleled and inexplicable, for only workers of the *Tetramorium* are found in company with the ♂ and ♀ *Anergates*; the community, in fact, consisting of males and females of one species and workers of another. The nests of *Anergates* are so rare that only a few naturalists have been able to observe them (Schenk, von Hagens, and Forel may be specially mentioned), but in the spots where they occur, nests of the *Tetramorium*, containing all the forms of that species, are numerous, and it therefore seems probable that a young fertile female of the *Anergates* may leave a nest in which it was born, enter a nest of the *Tetramorium*, and, destroying the queen thereof, substitute herself in the place of the victim; but if this be really the case, the larvae and pupae of the *Tetramorium* must also be destroyed, for no young of the *Tetramorium* are ever found in these strange associations. It is very difficult to believe that the *Tetramorium* workers should be willing to accept as their queen a creature that commenced her acquaintance with them by destroying their own queen or queens and a number of their young sisters; especially as the *Tetramorium* is a more powerful ant than the *Anergates*, and could readily dispose of the murderous intruder if it were disposed to do so. It is known, however, that colonies of *Tetramorium* completely destitute of queens sometimes occur, and Wasmann has suggested that the female *Anergates* may seek out one of these, and installing herself therein as a substitute, may be accepted by the orphaned colony. This plausible hypothesis has still to be verified.

The genus *Cardiocondyla* also exhibits the phenomenon of apterous, worker-like males, while in one species, *C. emeryi*, a winged male is also known to exist.

Tomognathus sublaevis is a little Myrmicid ant, found rarely in Denmark and Sweden, where its habits have recently been studied by Adlerz. A band of the *Tomognathus* attack the nest of another little Myrmicid, *Leptothorax acervorum*, and succeed by their own pertinacity and the fears of the *Leptothorax* in obtaining possession of it; the legitimate owners disappear, leaving the *Tomognathus* in possession of their larvae and pupae; these complete their development only to find themselves the slaves of *Tomognathus*. The subsequent relations of the two ants are friendly, the slaves even preventing their masters from wandering from the nest when they wish to do so. If an established mixed community of this nature is in want of additional servitors, the *Tomognathus* secure a supply by raids after the fashion of the Amazon-ant, bringing back to their abode larvae and pupae of *Leptothorax* to be developed as slaves. It was formerly supposed that the *Tomognathus* continued its species by perpetual parthenogenesis of the workers, for neither males nor females could be found. Adlerz [1] has, however, now discovered the sexual individuals. The male is an ordinary winged ant, and is so like that sex of the *Leptothorax*, that Adlerz had failed to distinguish the two before he reared them. The females are apterous, and in fact like the workers. It would perhaps be more correct to say that the workers of this species vary greatly but never become winged; some of them have ocelli and a structure of the thorax more or less similar to that of winged females, though none have been found with wings. Certain of these females possess a receptaculum seminis, and Adlerz treats this as the true distinction between female and worker. In accordance with this view the female of *Tomognathus* may be described as a worker-like individual possessing a receptaculum seminis, and having more or less of the external structures of winged females, though never being actually winged. It is probable that other workers reproduce parthenogenetically. The males of this species will not unite with females from the same nest, thus differing from many other ants, in which union between individuals of the same nest is the rule. Finally, to complete this curious history, we should remark that the larvae of the *Tomognathus* are so similar to those of the *Leptothorax* that Adlerz is quite unable to distinguish the two.

Strongylognathus testaceus and *S. huberi* live in association with *Tetramorium caespitum*, and are cared for by these latter ants; it is notable that as in the case of the slave-making *Polyergus rufescens* the mandibles of the *Strongylognathus* are cylindrical and pointed, and therefore unsuitable for industrial occupations.

[1] *Bih. Svenska Ak.* xxi. 1896, Afd. iv. No. 4.

S. testaceus is a weak little ant, and lives in small numbers in the nests with *T. caespitum*, which it is said to greatly resemble in appearance.   The proportions of the forms of the two species usually associated is peculiar, there being a great many workers of *T. caespitum* both in the perfect and pupal states, and also all the sexes of the *Strongylognathus*, of which, however, only a few are workers.   This would seem to suggest that *S. testaceus* attacks and pillages the nests of *T. caespitum* in order to carry off worker pupae, just as *Polyergus rufescens* does.   But the facts that *S. testaceus* is a weaker Insect than the *Tetramorium*, and that only a few of its worker-caste are present in a community where there are many workers of the *Tetramorium*, seem to negative the view that the latter were captured by the former; and the mode in which the associated communities of these two species are started and kept up is still therefore in need of explanation.

Strongylognathus huberi is a much stronger Insect than its congener, *S. testaceus*, and Forel has witnessed its attack on *Tetramorium caespitum*.   Here the raid is made in a similar manner to that of *Polyergus rufescens* on *Formica ;* the *Tetramorium* is attacked, and its pupae carried off to the abode of the *Strongylognathus* to serve in due time as its slaves.   The mandibles of *S. huberi*, being similar in form to those of *Polyergus rufescens*, are used in a similar manner.

Although *T. caespitum* is common enough in South-East England, it is to be regretted that none of the guests or associates we have mentioned in connection with it occur in this country.   It is a most variable species, and is distributed over a large part of the globe.

Our British species of Myrmicides, about ten in number, all belong to the group Myrmicini ; none of them are generally common except *Myrmica rubra*, which is a most abundant Insect, and forms numerous races that have been considered by some entomologists to be distinct species ; the two most abundant of these races are *M. ruginodis* and *M. scabrinodis*, which sometimes, at the time of the appearance of the winged individuals, form vast swarms.

The tiny *Monomorium pharaonis* is a species that has been introduced into Britain, but now occurs in houses in certain towns ; it sometimes accumulates on provisions in such numbers as to be a serious nuisance.   Seventeen thousand individuals weigh 1 gramme, and it is probable that a nest may include millions of specimens.

The genus *Aphaenogaster*[1] and its immediate allies include the harvesting ants of Europe and North America : they form subter-

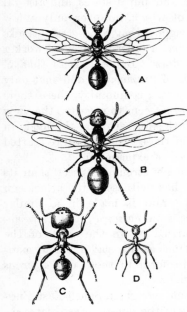

ranean nests consisting of isolated chambers connected by galleries ; some of the chambers are used as store-houses or granaries, considerable quantities of corn, grass, and other seeds being placed in them. *A. structor* and *A. barbarus* have been observed to do this in Southern Europe by Lespès, Moggridge, and others.

In the deserts about Algeria and Tunis a harvesting ant, *Aphaenogaster* (*Messor*) *arenarius*, is an important creature : its subterranean dwellings are very extensive, and are placed at a depth of several feet from the surface. Entrance to these dwellings is obtained by small holes, which are the orifices of galleries many feet in length : the holes are surrounded by pellets of sand projecting some-

Fig. 70.—*Aphaenogaster* (*Messor*) *barbarus*. Algeria. **A**, male ; **B**, winged female ; **C**, large worker or soldier ; **D**, small worker. × $\frac{3}{2}$.

what above the general surface, and consequently making the places conspicuous. The subterranean works occupy an area of fifty or a hundred square yards excavated at a depth of three to six feet. In these immense nests there exists a form of worker, of very small size, that never comes to the surface.[2]

Pogonomyrmex barbatus and other species have been observed to do harvesting in North America. After the workers of *P. barbatus* have taken the seeds into the nest they separate the husks and carry them out, depositing them on a heap or kitchen-

---

[1] Until recently this genus was generally known as *Atta*, but this name is now applied to the leaf-cutting ants, that were formerly called *Oecodoma*.

[2] Forel, *Bull. Soc. Vaudoise*, xxx. pp. 29-30, 1894.

midden, formed near by.   M'Cook has witnessed and described
the process of stripping the seeds.

Certain genera—e.g. *Aphaenogaster, Pheidole*—exhibit great
disparity in the forms of the workers, some of which are of
size much superior to the others, and possess disproportionately
large heads ; these large individuals are found in the same nest
as the smaller forms.   All the intermediate forms may frequently
be found, and at the same time, in the genus *Aphaenogaster ;* but
in *Pheidole* intermediates are of the utmost rarity.

The genus *Cremastogaster* is remarkable on account of the
shape of the hind body and its articulation, which give the
abdomen the appearance of being put on upside down.   This
mode of articulation may allow the Insect to threaten its enemies

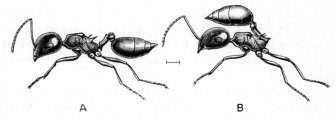

Fig. 71.—*Cremastogaster tricolor*, worker.   **A,** with abdomen extended ; **B,** uplifted.

when they are in front of it ; but it is doubtful whether the
Cremastogaster possesses an effective sting.

ii. The group ATTINI is distinguished by the presence of a
carina near the eye, by the antennae being inserted at a moderate
distance from one another, by the clypeus being prolonged backwards between them ; and by the absence of a sting.   The
group is not represented in Europe, but in Tropical America the
ants belonging to it are amongst the most important of natural
objects.   The species of the genus *Atta* (usually styled *Oecodoma*)
are the formidable leaf-cutting ants of America.   They occur in
enormous colonies in certain places, and will in a short time
completely strip a tree of its leaves.   As they appear to prefer
trees of a useful kind, especially those planted by man, their
ravages are often of the most serious nature.   The natives,
feeling it hopeless to contend with these Insect hordes, only too
frequently abandon all attempts to cultivate the trees and
vegetables the Insects are fond of.   Both Bates and Belt have

given accounts of some points in the economy of these ants. They are amongst the largest of the Formicidae, the females in some cases measuring about two and a half inches across their expanded wings; the males are much smaller, but are less dissimilar to their partners than is usual among ants. The workers, on the other hand, are so extremely different, that no one would suppose them to be at all related to the males and females (see vol. v. Fig. 339).

The mode of operation of these ants is to form paths from their formicary extending for a considerable distance in various directions, so that they have a ready access to any spot in a district of considerable extent; when a tree or bush is found bearing leaves suitable for their purposes, the worker ants ascend it in large numbers and cut up the leaves by biting out of them pieces similar in size and shape to a small coin; these pieces are then carried back in the jaws of the ants to their nests; the ant-paths are therefore constantly traversed by bands of little creatures carrying burdens homewards, or hurrying outwards in search of suitable trees.

The formicaries are of considerable size, and are described as consisting of low mounds of bare earth of considerable extent. Bates speaks of as great a circumference as forty yards; these accumulations of earth have frequently an appearance different from the adjoining soil, owing to their being formed of subsoil brought up from below; they are kept bare by the ants constantly bringing to and depositing on the surface fresh material resulting from their subterranean excavations. The true abodes, beneath the earth, are of greater extent than the mounds themselves, and extend to a considerable depth; they consist of chambers connected by galleries.

The leaf - cutting ants extend their range to North America, and M'Cook has recently called attention to a case there in which *A. fervens* made an underground route at an average depth of 18 inches, and at an occasional depth of 6 feet, extending 448 feet entirely beneath the earth, after which it was continued for 185 feet to reach a tree which the ants were engaged in defoliating. This route, extending altogether to a length of more than 600 feet, presented only a very slight deviation from a straight line drawn between the point of departure and the object to be attained. By what sense this ant was enabled to make a subterranean tunnel in a straight line to a desired object situated at so great a distance, we know not.

The use the leaf-cutting ants make of the enormous amount of material they gather was for long a subject of debate, and has only recently been ascertained by the observations of Möller. After being carried to the nest the pieces of leaves are cut into small fragments by another set of workers and formed into balls, which are packed in various parts of the nest, and amongst which the mycelium of a fungus—*Rozites gongylophora*—ramifies. This fungus the ants cultivate in the most skilful manner : they manage to keep it clear from mouldiness and bacterial agents, and to make it produce a modified form of growth in the shape of little white masses, each one formed by an agglomeration of swellings of the mycelium. These form the chief food of the colony. Möller ascertained by experiment that the results were due to a true cultivation on the part of the ants : when they were taken away from the nests, the mycelium produced two kinds of conidia instead of the ant-food.

Many details of the economy of these leaf-cutting ants are still very imperfectly known. The large-headed forms, called soldiers, have been the subject of contradictory statements ; Bates having concluded from his own observations that they are harmless, while Mr. J. H. Hart assures us that they are very fierce and vindictive, and inflict very serious wounds by biting (the Attini do not sting). We anticipate that the observations of both these naturalists will prove to be substantially correct, and that the differences in habits will be found to be owing to distinctions in the conditions of the community. In connection with this point we may remark that the function of the excessively large heads of certain kinds of soldier-ants is still obscure. In the East Indian *Pheidologeton diversus* the big soldiers are quite one hundred times as large as the smaller workers. As these latter bite viciously it would naturally be supposed that their gigantic *confrères* with enormous heads would be warriors of a most formidable nature ; but, as a matter of fact, the giants are unable to bite even when they try to do so. Aitken has somewhere suggested that these enormous individuals play the part of state elephants ; and we have been informed by Colonel Bingham that the small ants may frequently be seen riding in numbers on their unwieldy fellows. We anticipate however, that some other function will be found to exist for these forms with enormous heads. An examination of their organs of sense and of voice is very desirable.

Details of the modes in which the great communities of the leaf-cutting Attidae are maintained, are still wanting. The females do not, we have been informed by Mr. Hart, possess any considerable powers of aftergrowth, so that there is no reason to suppose them to be unusually prolific. At certain seasons great swarms of winged individuals are produced, and after leaving the nests pair in the manner of our European *Myrmica.* Possibly the females may, after losing their wings, again enter the large communities. Von Ihering states that the workers of *Atta lundi* are fertile.

iii. The group PSEUDOMYRMINI includes the genera *Pseudomyrma* and *Sima,* which are by some entomologists treated as but a single genus. The antennae are inserted near together on the front of the head ; there is no carina on the head external to their insertion, and the clypeus does not extend forwards between them. The Insects are usually of elongate form, possess a sting, and have a naked pupa. The group occurs in both hemispheres, but is exclusively exotic, and but little is known of the habits of its members. Forel has recently observed that numerous species live inside dried stems of grass or in hollow twigs, and are beautifully adapted for this mode of life by their elongate form, some of them being as slender as needles. Some interesting observations have been made in Nicaragua by Belt on *Pseudomyrma bicolor* and its relations with an acacia-tree, in the thorns of which it lives. The acacia in question is called the bull's-horn thorn, because the branches and trunk are armed with strong curved spines, set in pairs, and much resembling the horns of the quadruped whose name they bear. The ant takes possession of a thorn by boring a small hole near the distal extremity, and forms its nest inside. The leaves of this plant are provided with glands that secrete a honey-like fluid, which it appears forms the chief, if not the sole, subsistence of the ant. Belt considers that the presence of the ant is beneficial to the acacia ; he supposes that the ants assume the rights of proprietors, and will not allow caterpillars or leaf-cutting ants to meddle with their property ; the leaves are, he thinks, so preserved to the benefit of the tree.

Rothney has given some particulars of the habits of *Sima
rufo-nigra*, an ant of this group that appears to be not uncommon

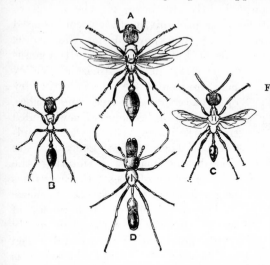

Fig. 72.—*Sima rufo-nigra* and
its associates. **A**, winged
female ; **B**, worker, of the
ant ; **C**, *Rhinopsis ruficornis*, a fossorial wasp of
the sub-family *Ampuli-
cides ;* **D**, a spider, *Salticus*
sp. The coloration is ex-
tremely similar in all these
creatures.

near Calcutta, where it lives on the trunks of trees in company
with a spider and a wasp that greatly resemble it in form and
in colour. The three creatures seem to associate together
on amicable terms ; indeed the wasp and the ant occasionally
indulge in wrestling matches without doing
one another any serious harm. In connection
with this fact we may observe that other
species of ants have been observed to indulge
in sports and feats of agility.

S. leviceps, an Australian species of this
genus, is furnished with a stridulating file
that has the appearance of being constructed
so as to produce two very different kinds of
sounds.

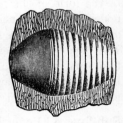

Fig. 73.—Stridulating file
of *Sima leviceps.*

iv. The CRYPTOCERINI are distinguished from other ants by their
antennae being inserted at the sides of the head, where they are
placed between ridges or in a groove into which they can be
withdrawn ; when in some cases they are entirely concealed.
These ants assume a great variety of shapes and forms, some of which
look almost as if they were the results of an extravagant imagination. The skeleton is usually much harder than it is in other

ants; the abdomen consists almost entirely of one very large segment, there being, however, three others visible at its extremity; these segments can be only slightly protruded, and the ants have no power of stinging. They are probably most of them arboreal in their habits. Nearly all of the known forms are exotic. According to the observations of Bates the species of the genus

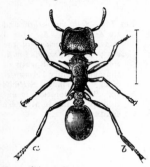

Cryptocerus in the Amazons Valley may frequently be observed in dry open places on low trees and bushes, or running on branches of newly felled trees; they also visit flowers abundantly. The species generally are wood-borers, usually perforating the dead branches of trees. *C. atratus* has been observed to construct its nests in the dead, suspended branches of woody climbers; a number of neatly drilled holes are all that can be seen externally; but, inside, the wood is freely perforated with intercommunicating galleries. Each community

FIG. 74. — *Cyrptocerus atratus*, worker. Amazons. The compressed first joint of the hind foot is shown at *a* and *b* in different positions.

appears to consist of a single female and two kinds of workers; the latter in some species are quite unlike each other, differing in the form of the head, and in the armature of the thorax and nodes of the peduncle. The species of *Cryptocerus* appear to be omnivorous, and are frequently attracted by the excrement of birds. The pupae are not enclosed in a cocoon. In the South of Europe two very minute ants, of the genera *Strumigenys* and *Epitritus*, belonging to this family, are met with under very large stones partly embedded in the earth. They are of the greatest rarity.

Sub-fam. 4. Ponerides. —*Hind body elongate, furnished with one node at the base, and having also great capacity of movement between the first and second segments, between which there is usually a slight constriction. Sting well developed.*

This sub-family includes numerous genera and about 400 species. The Ponerides have an elongate hind-body; the second segment behind the node is capable of great movement in and out of the preceding segment, and for this purpose is furnished with a basal portion slightly more slender than the apical part; this basal part is usually concealed within the more anterior segment, the hind margin of which embraces it very closely. On the middle of the dorsal aspect of this articulation there is usually placed a stridulating organ, consisting of an elongate band or patch of very fine lines; this gives out a sound when the second segment is moved in and out of the first at a time when the posterior edge of the latter is slightly depressed.

We follow Forel in including the Australian bull-dog ants— *Myrmecia*—in Ponerides, as well as the Odontomachi. The former have, however, a definite pedicel, consisting of two nodes (Fig. 76). In the Odontomachi the mandibles are approximate at their bases, being inserted on the middle of the front of the head (Fig. 77).

This sub-family includes a considerable number of species, and is found in all parts of the world. Extremely little is known as to the habits, but the true Ponerides do not, so far as is known, occur in large communities, and it seems probable that they are destitute of the powers of combined action that are so remarkable in the Camponotides, and in some of the Myrmicides and Dorylides. Most of the species that have been described are known by only one sex, so that very little knowledge exists as to the sexual distinctions; but from the little that is known it would appear that the three sexual forms are not so differentiated as they are in most of the Camponotides and Myrmicides.

The species of the genus *Leptogenys* are believed by Emery and Forel to possess an apterous female. Mr. Perkins has observed that the Hawaiian *L. falcigera* has workers with different kinds of sting, but no true female. Males of this species are, however, abundant. Wroughton has recently discovered that one member of this genus is of Termito-

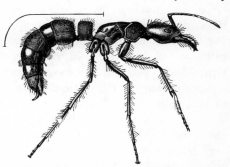

FIG. 75.—*Dinoponera grandis*, worker.   Amazons.

phagous habits, but this is not the case with *L. falcigera*. *Dinoponera grandis* (Fig. 75) is the largest of the Ponerides, its

workers attaining an inch and a quarter in length.   This Insect,
according to Bates, marches in single file in the thickets at Pará;
its colonies consist of a small number of individuals, and are
established at the roots of slender trees.   The effects of its
powerful sting are not so serious as is the·case with some of the
smaller ants.

In Britain we have only two representatives of the sub-family,
viz. *Ponera contracta,* a small ant of dirty-yellow colour, found
rarely in the Southern counties, living in moss or under stones.
Its colonies consist of only a few individuals; Forel giving fifty
as the highest number he has observed.   The second species, *P.
punctatissima,* presents the almost unique peculiarity of possessing two forms of the male sex, one of them resembling the
worker in most of its peculiarities, and in being destitute of
wings, while the other is winged, as is usual in male ants.   In
the island of St. Vincent another species of *Ponera* has been discovered having an apterous and worker-like male, and was named
by Forel *P. ergatandria.*[1]   The discovery of this form has led
him to express some doubt as to whether *Ponera punctatissima*
has two forms of males; but it seems probable that it really is
so, the ergatoid males being produced under somewhat different
circumstances from the normal males.   We have already said
that *Cardiocondyla* and a few other Myrmicides exhibit an
analogous peculiarity.

The genus *Myrmecia* is confined to the Australian continent
and Tasmania, and includes a considerable number of species of
large and moderate-sized ants, the classification of which has
been a subject of difference of opinion.   This has arisen from
the fact that the nodes of the abdominal pedicel are more similar
to those existing in the Myrmicides than to those of the typical
Ponerides.   There are, however, some American members of the
latter sub-family (*Paraponera clavata, e.g.*) that differ but little
in this point from *Myrmecia,* and, moreover, the pupae of *Myrmecia* are enclosed in a cocoon, while in the Myrmicides they
are usually naked.   On the other hand the nests are, it appears,
very large and populous, more like what exists in the Myrmicides; there is no true stridulating organ on the first abdominal
segment.   The genus is therefore one of those interesting
anomalies that form so large a proportion of the Australian

[1] *Tr. ent. Soc. London,* 1893, pp. 365-467.

fauna, and will probably be ultimately treated as a distinct sub-
family.   There are about thirty species.

The ants of this genus are well known to the residents in
Australia, where they are called " bull-
dog ants." They form large mounds of
earth for their nests.   The workers, and
females (Fig. 76) are much alike except
during the period when the latter are
still carrying their wings.   The males,
however, differ considerably, being of
more slender form, and possessing only
insignificant mandibles, and straight
antennae with a quite short basal joint.

Forel considers *Myrmecia* to be the
most formidable of all the ants ; the
hills are said to be sometimes five feet
high, and the colonies are immense in
numbers, while the Insect is an inch or

FIG. 76.—*Myrmecia pyriformis.*
Australia.   Female   after
casting wings.

more in length, and armed with a very powerful sting, the use
of which on the human body is said to give rise in some cases
to serious symptoms.   On the other hand, we have seen statements to the effect that the sting of *Myrmecia* has only very
evanescent sequelae ; it is also said that the ant-hills have only
a slight elevation, so that probably both these points differ
according to the species.   It appears from a communication of
Miss Shepherd's that the formidable *Myrmecia forficata* has its
larvae destroyed by a parasitic Hymenopteron (*Eucharis myr-
meciae*) of brilliant colour and considerable size, so that we have
the curious fact of the hordes of this most formidably armed ant,
which possesses also large eyes, falling a victim to a brilliant and
very conspicuous Insect.   Particulars of this case of parasitic attack
are still wanting.   There are other cases known of the larvae of
ants being destroyed by parasitic Diptera and Hymenoptera, but
in none of them have any sufficient observations been made as to
the mode in which the attack is made.   Lowne says that *M. gulosa*
itself attacks large beetles of the genus *Anoplognathus* and buries
them ; and he also adds the very curious statement that *M. nigrocincta*, when running, is able to take leaps of a foot in length.

The Odontomachi were formerly considered a distinct sub-
family, distinguished by the peculiar mandibles (Fig. 77).

Many of the Ponerides have elongate mandibles, but they are
inserted at the sides of the front of the head, not in the middle
of the front.   These organs in some species of Odontomachi
serve as levers, by aid of which the Insect can execute considerable
leaps.   In only a few species are the males known; Mayr and
Forel state that they are destitute of the peculiar mandibles
characteristic of the worker.

The unique European representative of the Odontomachi,
Anochetus ghiliani, occurs in Andalusia.   Near Tangier Mr.
George Lewis found it to be not uncommon; but the sexes are

not known, and it even appears doubtful whether there exists any well-
marked division between workers and
female.   Lewis observed, among the
ordinary forms, individuals with longer
bodies, usually one in a nest, and he
supposed these to be females; Saunders, on examining these examples,
found them to possess distinct ocelli,
and therefore agreed with Lewis as to
their being the female sex.   Dr. Emery
subsequently examined these same
specimens, and took what is scarcely
a different view, viz. that they are not

Fig. 77.—*Anochetus ghiliani*,
worker.   Tangier.

females but an intermediate form; and he also expressed the
opinion that "the true female may not exist."   The male of
Anochetus is not known.   The female of *A. mayri*, a Neotropical
species, has rudimentary wings.

Sub-fam. 5. Dorylides.—*Clypeus extremely small, the antennae
inserted very near the front margin of the head.   Hind
body usually elongate and subcylindrical, with an imperfect
pedicel formed by the constriction of the back of the first
segment, but occasionally there are two nodes in the workers.
Distinctions between the two sexes, and between the workers
and sexed forms, enormous, the queens truly wingless.   The
females and workers usually blind, or at any rate destitute of
facetted eyes.   (In Ecitonini the antennae are not inserted
quite at the front of the head, and there are two nodes in the
pedicel.)*

We have reserved to the end of the ants the consideration of the two groups Dorylides and Amblyoponides, recent investigations having rendered it somewhat doubtful whether they can be maintained as distinct from Ponerides. The chief character of the Dorylides is that the males are much less ant-like in form than they are in the other groups, and that the distinction between the females and workers are enormous. The little that is known as to the males and females of this group suggests the view that these sexes may offer sufficient reason for keeping the Dorylides as a group distinct from the other ants; but it must be admitted that it is very difficult to find satisfactory characters to distinguish the workers of the Dorylides in some cases from the Ponerides, in others (*Eciton*) from the Myrmicides.[1]

The Dorylides are of great interest, for they exhibit the remarkable phenomenon of a nomadic social life, accompanied by imperfect sight in the wanderers. The sub-family includes two apparently distinct groups: (1) the Ecitonini, peculiar to the New World, and having a close relationship with the Myrmicides; and (2) the Dorylini existing chiefly in the eastern hemisphere, and related closely by its workers to the Ponerides and Amblyoponides. (i.) The ECITONINI consist of the species of the genus *Eciton*, the wandering ants of America, and of *Labidus*, which there is now good reason for believing to consist of the males of *Eciton*.

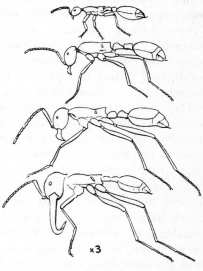

×3

FIG. 78.—Various forms of worker of *Eciton hamatum.* Guatemala.

The female is still uncertain. The *Eciton* are nomad ants having no fixed abode, but wandering from place to place in search of prey, and forming temporary resting-places. The

[1] For a valuable revision of *Dorylus* and its allies see Emery, *Zool. Jahrb. Syst.* viii. 1895, pp. 685, etc. We, however, doubt the wisdom of extending the sub-family so as to include *Cerapachys, Parasyscia*, etc.

species are rather numerous, and the habits of several have been described by Bates, who, however, was not acquainted with some of the most peculiar features in their biology, these having been since revealed by Belt and W. Müller.

These ants are predaceous in their habits, and some of the species travel in vast hordes; they occasionally enter houses and clear them of much of the vermin with which they may be infested. They have no facetted eyes, some of the forms being quite blind, while others have a pair of peculiar lenses in the position normally occupied by the compound eyes. Usually there are two castes of the workers, and in some species these are very different from one another, the mandibles being in the larger form very elongate, cylindrical and unfit for industrial purposes, while the individuals of the smaller caste have the outer jaws shorter, with their edges apposed and coadapted: in other species individuals with mandibles differentiated from the normal form do not exist. The nomad habits of these ants were described by Bates, but the detection of their temporary resting-places was reserved for Belt, who found that, after their plundering raids, they retired to a place of concealment, and there clustered together in a compact mass like a swarm of bees. Belt says: "They make their temporary habitations in hollow trees and sometimes underneath large fallen trunks that offer suitable hollows. A nest that I came across in the latter situation was open at one side. The ants were clustered together in a dense mass, like a great swarm of bees, hanging from the roof, but reaching to the ground below. Their innumerable long legs looked like brown threads binding together the mass, which must have been at least a cubic yard in bulk, and contained hundreds of thousands of individuals, although many columns were outside, some bringing in the pupae of ants, others the legs and dissected bodies of various Insects. I was surprised to see in this living nest tubular passages leading down to the centre of the mass, kept open, just as if it had been formed of inorganic materials. Down these holes the ants who were bringing in booty passed with their prey. I thrust a long stick down to the centre of the cluster and brought out clinging to it many ants holding larvae and pupae."

Turning now to the *Labidus* question: many American species of this genus have long been known, though all of them by the male sex only. The discoveries (to be subsequently alluded to) made in the Old World as to the relations between the driver ants and *Dorylus* raised a suspicion that *Labidus* might be the male of *Eciton*, the distinctions in the two cases being very analogous: this conjecture has been almost proved to be correct by the recent observations of Hetschko and W. Müller. The latter, who observed the temporary nests of *Eciton hamatum*, confirms Belt's statements as to the ants hanging together in clumps, like swarms of bees; he also states that the change from one temporary abode to another takes place at night, though, as is well known, the hunting forays of this ant are carried on in the daytime. The periods of migration appear to be determined by the time at which all the larvae have assumed the pupal state, this at any rate being the time chosen in the case observed by Müller. This naturalist bagged a part of one of the nests by the aid of ether, and found the larger portion to consist of pupae; there were also some larvae and eggs; a specimen of *Labidus* (*L. burchelli*) was also found on friendly terms with the *Eciton*-workers; and myrmecophilous Coleoptera were discovered. The pupae are enclosed in cocoons. Persistent search failed to reveal any female, but the examination was made under great difficulties. Müller also states that the earliest pupated larvae yield soldiers, the latest the smallest forms of workers. From observations made by Forel on a pupa, it seems probable that a wingless form of male may be found to exist. If therefore, as appears practically certain, *Labidus* is the winged male of *Eciton*, it is probable also that males of more or less worker-like form exist, as is now known to be the case in some other Formicidae.

We may here notice a peculiar apterous female ant recently described by André under the name of *Pseudodicthadia incerta*. He thought this might prove to be the female of *Eciton-Labidus;* but his description and figure are imperfect, and do not greatly support his idea of a connection between *Eciton* and *Pseudodicthadia*.

ii. The group DORYLINI includes the genus *Dorylus*, which was founded many years ago for Insects very like *Labidus*. As in the case of the American Insect named, males only were known; two or three allied genera, consisting exclusively of individuals of the sex mentioned, were subsequently described. In the

regions inhabited by these males

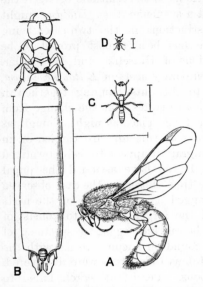

numerous species of blind ants are known, but only in the worker form, and were, or still are, referred to genera called *Typhlopone* and *Anomma*. Nothing that could be considered to be a female pertaining to any of these Insects was discovered until Gerstaecker described under the generic name *Dicthadia* an extraordinary apterous female ant found in Java, and it was suspected that it might be the long-expected female of the male *Dorylus* and of the worker *Typhlopone* or *Anomma*. This remained for many years without confirmation, but in 1880 Trimen announced the discovery in South Africa of an enormous apterous female ant, allied to *Dicthadia ;* it had

FIG. 79.—*Dorylus helvolus.* Africa. **A**, male; **B**, female (*Dicthadia*) ; **C**, worker major (*Typhlopone*) ; **D**, worker minor. (After Emery.)

been disinterred from a nest of small red ants believed (wrongly) to be *Anomma*. As *Dorylus* had been previously found in connection with allied worker ants it has since then been clear that notwithstanding the enormous differences existing between these three forms they may all pertain to one (or to closely allied) species. From this summary the student should understand that he will find in myrmecological literature many references to two or three genera that really belong to one species.

The workers of the Dorylini at present known are without exception quite blind, and are believed to be all of predaceous habits ; it is thought by some that they have no fixed abodes, but, like the Ecitonini, frequently change their residence, and it has been suggested that in doing so they make use of the nests of other ants as temporary abodes ; all these points are, however, still unsettled, and as there are several genera it is not unlikely that considerable variety will be found to prevail. The driver ants of Africa, belonging to the genus *Anomma*, are in some

respects similar to *Eciton* in habits, as they enter human habitations and cause nearly everything else to quit; it is probable
that they are also exclusively carnivorous.   Savage detected the
nests of *A. arcens,* but the account he has given of them is too
vague to permit one to decide whether the assemblages he saw
were of a nomad kind.   The workers of this species vary greatly

in size, and Emery has
recently stated that
he believes all the
supposed species of
the genus to be
merely varieties of *A.
burmeisteri.*   The
female of the driver
ants is still quite
unknown.   A *Dorylus*
has been ascertained

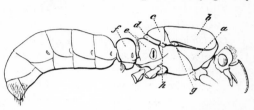

Fig. 80.—Body of male of *Dorylus* sp. Delagoa Bay.
a, pronotum; *b*, *c*, divisions of mesonotum; *d*,
metanotum; *e*, propodeum; *f*, first abdominal segment; *g*, *h*, points of insertion of anterior and posterior wings.

to be the male of *Typhlopone*.   The male *Dorylus* (Figs. 79, A,
and 80) is of great interest, for the propodeum is in a more primitive form than it is in any other petiolate Hymenopteron known to
us, while at the same time the pronotum and mesonotum are very
highly developed.   The genus *Typhlatta* Sm. has been recently
identified by Wroughton and Forel as the worker-condition of
which *Aenictus* is the winged male.   The genus *Alaopone* will
probably be found to have some species of *Dorylus* as its
male.

The females of the Dorylides are amongst the rarest of Insects,
and are also amongst the greatest of natural curiosities.   Although
worker ants and female ants are merely forms of one sex—the
female—yet in this sub-family of ants they have become so
totally different from one another in size, form, structure, and
habits that it is difficult to persuade oneself they can possibly
issue from similar eggs.   In the Insect world there are but few
cases in which males differ from females so greatly as the
workers of Dorylides do from the females, the phenomena finding
their only parallel in the soldiers and females of Termites; the
mode in which this difference is introduced into the life of the
individuals of one sex is unknown.   The largest of all the
Dorylides are the African Insects of the genus *Rhogmus*.   Only
the male is known.

The specimens of female Dorylides that have been detected may, after fifty or sixty years of research, be still counted on the fingers. As the greatest confusion exists in entomological literature owing to the forms of a single species having been described as two or three genera, the following summary of the principal names of genera of *Dorylides* may be useful :—

Eciton = the workers, *Labidus* = male : ♀ unknown.

Pseudodicthadia : female only known, possibly that of *Eciton.*

Cheliomyrmex : workers and soldiers only known.

Aenictus = the male, *Typhlatta* = worker : unknown.

Rhogmus : male ; female unknown. (According to Emery the worker is very small and like *Alaopone.*)

Anomma : only worker known ; male probably a *Dorylus.*

Dorylus = male ; *Dicthadia* = ♀ : *Alaopone* and *Typhlopone* = workers.

Sub-Fam. 6. Amblyoponides.—*Abdomen destitute of distinct pedicel ; the articulation between the first and second segments behind the true petiole being broad.*

We follow Forel in separating *Amblyopone* and a few allies from the Ponerides, because the abdominal pedicel is more

FIG. 81.—*Amblyopone,* worker. Tasmania.

imperfect than in any other ants. It is, indeed, very difficult to frame a definition that will include the Amblyoponides among ants, and at the same time separate Formicidae and Scoliidae. Forel considers the Amblyoponides to approach closely to certain divisions of the Scoliidae (Thynnides, *e.g.*). Little is known of these Insects, though they are widely distributed. *Amblyopone* is found in Australia and New Zealand ; the allied genus *Stigmatomma* has a wide distribution, occurring even in Europe. The social life is believed to be imperfect, and the habits subterranean and sedentary. The males and females are winged ; the latter much resemble the workers, which are nearly blind, and have a considerable general resemblance to *Anomma* in Dorylides.

Association of Ants with other kinds of Insects.—We have already alluded to the fact that a few species of ants are used by other species as attendants, and that the two kinds then live together quite amicably ; and we have also seen that a few ants live in association with other species on terms that are not yet understood.   One little ant, *Formicoxenus nitidulus,* lives only in the large nests of *Formica rufa ;* these ants tolerate the little *Formicoxenus,* which so far as is known does them neither good nor harm.   There are also a considerable number of species of small ants that are in the habit of choosing the neigh-bourhood of larger species for their dwelling-places ; in some cases the nests are constructed actually within a portion of the edifice of the more powerful species, and the rule then appears to be that these neighbours do not molest one another.   Not-withstanding the militant lives that many of them lead, ants cannot be considered as of generally ferocious disposition.

But the most remarkable point in connection with their toleration consists in the fact that the nests of many species are inhabited by quite a colony of foreign Insects of various Orders ; many of these, being found nowhere else, are spoken of as ants'-nest or Myrmecophilous Insects.[1]   The relations of ants with other Insects are of the most varied and complex character ; some of their guests live with them on terms of the most intimate association, being indeed absolutely dependent for their existence on the good offices of their hosts ; others of the ants'-nest Insects are enemies, while others are neutral or indifferent to the ants. We have already mentioned that the guests migrate in company with their hosts.

Many species of ants derive a considerable portion of their sustenance from the sweet substances excreted by Aphidae. Ants may constantly be seen occupied with clusters of Aphidae, and it is said that the ingenious little creatures defend from enemies the manufacturers of the sweet-stuff they are so fond of, even going so far as to form barricades and covered places for the isolation and protection of this peculiar kind of cattle ; a few ants keep some of the root-feeding Aphidae in their nests. Coccidae and other Homoptera, which also excrete much matter of a sugary nature, are likewise consorted with by ants ; as are also the larvae of some butterflies of the family Lycaenidae ; these latter being believed to furnish to the ants some substance

[1] A Catalogue of Myrmecophilous and Termitophilous Arthropods was pub-lished by Wasmann, Berlin 1894.

of a nutritious kind.   The Insects we have spoken of are, however, rather of the nature of ant-cattle, and the fondness of the
ants for them is not very remarkable.   The relations of the ants
to the peculiar species of Insects that live only in or around their
nests are much more extraordinary.   The greater number of these
guests belong to the Order Coleoptera, and of these there are many
hundreds—probably many thousands—of species that depend on
ants for their existence.   The family Pselaphidae furnishes a
large number of ants'-nest beetles, and it appears probable that
most of them excrete some
sugary substance of which the
ants are fond.   Many of these
Pselaphidae are of the most
fantastic shapes, more especially the members of the sub-
family Clavigerides.   But the
most curious of all the ant's-
nest beetles are the Paussidae,

Fig. 82.—The beetle, *Atemeles*, soliciting
food from an ant.   (After Wasmann.)

a family exclusively dependent on ants, and having the curious
faculty, when disturbed, of bombarding—that is, of discharging
a small quantity of vapour or liquid in a state of minute
subdivision accompanied by a detonation.   Many species of
Staphylinidae are peculiar to ant's-nests, and most of them are
indifferent or inimical to their hosts, but some of them, such as
Atemeles (Fig. 82) and *Lomechusa*, are doubtless producers of sweet
stuff that is liked by the ants.   The ants feed some of their special
favourites amongst these guests in the same manner as they feed
one another, viz. by opening the mouth, causing a drop of liquid
to appear on the lip, and remaining passive while the guest
partakes of the proffered *bonne bouche*.   This way of giving food
to other individuals is a most remarkable feature in the character
of ants ; it is not the same system that they adopt in feeding the
larvae, for they then make a series of actual movements, and
force the nutriment into the mouths of the grubs.   Besides the
Insects we have mentioned there are also Orthoptera, Hemiptera,
Poduridae and Thysanura, Acari, and small Isopod crustaceans
that live exclusively in company with ants.   We have mentioned
that a few Hymenopterous and Dipterous parasites have been
detected living at the expense of ants ; it is probable that
closer observation of the ant larvae and pupae in their nests

will disclose a greater number of the parasites of this latter class.

Much attention has been given to the relations between ants and their guests by Wasmann.[1] He arranges them in four categories ; 1, " Symphily " for the true guests, which are fed and tended by the ants, the guests often affording some substance the ants delight in ; 2, " Metochy," the class of tolerated guests, being so far as is known not disagreeable to the hosts ; 3, " Synecthry," including those Insects, etc., to which the ants are hostile, but which nevertheless maintain themselves in the midst of their foes ; 4, Parasites, dwelling in the bodies of the adult, or of the young ants. Many of these ants'-nest Insects present a more or less perfect resemblance to the ants in one or more points, such as sculpture, colour, size, or form. To these resemblances Wasmann attaches great importance. We should, too, notice that some of the inquilines [2] have become acquainted with the movements and habits of the ants, and stroke them (as the ants do one another) to induce them to disgorge food in the manner we have alluded to. According to Janet, ants of the genus *Lasius* are infested by Acari of the genus *Antennophorus*. The ants carry the mites, which assume positions so as not to cause greater inconvenience than is inevitable. Moreover, the ants give food to the mites when requested, and behave in a most obliging way to them, though there is not any reason for supposing that in this case the ants derive any benefit from the Symphily.

The relations between ants and plants have been of late years much discussed. We have already briefly alluded to the subject when speaking of the Pseudomyrmini. We will here only remark that ants frequent plants not only for the purpose of securing the sweet stuff excreted by the Aphidae that live on them, but also for the sake of getting the sweet products the plants themselves afford. Mr. Aitken, speaking of ants in India, says : " I have come to the conclusion that one of the most important sources of food-supply which ants have is the sacchariferous glands to be found at the bases of so many leaves." It is supposed that the ants are on the whole beneficial to the plants that thus afford them supply ; and this fact is considered by many to afford an adequate explanation of the existence of these interesting relations.

[1] For a summary of this subject see Wasmann, *Congr. internat. Zool.* iii. 1896, pp. 411-440.   [2] For explanation of this term see vol. v. p. 524.

CHAPTER V

Order V. Coleoptera.

Apparently wingless Insects when at rest, but really with four wings; the elytra, or anterior pair, shell-like, reposing on the back of the body and fitted together accurately along the middle by a straight suture; the posterior pair membranous, folded together under the elytra. Mouth with mandibles; lower lip not divided along the middle. Metamorphosis great and very abrupt; the larva being a grub or maggot, which changes to a pupa (usually soft) in which the external structure of the perfect Insect is conspicuous.

COLEOPTERA——or Beetles——are chiefly distinguished from other Insects by the solidity of their external integument, and by the peculiar nature of the first pair of their alar organs, which do not serve as instruments of flight, but as shells for protecting the upper face of the after-body, which, unlike the other parts, remains as a rule soft and membranous. These modifications of structure, though apparently slight, must be really extremely advantageous, for beetles are the predominant Order of Insects in the existing epoch. They depart from most other Insects in being less aerial in their habits; therefore, notwithstanding their enormous numbers, they do not meet the eye so frequently as flies, bees, or butterflies. The parts of the hard outer skeleton are beautifully fitted together, and as their modifications are easily appreciated they offer as fascinating a subject for study as do the skeletons of Vertebrata. The habits of beetles are so extremely varied that it is but little exaggeration to say that Coleoptera are to be found everywhere, when looked for. The number of species at present known is probably about 150,000. Of these somewhere about 3300 have been found in Britain. The structure

of the hard parts of the skeleton is of importance, as the classification of this enormous number of species is entirely based
thereon; it will be readily understood from the accompanying
diagram (Fig. 83). The general proportions of the chief parts
of the body call for a few remarks. The prothorax is remarkably
free, and is therefore capable of a much greater amount of movement independent of the after-body than it is in other Insects.
The mesothorax is, on the other hand, much reduced; its chief
function in the higher forms is to support the elytra, and to

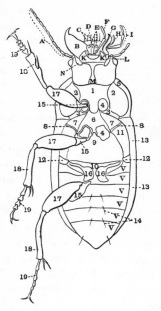

Fig. 83.—Under-surface of a beetle,
Harpalus caliginosus; legs and
antenna of one side, and some parts
of the mouth removed. **A**, antenna; **B**, mandible; **C**, labrum;
D, ligula; **E**, paraglossa; **F**, labial
palp; **G**, inner lobe of maxilla;
H, outer lobe (palpiform) of
maxilla; **I**, maxillary palp; **K**,
mentum; **L**, gena; **M**, gula; **N**,
buccal fissure; **V**, plates of ventral segments. 1, Prosternum;
2, prosternal episternum; 3, prosternal epimeron; 4, anterior and
middle coxal cavities; 5, inflexed
side of pronotum; 6, mesosternum;
7, mesosternal episternum; 8,
mesosternal epimeron; 9, metasternum; 10, posterior division of
metasternum or ante-coxal piece;
11, metasternal episternum; 12,
metasternal epimeron; 13, epi-
pleuron or inflexed margin of elytron; 14, ventral or ambulatory
setae; 15, trochanter; 16, posterior coxa; 17, femur; 18, tibia;
19, tarsus. (Modified from Leconte and Horn.)

help to keep them together by means of its scutellum. The
metathorax, on the contrary, is largely developed, except in the
rather numerous forms that are entirely deprived of powers of
flight. The composition of the abdomen has been a subject of
great difference of opinion. Its upper surface is usually entirely
covered by the elytra; the parts visible on the lower surface are
called ventral segments, and are usually five in number. Although
these five plates may constitute all that is superficially visible of
the abdomen, yet if the elytra are taken off it is found that a larger
number of segments—usually seven or eight—are visible on
the dorsum. This seeming discrepancy of number between the

dorsal and ventral plates is due to two facts ; 1, that the hind coxae have a great and complex development, so that they conceal the true base of the venter, which, moreover, remains membranous to a greater or less extent, and thus allows much mobility, and at the same time a very accurate coadaptation between the hard parts of the venter and the metasternum [1] ; 2, that the terminal segments are withdrawn into the interior of the body, and are correspondingly much modified, the modification being greater in the case of the ventral than in that of the dorsal plates. The anatomy of the parts of the abdomen that are not externally visible has not been adequately studied by coleopterists, but Verhoeff has inaugurated a careful study of the comparative anatomy of the terminal segments [2] ; unfortunately, however, he has not so thoroughly studied the modifications at the base, and as it is not clear that these are so uniform as he has taken for granted, it is possible that his numbering of the segments may have to be in some cases modified. The retracted plates or segments are so intimately connected with the internal copulatory organs that it is no easy matter to interpret them. For the nomenclature of these parts we must refer the student to Verhoeff's later works. He considers the abdomen as composed of ten segments, the dorsal plates being demonstrable, while the tenth ventral plate is usually absent. The anal orifice is placed immediately beneath the tenth dorsal plate, and above the genital orifice, which lies behind and above the ninth ventral plate. Peytoureau admits a diversity in both the number of segments and the position of the orifice. These studies in comparative anatomy are surrounded with difficulties, and no morphological conclusions based on them can be considered as final until they have been confirmed by observation of the development of the parts.

The elytra—or wing-cases—frequently have a remarkable sculpture, the use of which is unknown. According to Hofbauer there are between the outer and inner layers, glands secreting a

---

[1] An interesting exception occurs in the Malacodermidae, where this coadaptation is wanting, or is imperfect ; they are frequently considered to be the most primitive of existing beetles.

[2] In a series of memoirs in various German periodicals during the last five or six years (see especially *Deutsche ent. Zeit.* 1893 and 1894, also subsequent years of *Arch. Naturges.*). It should be noticed that in the course of his studies Verhoeff has modified some of his earlier views.

fluid that reaches the surface through small pores. Hicks supposed that he detected nerve cells. Meinert is of opinion that the elytra correspond to the tegulæ of Hymenoptera rather than to the wings of other Insects, but the little evidence that exists is not favourable to this view. The two elytra are usually, in repose, very perfectly fitted together by a complete coadaptation along the middle of the body, so that it is difficult to separate them; this line of junction is called the suture. There are forms in which the coadaptation is quite imperfect (Malacodermidae) and some in which it does not exist at all (*Meloë*). The wings proper of beetles correspond to the posterior pair in other Insects, and are much more irregular in nervuration than those of most other Insects, correlative, it is supposed, with the folding they are subjected to in order to get them beneath the wing-cases. There are large numbers of species, genera, and groups of genera, all the members of which have the wings so much reduced in size as to be quite useless for purposes of flight. These forms are called apterous, though they are not really so, for the elytra (which are really the anterior wings) are present, and even the posterior wings are not truly absent in these cases, though they are sometimes so extremely rudimentary as to elude all but the most careful observation. The number of forms in which the elytra are absent is extremely small; this condition occurs only in the female sex; it is usually confined to cases in which the female is larva-like in form; but in the extraordinary Mediterranean Lamellicorn genus, *Pachypus*, the females are destitute of wings and elytra, though the anterior parts of the body are normally formed: these individuals live underground and rarely or never emerge. When the wings are absent the elytra are frequently soldered; that is to say, united together along the suture by some sort of secondary exudation; this union occurs in every degree of firmness, and appears to be variable in the individuals of one species; probably in accordance with the age of the individual. In most beetles the elytra are not only themselves closely connected, but are also very accurately coadapted with the sides of the body, except at the tip. Sometimes a coadaptation occurs between the tips of the elytra and the body, but not at the tip of the latter. In such cases one or more dorsal plates are left exposed: the last of such exposed dorsal plates is termed pygidium; a similar plate anterior to the pygidium is called propygidium.

Larvae.—Owing to the difficulty of rearing Coleoptera, less is perhaps known of their life-histories than of those of other Insects. They exhibit, however, extreme diversity correlative with the great specialisation of so many beetles to particular kinds of life. Most beetles must have exactly the right conditions to live in. The larvae of many forms are known. They are composed of a head, three thoracic segments (usually very distinct), and a number of abdominal segments varying from eight to ten. Coleopterous larvae are usually described as having nine abdominal segments; and it is but rarely that ten can be readily detected; they are, however, visible in various forms, as is the case in the form figured (Fig. 84). A great many of them possess a peculiar pseudopod at the underside of the body near or at the extremity; it can in many cases be entirely retracted into the body, and is generally described as being the pro-

truded termination of the alimentary canal. Inspection of a series of larvae shows that it represents a body segment: it is sometimes armed with hooks. Three pairs of small thoracic legs are often present, but are very often completely absent. These

FIG. 84.—Larva of a beetle, Family Cerambycidae (? *Aromia moschata*). The first spiracle is placed just at the hind margin of the large prothoracic segment. (From La Massane.)

thoracic legs may be present in the young larva, but not in the older (*Bruchus*). The usual number of spiracles is nine pairs, one prothoracic, eight abdominal; but this is subject to many exceptions, and mesothoracic and metathoracic stigmata are occasionally found. The figures we give in the following pages will enable the student to form some idea of the variety of form exhibited by beetle larvae.

Pupation usually takes place in a cavity in the earth, or near the feeding-place, but a great many species form a cocoon, composed either of fragments of earth or of wood, and slightly cemented together. A few suspend themselves by the tail after the manner of butterfly caterpillars (Cassididae, Coccinellidae). The pupae are usually extremely soft, their appendages not being fastened to the body. But some pupae (Staphylinides) are truly obtected, having a hard shell and the rudimentary appendages fastened by exudation to the body, like Lepidopterous pupae, and others (Coccinellidae) are intermediate

between this state and the normal soft pupa. The pupal state
lasts but a short time, from one to three weeks being the usual
period. The perfect Insect is at first soft and almost colourless,
and it is often some days before it attains its complete coloration
and hardness.

Classification.—Owing to the hardness of the skeleton, beetles
shrivel but little after death, so that the form and relations of
the various sclerites can usually be detected with ease. These
sclerites seem to be remarkably constant (except in the case of
sexual distinctions) within the limits of each species, and are
very useful for the formation of genera and groups of genera ;
but they vary so much outside the limits mentioned that it is
very difficult to make use of them for defining the larger groups.
Hence it is not easy to frame accurate definitions of the
families, and still less so to arrange these families in more comprehensive series. The natural difficulty has been much increased
by the habit coleopterists have of framing their definitions
on what is visible without the aid of dissection. Nevertheless
considerable progress has been made. We are obliged at present
to adopt upwards of eighty families ; and we are able to distinguish on positive characters five series ; this leaves a large
number of forms still unclassified, and these we have here
associated as a sixth series, which we have called Coleoptera Polymorpha. This series corresponds with the two series called in
books Clavicornia and Serricornia. As it is admitted to be
impossible to define these two series, we think it much better to
act accordingly, and to establish for the present a great group
that can only be characterised by the fact that its members do
not belong to any of the other five series. No doubt a larger
knowledge of development, coupled with the advance of comparative anatomy, will ultimately bring about a better state of
affairs. The Strepsiptera, with one family Stylopidae, are only
provisionally included among the Coleoptera. These six series
are fairly equal as regards extent. Though the Polymorpha
includes the larger number of forms, yet a large part of them
belong to four great families (Staphylinidae, Buprestidae, Elateridae, Malacodermidae), which are easily recognisable, so that
the number of unmanageable forms is not really great. Indeed,
an acquaintance with the external anatomy of two or three
dozen species, selected as typical, would enable a student to classify

with tolerable certainty the vast majority of species that he would subsequently meet with.

Series 1. *Lamellicornia.*—Antennae with the terminal joints leaf-like (or broader than the others, if not actually leaf-like), and capable of separation and of accurate apposition.   Tarsi five-jointed.

Series 2. *Adephaga*—(*Caraboidea* of some authors).—Antennae never lamelliform, thin at the end ; all the tarsi five-jointed, with the fourth joint quite distinct.   Maxillae highly developed, with the outer lobe slender and divided into two segments so as to be palpiform.   Abdomen with six (or more) ventral segments visible.

Series 3. *Polymorpha.*—Antennae frequently with either a club, *i.e.* the distal joints broader [Clavicorn series of authors], or the joints from the third onwards more or less saw-like, the serrations being on the inner face [Serricorn series of authors]; but these and all the other characters, including the number of joints in the feet, very variable.

Series 4. *Heteromera.*—Front and middle tarsi five-jointed, hind tarsi four-jointed.   Other characters very variable.

Series 5. *Phytophaga.*—Tarsi four-jointed [apparently], but with a small additional joint at the base of the fourth joint : sole usually densely pubescent [sometimes the feet are bare beneath or bristly, and occasionally the small joint at the base of the fourth joint is more distinct].

Series 6. *Rhynchophora.*—Head prolonged in front to form a beak ; gula indistinguishable. [Palpi usually not evident.]   Tarsi four-jointed [apparently], but with a very minute additional joint at the extreme base of the fourth joint.

Strepsiptera (see p. 298).

The first and second series, with much of the third, form the Pentamera, the fifth and sixth the Tetramera [or Pseudotetramera [1]].   The term Isomera was applied by Leconte and Horn to a combination of series 1, 2, 3, and 5.

Series I. Lamellicornia.

Tarsi five-jointed ; antennae with the terminal joints (usually three, sometimes more), broader on one side, so as to form a peculiar club, the leaves of which are movable, and in repose are more or less perfectly coadapted so as to have the appearance of being but one piece.

This series includes three families, Passalidae, Lucanidae, and Scarabaeidae ; the latter includes an enormous majority of the species, and in them the structure of the antennae characteristic of the series is well developed ; but in the other two families

---

[1] We consider this term inferior to Tetramera for nomenclatorial purposes.

the form of the antennae is not so widely different from that of other Coleoptera. The larvae live on decaying vegetable matter, roots or dung. They have three pairs of legs, and are thick clumsy grubs with curved bodies, the last two segments being of larger size than usual. Many of them possess organs of stridulation, and the structure of their spiracles is very peculiar, each one being more or less completely surrounded by a chitinous plate. The spiracles usually form a system entirely closed, except at the moment when the

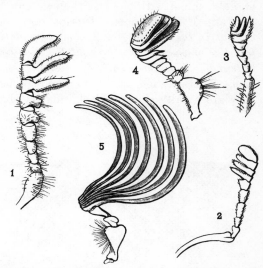

FIG. 85.—Antennae of Lamellicorns. 1, *Neleus interruptus*; 2, *Lucanus cervus* ♂; 3, *Phanaeus splendidulus* ♀; 4, *Phileurus didymus* ♀; 5, *Polyphylla fullo* ♂.

skin is shed and the tracheal exuviae are detached. Meinert[1] considers these spiracles to be organs of hearing. The life of the larvae is passed underground or in the decaying wood on which the Insect feeds.

Most of the members of this series are remarkable on account of the great concentration of the nerve-centres. This is extreme in *Rhizotrogus*, where there are only two great ganglia, viz. the supra-oesophageal and a great ganglion situate in the thorax, and consisting of the conjoined infra-oesophageal, thoracic, and abdominal ganglia. According to Brandt[2] there are several distinct forms of concentration in the series; the Lucanidae only participate in it to the extent that the perfect Insects exhibit fewer ganglia than the larvae; the latter possess two cephalic, three thoracic, and eight abdominal ganglia, while the perfect Insect has the abdominal ganglia reduced in number to six, and

[1] *Danske Selsk. Skr.* (6), viii. No. 1, 1895.
[2] *Horae Soc. ent. Ross.* xiv. 1879, p. 15.

they are placed partially in the thorax. The diminution in number takes place in this case by the amalgamation of the first two abdominal with the last thoracic ganglia.

Fam. 1. Passalidae.—*Labrum large, mobile ; mentum deeply cut out in the middle for the accommodation of the ligula ; the lamellae of the antenna brought together by the curling up of the antenna. The elytra entirely cover the dorsal surface of the abdomen.* There are four or five hundred species of this family known ; they are usually shining-black, unattractive beetles, of large size,

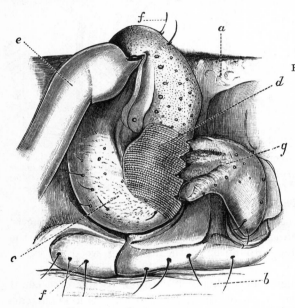

Fig. 86.—View of one side of meso- and metathorax of a Passalid larva from Borneo showing the stridulating organs. *a, b,* Portions of the metathorax ; *c,* coxa of 2nd leg ; *d,* striate or stridulating area thereon ; *e,* basal part of femur of middle leg ; *f,* hairs with chitinous process at base of each ; *g,* the diminutive 3rd leg modified for scratching the striated area. × 20.

and are abundant in the decaying wood of tropical forests. They are quite absent from Europe, and there is only one species in the United States of North America. The larvae are very interesting, from the fact that they appear to have only four legs. This arises from the posterior pair being present only as very short processes, the function of which is to scrape striated areas on the preceding pair of legs and so produce sound. In the species figured (Fig. 86) this short leg is a paw-like structure, bearing several hard digits ; but in other species it is more simple, and without the digits. The perfect Insect has no sound-producing organs, and it is very remarkable therefore to find the larvae provided with highly-developed stridulatory structures. No auditory organ is known, unless the peculiar spiracles be such.

Fam. 2. Lucanidae (*Stag-beetles*).—*Labrum indistinct, fixed ; mentum not excised ; antennae not curled in repose, with but little coadaptation of the terminal joints ; the elytra entirely cover the dorsal surface of the abdomen.* The Stag-beetles are well known on account of the extraordinary development of the mandibles in the male sex, these organs being in some cases nearly as long as the whole of the rest of the Insect, and armed with projections or teeth that give the Insects a most formidable appearance. So far as we have been able to discover, these structures are put to very little use, and in many cases are not capable of being of service even as weapons of offence. The males are usually very much larger than the females, and are remarkable on account of the great variation in the stature of different individuals of the same species ; correlative with these distinctions of individual size we find extreme differences in the development of the head and mandibles. Moreover, the small male specimens exhibit not merely reductions in the size of the mandibles, but also show considerable differences in the form of these parts, due, in some cases, apparently to the fact that only when a certain length of the mandible is attained is there any development of certain of the minor projections : in other cases it is not possible to adopt this view, as the small mandibles bear as many projections as the large forms do, or even more. In each species these variations fall, in the majority of cases, into distinct states, so that entomologists describe them as " forms," the largest developments being called teleodont, the smallest priodont ; the terms mesodont and amphiodont being applied to intermediate states. Leuthner, who has examined many specimens, states that in *Odontolabis sinensis,* no intermediates between the teleodont and mesodont forms occur, and as the

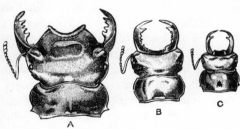

FIG. 87.—Head and prothorax of forms of the male of a stag-beetle ; *Homoeoderus mellyi* (Africa). **A,** Large, **B,** intermediate, **C,** small forms. (From a photograph by R. Oberthür.)

two forms are very different they are liable to be mistaken for distinct species.

There are at present between 500 and 600 species of stag-beetles known; the Indo-Malayan and Austro-Malayan regions being richest in them. Australia possesses many remarkable and aberrant forms. In the Ceratognathini—a group well represented in New Zealand as well as in Australia—the structure of the antennae is like that of the Scarabaeidae, rather than of the Lucanidae. The most aberrant form known is, however, our common *Sinodendron cylindricum;* this departs in numerous features from other Lucanidae, and instead of the mandibles of the male being more largely developed, there is a horn on the head; it is very doubtful whether this Insect should be allowed to remain in the family. Little is known of the habits and development of Lucanidæ, except in the case of three or four species that are common in Europe.

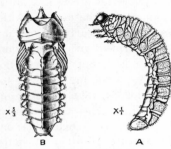

x⅔   x¼

B   A

Fig. 88.—*Sinodendron cylindricum.* A, Larva; B, pupa. New Forest.

The common stag-beetle, *Lucanus cervus,* is our largest British beetle. The larva much resembles that of *Melolontha vulgaris,* but attains a larger size, and the anal aperture is placed longitudinally instead of transversely; it lives in decaying wood, or eats the roots of trees without being injurious; its life in this state lasts about four years; the pupal period is passed through rapidly, and the perfect Insect may remain for months underground before it becomes active; this occurs in June and July. This larva stridulates by scraping certain hard tubercular ridges on the third pair of legs, over a specially adapted rough area at the base of the second pair.

The Passalidae and Lucanidae are united by some authorities as a group called Pectinicornia; the term Lamellicornia being then confined to the Scarabaeidae. The Passalidae appear, however, to be really more nearly allied to the Scarabaeidae than to the Lucanidae.

Fam. 3. Scarabaeidae (*Chafers*).—*The leaflets of the antennae are well coadapted, and are susceptible of separation. The elytra* *usually leave the pygidium uncovered. The number of visible ventral segments is usually six, or at the sides seven, not five, as in Lucanidae and Passalidae.* This is one of the most important families of Insects. About 13,000 species are already known; as some of them are highly remarkable creatures on account of the males being armed with horns, they are figured in many works on natural history. There is great variety of form, and the following five sub-families may be adopted, though authorities are by no means agreed as to the classification of this extensive family, which, moreover, be it remarked, is increasing by the discovery of about 300 new species every year.

Abdominal spiracles placed in a line on the connecting membranes, and entirely covered by the wing-cases (Laparosticti).   Sub-fam. 1. COPRIDES.[1]

Abdominal spiracles placed almost in a line, but only the basal three on the connecting membranes; the terminal one usually not covered by the wing-cases.   Sub-fam. 2. MELOLONTHIDES.

Abdominal spiracles placed in two lines, the basal three on the connecting membranes, the others on the ventral segments (Pleurosticti).

The claws of the tarsi unequal.   Sub-fam. 3. RUTELIDES.

The claws of the tarsi equal; the front coxae transverse, but little prominent in the descending axis.   Sub-fam. 4. DYNASTIDES.

The claws of the tarsi equal; the front coxae more prominent, shorter transversely.   Sub-fam. 5. CETONIIDES.

i. The COPRIDES form an immense group of about 5000 species; they differ somewhat in habits from other Lamellicorns, inasmuch as most of them live on dung, or decaying animal matter; the sub-family connects with the Lucanidae, so far as superficial characters go, by means of two of its groups, Trogini and Nicagini, the latter being very near to the Ceratognathini in Lucanidae. So little is known as to the morphology and development of these groups that it is not possible to pronounce an opinion as to the validity of this apparent alliance. *Trox* stridulates by rubbing two raised lines on the penultimate dorsal segment across two striate ribs on the inner face of the elytra; *Geotrupes,* on the other hand, produces an audible sound by rubbing together a file on the posterior coxa and a fine ridge on the contiguous ventral segment. The larva in this genus has a different organ

---

[1] In this sub-family there are numerous forms in which the elytra cover the pygidium, and in which the number of conspicuous ventral segments is reduced to five or even four. We use the term Coprides as equivalent to the "Laparosticti" of Lacordaire (*Gen. Col.* iii. 1856); it thus includes the "Coprini" and "Glaphyrini" of the *Catalogus Coleopterorum*, vol. iv. Munich, 1869.

for stridulation from the imago; it is placed on the second and third pairs of legs, the latter pair being much reduced in size.

The most interesting division of the Coprides is the group Scarabaeini. No member of this group inhabits the British islands, but in Southern Europe, and in still warmer lands, these Insects are well known from the curious habit many of the species have of rolling about balls of dung and earth. The long hind legs are chiefly used for this purpose, and it is on the peculiar structure of these limbs that the group has been established. Many of the stone Scarabaei found in Egyptian tombs represent some kind of Scarabaeini, and it has been said that the ancient Egyptians looked on these Insects as sacred because of their movements. These must certainly appear very strange to those who see them and are unacquainted with their object. It is stated that the dwellers in the valley of the Nile thought the actions of these Insects, when rolling their balls, were typical of the planetary and lunar revolutions; and that the sudden appearance of the beetles after a period of complete absence was emblematic of a future life. Many accounts have been given of the habits of members of this group, but according to Fabre all are more or less erroneous; and he has described the habits and life-history of *Scarabaeus sacer* (Fig. 89), as observed by him in Southern France. These Insects act the part of scavengers by breaking up and burying the droppings of cattle and other animals. The female *Scarabaeus* detaches a portion of the dung and forms it into a ball, sometimes as large as the fist; this it rolls along by means of its hind legs, by pushing when necessary with its broad head, or by walking backwards and dragging the ball with its front legs. The strength and patience displayed by the creature in the execution of this task are admirable. Frequently the owner of this small spherical property is joined, so Fabre informs us, by a friend, who is usually of the same sex and assists her in pushing along the ball till a suitable place is reached. When this is attained, the owner commences to excavate a chamber for the reception of the ball; sometimes the false friend takes advantage of the opportunity thus offered and carries off the ball for her own use. Should no disappointment of this sort occur, the *Scarabaeus* accomplishes the burying of the ball in its subterranean chamber, and accompanies it for the purpose of devouring it; the feast is continued without intermission till the food is entirely

exhausted, when the *Scarabaeus* seeks a fresh store of provender
to be treated in a similar manner.   According to M. Fabre's
account these events occur in the spring of the year, and when
the hot weather sets in the *Scarabaeus* passes through a period of
quiescence, emerging again in the autumn to recommence its
labours, which are now, however, directed immediately to the continuance of the species ; a larger subterranean chamber is formed,
and to this retreat the beetle carries dung till it has accumulated
a mass of the size of a
moderate apple ; this material is carefully arranged,
previous to the laying
of the egg, in such a
manner that the grub to
be hatched from the egg
shall find the softest and
most nutritive portions
close to it, while the
coarser and more innu-
tritious parts are arranged
so as to be reached by the
grub only after it has
acquired some strength ;
lastly, a still more delicate and nutritive paste
is prepared by the mother
beetle for a first meal for
the newly-hatched grub,
by some of the food being

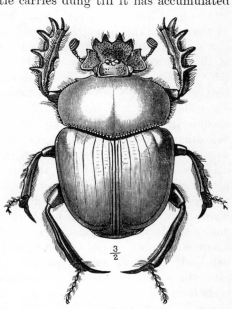

Fig. 89.—*Scarabaeus sacer.*   Portugal.

submitted to a partial digestion in her organs ; finally, the egg
is deposited in the selected spot, and the chamber closed. Certain
of the Coprides exhibit, according to Fabre, some extremely
exceptional features in their life-histories.   The mother, instead
of dying after oviposition, survives, and sees the growth of her
young to the perfect state, and then produces another generation.
No similar case can be pointed out in Insects, except in the Social
kinds ; but from these the Coprides observed by Fabre differ profoundly, inasmuch as the number of eggs produced by the mother
is extremely small ; *Copris hispanus,* for instance, producing in
each of its acts of oviposition only one, two, or three eggs.

ii. The MELOLONTHIDES are probably almost as numerous as the Coprides, some 4000 species being already known. The larvae are believed to feed chiefly on roots. *Melolontha vulgaris*, the common cockchafer, is very abundant in some parts of Europe, and owing to this and to the great damage it causes, has attracted much attention. The memoir by Straus-Durckheim [1] on its anatomy is one of the classical works of Entomology. This Insect is so injurious in some parts of France that money is paid by the local authorities for its destruction. M. Reiset informs us that under this arrangement 867,173,000 perfect cockchafers, and 647,000,000 larvae were destroyed in the Seine-inférieure in the four years from the middle of 1866 to 1870. Unlike the Coprides, the larval life in Melolonthides is prolonged, and that of the imago is of brief duration. In Central Europe the life-cycle of the individual in *M. vulgaris* occupies three years, though in dry periods it may be extended to four years. In Scandinavia the time occupied by the development appears to be usually five years. The fertile female enters the ground and deposits its eggs in two or three successive batches of about fifteen each. The eggs swell as the development of the embryo progresses; the larva emerges about five weeks after the eggs have been deposited, and is of relatively large size. When young the larvae can straighten themselves out and crawl, but when older they lose this power, and when above ground rest helplessly on their sides. In the winter they descend deeply into the earth to protect themselves from frost. The pupa state lasts only a few days, but after the final transformation the perfect Insect may remain motionless for as much as eight months underground before commencing its active life in the air.[2] In the perfect state the Insect is sometimes injurious from the large quantity of foliage it destroys. Schiödte [3] considered that these larvae (and those of numerous other Scarabaeidae) stridulate by rubbing certain projections on the stipes of the maxilla against the under-surface of the mandible. These surfaces appear, however, but little adapted for the purpose of producing sound.

iii. The RUTELIDES number about 1500 species; there are many

[1] *Considérations genérales sur l'anatomie comparée des animaux articulés*, etc., Paris 1828, 4to. xix. and 435 pp., and Atlas of ten (xx.) plates, and 36 pp.

[2] Raspail, *Mém. soc. zool. France*, vi. 1893, pp. 202-213.

[3] *Ann. soc. ent. France*, (v.) iv. 1874, p. 39.

Insects of brilliant metallic colours amongst them, but very little
is known as to their life-histories.   The larvae are very much
like those of Melolonthides.

iv. The DYNASTIDES are the smallest division in number of
species, there being scarcely 1000 known; but amongst them
we find in the genera *Dynastes* and *Megasoma* some of the
largest of existing Insects.   The horns and projections on the
heads and prothoraces of some of the males of these Insects are
truly extraordinary, and it does not appear possible to explain
their existence by any use they are to their possessors.   These
structures are but little used for fighting.   Baron von Hügel
informs the writer that in Java he has observed large numbers
of *Xylotrupes gideon;* he noticed that the males sometimes carry
the females by the aid of their horns; but this must be an exceptional case, for the shape of these instruments, in the majority of
Dynastides, would not allow of their being put to this use.   The
development of these horns varies greatly in most of the species,
but he did not find that the females exhibited any preference for
the highly armed males.   The fact that the males are very much
larger than the females, and that the armature is usually confined
to them, suggests, however, that some sexual reason exists for these
remarkable projections.   Many Dynastides possess organs of stridulation, consisting of lines of sculpture placed so as to form one or
two bands on the middle of the propygidium, and brought into
play by being rubbed by the extremities of the wing-cases.   This
apparatus is of a less perfect nature than the structures for the
same purpose found in numerous other beetles.   We have no
member of this sub-family in Britain, and there are scarcely a
dozen in all Europe.   Decaying vegetable matter is believed to
be the nutriment of Dynastides.   The European *Oryctes nasicornis*
is sometimes found in numbers in spent tan.   The growth and
development of the individual is believed to be but slow.

v. The CETONIIDES are renowned for the beauty of their colours
and the elegance of their forms; hence they are a favourite
group, and about 1600 species have been catalogued.   They are
specially fond of warm regions, but it is a peculiarity of the
sub-family that a large majority of the species are found in the
Old World; South America is inexplicably poor in these Insects,
notwithstanding its extensive forests.   In this sub-family the
mode of flight is peculiar; the elytra do not extend down the

sides of the body, so that, if they are elevated a little, the wings can be protruded. This is the mode of flight adopted by most Cetoniides, but the members of the group Trichiini fly in the usual manner. In Britain we have only four kinds of Cetoniides; they are called Rose-chafers. The larvae of *C. floricola* and some other species live in ants' nests made of vegetable refuse, and it is said that they eat the ants' progeny. Two North American species of *Euphoria* have similar habits. The group Cremasto-chilini includes numerous peculiar Insects that apparently have still closer relations with ants. Most of them are very aberrant as well as rare forms, and it has been several times observed in North America that species of *Cremastochilus* not only live in the nests of the ants, but are forcibly detained therein by the owners, who clearly derive some kind of satisfaction from the companionship of the beetles. The species of the genus *Lomaptera* stridulate in a peculiar manner, by rubbing the edges of the hind femora over a striate area on the ventral segments.

Series II.   Adephaga or Caraboidea.

All the tarsi five-jointed ; antennae filiform, or nearly so ; mouth-parts highly developed, the outer lobe of the maxilla nearly always divided into a two-jointed palpus ; supports of the labial palpi developed as joints of the palpi, and in some cases approximate at their bases. Abdomen with the exposed segments one more in number at the sides than along the middle, the number being usually five along the middle, six at each side.

THIS extensive series includes the tiger-beetles, ground-beetles, and true water-beetles; it consists of six families, and forms a natural assemblage. It is sometimes called Carnivora or Filicornia. The exceptions to the characters we have mentioned are but few. The supports of the labial palpi are frequently covered by the mentum, and then the palpi appear three-jointed; but when the joint-like palpiger is not covered these palps appear four-jointed. As a rule, approximation of these supports is indica-tive of high development. In some of the lower forms the trophi remain at a lower stage of development than is usual. This is especially the case with the genus *Amphizoa,* which forms of itself the family Amphizoidae.   The Bombardier-beetles make an exception as regards the abdominal structure, for in some of them no less than eight segments are visible, either along the middle line or at the sides of the venter.   In Hydroporides (one of the divisions of Dytiscidae) the front and middle feet have each only four joints.   Many naturalists unite the Gyrinidae with the Adephaga, and a few also associate with them the Paussidae and Rhyssodidae; but we think it better at present to exclude all these, though we believe that both Paussidae and Rhyssodidae will ultimately be assigned to the series.   The larvae are usually very active, and have a higher development of the legs than is usual in this Order.   Their tarsi possess two claws.

Fam. 4.   Cicindelidae (*Tiger-beetles*).——*Clypeus extending laterally in front of the insertion of the antennae.   Lower lip with the palpi usually greatly developed, but with the ligula and paraglossae very much reduced, often scarcely to be detected.   Maxillae with the outer lobe forming a two-jointed palp,[1] the inner lobe elongate, furnished at the tip with a hook-like process, which is usually articulated by a joint with the lobe itself.*   The tiger-beetles are very active Insects, running with extreme speed, and sometimes flying in a similar manner; they are all predaceous, and amongst the most voracious and fierce of the carnivorous beetles, so that they well deserve their name.   Bates, speaking of the Amazonian *Megacephala*, says " their powers of running exceed anything I have ever observed in this style of Insect locomotion ; they run in a serpentine course over the smooth sand, and when closely pursued by the hand they are apt to turn suddenly back and thus baffle the most practised hand and eye."   He further says that the species he observed (being of diverse colours) agreed in colour with the general colours of the " locale they inhabit."   The larvae of Cicindelidae live in deep burrows, sinking more or less vertically into the ground, and in these they take up a peculiar position, for which their shape is specially adapted; the head and prothorax are broad, the rest of the body slender, the fifth segment of the abdomen is furnished on the back with a pair of strong hooks; the ocelli on the sides of the head are very perfect.   Supporting itself at the top of the burrow by means of these hooks and of its terminal tube, the larva blocks the mouth of the burrow with its large head and prothorax, and

---

[1] In Theratides this outer lobe is in a rudimentary state, like a seta.

in this position waits for its prey. This consists of Insects that
may alight on the spot or run over it. When an Insect ventures
within reach, the head of the larva is thrown back with a rapid
jerk, the prey is seized by the long sharp mandibles, dragged to
the bottom of the burrow and devoured. The burrows are often
more than a foot deep, and are said to be excavated by the larva
itself, which carries up the earth on the shovel-like upper surface
of its head. The female tiger-beetle is endowed with powerful
and elongate excavating instruments at the termination of the
body, and it is probable that when placing the egg in the earth

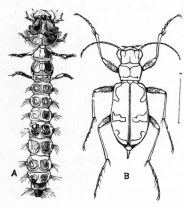

she facilitates the future operations of the larva by forming
the outlines of the burrow. Extremely few larvae of Cicindelidae are known, but they all
exhibit the type of structure
mentioned above, and apparently
have similar habits. Our little
British *Cicindela*, most of which
are so active on the wing, agree
in these respects with the African
species of *Manticora*, which are
entirely apterous, and are the
largest of the Cicindelidae. Péringuey found a breeding-ground
of *M. tuberculata* near Kimberley;

Fig. 90. — *Cicindela hybrida*. Britain.
A, larva (after Schiödte) ; B, imago,
male.

the larvae were living in the usual Cicindelid manner; but the
ground was so hard that he was not able to investigate the
burrows, and there were but few Insects that could serve as food
in the neighbourhood.

The Cicindelidae, although one of the smaller families of Coleoptera, now number about 1400 species; of these about one-half
belong to the great genus *Cicindela*, to which our four British
representatives of the Cicindelidae are all assigned. There is no
general work of much consequence on this important family, and
its classification is not thoroughly established.[1]

Tiger-beetles display considerable variety of structure, especially
as regards the mouth, which exhibits very remarkable develop-

[1] The first portion of a classification of Cicindelidae by Dr. Walther Horn,
Revision der Cicindeliden, Berlin, 1898, has appeared since this was written.

ments of the palpi and labrum (Fig. 91). The tiger-beetles, like most other Insects that capture living prey, do not consume their victims entire, but subsist chiefly on the juices they squeeze out of them; the hard and innutritious parts are rejected after the victim has been thoroughly lacerated and squeezed; the mouth forms both trap and press; the palpi spread out in order to facilitate the rapid engulfing of a victim, then close up under it and help to support it in the mouth; while the labrum above closes the cavity in the other direction. The mouth itself is a large cavity communicating very freely with the exterior, but so completely shut off from the following parts of the alimentary canal that it is difficult to find the orifice of communication; the labium being much modified to form the posterior wall. For the capture of the prey, always living but of various

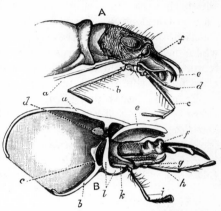

Fig. 91. — Mouth - parts of tiger - beetles. **A.** Profile of *Pogonostoma* sp. (Madagascar): *a*, antenna; *b*, labial palp; *c*, maxillary palp: *d*, palpiform lobe of maxilla; *e*, mandible; *f*, labrum. **B**, Section of head of *Manticora maxillosa* (South Africa): *a*, front of upper part of head-capsule; *b*, gula; *c*, tentorium; *d*, eye; *e*, labrum; *f*, left mandible; *g*, maxilla; *h*, maxillary palp; *i*, labial palp; *k*, support of this palp; *l*, labium.

kinds, a mechanism with great holding power and capable of rapid action is required. The mouth of the terrestrial *Manticora* (Fig. 91, B), exhibits great strength; some of the chitinous parts are extremely thick, the mandibles are enormous, the palpi, however, are comparatively low in development. In the arboreal genus *Pogonostoma* the palpary structures (Fig. 91, A) attain a development scarcely equalled elsewhere in the Insect world. The great majority of the Cicindelidae are inhabitants of the warmer, or of the tropical regions of the world, and very little is known as to their life-histories; they show great diversity in their modes of hunting their prey. Some are wingless; others are active on the wing; and of both of these divisions there are forms that are found only on trees or bushes. Some, it is believed, frequent only the mounds of Termites. The characteristic feature common

to all is great activity and excessive wariness. The genus
Pogonostoma, to which we have already alluded, is confined to
Madagascar, where the species are numerous, but are rare in
collections on account of the difficulty of securing them. Raffray
informs us that certain species frequent the trunks of trees, up
which they run in a spiral manner on the least alarm. The only
way he could obtain specimens was by the aid of an assistant;
the two approached a tree very quietly from opposite sides, and
when near it, made a rush, and joined hands as high up the
trunk as they could, so as to embrace the tree, when the *Pogonostoma* fell to the ground and was captured.

Fam. 5. Carabidae (*Ground-beetles*).—*Clypeus not extending
laterally in front of the antennae. Maxillae with the outer lobe
destitute of an articulated hook at the tip. Antennae covered
(except the basal joints) with a minute pubescence. Hind legs not
very different from the middle pair, formed for running, as usual
in beetles.* This is one of the largest and most important of the
families of Coleoptera, in-
cluding as it does 12,000
or 13,000 described
species. In this country
Carabidae are nearly
entirely terrestrial in
habits, and are scarcely
ever seen on the wing;
many of the species indeed
have merely rudimentary
wings; in the tropics
there are, however, many
arboreal forms that take
wing with more or less
alertness. The larvae (Fig.
92, A) are usually elon-
gate in form and run
freely; they may be known

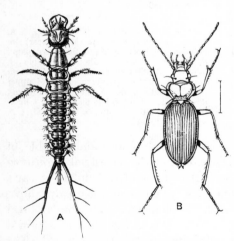

FIG. 92.—*Leistus spinibarbis.* **A**, Larva (after
Schiödte); **B**, imago. Britain.

by their tarsi ending in two claws, by the exserted, sharp, calliper-
like mandibles, by the body ending in two processes (sometimes
jointed) and a tube of varying length projecting backwards.
The pupae usually have the hind pair of legs so arranged that
the tips of the tarsi project behind, beyond the extremity of the

body. The Carabidae are carnivorous and predaceous both as larvae and perfect Insects ; they attack living Insects, worms, or other small, soft creatures, but do not disdain dead specimens. Some species of *Carabus*, found in North Africa where snails abound, are specially formed for attacking these molluscs, having the head long and slender so that it can be thrust into the shell of the snail.   A few species have been detected eating growing corn, and even the young seeds of some Umbelliferae ; these belong chiefly to the genera *Harpalus, Zabrus*, and *Amara.*   Some species of the abundant genera *Pterostichus* and *Harpalus*, are said to be fond of ripe strawberries.   The most anomalous forms of Carabidae are the Pseudomorphides, a sub-family almost peculiar to Australia, the members of which live under bark, and have but little resemblance to other Carabids owing to their compact forms and continuous outlines.   The genus *Mormolyce* is one of the wonders of the Insect world on account of the extraordinary shape of its members ; the sides of the elytra form large crinkled expansions, and the head is unusually elongate.   These Insects live on the underside of fallen trees in the Malay Archipelago and Peninsula ; no reason whatever can be at present assigned for their remarkable shape.

There are a considerable number of blind members of this family : some of them live in caverns ; these belong chiefly to the genus *Anophthalmus*, species of which have been detected in the caves of the Pyrenees, of Austria, and of North America. It has been shown that the optic nerves and lobes, as well as the external organs of vision, are entirely wanting in some of these cave Carabidae ; the tactile setae have, however, a larger development than usual, and the Insects are as skilful in running as if they possessed eyes.   *Anophthalmus* is closely related to our British genus *Trechus*, the species of which are very much given to living in deep crevices in the earth, or under large stones, and have some of them very small eyes.   In addition to these cavernicolous *Anophthalmus*, other blind Carabidae have been discovered during recent years in various parts of the world, where they live under great stones deeply embedded in the earth ; these blind lapidicolous Carabidae are of extremely minute size and of most sluggish habits ; the situations in which they are found suggest that many successive generations are probably passed under the same stone.   Not a single specimen has ever been found above ground.   The minute

Carabids of the genus *Aëpus*, that pass a large part of their
lives under stones below high-water mark (emerging only when
the tide uncovers them), on the borders of the English Channel
and elsewhere, are very closely allied to these blind Insects, and
have themselves only very small eyes, which, moreover, according
to Hammond and Miall, are covered in larger part by a peculiar
shield.[1]   A few Carabidae, of the genera *Glyptus* and *Orthogonius*,
are believed to live in the nests of Termites.   Savage found the
larva of *G. sculptilis* in the nests of *Termes bellicosus;* it has
been described by Horn, and is said to bear so great a resemblance to young queens of the Termites as to have been mistaken
for them.[2]   Mr. Haviland found *Rhopalomelus angusticollis* in
Termites' nests in South Africa.   Péringuey states that it emits
a very strong and disagreeable odour.   It is probable that it
preys on the Termites, and this also is believed to be the habit
of the Ceylonese *Helluodes taprobanae.*   Some species of the
Mediterranean genus *Siagona* stridulate by means of a file on
the under surface of the prothorax, rubbed by a striate area,
adapted in form, on the anterior femora.

A valuable memoir on the classification of this important
family is due to the late Dr. G. H. Horn ;[3] he arranges Carabidae
in three sub-families; we think it necessary to add a fourth for
Mormolyce :

1. Middle coxal cavities enclosed externally by the junction of the meso- and
        meta-sternum ; neither epimeron nor episternum attaining the
        cavity.
    Head beneath, with a deep groove on each side near the eye for
        the reception of the antennae or a part thereof.
                                    Sub-fam. 3. PSEUDOMORPHIDES.
    Head without antennal grooves.   Sub-fam. 2. HARPALIDES.
2. Middle coxal cavities attained on the outside by the tips of the episterna
        and epimera.   Sub-fam. 4. MORMOLYCIDES.
3. Middle coxal cavities attained on the outside by the tips of the epimera,
        but not by those of the episterna.   Sub-fam. 1. CARABIDES.

These four sub-families are of extremely different extent and
nature.   The Harpalides are the dominant forms, and include
upwards of 10,000 known species; while the various tribes
into which the sub-family is divided include, as a rule, each many

---

[1] *Natural History of aquatic Insects,* 1895, p. 376.
[2] *Tr. Amer. ent. Soc.* xv. 1888, p. 18.
[3] *Op. cit.* v. 1881, p. 91 ; cf. Sharp, *Tr. ent. Soc. London,* 1882, p. 61.

genera ; the Carabides are next in importance, with upwards of 2000 species, but are divided into a comparatively large number of tribes, each of which averages a much smaller number of genera than do the tribes of Harpalides ; Pseudomorphides includes only about 100 species ; and Mormolycides consists of the single genus *Mormolyce* with three species.

Fam. 6. Amphizoidae.—*Antennae destitute of pubescence : outer lobe of maxilla not jointed ; metasternum with a short transverse impressed line on the middle behind. Hind legs slender, not formed for swimming.*   This family is limited to the genus *Amphizoa ;* the species of which may be briefly de-scribed as lowly organised Carabidae that lead an aquatic life. The geo-graphical distribution is highly remarkable, there being but three species, two of which live in Western North America, the third in Eastern Tibet. The habits of American *Am-phizoa* are known ; they pass a life of little activity in very cold, rapid streams ; they do not swim, but cling to stones and timber.

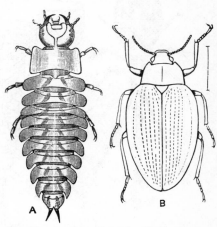

FIG. 93.—*Amphizoa lecontei.*   North America. A, Larva ; B, imago.

The larva was recently discovered in Utah by Messrs. Hubbard and Schwarz:[1] it has the same habits as the perfect Insect, and in general form resembles the larvae of the genus *Carabus ;* but it has no terminal tube to the body, the abdomen consisting of eight segments and a pair of short terminal appendages ; the spiracles are obsolete, with the exception of a pair placed near to one another at the termination of the eighth abdominal segment. As regards the mouth this larva is Carabid, as regards the abdomen and stigmata Dytiscid of a primitive type.

Fam. 7. Pelobiidae.—*Antennae destitute of pubescence : outer lobe of maxilla jointed, metasternum with a short transverse impressed line on the middle behind.   Hind legs rather slender,*

[1] *P. ent. Soc. Washington,* ii. 1892, p. 341.

formed for swimming, the tarsi longer than the tibiae.   This family
is limited to the one genus *Pelobius* (*Hygrobia* of some authors).
Like *Amphizoa,* to which it is in several respects analogous, it
has a singular geographical distribution; there are only four
known species, one lives in Britain and the Mediterranean region,
one in Chinese Tibet, two in Australia.   *Pelobius* may be briefly
described as a Carabid adapted to a considerable extent for
living in and swimming about in water; differing thus from

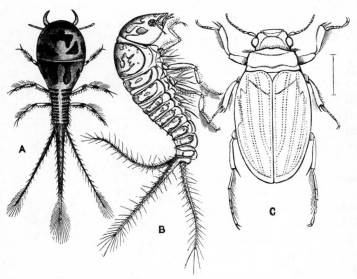

Fig. 94.—*Pelobius tardus.*   Britain.   **A,** Young larva ; **B,** adult larva ; **C,** imago.
(**A** and **B** after Schiödte.)

Amphizoa, which has no special adaptation for swimming.   The
larva of *Pelobius* is remarkable; it breathes by means of branchial
filaments on the under surface of the body, the spiracles being
present, though those of the abdomen are very minute and the
others small.   The head is very large, the mandibles are not
tube-like, the food being taken after the manner of the Carabidae ;
the 8th abdominal segment ends in three long processes ; the
small 9th segment is retracted beneath them.   The adult *Pelobius
tardus* is remarkable for its loud stridulation.   The sound is produced by an apparatus described correctly by Charles Darwin ;[1]

[1] *Descent of Man,* i. 1890, p. 338 ; The views of Landois and Recker, *Arch. f.
Naturgesch.* lvii. 1, 1891, p. 101, are erroneous.

there is a file on the inside of the wing-cases, and the Insect turns up the tip of the abdomen and scrapes the file therewith. The Insects are called squeakers in the Covent Garden market, where they are sold.

Fam. 8. Haliplidae.—*Antennae bare, ten-jointed; metasternum marked by a transverse line; posterior coxae prolonged as plates, covering a large part of the lower surface of the abdomen; the slender, but clubbed, hind femora move between these plates and the abdomen.* The Haliplidae are aquatic, and are all small, not exceeding four or five millimetres in length. The ventral plates are peculiar to the Insects of this family, but their function is not known. The larvae are remarkable on account of the fleshy processes disposed on their bodies; but they exhibit considerable variety in this respect; their mandibles are grooved so that they suck their prey. In the larva of *Haliplus*, according to Schiödte, there are eight pairs of abdominal spiracles, but in *Cnemidotus* (Fig. 95, B), there are no spiracles, and air is obtained by

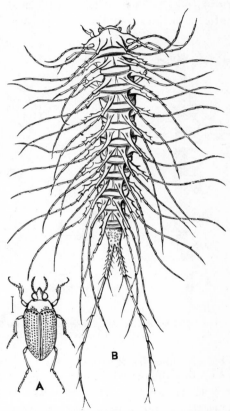

Fig. 95.—*Cnemidotus caesus.* England. **A**, Imago; **B**, larva, highly magnified. (After Schiödte.)

means of a trachea traversing each of the long filaments. The Insects of these two genera are so similar in the imaginal instar that it is well worthy of note that their larvae should be distinguished by such important characters. Haliplidae is a small family consisting of three genera, having about 100 species;

it is very widely distributed. We have 13 species in Britain, all the genera being represented.

Fam. 9. Dytiscidae (*Water-beetles*).—*Antennae bare; hind legs formed for swimming, not capable of ordinary walking : metasternum without a transverse line across it ; behind closely united with the extremely large coxae. Outer lobe of maxilla forming a two-jointed palpus.* The Dytiscidae, or true water-beetles, are of interest because—unlike the aquatic Neuroptera—they exist in water in both the larval and imaginal instars ; nevertheless there is reason for supposing that they are modified terrestrial Insects : these reasons are (1) that in their general organisation they are similar to the Carabidae, and they drown more quickly than the majority of land beetles do ; (2) though the larvae are very different from the larvae of terrestrial beetles, yet the imaginal instars are much less profoundly

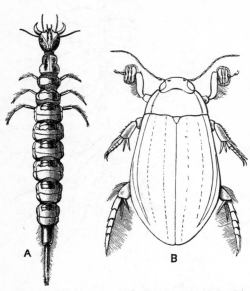

Fig. 96.—*Cybister roeseli* (=*laterimarginalis* De G.) Europe. **A**, Larva (after Schiödte) ; **B**, ♂ imago.

changed, and are capable of existing perfectly well on land, and of taking prolonged flights through the air ; (3) the pupa is, so far as known, always terrestrial. The larvae and imagos are perfectly at home in the water, except that they must come to the surface to get air. Some of them are capable, however, when quiescent, of living for hours together beneath the water, but there appears to be great diversity in this respect.[1] The hind pair of legs is the chief means of locomotion. These swimming-legs (Fig. 97) are deserving of admiration on account of their mechanical perfection ; this, however, is exhibited in various

[1] See *J. Linn. Soc. Zool.* xiii. 1876, p. 161.

degrees, the legs in the genera *Dytiscus* and *Hydroporus* being but slender, while those of *Cybister* are so broad and powerful, that a single stroke propels the Insect for a considerable distance.

The wing-cases fit perfectly to the body, except at the tip, so as to form an air-tight space between themselves and the back of the Insect; this space is utilised as a reservoir for air. When the *Dytiscus* feels the necessity for air it rises to the surface and exposes the tip of the body exactly at the level of the water, separating at the same time the abdomen from the wing-cases so as to open a broad chink at the spot where the parts were, during the Insect's submersion, so well held together as to be air- and water - tight. The ter-minal two pairs of spiracles are much enlarged, and by curving the abdomen the beetle brings them into con-tact with the atmosphere; respiration is effected by this means as well as by the store of air carried about under the wing - cases. The air that enters the space between the elytra and body is shut in there when the Insect closes

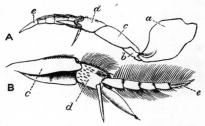

Fig. 97.—Hind- or swimming-leg of *Cybister tripunctatus*. **A,** The whole leg detached; **B,** the movable parts in the striking posi-tion. *a,* Coxa; *b,* trochanter; *c,* femur; *d,* tibia; *e,* last joint of tarsus.

the chink and again dives beneath the water. The enlargement of the terminal stigmata in *Dytiscus* is exceptional, and in forms more highly organised in other respects, such as *Cybister*, these spiracles remain minute; the presumption being that in this case respiration is carried on almost entirely by means of the supply the Insect carries in the space between the elytra and the base of the abdomen.[1] The structure of the front foot of the male *Dytiscus*, and of many other water-beetles, is highly remarkable, the foot being dilated to form a palette or saucer, covered beneath by sucker-like structures of great delicacy and beauty; by the aid of these the male is enabled to retain a position on the female for many hours, or even days, together. Lowne has shown that the

[1] For many particulars as to respiration of *Dytiscus*, and peculiarities of the larva see Miall, *Aquatic Insects*, 1895, pp. 39, etc. (In the figure given on p. 60 the large stigma on the terminal segment of the abdomen is omitted, though it is referred to in the text.)

suckers communicate with a sac in the interior of the foot containing fluid, which exudes under pressure. As the portions of the
skeleton of the female on which these suckers are brought to
bear is frequently covered with pores, or minute pits, it is probable that some correlation between the two organisms is brought
about by these structures. The females in many groups of
Dytiscidae bear on the upper surface of the body a peculiar
sculpture of various kinds, the exact use of which is unknown ;
in many species there are two forms of the female, one possessing
this peculiar sculpture, the other nearly, or quite, without it.
The larvae of Dytiscidae differ from those of Carabidae chiefly
by the structure of the mouth and of the abdomen. They are
excessively rapacious, and are indeed almost constantly engaged
in sucking the juices of soft and small aquatic animals, by no
means excluding their own kind. The mode of suction is not
thoroughly known, but so far as the details have been ascertained
they are correctly described, in the work on aquatic Insects, by
Professor Miall, we have previously referred to ; the mandibles
are hollow, with a hole near the tip and another at the base, and
being sharp at the tips are thrust into the body of a victim, and
then by their closure the other parts of the mouth, which are
very beautifully constructed for the purpose, are brought into
fitting mechanical positions for completing the work of emptying
the victim. Nagel states that the larva of *Dytiscus* injects a
digestive fluid into the body of its victim, and that this fluid
rapidly dissolves all the more solid parts of the prey, so that the
rapacious larva can easily absorb all its victim except the
insoluble outer skin. The abdomen consists of only eight
segments, and a pair of terminal processes ; the stigmata are all
more or less completely obsolete—according to species—with the
exception of the pair on the eighth segment at the tip of the
body ; the terminal segments are frequently fringed with hairs,
that serve not only as means of locomotion, but also to float the
pair of active stigmata at the surface when the creature rises to
get air. Although the larvae of Dytiscidae are but little known,
yet considerable diversity has already been found. Those of
Hyphydrus and some species of *Hydroporus* have the front of the
head produced into a horn, which is touched by the tips of the
mandibles.

Dytiscidae are peculiar inasmuch as they appear to flourish

best in the cooler waters of the earth.   Lapland is one of the parts of Europe richest in Dytiscidae, and the profusion of species in the tropics compared with those of Europe is not nearly so great as it is in the case of most of the other families of Coleoptera.   About 1800 species are at present known, and we have rather more than 100 species in Britain.[1]

Series III. Polymorpha.

Antennae frequently either thicker at the tip (clavicorn) or serrate along their inner edge (serricorn); but these characters, as well as the number of joints in the feet and other points, are very variable.

Upwards of fifty families are placed in this series ; many of these families are of very small extent, consisting of only a few species ; other families of the series are much larger, so that altogether about 40,000 species—speaking broadly, about one-fourth of the Coleoptera—are included in the series.   We have already (p. 189) alluded to the fact that it is formed by certain conventional series, Clavicornia, Serricornia, etc. united, because it has hitherto proved impossible to define them.

Fam. 10. Paussidae.—*Antennae of extraordinary form, usually two-jointed, sometimes six- or ten-jointed.   Elytra elongate, but truncate behind, leaving the pygidium exposed.   Tarsi five-jointed.*   The Paussidae have always been recognised as amongst the most remarkable of beetles, although they are of small size, the largest attaining scarcely half an inch in length.   They are found only in two ways ; either in ants' nests, or on the wing at night. They apparently live exclusively in ants' nests, but migrate much.   Paussidae usually live in the nests of terrestrial ants, but they have been found in nests of *Cremastogaster* in the spines of *Acacia fistulosa*.   They have the power of discharging, in an explosive manner, a volatile caustic fluid from the anus, which is said by Loman to contain free iodine.   Their relations to the ants are at present unexplained, though much attention has been given to the subject.   When observed in the nests they frequently appear as if asleep, and the ants do not take much notice of them.   On other occasions the ants endeavour to drag them into the interior of the nest, as if desirous of retaining their company :

[1] For classification and structure see Sharp, "On Dytiscidae," *Sci. Trans. R. Dublin Soc.* (2) ii. 1882.

the *Paussus* then makes no resistance to its hosts; if, however, it be touched, even very slightly, by an observer, it immediately bombards : the ants, as may be imagined, do not approve of this, and run away.   Nothing has ever been observed that would lead to the belief that the ants derive any benefit from the presence of the Paussi, except that these guests bear on some part of the body—frequently the great impressions on the pronotum—patches of the peculiar kind of pubescence that exists in many other kinds of ants'-nest beetles, and is known in some of them to secrete a substance the ants are fond of, and that the ants have been seen

to lick the beetles.   On the other hand, the Paussi have been observed to eat the eggs and larvae of the ants.   The larva of *Paussus* is not known,[1] and Raffray doubts whether it lives in the ants' nests.   There are about 200 species of Paussidae known, Africa, Asia and Australia being their chief countries; one species, *P. favieri*, is not uncommon in the Iberian peninsula and South France, and a single species was formerly found in Brazil.   The position the family should occupy has been much discussed; the only forms to which they make any real approximation are Carabidae, of the group

FIG. 98. — *Paussus cephalotes* ♂. El Hedjaz. (After Raffray.)

Ozaenides, a group of ground beetles that also crepitate.   Burmeister and others have therefore placed the Paussidae in the series Adephaga, but we follow Raffray's view (he being the most recent authority on the family),[2] who concludes that this is an anomalous group not intimately connected with any other family of Coleoptera, though having more affinity to Carabidae than to anything else.   The recently discovered genus *Protopaussus* has eleven joints to the antennae, and is said to come nearer to Carabidae than the previously known forms did, and we may anticipate that a more extensive knowledge will show that the family may find a natural place in the Adephaga.   The description of the abdomen given by Raffray is erroneous; in a specimen of the genus *Arthropterus* the writer has dissected, he finds that there

---

[1] Descriptions of larvae that may possibly be those of Paussids have been published by Xambeu, *Ann. Soc. Linn. Lyon*, xxxix. 1892, p. 137, and Erichson, *Arch. Naturgesch.* xiii. 1847, p. 275.

[2] *Arch. Mus. Paris* (2), viii. and ix. 1887.

are five ventral segments visible along the middle, six at the sides, as in the families of Adephaga generally.   There is said to be a great difference in the nervous systems of Carabidae and Paussidae, but so little is known on this point that we cannot judge whether it is really of importance.

Fam. 11. Gyrinidae (*Whirligig beetles*).—*Antennae very short; four eyes; middle and hind legs forming short broad paddles; abdomen with six segments visible along the middle, seven along each side.*   These Insects are known to all from their habit of floating lightly on the surface of water, and performing graceful complex curves round one another without colliding ; sometimes they may be met with in great congregations. They are admirably constructed for this mode of life, which is comparatively rare in the Insect world ; the Hydrometridae amongst the bugs, and a small number of different kinds of Diptera, being the only other Insects that are devoted to a life on the surface of the waters.   Of all these, Gyrinidae are in their construction the most adapted for such a career.   They are able to dive to escape danger,

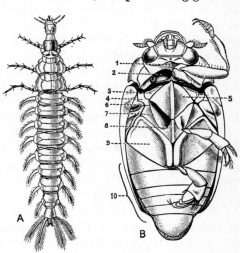

FIG. 99.—**A**, Larva of *Gyrinus* (after Schiödte); **B**, under side of *Gyrinus* sp. (after Ganglbauer). 1, Prosternum ; 2, anterior coxal cavity ; 3, mesothoracic episternum ; 4, mesoepimeron ; 5, mesosternum ; 6, metathoracic episternum ; 7, middle coxal cavity ; 8, metasternum ; 9, hind coxa ; 10, ventral segments. [N.B.—The first ventral segment really consists, at each side, of two segments united ; this may be distinctly seen in many Gyrinidae.]

and they then carry with them a small supply of air, but do not stay long beneath the surface.   Their two hind pairs of legs are beautifully constructed as paddles, expanding mechanically when moved in the backward direction, and collapsing into an extremely small space directly the resistance they meet with is in the other direction.   The front legs of these Insects are articulated to the thorax in a peculiar direction so that their soles do not look downwards but towards one another; hence the sensitive adhesive surface used during coupling is placed on the side of the foot, forming thus a false sole: a remarkable modification otherwise unknown in Insects. They breathe chiefly by means of the very large metathoracic spiracles.

The larvae (Fig. 99, A) are purely aquatic, and are highly modified for this life, being elongate creatures, with sharp, mandibles and nine abdominal segments, each segment bearing on each side a tracheal branchia; these gills assist to some extent in locomotion. The stigmata are quite obsolete, but the terminal segment bears four processes, one pair of which may be looked on as cerci, the other as a pair of gills corresponding with the pair on each of the preceding segments. The mandibles are not suctorial, but, according to Meinert, possess an orifice for the discharge of the secretion of a mandibular gland. Gyrinidae are chiefly carnivorous in both the larval and imaginal instars. Fully 300 species are known; they are generally distributed, though wanting in most of the islands of the world except those of large size. The finest forms are the Brazilian *Enhydrus* and the *Porrorhynchus* of tropical Asia.[1] In Britain we have nine species, eight of *Gyrinus*, one of *Orectochilus;* the latter form is rarely seen, as it hides during the day, and performs its rapid gyrations at night.

The Gyrinidae are one of the most distinct of all the families of Coleoptera: by some they are associated in the Adephagous series; but they have little or no affinity with the other members thereof. Without them the Adephaga form a natural series of evidently allied families, and we consider it a mistake to force the Gyrinidae therein because an objection is felt by many taxonomists to the maintenance of isolated families. Surely if there are in nature some families allied and others isolated, it is better for us to recognise the fact, though it makes our classifications look less neat and precise, and increases the difficulty of constructing " tables."

Fam. 12. Hydrophilidae.—*Tarsi five-jointed, the first joint in many cases so small as to be scarcely evident: antennae short, of less than eleven joints, not filiform, but consisting of*

---

[1] For classification and monograph of the family, see Régimbart, *Ann. Soc. ent. France*, 1882, 1883, and 1886. For a catalogue, Séverin, *Ann. Soc. ent. Belgique*, xxxiii. 1889.

*three parts, a basal part of one or two elongate joints, an inter-
mediate part of two or more small joints, and an apical part of
larger (or at any rate broader) joints, which are pubescent, the others
being bare. Outer lobe of maxillae usually complex, but not at
all palpiform, maxillary palpi often very long; the parts of the
labium much concealed behind the mentum, the labial palpi very
widely separated. Hind coxae extending the width of the
body, short, the lamina interior small in comparison with the
lamina exterior. Abdomen of five visible segments.* The Hydrophilidae are an extensive family of beetles, unattractive in colours
and appearance, and much neglected by collectors. A large part
of the family live in water, though most of them have only
feeble powers of aquatic locomotion, and the beetles appear
chiefly to devote their attention to economising the stock of air
each individual carries about. The best known forms of the
family are the species of *Hydrophilus.* They are, however, very
exceptional in many respects, and are far more active and predaceous than most of the other forms. Much has been written
about *Hydrophilus piceus,* one of the largest of British beetles.
This Insect breathes in a most peculiar manner : the spiracles
are placed near bands of delicate pubescence, forming tracts that
extend the whole length of the body, and in this particular
species cover most of the under surface of the body ; these
velvety tracts retain a coating of air even when the Insect is
submerged and moves quickly through the water. It would
appear rather difficult to invent a mechanism to supply these
tracts with fresh air without the Insect leaving the water ; but
nevertheless such a mechanism is provided by the antennae of
the beetle, the terminal joints of which form a pubescent scoop,
made by some longer hairs into a funnel sufficiently large to
convey a bubble of air. The Insect therefore rises to the surface, and by means of the antennae, which it exposes to the air,
obtains a supply with which it surrounds a large part of its
body ; for, according to Miall, it carries a supply on its back,
under the elytra, as well as on its ventral surface. From the
writer's own observations, made many years ago, he inclines to
the opinion that the way in which the *Hydrophilus* uses the
antennae to obtain air varies somewhat according to circumstances.

Many of the members of the sub-family Hydrophilides construct egg-cocoons. In the case of *Hydrophilus piceus,* the boat-

like structure is provided with a little mast, which is supposed by some to be for the purpose of securing air for the eggs. *Helochares* and *Spercheus* (Fig. 100) carry the cocoon of eggs attached to their own bodies. *Philydrus* constructs, one after the other, a number of these egg-bags, each containing about fifteen eggs, and fixes each bag to the leaf of some aquatic plant; the larvae as a rule hatch speedily, so that the advantage of the bag is somewhat problematic.

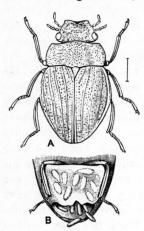

Fig. 100. — *Spercheus emarginatus* ♀. Britain. **A**, Upper surface of beetle; **B**, under surface of abdomen, with the egg-sac ruptured and some of the eggs escaping.

The larvae of the aquatic division of the family have been to a certain extent studied by Schiödte and others; those of the Sphaeridiides—the terrestrial group of the family—are but little known. All the larvae seem to be predaceous and carnivorous, even when the imago is of vegetable-feeding habits; and Duméril states that in *Hydrous caraboides* the alimentary canal undergoes a great change at the period of metamorphosis, becoming very elongate in the adult, though in the larva it was short. The legs are never so well developed as they are in the Adephaga, the tarsi being merely claw-like or altogether wanting; the mandibles are never suctorial. The respiratory arrangements show much diversity. In most of the Hydrophilides the process is carried on by a pair of terminal spiracles on the eighth abdominal segment, as in Dytiscidae, and these are either exposed or placed in a respiratory chamber. In *Berosus* the terminal stigmata are obsolete, and the sides of the body bear long branchial filaments. Cussac says that in *Spercheus* (Fig. 101) there are seven pairs of abdominal spiracles, and that the larva breathes by presenting these to the air;[1] but Schiödte states that in this form there are neither thoracic nor abdominal spiracles, except a pair placed in a respiratory chamber on the eighth segment of the abdomen, after the manner described by Miall as existing in *Hydrobius*. No doubt Cussac was wrong in supposing the peculiar lateral abdominal processes to be stig-

[1] *Ann. Soc. ent. France*, xxi. 1852, p. 619.

matiferous.   In *Berosus* there are patches of aëriferous, minute
pubescence on the body.   The pupae of Hydrophilides repose on
the dorsal surface, which is protected by
spinous processes on the pronotum, and
on the sides of the abdomen.

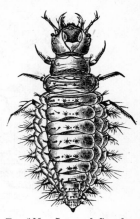

We have already remarked that this
is one of the most neglected of the
families of Coleoptera, and its classification is not satisfactory.   It is usually
divided into Hydrophilides and Sphaeridiides.   The Sphaeridiides are in large
part terrestrial, but their separation from
the purely aquatic Hydrophilides cannot
be maintained on any grounds yet pointed
out.   Altogether about 1000 species of
Hydrophilidae are known, but this probably is not a tenth part of those existing.   In Britain we have nearly ninety
species.   Some taxonomists treat the

Fig. 101.—Larva of *Spercheus
emarginatus.*   (After
Schiödte).

family as a series with the name Palpicornia.   The series Phil-
hydrida of older authors included these Insects and the Parnidae
and Heteroceridae.

Fam. 13. Platypsyllidae.—This consists of a single species.
It will be readily recognised from Fig. 102, attention being given
to the peculiar antennae, and to the fact that the mentum is tri-
lobed behind.   This curious species has been found only on the
beaver.   It was first found by Ritsema on American beavers
(*Castor canadensis*) in the Zoological Gardens at Amsterdam, but
it has since been found on wild beavers in the Rhone in France;
in America it appears to be commonly distributed on these
animals from Alaska to Texas.   It is very remarkable that a
wingless parasite of this kind should be found in both hemispheres.   The Insect was considered by Westwood to be a separate
Order called Achreioptera, but there can be no doubt that it is a
beetle.   It is also admitted that it shows some points of resemblance with Mallophaga, the habits of which are similar.   Its
Coleopterous nature is confirmed by the larva, which has been
described by both Horn and Riley.[1]   Little is known as to the
food and life-history.   Horn states that the eggs are placed on

[1] Horn, *Tr. Amer. ent. Soc.* xv. 1888, p. 23 ; Riley, *Insect Life*, i. 1889, p. 300.

the skin of the beaver amongst the densest hair ; the larvae move with a sinuous motion, like those of Staphylinidae.　It has been

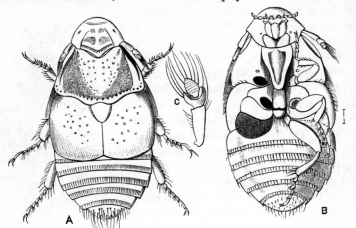

FIG. 102.—*Platypsyllus castoris.*　**A**, Upper side ; **B**, lower side, with legs of one side removed ; **C**, antenna.　(After Westwood.)

suggested that the Insect feeds on an Acarid, *Schizocarpus mingaudi ;* others have supposed that it eats scales of epithelium or hairs of the beaver.

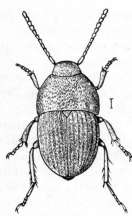

FIG. 103.—*Leptinus testaceus.* Britain.

Fam. 14. Leptinidae. — *Antennae rather long, eleven-jointed, without club, but a little thicker at the extremity.　Eyes absent or imperfect.　Tarsi five-jointed.　Elytra quite covering abdomen.　Mentum with the posterior angles spinously prolonged.* A family of only two genera and two species. Their natural history is obscure, but is apparently of an anomalous nature ; the inference that may be drawn from the little that is known being that they are parasitic on mammals.　There is little or nothing in their structure to indicate this except the condition of blindness ; and until recently the Insects were classified amongst Silphidae.　*Leptinus testaceus* (Fig. 103) is a British Insect, and besides occurring in Europe is well known in North America.　In Europe it has been found in curious places, including the nests of mice and bumble-bees. In America it has been found on the mice themselves by Dr. Ryder, and by Riley in the nests of a common field-mouse, together with its larva, which, however, has not been described. The allied genus *Leptinillus* is said by Riley to live on the beaver, in company with *Platypsyllus*.[1] It has been suggested that the natural home of the *Leptinus* is the bee's nest, and that perhaps the beetle merely makes use of the mouse as a means of getting from one nest of a bumble-bee to another.

Fam. 15. Silphidae.—*The mentum is usually a transverse plate, having in front a membranous hypoglottis, which bears the exposed labial palpi, and immediately behind them the so-called bilobed ligula. The anterior coxae are conical and contiguous : prothoracic epimera and episterna not distinct. Visible abdominal segments usually five, but sometimes only four, or as many as seven. Tarsi frequently five-jointed, but often with one joint less. Elytra usually covering the body and free at the tips, but occasionally shorter than the body, and even truncate behind so as to expose from one to four of the dorsal plates ; but there are at least three dorsal plates in a membranous condition at the base of the abdomen.* These beetles are extremely diverse in size and form, some being very minute, others upwards of an inch long, and there is also considerable range of structure. In this family are included the burying-beetles (*Necrophorus*), so well known from their habit of making excavations under the corpses of small Vertebrates, so as to bury them. Besides these and *Silpha*, the roving carrion-beetles, the family includes many other very different forms, amongst them being the larger part of the cave-beetles of Europe and North America. These belong mostly to the genera *Bathyscia* in Europe, and *Adelops* in North America ; but of late years quite a crowd of these eyeless cave-beetles of the group Leptoderini have been discovered, so that the European catalogue now includes about 20 genera and 150 species. The species of the genus *Catopomorphus* are found in the nests of ants of the genus *Aphaenogaster* in the Mediterranean region. Scarcely anything is known as to the lives of either the cave-Silphidae or the myrmecophilous forms.

The larvae of several of the larger forms of Silphidae are well known, but very little has been ascertained as to the smaller forms.

---

[1] *Insect Life*, i. 1889, pp. 200 and 306.

Those of the burying-beetles have spiny plates on the back of the body, and do not resemble the other known forms of the family. The rule is that the three thoracic segments are well developed, and that ten abdominal segments are also distinct; the ninth abdominal segment bears a pair of cerci, which are sometimes elongate.   Often the dorsal plates are harder and better developed than is usual in Coleopterous larvae.   This is especially the case

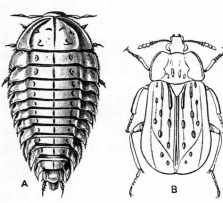

with some that are en-dowed with great powers of locomotion, such as *S. obscura* (Fig. 104).   The food of the larvae is as a rule decomposing animal or vegetable matter, but some are predaceous, and attack living objects. The larger *Silpha* larvae live, like the *Necro-phorus*, on decomposing animal matter, but run about to seek it; hence many specimens of some of these large larvae may

FIG. 104.—**A**, Larva of *Silpha obscura*. Europe. (After Schiödte). **B**, *Ptomaphila lacrymosa*, Australia.

sometimes be found amongst the bones of a very small dead bird. We have found the larva and imago of *S. thoracica* in birds' nests containing dead nestlings.   *S. atrata* and *S. laevigata* make war on snails.   *S. lapponica* enters the houses in Lapland and ravages the stores of animal provisions.   *S. opaca* departs in a very decided manner from the habits of its congeners, as it attacks beetroot and other similar crops in the growing state; it is sometimes the cause of serious loss to the growers of beet.   The larvae of the group Anisotomides are believed to be chiefly subterranean in habits; that of *A. cinnamomea* feeds on the truffle, and the beetle is known as the truffle-beetle.

The number of species of Silphidae known must be at present nearer 900 than 800.   Of these an unusually large proportion be-long to the European and North American regions; Silphidae being apparently far from numerous in the tropics.   Rather more than 100 species are natives of Britain.   The family reappears in con-siderable force in New Zealand, and is probably well represented

in South Australia and Tasmania.   The most remarkable form
known is perhaps the Australian genus *Ptomaphila* (Fig. 104, B).
The classification of the family is due to Dr. Horn.[1]   The
only change of importance that has since been suggested is
the removal of *Sphaerites* from this family to Synteliidae.
Anisotomidae and Clambidae have been considered distinct
families, but are now included in Silphidae.

Fam. 16. Scydmaenidae.—*Minute Insects allied to Silphidae,
but with the hind coxae separated, and the facets of the eyes coarser ;
the tarsi are five-jointed ; the number of visible abdominal segments is
six.*   These small beetles are widely spread over the earth's surface,
and about 700 species are now known, of which we have about a
score in Britain ; many live in ants' nests, but probably usually
rather as intruders than as guests that have friendly relations
with their hosts.   Nothing is known as to their life-histories, but
the food of the imago, so far as is known, consists of Acari. *Mastigus*
is a very aberrant form, found in moss and dead leaves in Southern
Europe.   By means of *Brathinus* the family is brought very near
to Silphidae ; Casey, however, considers *Brathinus* to belong to
Staphylinidae rather than to Scydmaenidae.   The South European
Leptomastax is remarkable on account of the slender, long, sickle-
shaped mandibles.   The Oriental genus *Clidicus* is the largest and
most remarkable form of the family ; it has a very slender neck
to its broad head, and is more than a quarter of an inch long.

Fam. 17. Gnostidae. — *Minute Insects with three-jointed
antennae, five-jointed tarsi, and three apparent ventral segments, the
first of which, however, is elongate, and consists of three united
plates.   Elytra entirely covering the after-body.*   The family consists of two species which have been found in the nests of ants,
of the genus *Cremastogaster*, in Brazil.[2]

Fam. 18. Pselaphidae.   *Very small Insects ; the elytra much
abbreviated, usually leaving as much as half the abdomen uncovered ;
the maxillary palpi usually greatly developed, and of a variety of
remarkable forms ; the segments of the abdomen not more than
seven in number, with little or no power of movement.   Tarsi with
not more than three joints.*   These small Coleoptera mostly live in
the nests of ants, and present a great diversity of extraordinary

---

[1] *Tr. Amer. ent. Soc.* viii. 1880, pp. 219-321.
[2] Westwood, *Tr. ent. Soc. London* (N.S.) iii. 1855, p. 90 ; Wasmann, *Krit.
Verzeichniss Myrmekoph. Arthropod.* 1894, p. 121.

shapes, and very peculiar structures of the antennae and maxillary palpi. Owing to the consolidation of some of its segments, the abdomen frequently appears to have less than the usual number. In the curious sub-family Clavigerides, the antennae may have the joints reduced to two or even, to all appearance, to one ; the tarsi suffer a similar reduction. There are about 2500 species of Pselaphidae known ; many of them have never been found outside the ants' nests ; very little, however, is known as to their natural history. It is certain that some of them excrete, from little tufts of peculiar pubescence, a substance that the ants are fond of. The secretory patches are found on very different parts of the body and appendages. *Claviger testaceus* is fed by the ants in the same way as these social Insects feed one another ; the *Claviger* has also been seen to eat the larvae of the ants. They ride about on the backs of the ants when so inclined. The family is allied to Staphylinidae, but is easily distinguished by the rigid abdomen. Only one larva—that of *Chennium bituberculatum*—is known. It appears to be very similar to the larvae of Staphylinidae. The best account of classification and structure is that given by M. Achille Raffray,[1] who has himself discovered and described a large part of the known species.

Fam. 19. Staphylinidae.—*Elytra very short, leaving always some of the abdominal segments exposed, and covering usually only two of the segments. Abdomen usually elongate, with ten dorsal, and seven or eight ventral segments ; of the latter six or seven are usually exposed ; the dorsal plates as hard as the ventral, except sometimes in the case of the first two segments ; the segments very mobile, so that the abdomen can be curled upwards. The number of tarsal joints very variable, often five, but frequently as few as three, and not always the same on all the feet.* Staphylinidae (formerly called Brachelytra or Microptera) is one of the most extensive of even the great families of Coleoptera ; notwithstanding their diversity, they may in nearly all cases be recognised by the more than usually mobile and uncovered abdomen, combined with the fact that the parts of the mouth are of the kind we have mentioned in Silphidae. The present state of the classification of this family has been recently discussed by Ganglbauer.[2] At present

---

[1] *Rev. ent. franc.* ix. 1890.

Die Käfer von Mitteleuropa : II. *Familienreihe, Staphylinoidea.* Vienna, 1895 and 1899.

about 9000 species are known, some of which are minute, while
scarcely any attain a size of more than an inch in length, our
common British black cock-tail, or " devil's coach-horse beetle,"
Ocypus olens, being amongst the largest.   Though the elytra
are short, the wings in many forms are as large as those of
the majority of beetles; indeed many Staphylinidae are more
apt at taking flight than is usual with Coleoptera; the wings
when not in use are packed away under the short elytra,
being transversely folded, and otherwise crumpled, in a complicated but orderly manner.   It is thought that the power

of curling up the abdomen is
connected with the packing
away of the wings after flight;
but this is not the case: for
though the Insect sometimes
experiences a difficulty in folding the wings under the elytra
after they have been expanded,
yet it overcomes this difficulty
by slight movements of the base
of the abdomen, rather than
by touching the wings with
the tip.   What the value of
this exceptional condition of
short elytra and corneous dorsal
abdominal segments to the
Insect may be is at present
quite mysterious.   The habits
of the members of the family

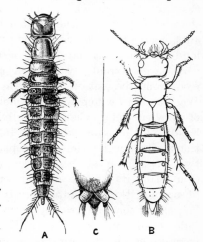

Fig. 105.—Staphylinidae. **A**, Larva of *Phi-
lonthus nitidus.* Britain. (After Schiödte.)
B, *Ocypus olens,* Britain ; **C**, tip of abdomen, of *O. olens* with stink-vessels.

are very varied; many run with great activity; the food is
very often small Insects, living or dead; a great many are
found in fungi of various kinds, and perhaps eat them.   It is
in this family that we meet with some of the most remarkable
cases of symbiosis, *i.e.* lives of two kinds of creatures mutually
accommodated with good will.   The relations between the
Staphylinidae of the genera *Atemeles* and *Lomechusa,* and certain
ants, in the habitations of which they dwell, are very interesting.
The beetles are never found out of the ants' nests, or at any rate
not very far from them.   The most friendly relations exist between
them and the ants : they have patches of yellow hairs, and these

apparently secrete some substance with a flavour agreeable to the ants, which lick the beetles from time to time. On the other hand, the ants feed the beetles; this they do by regurgitating food, at the request of the beetle, on to their lower lip, from which it is then taken by the beetle (Fig. 82). The beetles in many of their movements exactly resemble the ants, and their mode of requesting food, by stroking the ants in certain ways, is quite ant-like. So reciprocal is the friendship that if an ant is in want of food, the *Lomechusa* will in its turn disgorge for the benefit of its host. The young of the beetles are reared in the nests by the ants, who attend to them as carefully as they do to their own young. The beetles have a great fondness for the ants, and prefer to sit amongst a crowd thereof; they are fond of the ants' larvae as food, and indeed eat them to a very large extent, even when their own young are receiving food from the ants. The larva of *Lomechusa*, as described by Wasmann (to whom we are indebted for most of our knowledge of this subject),[1] when not fully grown, is very similar to the larvae of the ants; although it possesses legs it scarcely uses them: its development takes place with extraordinary rapidity, two days, at most, being occupied in the egg, and the larva completing its growth in fourteen days. Wasmann seems to be of opinion that the ants scarcely distinguish between the beetle-larvae and their own young; one unfortunate result for the beetle follows from this, viz. that in the pupal state the treatment that is suitable for the ant-larvae does not agree with the beetle-larvae: the ants are in the habit of digging up their own kind and lifting them out and cleaning them during their metamorphosis; they also do this with the beetle-larvae, with fatal results; so that only those that have the good fortune to be forgotten by the ants complete their development. Thus from thirty *Lomechusa* larvae Wasmann obtained a single imago, and from fifty *Atemeles* larvae not even one.

Many other Staphylinidae are exclusively attached to ants' nests, but most of them are either robbers, at warfare with the ants—as is the case with many species of *Myrmedonia* that lurk about the outskirts of the nests—or are merely tolerated by the ants, not receiving any direct support from them. The most

---

[1] *Vergleichende Studien über Ameisengäste*, Nijhoff, 1890 ; and *Tijdschr. ent.* xxxiii. 1890, pp. 93, etc. ; *Biol. Centralbl.* xv. 1895, p. 632.

remarkable Staphylinidae yet discovered are some viviparous species, forming the genera *Corotoca* and *Spirachtha*, that have very swollen abdomens, and live in the nests of Termites in Brazil :[1] very little is, however, known about them.   A very large and powerful Staphylinid, *Velleius dilatatus*, lives only in the nests of hornets and wasps.   It has been supposed to be a defender of the Hymenoptera, but the recent observations of Janet and Wasmann make it clear that this is not the case : the *Veileius* has the power of making itself disagreeable to the hornets by some odour, and they do not seriously attack it.   The *Velleius* finds its nutriment in larvae or pupae of the wasps that have fallen from their cells, or in other organic refuse.

The larvae of Staphylinidae are very similar to those of Carabidae, but their legs are less perfect, and are terminated only by a single claw ; there is no distinct labrum.   The pupae of some are obtected, *i.e.* covered by a secondary exudation that glues all the appendages together, and forms a hard coat, as in Lepidoptera.   We have about 800 species of Staphylinidae in Britain, and it is probable that the family will prove one of the most extensive of the Order.   It is probable that one hundred thousand species or even more are at present in existence.

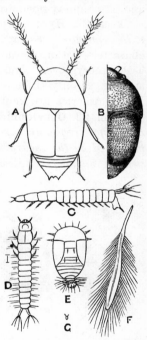

Fam.   20.   Sphaeriidae. — *Very minute.   Antennae eleven-jointed, clubbed. Tarsi three-jointed.   Abdomen with only three visible ventral segments.*   This family includes only three or four species of Insects about $\frac{1}{50}$ of an inch long.   They are very convex, and may be found walking on mud.   *S. acaroides* occurs in our fens. Mr. Matthews considers that they are most nearly allied to Hydrophilidae.[2]

Fig. 106.—*Trichopteryx fascicularis.*   Britain.   **A,** Outline of perfect Insect ; **B,** part of upper surface ; **C,** larva from side ; **D,** from above ; **E,** pupa ; **F,** wing ; **G,** natural size of imago.

Fam.   21.   Trichopterygidae.—*Extremely   minute : antennae*

---

[1] Schiödte, *Ann. Sci. Nat. Zool.* (4) v. 1857, p. 169.
[2] *Biol. Centr. Amer. Col.* ii. pt. i. 1888, p. 156.

*clavicorn (basal and apical joints thicker than middle joints) ; tarsi
three-jointed ; elytra sometimes covering abdomen, in other cases
leaving a variable number of segments exposed ; wings fringed.*
This family comprises the smallest Insects ; *Nanosella fungi* being
only $\frac{1}{100}$ of an inch long, while the largest Trichopterygid is
only $\frac{1}{12}$ of an inch. The small size is not accompanied by any
degeneration of structure, the minute, almost invisible forms, having
as much anatomical complexity as the largest Insects. Very little
is known as to the natural history. Probably these Insects exist in
all parts of the world, for we have about eighty species in England,
and Trichopterygidae are apparently numerous in the tropics.[1]

Fam. 22. Hydroscaphidae.—*Extremely minute aquatic Insects,
with elongate abdomen. Antennae eight-jointed.* The other
characters are much the same as those we have mentioned for
Trichopterygidae. The family is not likely to come before the
student, as only three or four species from Southern Europe and
North America are known.[2]

Fam. 23. Corylophidae.—*Minute beetles. Tarsi four-jointed,
but appearing only three-jointed, owing to the hind joint being
concealed by the emarginate (or notched) second joint. Six free
ventral segments. Maxillae with only one lobe. Antennae of
peculiar form.* There are about
200 species of these little Insects,
but the family is apparently represented all over the world, and will
probably prove to be much more
extensive. The peculiar larva of
Orthoperus brunnipes was found
abundantly by Perris in thatch in
France. Mr. Matthews proposes
to separate the genus *Aphanocephalus* as a distinct family, Pseudocory-
lophidae.[3] In Corylophidae the
wings are fringed with long hairs,
as is the case in so many small
Insects : the species of *Aphanocephalus* are rather larger Insects,
and the wings are not fringed ; the tarsi are only three-jointed.

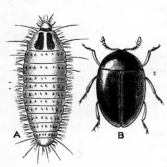

Fig. 107.—**A,** Larva of *Orthoperus
brunnipes* (after Perris); **B,** *O. ato-
marius,* perfect Insect. Britain.

---

[1] Monograph, *Trichopterygia illustrata,* by A. Matthews, London, 1872.
[2] For further information refer to Matthews, *An Essay on* Hydroscapha, London,
1876, 20 pp. 1 pl.   [3] *Ann. Nat. Hist.* (5) xix. 1887, p. 115.

Fam. 24. Scaphidiidae.—*Front coxae small, conical; prothorax very closely applied to the after-body ; hind coxae transverse, widely separated : abdomen with six or seven visible ventral plates ; antennae at the extremity with about five joints that become gradually broader. Tarsi five-jointed.* This family consists of a few beetles that live in fungi, and run with extreme rapidity ; they are all small, and usually rare in collections. Some of the exotic forms are remarkable for the extreme tenuity and fragility of the long antennae, which bear fine hairs. The number of described species does not at present reach 200, but the family is very widely distributed. We have three or four species in Britain. All we know of the larvae is a description of that of *Scaphisoma agaricinum* by Perris ;[1] it is like the larva of Staphylinidae, there are nine abdominal segments in addition to a very short, broad pseudopod, and very short cerci. This larva feeds on agarics ; it goes through its development in about three weeks ; unlike the adult it is not very active.

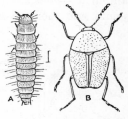

FIG. 108.—*Scaphisoma agaricinum.* Britain. **A** Larva (after Perris) ; **B** perfect Insect.

Fam. 25. Synteliidae.—*Antennae clavicorn, with very large club : labium, with hypoglottis and the parts beyond it, exposed. Front coxae transverse. Abdomen with five visible ventral segments, and eight or nine dorsal, the basal four of which are semi-corneous.*

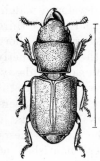

FIG. 109.—*Syntelia west-wcodi.* Mexico. (From *Biol. Centr. Amer.*)

This family includes only five species ; its classification has given rise to much difference of opinion. We have, after consideration of all its characters, established it as a distinct family [2] allied to Silphidae. The perfect Insects live on the sap running from trees : but nothing else is known of their natural history. Like so many others of the very small families of aberrant Coleoptera, it has a very wide distribution ; *Syntelia* being found in Eastern Asia and Mexico, while the sub-family Sphaeritides occurs, as a single species, in Europe and North America. The earlier instars are unknown.

[1] *Larves de Coléoptères,* 1878, p. 11, pl. i.   [2] *Biol. Centr. Amer. Col.* ii. pt. i. p. 438.

Fam. 26. Histeridae.—*Very compact beetles, with very hard integument, short, bent antennae, with a very compact club: no hypoglottis. Elytra closely applied to body, but straight behind, leaving two segments exposed. Abdomen with five visible ventral segments; with seven dorsal segments, all hard. Front coxae strongly transverse, hind coxae widely separated.* The extremely compact form, and hard integument, combined with the peculiar antennae—consisting of a long basal joint, six or seven small joints, and then a very solid club of three joints covered with minute pubescence — render these Insects unmistakable. The colour is usually shining black, but there are numerous departures from this. The way in which these Insects are put together so as to leave no chink in their hard exterior armour when in repose, is very remarkable. The mouth - parts are rather highly developed, and the family is entitled to a high rank; it consists at present of about 2000 species;[1] in Britain we have about 40. The larvae are without ocelli or labrum, but have well-developed mandibles, the second and third thoracic segments being short,

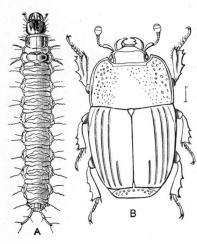

Fig. 110.—*Platysoma depressum.* Europe. **A**, Larva (after Schiödte); **B**, perfect Insect.

the ninth segment of the abdomen terminal, with two distinctly jointed cerci.[2] Histeridae are common in dung, in carcases, decaying fungi, etc., and some live under bark—these being, in the case of the genus *Hololepta*, very flat. Some are small cylinders, elaborately constructed, for entering the burrows of Insects in wood (*Trypanaeus*); a certain number are peculiar to ants' nests. Formerly it was supposed that the Insects were nourished on the decaying substances, but it is now believed, with good reason, that they are eminently predaceous, in both larval and imaginal

[1] The family was monographed by the Abbé de Marseul in *Ann. Soc. ent. France*, 1853-1862, but great additions have been made since then.

[2] For characters of larvae of various genera, see Perris, *Larves, etc.* p. 24.

instars, and devour the larvae of Diptera, etc.   The relations of the ants'-nest forms to the ants is not made out, but it is highly probable that they eat the ants' larvae, and furnish the ants with some dainty relish.   A few species live in company with Termites.

Fam. 27. Phalacridae.—*Body very compact; elytra entirely covering it; apical joints of antennae rather broader, usually long; front coxae globular; posterior coxae contiguous; abdomen with five visible ventral segments; tarsi five-jointed, fourth joint usually small and obscure.*   This family consists entirely of small Insects : the tarsal structure is very aberrant, and is also diverse, so that the student may without careful observation pass the Insects over as having only four-jointed tarsi; their structure, so far as the front two pairs are concerned, being very nearly that of many Phytophaga.   The larvae live in the heads of flowers, especially of the flowers of Compositae.   Having bored their way down the stems, they pupate in earthen cocoons. Heeger [1] says that he has observed in favourable seasons six generations; but the larvae die readily in unfavourable seasons, and are destroyed in vast numbers when the meadows are mowed.   Seven years ago very little was known as to the family, and the list of their species scarcely amounted to 100, but now probably 300 are described.   They occur in all parts of the world; we have fourteen in Britain.

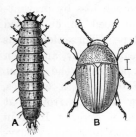

Fig.   111. — *Olibrus   bicolor.* Europe.   **A,** Larva (after Heeger) ; **B,** perfect Insect.

Fam. 28. Nitidulidae.—*Antennae with a three-jointed club; all the coxae separated, and each with an external prolongation; tarsi five-jointed, the fourth joint smaller than any of the others; abdomen with five visible plates.*   These Insects are numerous, about 1600 species being at present known; in many of them the elytra nearly or quite cover the hind body, but in many others they are more or less abbreviated; in this case the Insects may be distinguished from Staphylinidae by the form of their antennae, and the smaller number of visible ventral segments.   The habits are very varied, a great many are found on flowers, others are attracted by the sap of trees; some live in carcases.   We have about 90 species in Britain; several forms of

[1] *SB. Ak. Wien.* xxiv. 1857, p. 330.

the genera *Meligethes* and *Epuraea* are among the most abundant of our beetles. Most of what is known as to the larvae is due to Perris; several have been found living in flowers; that of *Pria* haunts the flower of *Solanum dulcamara* at the junction of the stamens with the corolla; the larva of *Meligethes aeneus*

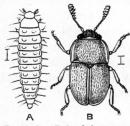

sometimes occasions much loss by preventing the formation of seed in cultivated Cruciferae, such as Rape. These floricolous larvae grow with great rapidity, and then leave the flowers to pupate in the ground. The larva of *Nitidula* lives in carcases, though it is not very different from that of *Pria*. The larva of *Soronia* lives in fermenting sap, and has four hooks curving upwards at the extremity of the body.

FIG. 112.—*Pria dulcamarae.* Britain. **A,** Larva (after Perris); **B,** perfect Insect.

The curious genus *Cybocephalus* consists of some very small, extremely convex Insects that live in flowers in Southern Europe; they have only four joints to the tarsi. The perfect Insects of the group Ipides are remarkable from having a stridulating organ on the front of the head. The classification of the well-known genus *Rhizophagus* has given rise to much discussion; although now usually placed in Nitidulidae, we think it undoubtedly belongs to Cucujidae.

Fam. 29. Trogositidae.—*Differs from Nitidulidae in the struc-*

ture of the tarsi; these appear to be four-jointed, with the third joint similar in size and form to the preceding; they are, however, really five-jointed, an extremely short basal joint being present. Hind coxae contiguous. The club of each antenna is bilaterally asymmetric, and the sensitive surface is confined to certain parts of the joints. There are some 400 or 500 species of Trogositidae, but nearly all of them are exotic. The larvae (Fig. 113, A), are predaceous, destroying other larvae in large numbers, and it is probable that the imagos do the same.

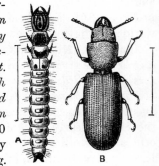

FIG. 113.—*Temnochila coerulea.* Europe. **A,** Larva (after Perris); **B,** perfect Insect.

The larva of *Tenebroides* (better known as *Trogosita*) *mauritanica* is found in corn and flour, and is said to have sometimes been very injurious by eating the embryo of the corn, but it is ascertained that it also devours certain other larvae that live on the corn. This beetle has been carried about by commerce, and is now nearly cosmopolitan. Our three British species of Trogositidae represent the three chief divisions of the family, viz. Nemosomides, Temnochilides, Peltides; they are very dissimilar in form, the Peltides being oval, with retracted head. It is doubtful whether the members of the latter group are carnivorous in any of their stages; it is more probable that they live on the fungi they frequent. Peltidae stand as a distinct family in many works.[1]

Fam. 30. Colydiidae.—*Antennae with a terminal club, tarsi four-jointed, none of the joints broad; front and middle coxae small, globose, embedded; hind coxae transverse, either contiguous or separated; five visible ventral segments, several of which have no movement.* This is a family of interest, owing to the great diversity of form, to the extraordinary sculpture and clothing exhibited by many of its members, and to the fact that most of its members are attached to the primitive forests, and disappear entirely when these are destroyed. We have fifteen species in Britain, but about half of them are of the greatest rarity. There are about 600 species known at present; New Zealand has produced the greatest variety of forms; the forests of Teneriffe are rich in the genus *Tarphius*. The sedentary lives of many of these beetles are very remarkable; the creatures concealing themselves in the crannies of fungus-covered wood, and scarcely ever leaving their retreats, so that it is the rarest circumstance to find them at any distance from their homes. *Langelandia anophthalma* lives entirely underground and is quite blind, the optic lobes being absent. Some Colydiidae are more active, and enter the burrows of wood-boring Insects to destroy the larvae (*Colydium*). Few of the larvae are known; but all appear to have the body terminated by peculiar hard corneous processes, as is the case with a great variety of Coleopterous larvae that live in wood.[2]

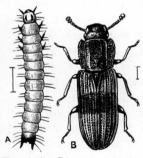

FIG. 114.—*Bitoma crenata.* Britain. **A,** Larva (after Perris); **B,** perfect Insect.

---

[1] Catalogue of Trogositidae, by Leveillé, in *Ann. Soc. ent. France*, 1888, p. 429.

[2] For classification, see Sharp, *Biol. Centr. Amer. Col.* ii. pt. i. 1894, p. 443.

Fam. 31. Rhysodidae. — *Tarsi four-jointed; mouth-parts covered by the large mentum; front tibiae notched on the inner edge.* This family consists only of a few species, but is found nearly all over the world in the warm and temperate regions. In many of their characters they resemble the Adephaga, but are very different in appearance and in the mouth. The larvae are not known. Some authorities think these Insects should be placed in the series Adephaga,[1] but it is more probable that they will prove to be amongst the numerous aberrant forms of Coleoptera that approach the various large natural series, without really belonging to them. The three families, Colydiidae, Cucujidae, and Rhysodidae, exhibit relations not only with other families of the Coleoptera Polymorpha, but also with most of the great series; Adephaga, Rhynchophora, Phytophaga, and Heteromera, being each closely approached.

Fam. 32. Cucujidae. — *Tarsi five- or four-jointed, the first joint often short: antennae sometimes clubbed, but more often quite thin at the tip; front and middle coxae deeply embedded, globular, but with an angular prolongation externally; abdomen with five visible ventral segments, all movable.* This family and the Cryptophagidae are amongst the most difficult families to define; indeed it is in this portion of the Clavicorns that an extended and thorough study is most urgently required. The Cucujidae include a great diversity of forms; they are mostly found under the bark of trees, and many of them are very flat. Many of the larvae are also very flat, but Perris says there is great diversity in their structure: they are probably chiefly carnivorous.

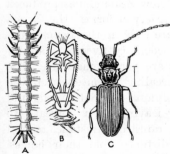

FIG. 115.—*Brontes planatus.* Britain. **A**, Larva; **B**, pupa; **C**, perfect Insect. (**A** and **B** after Perris.)

There are about 400 species described; we have nearly a score in Britain.

The family Cupesidae of certain taxonomists must be at present associated with Cucujidae, though the first joint of the tarsus is elongate.

---

[1] See Ganglbauer, *Käf. Mitteleuropas,* i. p. 530, as well as Leconte and Horn *Classification,* etc., p. 130.

Fam. 33. Cryptophagidae.—*Front and middle coxae very small and deeply embedded; antennae with enlarged terminal joints; tarsi five-jointed, the posterior sometimes in the male only four-jointed; abdomen with five visible ventral segments, capable of movement, the first much longer than any of the others.* A small family composed of obscure forms of minute size, which apparently have mould-eating habits, though very little is known on this point, and several of the genera (*Antherophagus, Telmatophilus*) are found chiefly on growing plants, especially in flowers. Although the imago of *Antherophagus* lives in flowers, yet the larva has only been found in the nests of bumble-bees; there is reason for believing that the imago makes use of the bee to transport

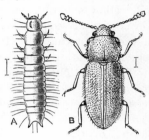

FIG. 116.—*Cryptophagus dentatus.* Britain. **A,** Larva (after Perris); **B,** perfect Insect.

it from the flowers it haunts to the nests in which it is to breed;[1] this it does by catching hold of the bee with its mandibles when the bee visits the flower in which the beetle is concealed. It is strange the beetle should adopt such a mode of getting to its future home, for it has ample wings. We must presume that its senses and instinct permit it to recognise the bee, but do not suffice to enable it to find the bee's nest. Some of the larvae of the genus *Cryptophagus* are found abundantly in the nests of various wasps, where they are probably useful as scavengers, others occur in the nests of social caterpillars, and they are sometimes common in loose straw; this being the habitat in which Perris found the one we figure.

Fam. 34. Helotidae.—*Front and middle coxal cavities round, with scarcely any angular prolongation externally; all the coxae widely separated; five visible ventral segments, all mobile.* The Insects of this family are closely allied to Trogositidae and Nitidulidae, and have the tarsal structure of the former family; but the Helotidae are different in appearance from any members of either of these two families, and are readily distinguished by the coxal character. They are frequently classified with the Erotylidae, from which they differ by the differently shaped feet, especially by the diminished basal joint.

[1] Perris, *Larves, etc.*, p. 75.

There is but one genus, and for a long time only two or three species were known, and were great rarities in collections; in the last few years the number has been raised to nearly forty.[1] They are remarkable beetles with oblong form, and a somewhat metallic upper surface, which is much sculptured, and possesses four yellow, smooth spots on the elytra. According to Mr. George Lewis they are found feeding at the running sap of trees, but the larvae are not known. Helotidae are peculiar to the Indo-Malayan region (including Japan) with one species in Eastern Africa.

Fam. 35. Thorictidae.—*Tarsi five-jointed, none of the joints broad; front coxae small, rather prominent, but not at all trans- verse; five visible ventral plates, all mobile; metasternum very short; antennae short, with a solid club.* This little family, con- sisting of the genus *Thorictus*, appears to be a distinct one, though the structure has only been very imperfectly studied. It is peculiar to the Mediterranean region, where the species live in ants' nests. They appear to be on terms of great intimacy with the ants; a favourite position of the beetle is on the scape of the antenna of an ant; here it hooks itself on firmly, and is carried about by the ant. Like so many other ants'-nest beetles, Thorictidae possess tufts of golden hair, which secrete some substance, the flavour of which is appreciated by the ants; these tufts in Thorictidae are situated either at the hind angles of the pronotum, or on the under surface of the body on each side of the breast; Wasmann thinks that when the beetles are riding about,

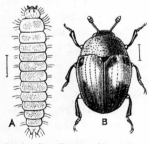

as above described, the ants have then an opportunity of getting at the patches on the under surface.

Fam. 36. Erotylidae.—*Tarsi five- jointed, but with the fourth usually very small, the first three more or less broad and pubescent beneath. Antennae strongly clubbed. Front and middle coxal aceta- bula round, without angular prolongation externally; five visible ventral segments.* This is now a large and important family of about 1800 species, but it is chiefly exotic and tropical, its members haunting the fungoid growths

Fig. 117.—*Tritoma bipustulata.* Erotylidae. Britain. **A,** Larva (after Perris); **B,** perfect Insect.

[1] Ritsema, *Catalogue of* Helota, *Notes Leyden Mus.* xiii. 1891, p. 223, and xv. 1893, p. 160.

in forests.   We have only six species in Britain, and the whole of Europe has only about two dozen, most of them insignificant (and in the case of the Dacnides aberrant, approaching the Cryptophagidae very closely).   The sub-family Languriides (quite wanting in Europe) consists of more elongate Insects, with front acetabula open behind; they have different habits from Erotylides proper; some are known to live as larvae in the stems of herbaceous plants.   They possess a highly developed stridulating organ on the front of the head.   The Clavicorn Polymorpha are very closely connected with the Phytophaga by Languriides.

Fam. 37. Mycetophagidae.—*Tarsi four-jointed, slender, the front feet of the male only three-jointed; coxae oval, not deeply embedded; abdomen with five ventral segments, all movable.* A small family, of interest chiefly because of the anomaly in the feet of the two sexes, for which it is impossible to assign any reason.   The species are small, uninteresting Insects that live chiefly on Cryptogams of various kinds, especially in connection with timber; the larvae being also found there.   There are about a dozen species in Britain, and scarcely 100 are described from all the world.   The Diphyllides, placed by Leconte and Horn in this family, seem to go better in Cryptophagidae.

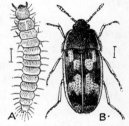

Fig. 118.—*Litargus bifasciatus.* Mycetophagidae. Britain. **A,** Larva (after Perris); **B,** perfect Insect.

Fam. 38. Coccinellidae (*Lady-birds*).—*Tarsi apparently three-jointed; the first two joints pubescent beneath; the third joint consisting really of two joints, the small true third joint being inserted near the base of the second joint, the upper surface of which is grooved to receive it.   Head much concealed by the thorax. Antennae feebly clubbed.* The lady-birds number fully 2000 species.   The structure of their feet distinguishes them from nearly all other Coleoptera except Endomychidae, which are much less rotund in form, and have larger antennae.   One genus of Endomychids—*Panomoea*—bears, however, a singular resemblance to lady-birds, both in form and style of coloration.   Several species of Coccinellidae are remarkable on account of the numerous variations in colour they present.   Coccinellidae frequently multiply to an enormous extent, and are of great value, as they destroy wholesale the plant-lice, scale-Insects, and Acari that are so injurious to cultivated plants. They also eat various other soft-bodied Insects that attack plants. As they are excessively voracious, and are themselves singularly free from enemies and multiply with great rapidity, all these features of their economy render them of inestimable value to the agriculturist and horticulturist. The species of the sub-family Epilachnides feed on plants, and one or two are occasionally injurious. The body-fluid of Coccinellidae has an unpleasant odour and taste. Many lady-birds have the power of exuding, when disturbed, small quantities of a yellow fluid. Lutz has shown that this is not a special secretion, but an exudation of the fluid of the body that takes place through a small orifice at the tip of the tibia, from pressure caused by contraction of the body and limb.[1]

The larvae are much more active than beetle-larvae usually are, and many of them are very conspicuous when running about on plants to hunt their prey. They usually cast their skins three times, and sometimes concomitantly change a good deal in colour and form ; the larval life does not usually exceed four or five weeks ; at the end of which time the larva suspends itself by the posterior extremity, which is glued by a secretion to some object ; the larval skin is pushed back to the anal extremity, disclosing the pupa ; this differs in several respects from the usual pupa of beetles ; it is harder, and is coloured, frequently conspicuously spotted, and dehisces to allow the escape of the beetle, so that the metamorphosis is altogether more like that of Lepidoptera than that of Coleoptera. There is much variety in the larvae; some of them bear large, complexly-spined, projections ; those of the group Scymnites have small depressions on the surface, from which it has been ascertained that waxy secretions exude ; but in *Scymnus minimus* no such excretions are formed. Certain species, when pupating, do not shuffle the skin to the extremity of the body, but retain it as a covering for the pupa. The larvae that feed on plants are much less active than the predaceous forms. We are well supplied with Coccinellidae in Britain, forty species being known here.

The systematic position of Coccinellidae amongst the Coleoptera has been for long a moot point. Formerly they were associated with various other beetles having three-jointed, or apparently three-jointed, feet, as a series with the name Trimera, or

[1] *Zool. Anz.* xviii. 1895, p. 244.

Pseudotrimera.   But they are generally placed in the Clavicorn series, near Endomychidae.   Verhoeff has recently made considerable morphological studies on the male genital organs of Coleoptera, and as the result, he concludes that Coccinellidae differ radically from all other Coleoptera as regards these structures, and he therefore treats them as a distinct series or sub-order, termed Siphonophora.   The genus *Lithophilus* has been considered doubtfully a member of Coccinellidae, as the tarsi possess only in a slight degree the shape characteristic of the family : Verhoeff finds that they are truly Coccinellidae, forming a distinct division, Lithophilini; and our little species of *Coccidula*, which have somewhat the same appearance as Lithophilini, he treats as another separate group, Coccidulini.

Fam. 39. Endomychidae.[1]—*Tarsi apparently three-jointed, the first two joints broad, the terminal joint elongate ; at the base of the terminal joint there is, however, a very small joint, so that the tarsi are pseudotetramerous ; antennae rather large, with a large club ; labium not at all retracted behind the mentum ; front and middle coxae globose ; abdomen with five movable ventral segments, and a sixth more or less visible at the tip.*   This family includes a considerable diversity of elegant Insects that frequent fungoid growths on wood.   It comprises at present fully 500 species, but nearly the whole of them are exotic, and inhabit the tropical forests.   We have only two British species, both of which are now rarities, but apparently were much commoner at the beginning of the century.   The larvae are broader than is usual in Coleoptera ; very few, however, are known.

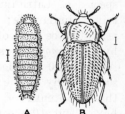

Fam. 40. Mycetaeidae.—*Tarsi four-jointed, the first two joints not very different from the third, usually slender ; abdomen with five visible ventral segments, which are movable ; front and middle coxae globular.*   The little Insects composing this family are by many placed as a division of Endomychidae, and Verhoeff is of opinion that the

Fig. 119.—*Mycetaea hirta.* Britain.   **A,** Larva (after Blisson) ; **B,** perfect Insect.

group is an altogether artificial one ; but we think, with Duval, it makes matters simpler to separate them.   There are only

[1] Gerstaecker, *Monographie der Endomychiden*, Leipzig, 858, 1433 pp.   Since this work was published, the species known have been multiplied two or three times.

some forty or fifty species, found chiefly in Europe and North America. We have three in Britain; one of these, *Mycetaea hirta* is very common, and may be found in abundance in cellars in the heart of London, as well as elsewhere; it is said to have injured the corks of wine-bottles, and to have caused leakage of the wine, but we think that it perhaps only increases some previous deficiency in the corkage, for its natural food is fungoid matters. The larva is remarkable on account of the clubbed hairs at the sides of the body.

Fam. 41. Latridiidae.—*Tarsi three-jointed; anterior coxal cavities round, not prolonged externally; abdomen with five visible and mobile ventral segments.* Very small Insects, species of which are numerous in most parts of the world, the individuals being sometimes very abundant. The larvae (Fig. 120, A) are said by Perris to have the mandibles replaced by fleshy appendages. The pupa of *Latridius* is remarkable, on account of the numerous long hairs with heads instead of points; the larva of *Corticaria* is very like that of *Latridius*, but some of the hairs are replaced by obconical projections. The sub-family Monotomides is by many treated as a distinct family; they have the elytra truncate behind, exposing the pygidium, and the coxae are very small and very deeply embedded. Most of the Latridiidae are believed to live on fungoid matters; species of *Monotoma* live in ants' nests, but probably have no relations with the ants. A few species of Latridiides proper also maintain a similar life; *Coluocera formicaria* is said to be fond of the stores laid up by *Aphaenogaster structor* in its nests. About 700 species are now known; scarcely any of the individuals are more than one-tenth of an inch long. We have about 40 species in Britain. The North American genus *Stephostethus* has

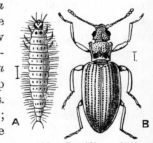

FIG. 120.—*Latridius minutus.* Britain. **A,** Larva (after Perris); **B,** perfect Insect.

the prosternum constructed behind the coxae, somewhat in the same manner as it is in the Rhynchophorous series of Coleoptera.

Fam. 42. Adimeridae.—*Tarsi appearing only two-jointed, a broad basal joint and an elongate claw-bearing joint, but between the two there are two very small joints.* This family consists only of the American genus *Adimerus;* nothing is known of

the life-history of these small Insects.   They are of some
interest, as this structure of the foot
is not found in any other beetles.

Fam. 43. Dermestidae.—*Tarsi
five-jointed; antennae usually short,
with the club frequently very large
in proportion, and with the under
side of the thorax bearing a hollow
for its reception.   Front coxae rather
long, oblique: hind coxa formed to
receive the femur when in repose.*
A family of 300 or 400 species of
small or moderate-sized beetles; the
surface, usually covered with fine
hair, forming a pattern, or with
scales.

FIG. 121. — *Adimerus setosus.*   Adimeridae. **A,** the Insect; **B,** one
foot more enlarged. Mexico. From
Biol. Centr. Amer. Col. ii. pt. i.

Byturus, the position of which has long been disputed,
has now been placed in this family; it has a more imperfectly
formed prosternum, and the third and fourth joints of the tarsi
are prolonged as membranous lobes beneath; the hind coxae leave
the femora quite free.   Dermestidae in the larval state nearly all
live on dried animal matter, and are sometimes very destructive;
some of them totally destroy zoological collections.   They are
very remarkable on account of the complex
clothing of hairs they bear; they have good
powers of locomotion, and many of them
have a peculiar gait, running for a short
distance, then stopping and vibrating some
of their hairs with extreme rapidity.   They
exhibit great variety of form.   Many of
them are capable of supporting life for long
periods on little or no food, and in such
cases moult an increased number of times:
pupation takes place in the larval skin.
Anthrenus fasciatus has been reared in large
numbers on a diet of dried horse-hair in
furniture.   The young larva of this species
observed by the writer did not possess

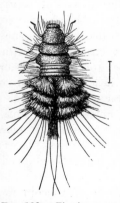

FIG. 122.—*Tiresias serra.*
Larva.   New Forest.

the remarkable, complex arrangement of hairs that appeared
when it was further grown.   The most curious of Dermestid
larvae is that of *Tiresias serra*, which lives amongst cobwebs in

old wood, and probably feeds on the remains of Insects therein, perhaps not disdaining the cobwebs themselves. Attention has been frequently called to the hairs of the larvae of these Insects, but they have never been adequately discussed, and their function is quite unknown.

Fam. 44. Byrrhidae (*Pill-beetles*).—*Oval or round, convex beetles; tarsi five-jointed, front coxae not exserted, transverse; hind coxa shielding the retracted femur. The whole of the appendages capable of a complete apposition to the body.* Although a small family of only 200 or 300 species, Byrrhidae are so heterogeneous that no characteristic definition that will apply to all the sub-families can be framed. Very little is known as to their life-histories. *Byrrhus pilula* is one of our commonest beetles, and may be found crawling on paths in early spring even in towns; it moves very slowly, and when disturbed, at once contracts the limbs so completely that it looks like an inanimate object. The larva is cylindrical, soft; the prothoracic and last two abdominal segments are larger than the others, the last bearing two pseudopods; its habits are unknown, and no good figure exists of it.

The chief groups of Byrrhidae are Nosodendrides, Byrrhides (including Amphicyrtides), Limnichides, and Chelonariides. The first consists of species frequenting the exuding sap of trees; they have an unusually large mentum, abruptly clubbed antennae, and the head cannot be retracted and concealed. The genus *Nosodendron* seems to be distributed over a large part of the world. The Byrrhides have the antennae gradually thicker towards the tip, the mentum small, and the head and thorax so formed that the former can be perfectly retracted. The species are rather numerous, and are found in the northern and antipodeal regions, being nearly completely absent from the tropics. The Limnichides are minute Insects living in very moist places; they have small delicate antennae, which are imperfectly clubbed. The group is very widely distributed.

The Chelonariides are a very peculiar form of Coleoptera: oval Insects of small size with the prothorax so formed that the head can be withdrawn under (rather than into) it, and then abruptly inflexed, so that the face then forms part of the under surface: the antennae have the basal three joints thicker than the others; these being not in the least clubbed, but having the

joints so delicately connected that the organs are rarely un-
mutilated. The modifications of the head and prothorax are
quite unlike those of other Byrrhidae, and if the Chelonariides
do not form a distinct family, they should be associated with
Dascillidae. Nothing is known as to the earlier stages. They
are chiefly tropical Insects, though one species is found in North
America.

Fam. 45. Cyathoceridae—*Minute Insects of broad form; parts
of the mouth concealed; antennae four-jointed; tarsi not divided
into joints; prosternum small.* The only species of this aberrant
family, *Cyathocerus horni*, has been found in Central America.
Nothing is known as to its life-history.

Fam. 46. Georyssidae.—*Antennae short, clubbed; tarsi four-
jointed; prosternum very small; front coxae exserted, but not
contiguous.* There are about two dozen species of these small
beetles known. Our British *Georyssus pygmaeus* lives in extremely
wet places, and covers itself with a coating of mud or fine ·sand
so that it can only be detected when in movement. Nothing
further is known as to its life-history or habits. Members of
the genus have been detected in widely-separated parts of the
globe.

Fam. 47. Heteroceridae.—*Labrum and mandibles projecting
forwards; antennae short, the terminal seven joints broad and short,
forming a sort of broad serrate club; legs armed with stout spines;
tarsi four-jointed.* The Heteroceridae are small beetles covered
with very dense but minute pubescence; they live in burrows
among mud or sand in wet places, and are found in many parts
of the world. They possess a stridulating organ in the form
of a slightly elevated curved line on each side of the base of the
abdomen, rubbed by the posterior femur. The larvae live in the
same places as the beetles; they have well-developed thoracic
legs, the mandibles are porrect, the three thoracic segments
rather large, and the body behind these becomes gradually
narrower; they are believed to eat the mud amongst which
they burrow. We have seven British species of Heteroceridae.

Fam. 48. Parnidae.—*Prosternum distinct in front of the coxae,
usually elongate, behind forming a process received into a definite
cavity on the mesosternum; head retractile, the mouth protected
by the prosternum. Tarsi five-jointed, terminal joint long.*

Although the characters of these Insects are not very different from those of Byrrhidae, of Dascillidae, and even of certain Elateridae, there is practically but little difficulty in distinguishing Parnidae. They are of aquatic habits, though many, in the perfect state, frequently desert the waters. There are about 300 or 400 species known, but the family is doubtless more extensive, as these small beetles attract but little notice. There are two groups:—1. Parnides, in which the front coxae have a considerable transverse extension, the antennae are frequently short and of peculiar structure, and the body is usually clothed with a peculiar, dense pubescence. 2. Elmides, with round front coxae, a bare, or feebly pubescent body, and simple antennae. *Parnus* is a genus commonly met with in Europe, and is less aquatic in habits than its congeners; it is said to enter the water carrying with it a coating of air attached to its pubescence. Its larvae are not well known; they live in damp earth near streams, and are said to much resemble the larvae of Elateridae. *Potamophilus acuminatus* has a very interesting larva, described by Dufour; it lives on decaying wood in the Adour. It is remarkable from the ocelli being arranged so as to form an almost true eye on each side of the head; there are eight pairs of abdominal spiracles, and also a pair on the mesothorax, though there are none on the pro- or meta-thorax; each of the stigmata has four elongate sacs between it and the main tracheal tube; the body is terminated by a process from which there can be protruded bunches of filamentous branchiae. The larvae of *Macronychus quadrituberculatus* is somewhat similar, though the features of its external structure are less remarkable. The Elmides live attached to stones in streams; the larva is rather broad, fringed at the sides of the body, and bears behind three elegant sets of fine filamentous branchiae. The North American genus *Psephenus* is placed in Parnidae, though instead of five, the male has seven, the female six, visible ventral segments; the larva is elliptical, with dilated margins to the body. Friederich, has given,[1] without mentioning any names, a detailed account of Brazilian Parnid larvae, that may perhaps be allied to *Psephenus*.

Fam. 49. Derodontidae.—*Tarsi five-jointed, slender, fourth joint rather small; front coxae prominent and transversely pro-*

[1] *Stettin. ent. Zeit.* xlii. 1881, pp. 104-112.

*longed ; middle coxae small ; abdomen with five visible segments,
all mobile, the first not elongated.*   One of the smallest and least
known of the families of Coleoptera ; it
consists of four or five species of small
Insects of the genera *Derodontus* and
Peltasticta, found in North America,
Europe, and Japan.   The distinction of the
family from Cleridae is by no means certain ; our European *Laricobius* apparently
possessing characters but little different.
Nothing is known as to the life-histories.

Fam. 50. Cioidae.—*Small or minute
beetles ; antennae short, terminal joints
thicker ; tarsi short, four-jointed ; anterior
and middle coxae small, oval, deeply embedded ; abdomen with five ventral segments, all mobile.*   The position of these

Fig. 123.—*Derodontus maculatus.*   North America.

obscure little Insects seems to be near Colydiidae and Cryptophagidae, though they are usually
placed near Bostrichidae.   So far as
known, they all live in fungi, or in
wood penetrated by fungoid growths.
The cylindrical larvae live also in
similar matter ; they usually have the
body terminated behind by one or two
hooks curved upwards ; that of *Cis
melliei* (Fig. 124) has, instead of these
hooks, a curious chitinous tube.   About
300 species of the family are now
known ; a score, or so, occurring in
Britain.   The Hawaiian Islands have
a remarkably rich and varied fauna of
Cioidae.

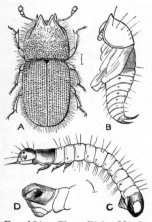

Fig. 124.—*Cis melliei.*   Martin-
ique.   **A,** Perfect Insect ; **B,**
pupa ; **C,** larva ; **D,** terminal
portion of body of larva.
(After Coquerel.)

Fam. 51. Sphindidae.—This family
of half a dozen species of rare and
small Insects, differs from Cioidae by
the tarsi being five-jointed at any rate on the front and middle
feet, opinions differing as to whether the number of joints of the
hind tarsi is four or five.   These Insects live in fungi growing
in wood, *e.g. Reticularia hortensis,* that are at first pulpy and

afterwards become powder. The larvae of both of our British genera, *Sphindus* and *Aspidiphorus*, have been described by Perris, who considers them allied to the fungivorous Silphidae and Latridiidae. The systematic position of these Insects has been the subject of doubt since the days of Latreille.

Fam. 52. Bostrichidae (**Apatidae** of some authors).—*Tarsi five-jointed, but the first joint very short and imperfectly separated from the second; front coxae prominent, contiguous, very little extended transversely; five visible ventral segments.* The Bostrichidae attack dry wood, and sometimes in such large numbers that timber is entirely destroyed by them; most of them make cylindrical burrows into the wood. The larvae have the posterior part of the body incurved, and resemble the wood-boring larvae of Anobiidae rather than the predaceous larvae of Cleridae. We follow Leconte and Horn in placing Lyctides as a division of Bostrichidae; although differing very much in appearance, they have similar habits and larvae. The typical Bostrichides are remarkable for their variety of sculpture and for the shapes of the posterior part of the body; this part is more or less conspicuously truncate, and furnished with small prominences. *Dinapate wrightii*, found in the stems of a species of *Yucca* in the Mojave desert of California, attains a length of nearly two inches; its larva is extremely similar to that of *A. capucina*. Some of the forms (*Phonapate*) stridulate in a manner peculiar to themselves, by rubbing the front leg against some projections at the hind angle of the prothorax. Upwards of 200 species of the family are known. In Britain we have only four small and aberrant forms.

FIG. 125.—*Apate capucina.* Europe. **A**, Larva (after Perris) ; **B**, perfect Insect.

Fam. 53. Ptinidae.—*Tarsi five-jointed, first joint not reduced in size, often longer than second; front and middle coxae small, not transversely extended, the former slightly prominent; five visible ventral segments; prosternum very short.* Here are included two sub-families, Ptinides and Anobiides; they are considered as distinct families by many authors, but in the present imperfect state of knowledge [1] it is not necessary to treat them separately. Ptinidae are sometimes very destructive to dried animal matter, and attack specimens in museums; Anobiides bore into wood, and apparently emerge as perfect Insects only for a very brief period; *Anobium (Sitodrepa) paniceum* is, however, by no means restricted in its tastes; it must possess extraordinary powers of digestion, as we have known it to pass several consecutive generations on a diet of opium; it has also been reported to thrive on tablets of dried compressed meat; in India it is said to disintegrate books; a more usual food of the Insect is, however, hard biscuits; weevilly biscuits are

Fig. 126.—"Biscuit-weevil." *Anobium paniceum*.

known to every sailor, and the so-called "weevil" is usually the larva of *A. paniceum* (Fig. 127, B). In the case of this Insect we have not detected more than one spiracle (situate on the first thoracic segment); the other known larvae of Anobiides are said to possess eight abdominal spiracles. The skeleton in some

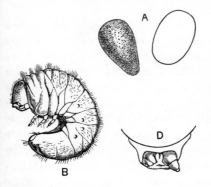

Fig. 127. — Early stages of *Anobium paniceum*. **A,** Eggs, variable in form; **B,** larva; **C,** pupa; **D,** asymmetrical processes terminating body of pupa. [This larva is probably the "bookworm" of librarians].

of this sub-family is extremely modified, so as to allow the Insects to pack themselves up in repose; the head is folded in over the chest, and a cavity existing on the breast is thus closed by the head; in this cavity the antennae and the prominent mouth-parts are received and protected; the legs shut together

---

[1] It is probable that we do not know more than the fiftieth part of the existing species, most of which lead lives that render them very difficult to find.

in an equally perfect manner, so that no roughness or chink remains, and the creature looks like a little hard seed. *Anobium striatum* is a common Insect in houses, and makes little round holes in furniture, which is then said to be " worm-eaten." *A. (Xestobium) tessellatum,* a much larger Insect, has proved very destructive to beams in churches, libraries, etc. These species

Fig. 128.—*Ectrephes kingi.* West Australia. (After Westwood.)

are the " death-watches " or " greater death-watches " that have been associated with the most ridiculous superstitions (as we have mentioned in Volume V., when speaking of the lesser death-watches, or Psocidae). The ticking of these Insects is really connected with sex, and is made by striking the head rapidly against the wood on which the Insect is standing.

The very anomalous genus *Ectrephes* (Fig. 128) is found in ants' nests in Australia. Westwood placed it in Ptinidae. Wasmann has recently treated it as a distinct family, Ectrephidae, associating it with *Polyplocotes* and *Diplocotes,* and treating them as allied to Scydmaenidae.

Fam. 54. Malacodermidae.—*Seven (or even eight) visible ventral segments, the basal one not co-adapted in form with the coxae; tarsi five-jointed. Integument softer than usual, the parts of the body not accurately co-adapted.* This important family includes a variety of forms : viz. Lycides, Drilides, Lampyrides, Telephorides; though they are very different in appearance, classifiers have not yet agreed on separating them as families. Of these the Lampyrides, or glow-worms, are of special interest, as most of their members give off a phosphorescent light when alive; in many of them the female is apterous and like a larva, and then the light it gives is usually conspicuous, frequently much more so than that of its mate ; in other cases the males are the most brilliant. The exact importance of these characters in the creatures' lives is not yet clear, but it appears probable that in the first class of cases the light of the female serves as an attraction to the male, while in the second class the very brilliant lights of the male serve as an amusement, or as an incitement to rivalry amongst the individuals of this sex. The well-known fire-flies

(*Luciola*) of Southern Europe are an example of the latter condition. They are gregarious, and on calm, warm nights crowds of them may be seen moving and sparkling in a charming manner. These individuals are all, or nearly all, males; so rare indeed is the female that few entomologists have even noticed it. The writer once assisted in a large gathering of *Luciola italica* in the Val Anzasca, which consisted of many hundreds of specimens; all of those he caught, either on the wing or displaying their lights on the bushes, were males, but he found a solitary female on the ground. This sex possesses ordinary, small eyes instead of the large, convex organs of the male, and its antennae and legs are much more feeble, so that though provided with elytra and wings it is altogether a more imperfect creature. Emery has given an account of his observations and experiments on this Insect, but they do not give any clear idea as to the exact function of the light.[1] In our British glow-worm the female is entirely apterous—hence the name glow-worm —but the male has elytra and ample wings, and frequently flies at night into lighted apartments.

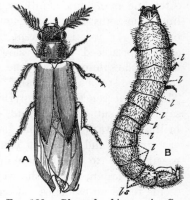

FIG. 129.—*Phengodes hieronymi.* Cordoba, South America. (After Haase.) **A**, Male; **B**, female. *l*, *l*, Positions of luminous spots; *ls*, spiracles. About × 3.

Although so little has been ascertained as to the light of Lampyridae, there are two facts that justify us in supposing that it is in some way of importance to the species. These are: (1) that in a great many species the eyes have a magnificent and unusual development; (2) that the habits of the creatures are in nearly all cases nocturnal. It is true that the little *Phosphaenus hemipterus* is said to be diurnal in habits, but it is altogether an exceptional form, being destitute of wings in both sexes, and possessed of only very feeble light-giving powers, and we have, moreover, very little real knowledge as to its natural history; it is said

---

[1] *Bull. ent. ital.* 1886, p. 406, and *Ent. Zeit. Stettin*, xliii. 1887, pp. 201-206. Emery does not mention the name of the species, but we presume it to be the common Italian fire-fly, *Luciola italica*.

that the female is of the utmost rarity, though the male is not uncommon.

The nature of the luminosity of *Lampyris* has given rise to many contradictory statements; the light looks somewhat like that given off by phosphorus, and is frequently spoken of as phosphorescence; but luminescence is a better term. The egg, larva, pupa, and male are luminous as well as the female (at any rate in *L. noctiluca*); the luminescence is, however, most marked in the female imago, in which it is concentrated near the extremity of the abdomen; here there are two strata of cells, and many fine capillary tracheae are scattered through the luminous substance. Wielowiejski concludes that the light-producing power is inherent in the cells of the luminous organ, and is produced by the slow oxidation of a substance formed under the influence of the nervous system. The cells are considered to be essentially similar to those of the fat-body.[1] The luminescence of Lampyridae is very intermittent, that is to say, it is subject to rapid diminutions and increases of its brilliancy; various reasons have been assigned for this, but all are guesses, and all that can be said is that the changes are possibly due to diminution or increase of the air-supply in the luminous organ, but of the way in which this is controlled there seems to be no evidence. Considerable difference of opinion has existed as to the luminescence of the eggs of *Lampyris*. If it exist in the matter contained in the egg, it is evident that it is independent of the existence of tracheae or of a nervous system. Newport and others believed that the light given by the egg depended merely on matter on its exterior. The observations of Dubois[2] show, however, that it exists in the matter in the egg; he has even found it in the interior of eggs that had been deposited unfertilised.

From time to time, since the commencement of the nineteenth century, there have appeared imperfect accounts of extraordinary light-giving larvae found in South America, of various sizes, but attaining in some cases a length, it is said, of three inches; they are reported as giving a strong red light from the two extremities of the body, and a green light from numerous points along the

---

[1] *Zeitschr. wiss. Zool.* xxxvii. 1882, p. 354; also Emery, *op. cit.* xl. 1884, p. 338. For another theory as to the luminescence, see p. 259.

[2] *Bull. Soc. Zool. France*, xii. 1887, p. 137, *postea*.

sides of the body, and hence are called, it is said, in Paraguay the railway-beetle. We may refer the reader to Haase's paper[1] on the subject of these " larvae," as we can here only say that it appears probable that most of these creatures may prove to be adult females of the extraordinary group Phengodini, in which it would appear that the imago of the female sex is in a more larva-like state than it is in any other Insects. The males, however, are well-developed beetles; unlike the males of Lampyrides, in general they have not peculiar eyes, but on the other hand they possess antennae which are amongst the most highly developed known, the joints being furnished on each side with a long appendage densely covered with pubescence of a remarkable character. There is no reason to doubt that Haase was correct in treating the Insect we figure (Fig. 129, B) as a perfect Insect; he is, indeed, corroborated by Riley.[2] The distinctions between the larva and female imago are that the latter has two claws on the feet instead of one, a greater number of joints in the antennae, and less imperfect eyes; the female is in fact a larva, making a slightly greater change at the last ecdysis, than at those previous. It is much to be regretted that we have so very small a know-ledge of these most interesting Insects. Malacodermidae are probably the most imperfect or primitive of all beetles, and it is a point of some interest to find that in one of them the phenomena of metamorphosis are reduced in one sex to a minimum, while in the other they are—presumably at least —normal in character.

Numerous larvae of most extraordinary, though diverse, shapes, bearing long processes at the sides of the body, and having a head capable of complete withdrawal into a slender cavity of the thorax, have long been known in several parts of the world, and Dr. Willey reeently found in New Britain a species having these body-processes articulated. Though they are doubtless larvae of Lampyrides, none of them have ever been reared or exactly identified.

A very remarkable Ceylonese Insect, *Dioptoma adamsi* Pascoe, is placed in Lampyrides, but can scarcely belong there, as apparently it has but five or six visible ventral segments; this Insect has two pairs of eyes, a large pair, with coarse facets on

---

[1] *Deutsche ent. Zeitschr.* xxxii. 1888, pp. 145-167.
[2] *Ent. Mag.* xxiv. 1887, p. 148.

the under side of the head, and a moderate-sized pair with fine facets on the upper side. Nothing is known as to the habits of this curiosity, not even whether it is luminous in one or both sexes.

It is believed that the perfect instar of Lampyrides takes no food at all. The larvae were formerly supposed to be vegetarian, but it appears probable that nearly all are carnivorous, the chief food being Mollusca either living or dead. The larvae are active, and in many species look almost as much like perfect Insects as do the imagos.

The other divisions of Malacodermidae—Lycides, Drilides, Telephorides—also have predaceous, carnivorous larvae. All these groups are extensive. Though much neglected by collectors and naturalists, some 1500 species of the family Malacodermidae have been detected. We have about 50 in Britain, and many of them are amongst the most widely distributed and abundant of our native Insects. Thus, however near they may be to the primitive condition of Coleoptera, it is highly probable that they will continue to exist alongside of the primitive Cockroaches and Aptera, long after the more highly endowed forms of Insect-life have been extinguished wholesale by the operations of mankind on the face of the earth.

Fam. 55. Melyridae (or **Malachiidae**).—*Six visible and move- able ventral abdominal segments; the basal part more or less distinctly co-adapted with the coxae.* These Insects are extremely numerous, but have been very little studied. In many works they are classified with Malacodermidae, but were correctly separated by Leconte and Horn, and this view is also taken by Dr. Verhoeff, the latest investigator. The smaller num- ber of visible ventral segments appears to be due to a change at the base correlative with an adaptation between the base of the abdomen and the hind coxae. The characters are singu- larly parallel with those of

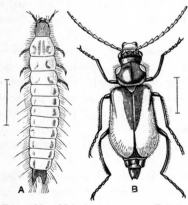

Fig. 130.—*Malachius aeneus.* Britain. **A**, Larva (after Perris); **B**, female imago.

Silphidae; but in Melyridae the antennae are filiform or serrate,

not clavate.   The habits in the two families are different, as the
Melyridae are frequenters of flowers.   Many of the Melyridae
have the integument soft, but in the forms placed at the end
of the family—*e.g. Zygia*—they are much firmer.   Thus these
Insects establish a transition from the Malacodermidae to ordinary Coleoptera.   Although the imagos are believed to consume
some products of the flowers they frequent, yet very little is
really known, and it is not improbable that they are to some
extent carnivorous.   This is the case with the larvae that are known
(Fig. 130, larva of *Malachius aeneus*).   These are said by Perris
to bear a great resemblance to those of the genus *Telephorus*,
belonging to the Malacodermidae.

Fam. 56. Cleridae.—*Tarsi five-jointed; but the basal joint of
the posterior very indistinct, usually very small above, and closely
united with the second by an oblique splice; the apices of joints
two to four usually prolonged as membranous flaps; anterior coxae
prominent, usually contiguous, rather large, but their cavities not
prolonged externally; labial palpi usually with large hatchet-
shaped terminal joint; ventral segments five or six, very mobile.*
The Cleridae are very varied in form and colours; the antennae
are usually more or less clubbed at the tip, and not at all serrate,
but in *Cylidrus* and a few others they are not clubbed, and in
Cylidrus have seven flattened joints.   The student should be
very cautious in deciding as to the number of joints in the feet
in this family, as the small basal joint is often scarcely dis-
tinguishable, owing to the obliteration of its suture with the
second joint.   The little Alpine *Laricobius* has the anterior coxal
cavities prolonged externally, and the coxae receive the femora to
some extent, so that it connects Cleridae and Derodontidae.   The
Cleridae are predaceous, and their larvae are very active; they
are specially fond of wood-boring Insects; that of *Tillus elongatus* (Fig. 131) enters the burrows of *Ptilinus pectinicornis* in
search of the larva.   The members of the group Corynetides
frequent animal matter, carcases, bones, etc., and, it is said, feed
thereon, but Perris's recent investigations [1] make it probable that
the larvae really eat the innumerable Dipterous larvae found in
such refuse; it is also said that the larvae of Cleridae spin
cocoons for their metamorphosis; but Perris has also shown
that the larvae of *Necrobia ruficollis* really use the puparia formed

[1] *Larves des Coléoptères*, 1878, p. 208.

by Diptera.　Some of the species of *Necrobia* have been spread
by commercial intercourse, and *N. rufipes* appears to be now one
of the most cosmopolitan of Insects.　The beautifully coloured
Corynetes coeruleus is often found in our houses, and is useful, as
it destroys the death-watches (*Anobium*) that are sometimes very
injurious.　*Trichodes apiarius,* a very lively-coloured red and
blue beetle, destroys the larvae of the honey-bee, and Lampert

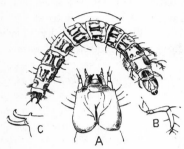

FIG. 131. — Larva of *Tillus elongatus.*
(New Forest).　**A,** Head ; **B,** front leg ;
C, termination of the body, more mag-
nified.

has reared *Trichodes alvearius*
from the nests of *Chalicodoma
muraria,* a mason-bee ; he records that one of its larvae,
after being full grown, remained
twenty - two months quiescent
and then transformed to a pupa.
Still more remarkable is a case
of fasting of the larva of *Trichodes ammios* recorded by
Mayet ;[1] this Insect, in its
immature form, destroys *Acri-
dium maroccanum ;* a larva sent
from Algeria to M. Mayet refused such food as was offered to
it for a period of two and a half years, and then accepted
mutton and beef as food ; after being fed for about a year and a
half thereon, it died.　Some Cleridae bear a great resemblance
to Insects of other families, and it appears probable that they
resemble in one or more points the Insects on which they feed.
The species are now very numerous, about 1000 being known,
but they are rare in collections ; in Britain we have only nine
species, and some of them are now scarcely ever met with.

Fam. 57. Lymexylonidae.—*Elongate beetles, with soft integuments, front and middle coxae exserted, longitudinal in position ;
tarsi slender, five-jointed ; antennae short, serrate, but rather broad.*
Although there are only twenty or thirty species of this family,
they occur in most parts of the world, and are remarkable on
account of their habit of drilling cylindrical holes in hard wood,
after the manner of Anobiidae.　The larva of *Lymexylon navale* was
formerly very injurious to timber used for constructing ships, but
of late years its ravages appear to have been of little importance.
The genus *Atractocerus* consists of a few species of very abnormal

[1] *Ann. Soc. ent. France,* 1894, p. 7.

Coleoptera, the body being elongate and vermiform, the elytra reduced to small, functionless appendages, while the wings are ample, not folded, but traversed by strong longitudinal nervures, and with only one or two transverse nervures.   Owing to the destruction of our forests the two British Lymexylonidae—*L. navale* and *Hylecoetus dermestoides*—are now very rarely met with.

Fam. 58. Dascillidae.—*Small or moderate-sized beetles, with rather flimsy integuments, antennae either serrate, filiform, or even made flabellate by long appen-*
dages ; front coxae elongate, greatly
exserted ; abdomen with five mobile
ventral segments ; tarsi five-jointed.
This is one of the most neglected
and least known of all the families
of Coleoptera, and one of the most
difficult to classify ; though always
placed amongst the Serricornia, it
is more nearly allied to Parnidae
and Byrrhidae, that are placed in
Clavicornia, than it is to any of the
ordinary families of Serricornia. It
is probable that careful study will

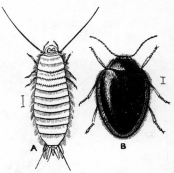

Fɪɢ. 132. — *Hydrocyphon deflexicollis.*
Britain.   **A,** Larva (after Tournier) ;
B, imago.

show that it is not natural as at present constituted, and that the old families, Dascillidae and Cyphonidae, now comprised in it, will have to be separated.   Only about 400 species are at present known ; but as nearly 100 of these have been detected in New Zealand, and 17 in Britain, doubtless the numbers in other parts of the world will prove very considerable, these Insects having been neglected on account of their unattractive exterior, and fragile structure.   The few larvae known are of three or four kinds.   That of *Dascillus cervinus* is subterranean, and is believed to live on roots ; in form it is somewhat like a Lamellicorn larva, but is straight, and has a large head.   Those of the Cyphonides are aquatic, and are remarkable for possessing antennae consisting of a great many joints (Fig. 132, A).   Tournier describes the larva of *Helodes* as possessing abdominal but not thoracic spiracles, and as breathing by coming to the surface of the water and carrying down a bubble of air adhering to the posterior part of the body; the larva of *Hydrocyphon* (Fig. 132, A)

possesses several finger-like pouches that can be exstulpated at
the end of the body. It is probable that these larvae are carnivorous. The imago of this Insect abounds on the bushes along
the banks of some of the rapid waters of Scotland; according to
Tournier, when alarmed, it enters the water and goes beneath it
for shelter. The third form of larva belongs to the genus *Eucinetus*, it lives on fungoid matter on wood, and has ordinary
antennae of only four joints.[1] It is very doubtful whether
Eucinetus is related to other Dascyllidae; some authorities indeed
place it in Silphidae.

Fam. 59. Rhipiceridae.—*Tarsi five-jointed, furnished with
a robust onychium (a straight chitinous process bearing hairs)*

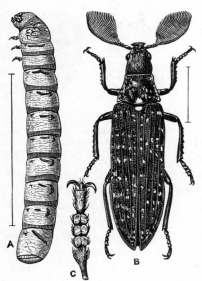

*between the claws; antennae of
the male bearing long processes,
and sometimes consisting of a
large number of joints. Mandibles robust, strongly curved,
and almost calliper-like in
form.* This small family of
less than 100 species is widely
distributed, though confined to
the warmer regions of the
earth, a single species occurring in the extreme south of
Eastern Europe. Very little
is known as to the natural
history. The larva of *Callirhipis dejeani* (Fig. 133, A) is
described by Schiödte as hard,
cylindrical in form, and pecu-

FIG. 133.—**A**, Larva of *Callirhipis dejeani*
(after Schiödte); **B**, *Rhipicera mystacina*
male, Australia; **C**, under side of its hind
foot.

liarly truncate behind, so that
there appear to be only eight
abdominal segments, the ninth
segment being so short as to

look like an operculum at the extremity of the body. It lives
in wood.

Fam. 60. Elateridae (*Click-beetles*).—*Antennae more or less
serrate along the inner margin, frequently pectinate, rarely
filiform. Front coxae small, spherical. Thorax usually with*

[1] Perris, *Ann. Soc. ent. France* (2) ix. 1851, p. 48.

*hind angles more or less prolonged backwards; with a prosternal
process that can be received in, and usually can move in, a
mesosternal cavity.   Hind coxa with a plate, above which the femur
can be received.   Visible ventral segments usually five, only the
terminal one being mobile.   Tarsi five-jointed.* This large family
of Coleoptera comprises about 7000
species.   Most of them are readily
known by their peculiar shape, and
by their faculty of resting on the
back, stretching themselves out
flat, and then suddenly going off
with a click, and thus jerking
themselves into the air.   Some,
however, do not possess this faculty,
and certain of these are extremely
difficult to recognise from a definition of the family.   According
to Bertkau[1] our British *Lacon
murinus* is provided near the
tip of the upper side of the abdomen with a pair of eversible

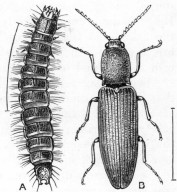

FIG. 134.—*Athous rhombeus.* New
Forest.   **A**, Larva; **B**, female
imago.

glands, comparable with those that are better known in Lepidopterous larvae.   He states that this Insect does not try
to escape by leaping, but shams death and "stinks away" its
enemy.   The glands, it would appear, become exhausted after the
operation has been repeated many times.   The extent of the leap
executed by click-beetles differs greatly; in some species it is
very slight, and only just sufficient to turn the Insect right side
up when it has been placed on its back.   In some cases the
Insects go through the clicking movements with little or no
appreciable result in the way of consequent propulsion.   Although
it is difficult to look on this clicking power as of very great value
to the Elateridae, yet their organisation is profoundly modified so
as to permit its accomplishment.   The junction of the prothorax
with the after-body involves a large number of pieces which are
all more or less changed, so that the joint is endowed with greater
mobility than usual; while in the position of repose, on the other
hand, the two parts are firmly locked together.   The thoracic
stigma is of a highly remarkable nature, and the extensive

[1] *Arch. Naturgesch.* xlviii. 1, 1882, p. 371.

membrane in which it is placed appears to be elastic. Although the mechanics of the act of leaping are still obscure, yet certain points are clear; the prosternal process possesses a projection, or notch, on its upper surface near the tip; as a preliminary to leaping, this projection catches against the edge of the meso-sternal cavity, and as long as this position is maintained the Insect is quiescent; suddenly, however, the projection slips over the catch, and the prosternal process is driven with force and rapidity into the mesosternal cavity pressing against the front wall thereof, and so giving rise to the leap.

Several larvae are well known; indeed the "wire-worms" that are sometimes so abundant in cultivated places are larvae of Elateridae. In this instar the form is usually elongate and nearly cylindrical; the thoracic segments differ but little from the others except that they bear rather short legs; the skin is rather hard, and usually bears punctuation or sculpture; the body frequently terminates in a very hard process, of irregular shape and bearing peculiar sculpture on its upper surface, while beneath it the prominent anal orifice is placed: this is sometimes furnished with hooks, the function of which has not yet been observed. The majority of these larvae live in decaying wood, but some are found in the earth; as a rule the growth is extremely slow, and the life of the larva may extend over two or more years. Some obscurity has prevailed as to their food; it is now considered to be chiefly flesh, though some species probably attack decaying roots; and it is understood that wire-worms destroy the living roots, or underground stems, of the crops they damage. Various kinds of Myriapods (see Vol. V. p. 29) are often called "wire-worm," but they may be recognised by possessing more than six legs. The larvae of the genus *Cardiophorus* are very different, being remarkably elongate without the peculiar terminal structure, but apparently composed of twenty-three segments.

The genus *Pyrophorus* includes some of the most remarkable of light-giving Insects. There are upwards of 100 species, exhibiting much diversity as to the luminous organs; some are not luminous at all; but all are peculiar to the New World, with the exception that there may possibly be luminous species, allied to the American forms, in the Fiji Islands and the New Hebrides. In the tropics of America the *Pyrophorus*, or Cucujos, form one of the most remarkable of the natural phenomena.

The earliest European travellers in the New World were so impressed by these Insects that descriptions of their wondrous display occupy a prominent position in the accounts of writers like Oviedo, whose works are nearly 400 years old.   Only one of the species has, however, been investigated.   *P. noctilucus* is one of the most abundant and largest of the *Pyrophorus*, and possesses on each side of the thorax a round polished space from which light is given forth ; these are the organs called eyes by the older writers. Besides these two eye-like lamps the Insect possesses a third source of light situate at the base of the ventral surface of the abdomen ; there is no trace of this latter lamp when the Insect is in repose ; but when on the wing the abdomen is bent away from the breast, and then this source of light is exposed ; hence, when flying, this central luminous body can be alternately displayed and concealed by means of slight movements of the abdomen. The young larva of *P. noctilucus* is luminous, having a light-giving centre at the junction of the head and thorax ; the older larva has also numerous luminous points along the sides of the body near the spiracles.   It is remarkable that there should be three successive seats of luminescence in the life of the same individual.   The eggs too are said to be luminous.   The light given off by these Insects is extremely pleasing, and is used by the natives on nocturnal excursions, and by the women for ornament.   The structure of the light-organs is essentially similar to that of the Lampyridae.   The light is said to be the most economical known ; all the energy that is used being converted into light, without any waste by the formation of heat or chemical rays.   The subject has been investigated by Dubois,[1] who comes, however, to conclusions as to the physiology of the luminous processes different from those that have been reached by Wielowiejski and others in their investigations on Glow-worms.   He considers that the light is produced by the reactions of two special substances, luciferase and luciferine.   Luciferase is of the nature of an enzyme, and exists only in the luminous organs, in the form, it is supposed, of extremely minute granules. Luciferine exists in the blood ; and the light is actually evoked by the entry of blood into the luminous organ.

We have given to this family the extension assigned to it by

[1] "Les Élatérides lumineux," *Bull. Soc. Zool. France*, xi. 1886 ; also *Leçons de Physiologie générale*, Paris, 1898, and *C.R. Ac. Sci.* cxxiii. 1896, p. 653.

Schiödte. Leconte and Horn also adopt this view, except that they treat Throscides as a distinct family. By most authors Eucnemides, Throscides, and Cebrionides are all considered distinct families, but at present it is almost impossible to separate them on satisfactory lines. The following table from Leconte and Horn exhibits the characters of the divisions so far as the imago is concerned :—

Posterior coxae laminate ; trochanters small.
    Labrum concealed ; antennae somewhat distant from the eyes, their
        insertion narrowing the front   .   .   .   EUCNEMIDES.
    Labrum visible, free ; antennae arising near the eyes under the frontal
        margin   .   .   .   .   .   ELATERIDES.
    Labrum transverse, connate with the front.
        Ventral segments six ; claws simple ; tibial spurs well developed.
                        CEBRIONIDES.
        Ventral segments five ; claws serrate ; tibial spurs moderate.
                        PEROTHOPIDES.
Posterior coxae not laminate ; trochanters of middle and posterior legs very
    long .   .   .   .   .   .   CEROPHYTIDES.

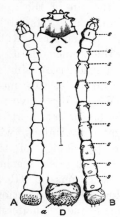

FIG. 135.—Larva of *Fornax* n. sp. Hawaii. **A**, Upper side ; **B**, under side : *s s*, position of spiracles ; **C**, head more enlarged ; **D**, under side of terminal segment ; *a*, anus.

Throscides are considered to be distinguished by the mesosternum being impressed on each side in front for the accommodation of the posterior face of the front coxae. The genus *Throscus* has the antennae clavate. The classification of the Elaterides and these forms is a matter of the greatest difficulty, and, if the larvae are also considered, becomes even more complex. Cebrionid larvae are different from those of any of the other divisions, and possess laminate, not calliper-like, mandibles. The larvae of Eucnemides (Fig. 135) are very little known, but are highly remarkable, inasmuch as it is very difficult to find any mouth-opening in some of them, and they have no legs. The other divisions possess very few species compared with Elaterides. In Britain we have about sixty species of Elaterides, four of Throscides and three of Eucnemides ; *Cerophytum* was probably a native many years ago. Neither Perothopides

nor Cebrionides are represented in our fauna ; the former of these
two groups consists only of four or five North American species,
and the Cerophytides are scarcely more numerous.

Fam. 61. Buprestidae.—*Antennae serrate, never elongate ;
prothorax fitting closely to the after-body, with a process received
into a cavity of the mesosternum so as to permit of no movements
of nutation.   Five visible ventral segments, the first usually
elongate, closely united with the second, the others mobile.   Tarsi
five-jointed, the first four joints usually with membranous pads
beneath.*   This family is also of large extent, about 5000 species
being known.   Many of them are remarkable for the magnificence
of their colour, which is usually metallic, and often of the greatest
brilliancy ; hence their wing-cases are
used by our own species for adornment.   The elytra of the eastern kinds
of the genus *Sternocera* are of a very
brilliant green colour, and are used
extensively as embroidery for the
dresses of ladies ; the bronze elytra
of *Buprestis* (*Euchroma*) *gigantea*
were used by the native chieftains in
South America as leg-ornaments, a
large number being strung so as to
form a circlet.   The integument of
the Buprestidae is very thick and hard,
so as to increase the resemblance to
metal.   The dorsal plates of the abdomen are usually soft and colourless in
beetles, but in Buprestidae they are
often extremely brilliant.   The metallic colour in these Insects is

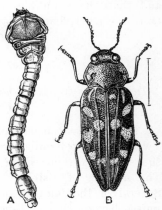

Fig. 136.—**A,** Larva of *Euchroma
goliath* (after Schiödte) ; **B,** imago
of *Melanophila decostigma.*
Europe.

not due to pigment, but to the nature of the surface.   Buprestidae
appear to enjoy the hottest sunshine, and are found only where there
is much summer heat.   Australia and Madagascar are very rich
in species and in remarkable forms of the family, while in Britain
we possess only ten species, all of which are of small size, and
nearly all are excessively rare.   The family is remarkably rich in
fossil forms ; no less than 28 per cent of the Mesozoic beetles
found by Heer in Switzerland are referred to Buprestidae.

The larvae (Fig. 136, A) find nourishment in living vegetable
matter, the rule being that they form galleries in or under the

bark of trees and bushes, or in roots thereof; some inhabit the stems of herbaceous plants and one or two of the smaller forms have been discovered to live in the parenchyma of leaves. A few are said to inhabit dead wood, and in Australia species of *Ethon* dwell in galls on various plants. Buprestid larvae are of very remarkable shape, the small head being almost entirely withdrawn into the very broad thorax, while the abdomen is slender.[1] A few, however, depart from this shape, and have the thoracic region but little or not at all broader than the other parts. The larvae of *Julodis*—a genus that inhabits desert or arid regions—are covered with hair; they have a great development of the mandibles; it is believed that they are of subterranean habits, and that the mandibles are used for burrowing in the earth. Only the newly hatched larva is, however, known.

Series IV. Heteromera.

Tarsi of the front and middle legs with five, those of the hind legs with four, joints.

This series consists of some 14,000 or 15,000 species. Twelve or more families are recognised in it, but the majority of the species are placed in the one great family, Tenebrionidae. The number of visible ventral segments is nearly always five. Several of the families of the series are of doubtful validity; indeed beyond that of Tenebrionidae the taxonomy of this series is scarcely more than a convention. The larvae may be considered as belonging to three classes; one in which the body is cylindrical and smooth and the integument harder than usual in larvae; a second in which it is softer, and frequently possesses more or less distinct pseudopods, in addition to the six thoracic legs; and a third group in which hypermetamorphosis prevails, the young larvae being the creatures long known as Triungulins, and living temporarily on the bodies of other Insects, so that they were formerly supposed to be parasites.

---

[1] It seems impossible to understand the morphology of the anterior segments by mere inspection; the anterior spiracle being seated on the segment behind the broad thorax. Considerable difference of opinion has prevailed as to what is head, what thorax; the aid of embryology is necessary to settle the point. The larva described by Westwood (*Mod. Classif.* i. 1839, p. 229), and figured as probably *Buprestis attenuata*, is doubtless a Passalid.

Fam. 62. Tenebrionidae.—*Front coxae short, not projecting from the cavities, enclosed behind. Feet destitute of lobed joints. Claws smooth.* This is one of the largest families of Coleoptera, about 10,000 species being already known. A very large portion of the Tenebrionidae are entirely terrestrial, wings suitable for flight being absent, and the elytra frequently more or less soldered. Such forms are described in systematic works as apterous. Unfortunately no comprehensive study has ever been made of the wings or their rudiments in these "apterous forms."[1] It is probable that the wings, or their rudiments or vestiges, always exist, but in various degrees of development according to the species, and that they are never used by the great majority of the terrestrial forms. Many of the wood-feeding Tenebrionidae, and the genera usually placed

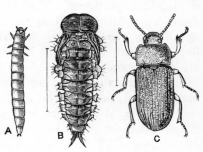

Fig. 137.—*Tenebrio molitor.* Europe, etc. **A**, Larva (meal-worm); **B**, pupa (after Schiödte); **C**, imago.

at the end of the family, possess wings well adapted for flight. The apterous forms are chiefly ground-beetles, living in dry places; they are very numerous in Africa, California, and North Mexico. Their colour is nearly always black, and this is probably of some physiological importance; the integuments are thick and hard, and if the wing-cases are taken off, it will be found that they are usually more or less yellow on the inner face, even when jet-black externally; the external skeleton is very closely fitted together, the parts that are covered consisting of very delicate membrane; the transition between the hard and the membranous portions of the external skeleton is remarkably abrupt. These ground-Tenebrionidae form a very interesting study, though, on account of their unattractive appearance, they have not received the attention they deserve.

Many of the Tenebrionidae, notwithstanding their dark

[1] Casey has examined the wings in the genus *Blapstinus* (an "apterous" genus), and found that the wings are extremely varied in development, according to the species; in no case, however, did they appear to be capable of giving more than a laboured and feeble flight.—*Ann. New York Ac.* v. 1890, p. 416.

In *Eleodes*, though the meso- and meta-notum are formed of delicate membrane, the wings exist as minute flaps, requiring some examination for their detection.

colours, are diurnal in habits, and some of them run with extreme velocity in places so bare and desert that the means of existence of the Insects is a mystery. Most of the Tenebrionidae, however, shun the light. The food is usually vegetable matter, and it is apparently preferred in a very dry state. Mr. Gahan has recently recorded that in *Praogena* the under surface of the head has the gular region striate for stridulating purposes. This is the only instance known of a voice-organ in this situation, and moreover is the only case in all the Tenebrionidae in which any sound-producing organ has been discovered. The larvae exhibit but little variety, they are elongate and cylindrical, with harder integument than is usual in Coleopterous larvae; they have six thoracic legs, and at the under side of the posterior extremity the anus serves as a very short pseudopod. The resemblance of these larvae to those of Elateridae is considerable; but though the body is terminated by one or two small processes, these never attain the complexity of the terminal segment of Elateridae. The common meal-worm—*i.e.* the larva of *Tenebrio molitor*—is a very characteristic example of the group. The pupae are remarkable on account of peculiar projections, of varied and irregular form, that exist on the sides of the abdominal segments. Britain is very poor in these Insects; our list of them scarcely attains the number of thirty species.

Fam. 63. Cistelidae.—*Claws comb-like.* The very obscure beetles forming this family are only separated from Tenebrionidae on account of their pectinate claws. About 500 species of Cistelidae are recorded; the early instars, so far as known, do not differ from those of Tenebrionidae; the larvae are believed to live on dead wood.

Fam. 64. Lagriidae.—*Anterior coxal cavities closed, tips of the front coxae free, claws smooth, penultimate joint of the tarsi broader, pubescent beneath.* This family has very little to distinguish it from Tenebrionidae, and the group Heterotarsini appears to connect the two. It is a small family of about 200 species, widely distributed, and represented in Britain by one species, *Lagria hirta*. The early instars are similar to those of the Tenebrionidae, except that the larva is less retiring in its habits and wanders about on foliage: it is of broader form than that of most of the Tenebrionidae. The pupa has long projections at the sides of the abdominal segments.

Fam. 65. Othniidae.—Only about ten species are known of this dubious family. They are small Insects with weak integument, and are said by Leconte and Horn to be distinguished from "degraded Tenebrionidae" by the more mobile abdominal segments, the hind-margins of which are semi-membranous. The antennae are of the clubbed shape, characteristic of "Clavicornia," but this also occurs in numerous undoubted Tenebrionidae. Species of *Othnius* have been found in Japan and Borneo, as well as in North America. Nothing is known as to their metamorphoses.

Fam. 66. Ægialitidae.—*All the coxae very widely separated; no co-adaptation between the sides of the abdomen and the edges of the wing-cases; five ventral segments and tip of a sixth visible.* Two minute and rare Insects from North-West America constitute this family. It is distinguished from Pythidae by the minute front coxae, widely separated, completely closed in, and deeply embedded in the prosternum.

Fam. 67. Monommidae.—This is a small family of less than 100 species, the members of which have the details of their external structure much modified, permitting the Insect to pack itself up in repose in a very perfect manner. They are of small size and oval form; and are absent from Europe and the Antipodes. Nothing appears to be known as to the metamorphosis.

Fam. 68. Nilionidae.—*Broad, circular Heteromera, of moderate size, with the front coxae but little separated, and the anterior acetabula closed, though having the appearance of being open in consequence of the tips of the epimera being free. The inflexed portion of the wing-cases remarkably broad.* A small family of less than fifty species, found on fungi, chiefly in South America. The metamorphoses are not known. It is of very doubtful validity.

Fam. 69. Melandryidae.—*Head not constricted behind the eyes; anterior acetabula not closed; claws smooth. Prothorax broad behind.* These are loosely-fitted-together Insects, of moderate or small size, frequenting dry wood or fungi. About 200 species are known, found chiefly in temperate regions. The few described larvae are rather varied in their details and cannot be generalised at present. The characters of the members of this family require fresh investigation.

Fam. 70. Pythidae.—Distinguished from Melandryidae by the prothorax being narrow behind.   This is a small family of about 100 species, found in temperate regions in connection with timber.   The species of *Rhinosimus* have the head prolonged in front of the antennae so as to form a beak.   The larva of *Pytho depressus* is flat and has parallel sides; the body is terminated by two widely-separated sharp processes.   It is found occasionally under the bark of firs in Scotland.

Fam. 71. Pyrochroidae.—Differs from Melandryidae by the head forming a very narrow neck behind, and by the penultimate tarsal joints being broad.   They are feeble Insects, though active on the wing.   They are destitute of any of the various remarkable structures found in Mordellidae.   Only about forty species are known, and the family is confined to the north temperate region, being best represented in Japan.   *Pyrochroa rubens* is common in some parts of England; the larva is found under the bark of tree-stumps; it is remarkably flat, and has the eighth abdominal segment unusually long, while the ninth terminates the body in the form of two long sharp processes.

Fam. 72. Anthicidae.—*Head with an abrupt narrow neck; prothorax narrower than the elytra.   Middle and hind coxae placed in definite acetabula.   Claws simple.*   These little Insects are numerous in species; they have little resemblance to Pyrochroidae, though the characters of the two families cause us to place them in proximity.   There are about 1000 species known; though we have only about 12 in Britain, they are very numerous in the Mediterranean region.   The family Pedilidae of Lacordaire and some others is now merged in Anthicidae. Thomson and Champion, on the other hand, separate some very minute Insects to form the family Xylophilidae, on account of certain differences in the form of the abdomen and tarsi.   The Xylophilidae live in dead wood; the Anthicidae, on the surface of the earth, after the manner of ground-beetles; very little is, however, known as to their natural history.

Fam. 73. Oedemeridae.—*Prothorax not forming sharp edges at the sides, head without a narrow neck.   Penultimate tarsal joint broad; claws smooth.*   These Insects usually have a feeble integument, and bear a certain resemblance to Malacodermidae. Less than 500 species are known, but they are widely distributed, and occur in both temperate and tropical regions.   The larvae live in old wood.   *Nacerdes melanura* is common on our

coasts, where its larva lives in timber cast up by the sea, or
brought down by floods, and it
is able to resist immersion by
the tide. It is remarkable from
the possession of five pairs of
dorsal false feet on the anterior
segments, and two pairs on
the ventral aspect. In *Asclera
caerulea* there are six dorsal and
three ventral pairs of these remarkable pseudopods. We have
six species of Oedemeridae in
Britain, including *Asclera* as
well as *Nacerdes*.

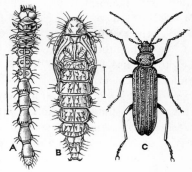

Fig. 138.—*Asclera caerulea*. **A**, Larva ;
B, pupa (after Schiödte) ; **C**, imago.
Cambridge.

Fam. 74. Mordellidae (incl.
Rhipiphoridae).—*Head peculiarly formed, vertex lobed or ridged
behind, so that in extension it reposes on the front edge of the pronotum ; capable of great inflection and then covering the prosternum ;
hind coxae with laminae forming a sharp edge behind, frequently
very large.* This family is a very distinct one, though it exhibits
great variety. Lacordaire has pointed out that Rhipiphoridae
cannot at present be satisfactorily distinguished from Mordellidae.
Leconte and Horn separate the two by the fact that the sides
of the prothorax form a sharp edge in Mordellidae, but not in
Rhipiphoridae. A better character would perhaps be found by a
study of the head, but as this would clearly result in a radical
change in the composition of the two families it is preferable to
treat them at present as only sub-families : if placed on a similar
basis to the preceding families, the group would however form,
not two, but several families. Besides the unusual shape of the
head (Fig. 139, D) the ventral region of the body is remarkably
formed, being very convex, and in many Mordellides terminating
in a strong spinous process (Fig. 139, C). The elytra are, in
several Rhipiphorids, of the groups Myoditini and Rhipidiini,
reduced to a very small size, and the wings are not folded. The
Mordellidae are remarkable for their activity ; in the perfect
state they usually frequent flowers, and fly and run with extreme
rapidity. Mordellides are amongst the most numerous and
abundant of the European Coleoptera, and in Britain the
Anaspini swarm on the flowers of bushes and Umbelliferae. The

life-histories appear to be singularly varied; but unfortunately they are incompletely known. The larvae of some of the Mordellids have been found in the stems of plants, and derive their nutriment therefrom. This is said by Schwarz to be undoubtedly the case with *Mordellistena floridensis.* Coquillett has found the larvae of *M. pustulata* in plant-stems under circumstances that render it highly probable that they were feeding on a Lepidopterous larva contained in the stems; and Osborn found a similar larva that was pretty certainly a *Mordellistena,* and fed voraciously on Dipterous larvae in the stems of a plant. The little that is known as to the meta-

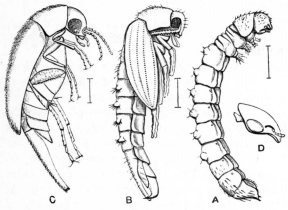

Fig. 139. — *Mordellistena floridensis.* America. (After Riley.) **A,** Larva; **B,** pupa; **C,** imago; **D,** outline of detached head of imago of *M. pumila,* to show the neck.

morphoses of *Mordella* and *Anaspis* shows that they live in old wood, but does not make clear the nature of their food.

Although it has been ascertained that the Rhipiphorides exhibit instances of remarkable metamorphosis, their life-histories are still very imperfectly known. Dr. Chapman has ascertained some particulars as to *Metoecus paradoxus,* which has long been known to prey in the larval state on the larvae of the common social wasps.[1] The eggs are apparently not deposited in the nests of the wasps, but in old wood. The young larva is a triungulin, similar to that of the Cantharidae, we shall subsequently describe. It is not known how it makes its way to the wasps' nests, but it is possible that when a wasp visits some old wood haunted by these larvae, some of them may attach themselves to it and be carried to the wasps' nests. When

[1] *Ann. Nat. Hist.* (4) vi. 1870, p. 314; and *Ent. Mag.* xxvii. 1891, p. 18.

access is gained to the cells the little *Metoecus* pierces the skin of one of the wasp-grubs, and entering in it feeds on the interior; after it has increased in size it emerges, changes its skin, and assumes a different form and habits; subsequently, as an external parasite, entirely devouring the wasp-larva, and then becoming a pupa, and finally a perfect *Metoecus*, in the cell of the wasp. The wasps, though they investigate the cells, do not apparently entertain any objection to the *Metoecus*, though there may be sometimes as many as twenty or thirty of the destroyers in a single nest. A few hours after the *Metoecus* has become a winged Insect and has escaped from the cells, it appears however, from the observations of Erné [1] on nests of wasps in captivity, that the wasps become hostile to the foreigners, and it is probable that in a state of nature these leave the nest as quickly as possible. *Emenadia flabellata*, a genus allied to *Metoecus*, has been discovered by Chobaut to have a similar life-history, except that it attacks a solitary wasp of the genus *Odynerus*.[2] An old record to the effect that a second species of *Emenadia, E. bimaculata*, lives in the stalks of *Eryngium campestre*, on the pith, is now thought to be erroneous. Fabre has found the larvae and pupae of another Rhipiphorid in the cells of a bee, *Halictus sexcinctus*.

The most remarkable of the Rhipiphorids, from the point of view of its habits, is certainly *Symbius blattarum*, which is now treated as the same as an Insect previously described by Thunberg from specimens found in amber and called *Ripidius pectinicornis*. This species is parasitic in cockroaches; the male and female are very different, the former being an active winged Insect, while the female is worm-like, differing but little from the larva, and never leaving the body of the cockroach. It is to be regretted that the life-history is not better known. The species has been found on board ship in vessels coming from India; the male has been met with in several European countries, but the female is excessively rare.

Fam. 75. Cantharidae or Meloidae (*Blister-beetles, Oil-beetles*). —*Head with an abrupt neck; elytra and sides of the abdomen without any coadaptation; each claw of the feet with a long appendage closely applied beneath it.* This distinct family consists of Heteromera with soft integument, and is remarkable for the fact that many of its members contain a substance that when extracted

---

[1] *Mitt. Schweiz. ent. Ges.* iv. 1876, p. 556.   [2] *Ann. Soc. ent. France*, lx. 1891, p. 447.

and applied to the human skin, possesses the power of raising blisters. The life-history is highly remarkable, the most complex forms of hyper-metamorphosis being exhibited. The species now known amount to about 1500; there can be no difficulty in recognising a member of the family by the above characters, except that in a very few cases each claw bears a projecting tooth, instead of an elongate appendage parallel with itself. The penultimate tarsal joint is scarcely ever broader than the preceding; the colour and style of markings are extremely varied. There are two very distinct sub-families, Cantharides and Meloides; the former are winged Insects, and are frequently found on flowers or foliage. The Meloides are wingless, and consequently terrestrial; they have a very short metasternum, so that the middle coxae touch the hind; and they also have very peculiar wing-cases, one of the two overlapping the other at the base; in a few Meloids the wing-cases are merely rudiments.

The post-embryonic development of these Insects is amongst the most remarkable of modern entomological discoveries. The first steps were made by Newport in 1851,[1] and the subject has since been greatly advanced by Fabre, Riley, and others. As an example of these peculiar histories, we may cite Riley's account [2] of *Epicauta vittata* (Fig. 140), a blister-beetle living at the expense of North American locusts of the genus *Caloptenus*. The locust lays its eggs underground, in masses surrounded by an irregular capsule, and the *Epicauta* deposits its eggs in spots frequented by the locust, but not in special proximity to the eggs thereof. In a few days the eggs of the blister-beetle hatch, giving rise to little larvae of the kind called triungulin (Fig. 140, A), because each leg is terminated by three tarsal spines or claws. In warm, sunny weather these triungulins become very active; they run about on the surface of the ground exploring all its cracks, penetrating various spots and burrowing, till an egg-pod of the locust is met with; into this the triungulin at once eats its way, and commences to devour an egg. Should two or more triungulins enter the same egg-pod, battles occur till only one is left. After a few days passed in

---

[1] "On the Natural History, Anatomy, and Development of the Oil-Beetle, *Meloe*," *Tr. Linn. Soc.* xx. 1851, p. 297; and xxi. 1853, p. 167.

[2] *Rep. U.S. ent. Commission*, i. 1878, p. 297.

devouring a couple of eggs, the triungulin sheds its skin and
appears as a different larva (Fig. 140, B), with soft skin, short
legs, small eyes, and different form and proportions; a second
moult takes place after about a week, but is not accompanied by
any very great change of form, though the larva is now curved,
less active, and in form like a larva of Scarabaeidae; when
another moult occurs the fourth instar appears as a still more
helpless form of larva (Fig. 140, D), which increases rapidly
in size, and when full grown leaves the remains of the egg-pod

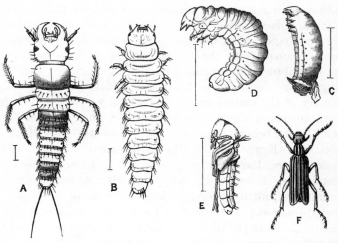

FIG. 140.—Hypermetamorphosis of *Epicauta vittata.* North America. (After Riley.)
A, Young larva or triungulin ; B, Caraboid instar or second larva ; C, coarctate
larva, or instar between the Scarabaeoid and Scolytoid larva ; D, Scarabaeoid larva,
from which the Scolytoid, or sixth, instar differs but little ; E, pupa ; F, imago.

it has been living on, and forms a small cavity near by ; here it
lies on one side motionless, but gradually contracting, till the
skin separates and is pushed down to the end of the body, disclosing a completely helpless creature that has been variously
called a semi-pupa, pseudo-pupa, or coarctate larva (Fig. 140, C) ;
in this state the winter is passed.   In spring the skin of the
coarctate larva bursts, and there crawls out of it a sixth instar
which resembles the fourth (Fig. 140, D), except in the somewhat
reduced size and greater whiteness.   It is worthy of remark that
the skin it has deserted retains its original form almost intact.
In this sixth instar the larva is rather active and burrows about,

but does not take food, and in the course of a few days again moults and discloses the true pupa (Fig. 140, E). As usual in Coleoptera this instar lasts but a short time, and in five or six days the perfect beetle appears (Fig. 140, F). It is extremely difficult to frame any explanation of this complex development; there are, it will be noticed, no less than five stages interposed between the first larval instar and the pupal instar, and the creature assumes in the penultimate one a quasi-pupal state, to again quit it for a return to a previous state. It is possible to look on the triungulin and the pupal instars as special adaptations to external conditions; but it is not possible to account for the intermediate instars in this way, and we must look on them as necessitated by the physiological processes going on internally. Nothing, how-ever, is known as to these. It may be well to mention that, after describing and figuring (*loc. cit.*) this series of instars, Riley changed his views as to their nomenclature.[1] The following summary of the metamorphosis, to which we have added the two nomenclatures of Riley—the original one, when different from the amended one, being given in square brackets—may therefore be useful, viz.—Egg; 1, triungulin-larva—moult; 2, Caraboid larva [second larva, Caraboid stage]—moult; 3, Scarabaeoid larva [second larva, Scarabaeoid stage]—moult; 4, Scarabaeoid larva [second larva, ultimate stage] (large amount of food and much growth)—moult; 5, coarctate larva [pseudo-pupa, or semipupa]; 6, Scolytoid larva [third larva] (active, but little or no food taken)—moult; 7, pupa—moult; 8, perfect Insect.

M. Fabre has succeeded in elucidating the history of *Sitaris humeralis,* a Cantharid that lives at the expense of bees of the genus *Anthophora.*[2] The eggs of the *Sitaris* are deposited in the earth in close proximity to the entrances to the bees' nests, about August. They are very numerous, a single female pro-ducing, it is believed, upwards of 2000 eggs. In about a month — towards the end of September — they hatch, producing a tiny triungulin of black colour; the larvae do not, however, move away, but, without taking any food, hibernate in a heap, remaining in this state till the following April or May, when they become active. Although they are close to the abodes of the bees they do not enter them, but seek to attach themselves

---

[1] *Amer. Nat.* xvii. 1883, p. 790.

[2] For illustration of this metamorphosis, see Vol. V. p. 159 of this work.

to any hairy object that may come near them, and thus a certain
number of them get on to the bodies of the *Anthophora* and are
carried to its nest.   They attach themselves with equal readiness
to any other hairy Insect, and it is probable that very large
numbers perish in consequence of attaching themselves to the
wrong Insects.   The bee in question is a species that nests in
the ground and forms cells, in each of which it places honey and
lays an egg, finally closing the receptacle.   It is worthy of
remark that in the case of the *Anthophora* observed by M.
Fabre, the male appears about a month before the female, and it
is probable that the vast majority of the predatory larvae attach
themselves to the male, but afterwards seize a favourable
opportunity, transfer themselves to the female, and so get
carried to the cells of the bee.   When she deposits an egg on
the honey, the triungulin glides from the body of the bee on to
the egg, and remains perched thereon as on a raft, floating on
the honey, and is then shut in by the bee closing the cell.   This
remarkable act of slipping on to the egg cannot be actually
witnessed, but the experiments and observations of the French
naturalist leave little room for doubt as to the matter really
happening in the way described.   The egg of the bee forms the
first nutriment of the tiny triungulin, which spends about eight
days in consuming its contents; never quitting it, because contact
with the surrounding honey is death to the little creature, which
is entirely unfitted for living thereon.   After this the triungulin
undergoes a moult and appears as a very different creature, being
now a sort of vesicle with the spiracles placed near the upper part ;
so that it is admirably fitted for floating on the honey (Vol. V.
Fig. 86, 10).   In about forty days, that is, towards the middle
of July, the honey is consumed, and the vesicular larva after a
few days of repose changes to a pseudo-pupa (11 of the fig.
cited) within the larval skin.   After remaining in this state for
about a month, some of the specimens go through the subsequent
changes, and appear as perfect Insects in August or September.
The majority delay this subsequent metamorphosis till the following spring, wintering as pseudo-pupae and continuing the series
of changes in June of the following year ; at that time the pseudo-
pupa returns to a larval form (12 of the fig. cited), differing comparatively little from the second instar.   The skin, though detached,
is again not shed, so that this ultimate larva is enclosed in two

dead skins; in this curious envelope it turns round, and in a couple of days, having thus reversed its position, becomes lethargic and changes to the true pupa, and in about a month subsequent to this appears as a perfect Insect, at about the same time of the year as it would have done had only one year, instead of two, been occupied by its metamorphosis. M. Fabre employs the term, third larva, for the instar designated by Riley Scolytoid larva, but this is clearly an inconvenient mode of naming the instar. *Sitaris humeralis* is now very rare in Britain, but it seems formerly to have been more common, and it is not improbable that its triungulin may have been the "*Pediculus melittae*," that was believed by Kirby to be a sort of bee-louse. Some species of the genus *Meloe* are still common in Britain, and the Insects may be seen with heavy distended abdomen grazing on herbage in the spring. The females are enormously prolific, a single one producing, it is believed, about 10,000 eggs. *Meloe* is also dependent on *Anthophora*, and its life-history seems on the whole to be similar to that of *Sitaris;* the eggs are, however, not necessarily deposited in the neighbourhood of the bees' nests, and the triungulins distribute themselves on all sorts of unsuitable Insects, so that it is possible that not more than one in a thousand succeeds in getting access to the *Anthophora* nest. It would be supposed that it would be a much better course for these bee-frequenting triungulins to act like those of *Epicauta*, and hunt for the prey they are to live on; but it must be remembered that they cannot live on honey; the one tiny egg is their object, and this apparently can only be reached by the method indicated by Fabre. The history of these Insects certainly forms a most remarkably instructive chapter in the department of animal instinct, and it is a matter for surprise that it should not yet have attracted the attention of comparative psychologists. The series of actions, to be performed once and once only in a lifetime by an uninstructed, inexperienced atom, is such that we should *a priori* have denounced it as an impossible means of existence, were it not shown that it is constantly successful. It is no wonder that the female *Meloe* produces 5000 times more eggs than are necessary to continue the species without diminution in the number of its individuals, for the first and most important act in the complex series of this life - history is accomplished by an extremely indiscriminating instinct; the

newly hatched *Meloe* has to get on to the body of the female of
one species of bee; but it has no discrimination whatever of the
kind of object it requires, and as a matter of fact, passes with
surprising rapidity on to any hairy object that touches it; hence
an enormous majority of the young are wasted by getting on to
all sorts of other Insects; these larvae have been found in
numbers on hairy Coleoptera as well as on flies and bees of wrong
kinds; the writer has ascertained by experiment that a camel's-
hair brush is as eagerly seized, and passed on to, by the young
Meloe as a living Insect is.

The histories of several other Cantharids have been more or
less completely discovered. Fabre has found the larva of
Cerocoma schaefferi attacking the stores of provisions laid up by
a fossorial wasp of the genus *Tachytes*, and consisting of
Orthoptera of the family Mantidae. The student who wishes
for further information may refer to M. Beauregard's work on
this family.[1]

Some half-dozen species of the genus *Cephaloon* found in
Siberia, Japan, and North America, have, by some authorities,
been separated as the family Cephaloidae. Nothing is known
as to the metamorphosis of these rare beetles; and at present it
is not necessary to distinguish them from Cantharidæ.

Fam. 76. Trictenotomidae.—*Large Heteromera, with powerful
free projecting mandibles; the antennae long, but with the terminal
three joints short, with angular projections on one side.* This
family includes only two genera and seven or eight species.
They are very remarkable Insects; *Autocrates aenea* being three
inches long. The family is of considerable interest, as it seems to
have no affinity with any other Coleoptera. The appearance of
the species somewhat reminds one of Lucanidae, or Prionides;
but Trictenotomidae have even less relation to those beetles than
they have to the members of the Heteromerous series. The
Trictenotomidae appear to be found only in the primitive forests
of the Indian and Indo-Malayan regions. Nothing is known as
to their life-histories.

[1] *Les Insectes Vésicants*, Paris 1890, 554 pp. Parts of this work were previously published in *J. de l'Anat. Phys.*, xxi. xxii. xxiii. 1886 and 1887.

Series V. Phytophaga.

Tarsi apparently four-jointed, the three basal joints usually densely set with cushion-like pubescence beneath; the third joint different in form, being divided into two lobes, or grooved on its upper surface so as to allow of the fourth joint being inserted near its base instead of at its extremity. Head not forming a definite prolonged beak; its labrum visible, the palpi rarely (and even then not completely) occluded in the mouth.

This great series of beetles includes something like 35,000 species.   It approaches, like all the other series, the Polymorpha, especially the family Erotylidae placed therein, but in the great majority of cases there is no difficulty in recognising its members.   The tarsi have never the Heteromerous formula, the head is not constructed like that of Rhynchophora, nor the mouth and feet like those of Adephaga; the antennae are different from those of the Lamellicorns.   The tarsi are really five-jointed, for careful inspection shows that the long claw-joint has at its extreme base a small nodule, which is undoubtedly the fourth joint (Fig. 142, B).   In speaking of the joints it is, however, customary not to refer to this small and functionally useless joint at all, and to call the claw-joint the fourth; when the little joint is referred to it may be called the true fourth joint.

Nearly the whole of the enormous number of species of this series are directly dependent on the vegetable kingdom for their nutriment; they are therefore well styled Phytophaga. This term is, however, restricted by some systematists to the family we have called Chrysomelidae.   Although there is enormous variety in this series, three families only can be at all naturally distinguished, and this with difficulty.   Of these the Bruchidae are seed-feeders, the Chrysomelidae, as a rule, leaf-feeders, the Cerambycidae wood and stem-feeders.   The number of exceptions to this rule is but small, though certain Cerambycidae and certain Chrysomelidae live on roots.

Fam. 77. Bruchidae.—*Prosternum extremely short; in front perpendicular; behind the coxae, forming merely a transverse lamina with pointed extremity.   Hind femora more or less*

thickened.   This comparatively small family includes about
700 species of small, unattractive beetles.   The larvae live in
seeds ; hence some of the species are liable to be transported by
means of commerce ; some of them do considerable injury ; peas
and beans being specially subject to their attacks.   They are
able to complete their growth with a very small amount of
nutriment, some of them consuming only a portion a little larger
than themselves of a bean or pea.   The larvae are fat maggots
without legs, but Riley has discovered that the young larvae of
Bruchus pisi and *B. fabae* have, when first hatched, three pairs
of legs which are subsequently lost.   They also have peculiar

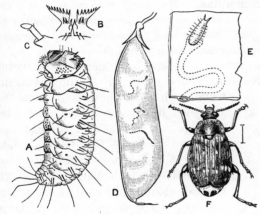

Fig. 141. — *Bruchus
pisi* or pea-weevil.
A, Young larva ;
B, prothoracic spin-
ous process ; C,
post-embryonic
leg, greatly magni-
fied ; D, pea-pod,
with tracks of
entry ; E, portion
of pod, with egg,
and the subse-
quently formed
track, magnified ;
F, imago. (After
Riley.)

spinous processes on the pronotum.   Both of these characteristics
may be correlative with the transient differences in the activities
of the larva, for the little creature is not at first located in the
pea, but mines a gallery in the pod, in which it moves about,
subsequently entering the pea and losing its legs.   There is a
good deal of difference in these respects between the two species
—*B. pisi* and *B. fabae*—examined by Riley, and as but little is
known of the life-histories of other Bruchidae it is probable that
still greater variety prevails.   Heeger has found that *Bruchus
lentis* sometimes requires two seeds to enable it to complete its
growth ; it is, notwithstanding its legless state when half-grown,
able to migrate by dropping to the earth, and dragging itself
along by its mandibles till it comes to another pod into which it
bites its way.

The family has, until recently, been placed in the Rhynchophorous series, with which it has, however, no direct connection. On the other hand, it is so closely connected with Chrysomelidae that it is not possible to indicate good characters to distinguish the two at present. The Australian genus *Carpophagus*, and the large South American species of *Caryoborus* appear to be quite indistinguishable as families, though Lacordaire and Chapuis placed one in Bruchidae, the other in Chrysomelidae. The definition we have given applies, therefore, to the majority of the family, but not to the aberrant forms just mentioned. The European genus *Urodon* appears to belong to Anthribidae, not to Bruchidae. The family Bruchidae is called Mylabridae by some.

Fam. 78. Chrysomelidae.—*Antennae moderately long ; eyes moderately large, usually not at all surrounding the insertion of the antennae ; upper surface usually bare, frequently brightly coloured and shining.* This enormous family comprises about 18,000 species of beetles, in which the form and details of structure are very varied. No satisfactory character for distinguishing Chrysomelidae from Cerambycidae has yet been discovered, although the two families are certainly distinct and natural. Most of the Chrysomelidae live on foliage ; few of them are more than half an inch long, whereas the Cerambycidae are wood - feeders and usually of more elongate form and larger size. The potato beetle, or Colorado beetle, that occasioned so much destruction in North America some thirty years ago, and the introduction of which into Europe was anticipated with much dread, is a good example of the Chrysomelidae. The turnip flea, a tiny hopping beetle, is among the smallest forms of the family, and is a member of another very exten-sive subdivision of Chrysomelidae, viz. Halticides. The term Phytophaga is by many naturalists limited to Chrysomelidae, the Cerambycidae being excluded. The classification of the family is but little advanced, but the enormous number of species of Chrysomelidae are placed in four divisions, viz. :—

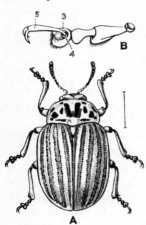

Fig. 142.—*Doryphora decem-lineata,* the potato beetle. North America. **A,** Imago ; **B,** hind - tarsus. 3, third joint ; 4, true fourth joint ; 5, so-called fourth joint.

Prothorax much narrower at the base than the elytra, and usually without side-margins (raised edges). Sub-fam. 1. EUPODA; with three divisions, Sagrides, Donaciides, Criocerides.

The basal ventral plates of the abdominal segments are somewhat shorter in the middle than at the sides, the fourth one being often invisible in the middle, while the fifth is very large. Sub-fam. 2. CAMPTOSOMES; with six divisions, Megascelides, Megalopides, Clythrides, Cryptocephalides, Chlamydes, Sphaerocarides.

In the other two groups there is no great disparity between the fourth and fifth ventral plates.

Prothorax not greatly narrower at the base than the elytra, and usually with distinct edges at the outsides. Sub-fam. 3. CYCLICA; with four divisions, Lamprosomides, Eumolpides, Chrysomelides, Galerucides.

Front of the head bent downwards or inflexed, so that the mouth is on the lower aspect. Antennae inserted close together on the most anterior part of the head, so that they are more forward than the mouth. Sub-fam. 4. CRYPTOSTOMES; with two divisions Hispides, Cassidides.

In the other three divisions the mouth is placed as usual, but the insertion of the antennae varies a good deal.

The larvae of about 100 species of the family are known; they are arranged in accordance with their habits, by Chapuis,[1] in six groups, viz. :

1. Elongate larvae, living under water, and there undergoing their metamorphosis. (Donaciides.)
2. Larvae mining in leaves, and undergoing their metamorphosis in the leaf. (Hispides and some Halticides.)
3. Short convex larvae, frequently with leathery and pigmented integuments, living exposed on plants. (Most of the Cyclica.)
4. Larvae of short form; covering the body with excrementitious matter. (Some Criocerides.)
5. Peculiar larvae of short form, spiny, and protecting their bodies by excrementitious matter attached by a special apparatus, the excrement itself being modified so as to be suitable for retention. (Cassidides.)
6. Elongate, pallid, larvae with curved abdomen; living in shell-like cases, and undergoing metamorphosis therein. (Most of the Camptosomes, the habits of which are known.)

Though our knowledge of these larvae extends to only about 100 out of 18,000 species, the above category by no means includes all the kinds of larvae; Captain Xambeu having recently discovered that the larva of *Chrysochus pretiosus* lives in the earth feeding on roots after the manner of a *Rhizotrogus* larva, which it resembles. The larva of *Sagra splendida* lives

[1] *Genera des Coléoptères (Suites à Buffon)*, x. Paris, 1874, p. 15.

inside the stems of *Dioscorea batatas*, in swellings; the group Sagrides, to which it belongs, is a very anomalous one.

i. EUPODA. The beetles of the genus *Donacia* are of special interest. They form, with the genus *Haemonia*, a peculiar group, well represented in Europe, and also in our own country. They are all connected with aquatic plants, the species of *Haemonia* living entirely under water, while the *Donacia* live in the imago-state an aërial life; though many of them enter the water with great readiness, and, it is said, are able to take wing from the surface. The larvae live on the roots of aquatic plants, and derive not only nutriment but air therefrom; they pass several months as pupae (or as resting larvae waiting for pupation), under water in cocoons which they construct, and which, incredible as it may seem, are filled with air, not water. Exact details as to the construction of these cocoons are wanting. It was formerly absurdly supposed that the larva swelled itself out to the size of the cocoon it was about to make, and so served as a mould, subsequently contracting. The observations of Schmidt-Schwedt [1] make it, however, more probable that the plant itself furnishes the air which, under pressure of the water (so he supposes), fills the cocoon; the larva wounds the root, piercing to an air-vessel and then constructs the cocoon on this spot, leaving to the last moment an orifice, according to Schmidt, as an exit for the water. The larva uses a similar artifice for obtaining air; it has no gills, but is provided near the extremity of the body with two sharp chitinous processes which it drives into the root of the plant till it penetrates an air-vessel. Schmidt thinks the processes serve as conduits to conduct the air to the tracheae, but Dewitz thinks the air enters the larva in a more normal manner, by means of a stigma placed at the base of the piercing process. A similar larva exists in *Haemonia;* which genus is additionally interesting from the fact that the imago lives entirely submerged. It is not known how it breathes. This genus is the only member of the Chrysomelidae that does not possess the structure of the feet that is characteristic of the Phytophaga. The late Professor Babington about sixty years ago found *H. curtisi* at Cley on the Norfolk coast on submerged *Potamogeton pectinatus*, but it has not been met with there for a great many years.

The larvae of Criocerides are of two kinds, in one of which the

---

[1] *Berlin. ent. Zeit.* 1887, p. 325, and 1889, p. 299.

body is peculiarly shaped in conformity with the curious habit of using the excrement as a covering. The larva is less elongate than usual, and has the anus placed on the upper surface, and formed so that the excrement when voided is pushed forward on to the Insect; here it is retained by means of a slimy matter, and a thick coat entirely covering the creature, is ultimately formed. The larva of *Lema melanopa* is not uncommon about Cambridge, where it feeds on the leaves of growing corn. It is a remarkable fact that even in one genus the species have some of them this habit, but others not. The species of *Crioceris* living on lilies—*C. merdigera,* *e.g.*—are noted for possessing it; while *C. asparagi* does not protect itself in this way, but emits fluid from its mouth when disturbed. This larva is a serious nuisance in some localities to the cultivators of asparagus. The eggs are deposited on the stems of the plant—as shown in our figure—sometimes in great numbers.

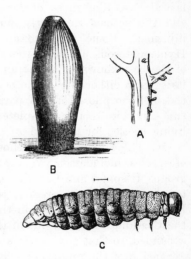

The perfect Insects of many of the Criocerides possess a stridulating organ. Two contiguous areas at the base of the last dorsal segment, where they can be rubbed by the tips of the elytra, are slightly elevated and bear very close and fine straight lines.

Fig. 143.—*Crioceris asparagi.* **A,** Eggs in position on stem of asparagus; **B,** one egg much enlarged; **C,** young larva. Cambridge.

ii. The CAMPTOSOMES, as we have already noticed, are distinguished by a peculiar structure of the abdomen. This character appears to be connected with a very remarkable habit, viz. the formation of a case to envelop the egg. The tip of the abdomen is somewhat curved downwards, and, in the female, bears a hollow near the extremity; when an egg is extruded the female holds it in this hollow by means of the hind legs, and envelops it with a covering said to be excrementitious. When the larva hatches, it remains within this case, and subsequently enlarges it by additions from its own body. The beautiful Insects of the genus *Cryptocephalus,* which is fairly well represented in Britain, belong to this division. The exotic group Megalopodes is incorrectly placed in Camptosomes ; the side pieces of the prothorax meet in it behind the middle coxae, as they do in Rhynchophora. The species of Megalopodes stridulate by means of an area on the base of the meso-scutellum rubbed by a ridge inside the pronotum, as in the Cerambycidæ.

iii. The division CYCLICA includes the great majority of Chryomelidae ; we have not less than 170 species in Britain. The larvae live, like those of Lepidoptera, at the expense of foliage, and the species frequently multiply to such an extent as to be injurious. Some of them are destroyed in great numbers by Hymenopterous parasites, the Braconid genus *Perilitus* being one of the best known of these ; in some cases the parasite deposits its eggs in either the larva or perfect Insect of the beetle, and the metamorphoses of the parasites in the latter case are sometimes, if not usually, completed, the larvae emerging from the living beetles for pupation.

iv. The CRYPTOSTOMES, though comparatively few in number of species, include some very remarkable beetles. There are two groups, Hispides and Cassidides. The former are almost peculiar to the tropics and are not represented by any species in the British fauna. The head in this group is not concealed ; but in the Cassidides the margins of the upper surface are more or less expanded, so that the head is usually completely hidden by the expansion of the pronotum. Both the groups are characterised by the antennae being inserted very near together, and by the short claw-joint of the feet. *Hispa* is one of the most extensive of the numerous genera of Hispides, and is remarkable from the imago being covered on the surface with long, sharp spines. But little is known as to the metamorphosis, beyond the fact already alluded to, that the larvae of several species mine the interior of leaves. The larva of *Hispa testacea,* according to Perris,[1] makes use of the leaves of *Cistus salvifolius* in Southern Europe ; it is broad and flat, and possessed of six short legs. The eggs are not deposited by the parents inside the leaves, but are probably attached to various parts of the plant. After hatching, the young larva enters a leaf, and feeds on the parenchyma without rupturing

---

[1] *Ann. Soc. Liége,* x. 1855, p. 260.

the epidermis; but when it has consumed about three-fourths of
the soft interior of the leaf it ruptures the epidermis of the upper
surface, and seeks another leaf; this found, it places itself on the
midrib, tears the upper epidermis, and lodges itself in the leaf.
In the case of this second leaf it attacks the parenchyma in the
neighbourhood of the petiole, and so forms an irregular tube
which has an open mouth, the point of entry. In this tube it
undergoes its metamorphosis. Each larva, it is said, always
makes use of two leaves, and of two opposed leaves. A knowledge of the habits of some of the larger of the exotic Hispides
would be of much interest.

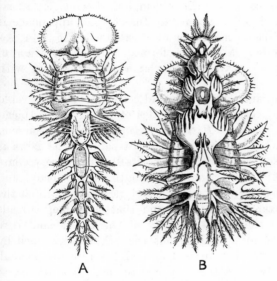

Fig. 144.—Pupa of
Cassidid beetle
(? *Aspidomorpha*
sp.). **A,** With
appendage ex-
tended; **B,** with
the appendage re-
posing on the back.
New Britain.

A   B

The Cassidides, in addition to the curious marginal expansion
of their upper surface, have the power of withdrawing the head
into the thorax, and hence they are often called shield or tortoise-
beetles. They exhibit considerable variety in form and colour,
and some of them display a peculiar metallic reflection of great
delicacy and beauty; this disappears entirely after death, but it
may be restored by thoroughly moistening the dead Insect. The
colour, therefore, probably depends on the presence of water in
the integument. The larvae of Cassidides are notorious on
account of their habit of covering their bodies with dried
excrement, for which purpose they are provided with a forked

process at the posterior extremity; this serves to place the protecting matter in a proper position and to retain it there. The
excrement assumes in various species forms so peculiar that they
cannot be considered merely incidental. In several species this
covering-matter is like lichen. This is the case with *Dolichotoma
palmarum*, the larva of which has, in place of the usual fork, a
more complex appendage on the back for the purpose of preparing and retaining its peculiar costume. The pupae, too, sometimes retain the larval skin. An extremely remarkable pupa of
a Cassidid—possibly of the genus *Aspidomorpha*—was recently
found by Dr. Arthur Willey in New Britain (Fig. 144). The
back of the pupa is covered with a complex appendage, so that
the creature has no resemblance to an Insect; this appendage is
perhaps capable of being moved, or even extended (Fig. 144, A),
during life. Whether it may be formed by the retention of
portions of the moulted skins of the larva we cannot say with
certainty.

The most remarkable of the Cassidid coverings yet discovered
are those formed by certain small beetles of the tropical American genus *Porphyraspis*. *P. tristis* is apparently a common
Insect at Bahia, where it lives on a cocoa-palm. The larva is
short and broad, and completely covers itself with a very dense
coat of fibres, each many times the length of the body, and
elaborately curved so as to form a round nest under which the
larva lives. On examination it is found that these long threads
are all attached to the anal extremity of the Insect, and there
seems no alternative to believing that each thread is formed by
small pieces of fibre that have passed through the alimentary canal,
and are subsequently stuck together, end to end. The process of

FIG. 145.—Nest of intes-
tinally-made filaments
under which the larva
of *Porphyraspis tristis*
lives.

forming these long fibres, each one from
scores of pieces of excrement, and giving
them the appropriate curve, is truly remarkable. The fibres nearest to the body of the
larva are abruptly curled so as to fit exactly,
and make an even surface; but the outside
fibres stand out in a somewhat bushy
fashion. The construction is much like that
of a tiny bird's nest. Señor Lacerda informed
the writer that the larva makes a nest as soon as it is hatched.
Another *Porphyraspis*—*P. palmarum*—has been recorded as

forming similar nests on a species of *Thrinax* in St. Domingo. Candèze says[1] that when it has completed its growth the larva ejects on to the leaf a quantity of semi-liquid matter, and this, on drying, sticks the nest to the leaf, so that the metamorphosis is effected under shelter.

Fam. 79. Cerambycidae (*Longicorns*).——*Form usually oblong, not much curved in outline at the sides; surface very frequently rendered dull by a very minute hairiness, which often forms a pattern; antennae usually long, and their insertion much embraced by the eyes.* This great family of beetles includes some 12,000 or 13,000 known species. The elegance and variety of their forms and the charm of their colours have caused them to attract much attention, so that it is probable that a larger proportion of the existing species have been obtained than is the case in any other of the great families of Coleoptera. Still it is not likely that one-half of the living forms are known. It is not possible at present to point out any one character of importance to distinguish Cerambycidae from Chrysomelidae, though the members of the two families have, as a rule, but little resemblance in external appearance. Most of them live on, or in, wood, though many are nourished in the stems of herbaceous plants. The larvae live a life of concealment, and are soft, whitish grubs with

Fig. 146.—*Saperda populnea.* Britain.

powerful mandibles, and usually with a comparatively small head, which is not much exserted from the thorax. Most of them are without legs, but a good many have three pairs of small legs, and there are numerous cases in which the surface of the body is furnished above or below with swellings believed to act as pseudopods (Fig. 84), and help the larvae to move about in their galleries; but this is probably not the sole function of these organs, as their surface is varied in character, and often not of a kind that appears specially adapted to assist in locomotion. There is a slight general resemblance between the larvae of Cerambycidae and those of Buprestidae, and when the thorax of a Longicorn larva is unusually broad, *e.g. Astyncmus,* this similarity is very pronounced.

[1] *Mem. Soc. Liége,* xvi. 1861, p. 387.

The modes of life of Cerambycid larvae exhibit considerable variety, and much perfection of instinct is displayed by the larvae, as well as by the mother beetles. The larvae of *Saperda populnea* are common in certain woods in the South of England in the stems of aspen; they consume only a small quantity of the interior of the stem, and are probably nourished by an afflux of sap to the spot where they are situated. *Elaphidion villosum* is called the oak-pruner in North America. The parent beetle lays an egg near the axilla of a leaf-stalk or small stem, and the young larva enters this and feeds on the tender material; as it grows it enters a larger limb, and makes an incision within this in such a manner that the wood falls to the ground with the larva within it, the dead wood serving subsequently as pabulum and as a shelter, within which the metamorphosis is completed. The species of the American genus *Oncideres* are called girdlers, because the parent beetle, after laying an egg in a small branch, girdles this round with a deep incision, so that the portion containing the larva sooner or later falls to the ground. The growth of a Longicorn larva frequently takes more than a year, and under certain circumstances it may be enormously prolonged. *Monohammus confusus* has been known to issue from wooden furniture in a dwelling-house when the furniture was fifteen years old. Individuals of another Longicorn have issued from the wood of a table, twenty and even twenty-eight years after the felling of the tree from which the furniture was made. Sereno Watson has related a case from which it appears probable that the life of a Longicorn beetle extended over at least forty-five years.[1] It is generally assumed that the prolongation of life in these cases is due to the beetle resting quiescent for long after it has completed the metamorphosis. Recent knowledge, however, renders it more probable that it is the larval life that is prolonged; the larva continuing to feed, but gaining little or no nutriment from the dry wood in these unnatural conditions. Mr. C. O. Waterhouse had for some years a Longicorn larva under observation, feeding in this way in the wood of a boot-tree;[2] the burrows in the wood contained a great deal of minute dust indicating that the larva passed much matter through the alimentary canal, probably with little result in the way of nutriment.

---

[1] Packard, 5th Rep. *U.S. Ent. Comm.* 1890, p. 689.
[2] Not a growing tree, but the instrument used for stretching boots.

There are numerous Longicorns that bear a great resemblance in form and colour to Insects to which they are not related. Haensch[1] has noticed that species of the genus *Odontocera* resemble various Hymenoptera, one species being called *O. braconoides;* he also observed that these Hymenoptera-like Longicorns, instead of withdrawing their underwings under the elytra as beetles generally do, vibrate them rapidly like Hymenoptera. A large number of Longicorns stridulate loudly by rubbing a ridge inside the pronotum on a highly specialised, striate surface at the base of the scutellum, and therefore covered up when the Insect is contracted in repose. A few produce noise by rubbing the hind femora against the edges of the elytra, somewhat after the fashion of grasshoppers. In this case there appears to be comparatively little speciality of structure, the femora bearing, however, more or less distinct small granules. The species of the Hawaiian genus *Plagithmysus* produce sound in both these manners, the thoracic stridulating organ being beautifully developed, while in some species the margin of the elytra and base of the femora are also well adapted for the purpose of sound-production, and in a few species of the genus there are also highly-developed stridulating surfaces on the hind and middle coxae. This is the only case in which a beetle is known to possess more than one set of sound-organs in the imago state.

Three divisions of this family are distinguished, viz.——

1. Front coxae large and transverse ; prothorax with distinct side margins.   Sub-fam. 1. PRIONIDES.

2. Front coxae not greatly extended transversely, thorax not margined ; last joint of maxillary palpus not pointed, usually broader (more or less) than the preceding joint.   Sub-fam. 2. CERAMBYCIDES.

3. Front coxae usually round and deeply embedded ; last joint of maxillary palpus pointed ; front tibiae with a more or less distinct, slanting groove on the inner side.   Sub-fam. 3. LAMIIDES.

The Prionides are on the average considerably larger in size than the members of the other divisions, and they include some of the largest of Insects. The Amazonian *Titanus giganteus* and the Fijian *Macrotoma heros* are amongst the most gigantic. Some of the Prionides have a great development of the mandibles in the male sex analogous to that we have already noticed in Lucanidae. The larvae of the large Prionides appear in various parts of the world to have been a favourite food with native

[1] *Berlin. ent. Zeitschr.* xli. 1896, SB. p. 22.

tribes, and Lumholz states that they are really good eating. In consequence of the destruction of forests that has progressed so largely of late years these gigantic Prionides have become much rarer.

Several aberrant forms are included in Prionides. The genus *Parandra* has five-jointed tarsi; the third joint being much smaller than usual, so that the fourth joint is not concealed by it. The Brazilian *Hypocephalus armatus* was for long a subject of dispute as to its natural position, and was placed by different authorities in widely-separated families of Coleoptera. The structure of this aberrant Longicorn seems to be only explicable on the hypothesis of warfare amongst the males.[1] Nothing is, however, known as to the habits and history of the Insect, and only one or two specimens of the female have yet been obtained.

The family Spondylidae has been proposed for some of these aberrant Longicorns, but as it includes but very few, and highly discrepant, species, it is neither natural nor of much use for systematic purposes.

The Lamiides are the most highly specialised division of the Longicorns, and includes the larger number of the species. The front of the head is usually placed at right angles to the vertex, and in some cases (groups Hippopsini, Spalacopsini) it is strongly inflexed, so that the mouth is placed on the under side of the head. The extension of the eyes round the antennae is accompanied by very curious shapes of those organs, and not infrequently each eye is divided into two more or less widely-separated parts, so that the Insect has, on the external surface, four eyes.

Series VI. Rhynchophora.

Head more or less prolonged in front to form a snout or beak, called rostrum. Tarsi four-jointed, usually at least the third joint broad and densely pubescent beneath.

This enormous series includes about 25,000 species, and as may well be imagined shows a great variety of structure amongst its forms. The vast majority may, however, be readily recognised by the two characters mentioned above. There are some cases in which the beak is indistinct, and others in which the tarsi are

[1] Sharp, *Ann. Soc. ent. Belgique*, xxviii. 1884, CR. p. cvii.

five-jointed (*Dryophthorus*), and even slender (Platypides). In these cases a close examination shows that the gular region on the middle of the back of the under surface of the head cannot be detected, and that the back of the prosternum is very strongly consolidated by the side-pieces of the thorax meeting together and being very firmly joined behind the coxae. The beak is in the great majority perfectly distinct, though it varies so extremely in form that it can only be briefly described by saying that it is a prolongation of the head in front of the eyes, or that the antennae are inserted on its sides near to, or far from, the tip. It has been ascertained in many cases that the rostrum is used by the female to assist in placing the eggs in suitable places, a hole being bored with it; in some cases it is also used to push the egg far into the hole in which it has previously been placed by the ovipositor; but there are many forms in which it is fairly certain that it is not so used. What purpose it serves in the male is totally unknown. In many members of the series, the rostrum differs in form in the two sexes, and in most, if not in all, these cases it is clear that the distinctions tend in the direction of making the beak of the female more efficient for the mechanical purpose we have mentioned.

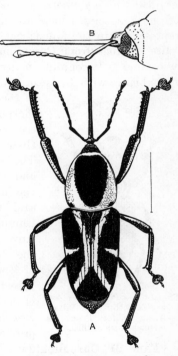

FIG. 147.—*Eugnoristus monachus* ♀. Madagascar. **A**, The imago; **B**, front of pronotum, head, and rostrum.

It was proposed by Leconte and Horn to separate this series from all the other Coleoptera as a primary division, and they looked on it as of lower or more imperfect structure. Packard has very properly protested against this interpretation; and there seems to be no reason whatever for considering the Rhynchophora as "lower" than other beetles; indeed we should be inclined to place such forms as Calandrides amongst the most perfect of Insects; their external structure (as shown by *Eugnoristus monachus,* Fig. 147) being truly admirable.

Only four families of Rhynchophora can be at present accepted as satisfactory; one of these—Curculionidae—includes an enormous majority of the whole series. Though it is probable that it will ultimately be divided into several families, the attempts to that end that have already been made are not satisfactory.

Fam. 80. Anthribidae.—*Palpi usually not covered, but distinct and flexible. Antennae often long, not elbowed, the first joint not very long. Third joint of tarsus small, usually much concealed by being embraced by the second joint. Pygidium exposed; propygidium deeply grooved in the middle.* This family includes 800 or more species, which are mostly tropical; it is very sparsely represented in the faunas of Europe and North America. It is quite distinct from Curculionidae with which it was formerly associated. It contains many graceful Insects having a certain resemblance with Longicorns on account of the large development

of the antennae. The habits and metamorphoses are but little known. It seems probable that many species find their nutriment in old wood or boleti. The larvae of some genera (*Cratoparis* and *Araeocerus*) have legs, but in others the legs are wanting, and the larvae are said to completely resemble those of Curculionidae. In the larva of our tiny British species, *Choragus sheppardi,* the legs are replaced by three pairs of thoracic, sac-like pseudopods. This Insect makes burrows in dead branches of hawthorn. The larvae of the genus *Brachytarsus* have been ascertained to prey on Coccidae.

Fig. 148. — *Platyrhinus latirostris,* Anthribidae. Britain. A, the perfect Insect; B, tarsus and tip of tibia.

Fam. 81. Curculionidae (*Weevils*).—*The beak of very variable length and thickness; the palpi small, nearly always concealed within the mouth, short, and rigid. Labrum absent. Antennae of the majority elbowed, i.e. with the basal joint longer, and so formed that when it is laterally extended the other joints can be placed in a forward direction.* This enormous family includes about 20,000 known species, and yet a large portion of the species yearly brought from the tropics still prove to be new. The rostrum or beak exhibits excessive variety in form, and is in many cases different in the sexes; in this case it is usually longer and thinner in the female. As the rostrum is one of the chief characters by which a member of the family may be recognised, it is necessary to inform the student that in certain forms (the Australian Amycterides, *e.g.*) the organ in question may be so short and thick that it is almost absent. In these cases the Insect may be identified as a Curculionid by the gular area being absent on the under side of the head, and by the concealment of the palpi. The tarsi are usually of the same nature as those of Phytophaga, already described, but the true fourth joint is less visible. In the Brachycerides this joint is not present, and the third joint is not lobed. The palpi are flexible and more or less exserted in a very few species (Rhynchitides); in Rhinomacerides there is also present a minute labrum. The front coxae are deeply embedded, and in many forms the prosternum is peculiar in structure; the side-pieces (epimera) meeting at the back of the prosternum in the middle line. This, however, is not universal in the family, and it occurs in some other beetles (*e.g.*, Megalopodides of the Phytophaga). The larvae are without legs. They are vegetarian, the eggs being deposited by the mother-beetle in the midst of the food. These larvae may be distinguished from those of Longicorns by the general form, which is sub-cylindric or rather convex, not flattened, and more particularly by the free, exserted head, the mouth being directed downwards; the attitude is generally a curve, and the anterior part of the body is a little the thicker. No part of plants is exempt from the attacks of the larvae of Curculionidae; buds, twigs, leaves, flowers, fruits, bark, pith, roots and galls may each be the special food of some Curculionid. Certain species of the sub-families Rhynchitides and Attelabides prepare leaves in an elaborate manner to serve as food and dwelling for their young. If young birches, or birch bushes from 5 to 10 feet in height, be looked at in the summer, one may often notice that some of the leaves are rolled so as to form, each one, a little funnel. This is the work of *Rhynchites* (or *Deporaus*) *betulae*, a little Curculionid beetle (Fig. 149). An inspection of one of these funnels will show that it is very skilfully constructed. The

whole of a leaf is not used in the formation of a funnel, cuts being
made across the leaf in suitable directions. The beetle standing on a leaf, as shown in the figure, proceeds to cut with its
mandibles an incision shaped like an erect S, commencing at a
certain part of the circumference, and ending at the midrib of the
leaf; the beetle then goes to the other side of the midrib, and
continues its incision so as to form another S-like curve considerably different from the first; being prostrate and less abrupt.
Thus the blade of the leaf is divided into two halves by certain
curved incisions, the midrib remaining intact. The little funnel-

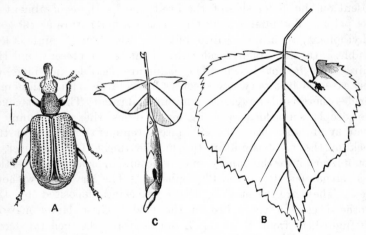

Fig. 149.—The leaf-rolling of *Rhynchites betulae*. Britain. **A**, Female beetle, magnified;
B, the beetle forming the first incision on a leaf; **C**, the completed roll. (**B** and **C**
after Debey.)

twister now commences to roll up the leaf to form the funnel;
and this part of the work is greatly facilitated by the shape of
the incisions. Going back to the spot where it commenced work,
by the aid of its legs it rolls one side of the leaf round an ideal
axis, somewhat on the same plan as that adopted by a grocer in forming a paper-funnel for sugar. The incisions are found to be just
of the right shape to make the overlaps in the rolling, and to retain them rolled-up with the least tendency to spring back. After
some other operations destined to facilitate subsequent parts of its
task, the beetle enters the rolled-up part of the leaf and brings it
more perfectly together; it again comes out and, pursuing a
different system, holds on with the legs of one side of the body

to the roll, and with the other legs drags to it the portion of the
leaf on the other side of the midrib so as to wrap this part (*i.e.*
the result of its second incision) round the part of the funnel
already constructed. This being done the Insect again enters
the funnel, bites three or four small cavities on the inside of the
leafy wall and deposits an egg in each. Afterwards it emerges
and fits the overlaps together in a more perfect manner so as to
somewhat contract the funnel and make it firmer; then proceeding
to the tip, this is operated on by another series of engineering
processes and made to close the orifice; this part of the operation being analogous to the closing by the grocer of his paper-
funnel after the sugar has been put in. The operation of the
beetle is, however, much more complex, for it actually makes a
sort of second small funnel of the tip of the leaf, bends this in, and
retains it by tucking in some little projections. The work, which
has probably lasted about an hour, being now completed, the creature
takes a longer or shorter rest before commencing another funnel.
We have given only a sketch of the chief points of the work,
omitting reference to smaller artifices of the craft master; but
we may remark that the curved incisions made by the beetle
have been examined by mathematicians and duly extolled as
being conducted on highly satisfactory mathematical principles.
It is impossible at present for us to form any conception as to the
beetle's conceptions in carrying out this complex set of operations.
Our perplexity is increased if we recollect its life-history, for we
then see that neither precept or example can have initiated its
proceedings, and that imitation is out of the question. The eggs
hatch in their dark place, giving rise to an eyeless maggot,
which ultimately leaves the funnel for the earth. The parts of
this maggot subsequently undergo complete change to produce
the motionless pupa of entirely different form, from which
emerges the perfect Insect. Hence the beetle cannot be considered to have ever seen a funnel, and certainly has never
witnessed the construction of one, though, when disclosed, it
almost immediately sets to work to make funnels on the complex
and perfect system we have so imperfectly described. More
general considerations only add to the perplexity we must feel
when reflecting on this subject. Why does the Insect construct
the funnel at all? As a matter of protection it appears to be
of little use, for the larvae are known to suffer from the attacks

of parasites as other Insects do. We have not the least reason for supposing that this mode of life for a larva is, so far as utility is concerned, better than a more simple and usual one. Indeed, extraordinary as this may appear, it is well known that other species of the same genus adopt a simple mode of life, laying their eggs in young fruits or buds. We think it possible, however, that a knowledge of the mode of feeding of this larva may show that a more perfect nutrition is obtained from a well-constructed cylinder, and if so this would to a slight extent satisfy our longing for explanation, though throwing no light whatever on the physiology or psychology of the artificer, and leaving us hopelessly perplexed as to why a beetle in ages long gone by should or could adopt a mode of life that by long processes of evolution should, after enormous difficulties have been overcome, attain the perfection we admire.[1]

Fam. 82. Scolytidae.—*Rostrum extremely short, broad ; tibiae frequently denticulate externally ; antennae short, with a broad club.* This family is not at all sharply distinguished from certain groups of Curculionidae (from Cossonides *e.g.*), but as the species have somewhat different habits, and in the majority of cases can be readily distinguished, it is an advantage to separate the two families. About 1400 species are at present known. Most of them are wood- and bark-feeders ; some bore into hard wood ; a few mine in twigs or small branches of trees, but the majority live in the inner layers of the bark ; and this also serves as the nidus of the larvae. A small number of species have been found to inhabit the stems of herbaceous plants, or to live in dry fruits. Owing to their retiring habits they are rarely seen except by those who seek them in their abodes, when they may often be found in great profusion. The mother-beetle bores into the suitable layer of the bark, forming a sort of tunnel and depositing eggs therein. The young larvae start each one a tunnel of its own, diverging from the parent tunnel ; hence each batch of larvae produces a system of tunnels, starting from the parents' burrow, and in many species these burrows are charac-

---

[1] For a more extensive account of *Rhynchites betulae* and others refer to Wasmann. *Der Trichterwickler*, Münster, 1884, and Debey, *Beiträge zur Lebens- und Entwickelungs-geschichte . . . der Attelabiden*, Bonn, 1846. The first includes an extensive philosophical discussion ; the second is a valuable collection of observations.

teristic in form and direction, so that the work of particular Scolytids can be recognised by the initiated.

The Platypides bore into the wood of trees and stumps; they are chiefly exotic, and little is known about them. They are the most aberrant of all Rhynchophora, the head being remarkably short, flat in front, with the mouth placed on the under surface of the head, there being no trace of a rostrum : the tarsi are elongate and slender, the third joint not being at all lobed, while the true fourth joint is visible. Hence they have not the appearance of Rhynchophora. Some authorities treat the Platypides as a distinct family.

Some of the members of the group Tomicides also bore into the wood. Recent observations have shown that there is an important feature in the economy of certain of these wood-borers, inasmuch as they live gregariously in the burrow, and feed on peculiar fungi that develop there, and are called ambrosia. According to Hubbard,[1] some species cultivate these fungi, making elaborate preparations to start their growth. The fungi, however, sometimes increase to such an extent as to seal up the burrows, and kill the Insects by suffocation.

Scolytidae sometimes multiply to an enormous extent, attacking and destroying the trees in wooded regions. Much discussion has taken place as to whether or not they are really injurious. It is contended by one set of partisans that they attack only timber that is in an unhealthy, dying, or dead condition. It may be admitted that this is usually the case; yet when they occur in enormous numbers they may attack timber that is in a sort of neutral state of health, and so diminish its vigour, and finally cause its destruction. Hence it is of great importance that they should be watched by competent foresters.

The larvae of Scolytidae are said to completely resemble those of Curculionidae : except in the group Platypides, where the body is straight and almost cylindrical, and terminates in an oblique truncation bearing a short hard spine.[2]

Fam. 83. Brenthidae.—*Form elongate ; rostrum straight, directly continuing the long axis of the body, often so thick as to form an elongate head ; antennae not elbowed.* The Brenthidae form a family of about 800 species, remarkable for the excessive

---

[1] *Bull. U.S. Dep. Agric. ent.* New series, No. 7, 1897.
[2] Perris, *Ann. Sci. Nat.* (2) xiv. 1840, p. 89, pl. iii.

length and slenderness of some of its forms, and for the
extreme difference in the sexes that frequently exists. It is

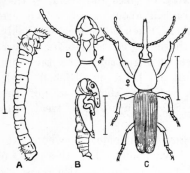

well represented in the tropics
only, and very little is known
as to the natural history and
development.   These beetles are
stated to be wood-feeders, and
no doubt this is correct in the
case of the majority of the
species ; but Mr. Lewis observed
in Japan that *Zemioses celtis* and
Cyphagogus segnipes are predaceous, and enter the burrows
of wood-boring Insects to search
for larvae as prey : they are
very much modified in structure
to permit this ; and as the other

FIG. 150. — *Eupsalis minuta.*   North
America.   **A,** Larva ; **B,** pupa ; **C,**
female imago ; **D,** head of male. (After
Riley.)

members of the group Taphroderides are similar in structure,
it is probable that they are all predaceous.   Nothing whatever is known as to the larval history of these carnivorous
forms.   Indeed an uncertainty, almost complete, prevails as to
the early stages of this family.   Riley has given a sketch of a
larva which he had no doubt was that of *Eupsalis minuta,* the
North American representative of the family ; if he is correct
the larva differs from those of Curculionidae by its elongate form,
and by the possession of thoracic legs : these, though small, are
three-jointed.   Descriptions, supposed to be those of Brenthid
larvae, were formerly published by Harris and Motschoulsky ;
but it is now clear that both were mistaken.

In the higher forms of Brenthidae the rostrum of the female
is perfectly cylindrical and polished, and the mandibles are
minute, hard, pointed processes placed at its tip.   This organ is
admirably adapted to its purpose ; it being used for boring a hole
in wood or bark, in which an egg is subsequently deposited.   The
males in these cases are extremely different, so that considerable
curiosity is felt as to why this should be so.   In some cases their
head is thick, and there may be no rostrum, while large powerful
mandibles are present.

In other cases the rostrum is slender, but of enormous
length, so that it may surpass in this respect the rest of

the body, although this itself is so drawn out as to be quite exceptional in the Insect world:[1] the antennae are inserted near the tip of the rostrum instead of near its base, as they are in the female. The size of the males is in these cases usually much larger than that of the female.[2] The males of some species fight; they do not, however, wound their opponent, but merely frighten him away. In *Eupsalis* it appears that the rostrum of the female is apt to become fixed in the wood during her boring operations; and the male then extricates her by pressing his heavy prosternum against the tip of her abdomen; the stout forelegs of the female serve as a fulcrum and her long body as a lever, so that the effort of the male, exerted at one extremity of the body of the female, produces the required result at the other end of her body. The New Zealand Brenthid, *Lasiorhynchus barbicornis*, exhibits sexual disparity in an extreme degree: the length of the male is usually nearly twice that of the female, and his rostrum is enormous. It is at present impossible to assign any reason for this; observations made at the request of the writer by Mr. Helms some years ago, elicited the information that the female is indefatigable in her boring efforts, and that the huge male stands near by as a witness, apparently of the most apathetic kind.

Coleoptera of uncertain position.

There are three small groups that it is impossible at present to place in any of the great series of beetles.

Fam. 84. Aglycyderidae. — *Tarsi three-jointed, the second joint lobed; head not prolonged to form a beak.* The two most important features of Rhynchophora are absent in these Insects, while the other structural characters are very imperfectly known, many parts of the external skeleton being so completely fused that the details of structure are difficult of appreciation. Westwood considered the tarsi to be really four-jointed, but it is not

---

[1] In the males of the genus *Cedeocera* the tips of the elytra are drawn out into processes almost as long as the elytra themselves, and rivalling the forceps of earwigs.

[2] The stature of the individuals of the same species is, in some of these Brenthidae, subject to extreme variation, especially in the males, some individuals of which—in the case of *Brenthus anchorago*—are five times as long as others.

at all clear that the minute knot he considered the third joint is more than the articulation of the elongate terminal joint. The family consists only of two or three species of *Aglycyderes,* one of which occurs in the Canary Islands, and one or two in New Zealand and New Caledonia. The former is believed to live in the stems of *Euphorbia canariensis ;* a New Zealand species has been found in connection with the tree-fern *Cyathea dealbata.*

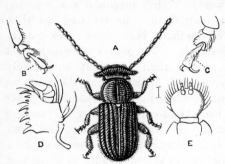

FIG. 151.—*Aglycyderes setifer.* Canary Islands. **A,** Imago ; **B,** tarsus according to Westwood ; **C,** according to nature ; **D,** maxilla ; **E,** labium.

Fam. 85. Proterhinidae.—*Tarsi three-jointed, the second joint lobed ; head of the male scarcely prolonged, but that of the female forming a definite rostrum,; maxillae and ligula entirely covered by the mentum.* As in the preceding family the sutures on the under side of the head and prosternum cannot be detected. The minute palpi are entirely enclosed in the buccal cavity. There is a very minute true third joint of the tarsus, at the base of the terminal joint, concealed between the lobes of the second joint. The family consists of the genus *Proterhinus* ; it is confined to the Hawaiian Islands, where these Insects live on dead wood in the native forests. The genus is numerous in species and individuals.

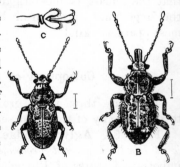

FIG. 152.—*Proterhinus lecontei.* Hawaiian Islands. **A,** Male ; **B,** female ; **C,** front foot, more magnified.

Strepsiptera (or **Rhipiptera,** Stylopidae).—*Male small or minute; prothorax extremely small ; mesothorax moderate, the elytra reduced to small, free slips ; metathorax and wings very large ; nervuration of the latter radiating, without cross nervules. Female a mere sac, with one extremity smaller and forming a sort of neck or head.* These curious Insects are parasitic in the interior of

other Insects, of the Orders Hymenoptera and Hemiptera.   Their
structure and their life-histories entitle them to be ranked as
the most abnormal of all Insects, and entomologists are not
agreed as to whether they are aberrant Coleoptera or a distinct
Order.   The newly-hatched larva is a minute triungulin (Fig.
154), somewhat like that of *Meloe*; it fixes itself to the skin
of the larva of a Hymenopterous Insect, penetrates into the
interior, and there undergoes its metamorphoses, the male emerging to enjoy a brief period of an abnormally active, indeed agitated,
existence, while the female never moves.   It is important to
note that these Strepsiptera do not, like most other internal
parasites, produce the death of their hosts; these complete their
metamorphosis, and the development of the parasite goes on
simultaneously with that of the host, so that the imago of the

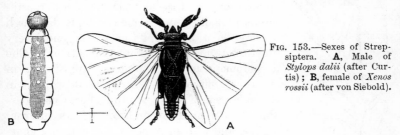

FIG. 153.—Sexes of Strep-
siptera.   **A,** Male of
Stylops dalii (after Cur-
tis); **B,** female of *Xenos
rossii* (after von Siebold).

Strepsipteron is found only in the imago of the host.[1]   After
the young *Stylops* has entered its host it feeds for a week or so
on the fat-body (apparently by a process of suction), then
moults and assumes the condition of a footless maggot, in which
state it remains till growth is completed.   At the latter part of
this period the history diverges according to sex; the female
undergoes only a slight metamorphic development of certain
parts, accompanied apparently by actual degradation of other
parts; while the male goes on to pupation, as is normal in Insects.
(We may remark that the great features of the development of
the sexes are parallel with those of Coccidae in Hemiptera.)
When the Hymenopterous larva changes to a pupa, the larva
of the Strepsipteron pushes one extremity of its body between two
of the abdominal rings of its host, so that this extremity becomes
external, and in this position it completes its metamorphosis, the

[1] This remark applies to the Strepsiptera parasitic on Hymenoptera : nothing
whatever is known as to the life-histories of the species that attack Hemiptera.

male emerging very soon after the host has become an active winged Insect, while the female undergoes no further change of position, but becomes a sac, in the interior of which young develop in enormous numbers, finally emerging from the mother-sac in the form of the little triungulins we have already mentioned. This is all that can be given at present as a general account; many points of the natural history are still obscure, others have been merely guessed; while some appear to differ greatly in the different forms. A few brief remarks as to these points must suffice.

Fig. 154.—Young larva of *Stylops* on a bee's-hair. Greatly magnified. (After Newport.)

Bees carrying, or that have carried, Strepsiptera, are said to be stylopised (it being a species of the genus *Stylops* that chiefly infests bees); the term is also used with a wider application, all Insects that carry a Strepsipterous parasite being termed stylopised, though it may be a Strepsipteron of a genus very different from *Stylops* that attacks them. The development of one or more Strepsiptera in an Insect usually causes some deformity in the abdomen of its host, and effects considerable changes in the condition of its internal organs, and also in some of the external characters. Great difference of opinion prevails as to what these changes are; it is clear, however, that they vary much according to the species, and also according to the extent of the stylopisation. Usually only one *Stylops* is developed in a bee; but two, three, and even four have been observed:[1] and in the case of the wasp, *Polistes*, Hubbard has observed that a single individual may bear eight or ten individuals of its Strepsipteron (*Xenos*, n. sp. ?).

There is no exact information as to how the young triungulins find their way to the bee-larvae they live in. Here again the discrepancy of opinion that prevails is probably due to great

---

[1] Although not an invariable, it seems that it is a general rule that the *Stylops* produced from the body of one individual are all of one sex; it has even been stated that female bees produce more especially female *Stylops*, and male bees male *Stylops*. If any correlation as to this latter point exist, it is far from general.

difference really existing as to the method. When a *Stylops* carried by an Insect (a Hymenopteron, be it noted, for we have no information whatever as to Hemiptera) produces young, they cover the body of the host as if it were powdered, being excessively minute and their numbers very great ; many hundreds, if not thousands, of young being produced by a single *Stylops*. The species of the wasp genus *Polistes* are specially subject to the attacks of *Stylops ;* they are social Insects, and a stylopised specimen being sickly does not as a rule leave the nest ; in this case the *Stylops* larva may therefore have but little difficulty in finding its way to a Hymenopterous larva, for even though it may have to live for months before it has the chance of attaching itself to a nest-building female, yet it is clearly in the right neighbourhood. The bee genus *Andrena* has, however, quite different habits ; normally a single female makes her nest under-ground ; but in the case of a stylopised female it is certain that no nest is built, and no larvae produced by a stylopised example, so that the young triungulins must leave the body of the bee in order to come near their prey. They can be active, and have great powers of leaping, so that it is perhaps in this way possible for them to attach themselves to a healthy female bee.

We have still only very imperfect knowledge as to the structure and development of Strepsip-tera. Indeed but little informa-tion has been obtained since 1843.[1] Before that time the mature female was supposed to be a larva, and the triungulins found in it to be parasites. Although the erroneous character of these views has been made clear, the problems that have been sug-gested present great difficulties. Apparently the change from the triungulin condition (Fig. 154) to the parasitic larvae (Fig. 155, A, B)

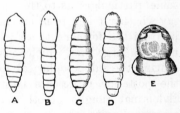

Fig. 155.—Portion of early stages of *Xenos rossii*. (After von Siebold.) **A**, Small male larva ; **B**, small female larva ; **C**, full-grown male larva ; **D**, full-grown female larva ; **E**, the so-called "cephalothorax" and adjacent segment of adult female. (The newly-hatched larva is very much like that of *Stylops* shown in Fig. 154.)

is extremely great and abrupt, and it appears also that during

---

[1] Von Siebold, *Arch. Naturges.* ix. 1843, pp. 137-161. Nassonoff's recent paper is in Russian, but so far as we can gather (cf. *Zool. Centralbl.* i. 1894, p. 766), it does not add greatly to the data furnished by von Siebold.

the larval growth considerable sexual differentiation occurs (Fig. 155, C, D); details are, however, wanting, and there exists but little information as to the later stages. Hence it is scarcely a matter for surprise that authorities differ as to which is the head and which the anal extremity of the adult female. Von Siebold apparently entertained no doubt as to the part of the female that is extruded being the anterior extremity; indeed he called it a cephalothorax. Supposing this view to be correct, we are met by the extraordinary facts that the female extrudes the head for copulatory purposes, that the genital orifice is placed thereon, and that the young escape by it. Meinert[1] contends that the so-called cephalothorax of the adult is the anal extremity, and that fertilisation and the escape of the young are effected by the natural passages, the anterior parts of the body being affected by a complete degeneration. Nassonoff, in controversion of Meinert, has recently pointed out that the "cephalothorax" of the young is shown by the nervous system to be the anterior extremity. It still remains, however, to be shewn that the "cephalothorax" of the adult female corresponds with that of the young, and we shall not be surprised if Meinert prove to be correct. The internal anatomy and the processes of oogenesis appear to be of a very unusual character, but their details are far from clear. Brandt has given some particulars as to the nervous system; though he does not say whether taken from the male or female, we may presume it to be from the former; there is a supra-oesophageal ganglion, and near it a large mass which consists of two parts, the anterior representing the sub-oesophageal and the first thoracic ganglia, while the posterior represents two of the thoracic and most of the abdominal ganglia of other Insects; at the posterior extremity, connected with the other ganglia by a very long and slender commissure, there is another abdominal ganglion.[2]

It is a matter of great difficulty to procure material for the prosecution of this study; the fact that the instars to be observed exist only in the interior of a few Hymenopterous larvae, which in the case of the bee, *Andrena*, are concealed under ground; and in the case of the wasps, *Polistes*, placed in cells in a nest of wasps, adds greatly to the difficulty. It is therefore of interest to know that Strepsiptera occur in Insects with incomplete

---

[1] *Ent. Meddel.* v. 1896. p. 148, and *Ov. Danske Selsk.* 1896, p. 67.
[2] *Horae Soc. ent. Ross.* xiv. 1879, p. 14.

metamorphosis.   They have been observed in several species of
Homoptera ; and the writer has a large Pentatomid bug of
the genus *Callidea*, which bears a female
Strepslpteron apparently of large size.   This
bug [1] is abundant and widely distributed in
Eastern Asia, and it may prove comparatively easy to keep stylopised examples
under observation.   Both v. Siebold and
Nassonoff think parthenogenesis occurs in
Strepsiptera, but there appear to be no facts
to warrant this supposition.   Von Siebold
speaks of the phenomena of Strepsipterous
reproduction as paedogenesis, or pseudo-
paedogenesis, but we must agree with
Meinert that they cannot be so classed.

Fig. 156.—Abdomen of a
wasp (*Polistes heb-
raeus*) with a Strep-
sipteron (*Xenos* ♀) in
position, one of the
dorsal plates of the
wasp's abdomen being
removed.   *a*, Projec-
tion of part of the
parasite ; *b*, line in-
dicating the position
of the removed dorsal
plate.

The males of Strepsiptera live for only a
very short time, and are very difficult of
observation.   According to Hubbard the
males of *Xenos* dash about so rapidly that the eye cannot see
them, and they create great agitation amongst the wasps in the
colonies of which they are bred.   Apparently they are produced in
great numbers, and their life consists of only fifteen or twenty
minutes of fiery energy.   The males of *Stylops* are not exposed
to such dangers as those of *Xenos*, and apparently live somewhat
longer—a day or two, and even three days are on record.   The
individuals of *Andrena* parasitised by *Stylops* are apparently
greatly affected in their economy and appear earlier in the season
than other individuals ; this perhaps may be a reason, coupled
with their short lives, for their being comparatively rarely met
with by entomologists.

It is not possible at present to form a valid opinion as to
whether Stylopidae are a division of Coleoptera or a separate
Order.   Von Siebold considered them a distinct Order, and
Nassonoff, who has recently discussed the question, is also of that
opinion.

---

[1] Named by Mr. Distant *Callidea baro ;* according to the Brussels catalogue of
Hemiptera, *Chrysocoris grandis* var. *baro*.

CHAPTER VI

LEPIDOPTERA—OR BUTTERFLIES AND MOTHS

Order VI. Lepidoptera.

*Wings four; body and wings covered with scales usually varie-
gate in colour, and on the body frequently more or less like
hair: nervures moderate in number, at the periphery of
one wing not exceeding fifteen, but little irregular; cross-
nervules not more than four, there being usually only one or
two closed cells on each wing, occasionally none. Imago
with mouth incapable of biting, usually forming a long
coiled proboscis capable of protrusion. Metamorphosis great
and abrupt; the wings developed inside the body; the larva
with large or moderate head and strong mandibles. Pupa
with the appendages usually adpressed and cemented to the
body so that it presents a more or less even, horny exterior,
occasionally varied by projections that are not the appendages
and that may make the form very irregular: in many
of the smaller forms the appendages are only imperfectly
cemented to the body.*

LEPIDOPTERA, or butterflies and moths, are so far as ornament is
concerned the highest of the Insect world. In respect of
intelligence the Order is inferior to the Hymenoptera, in the
mechanical adaptation of the parts of the body it is inferior to
Coleoptera, and in perfection of metamorphosis it is second to
Diptera. The mouth of Lepidoptera is quite peculiar; the proboscis—the part of the apparatus for the prehension of food—
is anatomically very different from the proboscis of the other
Insects that suck, and finds its nearest analogue in the extreme
elongation of the maxillae of certain Coleoptera, e.g. *Nemognatha.*

The female has no gonapophyses, though in certain exceptional forms of Tineidae, there are modifications of structure
connected with the terminal segments, that have as yet been
only imperfectly investigated.   As a rule, the egg is simply
deposited on some living vegetable and fastened thereto.
Lepidoptera are the most exclusively vegetarian of all the Orders
of Insects; a certain number of their larvae prey on Insects
that are themselves filled with vegetable juices (Coccidae,

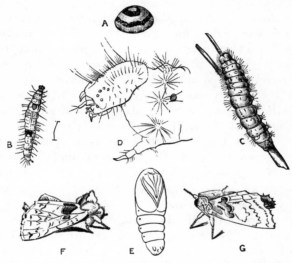

FIG. 157.—Metamorphosis of a Lepidopteron (*Rhegmatophila alpina*, Notodontidae).
(After Poujade, *Ann. Soc. ent. France*, 1891.)   Europe.   **A**, Egg; **B**, young larva,
about to moult; **C**, adult larva; **D**, head and first body-segment of adult larva,
magnified; **E**, pupa, ×$\frac{2}{1}$; **F**, male moth in repose; **G**, female moth in repose.

Aphidae) and a very small number (*Tinea,* etc.) eat animal
matter.   In general the nutriment appears to be drawn exclusively from the fluids of the vegetables, the solid matter
passing from the alimentary canal in large quantity in the form
of little pellets usually dry, and called frass.   Hence the
quantity of food ingested is large, and when the individuals
unduly increase in number, forest trees over large areas are
sometimes completely defoliated by the caterpillars.

Lepidoptera pass a larger portion of their lives in the pupal
stage than most other Insects do; frequently during nine months
of the year the Lepidopteron may be a pupa.   In other Orders of

Insects it would appear that the tendency of the higher forms is
to shorten the pupal period, and when much time has to be
passed between the end of the feeding up of the larva and the
appearance of the imago, to pass this time as much as possible
in the form of a resting-larva, and as little as may be in the
form of a pupa; in Lepidoptera the reverse is the case; the
resting-larva period being usually reduced to a day or two.
Hence we can understand the importance of a hard skin to the
pupa.   There are, however, numerous Lepidopterous pupae where
the skin does not attain the condition of hardness that is
secured for the higher forms by the chitinous exudation we
have mentioned; and there are also cases where there is a prolonged resting-larva period: for instance *Galleria mellonella*
spins a cocoon in the autumn and remains in it as a resting
larva all the winter, becoming a pupa only in the spring.   In
many of these cases the resting-larva is protected by a cocoon.
It is probable that the chief advantage of the perfect chitinous
exudation of the Lepidopterous pupa is to prevent the tiny,
complex organisation from the effects of undue transpiration.
Bataillon has suggested that the relation of the fluid contents of
the pupa to air and moisture are of great importance in the
physiology of metamorphosis.

The duration of life is very different in various forms
of Lepidoptera.   It is known that certain species (*Ephestia
kuehniella, e.g.*) may go through at least five generations a year.
On the other hand, certain species that feed on wood or roots
may take three years to complete their life-history; and it is
probable that some of the forms of Hepialidae are even longer
lived than this.

Lepidoptera have always been a favourite Order with entomologists, but no good list of the species has ever been made,
and it would be a difficult matter to say how many species are
at present known, but it can scarcely be less than 50,000.   In
Britain we have about 2000 species.

The close affinity of the Order with Trichoptera has long
been recognised: Réaumur considered the latter to be practically
Lepidoptera with aquatic habits, and Speyer pointed out the
existence of very numerous points of similarity between the
two.   Brauer emphasised the existence of mandibles in the
nymph of Trichoptera as an important distinction: the pupa

of *Micropteryx* (Fig. 211) has however been recently shown to be similar to that of Trichoptera, so that unless it should be decided to transfer *Micropteryx* to Trichoptera, and then define Lepidoptera and Trichoptera as distinguished by the condition of the pupa, it would appear to be very difficult to retain the two groups as distinct.

Structure of Imago.—The head of a Lepidopteron is in large part made up of the compound eyes; in addition to these it frequently bears at the top a pair of small, simple eyes so much concealed by the scales as to cause us to wonder if seeing be carried on by them. The larger part of the front of the head is formed by the clypeus, which is separated by a well-

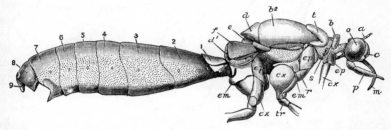

FIG. 158.—External structure of a female butterfly, *Anosia plexippus*. (After Scudder.)
a, Base of antenna ; *b*, pronotum ; *b²*, scutum of mesothorax ; *c*, clypeus ; *cx*, coxa ; *d*, scutellum ; *d¹*, scutellum of metathorax ; *e*, post-scutellum (= base of phragma) ; *em*, epimeron ; *ep*, episternum ; *f*, scutum of metathorax ; *m*, basal part of proboscis (= maxilla) ; *o*, eye ; *p*, labial palp ; *r*, mesosternum ; *s*, prothoracic spiracle ; *t*, tegula ; *tr*, trochanter ; 1-9, dorsal plates of abdomen.

marked line from the epicranium, the antennae being inserted on the latter near its point of junction with the former. There is sometimes (*Saturnia, Castnia*) on each side of the clypeus a deep pocket projecting into the head-cavity. The other parts of the head are but small. The occipital foramen is very large.[1]

The antennae are always conspicuous, and are very various in form ; they are composed of numerous segments, and in the males of many species attain a very complex structure, especially in Bombyces and Psychidae ; they doubtless function in such cases as sense-organs for the discovery of the female.

The largest and most important of the mouth-parts are the maxillae and the labial palpi, the other parts being so small as to render their detection difficult. The labrum is a very short,

[1] Kellogg, *Kansas Quarterly*, ii. 1893, p. 51, plate II.

comparatively broad piece, visible on the front edge of the clypeus; its lateral part usually forms a prominence which has often been mistaken for a mandible; Kellogg has applied the term "pilifer" to this part. In the middle of the labrum a small angular or tongue-like projection is seen just over the middle of the base of the proboscis; this little piece is considered by several authorities to be an epipharynx.

MANDIBLES.—Savigny, Westwood, and others considered the parts of the labrum recently designated pilifers by Kellogg to be the rudimentary mandibles, but Walter has shown that this

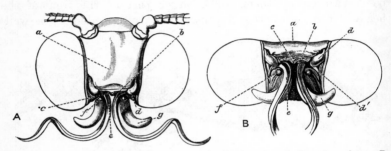

FIG. 159.—Mouth of Lepidoptera. Tiger-moth, *Arctia caja*. **A**, Seen from front; **B**, from front and below. *a*, Clypeus; *b*, labrum; *c*, epipharynx; *d*, mandibular area; *d'*, prominence beneath mandibular area; *e*, one side of haustellum or proboscis; *f*, maxillary palp; *g*, labial palp.

is not the case.[1] The mandibles are usually indistinguishable, though they, or some prominence possibly connected with them,[2] may frequently be detected in the neighbourhood of the pilifers; they are, according to Walter, largest and most perfectly developed in *Eriocephala*, a genus that was not distinguished by him from *Micropteryx* and was therefore termed "niedere Micropteryginen," *i.e.* lower Micropteryges. The opinion entertained by Walter that *Micropteryx* proper (his "höhere Micropteryginen") also possesses rudimentary mandibles is considered by Dr. Chapman, no doubt with reason, to be erroneous.[3] The mandibles, however, in the vast majority of Lepidoptera can scarcely be said to exist at all in the imago; there being only an obtuse projection — without trace of

[1] *Jena. Zeitschr. Naturw.* xviii. 1885, p. 751.

[2] The writer is not quite convinced that the supposed mandibles of these Macrolepidoptera are really entitled to be considered as such.

[3] *Tr. ent. Soc. London*, 1893, p. 263.

articulation——on each side of the labrum; and even this projection is usually absent. Meinert recognised these projections as
mandibles in *Smerinthus populi*, and Kellogg in *Protoparce caro-
lina*, another large Sphinx moth. They appear to be unusually
well developed in that group. In *Castnia* they are even more
definite than they are in Sphingidae.

The MAXILLAE are chiefly devoted to the formation of the
proboscis. Their basal portions are anatomically very indefinite,
though they exist very intimately connected with the labium.
Each usually bears a small tubercle or a segmented process, the
representative of the maxillary palpus. The proboscis itself consists of the terminal, or outer, parts of the two maxillae, which
parts are closely and beautifully coadapted to form the spirally
coiled organ, that is sometimes, though incorrectly, called the tongue.
The exact morphology of the Lepidopterous proboscis has not
been established. The condition existing in the curious family
Prodoxidae (see p. 432), where a proboscis coexists with another
structure called a maxillary tentacle, suggests a correspondence
between the latter and the galea of a typical maxilla; and
between the proboscis and the lacinia or inner lobe of a
maxilla: but J. B. Smith is of opinion that the tentacle in
question is a prolongation of the stipes. The condition of the
parts in this anomalous family (Prodoxidae) has not, however,
been thoroughly investigated, and Packard takes a different
view of the proboscis; he considers that "it is the two galeae
which become elongated, united and highly specialised to form
the so-called tongue or glossa of all Lepidoptera above the
Eriocephalidae."[1] The proboscis in some cases becomes very
remarkable, and in certain Sphingidae is said to attain, when
unrolled, a length of ten inches. In some cases the maxillary
lobes do not form a proboscis, but exist as delicate structures,
pendulous from the mouth, without coadaptation (*Zeuzera aesculi*,
the Wood-leopard moth). In other forms they are absent
altogether (*Cossus, e.g.*), and in *Hepialus* we have failed to detect
any evidence of the existence of the maxillae. On the other
hand, in *Micropteryx* the maxillae are much more like those of a
mandibulate Insect; and various other Microlepidoptera approach
more or less a similar condition. In the genus last mentioned

---

[1] *Amer. Natural.* xxix. 1895, p. 637. It should be recollected that many
Lepidoptera do not possess any proboscis.

the maxillary palpi are largely developed, flexible and slender. According to Walter various forms of palpus intermediate between that of *Micropteryx* and the condition of rudimentary tubercle may be found amongst the Microlepidoptera.[1]

LABIUM.—The labial palpi are usually largely developed, though but little flexible; they form conspicuous processes densely covered with scales or hairs, and curve forwards or upwards, rarely downwards, from the under side of the head, somewhat in the fashion of tusks. The other parts of the labium are frequently represented merely by a membranous structure, united with the maxillae and obstructing the cavity of the pharynx. Where the proboscis is absent it is difficult to find any orifice leading to the alimentary canal, such opening as may exist being concealed by the overhanging clypeus and labium. In some forms, *Saturnia, e.g.*, there appears to be no buccal orifice whatever. In *Hepialus* the labium is in a very unusual condition; it projects externally in the position usually occupied by the labial palpi, these organs being themselves extremely short. It is very difficult to form an opinion as to the structure of the labium and other mouth-parts when the maxillae are not developed, as in these cases the parts are of a delicate membranous nature, and shrivel after death. This is the explanation of the fact that in descriptive works we find vague terms in use such as " mouth aborted " or " tongue absent."

The mouth of the Lepidopterous imago is a paradoxical structure; it differs very greatly from that of the larva, the changes during metamorphosis being extreme. We should thus be led to infer that it is of great importance to the creatures; but, on the other hand, the various structures that make up the mouth, as we have remarked, are frequently absent or reduced to insignificant proportions; and even in forms where the apparatus is highly developed the individuals seem to be able to accomplish oviposition without taking food, or after taking only very minute quantities. It is therefore difficult to understand why so great a change should occur during the metamorphosis of the Insects of this Order. It has been ascertained that in some forms where the mouth is atrophied the stomach is in a correlative condition; but we are not aware that any investigations have been made as to whether this correspondence is general or exceptional.

[1] *Jena. Zeitschr. Naturw.* xviii. 1885, p. 168.

The exact mode in which the proboscis acts is in several respects still obscure, the views of Burmeister and Newport being in some points erroneous. Towards the tip of the proboscis there are some minute but complex structures considered by Fritz Müller to be sense-organs, and by Breitenbach to be mechanical instruments for irritating or lacerating the delicate tissues of blossoms. It is probable that Müller's view will prove to be correct. Nevertheless the proboscis has considerable power of penetration; there being a moth, "*Ophideres fullonica*," that causes considerable damage to crops of oranges by inserting its trunk through the peel so as to suck the juices.[1] The canal formed by each maxilla opens into a cavity inside the front part of the head. This cavity, according to Burgess,[2] is a sort of sac connected with five muscles, and by the aid of this apparatus the act of suction is performed: the diverticulum of the alimentary canal, usually called a sucking-stomach, not really possessing the function formerly attributed to it.

The PROTHORAX is very small, being reduced to a collar, between the head and the alitrunk, of just sufficient size to bear the front pair of legs. Its most remarkable feature is a pair of processes, frequently existing on the upper surface, called " patagia." These in many cases (especially in Noctuidae) are lobes capable of considerable movement, being attached only by a narrow base. In *Hepialus*, on the contrary, they are not free, but are merely indicated by curved marks on the dorsum. The patagia are styled by many writers " tegulae." They are of some interest in connection with the question of wing-like appendages on the prothorax of Palaeozoic insects, and they have been considered by some writers[3] to be the equivalents of true wings. The MESOTHORAX is very large, especially its upper face, the notum, which is more or less convex, and in the higher forms attains a great extension from before backwards. The notum consists in greater part of a large anterior piece, the meso-scutum, and a

---

[1] *Amer. Natural.* xiv. 1880, p. 313.

[2] For an account of the structures at the tip of the proboscis of this moth, and of the beautiful manner in which the lobes of the maxillae are dovetailed together, see Francis Darwin, *Quart. J. Micr. Sci.* xv. 1875, p. 385. For details as to numerous proboscides, and as to the difficulties that exist in comprehending the exact mode of action of the organ, refer to Breitenbach's papers, especially *Jena. Zeitschr. Naturw.* xv. 1882, p. 151.

[3] See Cholodkovsky, *Zool. Anz.* ix. p. 615 ; Haase, *t.c.* p. 711 ; also Riley, *P. ent. Soc. Washington*, ii. 1892, p. 310.

smaller part, the meso-scutellum behind.   In front of the scutum
there is a piece termed prae-scutum by Burgess.   It is usually
small and concealed by the front part of the scutum ; but
in *Hepialus* it is large and horizontal in position.   It is of
importance as being the chief point of articulation with the prothorax.   The scutellum is more or less irregularly rhomboidal in
form ; its hinder margin usually looks as if it were a lobe or fold
placed in front of the base of the abdomen or metathorax, according to whether the latter is concealed or visible.   In some of the
higher forms this meso-scutellar lobe is prominent, and there
may be seen under its projection a piece that has been called
the post-scutellum, and is really the base of the great mesophragma, a chitinous piece that descends far down into the
interior of the body.   In addition to the front pair of wings the
mesothorax bears on its upper surface another pair of appendages,
the tegulae : in the higher forms they are of large size ; they are
fastened on the front of the mesothorax, and extend backwards
over the joint of the wing with the body, being densely covered
with scales so that they are but little conspicuous.   These
appendages are frequently erroneously called patagia, but have
also been called scapulae, pterygodes, paraptera, and shoulder-
tufts, or shoulder-lappets.   The lower surface of the mesothorax
is much concealed by the large and prominent coxae, but the
sternum and the two pleural pieces on each side, episternum and
epimeron, are easily detected.   The area for attachment of the
anterior wing on each side is considerable, and appears to be of
rather complex structure ; its anatomy has been, however, but
little studied.

   The METATHORAX is small in comparison with the preceding
segment, to which it is intimately co-adapted, though the two
are really connected only by delicate membrane, and can consequently be separated with ease by dissection.   The metanotum
consists of (1) the scutum, which usually appears externally as
an anterior piece on each side ; (2) the scutellum, forming a
median piece placed behind the scutum, which it tends to
separate into two parts by its own extension forwards.   In order
to understand the structure of the metathorax it is desirable to
dissect it off from the larger anterior segment, and it will then
be found that its appearance when undissected is deceptive,
owing to its being greatly arched, or folded in the antero-

posterior direction. A broad, but short phragma descends from the hind margin of the metascutellum into the interior of the body. It should be noted that though the metanotum is forced, as it were, backwards by the great extension of the mesonotum in the middle line of the body, yet at the sides the metanotum creeps forward so as to keep the points of attachment of the hind wings near to those of the front wings. In many forms of Hesperiidae, Sphingidae, Noctuidae, etc. the true structure of the metanotum is further concealed by the back of the mesoscutellum reposing on, and covering it.

Difference of opinion exists as to the thoracic SPIRACLES; there is one conspicuous enough in the membrane behind the pronotum, and it is thought by some writers that no other exists. Westwood and Scudder, however, speak of a mesothoracic spiracle, and Dr. Chapman considers that one exists. Minot describes[1] a structure behind the anterior wing, and thinks it may be an imperfect spiracle, and we have found a similar stigma in *Saturnia pavonia*. At the back of the thorax there is on each side in some Lepidoptera (Noctuidae, *Arctia*, etc.), a curious large cavity formed by a projection backwards from the sides of the metasternum, and a corresponding development of the pleura of the first abdominal segment. Minot and others have suggested that this may be an organ of hearing.

The ABDOMEN differs according to the sex. In the female seven segments are conspicuous dorsally, but only six ventrally, because the first segment is entirely membranous beneath, and is concealed between the second abdominal ventral plate and the posterior coxae. Besides these segments there are at the hind end two others smaller, more or less completely withdrawn into the body, and in certain cases forming an ovipositor. These nine segments are usually considered to constitute the abdomen; but according to Peytoureau,[2] a tenth dorsal plate is represented on either side of the anal orifice, though there is no trace of a corresponding ventral plate. In the male the segments, externally conspicuous, are one more than in the female. According to the authority quoted,[3] this sex has also truly ten abdominal segments, the ninth segment being withdrawn to a greater or

---

[1] *Fourth Rep. U.S. Entom. Commission*, 1885, p. 49.
[2] *C.R. Ac. Sci. Paris*, cxviii. 1894, p. 360; and his *Thesis*, Bordeaux, 1895.
[3] *C.R. Ac. Sci. Paris*, cxviii. 1894, p. 542.

less extent to the inside of the body, and modified to form part of a copulatory apparatus; its dorsal portion bears a process called the "uncus"; the anal orifice opens on the inner face of this process, and below it there is another process—developed to a greater or less extent—called the "scaphium." The ventral portion of the ninth segment bears a lobe, the "saccus" (Peytoureau, *l.c.*). On each side of the ninth abdominal segment there is a process called the "valve," the internal wall of which bears some hook-like or other processes called "harpes"; it is continued as a membrane surrounding the "oedeagus," or penis, and—bearing more or less distinct prominences—connects with the scaphium. In many forms the parts alluded to, other than the valves, are concealed by the latter, which come together when closed, and may be covered externally with scales like the rest of the abdomen. Peytoureau considers that the uncus is really the dorsal plate of a tenth segment, and that the scaphium is the tenth ventral plate. Thus, according to this view, the ninth segment is extensive and complex, being very highly modified in all

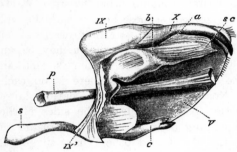

Fig. 160.—*Acherontia atropos.* · The termination of ♂ body, one side removed. *IX*, Ninth dorsal plate; *IX'*, ninth ventral; *s*, lobe, saccus, of ninth ventral plate; *X*, tenth dorsal plate, or uncus; *sc*, scaphium, or tenth ventral plate; *a*, position of anus; *b*, chitinised band of scaphium; *V*, valve or clasper; *c*, hooks, or harpes, of clasper; *p*, penis (or oedeagus). (After Peytoureau.)

its parts: while the tenth segment is greatly reduced. The structure of the male organs is simpler in Lepidoptera, and less varied than it is in the other great Orders of Insects. There are seven pairs of abdominal spiracles on the upper parts of the membranous pleurae.

LEGS.—The legs are long, slender, covered with scales, and chiefly remarkable from the fact that the tibiae sometimes bear articulated spurs on their middle as well as at the tip. The front tibia usually possesses on its inner aspect a peculiar mobile pad; this seems to be in some cases a combing organ; it also often acts as a cover to peculiar scales. The tarsi are five-jointed, with two small claws and a small apparatus, the functional importance of which is unknown, between the claws.

Wings.—The wings are the most remarkable feature of this Order ; it is to them that butterflies owe their beauty, the surfaces of the wings being frequently adorned with colours and patterns of the most charming and effective nature. These effects are due to minute scales that are implanted in the wing-membrane in an overlapping manner, somewhat similar to the arrangement of slates on the roof of a house. The scales are very readily displaced, and have the appearance of a silky dust. We shall describe their structure and allude to their development subsequently. The wings are usually of large size in comparison with the Insect's body : in the genus *Morpho,* the most gorgeous of the butterflies, they are enormous, though the body is small ; so that when deprived of these floats the Insect is insignificant. The great expanse of wing is not correlative with great powers of flight, though it is perhaps indicative of flying with little exertion ; for the small-winged Lepidoptera, Sphingidae, etc., have much greater powers of aërial evolution than the large-winged forms. The area of the wing is increased somewhat by the fact that the scales on the outer margin, and on a part or on the whole of the inner margin, project beyond the edges of the membrane that bears them : these projecting marginal scales are called fringes. In many of the very small moths the actual size of the wing-membranes is much reduced, but in such cases the fringes may be very long, so as to form the larger part of the surface, especially of that of the hind wings. Frequently the hind wings are of remarkable shape, being prolonged into processes or tails, some of which are almost as remarkable as those of *Nemoptera* in the Order Neuroptera.

The wings are very rarely absent in Lepidoptera ; this occurs only in the female sex, no male Lepidopterous imago destitute of wings having been discovered. Although but little is known of the physiology of flight of Lepidoptera, yet it is clearly important that the two wings of the same side should be perfectly coadapted or correlated. This is effected largely by the front wing overlapping the hind one to a considerable extent, and by the two contiguous surfaces being pressed, as it were, together. This is the system found in butterflies and in some of the large moths, such as Lasiocampidae and Saturniidae ; in these cases the hind

wing always has a large shoulder, or area, anterior to its point
of insertion. In most moths this shoulder is absent, but in its
place there are one or more stiff bristles projecting forwards and
outwards, and passing under a little membranous flap, or a tuft
of thick scales on the under face of the front wing ; the bristle is
called the " frenulum," the structure that retains it a " retinaculum."
In *Castnia* (Fig. 162) and in some Sphingidae there is the unusual condition of a highly-developed shoulder (*s*) coexisting with
a perfect frenulum (*f*) and retinaculum (*r*). The frenulum and
retinaculum usually differ in structure, and the retinaculum in
position, in the two sexes of the same moth ; the male, which
in moths has superior powers of flight, having the better retaining
organs. Hampson says " the form of the frenulum is of great
use in determining sex, as in the males of all the forms that
possess it, it consists of hairs firmly soldered together so as to
form a single bristle, whilst in nearly all females it consists of
three or more bristles which are shorter than that of the male ;
in one female Cossid I have found as many as nine. Also in the
large majority of moths the retinaculum descends from the costal
nervure in the male, while in the female it ascends from the
median nervure." [1] This sexual difference in a structure for the
discharge of a function common to the two sexes is a very remarkable fact. There are a few—very few—moths in which the
bases of the hind wings are not well coadapted with the front
wings, and do not possess a frenulum, and these species possess
a small more or less free lobe at the base of the front wing that
droops towards the hind wing, and may thus help to keep up an
imperfect connexion between the pair ; this lobe has been named
a jugum by Professor Comstock. Occasionally there is a jugum
on the hind as well as on the front wing. There is usually a
very great difference between the front and the hind wings ; for
whereas in the front wing the anterior portion is doubtless of
great importance in the act of flight and is provided with
numerous veins, in the hind wing, on the other hand, the corresponding part has not a similar function, being covered by the
front wing ; hence the hind wing is provided with fewer nervures
in the anterior region, the divisions of the subcostal being less
numerous than they are in the front wing. In the moths
possessing a jugum the two wings differ but little from one

[1] *Fauna of British India*, Moths, i. 1892, p. 6.

another, and it is probable that they function almost as four separate wings instead of as two pairs.

WING-NERVURES.—The nervures or ribs of the wings are of great importance in Lepidoptera, as at present they furnish the chief characters for classification and for the discussions of phylogeny that are so numerous in entomological literature. On looking at wings that have been deprived of their scales it will be noticed (Fig. 161) that the ribs are much more numerous at the outer margins than they are near the points of attachment of the wings, and that there is usually but one cell (or area completely enclosed by ribs). This latter point is one of the chief peculiarities of the Lepidopterous wing; in Insect-wings generally the number of cells in proportion to the area of the wings and to the number of nervures is greater than it is in Lepidoptera, for in the latter there are few or no cross-nervures. Hence there is sometimes no closed cell at all on the wing (Fig. 161, II. B). The maximum number of closed cells is six; this is found in some species of *Micropteryx*, while in *Hepialus* there may be three or four; but the rule is that there is only one cell in the Lepidopterous wing. When the number of cells is increased this is not necessarily due to an increase in the cross-nervures; and in fact it is generally due to irregular forking or to the sinuous form of the longitudinal nervures themselves (see wing of *Castnia*, Fig. 162, A.). Some authorities consider that all transverse or cross-veins in Lepidoptera are merely portions of longitudinal veins having diverted courses. When a portion of a nervure beyond the basal or primary portion serves as a common piece to two forked parts external to it, it is called a stalk (Fig. 162, A, *e*). There are cases in which the furcation takes place in the opposite direction, so that a nervure is double at the base of the wing (Fig. 161, I, A, 1*a*, and B, 1*b*). This important condition has not yet been adequately discussed.

Turning to the mode of designation of the nervures,[1] we may

---

[1] It is impossible for us to treat of the difficulties that exist on this point, and we must refer the student to the pamphlet, "The Venation of the Wings of Insects," by Prof. Comstock, Ithaca, 1895, being a reprint, with an important prefatory note, from the *Elements of Insect Anatomy*, by J. H. Comstock and V. L. Kellogg, also to Packard's discussion of the subject in *Mem. Ac. Sci. Washington*, vii. 1895, pp. 84-86. The method of Spuler, alluded to in these two memoirs, is based on development, and, when extended, will doubtless have very valuable results. See Spuler, *Zeitschr. wiss. Zool.* liii. 1892, p. 597.

commence by remarking that no system satisfactory from a
practical as well as from a theoretical point of view has yet been
devised. The diagrams given in figure 161 will enable us to
explain the methods actually in vogue ; I. representing the system,
dating from the time of Herrich-Schaeffer, chiefly used by
British naturalists, and II. that adopted by Staudinger and
Schatz in their recent great work on the Butterflies of the world.
The three anterior nervures in both front and hind wings
correspond fairly well, and are called, looking at them where
they commence at the base of the wing, " costal," " subcostal," and

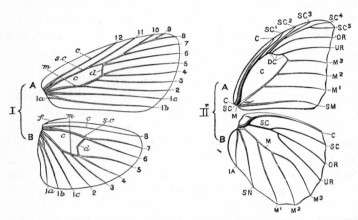

Fig. 161.—Wing-nervuration of Lepidoptera. I, Diagram of moths' wings (after Hampson) ; II, of a butterfly's wings (*Morpho menelaus* ♂, after Staudinger and Schatz).
A, front, **B**, hind wing. I.—*c*, costal ; *sc*, subcostal ; *m*, median ; 1*a*, 1*b*, 1*c*, internal nervures ; *f*, frenulum ; 2, 3, 4, branches of median nervure ; 5, lower
radial ; 6, upper radial· ; 7-11, divisions of the subcostal ; 12, termination of
costal ; *c*, cell ; *d*, discocellular nervure. II.—**C**, costal ; **SC**, subcostal ; **M**, median ;
SM and **SN**, submedian nervures ; **1A**, inner-margin nervure ; **UR**, lower radial ;
OR, upper radial ; **SC**^{1} to **SC**^{5}, divisions of subcostal ; **M**^{1} to **M**^{3}, divisions of median
nervure ; **C**, cell ; **DC**, discocellulars.

" median " nervures. The nervures near the inner margin of the
wing (that is the lower part in our figures) differ much in the front
and hind wings, consisting either of two or of three separate
portions not joined even at the base. British entomologists call
these " branches or divisions of the internal nervure " : the
Germans call the more anterior of them the " submedian," and the
more internal the " inner-margin nervure " ; they are also frequently
called anal nervures. The cross-nervure that closes the cell is
called discocellular ; when apparently composed of two or three

parts joined so as to form angles, the parts are called, according to position, upper, lower, and middle discocellulars. One or more short spurs may exist on the front part of the basal portion of the hind wing; these are called praecostal. The branches or terminal divisions of the nervures should be called nervules; they are usually mentioned by the numbers shewn in the diagram (Fig. 161, I.). In addition to this, it is only necessary to remember that number 2 is always assigned to the posterior division of the median nervure, the nervules below this being all called 1, and distinguished by the addition of a, b, c when requisite. This course is necessary, because if it were not adopted the corresponding nervules on the front and hind wings would bear different numbers.

The use of this system of numbers for the nervules is becoming general, and it answers fairly well for practical purposes. On the other hand, extreme discrepancy exists as to the nomenclature of the nervures and nervules, and there are almost as many systems as there are authorities.

The normal number of nervules is, on the front wing, $11 + 1$ or 2 inner marginal, and on the hind wing $7 + 2$ or 3 inner marginal. In the aberrant moths of the genus *Castnia* the nervuration is unusually complex and irregular (Fig. 162), and an analogous condition occurs in our common Goat-moth (*Cossus ligniperda*). In *Hepialus* and *Micropteryx* (the jugate moths of Comstock) the hind wings are less dissimilar in nervuration from the front wings than they are in other Lepidoptera.[1]

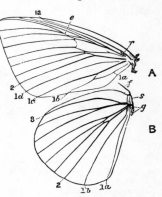

Fig. 162. — Wing - nervuration of *Castnia*. Undersides of, **A**, front, **B**, hind wings. 1*a*, 1*b*, 1*c*, 1*d*, Inner marginal nervures; 2, lower branch of median; 8, subcostal of hind wing; 12, subcostal of front wing; *e*, "stalk" of 8 and 9; *f*, frenulum; *r*, retinaculum; *s*, shoulder; *g*, articulation of wing.

Internal Anatomy.[2]—The alimentary canal extends as a long,

[1] The structure and development of scales and nervures is dealt with as part of the brief study of the development of the wing, on p. 329, etc.

[2] The internal anatomy of Lepidoptera has not been extensively studied. For information refer to Dufour, *C.R. Ac. Paris*, xxxiv. 1852, p. 748; Scudder, *Butt. New England*, i. 1889, p. 47; Minot and Burgess, *Fourth Rep. U. S. Entom. Comm.* 1885, p. 53.

slender oesophagus through the length of the thorax, dilating when it reaches the abdomen to form a tubular stomach; before this it is somewhat enlarged to form an indistinct crop, and gives off a large diverticulum usually called a sucking stomach. According to Burgess, this structure does not possess the function ascribed to it by this name, and he terms it a food-reservoir. The Malpighian tubes are six in number, three on each side, and each set of three unite to form a common tube opening into the posterior extremity of the stomach; behind them the alimentary canal continues in the form of a slender, tortuous intestine, expanding

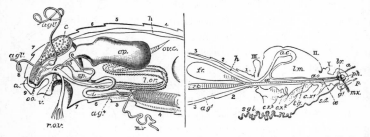

Fig. 163.—Internal anatomy of Lepidoptera. Section of the body of a female butterfly, *Anosia plexippus*. (After Scudder.) The portion to the left of the vertical line more magnified. I. II. III. thoracic segments; 1-9, abdominal segments; *a*, antenna; *a*, anus; *ac*, aortal chamber; *agl*, etc., abdominal ganglia; *agl¹*, *agl²*, accessory glands; *ao*, aorta; *br*, brain; *c*, colon; *cp*, copulatory pouch; *cx¹*, *cx²*, *cx³*, coxae; *fr*, food-reservoir; *g¹*, suboesophageal ganglion; *h*, dorsal vessel; *i*, intestine; *lm*, area filled by wing muscles; *l.or*, ovary, or egg-tubes of left side; *mv*, Malpighian tube (the two others of the right side cut away, except small portions); *mx*, maxilla; *o*, oviduct; *oo*, its orifice; *oe*, oesophagus; *ov.c*, end of left ovary; *p*, labial palp; *ph*, pharynx; *r.ov*, terminal parts of right ovarian tubes, turned to one side, after the tubes have been cut away; *sd*, salivary duct; *sgl*, salivary gland; *sp*, spermatheca; *st*, stomach; *tg*, thoracic ganglia; *v*, copulatory orifice.

at the extremity of the body to form a rectum. The dorsal or circulatory vessel commences near the posterior extremity of the body, but in the front part of the abdomen is deflexed to pass under the great phragma into the thorax, where it rises abruptly to the dorsal wall, but is again abruptly deflexed, forming a loop, and is then prolonged above the oesophagus into the head: at the summit of the thoracic loop there may be a dilatation called the aortal chamber. The supra- and infra-oesophageal ganglia are consolidated into a mass pierced by the oesophagus: there is a minute frontal ganglion; the ventral chain consists of three much approximated thoracic ganglia and four abdominal ganglia separated from the thoracic by a long interval.

The male sexual organs consist of the two testes placed in a common capsule, from which proceed a pair of contiguous vasa deferentia (dilated soon after their origin to form the vesiculae seminales); into each vas there opens a long, tubular gland; the two vasa subsequently unite to form a long, coiled, ejaculatory duct. It is in the structure of the female sexual organs that the most remarkable of the anatomical characters of Lepidoptera is found, there being two external sexual orifices. The imago has, in the great majority of cases, four egg-tubes in each ovary; the pair of oviducts proceeding from them unite to form a single un-paired (azygos) oviduct which terminates by an orifice quite at the posterior extremity of the body. There is a sac, the bursa copulatrix or copulatory pouch, which is prolonged in a tubular manner, to open externally on the eighth ventral plate : a tube, the seminal duct, connects the bursa with the oviduct, and on this tube there may be a dilatation—the spermatheca. Besides these structures two sets of accessory glands open into the oviduct, an unpaired gland, and a pair of glands. The development of these structures has been described by Hatchett Jackson,[1] and exhibits some very interesting features. The exact functions of the bursa copulatrix and of the other structures are by no means clear. According to Riley,[2] the spermatheca in *Pronuba* contains some curious radiate bodies, and Godman and Salvin describe some-thing of the same sort as existing in butterflies. Several varia-tions in the details of the structure of these remarkably complex passages have been described, and the various ducts are some-times rendered more complex by diverticula attached to them. Some noteworthy diversities in the main anatomical features exist. According to Cholodkovsky, there is but one sexual aperture—the posterior one—in *Nematois metallicus;* while, according to Brandt, the number of egg-tubes in a few cases exceeds the normal—four—being in *Sesia scoliaeformis* fourteen. In *Nematois metallicus* there is individual variation, the number of tubes varying from twelve to twenty.

The **egg** has been more extensively studied in Lepidoptera than in any other Order of Insects. It displays great variety : we meet with elongate forms (Fig. 164) and flat forms like buttons, while in *Limacodes* (Fig. 83, Vol. V.) the egg is a

---

[1] *Tr. Linn. Soc. London* (2), v. 1890, p. 143.
[2] *P. ent. Soc. Washington*, ii. 1892, p. 305.

transparent scale of somewhat inconstant outline.   Some are
coloured and mottled somewhat after the fashion of birds'-eggs;
this is the case with some eggs of Lasiocampidae and Liparidae; in
some the sculpture of the egg-shell is of the most elaborate character (Figs. 77, 78, Vol. V.).   The egg-shell or chorion is, according to Korschelt [1] and others, a cuticular product of the epithelium
of the egg-chambers of the ovaries.   The number of eggs deposited
by an individual differs greatly in different species, and has been
ascertained to be variable within certain limits in the same
species.   Speyer thought about 250 to be the average number
of eggs deposited by an individual.   The number in the case of
Aporia crataegi is believed to be from 60 to 100, and in some
Hepialus to be several thousands.   The mode of deposition also

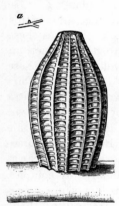

Fig. 164.—Egg of Orange-
tip butterfly, *Euchloe
cardamines*, magni-
fied. *a*, The egg of
natural size on a stalk.

differs greatly; where the eggs are very
numerous they seem to be discharged almost
at random in suitable spots; but moths such
as *Clisiocampa neustria* fasten their eggs
round the stems of the food-plant in a very
perfect and artistic manner.   Butterflies
seem as a rule to prefer to oviposit by placing
an egg here and there rather than risk many
in one situation; but to this there are many
conspicuous exceptions especially in the cases
where the larvae live gregariously, as in the
Vanessae.   Some moths cover the eggs with
fur from their own body, which, in the case
of certain of the Eggers (Lasiocampidae),
seems to have a special supply for the purpose.   The period that intervenes between
deposition and hatching of the eggs varies
from a few days to many months.   There
seems to be, as a rule, comparatively little power of extending the
period of latency beyond a single season; though certain facts
have been recorded that would lead us to believe that in
Australia eggs may last over the proper time during a drought,
and be hatched as soon as rain falls.

Larva.—The young condition or larva of the Lepidopterous
Insect is commonly called a caterpillar.   It is a somewhat
worm-like creature—in old English it was sometimes called

[1] *Acta Ac. German.* li. 1887, p. 238.

palmer-worm——and is composed of a head and thirteen divisions
or segments of the body ; the first three of the latter are called
thoracic, the other ten, abdominal segments ; in most caterpillars
the terminal two or three abdominal segments are more or less
run together, and the ninth may be very small, so that the true
number is indistinct.   The first three segments bear each, on
either side, a short limb, ending in a curved spine ; the next
two (or three or more) segments are destitute of legs, but on
some of the following divisions another kind of leg of a more
fleshy character appears, while the body is terminated by a pair
of these thick legs of somewhat different form.   The front legs
are usually called the true legs, the others prolegs, but this latter
designation is a most unfortunate one, the term " pro " being in
entomology used to signify anterior ; it is therefore better to
call the three anterior pairs thoracic legs, and the others abdominal
feet, distinguishing the hind pair of these latter as claspers.
There is, too, an unfortunate discrepancy amongst entomologists in
their manner of counting the body-segments, some count the head
as the first segment, while others apply this term to the first
thoracic segment.   The latter is the more correct course, for, as
the head is not a single segment it should not be called such in
a terminology that affects to be morphologically exact, not simply
descriptive.   The thoracic legs are transversely jointed (Fig. 165,
B), but this is not the case with the abdominal feet, which are
usually armed beneath with a circle, or with rows, of little hooks.
The thoracic legs are, independent of their form, of a different
nature from the abdominal, for these latter disappear subsequently,
while the former give rise to the legs of the imago.   The number
of thoracic legs is always six, except in a few cases where there
are none at all ; the abdominal feet are much more variable, and
exhibit so many distinctions that we cannot here attempt to
deal with them.   M. Goossens has given a concise and interesting account of this subject,[1] and Speyer [2] a summary of the variety
in number and position.

   The anatomy of the larva is simple in comparison with that
of the perfect Insect ; its main features will be appreciated from
Fig. 165, from which it will be seen that the stomach is
enormous, and the silk-vessels are also very extensive.   There
are three sets of glands opening by canals on the head, viz. the

[1] *Ann. Soc. ent. France*, 1887, pp. 384-404, Pl. 7.   [2] *Isis*, 1845, p. 835.

salivary glands proper, which open into the cavity of the mouth, one close to the base of each mandible; the silk-glands, which terminate by a common canal, continued externally as the spinneret; and the glands of Filippi situate in the head itself, and opening into the ducts of the silk-glands, near their union into a common duct. It should be recollected that Fig. 165 does not indicate all the details of the anatomy; the muscular system, for instance, being entirely omitted, though there are an enormous number of muscles; these however are not very complex, they being mostly repetitions in the successive segments.[1] The mouth-parts are very different from those of the

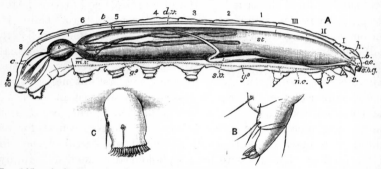

Fig. 165.—**A**, Section of male caterpillar of *Anosia plexippus*—muscular and tracheal systems and fat-body not shown: I, pro-, II, meso-, III, meta-thorax; 1-10, abdominal segments; *b*, supra-oesophageal ganglion; *c*, rectum; *d.v*, dorsal vessel; *g³-g⁹*, ganglia of ventral chain; *h*, head; *i*, intestine; *m.v*, Malpighian tube; *n.c*, nerve-cord of ventral chain; *oe*, oesophagus; *s*, spinneret; *s.o.g*, infra-oesophageal ganglion; *st*, stomach; *s.v*, silk-vessel; *t*, testis. **B**, One of the jointed prothoracic legs. **C**, An abdominal foot with its hooks. (After Scudder and Burgess, magnification about ⅔.)

perfect Insect, inasmuch as the maxillae and labial palpi, which are the most remarkable structures of the imago, are small, and are differently constructed in the caterpillar, while the mandibles, which are the largest organs of the caterpillar, disappear in the adult. The little organ by which the caterpillar exudes its silk is called a spinneret; according to Packard it is a "homologue of the hypopharynx." It is a more or less prominent point on the middle of the labium (Fig. 166, *g*) and sometimes forms a conspicuous spine projecting downwards. The eyes are extremely imperfect organs, consisting merely of six, in some cases

[1] For anatomy of caterpillars refer to Lyonnet's famous work, *Traité anatomique de la chenille qui ronge le bois de saule*, La Haye, 1762.

fewer, transparent, somewhat prominent, little spaces placed on
each side of the lower part of the head; they are called "ocelli,"
by Landois "ocelli compositi." Under each of these external
facets there are placed percipient
structures, apparently very imperfect
functionally, the caterpillar's sight
being of the poorest character.[1] The
spiracles of the caterpillar are nine
on each side, placed one on the first
thoracic segment and one on each of
the first eight abdominal segments;
there are no true stigmata on the
second and third thoracic segments,
though traces of their rudiments or
vestiges are sometimes visible.

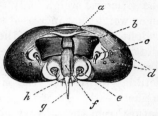

Fig. 166.—Front view of head of
a caterpillar, with the jaws
partially opened. *a*, Labrum;
b, mandible; *c*, antenna; *d*,
ocelli; *e*, maxilla; *f*, lingua; *g*,
spinneret; *h*, labial palp.

In the caterpillar there are no traces of the external sexual
organs, so that the two sexes cannot be distinguished on superficial inspection; it was however long ago demonstrated by
Herold[2] that the ovaries and testes exist in the youngest caterpillars, and undergo a certain amount of growth and development
in the larval instars; the most important feature of which is
that the testes are originally separate but subsequently coalesce
in the middle line of the body, and become enclosed in a common
capsule. In a few forms—especially of Liparidae—(Lymantriidae
of modern authors)—the caterpillars are said to be of different
colours in the two sexes. Most of what is known on this point
has been referred to by Hatchett Jackson.[3]

The SILK-GLANDS of Lepidoptera are of great interest from the
physiological point of view, as well as from the fact that they
have furnished for many ages one of the most beautiful of the
adornments made use of by our own species. The sericteria, or
vessels that secrete silk, are of simple structure, and differ greatly
in their size in the various forms of the Order; they sometimes
become of great length; in the Silk-worm each of the two
vessels is nearly five times as long as the body, while in
Bombyx yamamai and others, even this is exceeded. They

---

[1] See Plateau, *Bull. Ac. Belgique*, xv. 1888, p. 28; in reference to structure of
ocelli, Blanc, *Tête du Bombyx mori* . . . 1891, pp. 163, etc.; and Landois in
Zeitschr. wiss. Zool. xvi. 1866, p. 27.

[2] *Entwickelungsgeschichte der Schmetterlinge*, Cassel, 1815.

[3] *Tr. Linn. Soc. London, Zool.* 2nd Ser., v. 1890, pp. 147, 148.

grow with remarkable rapidity, being in the young silk-worm only 3 mm. long, in the adult 22 mm. The increase in weight is still more remarkable; when the silk-worm is thirty-one days old, the sericteria weigh only 3 mgr., but when the age is fifty days their weight has increased to 541 mgr., being then $\frac{2}{5}$ of the whole weight of the body. In the pupa they undergo a gradual atrophy, and in the moth they are, according to Helm, no longer to be found, though earlier authors were of a contrary opinion.[1] According to Joseph,[2] the silk-vessels begin to develop at an extremely early age of the embryo, and are very different in their nature from the salivary glands, the former being derivatives of the external integument (ectoderm), while the salivary glands belong to the alimentary system. This view is to some extent confirmed by the observations of Gilson as to the different manner in which these two sets of glands discharge their functions.

The chief feature in the anatomy of the larva is the great size of the stomach. There is a very short oesophagus and crop; the latter becomes enlarged, spreading out so as to form the stomach, a great sac occupying the larger part of the body-cavity (Fig. 165). On the hinder end of this sac the Malpighian tubes open; they are similar in their disposition to those of the imago; behind the stomach the canal expands into two successive, short dilatations, the first called an intestine, the second a rectum; they are connected by very short isthmuses. The dorsal vessel is a simple, slender tube, extending from the eighth abdominal segment to the head. The main nervous system consists of supra- and infra-oesophageal ganglia, a small frontal ganglion, and a ventral chain of eleven ganglia, three thoracic and eight abdominal, the last of these latter being double. The sexual organs are quite rudimentary, and the passages connected with them very incompletely developed.

Pupa.—The pupa, which is one of the most remarkable of the instars of an Insect's life, attains its highest development in Lepidoptera. The Lepidopterous pupa is frequently called a " chrysalis," a term originally applied to certain metallic butterfly pupae. The Lepidopterous pupa differs from that of other Insects in the fact that its outer skin forms a hard shell, all the appendages of

---

[1] For information as to the structure and function of the silk-vessels, refer to Helm, *Zeitschr. wiss. Zool.* xxvi. 1876, p. 434; and Gilson, *La Cellule*, vi. 1890, p. 116.   [2] *Jahresber. Schlesisch. Ges.* lviii. 1881, p. 116.

the body being glued together by an exudation so as to form a single continuous outer skin. This form of perfect pupa is called " pupa obtecta." The obtected pupa is exhibited in various stages of perfection in the Lepidoptera ; the maximum of perfection is attained by the pupae of such butterflies as are exposed without protection or concealment ; on the other hand, we find in various small moths conditions of the pupa that do not differ in any marked manner from the pupae of Insects of other Orders. Moreover, certain Coleoptera and Diptera exhibit obtected pupae of a more or less perfect kind. Hence the pupa obtecta is to be considered as a perfected condition that exists more frequently in the Lepidoptera than in other Orders.

The pupa has no orifices to the alimentary canal or sexual

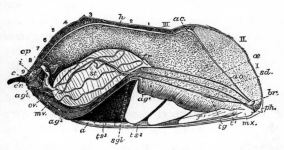

Fig. 167.—Section of female pupa of *Anosia plexippus*, 3-4 days old. I, pro-, II, meso-, III, meta-thorax ; 1-9, abdominal segments ; *a*, antenna (?) ; *ac*, aortal chamber ; *ag¹ - ag⁵*, abdominal ganglia ; *a g l*, accessory glands ; *ao*, aorta ; *br*, brain ; *c*, colon ; *cp*, bursa copulatrix ; *cr*, cremaster ; *f¹*, first femur ; *fr*, food-reservoir ; *h*, dorsal vessel ; *i*, part of intestine ; *mv*, Malpighian tube ; *mx*, base of maxilla ; *oe*, oesophagus ; *ov*, ovary ; *ph*, pharynx ; *sd*, salivary duct ; *sgl*, salivary gland ; *st*, stomach ; *t¹*, first tarsus ; *tg*, compound thoracic ganglion ; *ts²*, *ts³*, second and third tarsus.. (After Scudder.)

organs, but the respiratory openings are pervious. It has no means of locomotion, but it can move a certain number of the posterior segments (the number variable according to kind). In some cases it is provided with spines, " adminicula," by means of which, aided by the wriggling movements of the abdominal segments, considerable changes of position can be effected. The pupae of the genus *Micropteryx* apparently use the legs for locomotion, as do the pupae of Trichoptera.

The study of the pupa of Lepidoptera is less advanced than that of the imago and larva, between which it is, in many points of structure, intermediate.[1] The interior of the pupa contains a

---

[1] The student will find important information as to the varieties of external form of pupae in Dr. T. A. Chapman's writings ; see especially *Tr. ent. Soc. London*, 1893, 1894, and 1896.

quantity of cream-like matter, including the results of histolysis
—but this, as well as the condition of the internal organs, differs
much according to whether the change from the caterpillar to
the moth is much or little advanced.

Many pupae are protected by cocoons. These are masses of silk
—very various in form—disposed by the caterpillar around itself
during the last stage of its existence. Some of these cocoons are
so perfect that the moth has considerable difficulty in escaping
when the metamorphosis is complete. Various devices are used
for the purpose of emergence ; the Puss-moth excretes a corrosive
fluid, containing potassium hydroxide, and then protects itself
from this by retaining on the head while passing through it a
shield formed of a portion of the pupa-skin.[1] Lepidopterous pupae
usually have the body terminated by a projection of very various
and peculiar form called "cremaster." In certain cases these
projections are used for the suspension of the pupa, and are then
frequently provided with hooks (Fig. 177, C, D). In other cases
the cremaster is frequently called the anal armature (Fig. 205, B).

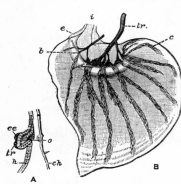

FIG. 168.—Wing-rudiments of *Pieris
brassicae.* **A,** Rudiments of a wing
before the first moult of the caterpillar : *ce,* embryonic cells ; *ch,* external cuticle ; *h,* hypodermis ; *o,*
opening of the invagination ; *tr,*
trachea. **B,** posterior wing-rudiment
of full-grown caterpillar ; *b,* semi-
circular pad ; *c,* a bundle of the
rolled tracheae ; *e,* envelope ; *i,* pedicel ; *tr,* trachea. (After Gonin.)

The **development** of the **wings**
of Lepidoptera has recently been
much studied. It has been known
since the time of Lyonnet, that
the rudiments of the wings exist
inside the body of the caterpillar
when it is nearly adult. Verson
considers that he has detected the
rudiments in the silk-worm larva
even before hatching, and he
attributes their origin to a
modification of form of those
hypodermal cells that occupy
the spots where the spiracles
of the second and third thoracic segments might be looked
for. (It will be recollected that
there are no spiracles on these
two thoracic segments in Lepidopterous larvae). Gonin has
examined the wing-rudiments in the caterpillar, a few days old, of

[1] Latter, *Tr. ent. Soc. London,* 1895, p. 399.

Pieris brassicae,[1] and finds that the future wing is then indicated by a thickening and bagging inwards of the hypodermis, and by some embryonic cells and a trachea in close relation with this mass (Fig. 168, A). The structure grows so as to form a sac projecting to the interior of the body, connected with the body-wall by a pedicel, and penetrated by a trachea forming branches consisting of rolled and contorted small tracheae (Fig. 168, B). If the body-wall be dissected off the caterpillar immediately before pupation the wings appear in crumpled form, as shown in Fig. 169. This fact was known to the older entomologists, and gave rise to the idea that the butterfly could be detected in a caterpillar by merely stripping off the integument.

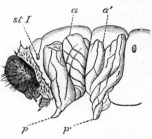

FIG. 169.—Anterior parts of a caterpillar of *P. brassicae,* the body-wall having been dissected off, immediately before pupation. *a, a',* Anterior and posterior wings; *st I,* first spiracle; *p, p',* second and third legs. (After Gonin.)

The exact mode by which the wings become external at the time of appearance of the chrysalis is not ascertained; but it would appear from Gonin's observations that it is not by a process of evagination, but by destruction of the hypodermis lying outside the wing. However this may be, it is well known that, when the caterpillar's skin is finally shed and the chrysalis appears, the wings are free, external appendages, and soon become fastened down to the body by an exudation that hardens so as to form the shell of the chrysalis.

Scales and nervures.——Before tracing the further development it will be well to discuss the structure of the scales and nervures that form such important features in the Lepidopterous wing.

If a section be made of the perfect wing of a Lepidopteron, it is found that the two layers or walls of the wing are firmly held together by material irregularly arranged, in a somewhat columnar manner. The thickness of the wing is much greater where the section cuts through a nervure (Fig. 170, A). The nervures apparently differ as to the structures found in them. Spuler observed in a nervure of *Triphaena pronuba,* a body having in section a considerable diameter, that he considered to be a

[1] *Bull. Soc. Vaudoise,* xxx. 1894, No. 115.

trachea, and also a " wing-rib " and blood-cells. He remarks that even in nervures, perfectly formed as to their chitinous parts, either wing-rib or trachea or both may be absent.[1] Schäffer[2] was unable to find any tracheae in the completed wings he examined, and he states that the matrix of the tracheae and even their inner linings disappear. The wing-ribs were, however, found by him to be present (Fig. 170, A and B).

The scales that form so conspicuous a feature in Lepidoptera exist in surprising profusion, and

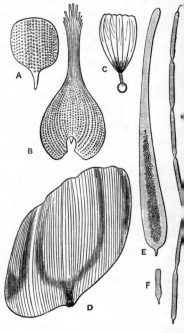

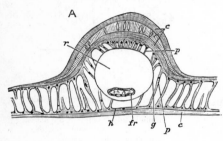

FIG. 170.—Structure of wing of imago. **A,** Transverse section of basal portion of wing [of *Vanessa ?*] containing a nervure ; *c,* cuticle ; *fr,* wing-rib ; *g,* wall of nervure ("Grundmembran") ; *h,* hypodermis ; *p,* connecting columns : *r,* lumen of nervure ; **B,** section of a rib ; *b,* one of the chitinous projections ; *str,* central rod. (After Schäffer.)

FIG. 171.—Scales of male *Lepidoptera.* **A,** Scale from upper surface of *Everes comyntas ;* **B,** from upper surface of *Pieris rapae ;* **C,** from inner side of fold of inner margin of hind wing of *Laertias philenor ;* **D,** one of the cover-scales from the costal androconium of *Eudamus proteus ;* **E, F, G,** scales from androconium of *Thorybes pylades.* (After Scudder).

are of the most varied forms. They may be briefly described as delicate, chitinous bags ; in the completed state these bags are flattened, so as to bring the sides quite, or very nearly, together. Their colour is due to contained pigments, or to striation of the exposed surface of the scale ; the latter condition

[1] *Zeitschr. wiss. Zool.* liii. 1892, p. 623. [2] *Zool. Jahrb. Anat.* iii. 1889, p. 646.

giving rise to metallic "interference-colours." The walls of the
scales are themselves, in some cases, tinted with pigment. It is
said that some of the scales contain air, and that the glistening
whiteness of certain scales is due to this. The exposed surface of
the scale usually differs from the
surface that is pressed down on
the wing in being delicately and
regularly striated; the colours
of the upper and under surfaces
of a scale may also be quite
different. Scales are essentially
of the nature of hairs, and all
the transitions between hairs and
true scales may be found on the
wings of certain Lepidoptera that
bear both hairs and scales, e.g.
Ithomia. It has been calculated

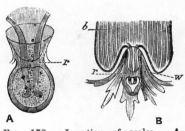

FIG. 172. — Insertion of scales. **A,**
Socket holding the stalk in *Galleria
mellonella;* **B,** insertion of the scale
of *Polyommatus phloeas.* *b,* Base of
scale ; *r,* holding-ring ; *w,* surface of
wing. (After Spuler.)

that there are a million and a half of scales on the wings of an
individual of the genus *Morpho.* The scales are arranged on
the wing in an overlapping manner, somewhat like slates on the
roof of a house. Each scale has a short stalk, and is maintained
in position by the stalk fitting into a cavity in a projection of
the wing-membrane (Fig. 172).

Androconia. — The males of numerous butterflies possess
scales peculiar in kind and various in arrangement. They may
be either irregularly scattered over the wing, or they may form
very complex definite structures (Fig. 173). They were formerly
called " plumules," but Scudder has replaced this name by the
better one, " androconia." The function of the androconia is
still obscure. An odour is believed to be connected with them.
Thomas supposes [1] that these scales are hollow tubes in connection with glands at their bases, and that matter secreted by the
glands passes through the scales and becomes diffused. In
nearly all Lepidoptera it is the male that seeks the female ; if
therefore odorous scales were present in one sex only we should
have supposed that this would have been the female rather than
the male. As, however, the reverse is the case, the function of
the androconia is supposed to be that of charming the female.
Scudder considers that the covering part of the androconial

---

[1] *Amer. Natural.,* xxvii. 1893, p. 1018.

structures is sometimes ornamental. As a rule, however, the
"brands" of male Lepidoptera detract from their beauty to
our eyes.

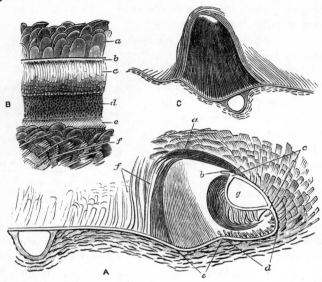

FIG. 173.—**A**, section of part of wing showing the complex androconia of *Thanaos tages*,
a Skipper butterfly. The turning over of the costal margin of the wing is in this
case part of the arrangement. *a*, Upper covering-scales attached to the costal
portion of the under surface of the wing ; *b*, edge of costal margin of the wing ;
c, costal nervure with its scales ; *d*, field of the wing next the costal nervure, bearing
stunted scales ; *e*, the androconia proper, or male scales ; *f*, posterior covering
scales ; *g*, lumen of the costal nervure : **B**, a portion of the costal area flattened
out and seen from above ; lettering as before : **C**, section of androconium on the
second nervure of *Argynnis paphia*. (After Aurivillius.)

Resuming our consideration of the **development** of the **wings,**
we may remark that the history of the changes during the
pupal state is still imperfect. By the changes of relative size
of the thoracic segments the hind wing is brought to lie under
the anterior one (*i.e.* between it and the body), so that in the
newly formed pupa the arrangement is that shown in Fig. 174.
The wings are two sacs filled with material surrounding peritracheal spaces in which run tracheae. The subsequent history
of the tracheae is very obscure, and contrary opinions have been
expressed as to their growth and disappearance. We have
alluded to the fact that in some nervures tracheae are present,
while in others they are absent ; so that it is quite possible that

the histories of the formation of the nervures and of their
relation to tracheae are different in various Lepidoptera.   This
conclusion is rendered more probable by the statement of Comstock and Needham,[1] that in some Insects the "peritracheal
spaces" that mark out the position of
the future nervures are destitute of
tracheae.   Gonin thinks the nervures
are derived from the sheaths of the
peritracheal spaces, and a review of all
the facts suggests that the tracheae
have only a secondary relation to the
nervures, and that the view that a
study of the pupal tracheae may be
looked on as a study of the preliminary state of the nervures is not
sufficiently exact.   It is, however,
probable that in Lepidoptera the
pupal tracheae play an important
though not a primary part in the
formation of the nervures ; possibly
this may be by setting up changes in
the cells near them by means of the
air they supply.   Semper long ago
discovered hypodermal cylinders traversed by a string (Fig. 170, B),
placed near the tracheae in the

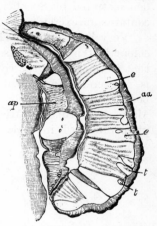

Fig. 174.—Transverse section of
part of the newly disclosed
chrysalis of *Pieris brassicae*,
showing the position and structure of the wings, hanging
from one side of the body.
aa, Anterior wing ; *ap*, posterior wing ; *e, e,* peritracheal
spaces ; *t, t,* tracheae. (After
Gonin.)

pupa.[2]   It appears probable that the "wing-ribs" found in
the nervures (Fig. 170, A *fr* and B) are the final state of these
cylinders, but the origin and import of the cylinders are still
unknown.

The formation of the scales of the wing commences very
early—apparently soon after the casting of the larval skin—
though the completion of the scales and their pigmentation is
delayed to a late period of the pupal life.   The scales are formed
by special cells of the hypodermis that are placed deeper in the
interior of the wing than the other hypodermal cells.   Each
scale is formed by one cell, and protrudes through the over-
lying hypodermis ; the membrane into which the scales are
inserted is a subsequently developed structure, and the beautiful

[1] *Amer. Natural.*, xxxii. 1898, p. 256.   [2] *Zeitschr. wiss. Zool.* viii. 1857, p. 326.

articulation of the scale with the wing takes place by a division
of the stalk of the scale where it is encompassed by the membrane.   Semper was not able to show that the scale-forming
cells are certainly hypodermal cells, but this has since been
demonstrated by Schäffer, who also shows that each of the cells
contains an excretory vesicle.

Very little is positively known as to the development of the
colour in the wing-scales.   It has been pointed out by Hopkins [1]
that in some cases the colours are of the nature of urates ; that
is, of excretory matter of the kind that usually passes from the
body by direct channels, and in the case of Lepidoptera, by the
Malpighian tubes.   Miss Newbigin suggests that the organic
pigments used in scale-coloration will be found to be of two

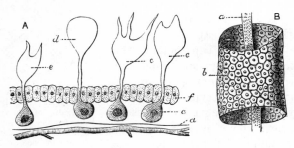

FIG. 175.—Early condition of scales and nervures.   (After Semper.)   **A**, Section of
portion of wing of pupa of *Sphinx pinastri* ; *a*, basal membrane with trachea
beneath it ; *c*, scale-forming cell ; *d*, early state of a scale ; *e, e*, more advanced
stages ; *f*, hypodermal cells.   **B**, part of a cellular cylinder that excretes the
nervure [or more probably the rib or "Rippe" of Schäffer ; cf. Fig. 170, B] ; *b*.
epithelial [hypodermal] cells ; *a*, central string [supposed by Semper to be a nerve].

kinds, urates and melanins, the urates being derivatives from nitro-
genous, the melanins from carbonaceous, matters.[2]   Marchal, who
has devoted a great deal of attention to the study of the Malpighian tubes, informs us that the subdermal pigments of caterpillars are frequently in large part deposits of urates, and he is
of opinion that, the function of the Malpighian tubes being
arrested at certain periods of the metamorphosis, elimination of
the matter they separate when functionally active then takes
place in a variety of other ways.[3]   A similar condition as to
the melanin-pigments and the respiratory functions appears also

[1] *Phil. Trans.* 186 B, 1896, No. 15.   [2] *Natural Science*, viii. 1896, p. 94.
[3] *Bull. Soc. ent. France*, 1896, p. 257.

probable.   The scales when first formed are pallid, and the physiology of their pigmentation is not fully ascertained; it is, however, known that when the scales are pallid the hypodermis is
either pigmented or in close contact with pigmentary matter,
and that as the scales become coloured this pigmentation of the
hypodermis diminishes; so that it is clear that the colour of
the scales is obtained from matter in the interior of the developing wing, and probably by the agency of the hypodermis.

The pattern on the wings of Lepidoptera is formed before
the emergence from the pupa.   In the Tortoiseshell butterfly,
according to Schäffer, it commences to appear about the ninth
day of the pupal life, and the pattern is completed about the
eleventh or twelfth day.   He also states that the process varies
in its rapidity, and this, he thinks, may depend on the previous
condition of the larva.   According to Buckell the pupa of
Nemeobius lucina is sufficiently transparent to allow the development of the colour of the imago to be watched.   He says that
the coloration occurred first in front; that its entire production
occupied less than twenty-four hours, and only commenced about
forty-eight hours before the imago emerged.[1]   When the butterfly leaves the pupal skin the wings are soft, crumpled sacs, of
comparatively small size, but, as everyone knows, they rapidly
expand and become rigid; the physiology of this process is
apparently still unknown.

A great deal of evidence, both direct and indirect, has
accumulated showing that the organisation of many Lepidoptera
is excessively sensitive, so that slight changes of condition produce remarkable results; and it has also been shown that in the
early part of the life this sensitiveness is especially great at the
period of ecdysis.   Numerous butterflies produce more than one
generation a year, and sometimes the generations are so different
that they have passed current with entomologists as distinct
species.   The phenomena of this character are styled " seasonal
variations " or " seasonal dimorphism."   It has, however, been
shown that, by careful management, the eggs of a generation (say
form *a*) may be made to produce form *a*, whereas in the usual
course of nature they would produce form *b*.   A very remarkable
condition is exhibited by the North American *Papilio ajax*.   There
are three forms of the species, known as *P. ajax, P. telamonides,*

[1] *Ent. Record*, vi. 1895, p. 258.

and *P. marcellus.* It is uncertain how many generations there may be in one year of this species, as the length of the life-cycle varies greatly according to circumstances. But in West Virginia all the butterflies of this species that emerge from the chrysalis before the middle of April are the form *marcellus;* those produced between the middle of April and the end of May are *telamonides;* while those that appear after this are *ajax.* *P. telamonides* is not, however, the offspring of *marcellus,* for both forms emerge from pupae that have passed through the winter (and are the offspring of *ajax*), those that emerge early being *marcellus,* those that appear later *telamonides.*

In various parts of Asia and Africa the butterflies produced during the wet season differ more or less markedly from those of the same species produced during the dry season. These are called " wet " and " dry season " forms. Their aetiology has not been investigated, this discovery being comparatively recent.

Turning to the early life we find that some larvae vary in colour, and that this variation is sometimes of a definite character, the larva being one of two different colours—green or brown. In other cases the variation of the species is less definitely dimorphic, a considerable range of variation being exhibited by the species. In tracing the life-histories of Lepidopterous larvae it is not rare to find species in which the larva abruptly changes its form and colour in the middle of its life, and so completely that no one would believe the identity of the individual in the two successive conditions had it not been shown by direct observation; in these cases the change in appearance is usually associated with a change in habits, the larva being, perhaps, a miner in leaves in its first stages, and an external feeder subsequently. In the case of the larval variation we have alluded to above, it is understood that there is no marked change of habits. Poulton has shown [1] that it is not infrequent for some of these latter kinds of variable larvae to change colour during life, and he considers that light or conditions of illumination, that he speaks of as " phytoscopic," are the inducing causes. Great difference is, however, exhibited according to species, some variable species not being so amenable to these influences as others are. In dimorphic forms the change was observed to take place at a moult, the larva changing its skin

---

[1] *Trans. ent. Soc. London,* 1892, p. 293, etc.

and appearing of another colour. In some cases the result of the change was to bring the colour of the larva into harmony with its surroundings, but in others it was not so. During the final stage many larvae are susceptible, the result being made evident only when the pupa is disclosed. Variably coloured pupae of certain species of butterflies have long been known, and it has been shown that some of the varieties can be induced by changing the surroundings. The result of the changes is in certain cases correspondence between the colour of the individual and its surroundings. In the case of other species having pupae of variable colour, the colour of the pupa is without relation to, or harmony with, the surroundings.

Experiments have been made on pupae by Merrifield and others, with the result of showing that by changes of temperature applied at certain moments some of the colours or marks of the butterfly that will emerge can be altered.

It is found that in certain localities the colour of various kinds of butterflies more or less agrees, while it differs from that of the same butterflies found in other localities. Thus Weir speaks of a duskiness common to various butterflies in Java, and calls it "phaeism"; and Bates states that in the Amazon valley numerous species of butterflies vary in a similar manner, as regards colour, in a locality. This phenomenon is now called " homoeochromatism," and is supposed to be due to the effect of local conditions on a susceptible organisation, though there is no experimental evidence of this.

Mimicry.—There are many cases in Lepidoptera of species that depart more or less strongly in appearance from those forms to which they are considered to be allied, and at the same time resemble more or less closely species to which they are less allied. This phenomenon is called mimicry.[1] Usually the resembling forms are actually associated during life. Bates, who observed this phenomenon in the Amazon valley, thought that it might be accounted for by the advantage resulting to the exceptionally coloured forms from the resemblance;[2] it being assumed that these were unprotected, while the forms they resembled were

---

[1] The term mimicry is sometimes used in a wider sense; but we think it better to limit it to its original meaning. The word is a most unfortunate one, being both inadequate and inaccurate.

[2] *Trans. Linn. Soc.* xxiii. 1862, p. 507.

believed to be specially protected by nauseous odours or taste. It was, in fact, thought that the destroying enemies were deceived by the resemblance into supposing that the forms that were in reality edible were inedible. This subject has been greatly discussed, and in the course of the discussion numerous cases that could not be accounted for by Bates's hypothesis have been revealed. One of these is the fact that resemblances of the kind alluded to very frequently occur amongst inedible forms. This also has been thought to be accounted for by a supposed advantage to the Insects; it being argued that a certain number of " protected " forms are destroyed by enemies the instincts of which are faulty, and which therefore always require to learn by individual experience that a certain sort of colour is associated with a nasty taste. The next step of the argument is that it will be an advantage to a protected butterfly to form part of a large association of forms having one coloration, because the ignorant enemies will more easily learn the association of a certain form of coloration with nastiness ; moreover such destruction as does occur will be distributed over a larger number of species, so that each species of a large, similarly coloured, inedible association will have a less number of its individuals destroyed. It is scarcely a matter for surprise that many naturalists are very sceptical as to these explanations ; especially as the phenomena are supposed to have occurred in the past, so that they cannot be directly verified or disproved. It has not, however, been found, as a matter of fact, that even unprotected butterflies are much destroyed in the perfect state by birds. Moreover, in endeavouring to realise the steps of the process of development of the resemblance, we meet with the difficulty that the amount of resemblance to the model that is assumed to be efficient at one step of the development, and to bring safety, is at the next step supposed to be inefficient and to involve destruction. In other words, while analysis of the explanation shows that it postulates a peculiar and well-directed discriminative power, and a persistent selection on the part of the birds, observation leads to the belief that birds have been but little concerned in the matter. If we add to this that there is no sufficient evidence that the species now similar were ever dissimilar (as it is supposed they were by the advocates of the hypothesis), we think it is clear that the explanation from our point of view is of but little importance.[1]   The comparatively simple, hypothetical explanation, originally promulgated by Bates, is sometimes called Batesian mimicry; while the "inedible association" hypothesis is termed Müllerian mimicry.

There is one branch of the subject of mimicry that we think of great interest.   This is the resemblance between Insects of different Orders; or between Insects of the same Order, but belonging to groups that are essentially different in form and appearance.   It is not infrequent for beetles to resemble Hymenoptera, and it is still more frequent for Lepidoptera to resemble Hymenoptera, and that not only in colour and form, but also in movements and attitude.   Druce says: "Many of the species of Zygaenidae are the most wonderful of all the moths; in some cases they so closely resemble Hymenoptera that at first sight it is almost impossible to determine to which Order they belong."[2] W. Müller says: "The little Lepidoptera of the family Glaucopides, that are so like certain wasps as to completely deceive us, have when alive exactly the same manner of holding their wings, the same restless movements, the same irregular flight as a wasp."[3] Seitz and others record a case in which a Brazilian *Macroglossa* exactly resembles a humming-bird, in company with which it flies; and the same naturalist also tells us [4] of a Skipper butterfly that greatly resembles a grasshopper of the genus *Tettix*, and that moreover makes movements like the jumping of grasshoppers. In most of these cases the probabilities of either original similarity, arrested evolution, or the action of similar conditions are excluded: and the hypothesis of the influence, by some means or other, of one organism on another is strongly suggested.

The **classification** of Lepidoptera was said by Latreille a century ago to be a reproach to entomologists.   Since that time an enormous number of new species and genera have been described, but only recently has much advance been made in

[1] A summary of the chief aspects of the question is contained in Beddard's *Animal Coloration*, London, 1892.   An account of the subject with numerous illustrations has been given by Haase, "Untersuchungen über die Mimicry," *Bibl. Zool.* iii. 1893, Heft viii.   Those who wish to see the case as stated by an advocate may refer to Professor Poulton's work, *The Colours of Animals* (International Scientific Series), lxviii. London, 1890.

[2] *P. Zool. Soc. London*, 1883, p. 372.

[3] *Kosmos*, xix. 1886, p. 353.   The Insects alluded to by both these naturalists are now, we believe, placed in the Family Syntomidae (see p. 388).

[4] *Stett. ent. Zeit.* li. 1891, p. 264 ; and lvi. 1895, p. 234.

the way of improvement of classification. The progress made has been limited to a better comprehension and definition of the families. The nervuration of the wings is the character most in vogue for this purpose. As regards the larger groups, and Phylogeny, there is a general opinion prevalent to the effect that Micropterygidae, Eriocephalidae and Hepialidae are in a comparatively primitive condition, but as to the relations of these families one with the other, or with other Lepidoptera, there is a wide difference of opinion.

The primary divisions of the family most often met with in literature are :—either Rhopalocera (= butterflies) and Hetero-

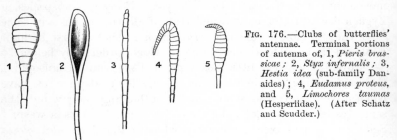

Fig. 176.—Clubs of butterflies' antennae. Terminal portions of antenna of, 1, *Pieris brassicae* ; 2, *Styx infernalis* ; 3, *Hestia idea* (sub-family Danaides) ; 4, *Eudamus proteus*, and 5, *Limochores taumas* (Hesperiidae). (After Schatz and Scudder.)

cera (= moths); or Macrolepidoptera and Microlepidoptera; the Macrolepidoptera including the butterflies and large moths, the Microlepidoptera being limited to the families Tineidae (now itself in process of division into numerous families) and Tortricidae ; some entomologists including also Pyralidae, Pterophoridae and Orneodidae in Microlepidoptera. The division of all Lepidoptera into two series is merely a temporary device necessitated by imperfect acquaintance with morphology. The division into Macro- and Micro- lepidoptera is entirely unscientific.

Series 1. *Rhopalocera* or Butterflies.—Antennae knobbed at the tip or thickened a little before the tip, without pectinations, projecting processes, or conspicuous arrangements of cilia. Hind wings without a frenulum, but with the costal nervure strongly curved at the base (Fig. 161, II, B).

Series II. *Heterocera* or Moths.—Antennae various in form, only rarely knobbed at the tip, and in such cases a frenulum present. In the large majority a frenulum is present, and the costal nervure of the hind-wing is either but little arched at the base (as in Fig. 161, I, B) or it has a large area between it and the front margin ; but in certain families the hind wing is formed much as in Rhopalocera.

It may be inferred from these definitions that the distinction between the two sub-Orders is neither sharply defined nor of great importance. The club of the antenna of the Rhopalocera exhibits considerable variety in form (Fig. 176).[1] Butterflies are as a rule diurnal in their activity and moths nocturnal; but in the tropics there are numerous Heterocera that are diurnal, and many of these resemble butterflies not only in colour but even in the shapes of their wings.

Series I. Rhopalocera. Butterflies.

Classification and Families of Butterflies. — Although considerable unanimity exists as to the natural groups of butterflies, there is much diversity of opinion as to what divisions are of equivalent value—some treating as sub-families groups that others call families—and as to the way the families should be combined. There is, however, a general agreement that the Hesperiidae are the most distinct of the families, and E. Reuter considers them a distinct sub-Order with the name Grypocera.[2]

Four categories may be readily distinguished, as follows, viz. :—

1. The majority of butterflies ; having the first pair of legs more or less strikingly different from the other pairs ; frequently very much smaller and not used as legs ; when not very small, then differing according to sex of the same species, being smaller in the male than in the female ; the part most peculiar is the tarsus, which is modified in various manners, but in the males of this great series is always destitute of its natural form of a succession of simple joints five in number. There is no pad on the front tibia.
    Fam. NYMPHALIDAE, ERYCINIDAE, LYCAENIDAE.
    [The distinctions between these three families are found in the amount and kind of the abortion of the front legs ; for definition refer to the heading of each of the families.]
2. The front legs are in general form like the other pairs ; their tibiae have no pads ; the claws of all the feet are bifid, and there is an empodium in connection with them.   Fam. PIERIDAE.

---

[1] For an account of the antennæ of butterflies, see Jordan, *Nov. Zool.* v. 1898, pp. 374-415.

[2] Haase first proposed the name Netrocera (*Deutsche ent. Zeit. Lep.* iv. 1891, p. 1) for Hesperiidae, as a division distinct from all other butterflies ; Karsch replaced the name in the following year by Grypocera, because *Netrocera* is the name of a genus.

3. The front legs are like the other pairs; their tibiae however possess
   pads; the claws are large, not bifid, and there is no empodium;
   the metanotum is completely exposed at the base of the abdomen.
                                             Fam. PAPILIONIDAE.
4. The front legs are like the other pairs; their tibiae however possess
   pads; the claws are small, toothed at the base, and there is an
   empodium; the metanotum is concealed by the prolonged and
   overhanging mesonotum.   Fam. HESPERIIDAE.

The relations between the families Erycinidae, Lycaenidae,
and Nymphalidae are very intimate. All these have the front
legs more or less modified, and the distinctions between the
families depend almost entirely on generalisations as to these
modifications. These facts have led Scudder to associate the
Lycaenidae and Erycinidae in one group, which he terms
"Rurales." It is however difficult to go so far and no farther;
for the relations between both divisions of Rurales and the
Nymphalidae are considerable. We shall subsequently find that
the genus *Libythea* is by many retained as a separate family,
chiefly because it is difficult to decide whether it should be
placed in Erycinidae or in Nymphalidae. Hence it is difficult to
see in this enormous complex of seven or eight thousand species
more than a single great Nymphalo-Lycaenid alliance. The
forms really cognate in the three families are however so few,
and the number of species in the whole is so very large, that it
is a matter of great convenience in practice to keep the three
families apart. It is sufficient for larger purposes to bear in
mind their intimate connexions.

The Papilionidae and Pieridae are treated by many as two
sub-divisions of one group. But we have not been able to find
any justification for this in the existence of forms with connecting characters. Indeed it would, from this point of view,
appear that the Pieridae are more closely connected with the
Lycaenidae and Erycinidae than they are with Papilionidae;
in one important character, the absence of the pad of the front
tibia, the Nymphalo-Lycaenids and the Pierids agree. It has
also been frequently suggested that the Papilionidae (in the
larger sense just mentioned) might be associated with the
Hesperiidae. But no satisfactory links have been brought to
light; and if one of the more lowly Hesperiids, such as *Thanaos*,
be compared with one of the lower Papilionidae, such as
Parnassius, very little approximation can be perceived.

It appears, therefore, at present that Hesperiidae, Papilionidae, Pieridae, and the Nymphalo-Lycaenid complex are naturally distinct. But in the following review of the families and sub-families of butterflies, we shall, in accordance with the views of the majority of Lepidopterists, treat the Lycaenidae and Erycinidae as families distinct from both Nymphalidae and Pieridae.[1]

The number of described species of butterflies is probably about 13,000; but the list is at present far from complete; forms of the largest size and most striking appearance being still occasionally discovered. Forty years ago the number known was not more than one-third or one-fourth of what it is at present, and a crowd of novelties of the less conspicuous kinds is brought to light every year. Hence it is not too much to anticipate that 30,000, or even 40,000 forms may be acquired if entomologists continue to seek them with the enthusiasm and industry that have been manifested of late. On the other hand, the species of Rhopalocera seem to be peculiarly liable to dimorphic, to seasonal and to local variation; so that it is possible that ultimately the number of true species—that is, forms that do not breed together actually or by means of intermediates, morphological or chronological—may have to be considerably reduced.

In Britain we have a list of only sixty-eight native butterflies, and some even of these are things of the past, while others are only too certainly disappearing. New Zealand is still poorer, possessing only eighteen; and this number will probably be but little increased by future discoveries. South America is the richest part of the world, and Wallace informs us that 600 species of butterflies could, forty years ago, be found in the environs of the city of Pará.

Fam. 1. Nymphalidae.—*The front pair of legs much reduced in size in each sex, their tarsi in the male with but one joint,*

---

[1] The literature of butterflies has become extremely extensive. The following works contain information as to general questions : 1, Scudder's *Butterflies of New England,* a beautifully illustrated work completed in 1889, and replete with interesting discussions. 2, Staudinger, Schatz and Röber, *Exotische Tagfalter,* in three folio volumes (Fürth, 1884-1887), with illustrations of exotic butterflies and a detailed sketch of their characters. 3, Enzio Reuter, "Uber die Palpen der Rhopaloceren," in *Acta Soc. Sci. Fenn.* xxii. 1896, treating fully of classification and phylogeny.

though in the female there are usually five but without any claws.
Pupa suspended by the tail so as to hang down freely. We
include in this family several sub-families treated by some
taxonomists as families; in this respect we follow Bates, whose
arrangement [1] still remains the basis of butterfly classification.
With this extension the Nymphalidae is the most important of
the families of butterflies, and includes upwards of 250 genera,
and between 4000 and 5000 species.   There are eight sub-
families.

It is in Nymphalidae that the act of pupation reaches its
acme of complication and perfection; the pupae hang suspended
by the tail, and the cremaster, that is the process at the end
of the body, bears highly-
developed hooks (Fig. 177,
C, D).   The variety in
form of the chrysalids is
extraordinary; humps or
processes often project
from the body, making
the Insect a fantastic
object; the strange ap-
pearance is frequently increased by patches like
gold or silver, placed on
various parts of the body.
It is believed that the

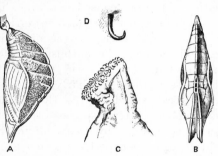

FIG. 177.—Pupa of the Purple Emperor butterfly,
Apatura iris. New Forest. **A**, Lateral, **B**,
dorsal aspect; **C**, enlarged view of cremaster
with the suspensory hook; **D**, one hook still
more enlarged.

term chrysalid was first suggested by these golden pupæ.
The Purple Emperor, *Apatura iris*, differs strikingly in the pupa-
as well as in the larva-stage from all our other Nymphalids; it
is of green colour, very broad along the sides, but narrow on
the dorsal and ventral aspects (Fig. 177).   The skin of this
pupa is less hard than usual, and the pupa seems to be of a
very delicate constitution.   The Purple Emperor, like some of
the Satyrides as well as some of its more immediate congeners,
hibernates in our climate as a partially grown larva and passes
consequently only a very brief period of its existence in the
form of a pupa.

Sub-Fam. 1. Danaides.—*Front wing with inner-margin*

[1] *Journal of Entomology*, i. 1862, p. 218 : for early instars of South American
Nymphalidae see Müller, *Zool. Jahrb. Syst.* i. 1886, p. 417.

(*submedian*) *nervure, with a short fork at the base. Cell of hind wing closed. Front foot of the female ending in a corrugate knob. Caterpillars smooth, provided with a few long fleshy processes.* The claws are in a variable state, being sometimes simple, as in Papilionidae, sometimes with an empodium, apparently of an imperfect kind. The Danaides are usually large Insects with an imperfect style of ornament and colour ; they have a great deal of black or very dark scaling, and in some *Euploea* this is agreeably relieved by a violet or purple suffusion, and these are really fine Insects. Usually there are large pale spaces, of some neutral indefinite tint, on which black blotches are distributed in a striking but inartistic manner. In many of the species the markings are almost spot for spot the same on the upper and under sides. About seven genera and 250 species are recognised. Danaides occur in all the warmer parts of the world, but are most numerous in the Eastern tropics. In Europe the family is represented only by an Asiatic and African species, *Limnas chrysippus*, that has extended its range to Greece. Besides this another species, *Anosia erippus*, Cr. (unfortunately also called *Anosia menippe*, Hb., and *Danais archippus* or even *D. plexippus*) has in the last two or three decades extended its range to various islands and distant localities, concomitantly, it is believed, with an extension of the distribution of its food-plant, *Asclepias*. This Insect has several times been taken in this country, and may probably be a natural immigrant. It is a common butterfly in North America, where it is called the Monarch.[1]

Some, at least, of the Danaides are unpleasant to birds in odour or in taste, or both. Among them there occur, according to Moore[2] and others, numerous cases of resemblance between forms that are thus protected. It is possible that the odour and taste are of some value to the Insects ;[3] as, however, butterflies of any kind appear to be but rarely attacked in the imago-state by birds, and as their chief enemies are parasitic Insects that attack the larval instar, it is impossible to consider this protection of such prime importance to the species as many theorists assume it to be.

[1] This is the subject of Scudder's *Life of a Butterfly*, 1893.
[2] *P. Zool. Soc. London*, 1883, p. 205.
[3] Finn, *J. Asiat. Soc. Bengal*, lxvi. 1896, p. 528 ; lxvii. 1897, p. 213.

Sub-Fam. 2. Ithomiides.—*Differs from Danaides by the female front foot having a true, though somewhat abbreviate tarsus. The caterpillers have no long processes.* There has been considerable difference of opinion as to this division of butterflies. It is the family Neotropidae of Schatz, the Mechanitidae of Berg; also the "Danaioid Heliconiidae" of several previous writers, except that *Ituna* and *Lycorea* do not belong here but to Danaides. Godman and Salvin treat it as a group of the Danaid sub-family. The Ithomiides are peculiar to tropical America, where some 20 or 30 genera and about 500

FIG. 178.—*Ithomia pusio.* Brazil.

species have been discovered. There is considerable variety amongst them. *Ithomia* and *Hymenitis* are remarkable for the small area of their wings, which bear remarkably few scales, these ornaments being in many cases limited to narrow bands along the margins of the wings, and a mark extending along the discocellular nervule. Wallace says they prefer the shades of the forest and flit, almost invisible, among the dark foliage. Many of these species have the hind-wings differently veined in the two sexes on the anterior part, in connection with the existence in the male of peculiar fine hairs, placed near the costal and subcostal veins. *Tithorea* and other forms are, however, heavily scaled insects of stronger build, their colours usually being black, tawny-red or brown, yellow, and white. In the sub-fam. Danaides, according to Fritz Müller, the male has scent-tufts at the extremity of the abdomen, whereas in Ithomiides analogous structures exist on the upper side of the hind-wing. Ithomiides have various colour-resemblances with members of the Heliconiides and Pieridae; *Tithorea* has colour analogues in *Heliconius*, and *Ithomia* in *Dismorphia* (formerly called *Leptalis*). Crowds of individuals of certain species of *Ithomia* are occasionally met with, and mixed with them there are found a small number of examples of *Dismorphia* coloured like themselves. They are placed by Haase in his category of secondary models. Belt states that some Ithomiides are distasteful to monkeys and spiders, but are destroyed by Fossorial Hymenoptera, which use the butterflies as food for their young; and he also says that they are very wary when the wasp is near, and rise off their perches into the air, as if aware that the wasp will not then endeavour to seize them. " Much information is given about the habits by Bates in the paper in which he first propounded the "theory of mimicry." [1] The larvae are said to live on Solanaceae.

The genus *Hamadryas* is placed by some writers in Danaides, by others in Ithomiides; and Haase has proposed to make it the group " Palaeotropinae." The species are small, black and white Insects, somewhat like Pierids. They are apparently hardy Insects, and are abundant in certain parts of the Austro-Malay region.

Sub-Fam. 3. Satyrides.—*Palpi strongly pressed together, set in front with long, stiff hairs. Front wings frequently with one or more of the nervures swollen or bladder-like at the base of the wing. Cells of both wings closed. Caterpillar thickest at the middle, the hind end of the body bifid. Pupa generally suspended by the cremaster, without girth: but sometimes terrestrial.* This is a very extensive group, consisting of upwards of 1000 species. The Insects are usually of small size, of various shades of brown or greyish colours, with circular or ringed marks on the under sides of the wings. It is found all over the world, and is well represented in Europe; our Meadow-browns, Heaths, and Marbled-whites, as well as the great genus *Erebia* of the highlands and mountains belonging to it. Most of these Insects have but feeble powers of flight, and rise but little from the surface of the ground. The caterpillars live on various grasses. They are usually green or brown, destitute of armature, and a good deal like the caterpillars of Noctuid moths, but the hind end of the body is thinner and divided to form two corners, while the head is more or less free, or outstanding. The pupae are of great interest, inasmuch as in a few cases they do not suspend themselves in any way, but lie on the ground; sometimes in a very feeble cocoon or cell. There are no cremasteral hooks. The pupae of the Grayling butterfly, *Hipparchia semele,* has been found in loose soil a quarter of an inch below the surface. The chrysalis of the Scotch Argus, *Erebia aethiops,* was found by Mr. Buckler to be neither suspended nor attached, but placed iu a perpendicular position, head upwards, amongst the grass.

[1] *Trans. Linn. Soc.* xxiii, 1862, p. 495.

In the majority of cases the pupa is, however, suspended as is usual in Nymphalidae. Nothing is known as to the nature of the peculiar inflation of the bases of the nervures of the front wings; it is well shown in our common species of *Coenonympha*; this character is not, however, constant throughout the family. There is in South America a very remarkable group of Satyrides consisting of the genera *Cithaerias* and *Haetera*, in which the wings are very delicate and transparent, bearing on the greater part of their area remote fine hairs instead of scales; there are nevertheless some scaled patches about the margins, and one or more of the ringed marks characteristic of the Satyrides; while in some species the distal portions of the hind wings are tinted with carmine. The species of the genus *Pierella* connect these transparent Satyrids with the more ordinary forms. According to Wallace the habits of these fairy-like forms are those characteristic of the family in general. The genus *Elymnias* has been separated by some authorities as a sub-family, or even as a family, Elymniidae, chiefly on the ground of a slight peculiarity in the termination of the branches of the veins at the outer angle of the front wings. The *Elymnias* are said to be of a mimetic nature, having a greater or less resemblance to butterflies of various other divisions; there is also a considerable difference in appearance between their own sexes. The larva of *E. undularis* is known; it is of the form usual in Satyrides, and lives on the palm *Corypha*. About 50 species, ranging from India to Australia, with two in Africa, are known of this interesting group.

Sub-Fam. 4. Morphides.—*There is no cell on the hind wing, the discocellular nervule being absent* (Fig. 161, II. B). *Caterpillars smooth or spiny, with the extremity of the body divided; frequently gregarious.* These Insects have become notorious from the extraordinary brilliancy of blue colour exhibited by the upper surface of the wings of the typical genus *Morpho*. The species of *Morpho* are all Insects of large size, but with wings enormous in proportion to the body; this latter part is carried in a sort of cradle formed by the inner parts of the margins of the hind wings. Although an arrangement of this kind is seen in numerous other butterflies, yet there is perhaps none in which it is carried to quite such a pitch of perfection as it is in *Morpho*, where, on the under surface no part of the body behind the posterior legs can

be seen.   There are only about 100 species of Morphides, and
50 of these are included in *Morpho*, which is peculiar to tropical
and sub-tropical America ; the other half of the family is divided
among ten or twelve genera, found in the Indo-Malay region ;
there being none in Africa.   The eastern Morphides, though
fine Insects, are not to be compared, either in size or brilliancy,
with their American allies.   The species of *Morpho* are apparently found only in the great forests of South America,
where they are far from rare ; some have a flapping and undulating flight, straight onwards along the alleys of the forest, and
near the ground ; others are never seen except steadily gliding
with outstretched wings from 20 to 100 feet above the ground,
where they move across sunny spaces between the crowns of the
taller trees ; the low-flyers settle frequently on the ground
to suck the juices from fallen fruit, but the members of the
other section never descend to the ground.   As regards the
caterpillars, W. Müller tells us [1] that the spines they are armed
with break off, and enter the skin, if the creatures are carelessly
handled.   Four of the five species known to him are conspicuously coloured with black, red, yellow and white.   The individuals
are gregarious.   The larvae of *M. achilles* sit in companies, often
of more than 100 individuals, on trunks of trees, and so form a
conspicuous patch.   The caterpillars of *M. epistrophis* hang together as red clumps on the twigs of their food-plants.   Hence
it appears that in this genus we have an exception to the rule
that night-feeding caterpillars rest in a hidden manner during
the day.

Sub-Fam. 5. Brassolides.—*Large butterflies, with the cell of
the hind wing closed, and usually with a small adjoining predis-
coidal cell.   Larva not very spiny ; thinner at the two ends, the tail
bifid, the head perpendicular and margined with spines.*   This
small sub-family includes less than 100 species arranged in about
eight genera, all South American.   They have the very unusual
habit of resting during the day like moths, becoming active only
late in the afternoon.   They are truly noble Insects ; although
not possessed of the brilliant colours of *Morpho*, they are
adorned, especially on the under surface, with intricate lines
and shades most harmoniously combined, while the upper surface
is frequently suffused with blue or purple.   This sub-family

[1] *Kosmos*, xix. 1886, p. 355.

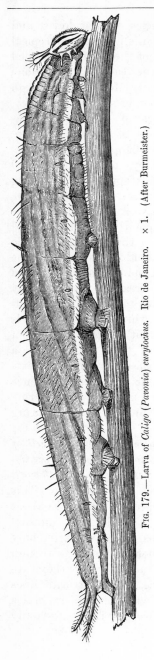

FIG. 179.—Larva of *Caligo (Pavonia) eurylochus*. Rio de Janeiro. × 1. (After Burmeister.)

attains its highest perfection in the genus *Caligo;* they are enormous Insects, and some of them not rare. The larva of *C. eurylochus* (Fig. 179) during early life is green, and sits on the leaf of a *Musa,* but after the third moult it becomes brown and hides itself among the dry leaves. It is common in the gardens of Rio de Janeiro, where its pupae are found on the walls, like those of our white butterflies here.

Sub - Fam. 6. Acraeides. — *Submedian nervure of fore wings not forked at the base; the median without spur. Cells closed. Palpi in section cylindric, sparingly set with hairs. Larva armed with branched spines.* A somewhat monotonous and uninteresting division ; the size is moderate or small, and the colours not artistic, but consisting of ill-arranged spots; the under side of the hind wings very frequently diversified by numerous line-like marks, radiately arranged, and giving place at the base to a few spots. There are about 200 species known, of which the majority are African; there are but few Oriental or South American species. Some authorities consider there is only one Eastern genus, but others prefer to adopt seven or eight divisions. *Alaena* is now placed in Lycaenidae, though until recently it was considered to belong here. The females of some species possess an abdominal pouch somewhat similar to that of *Parnassius.*

The members of this sub-family are considered to be of the protected kind.

Sub-Fam. 7. Heliconiides.—*Submedian nervure of front wing not forked ; median with a short spur near the base.   Cell of hind wing closed by a perfect nervule.   Palpi compressed, with scales at the sides, in front covered with hairs.   Male with an elongate unjointed, female with a four-jointed, front tarsus.   Caterpillars set with branched spines.*   This family is peculiar to tropical America and consists of only two genera, *Heliconius* and *Eueides*, with about 150 species ; but it is one of the most characteristic of the South American groups of Butterflies.   It is very closely allied to the Nymphalides, especially to the genera *Metamorpha* and *Colaenis*, but is readily distinguished by the perfectly-formed nervules that close the wing-cells.   The wings are longer and narrower than in Nymphalides, and the colour, though exhibiting much diversity, is on the whole similar to that of the heavily-scaled forms of Ithomiides of the genera *Tithorea, Melinaea, Melanitis ;* there being in several cases a great resemblance between species of the two groups.   A frequent feature in one group of *Heliconius* is that the hind wing bears a patch of red prolonged outwards by angular radiating marks.   The individuals of certain species—*H. melpomene* and *H. rhea*—are known to execute concerted dances, rising and falling in the air like gnats ; when some of them withdraw from the concert others fill their places.   *H. erato* exhibits the very rare condition of trichroism, the hind wings being either red, blue, or green.   Schatz states that the different forms have been reared from a single brood of larvae.   The caterpillars of Heliconiides live on Passiflorae, and are said to be very similar to our European *Argynnis*-caterpillars.   The chrysalids are very spinous.   We may here remark that considerable confusion exists in entomological literature in consequence of Ithomiides having been formerly included in this sub-family ; for remarks formerly made as to " Heliconiides," but that really referred only to Ithomiides, have been interpreted as referring to Heliconiides of the present system.

The Heliconiides seem remarkably plastic as regards colour, and are therefore exponents of " homoeochromatism."   Bates says, as regards them : " In tropical South America a numerous series of gaily-coloured butterflies and moths, of very different families, which occur in abundance in almost every locality a naturalist may visit, are found all to change their hues and markings together, as if by the touch of an enchanter's wand, at every few hundred miles, the distances being shorter near the eastern slopes of the Andes than nearer the Atlantic. So close is the accord of some half-dozen species (of widely different genera) in each change, that he had seen them in large collections classed and named respectively as one species." [1] Many of them are believed to be permeated by nauseous fluids, or to possess glands producing ill-smelling secretions.

Sub-Fam. 8. Nymphalides.—*Cells, of both front and hind wing, either closed only by imperfect transverse nervules or entirely open. Front tarsus of the male unjointed and without spines, of the female four- or five-jointed. Caterpillar either spined or smooth ; in the latter case the head more or less strongly horned or spined, and the apex of the body bifid.* This sub-family is specially characterised by the open cells of the wings ; the discocellulars, even when present, being frequently so imperfect as to escape all but the most careful observation. The Nymphalides include upwards of 150 genera and 2000 species. The divisions having smooth larvae are separated by Kirby [2] and others as a distinct sub-family (Apaturides). In Britain, as in most other parts of the world, Nymphalides is the predominant group of butterflies. We have eighteen species, among which are included the Fritillaries, Admirals, Purple Emperor, and the various *Vanessa*—Peacock, Camberwell Beauty, Red Admiral, Tortoise-shells, and Painted Lady. All have spined caterpillars except the Emperor. In the temperate regions of the northern hemisphere *Vanessa* may be considered the dominant butter-flies, they being very numerous in individuals, though not in species, and being, many of them, in no wise discomfited by the neighbourhood of our own species. Several of them are capable of prolonging and interrupting their lives in the winged condition to suit our climate ; and this in a manner that can scarcely be called hibernation, for they frequently take up the position of repose when the weather is still warm, and on the other hand recommence their activity in the spring at a very early period. This phenomenon may frequently be noticed in the Tortoise-shell butterfly ; it is as if the creature knew that however warm it may be in the autumn there will be no more growth of food for its young, and that in the spring vegetation

---

[1] *P. ent. Soc. London*, 1879, p. xxix.
[2] Allen's Naturalists' Library, *Butterflies*, i. 1896.

is sure to be forthcoming and abundant before long, although there may be little or none at the time the creature resumes its activity. It is probable that the habit may be in some way connected with an imperfect activity of the sexual organs. It should, however, be recollected that many larvae of butterflies hibernate as young larvae after hatching, and, sometimes, without taking any food. *Pyrameis cardui*, the Painted Lady, is, taking all into consideration, entitled to be considered the most ubiquitous of the butterfly tribe. Its distribution is very wide, and is probably still extending. The creature is found in enormous numbers in some localities, especially in Northern and Eastern Africa; and when its numbers increase greatly, migration takes place, and the Insect spreads even to localities where it cannot maintain itself permanently. In Britain it is probably during some years nearly or quite absent, but may suddenly appear in large numbers as an immigrant. The favourite food of the larva is thistles, but many other plants serve the Insect at times.

Vanessa, or *Pyrameis*,[1] *atalanta*, the Red Admiral, is common in the Palaearctic and Nearctic regions, and extends its range to various outlying spots. The most remarkable of these is the remote Hawaiian Islands, where the Insect appears really to be now at home, though it is associated with a larger and more powerful congener, *P. tameamea*. Another interesting Vanessid is *Araschnia levana*, which is peculiar to Europe, where it produces annually two generations so dissimilar to one another that they passed current as two species, *V. levana* and *V. prorsa*. Although intermediate forms are rare in nature they can be induced by certain treatments applied to the larvae under human control.

The dead-leaf butterflies of the genus *Kallima* belong to Nymphalides. They are so shaped and coloured that when settled, with wings closed, on a twig, the appearance is exactly that of a dry leaf; the exposed surface is mottled with spots that look just like the patches of minute fungi, etc. that are so common on decaying vegetation. The colour and the spots on the under surface of this butterfly are very variable. According to Mr. Skertchly,[2] we may presume that in the minute details of

---

[1] A most unfortunate diversity exists in the generic names applied to these *Vanessa*, as well as in those of many other Lepidoptera.

[2] *Ann. Nat. Hist.* (6), iv. 1889, p. 212.

these resemblances we have a case of hypertely similar to that of the resemblance to Insects' minings exhibited by certain marks on the tegmina of *Pterochroza* (mentioned in Vol. V. p. 322).

In South America there is a somewhat peculiar genus of Nymphalides—*Ageronia*—that delights in settling on the trunks of trees rather than on flowers or leaves.   It was long since noticed that the species of *Ageronia* make a clicking noise ; in some cases when on the wing, in other cases by moving the wings when the Insect is settled.   The object of the noise is quite uncertain ; it has been suggested that it is done in rivalry or courtship, or to frighten away enemies.   Bigg-Wether found, however, that in South Brazil there is a lazy little bird to which this sound serves as a signal, inducing it to descend from its perch and eat the clicker. The mode in which the noise is produced is not quite clear.   Sir George Hampson has pointed out [1] that the fore wing bears at the extreme base a small appendage bearing two hooks, and that two other processes on the thorax play on these when the wing moves.   His suggestion that these hooks are the source of the sound seems highly probable.

There is a great variety in the larvae of Nymphalides.   In the *Vanessa* group the body is armed with spines, each one of which bears shorter thorns, the head being unadorned.   The Fritillaries (*Argynnis, Melitaea*) also have caterpillars of this kind. In many other forms the head itself is armed with horns or spines of diverse, and frequently remarkable, character.   In *Apatura* and its allies the body is without armature, but the head is perpendicular, the vertex bifid and more or less prolonged.   The caterpillar of our Purple Emperor, *Apatura iris*, is quite unlike any other British caterpillar ; in colour it is like a Sphingid larva—green with oblique lateral stripes of yellow and red—but in form it is slug-like, pointed behind, and it has on the head two rather long tentacle-like horns.   In the South American genus *Prepona*, the larva of which in general form resembles that of *Apatura*, there are no anal claspers, but the extremity of the body is prolonged, forming a sort of tail.

Fam. 2. Erycinidae (**Lemoniidae** of some authors).—*The female has six perfectly formed legs, though the front pair is smaller. The male has the coxae of the front legs forming a spine, and the tarsi unjointed, without claws.*   This family consists of about 1000

[1] *P. Zool. Soc. London*, 1892, p. 191.

species, usually of rather small size, exhibiting a great variety of shape and coloration, some of them being remarkably similar to some of the gay, diurnal moths of South America. The palpi are usually small, but in *Ourocnemis* they are large and porrect. The family is specially characteristic of tropical America, but there is one small group of 30 or 40 species, *Nemeobiides*, in the Eastern Hemisphere. We have one species in Britain, *Nemeobius lucina*, the Duke of Burgundy Fritillary. Neither the larvae nor the pupae of Erycinidae present any well-marked characteristic feature, but exhibit considerable variety. According to Bar,[1] some of the larvae are like those of moths ; the caterpillar of *Meliboeus* is said to be like that of a *Liparis :* the chrysalis has the short, rounded form of that of the *Lycaenidae,* and is suspended with the head down, and without a band round the body. The larvae of *Eurygona* are gregarious. The pupae of some other forms adhere, heads downwards, to branches. Scudder considers that this family is not distinct from Lycaenidae, and that the Central American genus *Eumaeus* connects the two. Reuter also treats Erycinidae as a division of Lycaenidae.

Sub-Fam. 1. Erycinides.—[*Characters of the family.*] *Palpi not unusually large.* We place all the Erycinidae in this subfamily except the following—

Sub-Fam. 2. Libytheides.—*Butterflies of average size, with the palpi large and porrect : the front legs of the male small, the tarsus reduced to one joint : the front leg of the female of the normal structure, and but little reduced in size.* This division consists of the single genus *Libythea*, with only a score of species. They are Insects somewhat like *Vanessa* in appearance, but cannot fail to be recognised on account of the peculiar palpi. The genus is of very wide distribution, occurring in most parts of the warm and temperate continental regions, and it also occurs in Mauritius and the Antilles.

The Libytheides have given rise to much difference of opinion amongst systematists, some of whom assign them as a subfamily to the Erycinidae, some to the Nymphalidae ; while others treat them as a family apart. The families Nymphalidae, Erycinidae and Lycaenidae are so intimately allied, that Scudder is probably correct in considering them to form really one huge family ; if this view were adopted there would be no difficulty

[1] *Bull. Soc. ent. France*, 1856, pp. c, ci.

iu locating *Libythea* therein. If they be kept apart, it is almost necessary to separate *Libythea* also; though possibly its claims to be placed in Erycinidae slightly preponderate. The recently described genus *Ourocnemis* to some extent connects Erycinides with Libythaeides.[1]

Fam. 3. Lycaenidae.—*The front legs but little smaller than the others : in the male, however, the tarsus, though elongate, is only of one joint, and is terminated by a single claw. No pad on the front tibia. Claws not toothed.* The Lycaenidae, or Blues, are, as a rule, of small size, but in the tropics there are many that reach the average size of butterflies, *i.e.* something about the stature of the Tortoise-shell butterfly. The family is one of the larger of the divisions of butterflies, considerably more than 2000 species being at present known, and this number is still rapidly increasing. Although blue on a part of the upper surface is a very common feature in the group, it is by no means universal, for there are many " Coppers," as well as yellow and white Lycaenidae. Many species have delicate, flimsy appendages—tails— to the hind wings, but in many others these are quite absent ; and there are even tailed and tailless forms of the same species. The members of the group Lipteninae (*Liptena, Vanessula, Mimacraea*, etc.) resemble members of other sub-families of Nymphalidae, and even of Pieridae. Lycaenidae are well represented wherever there are butterflies ; in Britain we have 18 species.

The larvae of this family are very peculiar, being short, thicker in the middle, and destitute of the armature of spines so remarkable in many other caterpillars. It has of late years been frequently recorded that some of these larvae are attended by ants, which use their antennae to stroke the caterpillars and induce them to yield a fluid of which the ants are fond. Guénée had previously called attention [2] to the existence of peculiar structures contained in small cavities on the posterior part of the caterpillar of *Lycaena baetica*. These structures can be evaginated, and, it is believed, secrete a fluid ; Edwards and M‘Cook are of opinion that they are the source of the matter coveted by the ants. The larvae are without spines.

The caterpillars of the Blues have some of them strange tastes ; more than one has been recorded as habitually feeding on Aphidae

---

[1] Baker, *Tr. ent. Soc. London*, 1887, p. 175, Pl. ix.
[2] *Ann. Soc. ent. France* (4), vii. 1867, p. 665, Pl. xiii.

and scale-Insects. The pupae are, like the larvae, of short inflated form. By a remarkable coincidence, the pupae of two species bear a considerable resemblance to the heads of monkeys, or mummies. The Lycaenid pupa is usually extremely consolidated, destitute of movement, and is supported—in addition to the attachment by the cremaster—by a silk thread girdling the middle. There are exceptions to these rules, and according to Mr. Robson the pupa of *Tajuria diaeus* hangs free, suspended from a leaf, and can move the body at the spot where the abdominal segments meet the wing-cases in the dorsal line.[1]

Fam. 4. Pieridae.—*The six legs well developed, and similar in the sexes; there is no pad on the front tibia. The claws of all the feet are bifid, or toothed, and there is an empodium.* There are upwards of 1000 species of Pieridae already known. Although several taxonomists treat the Pieridae and Papilionidae as only subdivisions of one family, yet they appear to be quite distinct, and the relationships of the former to be rather with Lycaenidae. In Pieridae, white, yellow, and red are the predominant colours, though there is much black also. It has recently been ascertained that the yellow and red pigments, as well as the white, are uric acid or derivatives therefrom.[2] The physiology of this peculiarity has not yet been elucidated, so that we do not know whether it may be connected with some state of the Malpighian vessels during metamorphosis.

Our Garden-White, Brimstone, Clouded-yellows and Orange-tip butterflies belong to this family; as does also the South American genus formerly called *Leptalis*. This generic name, which is much mentioned in literature owing to the resemblance of the species of the genus to *Heliconiides*, has now disappeared; *Leptalis* having been divided into various genera, while the name itself is now considered merely a synonym of *Dismorphia*.

The African Insect, *Pseudopontia paradoxa*, has nearly transparent wings, no club to the antennae, a remarkably small cell on the wing, and an arrangement of the nervules not found in any other butterfly; there being only ten nervules at the periphery of the front wing, and both upper and lower radial nervules uniting with the posterior branch of the subcostal. It has been treated as a moth by several entomologists. Aurivillius considers that it

---

[1] *J. Bombay Soc.* ix. 1895, pp. 338-341.
[2] Hopkins, *Phil. Trans.* 186 B, 1895, p. 661.

is certainly a butterfly; but as the metamorphoses are unknown, we cannot yet form a final opinion as to this curious form. The extraordinary Peruvian Insect, *Styx infernalis*, is also placed in this family by Staudinger; it is a small, pale Insect, almost white, and with imperfect scales; a little recalling a Satyrid. It appears to be synthetic to Pieridae and Erycinidae.

The caterpillars of Pieridae are perhaps the least remarkable or attractive of all butterfly-caterpillars; their skins are as a

rule bare, or covered only with fine, short down or hair; their prevalent colour is green, more or less speckled with black and yellow, and they are destitute of any prominent peculiarities of external structure. Pupation is accomplished by the larva fixing itself to some solid body by the posterior extremity, with the head upwards (or the position may be horizontal), and then placing a girdle round the middle of the body. The pupa never hangs down freely as it does in Nymphalidae. It has been ascertained by experiment that if the girdle round the larva be cut, the pupation can nevertheless be accomplished by a considerable proportion of larvae. Some of the pupae are of very peculiar form, as is the case in the Orange-tip (Fig. 180, A) and Brimstone butterflies. The Orange-

FIG. 180.—Pupation of the Orange-tip butterfly, *Euchloe cardamines*. **A**, The completed pupa; **B**, the larva, with its girdle, prepared for the change.

tip butterfly passes nine or ten months of each year as a pupa, which is variable in colour; perhaps to some extent in conformity with its surroundings. The North American *E. genutia* has a similar life-history, but the larva leaves its Cruciferous food-plant, wanders to an oak tree, and there turns to a pupa, resembling in colour the bark of the tree.

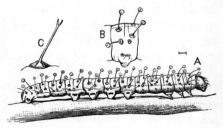

FIG. 181.—Newly-hatched larva of *Euchloe cardamines*. **A**, The larva in profile; **B**, one segment more magnified, showing the liquid-bearing setae; **C**, one of the setae still more magnified, and without liquid.

It is not unusual for caterpillars to change their habits and

appearance in a definite manner in the course of the larval life.
The caterpillar of *Euchloe cardamines* exhibits a larval metamorphosis of a well-marked character.   The young larva (Fig.
181) is armed with peculiar setae, furcate at the tip, each of
which bears a tiny
ball of fluid.   In this
stage the caterpillar
makes scarcely any
movement.   In the
middle of the cater-
pillar's life a new
vestiture   appears
after   an   ecdysis ;
numerous fine hairs
are present, and the
fluid - bearing spines

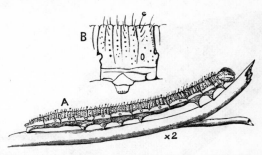

Fig. 182.—Larva of *Euchloe cardamines* in middle life.
A, the larva in profile ; B, one segment more magnified.

nearly disappear, being reduced to a single series of spines of a
comparatively small size on each side of the upper middle region
of the body (Fig. 182).   The colour is also a good deal
changed, and concomitantly there is a much greater voracity
and restlessness.

Fam. 5. Papilionidae.—*All the legs well developed.   Claws
large, simple, without empodium.   Front tibiae with a pad.   The
metanotum free, conspicuously exposed between mesonotum and
abdomen.*   This series of butterflies includes some of the most
magnificent of the members of the Insect world.   It is considered
by some authorities to be the highest family of butterflies ; and
in one very important feature—sexual differentiation—it certainly is entitled to the rank.   There are about 700 recorded
species, the larger portion of which are included in the genus
Papilio.   The great variety of form has led to this genus being
divided ; the attempts have, however, been partial, with the
exception of an arrangement made by Felder, who adopted 75
sections, and a recent consideration of the subject by Haase, who
arranges Felder's sections into three sub-genera.   Many of the
sections have received names, and are treated by some authors as
genera, so that an unfortunate diversity exists as to the names
used for these much-admired Insects.   The genus is distributed
all over the world, but is perhaps nowhere more numerous in
species than in South America.   Wallace informs us that the great

majority of the species of the Amazon valley frequent the shady groves of the virgin forest. In many cases the sexes are extremely different in appearance and habits, and are but rarely found together in one spot. The genus *Ornithoptera* is closely

FIG. 183.—*Ornithoptera* (*Schoenbergia*) *paradisea*, male. New Guinea. × 1. (Colours, velvet-black, golden-yellow and green.)

allied to *Papilio*, and contains some of the most remarkable of butterflies, the homes of the species being the islands of the Malay Archipelago, and outlying groups of islands, there being a smaller number of species in the neighbouring continents. The females are of great size, and are so excessively different from their

Fig. 184.— *Ornithoptera (Schoenbergia) paradisea*, female, × 1. (The wings, on the right side, detached, showing the under surface. Colours, black, white, and gray.)

consorts of the other sex, as to arouse in the student a feeling of surprise, and a strong desire to fathom the mysteries involved. It would be difficult to surpass the effective coloration of the males in many of the species of *Ornithoptera*; they are, too, very diverse in this respect; *O. brookiana* is of an intense black colour, with a band of angular green marks extending the whole length of its wings, while behind the head there is a broad collar of crimson colour. Perhaps the most remarkable of all is the *O. paradisea*, recently discovered in New Guinea; in this species the sexual disparity reaches its maximum. The female (Fig. 184) is a large, sombre creature of black, white and grey colours, but the male (Fig. 183) is brilliant with gold and green, and is made additionally remarkable by a long tail of unusual form on each hind wing.

We may anticipate that these extraordinary cases of sexual total dissimilarity in appearance are accompanied by equally remarkable habits and physiological phenomena. In the case of *O. brookiana* the female is extremely rare, so that the collector, Künstler, could only obtain fifteen females to a thousand males. According to Mr. Skertchly, instead of the crowd of males being eager to compete for the females, the reverse is the case; the female diligently woos the male, who exhibits a reluctance to coupling. This observer apparently considered that the "emerald feathers" of the male are a guide or incitement to the female.[1]

In Africa *Ornithoptera* is to a certain extent represented by two extremely remarkable forms, *Papilio zalmoxis* and *P. (Drurya) antimachus*. There are about a dozen other genera of Papilionidae; most of them contain but few species. *Parnassius*, however, is rich in species inhabiting the mountains and elevated plateaus of the northern hemisphere in both the Old and New Worlds; it is remarkable for the small amount of scales on the wings, and for the numerous variations of the species. The female possesses a peculiar pouch at the end of the body; although only formed during the process of coupling, it has a special and characteristic form in most of the species. The curious Indian genus *Leptocircus* has parts of the front wings transparent, while the hind pair form long tails. This genus is of interest in that

---

[1] *Ann. Nat. Hist.* (6), iv. 1889, p. 213. We trust there will not be many more Künstlers, as this beautiful butterfly must certainly become extinct, if the female be really as rare as is supposed.

it is said to connect Papilionidae to some extent with Hesperiidae. The larvae of this family are remarkable on account of a curious process on the thoracic segment called an " osmeterium." It is usually retracted, but at the will of the caterpillar can be everted in the form of a long furcate or Y-shaped process; there is a gland in the osmeterium, and as a result a strong odour is emitted when the exstulpation occurs.

The pupation of Papilionidae is similar to that of Pieridae, the pupa being placed with the head upwards, fixed by the tail, and girt round the middle. A very curious diversity of pupation occurs in the genus *Thais*, in which the pupa is attached by the tail as usual, and—which is quite exceptional—also by a thread placed at the top of the head. Scudder thinks there is also a girdle round the middle, but Dr. Chapman inclines to the view that the thread attaching the head is really the median girdle slipped upwards. The pupation of *Parnassius* is exceptional, inasmuch as, like Satyrides, it is terrestrial, in a slight construction of silk.

Fam. 6. Hesperiidae (*Skippers*).—*Six perfect legs: metanotum not free, largely covered by the mesonotum. A pad on the front tibia. Claws short and thick; empodium present.* Although this family has been comparatively neglected by entomologists, upwards of 2000 species and more than 200 genera are known, and it is not improbable that it may prove to be as extensive as Nymphalidae. We have already said that Hesperiidae is generally admitted to be the most distinct of the butterfly groups. It has been thought by some taxonomists to be allied to Papilionidae, but this is a mistake. It is undoubtedly more nearly allied to Heterocera, and when the classification of Lepidoptera is more advanced, so that the various natural groups placed in that sub-Order are satisfactorily distinguished, it is probable that Hesperiidae will be altogether separated from Rhopalocera. We have already mentioned that E. Reuter considers the Hesperiidae to be phylogenetically unconnected with Rhopalocera proper; but though quite ready to admit that he will probably prove correct in this, we think Lepidopterists will not be willing to recognise the family as a sub-Order equivalent in value to all Heterocera.

The body is shorter and thicker than it is in most butterflies, and is pointed at the tip rather than knobbed or bent downwards; the wings are less ample; the antennae are not truly knobbed, but are thicker before the actual tip, which is itself pointed and more or less bent backwards, so that the antennae are somewhat hook-shaped.

In habits as well as structure the family is markedly distinct from butterflies; the pupation is peculiar, and the name Skipper has been applied to the perfect Insects, because so many of them indulge in a brief, jerky flight, instead of the prolonged aerial courses characteristic of the higher butterflies.

There is great difference among the members of the family, and some of them possess a very high development of the powers of locomotion, with a correspondingly perfect structure of the thoracic region, so that, after inspection of these parts, we can quite believe Wallace's statement that the larger and strong-bodied kinds are remarkable for the excessive rapidity of their flight, which, indeed, he was inclined to consider surpassed that of any other Insects. "The eye cannot follow them as they dart past; and the air, forcibly divided, gives out a deep sound louder than that produced by the humming-bird itself. If power of wing and rapidity of flight could place them in that rank, they should be considered the most highly organised of butterflies." It was probably to the genera *Pyrrhopyge*, *Erycides*, etc., that Mr. Wallace alluded in the above remarks. Although the Hesperiidae are not as a rule beautifully coloured, yet many of these higher forms are most tastefully ornamented; parts of the wings, wing-fringes, and even the bodies being set with bright but agreeable colours. We mention these facts because it is a fashion to attribute a lowly organisation to the family, and to place it as ancestral to other butterflies. Some of them have crepuscular habits, but this is also the case with a variety of other Rhopalocera in the tropics.

In their early stages the Skippers—so far as at present known —depart considerably from the majority of butterflies, inasmuch as they possess in both the larval and pupal instars habits of concealment and retirement. The caterpillars have the body nearly bare, thicker in the middle, the head free, and more or less notched above. They make much greater use of silk than other butterfly-larvae do, and draw together leaves to form caves for concealment, and even make webs and galleries. Thus the habits are almost those of the Tortricid moths. Pupation takes place under similar conditions; and it is interesting to find that Chap-

man considers that the pupa in several points of structure resembles that of the small moths. Not only does the larva draw
together leaves or stalks to make a shelter for the pupa, but it
frequently also forms a rudimentary cocoon. These arrangements
are, however, very variable, and the accounts that have been
given indicate that even the same species may exhibit some
amount of variation in its pupation. Scudder considers that, in
the North American Skippers, the cremaster is attached to a single
Y-like thread. In other cases there is a silk pad on the leaf for
the cremaster to hook on. An interesting account given by Mr.
Dudgeon of the pupation of a common Indian Skipper, *Badamia
exclamationis*, shows that this Insect exercises considerable in-

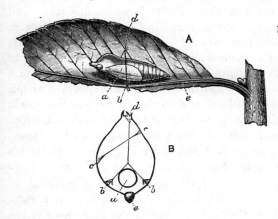

Fig. 185. — Pupation of
Badamia exclamationis.
(After Dudgeon. *J.
Bombay Soc.* x. 1895,
p. 144). **A,** One side
of the leaf-cradle, the
other (nearest to the
observer) being broken
away ; **B,** transverse section of entire cradle. *a,*
The pupa ; *b,* fastenings
of perpendicular threads
round pupa ; *c,* cross
thread retaining the leaf
in cradle form ; *d,* margins of the leaf ; *e,* midrib of leaf.

genuity in the structure of the puparium, and also that the
arrangements it adopts facilitate one of the acts of pupation most
difficult for such pupae as suspend themselves, viz. the hooking the
cremasters on to the pad above them. *Badamia* uses a rolled-up
leaf (Fig. 185) ; the edges of the leaf are fastened together by
silk at *d ;* from this spot there descends a thread which, when
it reaches the pupa, *a,* forks so as to form an inverted Y, and is
fastened to the leaf on either side ; the two sides of the leaf are kept
together by a cross thread, *cc.* Mr. Dudgeon was fortunate enough
to observe the act of pupation, and saw that " although the anal
prolegs of the larva were attached to a tuft or pad of silk in the
usual way, and remained so until nearly the whole skin had been
shuffled off, yet when the last segment had to be taken out, the
pupa drew it entirely away from the skin and lifted it over the

empty skin, and by a series of contortions similar to those made by an Insect in depositing an egg, it soon re-attached its anal segment or cremaster to the web, throwing away the cast-off skin by wriggling its body about."

Series II. Heterocera. Moths.

Although Rhopalocera—if exclusion be made of the Hesperiidae—is probably a natural group, yet this is not the case with Heterocera. The only definition that can be given of Heterocera is the practical one that all Lepidoptera that are not butterflies are Heterocera. Numerous divisions of the Heterocera have been long current, but their limits have become more and more uncertain, so that at the present time no divisions of greater value than the family command a recognition at all general. This is not really a matter of reproach, for it arises from the desire to recognise only groups that are capable of satisfactory definition.

Several attempts have recently been made to form a rough forecast of the future classification of moths. Professor Comstock, struck by some peculiarities presented by the Hepialidae, Micropterygidae (and Eriocephalidae), recently proposed to separate them from all other Lepidoptera as a sub-order Jugatae. Comstock's discrimination in making this separation met with general approval. The character on which the group Jugatae is based is, however, comparatively trivial, and its possession is not sufficient, as pointed out by Packard,[1] to justify the close association of Hepialidae and Micropterygidae, which, in certain important respects, are the most dissimilar of moths. The characters possessed by the two families in common may be summarised by saying that the wings and wing-bearing segments remain in a low stage of development. In nearly all other characters the two families are widely different. Packard has therefore, while accepting Comstock's separation of the families in question, proposed a different combination. He considers that Eriocephalidae should be separated from all others as " Protolepidoptera " or " Lepidoptera Laciniata," while the whole of the other Lepidoptera, comprised under the term " Lepidoptera Haustellata," are divided into Palaeolepidoptera (consisting only of Micropterygidae) and Neolepidoptera, comprising all Lepidoptera (in-

[1] *Mem. Ac. Washington*, vii. 1895, p. 57.

clusive of Hepialidae) except the Eriocephalidae and Micropterygidae. The question is rendered more difficult by the very close relations that exist between Micropterygidae and a sub-Order, Trichoptera, of Neuroptera. Dr. Chapman, by a sketch of the classification of pupae,[1] and Dyar, by one on larval stages,[2] have made contributions to the subject; but the knowledge of early stages and metamorphosis is so very imperfect that the last two memoirs can be considered only as preliminary sketches; as indeed seem to have been the wishes of the authors themselves.

Simultaneously with the works above alluded to, Mr. Meyrick has given[3] a new classification of the Order. We allude, in other pages, to various points in Mr. Meyrick's classification, which is made to appear more revolutionary than it really is, in consequence of the radical changes in nomenclature combined with it.

As regards the various aggregates of families that are widely known in literature by the names Bombyces, Sphinges, Noctuae, Geometres, Pyrales, we need only remark that they are still regarded as to some extent natural. Their various limits being the subject of discussion and at present undecided, the groups are made to appear more uncertain than is really the case. The group that has to suffer the greatest changes is the old Bombyces. This series comprises the great majority of those moths that have diurnal habits. In it there were also included several groups of moths the larvae of which feed in trunks of trees or in the stems of plants, such as Cossidae, that will doubtless prove to have but little connection with the forms with which they were formerly associated. These groups with aberrant habits are those that give rise to the greatest difficulties of the taxonomist.

The following key to the families of Heterocera is taken from Sir G. F. Hampson's recent work, *Fauna of British India—Moths*.[4] It includes nearly all the families at present recognised among the larger Lepidoptera; certain families [5] not mentioned in this key are alluded to in our subsequent remarks on the families :—

[1] *Tr. ent. Soc. London*, 1893, p. 97, with Suppl. *op. cit.* 1896, pp. 129 and 567.
[2] *Amer. Natural.* xxix. 1895, p. 1066. See also *Ann. N. York Ac.* viii. 1895, p. 194, and *Ent. Record*, 1897, pp. 136 and 196.
[3] *Handbook of British Lepidoptera*, 1895.
[4] London, 1892. Published under the authority of the Secretary of State for India in Council.
[5] Those numbered 2, 8, 10, 17, 22, 27, 44, and 46 in our arrangement.

KEY TO THE FAMILIES OF MOTHS [1]

N.B.—*This table is not simply dichotomic ; three contrasted categories are used in the case of the primary divisions,* A, B, C, *and the secondary divisions,* I, II, III.

A. Fore wing with nervule 5 coming from the middle of the discocellulars, or nearer 6 than 4 (Categories I, II, III = 1-18).

    I. Frenulum rudimentary .   . Fam. 38. **Epicopeiidae,** see p. 418

    II. Frenulum absent (Categories 1-8).

        1. Proboscis present, legs with spurs (Cat. 2-5).

          2. Hind wing with nervule 8 remote from 7 (Cat. 3 and 4).

            3. Fore wing with nervule 6 and 7 stalked

                Fam. 39. **Uraniidae,** see p. 419.

            4. Fore wing with nervules 6 and 7 not stalked

                Fam. 5. **Ceratocampidae,** see p. 375.

          5. Hind wing with nervule 8 nearly touching 7 beyond end of cell

                Fam. 4. **Brahmaeidae,** see p. 374.

        6. Proboscis absent, legs without spurs (Cat. 7 and 8).

          7. Hind wing with one internal nervure

                Fam. 3. **Saturniidae,** see p. 372.

          8. Hind wing with two or three internal nervures

                Fam. 6. **Bombycidae,** see p. 375.

   III. Frenulum present (Cat. 9-18).

        9. Antennae fusiform [spindle-shaped] Fam. 9. **Sphingidae,** see p. 380.

        10. Antennae not fusiform (Cat. 11-18).

          11. Proboscis absent .   . Fam. 7. **Eupterotidae,** see p. 376.

          12. Proboscis present (Cat. 13-18).

            13. Hind wing with nervule 8 curved and almost touching 7 after end of cell ; nervure 1a reaching anal angle

                Fam. 12. **Cymatophoridae,** see p. 386.

          14. Hind wing with nervule 8 remote from 7 after end of cell (Cat. 15-18).

            15. Tarsi as short as tibia, hairy ; stoutly built moths

                Fam. 11. **Notodontidae,**[2] see p. 383.

            16. Tarsi long and naked ; slightly built moths (Cat. 17 and 18)

              17. Fore wing with nervule 7 remote from 8, and generally stalked with 6

                Fam. 40. **Epiplemidae,** see p. 420.

              18. Fore wing with nervule 7 given off from 8 ; hind wing with nervure 1a short or absent

                Fam. 36. **Geometridae,** see p. 411.

---

[1] For explanatory diagram of the wings, see Fig. 161, I. When the nervuration is obscured by the wing-scales, it may be rendered temporarily visible by the application, with a camel's-hair brush, of a little benzine. The wings may be permanently denuded of their scales by being placed for a short time in Eau de Javelle (hypochlorite of potash).

[2] The genus *Cyphanta* (one species from India) has nervule 5 of the fore wing proceeding from the lower angle of the cell.

B. Fore wing with nervule 5 coming from lower angle of cell or nearer 4 than 6 [see figures 161 and 162, pp. 318, 319] (Categories 19-58).

  19. Hind wing with more than 8 nervules (Cat. 20, 21).

    20. Proboscis absent, no mandibles nor ligula ; size not very small
Fam. 23. **Hepialidae,** see p. 396.

    21. Mandibles, long palpi and ligula present ; size very small
Fam. 47. **Micropterygidae,** see p. 435.

  22. Hind wing with not more than 8 nervules (Cat. 23-58).

    23. Hind wing with nervule 8 remote from 7 after origin of nervules 6 and 7 (Cat. 24-51).

      24. Frenulum absent (Cat. 25-29).

        25. Hind wing with one internal nervure ; nervule 8 with a precostal spur, Fam. 31. **Pterothysanidae,** see p. 406.

        26. Hind wing with two internal nervures (Cat. 27 and 28).

          27. Hind wing with a bar between nervules 7 and 8 near the base; nervure 1a directed to middle of inner margin   Fam. 30. **Endromidae,** see p. 406.

          28. Hind wing with no bar between nervules 7 and 8 ; nervure 1a directed to anal angle
Fam. 29. **Lasiocampidae,** see p. 405.

        29. Hind wing with three internal nervures
Fam. 21. **Arbelidae,** see p. 396.

      30. Frenulum present (Cat. 31-51).

        31. Hind wing with nervule 8 aborted,
Fam. 15. **Syntomidae,** see p. 388.

        32. Hind wing with nervule 8 present (Cat. 33-51).

          33. Antennae knobbed Fam. 1. **Castniidae,** see p. 371.

          34. Antennae filiform, or (rarely) dilated a little towards the tip (Cat. 35-51).

            35. Fore wing with nervure 1c present (Cat. 36-43).

              36. Hind wing with nervule 8 free from the base or connected with 7 by a bar (Cat. 37-42).

                37. Proboscis present
Fam. 16. **Zygaenidae,** see p. 390.

                38. Proboscis absent (Cat. 39-42).

                  39. Palpi rarely absent; ♀ winged ; larvae wood-borers
Fam. 20. **Cossidae,** see p. 395.

                  40. Palpi absent ; ♀ apterous (Cat. 41, 42).

                    41. ♀ rarely with legs ; ♀ and larvae case-dwellers
Fam. 19. **Psychidae,** see p. 392.

                    42. ♀ and larvae free [1]
Fam. 18. **Heterogynidae,** see p. 392.

---

[1] This is a mistake of Sir George Hampson's. It has long been known that the female of *Heterogynis* does not leave the cocoon (for references see p. 392) ; the larvae, however, do not live in cases, as those of Psychidae do.

43. Hind wing with nervule 8 anastomosing
shortly with 7

> Fam. 26. **Limacodidae,** see. p. 401.

44. Fore wing with nervure 1c absent (Cat. 45-51).

45. Hind wing with nervule 8 rising out of 7

> Fam. 34. **Arctiidae,** see p. 408.

46. Hind wing with nervule 8 connected with 7
by a bar, or touching it near middle of
cell (Cat. 47, 48).

47. Palpi with the third joint naked and
reaching far above vertex of head ;
proboscis present

> Fam. 33. **Hypsidae,** see p. 408.

48. Palpi not reaching above vertex of
head ; proboscis absent or very minute

> Fam. 32. **Lymantriidae,** see p. 406.

49. Hind wing with nervule 8 anastomosing
shortly with 7 near the base ; proboscis
well developed (Cat. 50, 51).

50. Antennae more or less thick towards tip

> Fam. 35. **Agaristidae,** see p. 410.

51. Antennae filiform

> Fam. 37. **Noctuidae,** see p. 414.

52. Hind wing with nervule 8 curved and nearly or quite
touching nervule 7, or anastomosing with it after origin of
nervules 6 and 7 (Cat. 53-58).

53. Hind wing with nervure 1c absent (Cat. 54-57).

54. Hind wing with nervule 8 with a precostal spur

> Fam. 24. **Callidulidae,** see p. 400.

55. Hind wing with nervule 8 with no precostal spur
(Cat. 56, 57).

56. Hind wing with nervure 1a absent or very short

> Fam. 25. **Drepanidae,** see p. 400.

57. Hind wing with nervure 1a almost or quite
reaching anal angle

> Fam. 28. **Thyrididae,** see p. 404.

58. Hind wing with nervure 1c present

> Fam. 41. **Pyralidae,** see p. 420.

C. Fore wing with 4 nervules arising from the cell at almost even distances apart (Cat. 59-66).

59. Wings not divided into plumes (Cat. 60-63).

60. Hind wing with nervule 8 coincident with 7

> Fam. 13. **Sesiidae,** see p. 386.

61. Hind wing with nervule 8 free (Cat. 62, 63).

62. Fore wing with nervure 1b simple or with a very
minute fork at base

> Fam. 14. **Tinaegeriidae,** see p. 387.

63. Fore wing with nervure 1a forming a large fork
with 1b at base   Fam. 45. **Tineidae,** see p. 428.

64. Wings divided into plumes (Cat. 65, 66).
65. Fore wing divided into at most two, hind wing into three plumes . . . Fam. 42. **Pterophoridae**, see p. 426.
66. Fore wing and hind wing each divided into three plumes Fam. 43. **Alucitidae** (= **Orneodidae**), see p. 426.

Fam. 1. Castniidae.——*The Insects of this family combine to a large extent the characters of butterflies and moths. The antennae are knobbed or hooked at the tip, there is a large precostal area to the hind wing. The nervules of the front wing are complex and anastomose so as to form one or more accessory cells* (Fig. 162). This important, but not extensive, family consists chiefly of forms found in tropical America and Australia. The diversity of size, form and appearance is very great, and it is probable that the members of the family will be separated; indeed, taxonomists are by no means in agreement as to the limits of the family. The Castniidae are diurnal Insects, and the North American genus *Megathymus* is by many considered to belong to the Rhopalo-cera. *Euschemon rafflesiae* (Fig. 186) is extremely like a large Skipper with long antennae, but has a well-marked frenulum. The members of the Australian genus

FIG. 186.——*Euschemon rafflesiae.* Australia. (After Doubleday.)

Synemon are much smaller, but they also look like Skippers. Their habits are very like those of the Hesperiidae; they flit about in the hot sunshine, and when settling after their brief flights, the fore wings are spread out at right angles to the body, so as to display the more gaily coloured hind wings; at night, or in cloudy weather, the Insect rests on blades of grass with the wings erect, meeting vertically over the back, like a butterfly. *Hecatesia*, another Australian genus, is now usually assigned to Agaristidae; its members look like moths. The male of *H. fenestrata* is provided with a sound-producing organ similar to that of the Agaristid genus *Aegocera*. The *Castnia* of South America are many of them like

Nymphalid butterflies, but exhibit great diversity, and resemble butterflies of several different divisions of the family.[1]

The species are apparently great lovers of heat and can tolerate a very dry atmosphere.[2] The transformations of very few have been observed; so far as is known the larvae feed in stems; and somewhat resemble those of Goat-moths or Leopard-moths (Cossidae); the caterpillar of *C. therapon* lives in the stems of Brazilian orchids, and as a consequence has been brought to Europe, and the moth there disclosed. The pupae are in general structure of the incomplete character, and have transverse rows of spines, as is the case with other moths of different families, but having larvae with similar habits.[3] *Castnia eudesmia* forms a large cocoon of fragments of vegetable matter knitted together with silk. These Insects are rare in collections; they do not ever appear in numbers, and are generally very difficult to capture.

Fam. 2. Neocastniidae. — The Oriental genus *Tascina* formerly placed in Castniidae has recently been separated by Sir G. Hampson and associated with *Neocastnia nicevillei*, from East India, to form this family. These Insects have the appearance of Nymphalid butterflies. They differ from Castniidae by the want of a proboscis.

Fam. 3. Saturniidae.—This is a large and varied assemblage of moths; the larvae construct cocoons; the products of several species being used as silk. These moths have no frenulum and no proboscis. The hind wings have a very large shoulder, so that the anterior margin or costa stretches far forward beneath the front wing, as it does in butterflies. The antennae of the males are strongly bipectinated and frequently attain a magnificent development. The family includes some of the largest and most remarkable forms of the Insect-world. *Coscinocera hercules*, inhabiting North Australia, is a huge moth which, with its expanded wings and the long tails thereof, covers a space of about 70 square inches. One of the striking features of the family is the occurrence in numerous forms of remarkable transparent spaces on the wings; these window-like areas usually occur in the middle of the wing and form a most remarkable contrast to the rest of the surface, which is very densely

---

[1] See Westwood, *Tr. Linn. Soc. London* (2), i. 1877, p. 165, etc.

[2] For habits of some Brazilian Castnia see Seitz, *Ent. Zeit. Stettin*, li. 1890, p. 258.

[3] For pupa see Chapman, *Ent. Rec.* vi. 1895, pp. 286, 288.

scaled.   In *Attacus* these attain a large size.   In other species,
such as the South African *Ludia delegorguei*, there is a small
letter-like, or symboliform, transparent mark towards the tip of
each front wing.   We have at present no clue to the nature
or importance of these remarkable markings.   In the genus
Automeris, and in other forms, instead of transparent spaces
there are large and staring ocellate marks or eyes, which are
concealed when the Insect is reposing.   In *Arceina, Copiopteryx,
Eudaemonia* and others, the hind wings are prolonged into very
long tails, perhaps exceeding in length those of any other moths.

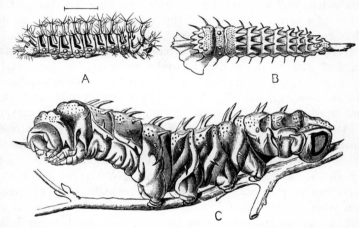

Fig. 187.—Larva of *Attacus atlas*.   India.   **A**, at end of 1st instar, profile ; **B**, 4th
instar, dorsal view ; **C**, full-grown larva, in repose.   (After Poujade.)

The cocoons are exceedingly various, ranging from a slight
open network to a dense elaborate structure arranged as in our
Emperor moth ; in this latter case an opening is left by the
larva for its exit after it has become a moth, but by an ingenious,
chevaux-de-frise work, this opening is closed against external
enemies, though the structure offers no resistance at all to the
escape of the moth.   Fabre has recorded some observations and
experiments which seem to show that the instinct predominating
over the formation of the cocoon is not cognoscent.   The Insect,
if interfered with, displays a profound stupidity.   Its method is
blind perseverance in the customary.[1]   The cocoon of Saturniidae
is more often continuous, *i.e.* entirely closed.   Packard says that

---

[1] *Souvenirs entomologiques*, quatrième série, 1891, pp. 39-46.

Actias luna effects its escape by cutting through the strong cocoon with an instrument situate at the base of the front wing. Other species were examined and were found to possess the instrument; but Packard is convinced that the majority of the species possessing the instrument do not use it, but escape by emitting a fluid that softens the cocoon and enables the moth to push itself through.[1] The cocoons of the species of *Ceranchia* have a beautiful appearance, like masses of filagree-work in silver. The pupa in *Ceranchia* is very peculiar, being terminated by a long, spine-like process. In *Loepa newara* the cocoon is of a green colour and suspended by a stalk; looking like the pod, or pitcher, of a plant. The silk of the Saturniidae is usually coarse, and is known as Tusser or Tussore [2] silk.

The larvae of this family are as remarkable as the imagos, being furnished with spine-bearing tubercles or warts, or long fleshy processes; the colours are frequently beautiful. The caterpillar of *Attacus atlas* (Fig. 187) is pale olive-green and lavender, and has a peculiar, conspicuous, red mark on each flank close to the clasper.

About seventy genera and several hundred species are already known of this interesting family. They are widely distributed on the globe, though there are but few in Australia. Our only British species, the Emperor moth, *Saturnia pavonia*, is by no means rare, and its larva is a beautiful object; bright green with conspicuous tubercles of a rosy, or yellow, colour. It affects an unusual variety of food-plants, sloe and heather being favourites; the writer has found it at Wicken flourishing on the leaves of the yellow water-lily. Although the Emperor moth is one of the largest of our native Lepidopterous Insects, it is one of the smallest of the Saturniidae.

The family Hemileucidae of Packard is included at present in Saturniidae.

Fam. 4. Brahmaeidae.—The species forming the genus *Brahmaea* have been placed in various families, and are now treated by Hampson as a family apart, distinguished from Saturniidae by the presence of a proboscis. They are magnificent, large moths, of sombre colours, but with complex patterns on the wings, looking as if intended as designs for

---

[1] *Amer. Natural.* xii. 1878, p. 379.
[2] Cotes, "Wild Silk Insects of India," *Ind. Mus. Notes*, ii. No. 2, 1891, 15 plates.

upholstery.   About fifteen species are recognised; the geographical distribution is remarkable; consisting of a comparatively
narrow belt extending across the Old World from Japan to West
Africa, including Asia Minor and the shores of the Caspian Sea.
Little has been recorded as to the life-histories of these Insects.
The larva is said to have the second and third segments swollen
and armed with a pair of lateral spines projecting forwards.   A
cocoon is not formed.

Fam. 5. Ceratocampidae.——This is a small family.   They are
fine moths peculiar to the New World, and known principally by
scattered notices in the works of North American entomologists.
Seven genera and about sixty species are known.   The chief
genus is *Citheronia*.   Some of the larvae are remarkable, being
armed with large and complex spines.   A cocoon is not formed.

Fam. 6. Bombycidae. — In entomological literature this
name has a very uncertain meaning, as it has been applied to
diverse groups; even at present the name is frequently used for
the Lasiocampidae.   We apply it to the inconsiderable family
of true silkworm moths.   They are comparatively small and
uninteresting Insects in both the larval and imaginal instars;
but the cocoons formed by the well-known silkworm are of great
value, and some other species form similar structures that are of
more or less value for commercial purposes.   The silkworm has
been domesticated for an enormous period, and is consequently
now very widely spread over the earth's surface; opinions differ
as to its real home, some thinking it came originally from
Northern China, while others believe Bengal to have been its
native habitat.   The silkworm is properly called *Bombyx mori*,
but perhaps it is as often styled *Sericaria mori*.   Besides being
of so great a value in commerce, this Insect has become an
important object of investigation as to anatomy, physiology and
development.   Its domestication has probably been accompanied
by a certain amount of change in habits and instincts, the
creature having apparently lost its appreciation of freedom and
its power of flight; it is also said to be helpless in certain
respects when placed on trees in the larval state; but the importance of these points has been perhaps somewhat exaggerated.[1]

Although the family Bombycidae is very widely distributed
in the warmer regions of the world, it includes only 15 or 20

---

[1] See on this subject Pérez, *Act. Soc. Bordeaux*, xlvii. 1894, p. 236, etc.

genera, and none of them have many species. The Mustiliidae of some entomologists are included here. Like the Saturniidae, the Bombycidae are destitute of proboscis and of frenulum to the wings, but they possess two or three internal nervures on the hind wing instead of the single one existing in Saturniidae.

Fam. 7. Eupterotidae (Striphnopterygidae of Aurivillius).— This family has only recently been separated from Lasiocampidae ; its members, however, possess a frenulum ; while none is present in the larger family mentioned. Its limits are still uncertain, but it includes several extremely interesting forms. The larvae of the European processionary moth, *Cnethocampa processionea,* are social in habits ; they sometimes occur in very large numbers, and march in columns of peculiar form, each band being headed by a leader in front, and the column gradually becoming broader. It is thought that the leader spins a thread as he goes on, and that the lateral leaders of the succeeding files fasten the threads they spin to that of the first individual, and in this way all are brought into unison. The hairs of these caterpillars are abundant, and produce great irritation to the skin and mucous membrane of any one unlucky enough to come into too close contact with the creatures. This property is, however, not confined to the hairs of the processionary moths, but is shared to a greater or less extent by the hairs of various other caterpillars of this division of Lepidoptera. In some cases the irritation is believed to be due to the form of the hair or spine, which may be barbed or otherwise peculiar in form. It is also thought that in some cases a poisonous liquid is contained in the spine.

The larvae of other forms have the habit of forming dense webs, more or less baglike, for common habitation by a great number of caterpillars, and they afterwards spin their cocoons inside these receptacles. This has been ascertained to occur in the case of several species of the genus *Anaphe,* as has been described and illustrated by Dr. Fischer,[1] Lord Walsingham,[2] and Dr. Holland.[3] The structures are said to be conspicuous objects on trees in some parts of Africa. The common dwelling of this kind formed by the caterpillars of *Hypsoides radama* in Madagascar is said to be several feet in length ; but the structures of most of the other species are of much smaller size.

---

[1] *Berlin. ent. Zeitschr.* xxvii. 1883, p. 9.
[2] *Tr. Linn. Soc.* ser. 2, ii. 1885, p. 421.　　　　[3] *Psyche,* vi. 1893, p. 385.

The larvae of the South American genus *Palustra*, though hairy like other Eupterotid caterpillars, are aquatic in their habits, and swim by coiling themselves and making movements of extension; the hair on the back is in the form of dense brushes, but at the sides of the body it is longer and more remote; when the creatures come to the surface—which is but rarely—the dorsal brushes are quite dry, while the lateral hairs are wet. The stigmata are extremely small, and the mode of respiration is not fully known. It was noticed that when taken out of the water, and walking in the open air, these caterpillars have but little power of maintaining their equilibrium. They pupate beneath the water in a singular manner: a first one having formed its cocoon, others come successively and add theirs to it so as to form a mass.[1] Another species of *Palustra, P. burmeisteri*, Berg,[2] is also believed to breathe by means of air entangled in its long clothing; it comes to the surface occasionally, to renew the supply; the hairs of the shorter brushes are each swollen at the extremity, but whether this may be in connexion with respiration is not known. This species pupates out of the water, between the leaves of plants.

Dirphia tarquinia is remarkable on account of the great difference of colour and appearance in the two sexes. In the Australian genus *Marane* the abdomen is densely tufted at the extremity with hair of a different colour.

Fam. 8. Perophoridae.—The moths of the genus *Perophora* have for long been an enigma to systematists, and have been placed as abnormal members of Psychidae or of Drepanidae, but Packard now treats them as a distinct family. The larvae display no signs of any social instincts, but, on the contrary, each one forms a little dwelling for itself. Some twenty species of *Perophora* are now known; they inhabit a large part of the New World, extending from Minnesota to Buenos Aires. The habits of *P. melsheimeri* have been described by Harris, Packard[3] and Newman, and those of *P. batesi* by Newman.[4] The larva is very peculiar; there is a flexible pair of appendages on the

[1] Bar and Laboulbène, *Ann. Soc. ent. France*, (v.) iii. 1873, p. 300.
[2] *Op cit.* (5), vii. 1877, p. 181; and *Ent. Zeit. Stettin*, xxxix. 1878, p. 221; and xliv. 1883, p. 402.
[3] *Ann. New York Ac.* viii. 1893, p. 48.
[4] *Tr. ent. Soc. London*, n.s. iii. 1854, p. 1.

head, the use of which is unknown ;[1] they arise by slender stalks
behind and above the eyes, are about as long as the head, and
are easily broken off.   After hatching, the young larva, when it
begins to feed, fastens two leaves together with silk threads, and
so feeds after the fashion of a Tortricid, rather than a case-making,
larva.   Subsequently, however, the caterpillar entirely detaches
two pieces of leaves and fastens them together at the edges, thus
constructing a case that it lives in, and carries about ; it can
readily leave the case and afterwards return to it.   When at
rest, the larva relieves itself from the effort of supporting this
case by the device of fastening it to a leaf with a few silken
threads ; when the creature wished to start again, " it came out
and bit off these threads close to the case."   Subsequently it
changes inside the case to a pupa armed with transverse rows of
teeth, like so many other pupae that are capable of a certain
amount of movement.   The larva is of broad, short, peculiar
form, and is said to be very bold in defending itself when attacked.   The moth is somewhat like the silkworm moth, though
of a more tawny colour.   Newman does not allude to any
cephalic appendages as existing in the larva of *P. batesi*.
If we accept the eggs figured and described by Snellen,[2] as those
of *P. batesi*, it is possible that this Insect possesses a peculiar
mode of oviposition, the eggs being placed one on the other, so
as to form an outstanding string ; but we think this example
probably abnormal ; the mode is not shared by *P. melsheimeri*.
The genus *Lacosoma* is considered by Packard to be an ally of
Perophora.   The caterpillar of *L. chiridota* doubles a leaf at the
mid-rib and fastens the two edges together, thus forming an un-
symmetrical case.   Many larvae of Microlepidoptera do something
like this, but the *Lacosoma* cuts off the habitation thus formed and
carries it about.   Packard says it may have descended from
ancestors with ordinary habits and that certain peculiar obsolete
markings on the body of the caterpillar may be indications of this.[3]
The Argentinian Insect *Mamillo curtisea* [4] is also probably an ally

---

[1] Dyar says, " We may surmise that it is to present a terrifying appearance to-
ward small enemies."   He calls the Insect both *Perophora* and *Cicinnus, melsheimeri*, and states that it belongs [according to the larva] to Tineidae ; the appendages
he considers to be enormously developed setae.   *J. N. York ent. Soc.* iv. 1896, p. 92.

[2] *Tijdschr. Ent.* xxxviii. 1895, p. 56, Pl. 4.

[3] *Ann. New York Ac.* viii. 1893, p. 48.

[4] Weyenbergh, *Tijdschr. Ent.* xvii. 1874, p. 220, Pl. xiii.

of *Lacosoma*.   The caterpillar of this moth spins a dwelling
for itself, and is remarkable from the bright colour of the
thoracic segments, the following somites being colourless ; the
head bears a pair of large processes, quite different from
those figured by Harris.   The moth itself is very Geometrid-
like in colour and form.   This species is now assigned to *Pero-*

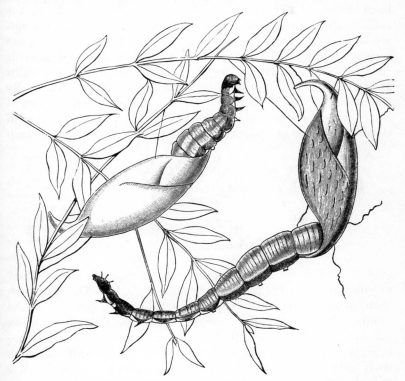

Fig. 188.—Larvae of Hammock-moth, *Perophora sanguinolenta*, projecting from their
    Hammocks, built from their own excrement.   South America.   (After Jones.)

phora, but it seems to be very doubtful whether many of the
species placed in this genus really belong to it.   The diversity
of habits and instincts evinced by these moths of exceptional
modes of life, but considered to be closely allied, is very interesting.   The most remarkable of all is the Hammock-moth, *Pero-*
phora sanguinolenta, of the centre of South America, the larva of
which constructs its portable habitations out of its own excre-

ment, which is of peculiar form, specially suitable for the purpose. The caterpillar, when wishing to enlarge its case, builds it up from excrement "flattened at the sides, so as to adapt it for building purposes." [1]

Fam. 9. Sphingidae (*Hawk-moths*).—A very important family of moths of large or moderate size. They have a proboscis which is frequently very long; there is a frenulum; the body is stouter than in most other Lepidoptera, and the wings are of small superficies in comparison with it; the antennae are somewhat peculiar, having a thick, solid appearance, pointed at the tip. This is usually somewhat hooked, and bears a few hairs. In the males the antennae are formed in a manner specially characteristic of the family. In section, each joint shows a chitinous process on the under side (Fig. 189, A), forming with that of the other joints a continuous ridge, and on each

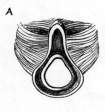 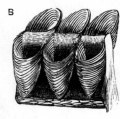

FIG. 189. — Antennae of Sphingidae. **A,** One joint of antenna of *Choerocampa elpenor* ♂, enlarged; **B,** three joints of antenna of *Sphinx ligustri,* seen from one side, and enlarged.

side of this ridge there exists a series of short, delicate "cilia" arranged in a very beautiful manner (Fig. 189, B). This structure, with some modifications, appears to be usually present in the family; it attains a very perfect development in cases where the tips of two rows of cilia bend towards one another, meeting so as to form an arched cavity. This structure is different from what occurs in the males of other families of Lepidoptera, for though cilia are very common, they are usually placed either on two projections from the body of the antennae (instead of on the two sides of a single projection), or there is but a single whorl, or set, of them on each joint (*Catocala,* etc.). The front wings are usually pointed at the tip, and are long in proportion to their width; but in the Smerinthini they are of different form, with the outer margin scalloped; the hind wings are remarkably small; the abdomen is frequently pointed, but in the Macroglossini, or Humming-bird hawk-moths, it is furnished at the

[1] Jones, *P. Liverpool Soc.* xxxiii. 1879, p. lxxvii.

tip with a tuft, or with two tufts, of dense, long scales, capable of expansion.

The larvae are remarkable for their colours and form. The anterior segments are attenuated, but are capable of great retraction, so that in repose (Fig. 190, A) this shape is concealed by the curious attitudes that are assumed. There is in nearly all cases a conspicuous horn on the eleventh segment, and the body at the extremity behind the horn is so much modified that the terminal two segments look like little more than a pair of large claspers. In the Choerocampini, the thoracic segments are retractile, and can be withdrawn into the more or less inflated fourth segment, and give the creature somewhat the appearance

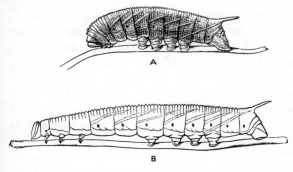

FIG. 190.—Larva of the Poplar Hawk-moth, *Smerinthus populi*. × 1. **A,** in repose ; **B,** in movement.

of a miniature hooded snake. The larvae of Sphingidae do not bear any conspicuous hairs—except during the first instar. They do not spin cocoons, but bury themselves in the earth. The pupa is remarkable from the deep cleft that exists to admit air to the first spiracle, and for a deep depression on each side of the anterior part of abdominal segments 5-7 ; in some cases the proboscis projects on the breast somewhat like the handle of a pitcher.

A great deal has been written on the colours, markings, and attitudes of Sphingid larvae, and many interesting facts have been brought to light. We may refer the reader to the writings of Weismann[1] and Poulton,[2] without, however, recommending him to place an implicit confidence in their somewhat metaphysical disquisitions ; for the views there shadowed will

[1] *Studies in the Theory of Descent*, part 2, London, 1881.
[2] *Tr. ent. Soc. London*, 1885 and 1886.

necessarily became much modified with the advance of exact knowledge. It is certain that the position assumed by the same individual varies much according to age, and to the interval since the last moult; sometimes the attitude is much more remarkable than that shown in Figure 190, A, for the anterior segments are held erect, as well as contracted, the front part of the body being curled, and the Insect supported by the claspers and two pairs only of the abdominal feet. There is, too, a considerable difference in colour before and after an ecdysis. Piepers, who has had a long experience among Sphingid larvae in Java, considers that much of what has been written as to the protective value of their colours and attitudes, is mere fancy, and wild generalisation.[1]

Sphingidae have been recorded as capable of producing sounds in the larval and pupal, as well as in the perfect, instars; but the method in which this is done has not been ascertained, except in the case of the imago of the Death's-head moth, which is well known to emit a very audible cry when not on the wing; in this case it is highly probable that the method is the friction of the palpi against the proboscis, as stated by Réaumur and Landois; the inner face of the palp is said to be marked in this case with fine ridges or striae.

Fam. 10. Cocytiidae.—A single genus constitutes this family, and there are only three or four species known; they come from

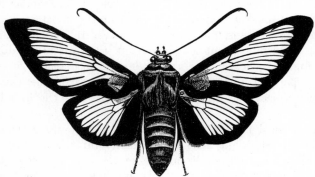

Fig. 191.—*Cocytia durvillii.* New Guinea. (After Boisduval.)

the region of New Guinea, whence the first was brought by D'Urville nearly a hundred years ago. They are still amongst

[1] *Tijdschr. Ent.* xl. 1897, pp. 27-103, 4 plates.

the rarest of Insects.   Nothing is known as to their life-histories.
In appearance they somewhat remind us of the Bee-hawk moths and
Zygaenidae.   Butler says [1] the family is characterised by the palpi,
which differ much in the two sexes, and by the antennae resembling those of Castniidae or Hesperiidae.   The form, transparency,
and coloration of the wings reminds one vividly of the Sphingid
genus *Hemaris ;* the nervuration is somewhat like that of *Hemaris*,
but has certain features of Zygaenidae.   Butler places the family
between Agaristidae and Zygaenidae.

Fam. 11. Notodontidae (*Prominents, Puss-moths,* etc.).——This
is one of the most extensive of the families of Bombyces ; it consists in larger part of obscure-coloured moths, somewhat like the
ordinary Noctuidae of temperate regions; to which family the Noto-
donts are indeed considered to be very closely allied.   The family
contains, however, some very remarkable forms.   *Tarsolepis* has
an elongate body,
terminated (in the
female of *T. ful-
gurifera*) by a very
conspicuous   tuft
of   enormously
long,   battledore
scales ;   while   in
the   male   of   *T.
sommeri* the hind
legs are provided
with an append-
age   of   beautiful,
roseate hairs.   A
few   of   the   larger
kinds   bear   a   considerable   resem-
blance in form and

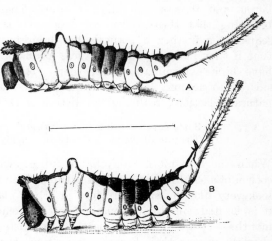

FIG. 192.——*Cerura vinula* (Puss-moth) caterpillar.   **A,** Moulting ;   **B,** the same individual a few hours after the moult.

proportions to the Sphingidae.   Some of the larvae are most interesting objects ; the Puss-moth caterpillar, the Lobster, and the
Dragon larvae are of such strange forms that they have already
interested several generations of observers.   The Puss-moth is
common in the southern half of England ; its caterpillar (Fig. 192)
has, instead of the claspers, a pair of tubes in which are concealed

[1] *Tr. ent. Soc. London*, 1884, p. 351.

two long, flexible whips, capable of being thrust out, and with-drawn, with rapidity. The structure and the mode of action of these flagella have been well elucidated by Professor Poulton.[1] The flagella are to be considered as actual prolongations of the receptacle in which each is placed, though they are of very different texture therefrom; they are everted by blood-pressure and drawn in by muscular action; this latter function is very perfectly accomplished, the amount of relaxation and contraction of the muscle being very great. It has been maintained that the whips have arisen as arms of protection against the attacks of Ichneumon flies; observation shows, however, that the pro-portion of these "protected" Insects destroyed by enemies of this sort is quite as large as it is in the case of forms that are not so protected. The Puss-moth larva is also believed to be protected by terrifying attitudes,[2] as well as by ejection (like so many other larvae and insects generally) of fluid. There is no reason for believing that these larvae are less eaten than others, and con-sequently a further hypothesis has been proposed, to the effect that if they had not acquired these means of defence they would have been exterminated altogether. This supposition is con-sidered to account for their acquiring the defence by means of natural selection; realising the dictum of D. O'Phace, Esq.—

> Some flossifers think that a fakkilty's granted,
> The minnit it's proved to be thoroughly wanted.

When the Puss-moth caterpillar is full grown it spins a peculiar cocoon of a solid and impervious nature, which it manages to make look very like the spots, crevices, or other places amongst which it is located; in this prison the creature remains for nine or ten months—by far the larger part of its existence. When it has changed to a moth it has to escape from the cell in which it so effectually confined itself. This is effected by the cocoon being thinner in front of the head of the moth, and by the emission from the alimentary canal of a fluid that softens the cocoon at the spot alluded to. Mr. Latter has ascertained[3] that this fluid is strongly alkaline, and contains potassium hydroxide. The front of the head of the moth is provided with a shield, consist-ing of a portion of the pupa shell, which enables the moth to

---

[1] *Tr. ent. Soc. London*, 1887, p. 297, Pl. x.

[2] See Poulton, *Tr. ent. Soc. London*, 1886, etc.   [3] *Op. cit.* 1895, p. 399.

push through in safety, and at the same time protects the head
from the emitted fluid. Figure 192 shows the great change that
occurs in the period of a few hours in the size of the head of the
larva, as well as in that of the spiracles: in A the old spiracles
are seen surrounded by the much larger new orifices, which are
at the moment of moulting quite visible through the skin that is
about to be cast off.

The caterpillar of the Lobster-moth, *Stauropus fagi*, is more
remarkable than that of the Puss-moth, but is unfortunately
very rare. It has remarkably long thoracic legs, the abdomen is
swollen at the tip, and instead of the terminal claspers has two
long slender processes. The effect of these peculiarities is greatly
enhanced by the extraordinary attitude assumed by the caterpillar, which holds the first five segments erect, with the second
and third pairs of thoracic legs outstretched; the swollen terminal
segment is also held erect. Hermann Müller states [1] that when
seen from the front this caterpillar looks like a spider, and also
that when alarmed it moves the long legs after the fashion of
an Arachnid. He believes that it is thus effectually protected
from the attacks of Ichneumons. Birchall says [2] that the young
larva, when at rest, closely resembles, in colour and outline,
one of the twigs of beech with unopened buds, on which it
frequently stations itself; and that, when feeding, its likeness
to a great earwig or to a *Staphylinus* is very striking. Others
say that this caterpillar resembles a dead and crumpled beech
leaf.

The larva of *Hybocampa milhauseri*—the Dragon of old Sepp
—is highly remarkable. When young it has grand lateral
horns in front, and a dorsal row; as it grows the lateral
horns disappear. Dr. Chapman says [3] that he could not understand at first why any larva should have such remarkable angular
outlines, curiously conspicuous corners and humps. But he afterwards found that the creature exactly resembled a curled oak
leaf, eaten and abandoned by a *Tortrix* larva. This caterpillar
also constructs an elaborate cocoon from which the moth escapes
by an operation performed by the pupa, which is provided with
two hard spines, called by Dr. Chapman sardine-openers. " By
a lateral rotatory movement of the pupa, which obtains its fulcrum

[1] *P. ent. Soc. London*, 1880, p. iii.   [2] *Ent. Monthly Mag.* xiii. 1877, p. 231.
[3] *Entomologist*, xxiii. 1890, p. 92.

from the tightness with which it is grasped by the cocoon, it traverses over and over again " the same part of the cocoon till it is cut through ; at the same time the spines act as guides to a fluid which is emitted so as to soften the part that has to be sundered.

Though many other larvae of Notodontidae are of most curious form and assume remarkable attitudes, yet this is not the case with all, and some are quite ordinary and like the caterpillars of common Noctuidae. This is the case with the species *Rhegmatophila alpina* we have selected to illustrate the metamorphosis of the Order (Fig. 157). Those who wish to form an idea of the variety of larval forms in this family will do well to refer to Packard's beautiful volume on the North American forms.[1] The family has a very wide distribution, but is absent from New Zealand and Polynesia, and appears to be but poorly represented in Australia. In Britain we have about two dozen species.

Fam. 12. Cymatophoridae.—A small family of nocturnal moths that connect the Bombyces with the Noctuids ; they are usually associated with the latter, but are widely separated in Hampson's arrangement because of a slight difference of nervuration, nervule 5 being nearer to 6 than to 4, whereas in Noctuidae the reverse is the case. The Insects, however, in certain respects approach the Notodontidae, and are of interest if only as showing that the linear sequences we adopt in books are necessarily conventional, and to some extent deceptive. We have three genera in Britain ; our pretty Peach-blossom, *Thyatira batis*, and the very different Buff-arches, *T. derasa*, being among them. Meyrick denies any connexion of this group with Noctuidae, and in his nomenclature *Cymatophora* becomes *Polyploca*, and the family, consequently, Polyplocidae.

Fam. 13. Sesiidae or **Aegeriidae** (*Clear-wings*).—A family of comparatively small extent ; its members have frequently one or both pairs of wings in large part free from scales, the tip of the body tufted, the hind legs of one sex peculiar. The size is usually small, but in the largest forms the measurement may be but little less than two inches across the expanded wings. The pupa is of the kind classed as " incompletae " by Chapman, the appendages not being firmly glued to the body, and much

---

[1] *Mem. Ac. Washington*, vii. 1895, 290 pp., 49 plates.

mobility existing; an "eye-collar" is present, and the segments
of the abdomen are armed with series of teeth. The larva
is a concealed feeder, nearly naked and colourless, but with
the legs normal in number—three thoracic, four abdominal pairs
of feet, and the terminal claspers; these are sometimes but
poorly developed; the larvae have a greater or less resemblance
to those of Longicorn beetles, the habits of which they share. The
family was formerly associated with the Sphingidae, with which
it has no true relationship; it is more closely allied to the
Tineidae. Some of the species have a certain resemblance to
Hymenoptera, which is probably in most, if not in all cases
merely incidental. The proper position of the family was pointed
out by Butler,[1] but he did not distinguish it from Tinaegeriidae.
Meyrick calls the family Aegeriadae, and places it in his series
Tineina.

We have two genera of these Clear-wings in Britain.
They are *Trochilium* (called variously *Sesia*, *Sphecia*, and
Aegeria), with two species of comparatively large size, and *Sesia*
(called variously *Trochilium* and
Aegeria), with nearly a dozen species
of smaller size. A third genus,
Sciapteron, is doubtfully native with
us. They are much prized by collectors on account of the rarity of
the Insects and their great difference in appearance from our other
native Lepidoptera.

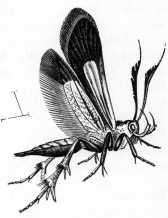

Fam. 14. Tinaegeriidae.—This
is one of the least known of the
families of Lepidoptera, and has only
recently been distinguished from
Sesiidae. It is entirely exotic, and
our knowledge of it is principally
due to Lord Walsingham.[2] Nothing

FIG. 193.—*Oedematopoda princeps.*
Africa. (After Walsingham.)

is known as to the life-histories, except that it has been stated
by Stainton that a larva feeds in webs on shoots of a shrub of
the genus *Clerodendron*. The family is widely distributed, but
its metropolis will probably prove to be the tropics of Africa. It
is of considerable interest as showing that the Sesiidae really

[1] *Tr. ent. Soc. London*, 1878, p. 121, Pl. v.   [2] *Op. cit.* 1889, pp. 1-40, 6 plates.

belong to the Tineid series of moths. The species we figure (Fig. 193) has a character otherwise peculiar to Sesiidae in the wings being inserted on the thorax remote from the head—a feature we do not find in the Tineidae proper; while on the other hand it has the long wing-fringes, and the shape of the wings that are characteristic of Tineidae. It is worth mentioning that though these Insects are of excessive rarity and very peculiar, there exists in the Solomon Islands [1] a species distinct from, though at first sight excessively similar to, the S. African one we figure.

Fam. 15. Syntomidae.—This family has usually been associated with the Zygaenidae. It includes a large number of moths having, as a rule, in external appearance little to distinguish them from the family named. Many of them are of gaudy colours, and probably of diurnal, but somewhat sedentary, habits. The wings are less ample than usual, the hind pair frequently very small, so that the Insects have somewhat the proportions of Hymenoptera. In some cases the resemblance is made more remarkable by the fact that the wings are transparent and bare of scales, or have scales only at the margins, so as to be like the wings of Hymenoptera. Not less remarkable is the fact that these Insects use the body itself for the purposes of adornment or display; thus adopting a system prevalent in the Hymenoptera, rather than that of their own Order, where the rule is that the wings are more ornamented than the body. In many cases the shape of the body is so very different from the normal that the disposition of the organs of life in the interior of the body must be materially affected. In some genera, such as *Andrenimorpha*, the form, colour and attitude of the body and some of the limbs are plainly similar to Hymenoptera. These Insects have a highly-developed frenulum, retinaculum, and proboscis; bipectinate antennae in the male, a complex organ at the base of the abdomen on each side, and are in fact highly-developed forms, except perhaps as regards the structures in connexion with flight.

Unfortunately little or nothing is known as to the habits and metamorphoses of these extraordinary creatures, but it is no doubt to them Seitz referred in saying, " How far one may be deceived by appearances of a mimetic nature can only be comprehended by visiting the tropics; in this part of the world

[1] Walsingham, *Op. cit.*, 1889. *c.* p. 21.

[Europe] one is prepared by knowledge gained from books for the appearance *Sesia* presents. Had one no knowledge of this sort as to Sesiidae he would actually in the field [in Brazil] overlook dozens of these little creatures without being aware of his deception. The surprise at finding a quite different being in the net from what one believes he has caught occurs daily in Brazil, so rich in Lepidoptera." [1] The same intelligent observer says [2] that a species of *Macrocneme* was observed by him to be exactly like one of the blue wasps of the genus *Pepsis*.

One remarkable point in these Hymenopteroid Syntomids is their complete dissimilarity from their immediate allies. They resemble very different Hymenoptera; and not only stinging Hymenoptera; the Sessiliventres have a large share of their attentions; the numerous species of *Dycladia* partaking the appearance of the South American Sawflies in a wonderful manner. Bees, Wasps of the most different kinds, and a variety of Sawflies are beautifully paralleled, if one may use such an expression, by these Syntomids. That shown in Fig. 194 has the abdomen formed like that of a Petiolate Hymenopteron; the base of this part, moreover, resembles in a remarkable manner the "median segment" of that Order. The constriction is, however, placed not at the base of the abdomen but beyond the second segment. Thus the structure is not morphologically similar to that of the Hymenoptera, for the median segment of Aculeate Hymenoptera consists of only one abdominal segment, while in this moth the corresponding part is formed of two segments. Though anatomically inexact, the resemblance is, as to proportions, correct; and those who delight in the use of the imagination will see that had the moth used only one segment for the imitation, the result would have been less successful owing to insufficient size. In his very interesting account of some Brazilian Syntomids, [3] Seitz describes a species of *Trichura* provided with a long appendage that is held straight backwards during life; and he informs us that this creature resembles a female Ichneumon, the long process looking like the elongate ovipositor of the Hymenopteron. Possibly the species from Demerara we figure may resemble an Ichneumon we are not acquainted with, though its colour and form rather suggest a likeness to an Aculeate.

---

[1] *Ent. Zeit. Stettin*, lvi. 1895, p. 233.   [2] *Op. cit.* li. 1890, p. 261.
[3] *Ent. Zeit. Stettin*, li., 1890, p. 263.

This case of resemblance is of the most noteworthy character, for an appendage of this kind in a Lepidopterous Insect is without parallel, and is almost equivalent to the production of a new structure.   An interesting feature of the case is that Ichneumonidae do not sting, and there is no evident reason why the enemies of the moth should be particularly afraid of an ovipositor.

The larvae appear to be in form somewhat like those of Zygaenidae; but with the same sort of remarkable clothing, in the form of tufts and brushes, that we find in Lymantriidae.   A

Fig. 194.—*Trichura*, sp. × ⅔.   Demerara.

cocoon is formed.   In Britain no member of this family is to be met with, but *Naclia ancilla* may formerly have been a native ; *Syntomis phegea* has occurred here ; probably an escaped example that had been introduced in one of its earlier stages.

Fam. 16. Zygaenidae (*Burnet-Moths*).—This family is one about the limits and characters of which much difference of opinion prevails.   As exemplified by our Burnet-moths it is characterised (in addition to the points given in the table) by the peculiar, flexible antennae; these are a little thicker before the tip, but are curved and pointed at the extremity, and without pectinations in the male.   There is an elongate proboscis ; bladder-like organs at the sides of the first abdominal segment are not present.   The pupa is softer than is usual in the Macrolepidoptera, and the parts are less firmly fixed together, so that unusual mobility exists ; six of the intersegmental membranes

are free, and the abdomen has much power of movement; there
is no eye-collar; the antennae, hind legs, and proboscis-tips
stretch backwards as far as the fifth or sixth abdominal segment, the tips being quite free; on the dorsal plates of the
abdomen there are rows of minute elevations reminding one of
the teeth existing in pupae that live in stems or galleries.   This
is altogether a peculiar pupa; it lives closely enclosed in a small
hard cocoon, and its great capacity for movement is perhaps connected with the fact that the pupa itself manages to force its
way through the cocoon in anticipation of the emergence of the
moth.   This cocoon is fastened tightly to a stem, and is covered
with a substance that gives it a glazed appearance.   The larvae
are objects of a baggy nature, with inferior coloration, consisting
of large dark blotches on a light ground, and without any
remarkable development of their somewhat feeble system of
hairs.   Numerous small moths from the tropics are assigned
to the family; they are most of them conspicuously marked
and coloured, and like our Burnets are probably diurnal.

The family Chalcosiidae is reduced by Hampson to the
position of a sub-family of Zygaenidae.   It consists of a large
variety of diurnal moths of varied and brilliant colours, with an
expanse of wing large in
comparison with the typi-
cal Zygaenae, and with
the antennae pectinate or
flabellate to the tip. Some
of these Insects (which are
as conspicuous as possible
in appearance, at any rate
in a cabinet, the East
Indian *Cadphises moorei*

Fig. 195.—*Hampsonia pulcherrima.*   Wings on
right side detached and denuded to show
nervuration.   India.   (After Swinhoe.)

e.g.) are considered to be destitute of any special " protection."
Histia is a genus of remarkable cruciform moths, of a mixture
of black and metallic colours, with carmine-tinted bodies.
Hampsonia pulcherrima (East India) is a curious moth of butterfly form and coloration, red and black with yellow patches, and
with some of the nervules distorted, as if they had been forced
apart in certain spots in order to accommodate these patches.

Two or three hundred species of Chalcosiidae are recorded.
They are specially characteristic of the Indo-Malayan region.

Fam. 17. Himantopteridae (**Thymaridae** of some authorities) are placed by Hampson in the sub-family Phaudinae of Zygaenidae characterised by the absence of the mouth-parts. The Himantopteridae are small moths, and have the scales on the wings very imperfect and hair-like; the hind wings form long slender tails, so that the Insects scarcely look like moths. They are peculiar to India and Africa. In the South African genus *Dianeura* (belonging really to Phaudinae) also the wings are scaleless and nearly transparent.

Fam. 18. Heterogynidae.—Consists of the single genus *Heterogynis* which has hitherto been found only in the south of Europe. This is an important form connecting Zygaenidae and Psychidae. The larvae resemble those of Zygaena, and construct an oval cocoon for their metamorphosis. The male issues as a small moth of smoky colour, the scales being but imperfect; the female chrysalis shows no trace of any appendages, and the imago is practically a maggot, and never leaves the cocoon; in it she deposits her eggs, and the young larvae hatch there.[1]

Fam. 19. Psychidae.—Small, or moderate-sized moths, with imperfect scales, and little or no colour beyond certain shades of duskiness; the sexes very different, the female being wingless and sometimes quite maggot-like; the male often with remarkable, bipectinate antennae, the branches sometimes very long and flexible. Larva inhabiting a case that it carries about. This family consists of Insects unattractive in appearance but presenting some points of great interest. It is frequently stated that the Psychidae are destitute of scales, but Heylaerts states[2] that, in addition to hairs, scales of a more or less imperfect formation are present in all, but that they are, like those of some Sphingidae (*Macroglossa*), very easily detached. There is much difference in the females, some having well-developed legs, while others are not only apterous, but are bare and destitute of appendages like a maggot, while in certain cases (Fig. 196, G), the head is reduced in size and is of peculiar form so as to make the Insect look really like the larva of one of the parasitic Diptera. These females never leave their cases, but deposit their eggs

---

[1] For details as to habits, etc., see Rambur, *Ann. Soc. ent. France*, v. 1836, p. 577 ; and Graslin, *op. cit.* xix. 1850, p. 396.

[2] Monograph of European Psychidae, *Ann. Soc. ent. Belgique*, xxv. 1881, p. 29, etc.

therein, and inside, also, their former pupa-skin; and here the
young hatch; the peculiar little larvae are very numerous, and it is
suggested that they make a first meal on the body of their parent,
but this we believe has not been satisfactorily ascertained.
Great differences as to the condition of the legs, antennae, etc.,
are said to exist in species of the same genus.   There is also a
remarkable diversity in the pupae of the females; the male sex
being normal in this respect.   Some of the female pupae are
destitute of wing-sheaths and all other appendages, while others
are said to possess them, though there are no wings at all in
the imago (*Fumea, e.g.*).[1]   Great difficulties attend the study of
these case-bearing Insects, and several points require careful

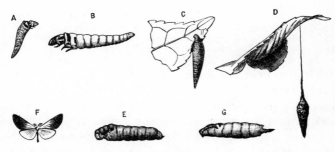

Fig. 196.—Metamorphosis of *Monda rhabdophora*.   Ceylon.   **A**, Larva in case, nat.
size ; **B**, larva itself, magnified ; **C**, case of female during pupation ; **D**, case of male
during pupation ; **E**, female pupa, magnified ; **F**, male moth, nat. size ; **G**, female
moth, magnified.   (From unpublished drawings by Mr. E. E. Green).

reconsideration, amongst them the one we have just mentioned.
The males fly rapidly in a wild manner, and may sometimes
be met with in swarms; their lives are believed to be very brief,
rarely exceeding a couple of days, and sometimes being limited
to a few hours.

The larvae are called basket-worms, and their baskets or
cases are well worthy of attention.   Their variety is remarkable; the most extraordinary are some of the genus *Apterona*
Fig. 197, B, which perfectly resemble the shells of Molluscs
such as snails; indeed, the specimens in the collection at
the British Museum were sent there as shells.   This case is not,
like those of other Psychidae, constructed of earth or vegetable
matter, but is of silk and is in texture and appearance exactly

[1] Heylaerts, *op. cit.* p. 55.

like the surface of a shell.　*Psyche helix* is, according to Ingenitzky,[1] found in great numbers near Lake Issyk-kul in Central Asia, where the larvae feed, in their snail-shell-like cases, on a grass, just like snails.　Only females could be reared from these larvae.　The case of *Chalia hockingii* (Fig. 197, C) consists of little pieces of wood cut to the proper lengths, and spirally arranged, so as to form a construction that would be quite a credit to our own species.　In some of the Canephorinae we

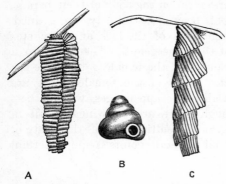

A　　　　　　　　B　　　　　　　C

FIG. 197.—Baskets, or cases, of Psychidae.　**A,** *Amicta quadrangularis;* **B,** *Apterona* (or *Cochlophora*) *valvata;* **C,** *Chalia hockingi.*

meet with long cylindrical cases, like those of Caddis-worms, or of Tineid larvae.

Riley has given an account of several points in the structure and natural history of one of the North American basket- or bag-worms, *Thyridopteryx ephemeraeformis;* one of his points being the manner in which the newly hatched larva forms its case.[2]　This question has also been discussed by Packard.[3]　The larvae when hatched in unnatural conditions will make use of fragments of paper, cork, etc., for the case; the act of construction takes one or two hours, and the larva does not eat till the case is completed.　It walks in a peculiar manner, the legs of the third pair being moved forwards together, as if they were the prongs of a fork.

This family is already one of considerable extent, but its study, as already remarked, is but little advanced.　Some naturalists are inclined to place it among the Tineidae, but it is connected with Zygaenidae by means of Heterogynidae.　Mr. Meyrick divides it, placing *Psyche* and *Sterrhopteryx* (the forms representing, according to his ideas, the family Psychidae in Britain) in the series Psychina which includes Zygaenidae.　He

---

[1] *Zool. Anz.* xx. 1897, p. 473.　This is probably *Apterona crenulella,* or one of its varieties.　　　　[2] *Bull. U.S. Dep. Agric. Ent.* x. 1887, p. 22.
[3] *Ann. New York Ac.* viii. 1893, p. 54.

removes the other British genera, *Fumea* and *Epichnopteryx*, to Tineidae near *Solenobia* and *Taleporia*. The group Canephorinae, to which the two genera in question belong, was long since separated from Psychidae by Herrich-Schäffer, but this course was condemned by Heylaerts. Parthenogenesis has been thought by some to occur in numerous species in this family, but Heylaerts says that it is limited to *Apterona crenulella* var. *helix*, and even of this species males are found in certain localities.

Fam. 20. Cossidae (*Goat-Moths*, or *Carpenter-Worms*).—— Moths of moderate, or rather large size, without proboscis, frequently with a dense covering of matted, imperfect scales; the pattern being vague. The larvae bore into trees in which they often make large burrows, leaving holes from which sap exudes. Our common Goat-moth is a good specimen of this family, which is a very widely distributed one. The Australian genus *Ptilomacra* has very large, pectinated antennae in the male. The larvae of Cossidae are nearly bare of clothing and are unadorned ; they form a slight cocoon of silk mixed with gnawed wood. The pupa of the Goat-moth is remarkable for the great development of the rows of teeth on the dorsal aspects of the segments of the abdomen, and for the absence of consolidation in this part, six of the intersegmental incisions being free, and the ventral aspect almost membranous. Very little is known as to other pupae of the family. It is believed that the generations of these Insects are fewer than usual, the growth of the larva occupying a period of two or three years. The larva of *Zeuzera aesculi* forms a temporary cocoon in which it passes a winter-sleep, before again feeding in the spring.[1] It is a moot question whether the Zeuzeridae should be separated from the Cossidae or not. The group includes our Wood-leopard moth, which, like many other Zeuzerids, is spotted in a very striking but inartistic manner. The position the family Cossidae should occupy in an arrangement of the Lepidoptera is a very difficult question. Some consider the Insects to be allied to Tortricidae. The wing-nervuration of *Cossus* is very peculiar and complex, there being four or five cells on the front wing, and three on the hind one. Meyrick places Zeuzeridae as a family of his series Psychina, but separates Cossidae proper (he calls them Trypanidae) as a family of the series Tortricina.

---

[1] Kalender, *Ent. Zeit. Stettin*, xxxv. 1874, p. 203.

Fam. 21. Arbelidae.—Closely allied to Cossidae, but without frenulum, and with less complex wing-nervures. A small
family believed to be similar to Cossidae in the life-history.
The tropical African Arbelidae are considered by Karsch to be
a distinct family, Hollandiidae.

Fam. 22. Chrysopolomidae.—This family has been established by Dr. Aurivillius[1] for an African genus, allied in wing-
nervuration to Cossidae ; the Insects are like Lasiocampidae.

Fam. 23. Hepialidae (*Ghost- and Swift-Moths*).—Moths of
very diverse size, some gigantic ; wings not fitting together well
at the bases ; without a frenulum ; no proboscis ; the scales
imperfect ; the nervures complex. The Hepialidae are extremely
isolated amongst the Lepidoptera ; indeed, they have really no
allies ; the conclusion that they are connected with the Micropterygidae being certainly erroneous. Although but small in
numbers—only about 150 species being known—they exhibit a
remarkable variety in size and colour. Many are small obscure
moths, while others are of gigantic size—six or seven inches
across the wings—and are amongst the most remarkably coloured
of existing Insects. The great *Charagia* of Australia, with
colours of green and rose, bearing white spots, are remarkable.
The South African *Leto venus* is of large size, and has an
astonishing supply of glittering metallic splashes on the wings,
making a barbaric but effective display. The South Australian
Zelotypia staceyi, of enormous size, is also a handsome moth ;
but the majority of species of the family are adorned only in
the feeblest manner.

Very little is known as to the larvae ; they are either subterranean, feeding on roots, or they live in the wood of trees and
shrubs. They are nearly bare, and are apparently the lowest type
of Bombycid larva. At the same time, it would appear there is
considerable variety amongst them. Packard says[2] the young
larva of *Hepialus mustelinus* has the arrangement of setae that is
normal in Tineidae. The larva of *H. humuli* seems to be a very
simple form, but *H. hectus* shows a considerable amount of
divergence from it. They probably live for several years ; the
larva of *H. argenteo-maculatus* in North America lives for three
years, at first eating the roots of Alder and then entering the

---

[1] *Ent. Tidskr.* xvi. 1895, p. 116.

[2] On larvae of Hepialidae, *J. New York ent. Soc.* iii. 1895, p. 69, Plates III. IV.

stems. The pupae are also peculiar. They are of unusually elongate, cylindrical form, with comparatively feeble integument, but with a considerable development of chitinous, elevated, toothed ridges, on the dorsal aspect, and a very strong ridge of this kind

on the ventral surface of the seventh segment; the wing-sheaths are short; it is very difficult to distinguish the full number of abdominal segments. These pupae are remarkably agile, and by wriggling and kicking are able to move a considerable distance; it is said that they can force themselves to the surface even when the superficial soil is quite hard. We cannot consider this pupa naturally placed amongst either the pupae obtectae or incompletae of Chapman.

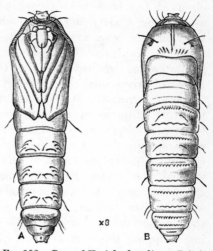

FIG. 198.—Pupa of *Hepialus lupulinus*. Britain. **A,** Ventral ; **B,** dorsal aspect.

We have already remarked that little is known as to the life-histories. The species are probably prolific, a female of *H. thule* having been known to deposit more than 2000 eggs. Of the Australian forms little more is known [1] than that they live in the wood of trees and shrubs, and are rapidly disappearing ; we may fear that some are extinct without ever having been discovered, and others, also unknown but still existing, may disappear only too soon ; the wasteful destruction of timber in Australia having been deplorable.

The peculiar habits of the Hepialidae are not likely to bring the Insects to the net of the ordinary collector, and we believe they never fly to light, hence it is probable that we are acquainted with only a small portion of the existing species; their distribution is very wide, but Australia seems to be their metropolis, and in New Zealand twelve species are known. The genera as at present accepted are remarkable for their wide distribution. *Leto* is said to occur in South Africa and in the

---

[1] Olliff, *Australian Hepialidae, Entomologist*, xxviii. 1895, p. 114.

Fiji Islands; but we must repeat that the study of these interesting Insects is in a very primitive state, and our present knowledge of their distribution may be somewhat misleading.

The habits of the European *Hepialus* in courtship have been observed to a considerable extent and are of great interest, an astonishing variety and a profound distinction in the methods by which the sexes are brought together having been revealed. *H. humuli*, our Ghost-moth, is the most peculiar. Its habits were detected by Dr. Chapman.[1] The male is an Insect of exceptional colour, being white above, in consequence of a dense formation of imperfect scales; the female is of the brownish tints usual in Swift-moths. In the month of June the male selects a spot where he is conspicuous, and hovers persistently there for a period of about twenty minutes in the twilight; his colour has a silvery-white, glistening appearance, so that the Insect is really conspicuous notwithstanding the advanced hour. Females may be detected hovering in a somewhat similar manner, but are not conspicuous like the male, their colour being obscure; while so hovering they are ovipositing, dropping the eggs amongst the grass. Females that have not been fertilised move very differently and dash about in an erratic manner till they see a male; they apparently have no better means of informing the hovering male of their presence than by buzzing near, or colliding with him. Immediately this is done, the male abandons his hovering, and coupling occurs. There can be little doubt that the colour of the male attracts the female; but there is a variety, *hethlandica*, of the former sex coloured much like the female, and in some localities varieties of this sort are very prevalent, though in others the species is quite constant. This variation in the colour of the males is very great in Shetland,[2] some being quite like the females. In *H. hectus* the two sexes are inconspicuously and similarly coloured. The male hovers in the afternoon or evening in a protected spot, and while doing so diffuses an agreeable odour—said by Barrett to be like pine-apple—and this brings the female to him, much in the same manner as the colour of *H. humuli* brings its female. The hind legs of the male

---

[1] *Ent. Mag.* xiii. 1876, p. 63 ; and xxiii. 1886, p. 164.

[2] Weir, *Entomologist*, xiii. 1880, p. 249, plate ; King, *Ent. Record*, vii. 1895, p. 111.

are swollen, being filled with glands for secreting the odorous matter.[1]   This structure has led to the suggestion of the generic name *Phymatopus* for the Insect.   Turning to other species of the genus, we find that the normal relative rôles of the sexes are exhibĭted, but with considerable diversity in the species.   In *H. lupulinus* the males fly about with rapidity, while the female sits on a stem and vibrates her wings ; she thus attracts the males, but they do not perceive her unless happening to come within three or four feet, when they become aware of her proximity, search for and find her.   It is doubtful whether the attraction is in this case the result of an odour ; it would appear more probable that it may be sound, or that the vibration of the wings may be felt by the male.

In *H. sylvinus, H. velleda* and *H. pyrenaicus* less abnormal modes of attracting the males occur, the individuals of this latter sex assembling in great numbers at a spot where there is a female. In the first of the three species mentioned the female sits in the twilight on the stem of some plant and vibrates the wings with rapidity ; she does not fly ; indeed, according to Mr. Robson, she does not till after fertilisation move from the spot where she emerged.   In *H. pyrenaicus* the female is quite apterous, but is very attractive to the males, which as we have said, assemble in large numbers near her.   Thus within the limits of these few allied forms we find radically different relations of the sexes.

1. The male attracts the female—(A) by sight (*H. humuli*) ; (B) by odour (*H. hectus*).
2. The female attracts the male—(A) by vibration of wings (*H. lupulinus* and *H. sylvinus*) ; (B) without vibration, but by some means acting at a distance (*H. velleda, H. pyrenaicus*).

Little or nothing is known as to the habits of the great majority of the more remarkable forms of the family.   The gigantic Australian forms are believed to be scarcely ever seen on the wing.

The Hepialidae differ from other Lepidoptera by very important anatomical characters.   The absence of most of the

---

[1] Bertkau, *SB. Ver. Rheinland*, xxxvi. 1879, p. 288 ; and *Arch. Naturg.* xlviii. i. 1882, p. 362.

mouth-parts is a character common to them and several other divisions of Lepidoptera; but the labial palpi are peculiarly formed in this family, being short and the greater portion of their length consisting of an undivided base, which probably represents some part of the labium that is membranous in normal Lepidoptera. The thoracic segments are remarkably simple, the three differing less from one another than usual, and both meso- and meta-notum being much less infolded and co-ordinated. The wings are remarkable for the similarity of the nervuration of the front and hind wings, and by the cell being divided by longitudinal nervules so as to form three or four cells. On the inner margin of the front wing there is near the base an incision marking off a small prominent lobe, the jugum of Prof. Comstock. Brandt mentions the following anatomical peculiarities,[1] viz. the anterior part of the alimentary canal is comparatively simple; the respiratory system is in some points like that of the larva; the heart is composed of eight chambers; the appendicular glands of the female genitalia are wanting. The testes remain separate organs throughout life. The chain of nerve ganglia consists of the supra- and infra-oesophageal, three thoracic, and five abdominal, ganglia, while other Lepidoptera have four abdominal.

Fam. 24. Callidulidae.—A small family of light - bodied diurnal moths having a great resemblance to butterflies. In some the frenulum is present in a very rudimentary condition, and in others it is apparently absent. *Cleosiris* and *Pterodecta* are very like butterflies of the Lycaenid genus *Thecla*. Although fifty species and seven or eight genera are known, we are quite ignorant of the metamorphoses. Most of the species are found in the islands of the Malay Archipelago, but there are a few in East India.

Fam. 25. Drepanidae (or **Drepanulidae**). (*Hook-tips*).—The larger moths of this family are of moderate size; many of the species have the apex of the front wing pointed or even hooked; some have very much the appearance of Geometrid moths; they resemble very different members of that family. *Oreta hyalodisca* is remarkable on account of the very large, transparent patch on each front wing, though the other species of the genus have nothing of the sort. In the genus *Deroca* we

---

[1] *Zool. Anz.* iii. 1880, p. 186.

find Insects with the scales imperfect, they being few and small and approximating in form to hairs; in *D. hyalina* scales are nearly entirely absent.   In other genera, *e.g. Peridrepana, Streptoperas,* there is only a very inferior state of scale-formation. The few larvae that are known are peculiar; they are nearly bare of hair, without the pair of terminal claspers, while the body is terminated by a long tubular process.   They form a slight cocoon among leaves.

The members of the family were formerly much misunderstood, and were assigned to various positions in the Order. There are now about 30 genera, and 150 species known, the geographical distribution of the family being very wide.   In Britain we have half a dozen species.   *Cilix glaucata* (better known as *C. spinula*) is said " to undoubtedly imitate" the excrement of birds.   No doubt the Insect resembles that substance so as to be readily mistaken for it.   This Insect has a very wide distribution in North America, Europe and East India, and is said to vary so much in the structure of its organs as to justify us in saying that the one species belongs to two or three genera.

Fam. 26. Limacodidae (or **Eucleidae**).—These are somewhat small moths, of stout formation, sometimes very short in the body, and with rather small wing-area.   The family includes however at present many Insects of diverse appearance; there are numerous forms in which apple-green is a prominent colour; some bear a certain resemblance to the Swifts, others to Noctuids; some, *Rosema* and *Staetherinia,* are of extraordinary shapes; certain very small forms, *Gavara, Ceratonema,* resemble Tortricids or Tineids; a few even remind one of Insects of other Orders; so that the group is

Fig. 199.—Mature larva of *Apoda testudo,* on beech-leaf.   Britain.

a mimetic one.   *Nagoda nigricans* (Ceylon) has the male somewhat like a Psychid, while the female has a different system of coloration and wing-form.   In *Scopelodes* the palpi are in both sexes remarkable; elongated, stiff, directed upwards and brush-like at the tip.   Altogether there are about 100 genera and 400 species known; the distribution of the family is very wide in both hemispheres, but these Insects do not occur in insular faunas. In Britain we have two genera, *Heterogenea* and *Apoda* (better known as *Limacodes* [1]), each with a single species.

The early stages of these Insects are of great interest. The eggs, so far as known, are peculiar flat oval scales, of irregular outline and transparent; we have figured an example in Vol. V. Fig. 83. The eggs of the same moth are said to vary much in size, though the larvae that emerge from them differ little from one another in this respect. The latter are peculiar, inasmuch as they have no abdominal feet, and the thoracic legs are but small; hence the caterpillars move in an imperceptible gliding manner that has suggested for some of them the name of slug-worms. The metamorphoses of a few are known. They may be arranged in two groups; one in which the larva is spinose or armed with a series of projections and appendages persisting throughout life; while in the members of the second group the spines have only a temporary existence. At the moment the young larva of *Apoda testudo* emerges from the egg it has no conspicuous spines or processes, and is an extremely soft, colourless creature,[2] but it almost immediately displays a remarkable system of complex spines. These really exist in the larva when it is hatched, and are thrust out from pits, as explained by Dr. Chapman. In the succeeding stages, the spines become modified in form, and the colour of the body and the nature of

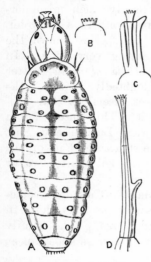

Fig. 200.—Larva of *Apoda testudo* just hatched. **A,** Dorsal view of larva; **B, C, D,** a spine in different states of evagination. All magnified. (After Chapman.)

---

[1] It is much to be regretted that, as in so many other Lepidoptera, no satisfactory agreement as to names has been attained; our British *A. testudo* is variously styled *Limacodes testudo* (by Chapman and most naturalists), *Apoda limacodes* (by Meyrick), or *Apoda avellana* (Kirby, *Catalogue of Moths*). The family is called either Limacodidae, Apodidae, Cochliopodidae, or Heterogeneidae.

[2] See Chapman, *Tr. ent. Soc. London*, 1894, p. 345, Plate VII., for our British species; for North American forms, Dyar, *Life-histories of the New York Slug-caterpillars* (in progress, with numerous plates), *J. New York ent. Soc.* iii. etc., 1895.

the integument are much changed, so that in the adult
larva (Fig. 199) the spines have subsided into the condition
of mere prominences, different in colour from the rest of
the surface. These larvae appear to be destitute of a head,
but there really exists a large one which is retracted, except
during feeding, into the body; the five pairs of abdominal feet of
the larvae of allied families are replaced by sucker-like structures
on the first eight abdominal segments. The spinneret of the
mouth is not a pointed tubular organ, but is fish-tailed in shape,
and hence disposes the silky matter, that aids the larva in moving on the leaves, in the form of a ribbon instead of that of a
thread. It has been stated that these peculiar larvae " imitate "
the coloured galls frequently found on the leaves of trees. The
North American forms of this family have very varied and most
extraordinary larvae.[1] In the pretty and conspicuous larva of
Empretia stimulea, the tubercles or processes of the body are, in
the later stages, armed with hairs, that contain a poisonous or
irritating fluid, said to be secreted by glands at the bases of the
processes. These hairs are readily detached and enter the skin
of persons handling the caterpillars. The larva of the North
American Hag-moth, *Phobetron pithecium*, is a curious object,
bearing long, fleshy appendages covered with down. Hubbard
makes the following statement as to the instincts of this larva : [2]—
" The hag-moth larvae do not seek to hide away their cocoons,
but attach them to leaves and twigs fully exposed to view, with,
however, such artful management as to surroundings and har-
monising colours that they are of all the group the most difficult
to discover. A device to which this Insect frequently resorts
exhibits the extreme of instinctive sagacity. If the caterpillar
cannot find at hand a suitable place in which to weave its
cocoon, it frequently makes for itself more satisfactory surroundings by killing the leaves, upon which, after they have become
dry and brown in colour, it places its cocoon. Several of these
caterpillars unite together, and selecting a long and vigorous
immature shoot or leader of the orange tree, they kill it by
cutting into its base until it wilts and bends over. The
leaves of a young shoot in drying turn a light tan-color, which

[1] See Packard, *P. Amer. Phil. Soc.* xxxi. 1893, pp. 83, 108, Plates. (He uses
the term Cochliopodidae instead of Limacodidae) ; also Dyar, as above.
[2] *Insects affecting the Orange*, Washington, 1885, p. 143.

harmonises most perfectly with the hairy locks of the caterpillar covering the cocoon. The latter is, consequently, not easily detected, even when placed upon the exposed and upturned surface of the leaf."

The cocoons of Limacodidae are unusually elaborate, the larva forming a perfect lid in order to permit itself to escape when a moth. Chapman states that the larva lies unchanged in the cocoon all winter, moulting to a pupa in the spring, and that the pupa escapes from the cocoon previous to the emergence of the moth.[1] Both Chapman and Packard look on the family as really nearer to Microlepidoptera than to Bombyces; Meyrick (calling it Heterogeneidae) places it at the end of his series Psychina next Zygaenidae.

We may allude here to the little moths, described by Westwood under the name of *Epipyrops*,[2] that have the extraordinary habit of living on the bodies of live Homopterous Insects of the family Fulgoridae in India. What their nutriment may be is not known. The larva exudes a white flocculent matter, which becomes a considerable mass, in the midst of which the caterpillar changes to a pupa. Westwood placed the Insect in Arctiidae; Sir George Hampson suggests it may be a Limacodid, and this appears probable.

Fam. 27. Megalopygidae (or **Lagoidae**).—The American genera, *Megalopyge* and *Lagoa*, are treated by Berg and by Packard[3] as a distinct family intermediate between Saturniidae and Limacodidae. The larva is said by the latter authority to have seven pairs of abdominal feet instead of five pairs—the usual number in Lepidoptera. When young the caterpillars of *Lagoa opercularis* are white and resemble a flock of cotton wool. When full grown the larva presents the singular appearance of a lock of hair, moving in a gliding, slug-like manner. Under the long silky hair there are short, stiff, poison-hairs. The larva forms a cocoon, fitted with a hinged trap-door for the escape of the future moth. This curious larva is destroyed by both Dipterous and Hymenopterous parasites.

Fam. 28. Thyrididae.—A small family of Pyraloid moths, exhibiting considerable variety of form and colour, frequently with hyaline patches on the wings. They are mostly small

---

[1] *Tr. ent. Soc. London*, 1894, p. 348.　　[2] *Op. cit.* 1876, p. 522 ; and 1877, p. 433.
[3] *P. Amer. Phil. Soc.* xxxii. 1894, p. 275.

Insects, and contain no very striking forms.   Some of them look like Geometrids of various groups.   The family is widely distributed in the tropical zone, and includes 25 genera, of which *Rhodoneura*, with upwards of 100 species, is the chief one.   The larvae are said to be similar to those of Pyralidae. This family is considered by Hampson and Meyrick to be ancestral to butterflies.[1]

Fam. 29. Lasiocampidae (*Eggers, Lappet-moths*).—Usually large Insects densely covered with scales, without frenulum, but with the costal area of the hind wing largely developed, and the male antennae beautifully pectinate, Lasiocampids are easily recognised.   They are well known in Britain, though we have but few species.   The flight of some of the species is powerful, but ill-directed, and the males especially, dash about as if their flight were quite undirected ;   as indeed it probably is.   The differ-ence in the flight of the two sexes is great in some species.   In the genus *Suana* and its allies we meet with moths in which the difference in size of the two sexes is extreme ; the

FIG. 201.—Lappet-moth, *Gastropacha querci-folia*, ♀.   Britain.

males may be but 1½ inches across the wings, while the very heavy females may have three times as great an expanse.   Kirby separates these Insects to form the family Pinaridae ; it in-cludes the ' Madagascar silkworm, *Borocera madagascariensis*. The African genus *Hilbrides* is remarkable for the wings being destitute of scales, and consequently transparent, and for being of very slender form like a butterfly.   The eggs of Lasiocampidae are smooth, in certain cases spotted in an irregular manner like birds' eggs.   Sometimes the parent covers them with hair. The larvae are clothed with a soft, woolly hair, as well as with a shorter and stiffer kind, neither beautifully arranged nor highly coloured, and thus differing from the caterpillars of Lyman-triidae ; this hair in some cases has very irritating pro-perties.   Cocoons of a close and compact nature are formed, and hairs from the body are frequently mixed with the cocoon.   In

[1] Revision of the Thyrididae ; Hampson, *P. Zool. Soc. London*, 1897, p. 603.

some species the walls of the cocoons have a firm appearance, looking very like egg-shell—a fact which is supposed to
have given rise to the name of Eggers. Professors Poulton
and Meldola have informed us that this appearance is produced
by spreading calcium oxalate on a slight framework of silk,
the substance in question being a product of the Malpighian
tubes.[1] In various families of Lepidoptera it happens that
occasionally the pupa exists longer than usual before the appearance of the perfect Insect, and in certain members of this family
—notoriously in *Poecilocampa populi*, the December moth—this
interval may be prolonged for several years. There is not at
present any explanation of this fact. It may be of interest to
mention the following case :—From a batch of about 100 eggs
deposited by one moth, in the year 1891 (the Puss-Moth of the
family Notodontidae), some sixty or seventy cocoons were obtained,
the feeding up of all the larvae having been effected within
fourteen days of one another; fourteen of the Insects emerged
as moths in 1892; about the same number in 1893; in 1894,
twenty-five; and in 1895, eleven emerged. Lasiocampidae is a
large family, consisting of some 100 genera and 500 or more
species, and is widely distributed. It is unfortunately styled
Bombycidae by some naturalists.

Fam. 30. Endromidae.—The " Kentish glory," *Endromis
versicolor*, forms this family; it is a large and strong moth, and
flies wildly in the daytime in birch-woods. The larva has but
few hairs, and is said when young to assume a peculiar position,
similar to that of saw-fly larvae, by bending the head and thorax
backwards over the rest of the body.

Fam. 31. Pterothysanidae.—Consists of the curious East
Indian genus *Pterothysanus*, in which the inner margins of the
hind wings are fringed with long hairs. They are moths of
slender build, with large wing-expanse, black and white in colour,
like Geometrids. There is no frenulum. Metamorphoses unknown.

Fam. 32. Lymantriidae.—(Better known as **Liparidae**).
These are mostly small or moderate-sized moths, without brilliant
colours; white, black, grey and brown being predominant; with
highly-developed, pectinated antennae in the male. The larva
is very hairy, and usually bears tufts or brushes of shorter hairs,

---

[1] *P. ent. Soc. London*, 1891, p. xv.

together with others much longer and softer, these being sometimes also amalgamated to form pencils; the coloration of these
larvae is in many cases very conspicuous, the tufts and pencils
being of vivid and strongly contrasted colours. Some of these
hairy larvae are poisonous. A cocoon, in which much hair is
mixed, is formed. The pupae are remarkable, inasmuch as they
too are frequently hairy, a very unusual condition in Lepidoptera.
The Lymantriidae is one of the largest families of the old group
Bombyces; it includes some 180 genera and 800 species, and is
largely represented in Australia. *Dasychira rossii* is found in the
Arctic regions. In Britain we have eight genera represented by
eleven species; the Gold-tails, Brown-tails and Vapourer-moths
being our commonest Bombyces, and the latter being specially fond
of the London squares and gardens, where its beautiful larva may
be observed on the leaves of roses. Most of the Lymantriidae are
nocturnal, but the male Vapourer-moth flies in the daytime. In
this family there are various species whose females have the
wings small and unfit for flight, the Insects being very sluggish,
and their bodies very heavy. This is the state of the female of
the Vapourer-moth. The males in these cases are generally remarkably active, and very rapid on the wing.

Some of these moths increase in numbers to an enormous
extent, and commit great ravages. *Psilura monacha*—the Nun,
" die Nonne " of the Germans,[1]—is one of the principal troubles of
the conservators of forests in Germany, and great sums of money
are expended in combating it; all sorts of means for repressing
it, including its infection by fungi, have been tried in vain. The
caterpillars are, however, very subject to a fungoid disease, communicated by natural means. It is believed, too, that its continuance in any locality is checked after a time by a change
in the ratio of the two sexes. It is not a prolific moth, for it
lays only about 100 eggs, but it has been shown that after
making allowance for the numerous individuals destroyed by
various enemies, the produce of one moth amounts in five generations to between four and five million individuals. The larva
feeds on Coniferae, and on many leafy trees and shrubs. The young

---

[1] This moth is known under several generic names—*Psilura, Liparis, Ocneria,
Lymantria;* there is now a very extensive literature connected with it. A good
general account by Wachtl may be found in *Wien. ent. Zeit.* x. 1891, pp. 149-180,
2 Plates.

larva is provided with two sets of setae, one set consisting of very long hairs, the other of setae radiating from warts ; each one of this second set of spines has a small bladder in the middle, and it has been suggested that these assist in the dissemination of the young caterpillars by atmospheric means.[1]   These aerostatic setae exist only in the young larva.   The markings of the moth are very variable ; melanism is very common both in the larva and imago ; it has been shown conclusively that these variations are not connected, as black larvae do not give a larger proportion of black moths than light-coloured caterpillars do.   In England this moth is never injurious.   A closely allied form, *Ocneria dispar*, was introduced by an accident into North America from Europe about thirty years ago ; for twenty years after its introduction it did no harm, and attracted but little attention ; it has, however, now increased so much in certain districts that large sums of money have been expended in attempting its extirpation.

Dasychira pudibunda has occasionally increased locally to an enormous extent, but in the limited forests of Alsace the evil was cured by the fact that the caterpillars, having eaten up all the foliage, then died of starvation.[2]   *Teara melanosticta* is said to produce columns of processionary caterpillars in Australia.

Fam. 33. Hypsidae (or **Aganaidae**).—A family of comparatively small extent, confined to the tropical and sub-tropical regions of the Eastern hemisphere.   The colours are frequently buff and grey, with white streaks on the outer parts of the wings. We have nothing very like them in the European fauna, our species of *Spilosoma* are perhaps the nearest approach.   In *Euplocia* the male has a pouch that can be unfolded in front of the costa at the base of the anterior wing ; it is filled with very long, peculiar, hair-like scales growing from the costal margin ; both sexes have on each side of the second abdominal segment a small, projecting structure that may be a sense-organ.   The female is more gaily coloured than the male.

Fam. 34. Arctiidae.—With the addition recently made to it of the formerly separate family Lithosiidae, Arctiidae has become the most extensive family of the old Bombycid series of moths, comprising something like 500 genera and 3000 species. Hampson recognises four sub-families—Arctiinae, Lithosiinae,

---

[1] Wachtl and Kornauth, *Mitt. forst. Versuchswesen Österreichs*, Heft xvi. 1893.
[2] Crahay, *Ann. Soc. ent. Belgique*, xxxvii. 1893, p. 282.

Nolinae, Nycteolinae,—to which may be added others from America—Pericopinae, Dioptinae, Ctenuchinae; these sub-families being treated as families by various authors.   The sub-family Arctiinae includes our Tiger- and Ermine-moths, and a great many exotic forms of very diverse colours and patterns; the species of this division are, on the whole, probably more variable in colour and markings than in any other group of Lepidoptera. There are many cases of great difference of the sexes; in the South American genus *Ambryllis* the male is remarkable for its hyaline wings with a few spots; while the female is densely scaled, and very variegate in colour.   There are some cases (the South European genus *Ocnogyna*) where the female is wingless and moves but little, while the male flies with great rapidity. *Epicausis smithi*, from Madagascar, one of the most remarkable of moths, is placed in this division of Arctiidae ; it is of a tawny colour, variegate with black ; the abdomen of this latter colour is terminated by a large tuft of long scarlet hairs ; the Insect has somewhat the appearance of a Hummingbird-hawkmoth. *Ecpantheria* is an extensive genus of tropical American moths (having one or two species in North America), of black and white or grey colours, with very complex markings ; the male in some species has a part of the hind wing produced as a tail, or lobe, of a different colour.

The sub-family Pericopinae are almost peculiar to South America (two species of *Gnophaela* exist in North America) ; some of this sub-family bear a great resemblance to Heliconiid butterflies.

The Dioptinae are likewise American moths of diurnal habits, and many of them bear a striking resemblance to the Ithomiid butterflies they associate with when alive.

The sub-family Lithosiinae is of great extent; our native " Footmen " give a very good idea of it; the moths are generally of light structure, with long, narrow front wings ; a simple system of yellow and black colour is of frequent occurrence.   Many of this group feed in the larval state on lichens.   Hampson includes in this group the Nyctemeridae—light-bodied diurnal moths, almost exclusively of black and white colours, of Geometrid form, frequently treated as a distinct family.

The sub-family Nolinae is a small group of rather insignificant Insects, in appearance like Pyralids or Geometrids; four or five species are native in Britain. Packard maintains the family Nolidae as distinct.[1]

The sub-family Nycteolinae consists of a few small moths the position of which has always been uncertain ; *Nycteola* (better known as *Sarrothripus*), *Halias*, and *Earias* are all British genera that have been placed amongst Tortrices, to which they bear a considerable resemblance. *Sarrothripus* is at present placed by Hampson in Noctuidae, by others in Lithosiidae, by Meyrick in Arctiidae. The sub-family forms the family Cymbidae of Kirby;[2] it includes at present only about 70 species, all belonging to the Eastern hemisphere. Two types of larvae are known in it : one bare, living exposed on leaves ; the other, *Earias*, hairy, living among rolled-up leaves. *Halias prasinana* is known from the testimony of numerous auditors to produce a sound when on the wing, but the *modus operandi* has not been satisfactorily ascertained. Sound-production seems to be of more frequent occurrence in Arctiidae than it is in any other family of Lepidoptera ; *Dionychopus niveus* produces a sound by, it is believed, friction of the wings. In the case of the genera *Setina* and *Chelonia* the process is said to be peculiar to the male sex : Laboulbène believes it to proceed from drum-like vesicles situate one on each side of the base of the metathorax.[3]

Fam. 35. Agaristidae.—An interesting assemblage of moths, many of them diurnal and of vivid colours, others crepuscular. There is considerable variety of appearance in the family, although it is but a small one, and many of its members remind one of other and widely separated families of Lepidoptera. The style and colour of the Japanese *Eusemia villicoides* are remarkably like our *Arctia villica*. In some forms the antennae are somewhat thickened towards the tip and hooked, like those of the Skipper butterflies. The family consists at present of about 250 species, but we doubt its being a sufficiently natural one. It is very widely distributed, with the exception that it is quite absent from Europe and the neighbourhood of the Mediterranean Sea. In North America it is well represented. The larvae, so far as known, are not very remarkable ; they have some lateral tufts of hair, as well as longer hairs scattered over the body.

[1] *Amer. Natural.* xxix. 1895, p. 801.
[2] *Catalogue of Lepidoptera Heterocera*, i. 1892.
[3] *Ann. Soc. ent. France* (4), iv. 1864, p. 689.

The male of the Indian *Aegocera tripartita* has been noticed to produce a clicking sound when flying, and Sir G. Hampson has shown [1] that there is a peculiar structure on the anterior wing ; he considers that this is rubbed against some spines on the front feet, and that the sound is produced by the friction. Though this structure is wanting in the acknowledged congeners of *A. tripartita*, yet it occurs in a very similar form in the genus *Hecatesia*, already noticed under Castniidae.

Fam. 36. Geometridae (*Carpets, Pugs, etc.*) — This very extensive family consists of fragile moths, only a small number being moderately stout forms ; they have a large wing-area ; the antennae are frequently highly developed in the males, but on this point there is much diversity. Either the frenulum or the proboscis is absent in a few cases. The caterpillars are elongate and slender, with only one pair of abdominal feet— placed on the ninth segment—in addition to the anal pair, or claspers. They progress by moving these two pairs of feet up to the thoracic legs, so that the body is thrown into a large loop, and they are hence called Loopers or Geometers. The family is universally distributed, and occurs even in remote islands and high latitudes ; in Britain we have about 270 species. The family was formerly considered to be closely connected with Noctuidae, but at present the opinion that it has more intimate relations with the families we have previously considered is prevalent. Packard considers it near to Lithosiidae, while Meyrick merely places the six families, of which he treats it as composed, in his series Notodontina. Hampson adopts Meyrick's six families as sub-families, but gives them different names, being in this respect more conservative than Meyrick, whose recent revision of the European forms resulted in drastic changes in nomenclature.[2] This classification is based almost exclusively on wing-nervuration. The number of larval legs and the consequent mode of walking is one of the most constant characters of the group ; the few exceptions that have been detected are therefore of interest. *Anisopteryx aescularia* has a pair of undeveloped feet on the eighth segment, and, according to Meyrick, its allies " sometimes show rudiments of the other two pairs." The larva of *Himera*

---

[1] *P. Zool. Soc. London*, 1892, p. 188.

[2] *Tr. ent. Soc. London*, 1892, pp. 53-140 ; for criticism on the nomenclature, see Rebel, *Ent. Zeit. Stettin*, liii. 1892, p. 247.

pennaria is said to have in early life a pair of imperfect feet on the eighth segment, which disappear as the larva approaches maturity.

The position of the abdominal feet and claspers throws the holding power of the larva to the posterior part of the body, instead of to the middle, as in other caterpillars. This, combined with the elongate form, causes these larvae when reposing to assume attitudes more or less different from those of other larvae ; holding on by the claspers, some of these Insects allow all the anterior parts of the body to project in a twig-like manner. The front parts are not, however, really free in such cases, but are supported by a thread of silk extending from the mouth to some point near-by. Another plan adopted is to prop the front part of the body against a twig placed at right angles to the supporting leaf, so that the caterpillar is in a diagonal line between the two (Fig. 202). Other Geometers assume peculiar coiled or spiral attitudes during a whole or a portion of their lives ; some doing this on a supporting object —leaf or twig—while others hang down (*Ephyra pendularia*). Certain of the larvae of Geometridae vary in colour, from shades of brown to green ; there is much diversity in this variation. In some

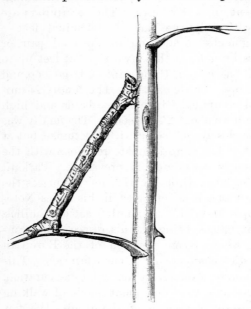

Fig. 202.—Larva of *Amphidasis betularia*, reposing on a rose-twig. ×1. Cambridge.

species it is simple variation ; in others it is dimorphism, *i.e.* the larvae are either brown or green. In other cases the larvae are at first variable, subsequently dimorphic. In *Amphidasis betularia* it would appear that when the larva is hatched the dimorphism is potential, and that the future colour, whether green or brown, is settled by some determining condition during the first period of larval life and cannot be subsequently modified.[1] According to Poulton, the dark tint is due in *A. betularia* to colouring matter in the skin or immediately below it, and the green tint to a layer of fat between the hypodermis and the superficial muscles; this layer being always green, but more brightly green in the larvae that are of this colour externally. Much discussion has occurred about these larval attitudes and colours, and it seems probable that Professor Poulton has over-rated the value of protection from birds, mammals and ento-mologists; the chief destroying agents being other than these, and not liable to be thus deceived, even if the vertebrates are. In some cases such resemblance as undoubtedly exists is not made the best use of. The larva shown in figure 202 bore a wonderful resemblance, when examined, to the rose-twigs it lived on, but the effect of this as a concealing agent was entirely destroyed by the attitude; for this, being on different lines to those of the plant, attracted the eye at once. This larva, and we may add numerous other larvae, could have been perfectly con-cealed by adopting a different attitude, but never did so; the position represented being constantly maintained except while feeding.

In some species of this family the adult females are without wings, or have them so small that they can be of no use for flight. This curious condition occurs in various and widely-separated groups of the Geometridae; and it would be naturally supposed to have a great effect on the economy of the species exhibiting it, but this is not the case. Some of the flightless females affect the highest trees and, it is believed, ascend to their very summits to oviposit. It has been suggested that they are carried up by the winged males, but this is probably only an exceptional occurrence; while, as they are known to be capable of ascending with rapidity by means of crawling and running, it may be taken for granted that this is the usual method with them. Some of these wingless females have been found in numbers on gas-lamps, and are believed to have been attracted by the light, as is the case with very many of the winged forms.[2]

---

[1] See Poulton, *Tr. ent. Soc. London*, 1884, p. 51; *op. cit.* 1892, p. 293; and Bateson, p. 213; Gould, p. 215.

[2] Giraud, *Ann. Soc. ent. France* (4), v. 1865, p. 105; Fauvel, *l.c. Bull.* p. liii.

Neither is the geographical distribution limited by this inferior condition of the most important of the organs of locomotion, for *Cheimatobia brumata* (the Winter-moth) one of the species with flightless female, is a common and widely distributed Insect in Europe and North America.

Although the classification of this family is based almost entirely on wing-nervuration, yet there are some divisions of the Geometridae in which this character is remarkably variable, certain individuals frequently exhibiting considerable abnormality.[1] *Amphidasis betularia* is believed to have changed its variation considerably in the course of the last fifty years. Previous to that time a black variety of the species was unknown, but it has now become common ; and it is believed that other species of Geometridae are in process of exhibiting a similar phenomenon.[2]

Fam. 37. Noctuidae (*Owlet-Moths, Eulen* of the Germans). —This very extensive assemblage consists of moths rarely seen in the day-time, of generally sombre colours, with antennae destitute of remarkable developments in the male (except in a small number of forms) ; proboscis and frenulum both present ; a complex sense-organ on each side of the body at the junction of the metathorax and abdomen. The number of species already known can scarcely be less than 8000 ; owing to their large numbers and the great general resemblance of the forms, their classification is a matter of considerable difficulty. Although the peculiar structure at the base of the thorax was long since pointed out, it has never received any thorough investigation. Few other remarkable structures have yet been discovered : the most interesting is perhaps the peculiarity in the hind wings of the males of certain Ommatophorinae recently pointed out by Sir G. F. Hampson [3] : in the genera *Patula* and *Argiva* the form of the hind wings is normal in the females, but in the male the anterior one-half of each of these wings is aborted, and the position of the nervures changed ; this condition is connected with the development of a glandular patch or fold on the wing, and is remarkable as profoundly affecting a structure which is

[1] For a table, see Meyrick, *l.c.*

[2] Barrett, "Increasing Melanism in British Geometridae," *Ent. Monthly Mag.* 1895, p. 198.

[3] *P. Zool. Soc. London*, 1892, p. 192.

otherwise so constant that the classification of the family is largely based on it.

The larvae are as a rule destitute of the remarkable adornments of hairs and armatures of spines that are so common in many of the families we have previously considered; they are fond of concealing themselves during the day and coming out at night to feed; many of them pass most of their time at, or beneath, the surface of the ground, finding nourishment in roots or the lower parts of the stems of plants; this is notably the case in the genus *Agrotis,* which is perhaps the most widely distributed of all the genera of moths. Such caterpillars are known as Cut-worms in North America.[1] The great resemblance, *inter se,* of certain of these Cut-worms, much astonished the American naturalist Harris, who found that larvae almost perfectly similar produced very different moths. The majority of Noctuid larvae have the usual number of legs, viz., three pairs of thoracic legs, four pairs of abdominal feet and the terminal claspers. In some divisions of the family there is a departure from this arrangement, and the abdominal feet are reduced to three, or even to two, pairs. One or two larvae are known—e.g. *Euclidia mi*—in which the claspers have not the usual function, but are free terminal appendages. When the abdominal legs are reduced in number (*Plusia,* e.g.) the larvae are said to be Half-loopers, or Semi-loopers, as they assume to some extent the peculiar mode of progression of the Geometrid larvae, which are known as Loopers. In the case of certain larvae, e.g. *Triphaena,* that have the normal number of feet, it has been observed that when first hatched, the one or two anterior pairs of the abdominal set are ill developed, and the larvae do not use them for walking. This is the case with the young larva of our British *Brephos notha* (Fig. 203). Subsequently, however, this larva undergoes a considerable change, and appears in the form shown in Fig. 204. This interesting larva joins together two or three

FIG. 203.—*Brephos notha.* Larva, newly hatched. Britain.

---

[1] Although this term is widely used in North America, it is not in use in England, though it may possibly have originated in Scotland. See Slingerland, *Bull. Cornell University Exp. Stat.* 104, 1895, p, 555.

leaves of aspen and lives between them, an unusual habit for
Noctuid larvae.   When about to pupate it bores into bark or
soft wood to change to a pupa, Fig. 205 ;
the specimen represented closed the hole
of entry by placing two separate doors
of silk across the burrow, as shown at *d*.
The anal armature of this pupa is terminated by a curious transverse process.
The systematic position of this inter-

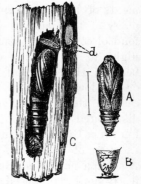

FIG. 205.—*Brephos notha*. **A,**
Pupa, ventral aspect ; **B,**
extremity of body, magni-
fied ; **C,** the pupa in wood ;
d, diaphragms constructed
by the larva.

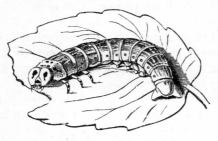

FIG. 204.—*Brephos notha*.   Adult larva.

esting Insect is very uncertain : Meyrick and others associate it
with the Geometridae.

The larva of *Leucania unipunctata* is the notorious Army-
worm that commits great ravages on grass and corn in North
America.   This species sometimes increases in numbers to a considerable extent without being observed, owing to the retiring
habits of the larvae ; when, however, the increase of numbers
has been so great that food becomes scarce, or for some other
cause—for the scarcity of food is supposed not to be the only
reason—the larvae become gregarious, and migrate in enormous
swarms : whence its popular name.   The Cotton-worm, *Aletia*
xylinae is even more notorious on account of its ravages.   Riley
states [1] that in bad years the mischief it commits on the cotton
crop causes a loss of £6,000,000, and that for a period
of fourteen successive years the annual loss averaged about
£3,000,000.   This caterpillar strips the cotton plants of all but
their branches.   It is assisted in its work by another highly
destructive Noctuid caterpillar, the Boll-worm, or larva of
Heliothis armigera, which bores into the buds and pods.   This

[1] *Fourth Rep. U.S Ent. Commission*, 1885, p. 3.

latter Insect attacks a great variety of plants, and has a very wide distribution, being found even in England, where happily it is always a rare Insect.

In Britain, as well as in parts of Northern Europe, a Noctuid moth, *Charaeas graminis,* occasionally increases to an enormous extent : its larva is called the Hill-grub and lives on the grass of pastures, frequently doing great damage in hill-lands. The increase of this moth seems to take place after the manner of an epidemic ; a considerable number of years may pass during which it is scarcely seen, and it will then appear in unusual numbers in widely separated localities. This moth lays a large number of eggs, and is not completely nocturnal in habits ; sometimes it may be seen on the wing in great numbers in the hottest sunshine, and it has been noticed that there is then a great disproportion of the sexes, the females being ten or twenty times as numerous as the males. In Australia, the Bugong moth, *Agrotis spina,* occurs in millions in certain localities in Victoria : this moth hibernates as an imago, and it formerly formed, in this instar, an important article of food with the aborigines. The powers of increase of another Noctuid moth—*Erastria scitula* —are of great value. Its habits have been described by Rouzaud.[1] On the shores of the Mediterranean the larva of this little moth lives on a Scale-Insect—*Lecanium oleae*—that infests the peach ; and as the moth may have as many as five generations in a year, it commits laudable havoc with the pest. The larva is of remarkable form, very short and convex, with small head, and only two pairs of abdominal feet. The scale of the *Lecanium* is of larger size than is usual in that group of Insects, and the young larva of the *Erastria* buries itself, as soon as hatched, in one of the scales ; it destroys successively numerous scales, and after having undergone several moults, it finds itself provided, for the first time, with a spinneret, when, with the aid of its silk, it adds to and adapts a Coccid scale, and thus forms a portable habitation ; this it holds on to by means of the pair of anal claspers, which are of unusual form. The case is afterwards subjected to further alteration, so that it may serve as a protection to the creature when it has changed to a pupa. This moth is said to be free from the attacks of parasites, and if this be the case it is probable that its increase is regulated by the fact that

[1] *Insect Life,* vi. 1894 p. 6.

when the creature becomes numerous it thus reduces the food supply, so that its own numbers are afterwards in consequence diminished.

One of the most remarkable genera of British Noctuidae is *Acronycta*,[1] the larvae of which exhibit so much diversity that it has been suggested that the genus should be dismembered and its fragments treated as allied to several different divisions of moths. There are many points of interest in connection with the natural history of these *Acronycta*. *A. psi* and *A. tridens* are practically indistinguishable as moths, though the larvae are easily separated : the former species is said to be destroyed to an amazing extent by parasites, yet it remains a common Insect. The genus *Apatela* is very closely allied to *Acronycta*, and Harris says that " *Apatela* signifies deceptive, and this name was probably given to the genus because the caterpillars appear in the dress of Arctians and Liparians, but produce true owlet-moths or Noctuas." [2] The species of another British genus, *Bryophila*, possess the exceptional habit of feeding on lichens. Some of the American group Erebides are amongst the largest Insects, measuring seven or eight inches across the expanded wings.

The Deltoid moths are frequently treated as a distinct family, Deltoidae, perhaps chiefly because of their resemblance to Pyralidae. At present, however, they are considered to be separated from Noctuidae by no valid characters.

Fam. 38—Epicopeiidae.—The genus *Epicopeia* consists of only a few moths, but they are amongst the most extraordinary known : at first sight they would be declared without hesitation to be large swallow-tail butterflies, and Hampson states that they " mimic " the Papilios of the *Polyxenus* group. Very little is known about these extremely rare Insects, but the larva is stated, on the authority of Mr. Dudgeon, to surpass the moths themselves in extravagance ; to be covered with long processes of snow-white efflorescence, like wax, exuded from the skin, and to " mimic " a colony of the larva of a Homopterous Insect. Some ten species of this genus are known from Java, India, China, and Japan. In this family there is said to be a rudimentary frenulum, but it is doubtful whether the hairs that have given rise to this definition really justify it.

---

[1] See Chapman, *The Genus* Acronycta *and its Allies*, London, 1893.
[2] *Insects Injurious, etc.*, Ed. 1862, Boston, p. 437.

Fam. 39. Uraniidae.—A family of small extent, including light-bodied moths with ample wings and thread-like antennae; most of them resemble Geometridae, but a few genera, *Urania* and *Nyctalemon,* are like Swallow-tail butterflies and have similar habits. The Madagascar moth, *Chrysiridia madagascar-iensis* (better known as *Urania rhipheus*), is a most elegant and beautiful Insect, whose only close allies (except an East African congener) are the tropical American species of *Urania,* which were till recently treated as undoubtedly congeneric with the Madagascar moth. The family consists of but six genera and some sixty species. The question of its affinities has given rise to much discussion, but on the whole it would appear that these Insects are least ill-placed near Noctuidae.[1] The larva of the South American genus *Coro-nidia* is in general form like a Noctuid larva, and has the normal number of legs; it possesses a few peculiar fleshy processes on the back. A description of the larva of *Chrysiridia madagascariensis* has been widely spread; but according to Camboué,[2] the account of the metamorphoses, first given by Boisduval, is erroneous. The larva, it appears, resembles in general form that of *Coronidia,* and has sixteen feet; it is, how-ever, armed with long, spatu-late black hairs; it changes to a pupa in a cocoon of open network.

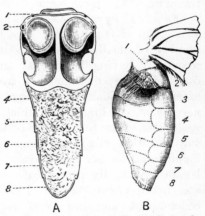

A   B

Fig. 206.—Abdomen of *Chrysiridia mada-gascariensis.* **A,** Horizontal section show-ing the lower part of the male abdomen : 1, first segment ; 2, spiracle of second segment ; 4-8, posterior segments. **B,** the abdomen seen from the side, with the segments numbered. The section is that of an old, dried specimen.

In all the species of this family we have examined, we have noticed the existence of a highly peculiar structure that seems hitherto to have escaped observation. On each side of the second abdominal segment there is an ear-like opening (usually

---

[1] See Westwood, *Tr. Zool. Soc. London,* x. pp. 507, etc., for discussion of this question and for figures ; also E. Reuter, *Act. Soc. Sci. Fenn.* xxii. 1896, p. 202.

[2] *Congr. Internat. Zool.* ii. 1892, pt. 2, p. 180.

much concealed by overlapping scales), giving entrance to a chamber in the body ; this chamber extends to the middle line, being separated from its fellow by only a thin partition. At its anterior and lateral part there is a second vesicle-like chamber, formed by a delicate membrane that extends as far forwards as the base of the abdomen. There can be little doubt that this is part of some kind of organ of sense, though it is much larger than is usual with Insect sense-organs.

Fam. 40. Epiplemidae.—Under this name Hampson has assembled certain Geometroid moths, some of them placed previously in Chalcosiidae, some in Geometridae. They form a varied group, apparently closely allied to Uraniidae, and having a similar peculiar sense-organ ; but are distinguished by the presence of a frenulum. The larva seems to be like that of Uraniidae.

Fam. 41. Pyralidae.—This division is to be considered rather as a group of families than as a family ; it includes a very large number of small or moderate-sized moths of fragile structure, frequently having long legs; antennae simple, only in a few cases pectinate ; distinguished from Noctuidae and all the other extensive divisions of moths by the peculiar course of the costal nervure of the hind wing, which either keeps, in the middle of its course, near to the sub-costal or actually unites with it, subsequently again separating. Members of the Pyralidae are found in all lands ; in Britain we have about 150 species. The larvae are usually nearly bare, with only short, scattered setae, and little coloration ; they have most varied habits, are fond of concealment, and are very lively and abrupt in movement, wriggling backwards as well as forwards, when disturbed ; a cocoon is formed for the metamorphosis.

The family as a whole consists of Insects of unattractive appearance, although it contains some very elegant and interesting moths and numerous forms of structural interest. In the genus *Thiridopteryx* little transparent spaces on the wings occur as a character peculiar to the males ; the spaces are correlative with a greater or less derangement of the wing-nervures. In some other forms there is a remarkable retinaculum, consisting of large scales, and this, too, is connected with a distortion of the wing-nervures. The Pyralidae—Pyralites of Ragonot,[1] Pyralidina of

---

[1] Ragonot, *Ann. Soc. ent. France*, 1890 and 1891 ; and Meyrick, *Tr. ent. Soc. London*, 1890, p. 429.

Meyrick——have recently been revised by two naturalists of distinction almost simultaneously; unfortunately their results are discrepant, Meyrick including Pterophoridae and Orneodidae, and yet admitting in all only eight families; while Ragonot does not include the two groups named, but defines seventeen tribes of the two families—Pyralidae and Crambidae—that he admits.

The Pyraustidae of Meyrick is an enormous division including the Hydrocampidae and Scopariidae of many authors, as well as the Pyraustinae proper and a small group of Ragonot's, the Homophysinae. The division Scopariinae is believed to be amongst the "most ancient" of Lepidoptera; the food of the larvae consists of moss and lichens. This group is widely distributed, being richly represented in Australia, New Zealand, and the Hawaiian Islands, as well as in Europe; and probably really occurs wherever their food-plants exist accompanied by a tolerable climate. The statistics of the distribution of this group, so far as at present known, have been furnished by Mr. Meyrick, as follows:——European region, about 25 species; Madeira, 3; St. Helena, 6; South Africa, 2 or 3; India, 9; Malayan region, 3 or 4; Australia, 24; New Zealand, 64; Hawaiian Islands, 50; North America, 17 (one of them European); South America, 10. The Hydrocampinae—the Chinamarks—are of great interest, as being amongst the few forms of Lepidoptera adapted for aquatic life. It is believed that all their larvae are aquatic, though of only a few is there much known. The diversity amongst these forms is of considerable interest. The habits of *Hydrocampa nymphaeata* were long since described by Réaumur, and have more recently been dealt with by Buckler,[1] W. Müller[2] and Prof. Miall.[3] Although there are some discrepancies in their accounts, due we believe to the observations being made at different periods of the life and under somewhat different circumstances, yet the account given by Müller is we feel no doubt substantially correct. The larvae when hatched mine in the leaves of a water-plant for a short time—thirty hours to three days according to Buckler—and are completely surrounded by water, which penetrates freely into their burrows; at this period the caterpillar breathes by its skin, the spiracles being very small, and the tubes leading from

---

[1] *Ent. Mag.* xii. 1876, p. 210, and xvii. 1881, p. 249.
[2] *Zool. Jahrb. Syst.* vi. 1892, p. 617.   [3] *Nat. Hist. Aquatic Insects*, London, 1895.

them closed and functionless. After this brief period of mining life, the larva moults and then constructs a habitation by cutting a piece out of a leaf, and fastening it to the under side of another leaf; it is thus provided with a habitation, but it is one into which the water freely enters, and the respiratory apparatus remains in the state we have described. The Insect passes through several moults, and then hibernates in the water. On its revival in the spring a change occurs, and the larva constructs a portable, or we should rather say free, habitation out of two large pieces of leaf of lens-shape, fastened together at the edges; but the larva has some method of managing matters so that the water can be kept out of this house; thus the creature lives in air though immersed in the water. A correlative change occurs in the structure of the skin and tracheal system. The former becomes studded with prominent points that help to maintain a coat of air round the Insect, like dry velvet immersed in water; the spiracles are larger than they were, and they and the tracheal tubes are open. One or two moults take place and the creature then pupates. There is a good deal of discrepancy in the accounts of this period, and it seems probable that the pupa is sometimes aerial, sometimes aquatic. Buckler's account of the formation of the case shows that the larva first cuts off, by an ingenious process, one piece of leaf, leaving itself on this, as on a raft; this it guides to a leaf suitable for a second piece, gets the raft underneath, and fastens it with silk to the upper portion, and then severs this, leaving the construction free; afterwards the larva goes through a curious process of changing its position and working at the two extremities of the case, apparently with the object of making it all right as regards its capacity for including air and keeping out water. He believes that Réaumur was correct in his idea that the larva regulates the admission of air or of water to the case in conformity with its needs for respiration. Müller calls special attention to the great changes in habit and in the structure of the integument during the life of this larva; but the reader will gather from what we relate as to various terrestrial Lepidopterous larvae, that these phenomena are not very dissimilar from what frequently take place in the latter; a change of habits at some particular moult, accompanied by great changes in the integument, and even in the size of the stigmata, being of frequent occurrence.

The larva of *Nymphula stagnata*, a close ally of *H. nymphaeata*, has aquatic habits of a somewhat similar but simpler nature; while *N. (Paraponyx) stratiotata* is very different. This larva is provided with eight rows of tufts of flexible branchiae, occupying the position of the spots or setigerous warts usual in caterpillars, and reminding one of the spines of certain butterfly-larvae, though they are undoubtedly respiratory filaments. These caterpillars protect themselves by forming silken webs or cases, or by adopting the case of some other larva, and are in the habit of holding on by the anal claspers, and rapidly and energetically moving the anterior parts of the body in an undulating fashion. The spiracles exist, but are functionless. The pupa lives under water, and has no branchiae; but three of the pairs of abdominal spiracles are open, and project from the body. Müller informs us that in a Brazilian *Paraponyx* these three pairs of spiracles were already large in the larva, though the other pairs were very small, or absent. He considers that the moth of this species descends beneath the water of a rapid stream, and fastens its eggs on the stems of plants therein. *Cataclysta lemnata* lives in a case of silk with leaves of duckweed attached to it, or in a piece of a hollow stem of some aquatic plant; it is believed to breathe, like *H. nymphaeata*, at first by the integument and subsequently by open stigmata; but particulars as to how it obtains the requisite air-supply are not forthcoming: the aquatic pupa breathes by three large abdominal spiracles like *Paraponyx.*

Musotimidae[1] is a small group of two or three genera found in Australia and Polynesia; and the Tineodidae also consist of only two Australian genera. Siculodidae is likewise a small Antarctic group, placed by Meyrick in Pyralidina; but his view is not accepted by Snellen and Ragonot. Epipaschiinae (formerly treated as a separate family) and Endotrichiinae are, according to Meyrick, subdivisions of the family Pyralidae proper, an enormous group of more than 100 genera. The Chrysauginae consist chiefly of American forms, and have not been treated by Meyrick; some of this group have been classed with Tortricidae or Deltoidae on account of the undulating costa of the front wings and the long, peculiar palpi. The Galleriidae are a small group including Insects that live in bees'-nests, and feed on the wax

---

[1] For Bibliographic references connected with the divisions of Pyralidae see Ragonot, *Ann. Soc. ent. France* (6), x. 1890, pp. 458, etc.

etc. ; others eat seeds, or dried vegetable substances. Three out of our five British species of this family occur (usually gregariously) in bee - hives, and have the peculiar habit of spinning their cocoons together. The mass of common cocoons formed in this manner by *Aphomia sociella* is remarkably tough and enduring ; portions of it are not infrequently picked up, and as the cocoons are of a peculiar tubular form their nature gives rise to some perplexity.

Phycitidae [1] is another very large assemblage of Insects with very diverse habits. The frenulum and retinaculum are similarly formed in the two sexes : the males frequently have the basal-joint of the antennae swollen ; hence the term " Knot-horns " applied by collectors to these moths. The larvae of the species of *Ephestia* infest groceries, and most children have become to a slight extent acquainted with them amongst dried figs ; that of *E. kuehniella* has become very injurious in flour-mills, its enormous increase being due in all probability to the fact that the favourable and equable temperature maintained in the mills promotes a rapid succession of generations, so that the Insect may increase to such an extent as to entirely block the machinery. Many of the Phycitidae feed on the bark of trees in galleries or tunnels constructed partially of silk. A very peculiar modification of this habit in *Cecidipta excoecaria* has been described by Berg. [2] In Argentina this Insect takes possession of the galls formed by a *Chermes* on *Excoecaria biglandulosa,* a Euphorbiaceous tree. The female moth lays an egg on a gall, and the resulting larva bores into the gall and nourishes itself on the interior till all is eaten except a thin external coat ; the caterpillar then pupates in this chamber. The galls vary in size and shape, and the larva displays much constructive ability in adapting its home to its needs by the addition of tubes of silk or by other modes. Sometimes the amount of food furnished by the interior of the gall is not sufficient ; the larva, in such cases, resorts to the leaves of the plant for a supplement, but does not eat them in the usual manner of a caterpillar ; it cuts off and carries a leaf to the entrance of its abode, fastens the leaf there with silk, and then itself entering, feeds, from the interior, on the food it has thus acquired. Another Phycitid, *Dakruma coccidivora,* is very

[1] Monograph, by Ragonot, in Romanoff, *Mem. Lep.* vii. 1893.
[2] *Ent. Zeit. Stettin,* 1878, p. 230.

beneficial in North America by eating large Scale-Insects of the *Lecanium* group, somewhat after the fashion of *Erastria scitula* ; it does not construct a case, but shelters itself when walking from one scale to another by means of silken tubes ; it suffers from the attacks of parasites.[1] Oxychirotinae, an Australian group, is interesting because, according to Meyrick, it possesses forms connecting the Pterophoridae with the more normal Pyralids.

Crambidae, or Grass-moths, are amongst the most abundant Lepidoptera in this country, as they include the little pale moths that fly for short distances amongst the grass of lawns and pastures ; they fold their wings tightly to their body, and have a head pointed in front, in consequence of the form and direction of the palpi. They sit in an upright position on the stems of grass, and it has been said that this is done because then they are not conspicuous. Perhaps : but it would be a somewhat difficult acrobatic performance to sit with six legs across a stem of grass. The larvae are feeders on grass, and construct silken tunnels about the roots at or near the surface. The Ancylolominae are included in Crambidae by Meyrick and Hampson. Schoenobiinae[2] are included by Meyrick in Pyraustidae, but this view appears not to meet with acceptance, and the group is more usually associated with the Crambidae. Most writers place the anomalous genus *Acentropus* as a separate tribe, but it is associated by both Meyrick and Hampson with *Schoenobius.* This Insect is apparently the most completely aquatic of all the Lepidoptera, and was for long associated with the Trichoptera in consequence of its habits and of the scaling of the wings being of a very inferior kind. The males may sometimes be found in large numbers fluttering over the surface of shallow, but large, bodies of water ; the females are rarely seen, and in some cases have no wings, or have these organs so small as to be useless. The female, it would appear, comes quite to the surface for coupling, and then takes the male beneath the water. The larvae have the usual number of Lepidopterous feet, and apparently feed on the leaves of plants below water just as Lepidopterous larvae ordinarily do in the air.[3] They have no trace of gills, and their

[1] Howard, *Insect Life*, vii. 1895, p. 402.
[2] Monograph by Hampson, *P. Zool. Soc. London*, 1895, p. 897-974.
[3] Disqué, *Ent. Zeit. Stettin*, li. 1890, p. 59. Cf. also Rebel, *Zool. Jahrb. Syst.* xii. 1898, p. 3.

mode of respiration is unknown. A great deal has been written about these Insects, but really very little is known. They are abundant, though local in many parts of North and Central Europe ; some of the females have, as we have said, abbreviated wings, but how many species there are, and whether the modifications existing in the development of the wings are constant in one species or locality, are unknown as yet.

Fam. 42. Pterophoridae [1] (*Plume-moths*).—Elegant Insects of small size, usually with the wings divided (after the fashion of a hand into fingers) so as to form feathers : the extent of this division is diverse, but the hind wings are more completely divided than the front, which indeed are sometimes almost entire. The group is placed by Meyrick in his Pyralidina, but there are many entomologists who look on it as distinct. It consists of two sub-families, Agdistinae and Pterophorinae, that have been treated as families by many entomologists. The Agdistinae (of which we have a British representative of the only genus *Agdistes*) have the wings undivided. Pterophorinae have the hind wings trifid or (rarely) quadrifid, the front wings bifid or (rarely) trifid. The larvae of the Pterophorinae are different from those of Pyralidae, being slow in movement and of heavy form, covered with hair and living exposed on leaves ; the pupae are highly remarkable, being soft, coloured somewhat like the larvae, and also hairy like the larvae, and are attached somewhat after the manner of butterfly-pupae by the cremaster : but in some cases there is a slight cocoon. There is, however, much variety in the larval and pupal habits of the Pterophoridae, many having habits of concealment of divers kinds. We have thirty species of these lovely Plume-moths in Britain. The family is widely distributed, and will probably prove numerous in species when the small and delicate Insects existing in the tropics are more appreciated by collectors.

Fam. 43. Alucitidae (Orneodidae of Meyrick and others).— The genus *Alucita* includes the only moths that have the front and hind wings divided each into six feathers. Species of it, though not numerous, occur in various regions. The larva and pupa are less anomalous than those of the Pterophoridae, though the imago is more anomalous. The caterpillar of our British *A. polydactyla* feeds on the flower-buds of honey-suckle, and forms a

---

[1] Classification ; Meyrick, *Tr. ent. Soc. London*, 1886, p. 1.

cocoon.   The moth with wings expanded is about an inch across, and is a lovely object.   It is not rare, though seldom numerous.

Fam. 44. Tortricidae.——Moths of small size, with a rather ample wing area, with the wing-fringes never as long as the wings are wide (long across), the hind wings without a pattern : the anterior nervure on the hind wings is simply divergent from that next to it, and the internal nervure, 1b, is very evidently forked at the base.   The larvae inhabit their food, which may be rolled up or twisted leaves, or the interior of fruits and herbs, or galls, or even roots ; they exhibit less diversity than is usual in other large series of moths ; all have the normal complement of sixteen legs.   This group is a very extensive one, but is much neglected owing to the great difficulties attending its study ; it is not recognised in Hampson's Table of families given on p. 370, being there merged in Tineidae.   It appears, however, to be a really natural group, and it is not desirable to merge it in the sufficiently enormous assemblage of the Tineidae till this has been shown to be necessary by the light of a greater knowledge of the external anatomy than we possess at present. The term Microlepidoptera is frequently met with in entomological literature, and should, we think, be confined to the two series Tortricidae and Tineidae.   The Pterophoridae, and even the Pyralidae, have been, and still sometimes are, included under this term, but at present it seems best to limit its application as is here suggested.

Three great divisions are at present recognised ; these were formerly called by Meyrick,[1] Tortricidae, Grapholithidae, Conchylidae ; subsequently,[2] he has adopted the names Tortricidae, Epiblemidae, Phaloniadae.   Lord Walsingham, who has devoted a great deal of time and study to the elucidation of this most difficult group, has suggested[3] that another change is desirable, and if so the nomenclature will be :——1. Tortricidae [or Torticinae, according to the view that may be taken as to the group being family or sub-family] ; 2. Phaloniidae [= the formerly used name, Conchylidae] ; 3. Olethreutidae [= the formerly used name Grapholithinae = Epiblemidae, Meyr.].   We have upwards of 300 species in Britain, nearly 200 of which belong to the last division.   The name Tortricidae refers to the habit the

---

[1] *P. Linn. Soc. N. S. Wales* (2), vi. 1881, p. 410.
[2] *Handbook Brit. Lep.* 1895, p. 493.   [3] *Tr. ent. Soc. London*, 1895, p. 495.

larvae of these moths possess of rolling up leaves, or twisting and distorting shoots and buds.

The mode in which leaves and shoots are twisted and rolled by the very small larvae has been much discussed and is probably the result of two or three distinct causes:—1, the immediate operations of the larva ; 2, the contraction of silk when drying ; 3, changes in the mode of growth of the parts of the vegetable, resulting from the interference of the caterpillar. The larvae of this family that live in fruits are only too widely (we will not say well) known.   Stainton gives as the habitat of *Epinotia funebrana*, " larva frequent in plum-pies " ; the caterpillar of *Carpocapsa pomonella* (the Codling-moth) mines in apples and pears, and its ravages are known only too well in widely distant parts of the world where fruit-trees of this kind are cultivated.   *C. splendana* lives in acorns and walnuts ; *C. juliana* in Spanish chestnuts.   Two, if not more, larvae live in the seeds of Euphorbiaceous plants, and have become notorious under the name of jumping-beans, on account of the movements they cause.   As these latter show no trace externally of being inhabited, the movements are supposed to be a mysterious property of the seed ; they are really due to its containing a large cavity, extending, in one direction of the seed, nearly or quite from skin to skin ; in this the larva makes a movement sufficient to alter the point of equilibrium of the quiescent seed, or as a free body to strike some part of it.   The exact nature of the movements of the larva have not, we believe, been ascertained. There are, at least, two species of these Insects, and two plants harbouring them, known in the United States and Mexico, viz. *Carpocapsa saltitans* living in the seeds of *Croton colliguaja* and *Grapholitha sebastianiae* living in the seeds of *Sebastiania bicapsularis*.

Fam. 45. Tineidae.—Small moths with the labial palpi more flexible and mobile than in other moths ; usually separated and pointed.   Hind wings frequently with very long fringes, the wing itself being proportionally reduced in size, and in consequence pointed at the tip.   Larvae very diverse, almost always with habits of concealment.   The series of forms included under this head is very numerous, the British species alone mounting up to 700, while the total described cannot be less than 4000. This number, however, must be but a fragment of what exists,

if Mr. Meyrick be correct in supposing that a single one of
the divisions of the family — Oecophoridae — comprises 2000
species in Australia and New Zealand alone. As the study
of these Insects is attended
with great difficulty on account of their fragility and
the minute size of the great
majority, it is not a matter
for surprise that their classification is in a comparatively
rudimentary state. We shall
not, therefore, deal with it here.
Neither can we attempt to give
any idea of the extreme diversity

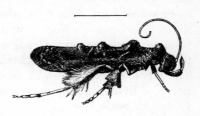

Fig. 207.—*Diplosara lignivora* (Gelechiides).
Hawaiian Islands.

in the colours, forms, and attitudes of these small Insects. The
one shown in Fig. 207, is remarkable on account of the great
accumulation of scales on the wings and legs. As regards the
pointed wings and the long fringes, we may remark that it is
probable that in many of these small forms the wings are
passive agents in locomotion ; a similar condition of the wings
is found in other very minute Insects, *e.g.* Thysanoptera and
Trichopterygidae ; in all these cases the framework of the wings is
nearly absent : in some forms of the Tineidae, *Opostega*, e.g. the
nervules are reduced to three or four in each wing. The
variety in habits is as great as that of the external form, and
the larvae exceed in diversity those of any other group of
Lepidoptera. No doubt a corresponding amount of diversity
will be discovered in the details of structure of the perfect
Insects, the anatomy of but few having been at present investigated. *Tinea pellionella* has two very important peculiarities in
its internal anatomy : the testes consist of four round follicles
on each side, and, contrary to the condition generally prevalent
in Lepidoptera, are not brought together in a common capsule : the
two groups are, however, not quite free (as they are in *Hepialus*),
but are connected by a loose tracheal network. Even more
remarkable is the fact also pointed out by Cholodkovsky[1] that
the adult Insect possesses only two Malpighian tubes instead of
six, the normal number in Lepidoptera ; in the larva there are,
however, six elongate tubes. The group of forms to which

[1] *Zool. Anz.* v. 1882. p. 262.

Tinea belongs is remarkable for the diversity and exceptional character of the food-habits of the larvae; species subsist on dried camel's dung, various kinds of clothes, furs, and hair, and even about horns of deer and horses' hoofs: one species has been found in abundance in the hair of a live sloth, *Bradypus cuculliger*, under circumstances that render it possible that the larva feeds on the creature's hair, though it may feed on minute vegetable matter found in the hair. The larva of *Tinea vastella* is occasionally found feeding on the horns of living antelopes. Several species of Tineidae are known to devour Scale-Insects.

Lita solanella is notorious for the ravages it commits on stored potatoes. Quite a number of species live on cryptogamic matter, or in old wood; *Oinophila v-flavum* feeds on the mould on the walls of cellars, and is reputed to be injurious by occasionally also attacking the corks of bottles containing wine. *Oecocecis guyonella* is said to be the cause of galls on *Limoniastrum guyonianum*, a plant that, growing in the deserts to the south of Algeria, is a favourite food of camels, and is frequently entirely covered with sand. The deposition of an egg by this moth is believed by Guénée [1] to give rise to a gall in which the larva is entirely enclosed (like the larvae of the gall-flies). Of Clothes-moths there are at least three species widely distributed. *Trichophaga tapetzella* is perhaps entitled to be considered the Clothes-moth; its caterpillar not only feeds on clothes, but spins webs and galleries amongst them. *Tinea pellionella* is also very common; its larva lives in a portable case, while that of the third species, *Tineola biselliella*, forms neither a case nor definite galleries. We have found this the most destructive of the three at Cambridge. Clothes or valuable furs may be completely protected by wrapping them in good sound paper in such a way that no crevices are left at the places where the edges of the paper meet. Garments that have become infested may be entirely cleared by free exposure to air and sunshine.

Two species of *Tinea* have been recorded as viviparous, viz. *Tinea vivipara* in Australia, and an undetermined species in South America. The species of the genus *Solenobia*—in which the female is apterous—are frequently parthenogenetic. The group Taleporiidae, to which this genus belongs, is by some

---

[1] *Ann. Soc. ent. France* (4), x. 1870, p. 1, pl. vii.

classified with Psychidae, in which family, as we have pointed out, one or two parthenogenetic forms are also known.

The larvae of Tineidae, though they do not exhibit the remarkable armature found in so many of the larger caterpillars, are exceedingly diverse.[1] Some are entirely destitute of feet (*Phyllocnistis*). Others are destitute of the thoracic legs ; *Nepticula* is in this case, but it is provided with an increased number of abdominal feet, in the form of more or less imperfect ventral processes. Some mine in leaves, others live in portable cases of various forms. Some are leaf-miners during their early life, and subsequently change their habits by constructing a portable case. The genus *Coleophora* affords numerous instances of this mode of life ; the habits of these case-bearers exhibit considerable variety, and there are many points of interest in their life-histories. Change of habit during the larval life has already been alluded to as occurring in many Lepidoptera and is nowhere more strikingly exemplified than in certain Tineidae. Meyrick mentions the following case as occurring in an Australian Insect, *Nematobola orthotricha ;*[2] the larva, until two-thirds grown, is without feet, and is almost colourless, and mines in the leaves of *Persoonia lanceolata ;* but when two-thirds grown it acquires sixteen feet, changes colour, becoming very variegate, and feeds externally, unprotected, on the leaves. The cases of the case-bearing Tineids are usually of small size, and do not attract attention like those of Psychidae. A very remarkable one was discovered by Mr. E. E. Green in Ceylon, and was at first believed to be formed by a Caddis-worm. It has now been ascertained that the Insect forming it is the caterpillar of *Pseudodoxia limulus,* a Tineid moth of the group Depressariidae ;[3] the case is composed of minute fragments of moss, sand, and lichens ; the anterior end is dilated into a shield-like hood that covers and protects the anterior parts of the larva when feeding ; the food is mosses and lichens on rocks and trees. Before pupating, the larva folds down the edges of the hood over the mouth of the tube, like an envelope, fastening them with silk. The case is fixed to the rock or other support and hangs there until the moth appears.

[1] For table of the larvae, according to number of feet and other characters, see Sorhagen, *Berlin. ent. Zeit.* xxvii. 1883, pp. 1-8.

[2] *P. Linn. Soc. N.S. Wales* (2) vii. 1892, p. 593.

[3] Durrant, *Ent. Mag.* xxxi. 1895, p. 107.

The family Prodoxidae consists of some Tineids, the larvae of which feed in the pods and stems of the Yuccas of south-western North America; they have the mouth of very unusual form (Fig. 208, E), and some of them, by aid of this peculiar mouth, exhibit a remarkable modification of instinct. The facts are chiefly known from the observations of Riley [1] on *Pronuba yuccasella*, a moth living on *Yucca filamentosa;* this plant has been introduced into our gardens in this country, where it never, we believe, produces seed. The Yuccas are not fitted for self-fertilisation or for fertilisation by Insect agency of an ordinary kind. The progeny of the moth develops in the pods of the plant, and as these cannot grow until the flowers have

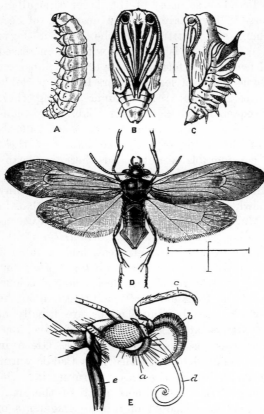

FIG. 208.—*Pronuba synthetica.* North America. **A**, Larva ; **B, C**, pupa, ventral and lateral aspects ; **D**, female moth ; **E**, head and part of thorax of the female moth : *a,* labial palp ; *b,* maxillary tentacle ; *c,* maxillary palp ; *d,* proboscis ; *e,* base of front leg. (After Riley.)

been fertilised, the moth has the habit of fertilising the flowers at the time she lays her egg in the part that is to develop into the pod, and to be the food for her own progeny. The female moth first visits the stamens, and collects, by the aid of the

[1] " The Yucca moth and Yucca Pollination," *Rep. Missouri Botanical Garden,* 1892, pp. 99-158.

maxillae (which in this sex are very remarkably formed),[1] a considerable mass of pollen, which she holds by means of the peculiar maxillary tentacles; she then lays an egg in the pistil, usually of some flower other than that from which she has gathered the pollen; and after she has accomplished this act she carefully applies the pollen she had previously collected to the pistil, so as to secure the fertilisation of the flower and the development of the pod.

The species of *Prodoxus* stand in a very peculiar relation to *Pronuba*. They also live in Yuccas, and have habits similar to those of *Pronuba*, with the important exception that, being destitute of the requisite apparatus, they do not fertilise the Yucca-flowers, and are thus dependent on *Pronuba* for the steps being taken that are necessary for the rearing of the progeny of the two kinds of moth. Hence the name of Yucca-moth has been bestowed on *Pronuba*, and that of " bogus Yucca-moth " on the *Prodoxus*. The *Pronuba* we figure is the largest and most remarkable species of the genus and fertilises *Yucca brevifolia;* the larva is destitute of abdominal feet, and in the pupa the spines on the back that exist in nearly all pupae that live in stems are developed to an extraordinary extent. The Yuccas do not flower every year, and the Prodoxidae have a corresponding uncertainty as to their periods of appearance, passing sometimes a year or two longer than usual in the pupal stage.

Fam. 46. Eriocephalidae.—This family has recently been proposed for some of the moths formerly included in the genus *Micropteryx*.[2] They are small, brilliant, metallic Insects, of diurnal habits, but are very rarely seen on the wing, and it is doubtful whether they can fly much. These little Insects are of peculiar interest, inasmuch as they differ from the great majority of the Lepidoptera in at least two very important points, viz. the structure of the wings and of the mouth-parts. The mouth shows that we may consider that the Lepidoptera belong to the mandibulate Insects, although in the great majority of them the mandibles in the final instar are insignificant, functionless structures, or are entirely absent, and although the maxillae are

---

[1] The maxillary tentacle is considered by Prof. J. B. Smith to be a prolongation of the stipes, cf. *antea*, p. 309 ; also *Insect Life*, v. 1893, p. 161.

[2] Chapman, *Tr. ent. Soc. London*, 1894, p. 366.

so highly adapted for the tasting of sweets that it is difficult to recognise in them the parts usually found in the maxilla of mandibulate Insects. *Eriocephala* in both these respects connects the Lepidoptera with Mandibulata : the mandibles have been shown by Walter[1] to be fairly well developed ; and the maxillae are not developed into a proboscis, but have each two separate, differentiated—not elongated—lobes, and an elongate, five-jointed, very flexible palpus. The moths feed on pollen, and use their maxillae for the purpose, somewhat in the style we have mentioned in Prodoxidae. The wings have no frenulum, neither have they any shoulder, and they probably function as separate organs instead of as a united pair on each side : the modification of the anterior parts of the hind wing—whereby this wing is reduced as a flying agent to the condition of a subordinate to the front wing—does not here exist : the hind wing differs little from the front wing in consequence of the parts in front of the cell being well developed. There is a small jugum. These characters have led Packard to suggest that the Eriocephalidae should be separated from all other Lepidoptera to form a distinct sub-Order, Lepidoptera Laciniata.[2] The wing-characters of *Eriocephala* are repeated—as to their main features—in Hepialidae and Micropterygidae ; but both these groups differ from *Eriocephala* as to the structure of the mouth-parts, and in their metamorphoses. Although *Erio-cephala calthella* is one of our most abundant moths, occurring in the spring nearly everywhere, and being easily found on account of its habit of sitting in buttercup-flowers, yet its metamorphoses were till recently completely unknown. Dr. Chapman has, however, been able to give us some information as to the habits and structure of the larvae, in both of which points the creature is most interesting.

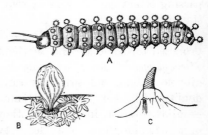

Fig. 209.—Larva of *Eriocephala calthella.* (After Chapman.) **A,** Young larva from side, × 50 ; **B,** portion of skin with a bulla or ball-like appendage : *c,* abdominal foot of larva.

The eggs and young larvae are " quite

[1] Walter, *Jena. Zeitschr. Naturw.* xviii. 1885. He did not distinguish *Eriocephala* as a genus, as we have explained on p. 308.
[2] *Amer. Natural.* xxix. 1895, pp. 636 and 803.

unlike our ideas of a Lepidopterous Insect ; " the former have a snowy or mealy appearance, owing to a close coating of minute rods standing vertically on the surface of the egg, and often tipped with a small bulb. The larva lives amongst wet moss and feeds on the growing parts thereof; it is not very similar to any other Lepidopterous larva: Dr. Chapman suggests a similarity to the Slug-worms (Limacodids), but Dyar is probably correct in thinking the resemblances between the two are unimportant : the larva of *Eriocephala* possesses three pairs of thoracic legs, and eight pairs of abdominal appendages, placed on the segments immediately following the thorax ; on the under-surface of the ninth and tenth abdominal segments there is a sucker, trifoliate in form ; this is probably really situate entirely on the tenth segment : the body bears rows of ball-appendages, and the integument is beautifully sculptured. The head is retractile and the antennae are longer than is usual in caterpillars. This larva is profoundly different from other Lepidopterous larvae inasmuch as the abdominal feet, or appendages, are placed on different segments to what is customary, and are of a different form. Unfortunately the pupa has not been procured, but there

is some reason for supposing that it will prove to be more like that of Tineidae than like that of Micropterygidae.

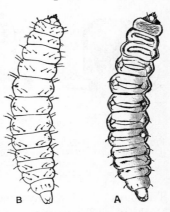

The New Zealand genus *Palaeomicra* is only imperfectly known. Meyrick considers it the "most ancient" Lepidopteron yet discovered; and it would appear that its relations are with *Eriocephala* rather than with *Micropteryx*. From information he has kindly given to us, we are able to say that this moth possesses mandibles but no proboscis.

Fɪɢ. 210.—Larva of *Micropteryx* sp. A, Ventral view of the larva, magnified ; B, the same, with setae unduly magnified. Britain.

Fam. 47. Micropterygidae.—Small moths of metallic colours, without mandibles, with elongate maxillary palpi : without frenulum : both wings with a complex system of wing-veins : on the hind wings the area anterior to the cell is large, and traversed by three or four elongate, parallel veins. There are no mandibles, but there is a short, imperfect proboscis. Larva (Fig. 210) without any legs, mining in leaves. The pupa (Fig. 211) is not a pupa obtecta, but has the head and appendages free, and it provided with enormous mandibles. Although these Insects in general appearance resemble *Erio-cephala* to such an extent that both have been placed in one genus, viz. *Micropteryx*, yet the two forms are radically distinct.

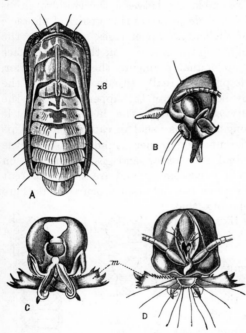

The most remarkable point in *Micropteryx* is the metamorphosis; the female moth is furnished with a cutting ovipositor, by the aid of which she deposits an egg between the two layers of a leaf after the manner of a saw-fly;[1] the larva mines the newly-opened leaves in the early spring, and feeds up with rapidity; it by some means reaches the ground, and there pupates in a firm but thin cocoon, with grains of earth fastened to it; in this it passes the greater part of its life as a larva, changing to a pupa very early in the following spring.

FIG. 211.—Pupa of *Micropteryx* (*semipurpurella ?*). **A,** Dorsal aspect; **B, C, D,** views of head dissected off; **B,** profile; **C,** posterior, **D,** anterior aspects; *m,* mandibles. Britain.

The pupa is unlike any other Lepidopterous pupa, but is similar to those of Trichoptera; neither the head nor the appendages are glued to the body or to one another, but are free, so that the pupa can use the appendages to a considerable extent; it is furnished with enormous mandibles (Fig. 211, C, D), which are detached and shed after emergence.[2] In the interval between

---

[1] Wood, *Ent. Mag.* xxvi. 1890, p. 148.
[2] See Chapman, *Tr. ent. Soc. London,* 1893, p. 255.

the larval period of feeding and the imaginal instar, the phenomena of life are essentially like those of Trichoptera. The larva
has not been at all satisfactorily studied; the spiracles appear
to be excessively minute, but have been ascertained by Dr.
Chapman to be normal in number and position.

All the information we possess points to profound distinctions
between *Micropteryx* and *Eriocephala*, for whereas in the former
the mandibles drop off from the pupa, so that the imago has no
mandibles, in the latter the mandibles exist, as they do in
several other true Lepidoptera. As the history of the mandibles is not known in other Lepidoptera (where they are present
in the larva but wanting in the imago), it is premature to
conclude that no other Lepidoptera suffer the actual loss of the
mandibles as *Micropteryx* does, though there is nothing to lead
us to believe that in any other Lepidopterous pupa are the
mandibles specially developed as they are in *Micropteryx*. This
pupa is in fact quite unique in this Order of Insects. When the
history of the pupal mandibles is known, we shall be able to
decide whether they are secondary structures, like the deciduous,
supplementary mandibles found in Otiorhynchides (Coleoptera,
Rhynchophora).

CHAPTER VII

Order VII. Diptera

*Wings two, membranous, usually transparent and never very large ;
behind the wings a pair of small erect capitate bodies—
halteres —frequently concealed under membranous hoods.
No distinct prothorax, all the divisions of the thorax being
united to form a large mass.   Mouth-parts very variable,
formed for suction not for biting, frequently assuming the
form of a proboscis that can be retracted and concealed in a
cleft of the under side of the head.   The metamorphosis is
very great, the larvae bearing no resemblance whatever to the
perfect Insects, but being usually footless grubs or maggots ;
frequently the head is indistinct, small, and retracted.
Pupa variable, either exposed and rather hard, with the
appendages of the body more or less adherent ; or enclosed
in a scaly capsule looking like a seed, and when extracted,
soft and delicate, with the appendages not fastened to the
body incapable of movement.*

THIS definition of the Diptera, or two-winged flies, is framed
without reference to the fleas, which are wingless, or to a few
other parasitic wingless Diptera, such as the sheep-tick.   Although
the Order is of enormous extent, these exceptional cases are
remarkably few.   About 40,000 species of Diptera have been
discovered, but these are only a tithe of what are still unknown
to science.   The Order is not a favourite one with entomologists,
and by the rest of the world it may be said to be detested.
Flies do not display the sort of intelligence we appreciate,

or the kind of beauty we admire, and as a few of the
creatures somewhat annoy us, the whole Order is only too
frequently included in the category of nuisances that we must
submit to.   Moreover, the scavenger-habits that are revealed,
when we begin to study their lives, are very repugnant to many
persons.   It is therefore no wonder that flies are not popular,

and that few are will-
ing to study them, or
to collect them for
observation.   Never-
theless, Diptera have
considerable claims to
be classed as actually
the highest of Insects
physiologically, for it
is certainly in them
that the processes of a
complete life-history
are carried on with the
greatest rapidity and
that the phenomena
of metamorphosis have
been most perfected.
A maggot, hatching
from an egg, is able

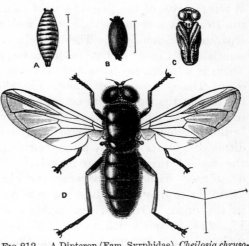

Fig. 212.—A Dipteron (Fam. Syrphidae), *Cheilosia chryso-
coma*. Britain. **A**, Adult larva ; **B**, the pupa ; **C**,
nymph, extracted from pupa ; **D**, imago. (From
Weyenbergh.)

to grow with such rapidity that the work of its life in this
respect is completed in a few days ; then forming an impenetrable skin it dissolves itself almost completely ; solidifying subsequently to a sort of jelly, it in a few days reconstructs itself
as a being of totally different appearance and habits, in all
its structures so profoundly changed from what it was that the
resources of science are severely taxed to demonstrate any
identity of the organs of the two instars.

A good study of the comparative anatomy of Diptera has never
been made ; Baron Osten Sacken, one of our most accomplished
Dipterologists, has recently stated that " the external characters
of the Diptera have as yet been very insufficiently studied."
We shall therefore only trouble the student with a few observations on points of structure that are of special importance, or
that he will find frequently alluded to.   The head is remarkable

for its mobility, and is connected with the thorax by a slender concealed neck that permits the head to undergo semi-rotation. A large part—sometimes nearly the whole—of the exposed surface of the head is occupied by the faceted eyes. It is usually the case that the eyes are larger in the male than in the female, and the sexual discrepancy in this respect may be very great. When the eyes of the two sides meet in a coadapted line of union the Insect is said to be " holoptic," and when the eyes are well separated " dichoptic." [1] The holoptic condition is specially characteristic of the male, but in some forms occurs in both sexes. There is no definite distinction between holoptic and dichoptic eyes. The eyes may be enormous, Fig. 238, without actually uniting, and in the cases where actual contiguity occurs, it takes place in different manners.[2] The eyes are frequently during life of brilliant colours and variegate with stripes or spots ; this condition disappears speedily after death, and it is uncertain what the use of this coloration may be.[3] The eyes are frequently densely set with hairs between the almost innumerable facets. These facets frequently differ in size according to their position in the organ. The curious double eye of the male *Bibio* (cf. Fig. 224) is well worth notice. There are usually three small ocelli placed very near together on the middle of the summit of the head.

The antennae are of considerable importance, as they offer one of the readiest means of classification. The families placed by systematists at the commencement of the Order have antennae similar to those of the majority of Insects, inasmuch as they consist of a series of segments approximately similar to one another, and arranged in a linear manner (Fig. 213, A). The number of these joints is never very great, but reaches sixteen in certain Tipulidae, and falls as low as eight in some Bibionidae. In certain cases where the antennae of the male are densely feathered (*Chironomus*, e.g.), the number of joints is in that sex greatly augmented, but they are imperfectly separated. This form of antenna gives the name Nemocera to the first series of Diptera. The majority of flies have antennae of another form,

---

[1] Osten Sacken, *Tr. ent. Soc. London*, 1884, p. 501, and *Berlin. ent. Zeitschr.* xxxvii. 1892, p. 423, etc.

[2] Osten Sacken has recently discussed the intermediate conditions, and proposed the name " pseudholoptic " for some of them, *Berlin. ent. Zeitschr.* xli. 1896, p. 367.

[3] Girschner, *Berlin. ent. Zeitschr.* xxxi. 1887, p. 155.

peculiar to the Order, viz. three segments, the outer one of which is of diverse form, according to the genus or species, and bears on its front a fine projecting bristle, frequently feathered, as in Fig. 213, F; and often distinctly divided into two or more joints. This form of antenna is found in the series Aschiza and Schizophora; it is well exemplified in the common house-fly, where the organs in question hang from the forehead, and are placed in a hollow formed for their reception on the front of the head. Flies with this form of antennae are called Athericerous. Between the two forms of antennae we have mentioned there exists what may, speaking roughly, be called an intermediate condition, or

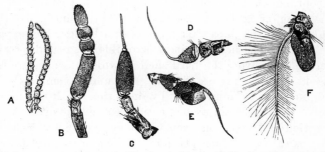

Fig. 213.—Antennae of flies. **A,** The two antennae of *Glaphyroptera picta* (Mycetophilidae); **B,** antenna of *Hexatoma pellucens* (Tabanidae); **C,** of *Asilus crabroniformis* (Asilidae); **D,** of *Leptis scolopacea* (Leptidae); **E,** of *Dolichopus undulatus* (Dolichopidae); **F,** of *Volucella bombylans* (Syrphidae). (After Wandolleck.)

rather a variety of intermediate conditions, associated in the series Brachycera (Fig. 213, B to D).[1] Here there are three (sometimes one or two) segments and a terminal appendage, but the appendage is usually compound (often so distinctly compound that it is evidently a series of partially, or even completely, separate joints, Fig. 213, B): the appendage in these cases is terminal, that is to say it is placed, not as in the Eumyiidae on the front of the joint that bears it, but (in the great majority of Brachycera) at the tip thereof; this appendage is often conical and pointed, often hair-like. Exceptional forms of antenna are found in the parasitic flies of the series Pupipara. In the Order generally the two basal joints of the antennae are evidently distinct in function from the others, and form the " scape "; the

---

[1] It may be well to remark that this name was formerly applied to all Diptera except Nemocera.

part of the antenna beyond the scape is called the "flagellum";
an appendage of the flagellum is called "arista" when bristle-
like, when thicker "style." In the basal joint of the antenna
there is a complex nervous structure known as Johnston's organ.
It is specially well developed in *Culex* and *Chironomus*, and is
larger in the male than it is in the female. Child has found
something of the kind present in all the Diptera he has
examined, and he considers that an analogous structure exists in
Insects of other Orders. He thinks it is concerned with the
perception of vibration, there being no sharp distinction between
auditory and tactile sensation.[1]

About one-half of the Diptera possess a peculiar structure
in the form of a head-vesicle called "ptilinum." In the fly
emerging from the pupa this appears as a bladder-like expansion
of the front of the head; being susceptible of great distension, it
is useful in rupturing the hard shell in which the creature is then
enclosed. In the mature fly the ptilinum is completely intro-
verted, and can be found only by dissection; a little space, the
"lunula," just under an arched suture, extending over the point
of insertion of the antenae remains, however, and offers evidence
of the existence of the ptilinum. This structure is also of
importance in classification, though, unfortunately, it is difficult
to verify.[2]

No point of Insect morphology has given rise to more difference of opinion than the mouth of Diptera; and the subject is
still very far from being completely understood. The anatomy
and morphology of the mandibulate Insect-mouth are comparatively simple (though not without greater difficulties than are
usually appreciated); and it has been the desire of morphologists
to homologise the sucking mouth of Diptera with the biting
mouth; hence the view that the appendages of three segments
are separate and distinct in the fly's mouth is taken for granted,
and it is further assumed that some of the secondary parts of the
appendages of the biting mouth can also be recognised in the
sucking mouth. The anatomy of the mouth-parts is, however,

[1] *Zool. Anz.* xvii. 1894, p. 35, and *Ann. Nat. Hist.* (6) xiii. 1894, p. 372; *Zeitschr. wiss. Zool.* lviii. 1895, p. 475.

[2] Cf. Osten Sacken, *Berlin. ent. Zeitschr.* xxxviii. 1893; and Becher, *Wien. ent. Zeit.* i. 1882, p. 49. For an account of the condition, with diagrammatic figures, of the fly emerging from the pupa, cf. Sasatti, *J. Coll. Japan,* i. 1887. p. 34, pl. vi.

subject to great diversity of structure within the limits of the
Order itself, even the two sexes in some species differing profoundly in this respect.[1]   In the majority of the family Oestridae
the mouth-parts are practically absent, and no definite entry to
the alimentary canal can be perceived (Fig. 245).   Besides this
condition and its antithesis (Fig. 214), the complex assemblage
of lancets seen in the Breeze-flies that draw blood, there is a
great variety of other anatomical conditions.

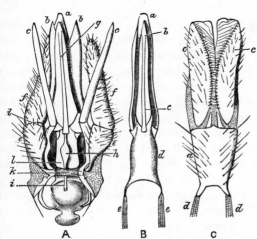

Fig. 214.—Mouth - parts of
the common blood-suck-
ing fly, *Haematopota
pluvialis* ♀. **A**, Viewed
from beneath, the pro-
boscis removed ; *a*,
labrum ; *b*, *b*, cultelli
(mandibles of other
anatomists) ; *c*, *c*, scal-
pella (maxillae of other
anatomists) ; *d*, part of
ventral scutum of second
metamere ; *e*, *e*,*f*,*f*, parts
of palpi ; *g*, hypopharynx
and pellucid salivary
duct ; *h*, salivary receptacle ; *i*, salivary duct ;
k, membranous part of
second metamere ; *l*,
pharynx : **B**, labrum,
pharynx, hypopharynx,
separated, seen from
beneath ; *a*, labrum ; *b*,

A   B   C

hypopharynx ; *c*, salivary duct ; *d*, pharynx ; *e*, protractor muscles : **C**, proboscis
(labium) from beneath ; *a*, scutum proboscidis ; *c*, *c*, labella ; *d*, *d*, retractor muscles.
(After Meinert).

Although, as we have said, great diversity of opinion
exists, yet on the whole the majority of Dipterologists accept a
view something to the following effect :—the labrum, or the
labrum combined with the epipharynx, is frequently much prolonged ; the tongue—hypopharynx—may also be much prolonged,
and may form, in apposition with the labrum, a more or less imperfect tube for ingestion of the nutriment ; the labium is more
or less membranous or fleshy, and acts as a sheathing organ, its
tips—called labella—being in some cases developed to a quite
extraordinary extent.   As to the other parts of the mouth there
is less agreement ; the pointed organs (Fig. 214, A, *b* *b*) are by

---

[1] It is frequently said that one sex of a single species may be dimorphic in this
respect, but we shall subsequently mention (in Blepharoceridae) that this is not
yet sufficiently established.

many identified as mandibles, while another pair of pointed processes (c c) are considered to be parts of a maxilla, and the palpi
(f f) are by some considered to be maxillary palps.   The Danish
entomologist, Meinert, has published the best anatomical description of many of the diverse kinds of Dipterous mouth.[1]   He,
however, takes a different view of the morphology; he considers
that not only may parts of the appendages of the mouth be much
modified during the early stages of the individual development,
but that they may be differently combined, even parts of the
appendages of two segments being brought together in intimate
combination.   He has also pointed out that the mandibulate and
sucking mouth are mechanical implements constructed on opposed
principles; the main object of a biting mouth being the fixing
and perfecting of the articulations of the mouth, so that great
power of holding may be attained with a limited but definite
power of movement.   In the sucking mouth the parts are intimately associated for simple protrusion.   Hence the two kinds
of mouth must have been distinguished very early in the
phylogeny, so that we must not expect to find a great correspondence between the parts of biting and sucking mouths.
He apparently also considers that not only the appendages of
a head-segment, but also part of the body of the segment, may
be used in the construction of the mouth-organs.   Meinert's
views allow a much greater latitude of interpretation of the parts
of the Dipterous mouth; had he contented himself with enun-
ciating them in the manner we have followed him in summarily
describing, they would have been recognised as a formidable
obstacle to the facile adoption of the ordinary views.   He has,
however, accompanied his general statement with a particular
interpretation and a distinct nomenclature, neither of which is it
possible to adopt at present, as they have no more justification
than the ordinary view.   So that instead of one set of doubtful
interpretations we have two.[2]   In so difficult a question as homo-
logising the trophi of different Orders of Insects we ought to use

[1] *Fluernes Munddele, Copenhagen*, 1881, 91 pp. 6 plates ; *Ent. Tidskr.* i. 1879,
p. 150 ; Becher having given (*Denk. Ak. Wien.* xlv. 1882, p. 123) an interpretation different from that of Meinert, this author set forth his general views in
Zool. Anz. v. 1882, pp. 570 and 599.

[2] The reader should not suppose that there are only two views as to the Dipterous
mouth, for actually there are several ; our object is here only to give a general idea
of the subject.

exhaustively every method of inquiry: and from this point of view the development is of great importance. This has, however, as yet thrown but little light on the subject, this study being a very difficult one owing to the profound changes that take place during metamorphosis, the diversity of the parts in the early stages of Diptera, and the possibility that the larval conditions may themselves have been greatly changed in the course of the phylogeny. Miall informs us, however, that in *Chironomus* as well as in *Corethra* the new parts of the mouth of the imago are developed within those of the larva.[1] This may permit of an identification of the main divisions of the mouth, at any rate in these cases. Lowne has to some extent traced the development in the blowfly, and he does not agree with the usual interpretation of the parts in the adult.

The mouth is of considerable importance in the classification of Diptera. The Nemocera are remarkable from the linear development and flexibility of the palpi, which are nearly always at least three- or four-jointed; this condition occurring in no other Diptera. The palpi attain an extraordinary development in some Culicidae; in the genus *Megarrhina* they are nearly as long as the body, and project in front of the head after the fashion of the palpi of Lepidoptera. In the Brachycera the sclerites or hard parts of the mouth reach a maximum of development, and in Tabanidae (Fig. 214), Nemestrinidae and Bombyliidae are often quite disproportionate to the size of the Insect. In many of the Eumyiid flies the soft parts are greatly developed, and capable of a variety of movement, the proboscis as a whole being protrusible, and having an elbow-joint in the middle.

The thorax is remarkable from the absence of distinct separation into the three divisions that may usually be so easily distinguished in Insects. The perfect combination of the three segments adds much to the difficulty of arriving at general conclusions as to the identification of the parts; hence considerable difference of opinion still prevails. It was formerly supposed that a segment from the abdomen was added to the thorax of Diptera as it is in Hymenoptera, but this has been shown by Brauer to be erroneous. Indeed, according to Lowne, the abdominal cavity is increased by the addition of the small posterior area of the thorax; it being the mesophragma that separates the

[1] *Tr. Linn. Soc. London* (2) v. 1892, p. 271.

second and third great divisions of the body-cavity. The prothorax is always small, except in a few of the abnormal wingless
forms (*Melophagus*); in *Nycteribia* (Fig. 248) the mesothorax
forms the anterior part of the body ; the head and such parts of
the prothorax as may be subsequently discovered to exist being
placed entirely on the dorsum of the body. The mesothorax in
all the winged Diptera forms by far the larger portion of the
thoracic mass, the prominent part of it, that projects backwards
to a greater or less extent over the base of the abdomen, being
the scutellum. The first or prothoracic stigma is remarkably large
and distinct, and is by some called mesothoracic. Another large
stigma is placed very near to the halter (or balancer); the metathorax being very small. An imperfect stigma is said by Lowne
to exist in the blowfly near the base of the wing. The number
of abdominal segments externally visible is very diverse ; there may
be as many as nine (in the male *Tipula*), or as few as five, or even
four, when the basal segment is much concealed ; the diminution is due to certain segments at the extremity being indrawn
and serving as a sort of tubular ovipositor in the female, or curled
under the body and altered in form in the other sex, so as to
constitute what is called a " hypopygium." In the female of
Tipulidae the body is terminated by some horny pieces forming
an external ovipositor. In nearly all Diptera the feet are five-
jointed ; the claws are well developed, there being placed under
each of them a free pad or membrane, the " pulvillus " ; there may
be also a median structure between each pair of claws, of diverse
form, the " empodium."

On the surface of the body of many flies there will be seen
an armature of pointed bristles; these flies are called " chaeto-
phorous "; where no regularly arranged system of such bristles
exists the fly is " eremochaetous." In some families the arrangement of these bristles is of importance in classification, and a
system of description has been drawn up by Baron Osten
Sacken : this branch of descriptive entomology is known as
chaetotaxy.[1]

The wings are of great importance in classifying Diptera ;
but unfortunately, like the other parts, they have not received an
exhaustive anatomical study, and Dipterologists are not agreed
as to the names that should be applied to their parts. We give

[1] *Tr. ent. Soc. London*, 1884, p. 497.

below figures of two systems that have been used by eminent Dipterologists for the description of the nervures and cells. The comprehension of these features of the Dipterous wing will be facilitated by noticing that the wing—being extended at right angles to the body—is divided by the longitudinal nervures into two great fields, anterior and posterior, with an interval between them: this interval is traversed only by a short cross-vein (marked x in Fig. 215 A, and i in B). This cross-vein may be placed near the base or nearer to the tip of the wing; it is of importance because no nervure in front of the median area traversed by it can corre-

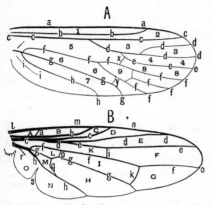

FIG. 215. — Nervuration of Dipterous wing. **A**, Wing of a Tipulid, according to Loew, who uses the following nomenclature : *a*, costal nervure ; *b*, mediastinal ; *c*, subcostal ; *d*, radial ; *e*, cubital ; *f*, discoidal ; *g*, postical ; *h*, anal ; *i*, axillar ; *x*, transverse, *y*, posterior transverse, nervure ; 1, 2, mediastinal areas ; 3, subcostal ; 4, cubital ; 5, anterior basal ; 6, posterior basal ; 7, anal ; 8, posterior marginal ; 9, discoidal. **B**, Wing of an Acalypterate Muscid (*Ortalis*), according to Schiner, who uses the following nomenclature : (nervures, small letters ; cells, capital letters) : *a*, transverse shoulder ; *b*, auxiliary ; *c* to *h*, first to sixth longitudinal ; *i*, middle transverse ; *k*, posterior transverse ; *l*, *m*, *n*, *o*, costa ; *p*, anterior basal transverse ; *q*, posterior basal transverse ; *r*, rudiment of a fourth nervure ; *s*, axillary incision : **A, B, C**, first, second, and third costal cells ; **D**, marginal ; **E**, sub-marginal ; **F, G, H**, first, second, and third posterior ; **I**, discal ; **K, L, M**, first, second, and third basal cells ; **N**, anal angle ; **O**, alula.

spond with a nervure placed behind it in another wing. The very different nature of the nervuration in the two wings we have figured will readily be appreciated by an inspection of the parts posterior to the little cross-vein. On the hind margin of the wing, near the base, there is often a more or less free lobe (Fig. 215, B, O) called the " alula " : still nearer to the base, or placed on the side of the body, may be seen one or two other lobes, of which the one nearer the alula is called the " tegula," or (when a lobe behind it is also present) the " upper tegula," (the " anti-tegula " of Osten Sacken); the other being the " lower tegula." These two terms are erroneous, the word tegula being definitely applied to another part of the Insect-body. In speaking of this structure in the following pages, we have preferred to call it the "squama."[1] Those Muscidae in which the squama covers the halter like a hood are called "calypterate." In Fig. 216, we

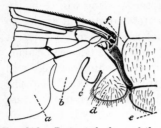

represent these structures, and in the explanation have mentioned the synonyms. The terms we think most applicable to the three lobes are alula, antisquama, squama. The squama may be called "calypter" when it covers the halter.

Fig. 216.—Parts at the base of the wing in *Calliphora*. *a*, Anal angle or lobe of the wing; *b*, alula; *c*, antisquama, squama alaris, or antitegula; *d*, squama, squama thoracicalis, tegula, calypter, or calyptron; *e*, posterior extremity (scutellum) of the mesothorax; *f*, scutum of mesothorax.

The halteres—commonly called balancers or poisers—are perhaps the most characteristic of all the Dipterous structures, though they are absent in most of the few wingless forms of the Order. Outside the Diptera similar organs appear to exist only in male Coccidae. The pair of halteres is placed on the metathorax, one on each of the pleural regions. They are believed to be the homologues of the hind wings; Weinland states [2] that certain canals existing in the interior of the halter correspond to wing-nervures. The halter may be described as a small rod-like body with a head like a pin, this terminal part being, however, rather variable in form. We have already stated that in many Diptera the squama forms a hood, the position of which leads to the belief that it is an important adjunct to the halter. Although the exact functions of the halteres are far from clear, it is certain that they are highly complex bodies, of extremely delicate structure : they are doubtless sense-organs, possessing as they do, groups of papillae on the exterior and a chordotonal organ (a structure for assisting the perception of sound) in the basal part; each halter is provided with four muscles at the base, and can, like the wings, execute most rapid vibrations. Seeing that they are the homologues of wings, it is a remarkable fact that in no Diptera are they replaced by wings, or by structures intermediate between these two kinds of organs.

Internal Structure.—Information about the internal anatomy

---

[1] Osten Sacken, although making use of the terms tegula and antitegula, suggested the propriety of using squama and antisquama, as we have done.

[2] *Zeitschr. wiss. Zool.* li. 1891, p. 55.

is by no means extensive. The tracheal system is highly developed, and has air-sacs connected with it ; a large pair at the base of the abdomen being called aërostats by Dufour.   Inside the thoracic spiracles there are peculiar structures supposed by some to be voice-organs, while the abdominal spiracles are said to be remarkably simple in structure.   Lowne says that there are ten or eleven pairs of spiracles in the Blow-fly ; one of these, near the base of the wing, is peculiar in structure, and may not be a true stigma ; he calls it a tympanic spiracle ; it seems doubtful whether there are more than seven abdominal pairs. The alimentary canal is very elongate, and is provided with a diverticulum, the crop; this is usually called the sucking stomach, though its function is extremely doubtful. The Malpighian tubes are four in number, and are very elongate ; in several groups of Nemocera there are, however, five Malpighian tubes, a number known to occur in only very few other Insects. The nervous system is remarkable on account of the concentration of ganglia in the thorax, so as to form a thoracic, in addition to the usual cephalic, brain.   For particulars as to the positions of the ganglia and the great changes that occur in the lifetime, the student should refer to Brandt, to Künckel, and to Brauer.[1] Much information as to the internal anatomy of the Blowfly is given by Lowne, but it is doubtful to what extent it is applicable to Diptera in general.[2]

The **larvae** of Diptera are—so far as the unaided eye is concerned—without exception destitute of any kind of adornment, the vast majority of them being of the kind known as maggots.   None of them have true thoracic legs ; though in the earlier groups, pseudopods or protuberances of the body that serve as aids in locomotion are common.   Unlike what occurs in other Orders

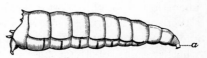

Fɪɢ. 217.—Acephalous larva or maggot of the blow-fly, with the head, *a*, extended. (After Lowne.)

the arrangement of these pseudopods on the body differs greatly in various forms ; in a few cases they are surmounted by

<hr/>

[1] Brandt, *Horae Soc. ent. Ross.* xiv. 1878, p. vii. ; xv. 1879, p. 20.   Brauer, *Denk. Ak. Wien*, xlvii. 1883, pp. 12–16.   Künckel, *C.R. Ac. Paris*, lxxxix. 1879, p. 491.
[2] *Blow-fly*, 1895 : in two vols.   For Anatomy of *Volucella*, see Künckel d'Herculais, *Recherches sur l'org. des Volucelles, Paris*, 1875 and 1881.

curved hairs.   The most important distinction in external form
in Dipterous larvae is that while those that are thorough maggots
possess no visible head, others have a well-marked one (Fig.
225); these are therefore called "eucephalous": they have a
mouth of the mandibulate type.   In some other Dipterous larvae
the head is more or less reduced in size, and in the acephalous forms
there is only a framework of a few chitinous rods to represent
it.   The nervous system in the most completely headless larvae
is very remarkable, all the ganglia being concentrated in a single
mass placed in the thorax.   The tracheal system exhibits a great
variety; some larvae have stigmata arranged along the sides of
the body after the fashion normal in Insect-larvae; these are
called "peripneustic"; as many as ten pairs of stigmata may be
present in these cases, but nine pairs is much more common.
Other larvae have a pair of stigmata placed at the termination of
the body, and another pair near the anterior extremity, the two
pairs communicating by large tracheal trunks extending the
length of the body; these larvae are said to be "amphipneustic":
this is the condition usual in the more completely acephalous
larvae.   Others have only the terminal pair of spiracles, and are
styled "metapneustic."   Some begin life in the metapneustic state
and afterwards become amphipneustic.   In the aquatic larva
of *Corethra* there are no spiracles, though there is an imperfect
tracheal system.   Many Dipterous larvae that live in water
or in conditions that prevent access of air to the body have
remarkable arrangements for keeping the tip of the body in
communication with the atmosphere.   The stigmata in metapneustic and amphipneustic larvae are very remarkable compound
structures, exhibiting however great diversity; their peculiarities
and uses are not well understood; it appears very doubtful
whether some of them have any external opening.   Reference
may be made, as to the variety of structure, to Meijere's paper [1]
from which we take the accompanying figure of a posterior
stigmatic apparatus in *Lipara lucens*.   It appears that there is a
compound chamber—" Filzkammer "—terminating externally in
lobes or fingers — " Knospen " and appearing as marks on the
outer surface: this chamber is seated on a tracheal tube, and is,
Meijere thinks, probably a secondary growth of the trachea
coming to the outer surface.   It is traversed by what may be

---

[1] *Tijdschr. Ent.* xxxviii. 1895, pp. 65–100.

considered the original tracheal tube, opening externally as an external stigmatic scar—" Stigmennarbe "—and with a second or inner scar placed internally. We may conclude from what is already known that these structures will be found to differ in the same larva according to the stage of its development.

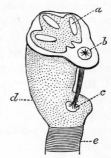

FIG. 218.—The posterior stigma of the larva of *Lipara lucens*. *a*, One of the three " Knospen " or lobes; *b*, external stigmatic scar; *c*, internal scar; *d*, stigmatic chamber (Filzkammer); *e*, trachea. (After Meijere.)

An extremely valuable summary of the characters and variety of Dipterous larvae has been given by Brauer,[1] from which it appears that the larvae of the first half of the family exhibit great variety and have been much studied, while the more purely maggot-like forms of the Muscidae have, with one or two exceptions, been little investigated.

The **pupal** instar is of two distinct kinds. First, we meet with a pupa like that of Lepidoptera, viz. a mummy-like object, or pupa obtecta, in which there is a crisp outer shell, formed in part by the adherent cases of the appendages of the future imago. This condition, with a few exceptions to be subsequently noticed, obtains in the Nemocera and Brachycera. It is exhibited in various degrees of perfection, being most complete in Tipulidae; in other forms the shell is softer and the appendages more protuberant. The second kind of pupa is found in the Cyclorrhaphous flies; it has externally no marks except some faint circular rings and, frequently, a pair of projections from near one extremity of the body; occasionally there is a single prominence at the other extremity of the body. This condition is due to the fact that the larva does not escape from the skin at the last ecdysis, but merely shrinks within it, so that the larval skin, itself contracted and altered by an excretion of chitin, remains and forms a perfect protection to the included organism. This kind of pupa looks like a seed, and is well exemplified by the common Blow-fly. The capacity for entering on such a condition is evidently correlative with the absence of a larval head. The metamorphosis in this curious little barrel goes on in a different manner to what it does in the pupa

[1] *Denk. Ak. Wien,* xlvii. 1883, pp. 1–100, pls. i.–v.

obtecta. A good name for the whole structure of this instar has not been found. Older authors called it "pupa coarctata," or "nympha inclusa"; Brauer speaks of it as a "compound pupa"; ordinarily in our language it is called a "puparium," a term which is more applicable to the case alone.

In species having a pupa obtecta the larval skin is cast after the chief processes of the external metamorphosis have occurred, and then an exudation of chitin hardens the general surface. In the "compound pupa" of the Blow-fly there is for a considerable period no formed pupa at all, but merely a shell or case containing the results of histolysis and the centres for regeneration of new organs; the chitin-exudation to the exterior of the larval skin occurs in the early part of the series of metamorphic changes, and the organism breaks down to a cream within the shell thus formed, and then gradually assumes therein the condition of a soft, nymphoid pupa. The exceptional conditions previously referred to as exhibited by a few forms are certain cases in which a more or less perfect pupa obtecta is found within the last larval skin, as is the case in *Stratiomys*. Another highly remarkable condition exists in the Hessian fly, and a few other Cecidomyiids, where the Insect apparently makes an exudation which it uses as a covering case, independent of the larval skin; this latter being subsequently shed inside the case, so that this condition of coarctate pupa differs from that we have described as existing in Cyclorrhaphous flies, although the two are superficially similar. In the Pupipara the larval stage is passed in the body of the mother, which produces a succession of young, nourished one at a time by the secretion of glands; this young is born as a full-grown larva that becomes at once a pupa.

Metamorphosis.—As it is in Diptera that the phenomena of Insect-metamorphosis have reached their highest development we endeavoured to give some idea of their nature in the previous volume, therefore we need give only a brief sketch of the chief features of Dipterous metamorphosis. The Blow-fly undergoes a rapid embryonic development, the later stages of which are, on the whole, of a retrogressive nature. On the emergence of the young maggot it feeds up rapidly, the rapidity varying greatly according to circumstances, and then when full-grown rests. While resting, a process of internal liquefaction, called histolysis, is going on, and the maggot contracts and exudes an excretion that hardens its skin. At the time this hard skin has become complete, or soon after, the maggot inside has dissolved into a cream contained in a sac inside the shell; this cream becomes reconstituted into a fly by a gradual process of growth and development of certain minute portions of the body—the imaginal discs or folds, the histoblasts and neuroblasts that were exempt from the histolytic process: in the early stages of the reconstitution the general structure is, of course, altogether vague, and this condition—purely one of transition—is called the pronymph; the nymph becomes gradually developed: it corresponds vaguely with the pupa obtecta of the early groups of Diptera, but is soft like the pupa of Hymenoptera. This nymph gradually develops into the fly itself, the external parts being first completed and the internal organs elaborated subsequently. The sexual organs do not undergo metamorphosis like other internal organs, there being a gradual (though irregular or interrupted) growth of them in the young larva, till they are completed some time after the emergence of the perfect fly. The processes in the Blow-fly have been studied by numerous able histologists of various nationalities, and have recently been described by Lowne in our own language.[1] Comparatively little has been done in studying the corresponding phenomena in other Diptera. Weismann has investigated the development of *Corethra*, and Miall that of *Chironomus*. These two flies belong to a division of Diptera different from that which includes the Blow-fly, and they display a condition of the metamorphic processes allied to what occurs in Lepidoptera, as well as to that which takes place in the Blow-fly. Imaginal folds are formed, but they only appear much later in the life, and they are much less distant from the positions they will, when developed, occupy in the imago. In *Chironomus*, according to Miall, the imaginal folds only appear in the last larval instar, but they grow with such rapidity that the legs and wings of the future fly can be distinguished in the larva, even before pupation; thus when the activity of the larva ceases but little change is required to complete the obtected pupa. In the Blow-fly some of the imaginal folds have been

---

[1] Since our brief and imperfect sketch of metamorphosis appeared in Vol. V. of this series, Packard has treated the subject more fully in his *Text-book of Entomology*, New York, 1898 ; and Pratt has summarised the state of knowledge as to imaginal discs in *Psyche*, viii. 1897, p. 15, étc.

traced back to the embryo; how many centres for the new growth there may be is uncertain, for though there are upwards of sixty for the outer body, the number of regenerative centres for the internal organs is not ascertained. The peculiar central nervous mass, mentioned in our remarks on the larva, consists of two kinds of tissue mixed together in a complex manner; one of these kinds is functionally active during the larval life and at the metamorphosis undergoes histolysis, while the other, or embryonic, portion develops into the nervous system of the fly.

It forms no part of our task to deal with general subjects, but we may be pardoned for calling attention to the bearing the metamorphosis of the higher Diptera has on our ideas of heredity in Insects. The fly bears no resemblance whatever to the larva, and is only obtained by the organic destruction of the latter, which occurs before the perfection of the sexual organs takes place, and yet the fly reproduces itself only secondarily, but primarily gives rise to the totally different larva. It is supposed that the larval structures have been gradually acquired, and yet they are transmitted with the utmost faithfulness by the totally different fly. We can only conclude that that which is bequeathed in each species is the early state of a particular process of development from which the subsequent stages follow necessarily if the developing organism be placed in conditions having on it influences like to those that influenced the ancestors.

Classification.—The classification of Diptera is as yet very imperfect. Formerly they were divided into two great groups, Nemocera and Brachycera, according to the structure of the antennae, as previously mentioned. This division has been abandoned, and the term Brachycera is now applied to only a small part of the old section that bore the name. The primary division usually adopted at present is into Orthorrhapha and Cyclorrhapha. The characters of these two groups are based on the nature of the metamorphosis, and have been gradually elaborated by Brauer in various memoirs.[1] The Orthorrhapha includes the forms with obtected pupae, the Cyclorrhapha those with a nymph-compound, as previously described. This distinction is of great importance, but unfortunately it is difficult to apply to the fly itself; the only character that can be used in connec-

---

[1] Monograph of Oestridae, *Verh. Ges. Wien*, 1863, and other papers *op. cit.* 1864, 1867, 1869 ; also *Denk. Ak. Wien*, xlii. 1880, xlvii. 1883.

tion with the imago is the existence of a suture over the insertion of the antennae in a portion, but not all, of the Cyclorrhapha.[1] The next set of divisions used by Brauer divides the Order into four sections, viz. 1. Orthorrhapha Nematocera, 2. O. Brachycera, 3. Cyclorrhapha Aschiza, 4. C. Schizophora. As these four groups are recognised more readily than the two major groups the student will do well at first to disregard the primary division and consider the Diptera as divisible into four great groups. To these four divisions we, however, add temporarily a fifth, viz. Pupipara. This is included by Brauer in Schizophora, but it appears to be really an unnatural complex, and had better be kept separate till it has been entirely reconsidered. These great sections may be thus summarised :—

Series 1. *Orthorrhapha Nemocera.*—Antennae with more than 6 segments, not terminated by an arista ; with the segments of the flagellum more or less similar to one another. Palpi slender and flexible, four- or five-jointed.[2]

Series 2. *Orthorrhapha Brachycera.* — Antennae variable, but never truly Nemocerous nor like those of Cyclorrhapha ; when an arista is present it is usually placed terminally, not superiorly ; when an arista is not present the flagellum terminates as an appendage consisting of a variable number of indistinctly separated segments ; thus the flagellum is not composed of similar joints ; [rarely are the antennae as many as seven-jointed]. Palpi only one- or two-jointed.[3] Around the insertion of the antennae there is no definite arched suture enclosing a small depressed space. The nervuration of the wings is usually more complex than in any of the other divisions.

Series 3. *Cyclorrhapha Aschiza.* Antennae composed of not more than three joints and an arista ; the latter is not terminal. Front of head without definite arched suture over the antennae, but frequently with a minute area of different colour or texture there. This group consists of the great family Syrphidae, and of four small families, viz. Conopidae, Pipunculidae, Phoridae, and Platypezidae. The section is supposed to be justified by its being Cyclorrhaphous in pupation, and by the members not possessing a ptilinum (or having no trace of one when quite mature). The Syrphidae are doubtless

---

[1] Becher, *Wien. Ent. Zeit.* i. 1882, p. 49 ; for observation on connecting forms see Brauer, *Verh. Ges. Wien*, xl. 1890, p. 272.

[2] The palpi are said to be of only one segment in some genera of Cecidomyiidae. The Cecidomyiidae are easily distinguished by the minute size—body not more than a line long—and by there not being more than six nervules at the periphery of the wing. *Aëdes* (Culicidae) has also short palpi.

[3] It is said by Schiner that in the anomalous genus *Nemestrina* the palpi are of three segments.

a natural group, but the association with them of the other families mentioned is a mere temporary device. The greatest difficulty is experienced in deciding on a position for Phoridae, as to which scarcely any two authorities are agreed.

Series 4. *Cyclorrhapha Schizophora*, or Eumyiid flies. The antennae consist of three joints and an arista. In the Calyptratae the frontal suture, or fold over the antennae, is well marked and extends downwards along each side of the face, leaving a distinct lunule over the antennae. In the Acalyptrate Muscids the form of the head and of the antennae vary much and are less characteristic, but the wings differ from those of Brachycera by their much less complex nervuration.

Series 5. *Pupipara*. These are flies of abnormal habits, and only found in connection with living Vertebrates, of which they suck the blood (one species, *Braula caeca*, lives on bees). Many are wingless, or have wings reduced in size. The young are produced alive, full grown, but having still to undergo a metamorphosis. This group consists of a small number of flies of which some are amongst the most aberrant known. This is specially the case with the Nycteribiidae. This Section will probably be greatly modified, as it is far from being a natural assemblage.[1]

The Sub-Order *Aphaniptera*, or Fleas, considered a distinct Order by many entomologists, may for the present be placed as a part of Diptera.

It must be admitted that these sections are far from satisfactory. Brauer divides them into Tribes, based on the nature of the larvae, but these tribes are even more unsatisfactory than the sections, hosts of species being entirely unknown in the larval state, and many of those that are known having been very inadequately studied. We must admit that the classification of Diptera has at present advanced but little beyond the stage of arranging them in natural families capable of exact definition. We may, however, draw attention to the attempt that is being made by Osten Sacken to remodel the classification of the Nemocera and Brachycera by the combination of families into super-families.[2] He proposes to divide the Nemocera into two super-families: 1. Nemocera Vera, including all the families from Cecidomyiidae to Tipulidae; 2. Nemocera Anomala, consisting of the small families Bibionidae, Simuliidae, Blepharoceridae, Rhyphidae and Orphnephilidae.

For Orthorrhapha Brachycera he adopts the following arrange-

[1] For tables of the families of flies the student may refer to Loew, *Smithson-Misc. Coll.* vi. Art. i. 1862; to Brauer, *Denk. Ak. Wien*, xlii. 1880, p. 110 (Orthorrhapha only); to Williston, *Manual of N. American Diptera*, 1896; to Schiner, *Fauna austriaca, Diptera*, Vienna, 1860, etc.

[2] *Berlin. ent. Zeitschr.* xxxvii. 1892, p. 365, and xli. 1897, p. 365.

ment : 1. Super-family Eremochaeta, for Stratiomyidae, Tabanidae, Acanthomeridae and Leptidae ; 2. Tromoptera, for Nemestrinidae, Acroceridae, Bombyliidae, Therevidae, and Scenopinidae ; 3. Energopoda, for Asilidae, Dolichopidae, Empidae and Lonchopteridae, Phoridae being included with doubt; 4. Mydaidae remains isolated.

This classification is based on the relations of the eyes and bristles of the upper surface, and on the powers of locomotion, aërial or terrestrial. At present it is not sufficiently precise to be of use to any but the very advanced student.

Blood-sucking Diptera.—The habit of blood-sucking from Vertebrates is, among Insects, of course confined to those with suctorial mouth, and is exhibited by various Diptera. It is, however, indulged in by but a small number of species, and these do not belong to any special division of the Order. It is remarkable that as a rule the habit is confined to the female sex, and that a large proportion of the species have aquatic larvae. This subject has many points of interest, but does not appear to have yet received the attention it merits. We give below a brief summary of the facts as to blood-sucking Diptera.

Series I. Nemocera.—In this section the habit occurs in no less than five families, viz. :

Blepharoceridae. *Curupira ;* in the female only ; larva aquatic.

Culicidae. *Culex*, Mosquitoes ; in the female only ; other genera, with one or two exceptions, do not suck blood ; larvae aquatic.

Chironomidae. *Ceratopogon*, Midge ; in the female only ; exceptional even in the genus, though the habit is said to exist in one or two less known, allied genera ; larval habits not certain ; often aquatic ; in *C. bipunctatus* the larva lives under moist bark.

Psychodidae. *Phlebotomus :* in the female only (?); quite exceptional in the family ; larva aquatic or in liquid filth.

Simuliidae. *Simulium*, sand-flies ; general in the family (?), which, however, is a very small one ; larva aquatic, food probably mixed vegetable and animal microscopic organisms.

Series II. Brachycera. Tabanidae. Gad-flies : apparently general in the females of this family ; the habits of the exotic forms but little known ; in the larval state, scarcely at all known ; some are aquatic.

Series IV. Cyclorrhapha Schizophora: *Stomoxys, Haematobia ;* both sexes (?); larvae in dung. [The Tse-tse flies, *Glossina,* are placed in this family, though their mode of parturition is that of the next section].

Series V. Pupipara. The habit of blood-sucking is probably common to all the group and to both sexes. The flies, with one exception, frequent Vertebrates; in many cases living entirely on their bodies, and apparently imbibing much blood ; the larvae are nourished inside the flies, not on the imbibed blood, but on a milky secretion from the mother.

Sub-Order Aphaniptera. Fleas. The habit of blood-sucking is common to all the members and to both sexes. The larvae live on dried animal matter.

Fossil Diptera.——A considerable variety of forms have been found in amber, and many in the tertiary beds ; very few members of the Cyclorrhaphous Sections are, however, among them ; the Tipulidae, on the other hand, are richly represented. In the Mesozoic epoch the Order is found as early as the Lias, the forms being exclusively Orthorrhaphous, both Nemocera and Brachycera being represented. All are referred to existing families. Nothing has been found tending to connect the Diptera with other Orders. No Palaeozoic Diptera are known.

Series 1. Orthorrhapha Nemocera

Fam. 1. Cecidomyiidae.——*An extensive family of very minute and fragile flies, the wings of which have very few nervures; the antennae are rather long, and are furnished with whorls of hair.* In the case of some species the antennae are beautiful objects; in *Xylodiplosis* some of the hairs have no free extremities, but form loops (Fig. 220). In the males of certain species the joints appear to be double, each one consisting of a neck and a body. Although comparatively little is known as to the flies themselves, yet these Insects are of importance on account of their preparatory stages. The larvae have very diverse habits ; the majority live in plants and form galls, or produce defor- mations of the leaves, flowers, stems, buds, or roots in a great variety of ways; others live under bark or in animal matter ; some are predaceous, killing Aphidae or Acari, and even other

Cecidomyiids. The North American *Diplosis resinicola* lives in the resin exuded as the results of the attacks of a caterpillar. The larva burrows in the semi-liquid resin, and, according to Osten Sacken,[1] is probably amphipneustic. Cecidomyiid larvae are short maggots, narrowed at the two ends, with a very small head, and between this and the first thoracic segment (this bears a stigma), a small supplementary segment; the total number of segments is thirteen, besides the head; there are eight pairs of stigmata

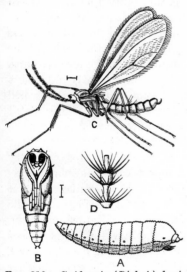

FIG. 219.—*Cecidomyia* (*Diplosis*) *buxi*. Britain. **A,** Larva, magnified; **B,** pupa; **C,** imago; **D,** portion of antenna. (After Laboulbene.)

FIG. 220.—One segment of antenna of *Xylodiplosis* sp.; *a,* Tip of one segment; *b,* base of another. (After Janet.)

on the posterior part of the body. Brauer defines the Cecidomyiid larva thus, "peripneustic, with nine pairs of stigmata, the first on the second segment behind the head; two to nine on fifth to twelfth segments; body as a whole fourteen-segmented without a fully-formed head." The most remarkable peculiarity of Cecidomyiid larvae is that those of many species possess a peculiar organ—called breast-bone, sternal spatula, or anchor-process—projecting from the back of the lower face of the prothoracic segment. The use of so peculiar a structure has been much discussed. According to Giard,[2] in addition to the part

<hr>

[1] *Tr. Amer. ent. Soc.* iii. 1871, p. 345.   [2] *Bull. Soc. ent. France,* 1893, p. lxxx.

that protrudes externally, as shown in Fig. 219, A, there is a longer portion concealed, forming a sort of handle, having muscles attached to it. Some of these larvae have the power of executing leaps, and he states that such larvae are provided on the terminal segment with a pair of corneous papillae ; bending itself almost into a circle, the larva hooks together the breast-bone and the papillae, and when this connection is broken the spring occurs. This faculty is only possessed by a few species, and it is probable that in other cases the spatula is used as a means for changing the position or as a perforator. Some of the larvae possess false feet on certain of the segments. Williston says they probably do not moult. In the pupal instar (Fig. 219, B), the Cecidomyiid greatly resembles a minute Lepidopterous pupa. The Hessian fly, *Cecidomyia destructor*, is frequently extremely injurious to crops of cereals, and in some parts of the world commits serious depredation. The larva is lodged at the point where a leaf enwraps the stem ; it produces a weakness of the stem, which consequently bends. This Insect and *C. tritici* (the larva of which attacks the flowers of wheat) pupate in a very curious manner : they form little compact cases like flax-seeds ; these have been supposed to be a form of pupa similar to what occurs in the Blow-fly ; but there are important distinctions. The larva, when about to undergo its change, exudes a substance from its skin, and this makes the flax-seed ; the larval skin itself does not form part of this curious kind of cocoon, for it may be found, as well as the pupa, in the interior of the " flax-seed." Other Cecidomyiids form cocoons of a more ordinary kind ; one species, described by Perris as living on *Pinus maritima*, has the very remarkable faculty of surrounding itself, by some means, with a cocoon of resin. Walsh describes the cocoon-forming process of certain Cecidomyiids as one of exudation and inflation ; Williston as somewhat of the nature of crystallisation. Some Cecidomyiids are said to possess, in common with certain other Diptera, the unusual number of five Malpighian tubes ; and Giard says that in the larva there is only a pair of these tubes, and that their extremities are united so as to form a single tube, which is twisted into an elegant double loop.

Thirty years or more ago the Russian naturalist, Wagner, made the very remarkable discovery that the larva of a Cecidomyiid produces young ; and it has since been found by Meinert and others that this kind of paedogenesis occurs in several species of the genera *Miastor* and *Oligarces*. The details are briefly as follows :—A female fly lays a few, very large, eggs, out of each of which comes a larva, that does not go on to the perfect state, but produces in its interior young larvae that, after consuming the interior of the body of the parent larva, escape by making a hole in the skin, and thereafter subsist externally in a natural manner. This larval reproduction may be continued for several generations, through autumn, winter, and spring till the following summer, when a generation of the larvae goes on to pupation and the mature, sexually perfect fly appears. Much discussion has taken place as to the mode of origination of the larvae ; Carus and others thought they were produced from the rudimental, or immature ovaries of the parent larva. Meinert, who has made a special study of the subject,[1] finds, however, that this is not the case ; in the reproducing larva of the autumn there is no ovary at all ; in the reproducing larvae of the spring-time rudimentary ovaries or testes, as the case may be, exist ; the young are not, however, produced from these, but from germs in close connection with the fat-body. In the larvae that go on to metamorphosis the ovaries continue their natural development. It would thus appear that the fat-body has, like the leaf of a *Begonia,* under certain circumstances, the power, usually limited to the ovaries, of producing complete and perfect individuals.

Owing to the minute size and excessive fragility of the Gall-midge flies it is extremely difficult to form a collection of them ; and as the larvae are also very difficult of preservation, nearly every species must have its life-history worked out as a special study before the name of the species can be ascertained. Notwithstanding the arduous nature of the subject it is, however, a favourite one with entomologists. The number of described and named forms cannot be very far short of 1000, and each year sees some 20 or 30 species added to the list. The number of undescribed forms is doubtless very large. The literature of the subject is extensive and of the most scattered and fragmentary character.

The Cecidomyiidae have but little relation to other Nemocera, and are sometimes called Oligoneura, on account of the reduced number of wing-nervures. Their larvae are of a peculiar type

---

[1] *Naturhist. Tidskr.* (3) viii. 1874, p. 34, pl. xii.

that does not agree with the larvae of the allied families having
well-marked heads (and therefore called Eucephala), nor with the
acephalous maggots of Eumyiidae.

Fam. 2. Mycetophilidae.—*These small flies are much less
delicate creatures than the Cecidomyiidae, and have more nervures
in the wings ; they possess ocelli, and frequently have the coxae
elongated, and in some cases the legs adorned with complex arrangements of spines : their antennae have not whorls of hair.* Although
very much neglected there are probably between 700 and 1000
species known ; owing to many of their larvae living in fungoid
matter the flies are called Fungus-gnats. We have more than
100 species in Britain. *Epidapus* is remarkable, inasmuch as
the female is entirely destitute of wings and halteres, while
the male has the halteres
developed but the wings of
very reduced size. *E. scabiei*
is an excessively minute fly,
smaller than a common flea,
and its larva is said to be
very imjurious to stored
potatoes. The larvae of
Mycetophilidae are usually
very elongate, worm - like
maggots, but have a distinct,
small head ; they are peripneustic, having, according to

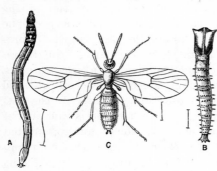

Fig. 221.—*Mycetobia pallipes.* Britain.
A, Larva ; B, pupa ; C, imago. (After Dufour.)

Osten Sacken, nine pairs of spiracles, one pair prothoracic, the others
on the first eight abdominal segments. They are usually worm-
like, and sometimes seem to consist of twenty segments. Some of
them have the faculty of constructing a true cocoon by some sort
of spinning process, and a few make earthen cases for the purpose of
pupation. The pupae themselves are free, the larval skin having
been shed. The Mycetophilidae are by no means completely
fungivorous, for many live in decaying vegetable, some even in
animal, matter.

The habits of many of the larvae are very peculiar, owing to
their spinning or exuding a mucus, that reminds one of snail-
slime ; they are frequently gregarious, and some of them have
likewise, as we shall subsequently mention, migratory habits.
Perris has described the very curious manner in which *Sciophila*

unimaculata forms its slimy tracks; [1] it stretches its head to one side, fixes the tip of a drop of the viscous matter from its mouth to the surface of the substance over which it is to progress, bends its head under itself so as to affix the matter to the lower face of its own body; then stretches its head to the other side and repeats the operation, thus forming a track on which it glides, or perhaps, as the mucus completely envelops its body, we should rather call it a tunnel through which the maggot slips along. According to the description of Hudson [2] the so-called New Zealand Glow-worm is the larva of *Boletophila luminosa;* it forms webs in dark ravines, along which it glides, giving a considerable amount of light from the peculiarly formed terminal segment of the body. This larva is figured as consisting of about twenty segments. The pupa is provided with a very long, curiously-branched dorsal structure: the fly issuing from the pupa is strongly luminous, though no use can be discovered for the property either in it or in the larva. The larva of the Australian *Ceroplatus mastersi* is also luminous. Another very exceptional larva is that of *Epicypta scatophora;* it is of short, thick form, like Cecidomyiid larvae, and has a very remarkable structure of the dorsal parts of the body; by means of this its excrement, which is of a peculiar nature, is spread out and forms a case for enveloping and sheltering the larva. Ultimately the larval case is converted into a cocoon for pupation. This larva is so different from that of other Mycetophilidae, that Perris was at first unable to believe that the fly he reared really came from this unusually formed larva. The larva of *Mycetobia pallipes* (Fig. 221) offers a still more remarkable phenomenon, inasmuch as it is amphipneustic instead of peripneustic (that is to say, it has a pair of stigmata at the termination of the body and a pair on the first thoracic segment instead of the lateral series of pairs we have described as normal in Mycetophilidae). This larva lives in company with the amphipneustic larva of *Rhyphus,* a fly of quite another family, and the *Mycetobia* larva so closely resembles that of the *Rhyphus,* that it is difficult to distinguish the two. This anomalous larva gives rise, like the exceptional larva of *Epicypta,* to an ordinary Mycetophilid fly.[3]

---

[1] *Ann. Soc. ent. France* (2) vii. 1849, p. 346.

[2] *Trans. New Zealand Inst.* xxiii. 1890, p. 48.

[3] Osten Sacken, *Berlin. ent. Zeitschr.* xxxvii. 1892, p. 442; and Perris, *Ann. Soc. ent. France* (2) vii. 1849, p. 202.

But the most remarkable of all the Mycetophilid larvae are those of certain species of *Sciara*, that migrate in columns, called by the Germans, Heerwurm. The larva of *Sciara militaris* lives under layers of decomposing leaves in forests, and under certain circumstances, migrates, sometimes perhaps in search of a fresh supply of food, though in some cases it is said this cannot be the reason. Millions of the larvae accumulate and form themselves by the aid of their viscous mucus into great strings or ribbons, and then glide along like serpents : these aggregates are said to be sometimes forty to a hundred feet long, five or six inches wide, and an inch in depth. It is said that if the two ends of one of these processions be brought into contact, they become joined, and the monstrous ring may writhe for many hours before it can again disengage itself and assume a columnar form. These processional maggots are met with in Northern Europe and the United States, and there is now an extensive literature about them.[1] Though they sometimes consist of almost incredible numbers of individuals, yet it appears that in the Carpathian mountains the assemblages are usually much smaller, being from four to twenty inches long. A species of *Sciara* is the " Yellow-fever fly " of the Southern United States. It appears that it has several times appeared in unusual numbers and in unwonted localities at the same time as the dreaded disease, with which it is popularly supposed to have some connection.

Fam. 3. Blepharoceridae.[2]—*Wings with no discal cell, but with a secondary set of crease-like lines.* The flies composing this small family are very little known, and appear to be obscure Insects with somewhat the appearance of Empidae, though with strongly iridescent wings ; they execute aerial dances, after the manner of midges, and are found in Europe (the Pyrenees, Alps and Harz mountains) as well as in North and South America. Their larvae are amongst the most remarkable of Insect forms ; indeed, no entomologist recognises them as belonging to a Hexapod Insect when he makes a first

[1] See Guérin-Méneville, *Ann. Soc. ent. France* (2) iv. 1846 ; *Bull.* p. 8 ; and Nowicki, *Verh. Ges. Wien*, xvii. 1867, *SB.* p. 23.

[2] For details as to the family cf. Osten Sacken, *Berlin. ent. Zeitschr.* xl. 1895, p. 148 ; and for the larvae F. Müller, *Arch. Mus. Rio-Jan.* iv. 1881, p. 47. The name "Liponeuridae" was formerly applied by some authorities to this family, but it is now generally recognised that Blepharoceridae is more legitimate.

acquaintance with them.   The larva of *Curupira* (Fig. 222)
lives in rapid streams in Brazil, fixed by its suckers to stones or
rocks.   It consists only of six or seven divisions, with projecting side-lobes ; the usual segmentation not being visible.   There
are small tracheal gills near the suckers, and peculiar scale-like
organs are placed about the edges of the lobes.   Müller considers
that the first lobe is " cephalothorax," corresponding to head,
thorax and first abdominal segment of other larvae, the next four
lobes he considers to correspond each to an
abdominal segment, and the terminal mass
to four segments.   He also says that
certain minute points existing on the surface, connected with the tracheal system by
minute strings, represent nine pairs of
spiracles.   These larvae and their pupae
can apparently live only a short time after
being taken out of the highly aërated
water in which they exist, but Müller
succeeded in rearing several flies from a
number of larvae and pupae that he
collected, and, believing them to be all one
species, he announced that the females
exhibited a highly developed dimorphism,
some of them being blood-suckers, others
honey-suckers.   It is however, more probable that these specimens belonged to two
or three distinct species or even genera.
This point remains to be cleared up.   The
larva we have figured is called by Müller
Paltostoma torrentium.   It is certain, however, that the Brazilian Insect does not

FIG. 222.—Under surface of
the larva of *Curupira*
(*Paltostoma*) *torrentium*,
showing the suckers along
the middle of the body,
much magnified.   Brazil.
(After Fritz Müller.)

belong to the genus *Paltostoma*, and it will no doubt bear the
name used by Osten Sacken, viz. *Curupira*.

The metamorphoses of the European *Liponeura brevirostris*
have been partially examined by Dewitz, who found the Insects
in the valley of the Ocker in September.[1]   He does not consider
the " cephalothorax " to include an abdominal segment ; and he
found that two little, horn-like projections from the thorax of the

---

[1] *Berlin. ent. Zeit.* xxv. 1881, p. 61 ; and cf. Brauer, *Wien. ent. Zeit.* i. 1882,
p. 1.

pupa are really each four-leaved. The pupa is formed within the larval skin, but the latter is subsequently cast so that the pupa is exposed ; its dorsal region is horny, but the under surface, by which it clings firmly to the stones of the rapid brook, is white and scarcely chitinised, and Dewitz considers that the chitinous exudation from this part is used as a means of fastening the pupa to the stones. Blepharoceridae possess, in common with *Culex, Psychoda* and *Ptychoptera,* the peculiar number of five Malpighian tubes, and it has been proposed by Müller to form these Insects into a group called Pentanephria.

Fam. 4. Culicidae (*Mosquitoes, Gnats*).—*Antennae with whorls of hair or plumes, which may be very dense and long in the male, though scanty in the female ; head with a long, projecting proboscis.* Although there are few Insects more often referred to in general literature than Mosquitoes, yet the ideas in vogue about them are of the vaguest character. The following are the chief points to be borne in mind as to the prevalence of Mosquitoes :—The gently humming Gnat that settles on us in our apartments, and then bites us, is a Mosquito ; there are a large number of species of Mosquitoes ; in some countries many in one locality ; in Britain we have ten or a dozen ; notwithstanding the multiplicity of species, certain Mosquitoes are very widely diffused ; the larvae are all aquatic, and specially frequent stagnant or quiet pools ; they are probably diffused by means of the water in ships, it being known that Mosquitoes were introduced for the first time to the Hawaiian Islands by a sailing vessel about the year 1828. Hence it is impossible to say what species the Mosquitoes of a given locality may be without a critical examination. No satisfactory work on the Mosquitoes of the world exists. Urich states that he is acquainted with at least ten species in Trinidad. The species common in our apartments in Central and Southern England is *Culex pipiens,* Linn., and this species is very widely distributed, being indeed one of the troublesome Mosquitoes of East India. The term Mosquito is a Spanish or Portuguese diminutive of Mosca. It is applied to a variety of small flies of other families than Culicidae, but should be restricted to these latter. The irritation occasioned by the bites of Mosquitoes varies according to several circumstances, viz. the condition of the biter, the condition or constitution of the bitten, and also the species of Mosquito. Réaumur and

others believed that some irritating fluid is injected by the Mosquito when it bites.   But why should it want to irritate as well
as to bite ?   Macloskie, considering that the Mosquito is really
a feeder on plant-substances, suggests that the fluid injected may
be for the purpose of preventing coagulation of the plant-juices
during the process of suction.   It is a rule that only the female
Mosquito bites, the male being an inoffensive creature, and provided with less effectual mouth-organs; it has, however, been
stated by various authors that male Mosquitoes do occasionally
bite.   It is difficult to understand the blood-sucking propensities
of these Insects ; we have already stated that it is only the
females that suck blood.   There is reason to suppose that it is an
acquired habit; and it would appear that the food so obtained
is not essential to their existence.   It has indeed been asserted
that the act is frequently attended with fatal consequences to
the individual that does it.   The proper method of mitigating
their nuisance is to examine the stagnant waters in localities
where they occur, and deal with them so as to destroy the larvae.
These little creatures are remarkable from the heads and thorax
being larger and more distinct than in other Dipterous larvae.
Their metamorphoses have been frequently described, and recently
the numerous interesting points connected with their life-histories
have been admirably portrayed by Professor Miall,[1] in an accessible
form, so that it is unnecessary for us to deal with them.
Corethra is placed in Culicidae, but the larva differs totally from
that of *Culex ;* it is predaceous in habits, is very transparent, has
only an imperfect tracheal system, without spiracles, and has two
pairs of air-sacs (perhaps we should rather say pigmented structures possibly for aerostatic purposes, but not suppliers of oxygen).
The kungu cake mentioned by Livingstone as used on Lake
Nyassa is made from an Insect which occurs in profusion there,
and is compressed into biscuit form.   It is believed to be a
Corethra.   One of the peculiarities of this family is the prevalence of scales on various parts of the body, and even on the
wings : the scales are essentially similar to those of Lepidoptera.
Though Mosquitoes are generally obscure plain Insects, there
are some—in the South American genus *Megarrhina*—that are
elegant, beautifully adorned creatures.   Swarms of various species
of Culicidae, consisting sometimes of almost incalculable numbers

---

[1] *Natural History of Aquatic Insects*, London, 1895, chap. ii.

of individuals, occur in various parts of the world ; one in New
Zealand is recorded as having been three-quarters of a mile long,
twenty feet high, and eighteen inches thick.   There is good
reason for supposing that Mosquitoes may act as disseminators
of disease, but there is no certain evidence on the subject.   The
minute *Filaria* that occurs in great numbers in some patients,
is found in the human body only in the embryonic and adult
conditions.   Manson considers that the intermediate stages are
passed in the bodies of certain Mosquitoes.[1]

Fam. 5. Chironomidae (*Gnats, Midges*).—*Small or minute
flies of slender form, with narrow wings, without projecting
rostrum, usually with densely feathered antennae in the male, and
long slender legs.*   The flies of this family bear a great general
resemblance to the Culicidae.   They are much more numerous
in species, and it is not improbable that we have in this country
200 species of the genus *Chironomus* alone.   They occur in
enormous numbers, and frequently form dancing swarms in the
neighbourhood of the waters they live in.   The species are
frequently extremely similar to one another, though distinguished
by good characters ; they are numerous about Cambridge.   Many
of them have the habit of using the front legs as feelers rather
than as means of support or locomotion.   This is the opposite of
what occurs in Culicidae, where many of the species have a habit
of holding up 'the hind legs as if they were feelers.   The eggs of
Chironomus are deposited as strings surrounded by mucus, and are
many of them so transparent that the development of the embryo
can be directly observed with the aid of the microscope.   They are
said to possess a pair of air-sacs.   The larvae, when born, are
aquatic in habits, and are destitute of tracheal system.   They
subsequently differ greatly from the larvae of *Culex*, inasmuch as
the tracheal system that develops is quite closed, and in some
cases remains rudimentary.   There is, however, much diversity
in the larvae and also in the pupae.   The little Blood-worms,
very common in many stagnant and dirty waters, and used by
anglers as bait, are larvae of *Chironomus*.   They are said to be
αἱ Ἐμπίδες of Aristotle.   The red colour of these larvae is due to
haemoglobin, a substance which has the power of attracting and
storing oxygen, and giving it off to the tissues as they require
it.   Such larvae are able to live in burrows they construct

[1] *Tr. Linn. Soc. Lond.* (2) ii. 1884, p. 367.

amongst the mud. Some of them, provided plentifully with haemoglobin, are in consequence able to live at great depths, it is said even at 1000 feet in Lake Superior, and come to the surface only occasionally. A few are able even to tolerate salt water, and have been fished up from considerable depths in the sea. It is a remarkable fact that these physiological capacities differ greatly within the limits of the one genus, *Chironomus*, for some of these species are destitute of haemoglobin, and have to live near the surface of the water; these have a superior development of the tracheal system. The pupae of *Chironomus* have the legs coiled, and the thorax, instead of being provided with the pair of tubes or trumpets for breathing that is so common in this division of Diptera, have a pair of large tufts of hair-like filaments.[1] A very curious form of parthenogenesis has been described by Grimm [2] as existing in an undetermined species of *Chironomus*, inasmuch as the pupa deposits eggs. Although this form of parthenogenesis is of much interest, it is not in any way to be compared with the case, already referred to, of *Miastor* (p. 461). The "pupa" is at the time of oviposition practically the imago still covered by the pupal integument; indeed Grimm informs us that in some cases, after depositing a small number of ova, the pupa became an imago. This parthenogenesis only occurs in the spring-generation; in the autumn the development goes on in the natural manner. The case is scarcely entitled to be considered as one of paedogenesis.

Gnats of this family, and believed to be a variety of *Chironomus plumosus*, are subject to a curious condition, inasmuch as individuals sometimes become luminous or "phosphorescent"; this has been noticed more specially in Eastern Europe and Western Asia. The whole of the body and legs may exhibit the luminous condition, but not the wings. It has been suggested by Schmidt that this condition is a disease due to bacteria in the body of the gnat.[3]

Ceratopogon is a very extensive genus, and is to some extent anomalous as a member of Chironomidae. The larvae exhibit considerable variety of form. Some of them are aquatic

---

[1] For an extremely interesting account of *Chironomus* refer to Miall's book, already cited, and, for the larva, to the valuable work of Meinert on Eucephalous larvae of Diptera, *Danske Selsk. Skr.* (6) iii. 1886, p. 436.

[2] *Ann. Nat. Hist.* (4) viii. 1871, p. 31.   [3] *Ibid.* (6) xv. 1895, p. 133.

in habits, but the great majority are terrestrial, frequenting trees, etc. The former larvae are very slender, and move after the manner of leeches; they give rise to imagos with naked wings, while the terrestrial larvae produce flies with hairy wings. There are also important distinctions in the pupae of the two kinds; the correlation between the habits, and the distinctions above referred to, is, however, far from being absolutely constant.[1] Certain species of midges are in this country amongst the most annoying of Insects; being of very minute size, scarcely visible, they settle on the exposed parts of the body in great numbers, and by sucking blood create an intolerable irritation. *Ceratopogon varius* is one of the most persistent of these annoyers in Scotland, where this form of pest is much worse than it is in England; in Cambridgeshire, according to Mr. G. H. Verrall, the two troublesome midges are the females of *C. pulicaris* and *C. bipunctatus*.

Fam. 6. Orphnephilidae.—*Small, brown or yellowish flies, bare of pubescence, with very large eyes contiguous in both sexes, and with antennae composed of two joints and a terminal bristle; both the second joint and the bristle are, however, really complex.* One of the smallest and least known of the families of Diptera, and said to be one of the most difficult to classify. The nervures of the wings are very distinct. Nothing is known of the habits and metamorphoses; there is only one genus—*Orphnephila*; it is widely distributed; we have one species in Britain.

Fam. 7. Psychodidae (*Moth-flies*).—*Extremely small, helpless flies, usually with thickish antennae, bearing much hair, with wings broader than is usual in small flies, and also densely clothed with hair, giving rise to a pattern more or less vague.* These flies are very fragile creatures, and are probably numerous in species. In Britain forty or fifty species have been recognised.[2] A South European form is a blood-sucker, and has received the appropriate name of *Phlebotomus*. The life-history of *Pericoma canescens* has recently been studied by Professor Miall.[3] The larva is of aquatic habits, but is amphibious, being capable of existing in the air; it has a pair of anterior spiracles, by means

---

[1] For metamorphoses of aquatic species of *Ceratopogon*, see Miall and Meinert, already quoted: for examples of the terrestrial species, and their illustrations, refer to Mik, *Wien. ent. Zeit.* vii. 1888, p. 183.

[2] Monograph, Eaton, *Ent. Mag.* xxix. and xxx. 1893, 1894: supplement *op. cit.* 1896, etc.   [3] *Tr. ent. Soc. London*, 1895, p. 141.

of which it breathes in the air, and a pair at the posterior
extremity of the body, surrounded by four ciliated processes,
with which it forms a sort of cup for holding air when it is
in the water.   The favourite position is amongst the filaments
of green algae on which it feeds.   A much more extraordinary
form of larva from South America, doubtless belonging to
this family, has recently been portrayed by Fritz Müller,
under the name of *Maruina*.[1]   These larvae live in rapid waters
in company with those of the genus *Curupira*, and like the
latter are provided with a series of suctorial ventral discs.
Fritz Müller's larvae belong to several species, and probably to
more than one genus, and the respiratory apparatus at the
extremity of the body exhibits considerable diversity among
them.

Fam. 8. Dixidae.—The genus *Dixa* must, it appears, form a
distinct family allying the Culicid series of families to the
Tipulidae.   The species are small, gnat-like Insects, fond of
damp places in forests.   We have four British species (*D.
maculata, D. nebulosa, D. aestivalis, D. aprilina*).   The genus is
very widely distributed, occurring even in Australia.   The
larvae are aquatic, and have been described by Réaumur,
Miall, and Meinert.   The pupa has the legs coiled as in the
Culicidae.

Fam. 9. Tipulidae (*Daddy-long-legs, or Crane-flies*).—*Slender
Insects with elongate legs, a system of wing-nervures, rather complex, especially at the tip ; an angulate, or open V-shaped, suture
on the dorsum of the thorax in front of the wings : the female
with the body terminated by a pair of hard, pointed processes,
concealing some other processes, and forming an ovipositor.*   The
curious, silly Insects called daddy-long-legs are known all
over the world, the family being a very large one, and found
everywhere, some of its members extending their range even
to the most inclement climates.   It includes a great variety
of forms that would not be recognised by the uninitiated,
but can be readily distinguished by the characters mentioned
above.   It is impossible to assign any reason of utility for
the extreme elongation of the legs of these Insects ; as
everyone knows, they break off with great ease, and the Insect
appears to get on perfectly well without them.   It is frequently

---

[1] *Tr. ent. Soc. London*, 1895, p. 479.

the case that they are much longer in the males than in
the females.   Other parts of the body exhibit a peculiar
elongation ; in some forms of the male the front of the head
may be prolonged into a rostrum.   In a few species the
head is separated by a great distance from the thorax, the
gap being filled by elongate, hard, cervical sclerites ; indeed
it is in these Insects that the phenomenon, so rare in Insect-
structure, of the elongation of these sclerites and their becoming a part of the actual external skeleton, reaches its
maximum.   In several species of *Eriocera* the male has the
antennae of extraordinary length, four or five times as long as
the body, and, strange to say, this elongation is accompanied
by a reduction in the number of the segments of which the
organ is composed, the number being in the male about six,
in the female ten, in place of the usual fourteen or sixteen.
In *Toxorrhina* and *Elephantomyia* the proboscis is as long as
the whole body.   In other forms the wings become elongated to
an unusual extent by means of a basal stalk.   It is probable
that the elongation of the rostrum may be useful to the Insects.
Gosse,[1] indeed, describes *Limnobia intermedia* as having a rostrum
half as long as the body, and as hovering like a Syrphid, but
this is a habit so foreign to Tipulidae, that we may be pardoned
for suspecting a mistake.   The larvae exhibit a great variety of
form, some being terrestrial and others aquatic, but the terrestrial forms seem all to delight in damp situations, such
as shaded turf or rotten tree-stems.   They are either amphipneustic or metapneustic, that is, with a pair of spiracles placed
at the posterior extremity of the body ; the aquatic species
frequently bear appendages or projections near these spiracles.
The pupae in general structure are very like those of Lepidoptera,
and have the legs extended straight along the body ; they possess
a pair of respiratory processes on the thorax in the form of
horns or tubes.

There are more than 1000 species of these flies known,
and many genera.   They form three sub-families, which are by
some considered distinct families, viz.: Ptychopterinae, Limnobiinae or Tipulidae Brevipalpi, Tipulinae or Tipulidae Longipalpi.

The Ptychopterinae are a small group in which the angulate

[1] *A Naturalist's Sojourn in Jamaica*, London, 1853, p. 284.

suture of the mesonotum is indistinct; the larvae are aquatic and
have the head free, the terminal two segments
of the body enormously prolonged (Fig. 223),
forming a long tail bearing, in the North
American *Bittacomorpha,* two respiratory filaments.   Hart [1] describes this tail as possessing
a stigmatal opening at the extremity ; no doubt
the structure is a compounded pair of spiracles.
The pupa (Fig. 223, B) has quite lost the respiratory tube at the posterior extremity of the
body, but has instead quite as long a one at
the anterior extremity, due to one tube of the
pair normal in Tipulidae being enormously
developed, while its fellow remains small.   This
is a most curious departure from the bilateral
symmetry that is so constantly exhibited in
Insect-structure.   Our British species of *Ptychoptera* have the pupal respiratory tube as extraordinary as it is in *Bittacomorpha,* though the
larval tail is less peculiar.[2]   This group should
perhaps be distinguished from the Tipulidae
as a separate family, but taxonomists are not
yet unanimous as to this.   Brauer considers
that the head of the larva, and the condition
of five Malpighian tubules in the imago,
require the association of Ptychopterinae with
the preceding families (Chironomidae, etc.),
rather than with the Tipulidae.

The great majority of the Tipulidae are comprised in the sub-family Limnobiinae—the
Tipulidae Brevipalpi of Osten Sacken :[3]   in
them the last joint of the palpi is shorter or
not much longer than the two preceding
together.   They exhibit great variety, and many
of them are types of fragility.   The common
winter gnats of the genus *Trichocera* are a
fair sample of this sub-family.   The species
of this genus mostly inhabit high latitudes, and delight in

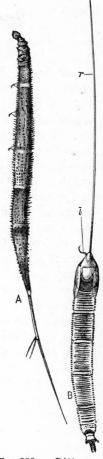

Fig. 223. — *Bittaco-
morpha   clavipes.*
North America × $\frac{2}{4}$.
(After Hart.)   **A,**
Larva ;   **B,** pupa :
l, the left, *r,* the
right   respiratory
tube.

---

[1] *Bull. Illinois Lab.,* iv. 1895, p. 193.   [2] Miall's *Aquatic Insects,* 1895, p. 174.
    [3] "Studies," etc., *Berlin. ent. Zeitschr.* xxxi. 1887.

a low temperature; it has been said that they may be seen on the wing in the depth of winter when the temperature is below freezing, but it is pretty certain that the spots chosen by the Insects are above that temperature, and Eaton states that the usual temperature during their evolutions is about 40° or 45° Fahr. They often appear in the damp conditions of a thaw when much snow is on the ground. *T. simonyi* was found at an elevation of 9000 feet in the Tyrol, crawling at a temperature below the freezing-point, when the ground was deeply covered with snow. *T. regelationis* occurs commonly in mines even when they are 500 feet or more deep. The most extraordinary of the Limnobiinae is the genus *Chionea*, the species of which are totally destitute of wings and require a low temperature. *C. araneoides* inhabits parts of northern Europe, but descends as far south as the mountains near Vienna; it is usually said to be only really active in the depth of winter and on the surface of the snow. More recently, however, a large number of specimens were found by Professor Thomas in the month of October in his garden in Thuringia; they were caught in little pit-falls constructed to entrap snails. The larva of this Insect is one of the interesting forms that display the transition from a condition with spiracles at the sides of the body to one where there is only a pair at the posterior extremity.

A very peculiar Fly, in which the wings are reduced to mere slips, *Halirytus amphibius*, was discovered by Eaton in Kerguelen Land, where it is habitually covered by the rising tide. Though placed in Tipulidae, it is probably a Chironomid.

The group Cylindrotomina is considered by Osten Sacken [1] to be to some extent a primitive one having relationship with the Tipulinae; it was, he says, represented by numerous species in North America during the Oligocene period. It is of great interest on account of the larvae, which are in several respects similar to caterpillars of Lepidoptera. The larva of *Cylindrotoma distincta* lives upon the leaves of plants—*Anemone*, *Viola*, *Stellaria*—almost like a caterpillar; it is green with a crest along the back consisting of a row of fleshy processes. Though this fly is found in Britain the larva has apparently not been observed here. The life-history of *Phalacrocera replicata* has been recently published by Miall and Shelford.[2] The larva eats

[1] *Tr. ent. Soc. London*, 1897, p. 362.   [2] *Tr. ent. Soc. London*, 1897, pp. 343-361.

submerged mosses in the South of England, and bears long forked
filaments, reminding one of those of caterpillars.   This species
has been simultaneously discussed by Bengtsson, who apparently
regards these Tipulids with caterpillar-like larvae—he calls them
Erucaeformia[1]—as the most primitive form of existing Diptera.

The Tipulinae—Tipulidae Longipalpi, Osten Sacken[2]—have
the terminal joint of the palpi remarkably long, longer than the
three preceding joints together.   The group includes the largest
forms, and the true daddy-long-legs, a Chinese species of which,
Tipula brobdignagia, measures four inches across the expanded
wings.   The group contains some of the finest Diptera.   Some
of the exotic forms allied to *Ctenophora* have the wings coloured
in the same manner as they are in certain Hymenoptera, and
bear a considerable resemblance to members of that Order.

Fam. 10. Bibionidae.—*Flies of moderate or small size, sometimes of different colours in the two sexes, with short, thick, straight,
antennae; front tibiae usually with a long pointed process;
coxae not elongate.   Eyes of male large, united, or contiguous in*

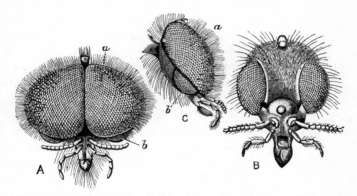

Fig. 224.—Head of *Bibio.*   × 10.   **A,** Of male, seen from the front ; **C,** from the side ;
a, upper, *b,* lower eye ; **B,** head of female.

front.   The flies of the genus *Bibio* usually appear in England
in the spring, and are frequently very abundant; they are of
sluggish habits and poor performers on the wing.   The difference in colour of the sexes is very remarkable, red or yellow
predominating in the female, intense black in the male; and

[1] *Acta Univ. Lund.* xxxiii. (2) No. 7, 1897.
[2] "Studies," etc., *Berlin. ent. Zeitschr.* xxx. 1886, p. 153.

it is a curious fact that the same sexual distinction of colour reappears in various parts of the world—England, America, India, and New Zealand; moreover, this occurs in genera that are by no means closely allied, although allied species frequently have concolorous sexes.   The eyes of the males are well worth study,

there being a very large upper portion, and, abruptly separated from this, a smaller, differently faceted lower portion, practically a separate eye; though so largely developed the upper eye is in some cases so hairy that it must greatly interfere with the formation of a continuous picture.   Carrière considers that the small lower eye of the male corresponds to the whole eye of the female. The larvae of *Bibio* (Fig. 225) are caterpillar-like in form, have a horny head, well developed, biting mouth-organs, and spine-like processes on the body-segments.   They are certified by good authorities[1] to possess the extremely unusual number of ten pairs of spiracles; a larva found at Cambridge, which we refer to *Bibio* (Fig. 225) has nine pairs of moderate spiracles, as well as a large terminal pair separated from the others by a segment without spiracles.   The genus *Dilophus* is closely allied to *Bibio*, the larvae of which (and those of Bibionidae in general) are believed to feed on vegetable substances; the parasitism of *Dilophus vulgaris* on the larva of a moth, *Epinotia (Chaetoptria) hypericana*, as recorded by Meade,[2] must therefore be an exceptional case.

FIG. 225. — Larva of *Bibio* sp. Cambridge.   × 5.

In the genus *Scatopse* there is a very important point to be cleared up as to the larval respiratory system; it is said by Dufour and Perris[3] to be amphipneustic; there are, however, nine projections on each side of the body that were considered by Bouché, and probably with good reason, to

[1] Osten Sacken, *Berlin. ent. Zeitschr.* xxxvii. 1892, p. 450.
[2] *Entomologist*, xiv. 1881, p. 287.   This observation has never, we believe, been confirmed.
[3] *Ann. Soc. ent. France* (2) v. 1847, p. 46.

be spiracles.   The food of *Scatopse* in the larval state is
principally vegetable.   The larva of *Scatopse* changes to a
pupa inside the larval
skin; the pupa is pro-
vided on the thorax with
two branched respiratory
processes that project
outside the larval skin.[1]
Lucas has given an in-
teresting account of the
occurrence of the larva
of *Bibio marci* in enormous numbers at Paris;
they lived together in
masses, there being ap-
parently some sort of
connection between the
individuals.[2]   In the following year the fly was almost equally
abundant.

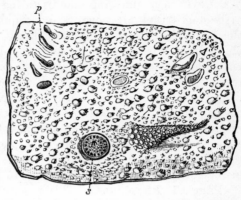

Fig. 226.—Portion of integument of *Bibio* sp.   Cambridge.   *p*, Intersegmental processes; *s*, spiracle.

Owing to the great numbers in which the species of Bibionidae
sometimes appear, these Insects have been supposed to be very
injurious.   Careful inquiry has, however, generally exculpated
them as doers of any serious injury, though *Dilophus febrilis*—a
so-called fever-fly—appears to be really injurious in this country
when it multiplies excessively, by eating the roots of the hop-
plant.

Fam. 11. Simuliidae (*Sand-flies, Buffalo-gnats*).—*Small obese
flies with humped back, rather short legs and broad wings, with short,
straight antennae destitute of setae; proboscis not projecting.*
There is only one genus, *Simulium*, of this family, but it is very
widely spread, and will probably prove to be nearly cosmopolitan.   Some of the species are notorious from their blood-sucking habits, and in certain seasons multiply to an enormous extent,
alight in thousands on cattle, and induce a disease that produces
death in a few hours; it is thought as the result of an instilled
poison.   *S. columbaczense* has occasioned great losses amongst
the herds near the Danube; in North America the Buffalo- and
Turkey-gnats attack a variety of mammals and birds.   In Britain

---

[1] Perris, in *Ann. Soc. ent. France* (2) v. 1847, p. 37, pl. i.
[2] *Ann. Soc. ent. France* (5) i. 1871, *Bull.* p. lxvii.

and other parts of the world they do not increase in numbers to an extent sufficient to render them seriously injurious : their bite is however very annoying and irritating to ourselves. In their early stages they are aquatic and require well aërated waters : the larvae hold themselves erect, fixed to a stone or some other object by the posterior extremity, and have on the head some beautiful fringes which are agitated in order to bring food within reach; the pupae are still more remarkable, each one being placed in a pouch or sort of watch-pocket, from which projects the upper part of the body provided with a pair of filamentous respiratory processes. For an account of the interesting circumstances connected with the metamorphoses of this species the reader should refer to Professor Miall's book; and for the life-history of the American Buffalo-gnat to Riley.[1]

Fam. 12. Rhyphidae.—This is another of the families that have only two or three genera, and yet are very widely distributed. These little flies are distinguished from other Nemocera Anomala (cf. p. 456) by *the presence of a discal cell ; the empodia of the feet are developed as if they were pulvilli, while the true pulvilli remain rudimentary.* The larvae are like little worms, being long and cylindric; they are amphipneustic, and have been found in decaying wood, in cow-dung, in rotten fruits, and even in dirty water. The "petite tipule," the metamorphoses of which were described and figured by Réaumur, is believed to be the common *Rhyphus fenestralis.*[2] *R. fenestralis* is often found on windows, as its name implies.

Series 2. Orthorrhapha Brachycera

Fam. 13. Stratiomyidae.—*Antennae with three segments and a terminal complex of obscure joints, frequently bearing an arista : tibiae not spined ; wings rather small, the anterior nervures usually much more strongly marked than those behind. The median cell small, placed near to the middle of the wing. Scutellum frequently spined ; terminal appendages of the tarsi small, but pulvilli and a pulvilliform empodium are*

---

[1] *Rep. Dep. Agric. Ent. Washington,* 1886, p. 492.
[2] Cf. Réaumur, *Mem.* v. 1740, p. 21 ; and Perris, *Ann. Soc. ent. France* (4) x. 1870, p. 190.

present.   This is a large family, whose members are very diversified, consequently definition of the whole is difficult.   The species of the typical sub-family Stratiomyinae generally have the margins of the body prettily marked with green or yellow, and the scutellum spined.   In the remarkable American genus, *Hermetia*, the abdomen is much constricted at the base, and the scutellum is not spined; in the division Sarginae the body is frequently of brilliant metallic colours.   The species all have an only imperfect proboscis, and are not blood-suckers.   The larvae are also of diverse habits; many of those of the Stratiomyinae are aquatic, and are noted for their capacity of living in salt, alkaline, or even very hot water.   Mr. J. C. Hamon found some of these larvae in a hot spring in Wyoming, where he could not keep his hand immersed, and he estimated the temperature at only 20° or 30° Fahr. below the boiling-point.   The larva of *Stratiomys* is of remarkably elongate, strap-like, form, much narrowed behind, with very small head; the terminal segment is very long and ends in a rosette of hairs which the creature allows to float at the surface.   After the larval skin is shed the pupa, though free, is contained therein; the skin alters but little in form, and has no organic connection with the pupa, which merely uses the skin as a shield or float.   These larvae have been very frequently described; they can live out of the water.   Brauer describes the larvae of the family as "peripneustic, some perhaps amphipneustic."   Miall says there are, in *Stratiomys*, nine pairs of spiracles on the sides of the body which are not open, though branches from the longitudinal air-tubes pass to them.   There are probably upwards of 1000 species of Stratiomyiidae known, and in Britain we have 40 or 50 kinds. The American genus *Chiromyza*, Wied., was formerly treated by Osten Sacken as a separate family, Chiromyzidae, but Williston places it in Stratiomyidae.

   Fam. 14. Leptidae, including **Xylophagidae** and **Coenomyi-idae.**—*The Leptidae proper are flies of feeble build; antennae with three joints and a terminal bristle; in the Xylophagidae the antennae are longer, and the third joint is complex.   The wings have five posterior cells, the middle tibiae are spined.   Pulvilli and a pulvilliform empodium present.*   The three families are considered distinct by most authors, but there has always been much difficulty about the Xylophagidae and Coenomyiidae, we therefore treat them

as sub-families.   The Xylophaginae are a small group of slender
Insects, perhaps most like the short-bodied kinds of Asilidae;
the third joint of the antenna is vaguely segmented, and there
is no terminal bristle.   *Rhachicerus* is a most anomalous
little fly with rather long stiff antennae of an almost nemocerous character, the segments of which give off a short
thick prolongation on each side, reminding one of a two-edged
saw.   The three or four British species of Xylophaginae
are forest Insects, the larvae of which live under bark, and
are provided with a spear-like head with which they pierce
other Insects.   The Coenomyiinae consist of the one genus
Coenomyia, with two or three European and North American
species.   They are remarkably thick-bodied, heavy flies, reminding
one somewhat of an imperfect Stratiomyid destitute of orna-
mentation.   The metamorphosis of *C. ferruginea* has been
described by Beling.[1]   The larva is not aquatic, but lives in
burrows or excavations in the earth where there are, or have
recently been, rotten logs; it is probably predaceous.   It is
cylindric, with an extremely small head and eleven other segments,
the stigma on the first thoracic segment distinct; the terminal
segment is rather broad, and the structures surrounding the
stigma are complex.   The pupa
has stigmata on each of abdominal segments 2 to 8.   Notwithstanding that the fly is so
different to *Xylophagus*, the
larvae indicate the two forms
as perhaps really allied.   One
of the Leptinae, *Atherix ibis*,
has a singular mode of oviposition (Fig. 227), the females
of the species deposit their eggs
in common, and, dying as they
do so, add their bodies to the
common mass, which becomes
an agglomeration, it may be
of thousands of individuals, and
of considerable size.   The mass is attached to a branch of a
bush or to a plant overhanging water, into which it ulti-

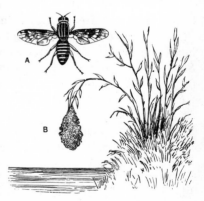

FIG. 227.—*Atherix ibis*.   **A,** The fly, nat.
size; **B,** mass of dead flies overhanging
water, much reduced.

[1] *Verh. Ges. Wien*, xxx. 1880, p. 343.

mately falls.   These curious accumulations are occasionally
found in England as well as on the Continent, but no reason
for so peculiar a habit is at present forthcoming.   Still more
remarkable are the habits of some European Leptids of the
genera *Vermileo* (*Psammorycter* of some authors) and *Lamp-
romyia*, slender rather small flies of Asilid-like appearance, the
larvae of which form pit-falls after the manner of the Ant-lion.
According to Beling[1] the larva of *Leptis* is very active, and is
distinguished by having the stigmatic orifice surrounded by four
quite equal, quadrangularly placed prominences ; and at the other

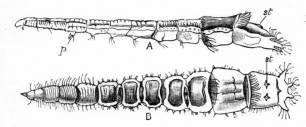

FIG. 228.—Larva of
Vermileo   degeeri
(*Psammorycter ver-
mileo*). **A**, lateral,
B, dorsal view :
p, an abdominal
pseudopod ; *st*,
stigma.   Europe.
(After   Réaumur
and Brauer.)

extremity of the body a blackish, naked, triangular plate ; on the
under side of each of seven of the abdominal segments there is a
band of spines.   The larva of *Atherix* has seven pairs of abdominal
feet.   Altogether there are some two or three hundred known
species of Leptidae ; our British species scarcely reach a score.
They are destitute of biting-powers and are harmless timid
creatures.   *Leptis scolopacea*, the most conspicuous of our native
species, a soft-bodied fly of rather large size, the wings much
marked with dark colour, and the thick, pointed body yellowish,
marked with a row of large black spots down the middle, is a
common Insect in meadows.

Fam. 15. Tabanidae (*Breeze - flies*, *Cleggs*, or *Horse - flies*,
also frequently called *Gad-flies*).—*Proboscis fleshy, distinct, enwrapping pointed horny processes, palpi distinct, terminal joint
inflated, pendent in front of proboscis.   Antennae projecting, four-
jointed, second joint very short, third variable in form, fourth
forming an indistinctly segmented continuation of the third, but
not ending in a bristle.   A perfect squama in front of the halter.
Eyes large, very large in the males, but laterally extending, rather
than globose.*   This large and important family of flies, of which

[1] *Arch. Naturges.* xli. i. 1875, p. 48.

Williston states that 1400 or 1500 species are named, is
well known to travellers on account of the blood-sucking

habits of its members; they have great powers
of flight, and alight on man and animals, and
draw blood by making an incision with the
proboscis; only the females do this, the
males wanting a pair of the lancets that
enable the other sex to inflict their formidable wounds.   They are comparatively large
Insects, some of our English species of *Tabanus*
attaining an inch in length.   The smaller, grey
Haematopota, is known to every one who has
walked in woods or meadows in the summer, as
it alights quietly on the hands or neck and
bites one without his having previously been
made aware of its presence.   The larger Tabani
hum so much that one always knows when an
individual is near.   The species of *Chrysops*, in
habits similar to *Haematopota*, are remarkable
for their beautifully coloured golden-green eyes.
In Brazil the Motuca fly, *Hadrus lepidotus*,
Perty, makes so large and deep a cut that considerable bleeding may follow, and as it sometimes settles in numbers on the body, it is
deservedly feared.   The most remarkable forms

Fig. 229.—*Pangonia*   of Tabanidae are the species of the widely dis-
longirostris.   ×
1. Nepal. (After   tributed genus *Pangonia* (Fig. 229).   The pro-
Hardwicke.)   boscis in the females of some of the species is
three or four times the length of the body, and as it is stiff and
needle-like the creature can use it while hovering on the wing, and
will pierce the human body even through clothing of considerable
thickness.   The males suck the juices of flowers.   The Seroot
fly, that renders some of the districts of Nubia uninhabitable
for about three months of the year, appears, from the figure and
description given by Sir Samuel Baker,. to be a *Pangonia*.
Tabanidae are a favourite food of the fossorial wasps of the
family Bembecidae.   These wasps are apparently aware of the
blood-sucking habits of their favourites, and attend on travellers
and pick up the flies as they are about to settle down to their
phlebotomic operations.   The larvae of the Tabanidae are some

of them aquatic, but others live in the earth or in decaying wood; they are of predaceous habits, attacking and sucking Insect-larvae, or worms. Their form is cylindric, attenuate at the two extremities; the slender small head is retractile, and armed with a pair of conspicuous, curved black hooks. The body is surrounded by several prominent rings. The breathing apparatus is apparently but little developed, and consists of a small tube at the extremity of the body, capable of being exserted or withdrawn; in this two closely approximated stigmata are placed. In a larva, probably of this family, found by the writer in the shingle of a shallow stream in the New Forest, the annuli are replaced by seven circles of prominent pseudopods, on the abdominal segments about eight in each circle, and each of these feet is surmounted by a crown of small hooks, so that there are fifty or sixty feet distributed equally over the middle part of the body without reference to upper or lower surface. The figures of the larva of *T. cordiger*, by Brauer, and of *Haematopota pluvialis*, by Perris, are something like this, but have no setae on the pseudopods. The meta

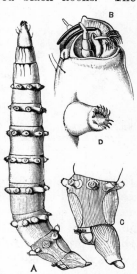

Fig. 230.—Larva of a Tabanid. [? *Atylotus fulvus*.] **A**, the larva, × 3; **B**, head; **C**, end of body; **D**, one of the pseudopods. New Forest.

morphoses of several Tabanidae are described and figured by Hart;[1] the pupa is remarkably like a Lepidopterous pupa. We have five genera and about a score of species of Tabanidae in Britain.

Fam. 16. Acanthomeridae.—A very small family of two genera (*Acanthomera* and *Rhaphiorhynchus*) confined to America, and including the largest Diptera, some being two inches long. The antenna is terminated by a compound of seven segments and a style; the proboscis is short, and the squama rudimentary. The general form reminds one of Tabanidae or Oestridae. A dried larva exists in the Vienna collection; it is amphipneustic, and very remarkable on account of the great size of the anterior stigma.

---

[1] *Bull. Illinois Lab.* iv. 1895.

Fam. 17. Therevidae.—*Moderate-sized flies, with somewhat the appearance of short Asilidae.* *They have, however, only a feeble fleshy proboscis, and minute claws, with pulvilli but no empodium ; the antennae project, are short, three-jointed, pointed.*—The flies of this family are believed to be predaceous like the Robber-flies, but they appear to be very feebly organised for such a life. We have about ten species in Britain, and there are only some 200 known from all the world. But little is known as to the metamorphoses. Meigen found larvae of *T. nobilitata* in rotten stumps, but other larvae have been recorded as devouring dead pupae or larvae of Lepidoptera. The larvae are said to be elongate, very slender, worm-like, and to have nineteen body-segments, the posterior pair of spiracles being placed on what looks like the seventeenth segment, but is really the eighth of the abdomen. The pupa is not enclosed in the larval skin ; that of *Psilocephala* is armed with setae and spinous processes, and was found in rotten wood by Frauenfeld.

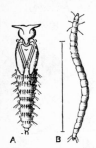

FIG. 231.—*Thereva (Psilo-cephala) confinis.* **A,** Pupa ; **B,** larva. Europe. (After Perris.)

Fam. 18. Scenopinidae.—*Rather small flies, without bristles. Antennae three-jointed, the third joint rather long, without appendage. Proboscis not projecting. Empodium absent.* These unattractive flies form one of the smallest families, and are chiefly found on windows. *S. fenestralis* looks like a tiny Stratiomyid, with a peculiar, dull, metallic surface. The larva of this species has been recorded as feeding on a variety of strange substances, but Osten Sacken is of opinion [1] that it is really predaceous, and frequents these substances in order to find the larvae that are developing in them. If so, *Scenopinus* is useful in a small way by destroying " moth," etc. The larva is a little slender, cylindrical, hard, pale worm of nineteen segments, with a small brown head placed like a hook at one extremity of the body and with two short, divergent processes at the other extremity, almost exactly like the larva of *Thereva.* Full references to the literature about this Insect are given by Osten Sacken.

Fam. 19. Nemestrinidae.—These Insects appear to be allied to the Bombyliidae. *They are of medium size, often pilose, and*

[1] *Ent. Mag.* xxiii. 1886, p. 51.

sometimes with excessively long proboscis; antennae short, with a simple third joint, and a jointed, slender, terminal appendage; the tibiae have no spurs, the empodium is pulvillus-like. The wing-nervuration is perhaps the most complex found in Diptera, there being numerous cells at the tip, almost after the fashion of Neuroptera. With this family we commence the aerial forms composing the Tromoptera of Osten Sacken. Nemestrinidae is a small family of about 100 species, but widely distributed. *Megistorhynchus longirostris* is about two-thirds of an inch long, but has a proboscis at least four times as long as itself. In South Africa it may be seen endeavouring to extract, with this proboscis, the honey from the flower of a *Gladiolus* that has a perianth just as long as its own rostrum ; as it attempts to do this when it is hovering on the wing, and as the proboscis is, unlike that of the Bombylii, fixed, the Insect can only succeed by controlling its movements with perfect accuracy ; hence it has great difficulty in attaining its purpose, especially when there is much wind, when it frequently strikes the earth instead of the flower. M. Westermann thinks [1] the life of the Insect and the appearance and duration of the flower of the *Gladiolus* are very closely connected. The life-history of *Hirmoneura obscura* has recently been studied in Austria by Handlirsch and Brauer.[2] The larva is parasitic on the larva of a Lamellicorn beetle (*Rhizotrogus solstitialis*); it is metapneustic, and the head is highly modified for predaceous purposes. The young larva apparently differs to a considerable extent from the matured form. The most curious fact is that the parent fly does not oviposit near the Lamellicorn-larva, but places her eggs in the burrows of some wood-boring Insect in logs ; the larvae when hatched come to the surface of the log, hold themselves up on their hinder extremity and are carried away by the wind ; in what manner they come into contact with the Lamellicorn larva, which feeds in turf, is unknown. The pupa is remarkable on account of the prominent, almost stalked stigmata, and of two pointed divergent processes at the extremity of the body. This life-history is of much interest, as it foreshadows to some extent the complex parasitic life-histories of Bombyliidae. The Nemestrinidae are not represented in the British fauna.

Fam. 20. Bombyliidae.—*Body frequently fringed with down,*

[1] *Ann. Soc. ent. France*, ii. 1833, p. 492.
[2] *Wien. ent. Zeit.* ii. 1883, pp. 11 and 24, pl. i.

*or covered in large part with hair.   Legs slender, claws small,
without distinct empodium, usually with only minute pulvilli.
Proboscis very long or moderate, antennae three-jointed, terminal
joint not distinctly divided, sometimes large, sometimes hair-like.*
This is a very large family, including 1500 species, and is of
great importance to both naturalist and economist.   Two well-
marked types, formerly treated as distinct families, are included in
it—(1) the Bombyliides with very long exserted rostrum, and
humped thorax ; and (2) Anthracides, with a short beak, and of
more slender and graceful form.   None of these flies are blood-
suckers, they frequent flowers only, and use their long rostrums in
a harmless manner.   The members of both of these groups usually
have the wings ornamented with a pattern, which in *Anthrax*
is frequently very remarkable ; in both, the clothing of the body
is frequently variegated.   Their powers of flight are very great,
and the hovering *Bombylius* of early spring is endowed with an
unsurpassed capacity for movement, remaining perfectly still on
the wing, and darting off with lightning rapidity ; *Anthrax* is
also most rapid on the wing.   In Britain we have but few
species of Bombyliidae, but in warm and dry climates they are
very numerous.   The life-history of these Insects was till recently

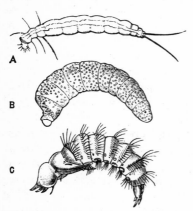

unknown, but that of *Argyromoeba* (*Anthrax*) *trifasciata* has
been described by the French
naturalist, Fabre, who ascertained
that the species is parasitic on the
Mason-bee, *Chalicodoma muraria*,
that forms nests of solid masonry.   He endeavoured to discover the egg, but failed ; the
parent-fly oviposits, it appears,
by merely dropping a minute
egg while flying over the surface
of the mass of masonry by which
the grubs of the *Chalicodoma* are
protected.   From this egg there
is hatched a minute delicate vermiform larva (Fig. 232, A).   In

FIG. 232.—*Argyromoeba trifasciata.* **A,**
Young larva ; **B,** adult larva ; **C,**
pupa.   France.   (After. Fabre.)
A, Greatly, **B, C,** slightly magnified.

order to obtain its food, it is necessary for this feeble creature to
penetrate the masonry ; apparently a hopeless task, the animal

being scarcely a twentieth of an inch long and very slender ; it is, however, provided with a deflexed horny head, armed in front with some stiff bristles, while on the under surface of the body there are four pairs of elongate setae serving as organs of loco-motion ; thus endowed, the frail creature hunts about the sur-face of the masonry, seeking to find an entrance ; frequently it is a long time before it is successful ; but though it has never taken any food it is possessed of great powers of endurance. Usually, after being disclosed from the egg, it remains about fifteen days without stirring ; and even after it commences its attempts to enter the nest it is still capable of a long life without taking any food. Possibly its organisation will not permit it to feed (supposing any food were obtainable by it) without its growing somewhat thereafter, and if so, its chance of obtaining entrance through the masonry would be diminished. Abstention, it would appear, is the best policy, whether inevitable or not ; so the starving little larva continues its endeavours to find a chink of entrance to the food contained in the interior of the masonry. It has plenty of time for this, because it is better for it not to get into the cell of the bee until the grub is quite full grown, and is about to assume the pupal form, when it is quite incapable of self-defence. Finally, after greater or less delay, the persevering little larva succeeds in finding some tiny gap in the masonry through which it can force itself. M. Fabre says that the root of a plant is not more persistent in descending into the soil that is to support it than is this little *Anthrax* in insinuating itself through some crack that may admit it to its food. Having once effected an entrance the organisation that has enabled it to do so is useless ; this primary form of the larva has, in fact, as its sole object to enable the creature to penetrate to its food. Having penetrated, it undergoes a complete change of form, and appears as a creature specially fitted for feeding on the quiescent larva of the bee without destroying it. To accomplish this requires an extreme delicacy of organisation and instinct ; to bite the prey would be to kill it, and if this were done, the *Anthrax* would, Fabre supposes, ensure its own death, for it cannot feed on the dead and putrefying grub ; accordingly, the part of its body that does duty as a mouth is merely a delicate sucker which it applies to the skin of the *Chalicodoma*-grub ; and thus without inflicting any perceptible wound it sucks day after day, changing its position frequently, until it has completely emptied the pupa of its contents, nothing being left but the skin. Although this is accomplished without any wound being inflicted, so effectual is the process that all the *Chalicodoma* is gradually absorbed. The time requisite for completely emptying the victim is from twelve to fifteen days; at the end of this time the *Anthrax*-larva is full grown, and the question arises, how is it to escape from the cell of solid masonry in which it is imprisoned ? It entered this cell as a tiny, slender worm through a minute orifice or crack, but it has now much increased in size, and exit for a creature of its organisation is not possible. For some months it remains a quiescent larva in the cell of the *Chalicodoma*, but in the spring of the succeeding year it undergoes another metamorphosis, and appears as a pupa provided with a formidable apparatus for breaking down the masonry by which it is imprisoned. The head is large and covered in front with six hard spines, to be used in striking and piercing the masonry, while the other extremity of the body bears some curious horns, the middle segments being armed with rigid hairs directed backwards, and thus facilitating movement in a forward direction and preventing slipping backwards. The pupa is strongly curved, and fixes itself by the aid of the posterior spines; then, unbending itself, it strikes with the armour of the other extremity against the opposing wall, which is thus destroyed piecemeal until a gallery of exit is formed; when this is completed the pupa-skin bursts and the perfect fly emerges, leaving the pupa-case still fixed in the gallery. Thus this species appears in four consecutive forms—in addition to the egg—each of which is highly specialised for the purposes of existence in that stage.

The habits of our British *Bombylius major* have been partially observed by Dr. Chapman,[1] and exhibit a close analogy with those of *Anthrax trifasciata*. The bee-larva that served as food was in this case *Andrena labialis*, and the egg was deposited by the fly, when hovering, by jerking it against the bank in which the nest of the bee was placed.

It has recently been discovered that the larvae of various species of Bombyliidae are of great service by devouring the eggs of locusts. Riley found that the egg-cases of *Caloptenus*

[1] *Ent. Mag.* xiv. 1878, p. 196.

spretus are emptied of their contents by the larvae of *Systoechus oreas* and *Triodites mus.* A similar observation has been made in the Troad by Mr. Calvert, who found that the Bombyliid, *Callostoma fascipennis,* destroys large quantities of the eggs of *Caloptenus italicus.* Still more recently M. Künckel d'Herculais has discovered that the destructive locust *Stauronotus maroccanus* is kept in check in Algeria in a similar manner, as many as 80 per cent of the eggs of the locust being thus destroyed in certain localities. He observes that the larva of the fly, after being full fed in the autumn, passes the winter in a state of lethargy—— he calls it "hypnody"——in the egg-case of the locust, and he further informs us that in the case of *Anthrax fenestralis,* which devours the eggs of the large

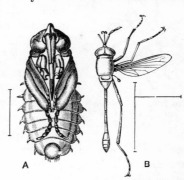

Fig. 233.—*Systropus crudelis.* South Africa. **A,** Pupa; **B,** imago, appendages of the left side removed. (After Westwood.)

Ocnerodes, the lethargy may be prolonged for a period of three years. After the pupa is formed it works a way out of the case by means of its armature, and then again becomes for some days immobile before the perfect fly appears. Lepidopterous larvae are also attacked by Bombyliid flies. A species of *Systropus* has been recorded as destroying the larva of *Limacodes.* Several of the Bombyliids of the genus just mentioned are remarkable for the great resemblance they display to various Hymenoptera, some of them being very slender flies, like the thin bodied fossorial Hymenoptera. The difference between the pupa and imago in this case is very remarkable (Fig. 233).

Fam. 21. Acroceridae or **Cyrtidae.**—*Flies of the average size, of peculiar form, the small head consisting almost entirely of the eyes, and bent down under the humped thorax: wings small, halteres entirely concealed by the very large horizontal squamae; antennae very diverse.* The peculiar shape of these flies is an exaggeration of that we have already noticed in *Bombylius.* The mouth in Acroceridae is very variable; there may be a very long, slender proboscis (*Acrocera*), or the mouth-parts may be so atrophied that it is doubtful whether even an orifice exists (*Ogcodes*). There are but few species known, and all of them are rare;[1] in Britain we have but two (*Ogcodes gibbosus, Acrocera globulus*).   The genus *Pterodontia,* found in North America and Australia, an inflated

bladder-like form with a minute head, is amongst the most extraordinary of all the forms of Diptera.   The habits are very peculiar, the larvae, so far as known, all living as parasites within the bodies of spiders or in their egg-bags.   It appears, however, that the flies do not oviposit in appropriate places, but place their eggs on stems of plants, and the young larvae have to find their way to the spiders.   Brauer has described the larva of the European *Asto-mella lindeni*,[2] which lives in the body of a spider, *Cteniza ariana ;* it is amphipneustic and maggot-like, the head being extremely small.   The larva leaves the body of the spider for pupation ; the pupa is much arched, and the head is destitute of the peculiar armature of the Bombyliidae, but has a serrate ridge on the thorax.   Emerton found the larvae of an *Acrocera* in the webs of a common North American spider, *Amaurobius sylvestris,* they having eaten, it was supposed, the makers of the cobwebs.

FIG. 234.—*Megalybus gra-cilis.* × 4. (Acroceridae.) Chili. (After Westwood.)

Fam. 22. Lonchopteridae.—*Small, slender flies, with pointed wings, short, porrect antennae, with a simple, circular third joint, bearing a bristle ; empodium very small, pulvilli absent.*—Only one genus of these little flies is known, but it is apparently widely distributed, and its members are common Insects.   They have the appearance of Acalyptrate Muscidae, and the nervuration of the wing is somewhat similar, the nervures being simple and parallel, and the minute cross-nervures placed near the base. The systematic position is somewhat doubtful, and the meta-morphoses are but incompletely known, very little having been added to what was discovered by Sir John Lubbock in 1862.[3] The larva lives on the earth under vegetable matter; it is very transparent, amphipneustic, with a peculiar head, and with fringes on the margins.   This larva changes to a semi-pupa or apterous maggot-like form, within the larval skin; the true pupa was

[1] For figures, etc., cf. Westwood, *Tr. ent. Soc. London,* 1876, p. 507, pls. v. vi.
[2] *Verh. Ges. Wien,* xix. 1869, p. 737, pl. xiii.
[3] *Tr. ent. Soc. London* (3) i. 1862, p. 338, pl. xi.

not noticed by Lubbock, but Frauenfeld[1] has since observed it, though he only mentions that it possesses differentiated limbs and segments. The metamorphoses appear to be very peculiar. This fly requires a thorough study.

Fam. 23. Mydaidae.—*Large flies of elongate form ; the hind femora long and toothed beneath ; the antennae knobbed at the tip, projecting, rather long, the basal joint definite, but the divisions of the subsequent joints more or less indistinct. Empodium small. Wings frequently heavily pigmented ; with a complex nervuration.* These fine flies are exotic ; a few species occur in the Mediterranean region, even in the South of Europe ; the chief genus, *Mydas*, is South American, but most of the other genera are Australian or African. But little is known as to the life-histories. The larvae are thought to live in wood, and to prey on Coleopterous larvae.

Fam. 24. Asilidae (*Robber-flies*).—*Mouth forming a short, projecting horny beak, the palpi usually only small ; the feet generally largely developed ; the claws large, frequently thick and blunt, the pulvilli generally elongate, the empodium a bristle ; halteres free ; no squama.* The Asilidae is one of the largest families of flies, and probably includes about 3000 described species : as will readily be believed, there is much variety of form ; some are short and thick and extremely hairy, superficially resembling hairy bees, but the majority are more or less elongate, the abdomen being specially long, and having eight segments conspicuously displayed. The antennae are variable, but are three-jointed with a terminal appendage of diverse form and structure. They belong to the super-family Energopoda of Osten Sacken, but the association of Empidae and Dolichopidae with them does not seem to be very natural. In their perfect state these flies are most voracious, their prey being Insects, which they seize alive and impale with the rostrum. They are amongst the most formidable of foes and fear nothing, wasps or other stinging Insects being attacked and mastered by the stronger species without difficulty. They have been observed to capture even dragon-flies and tiger-beetles. As is the case with so many other Insects that prey on living Insects, the appetite in the Asilidae seems to be insatiable ; a single individual has been observed to kill eight moths in twenty minutes. They have

---

[1] *Verh. Ges. Wien*, xix. 1869, p. 941.

been said to suck blood from Vertebrates, but this appears to be
erroneous. The metamorphoses of a few species have been observed. Perris has called attention to the close alliance between
the larvae of Tabanidae and of Asilidae,[1] and it seems at present
impossible to draw a line of distinction between the two. So
far as is known, the larvae of Asilidae are terrestrial and
predaceous, attacking more particularly the larvae of Coleoptera,
into which they sometimes bore; in *Laphria* there are numerous
pseudopods, somewhat of the kind shown in Fig. 230, but less
perfect and without hairs; the head and breathing organs appear
to be very different. According to Beling's descriptions of the
larvae of *Asilus*, the head in this case is more like that of the
figure, but there are no pseudopods. The flies of Asilidae and
Tabanidae are so very distinct that these resemblances between
their larvae are worthy of note.

  Fam. 25. Apioceridae.—*Moderate-sized flies marked with black
and white, with an appearance like that of some Muscidae and
Asilidae; with clear wings, the veins not deeply coloured; antennae
short, with a short, simple appendage; no empodium.* But little
is known as to the flies of this family, of which only two genera,
consisting of about a dozen species, are found in North America,
Chili, and Australia. Osten Sacken is inclined to treat them
as an aberrant division of Asilidae. Brauer looks on them as
primitive or synthetic forms of much interest, and has briefly
described a larva which he considers may be that of *Apiocera*,
but this is doubtful; it is a twenty-segmented form, and may be
that of a *Thereva*.[2]

  Fam. 26. Empidae.—*Small or moderate-sized flies of obscure
colours, grey, rusty, or black, with small head, somewhat globular
in form, with three-jointed antennae, the terminal joint long and
pointed; usually there is a long slender beak; the legs are elongate,
frequently hairy; the tarsi bear long pulvilli and a small empodium.* The Empidae are an extensive family of flies, with
predaceous habits, the rostrum being used by the female as
an instrument for impaling and sucking other flies. They are
occasionally very numerous in individuals, especially in wooded
districts. There is great variety; there are nearly 200 species
in Britain. The forms placed in the sub-family Hybotinae are
curious slender little Insects, with very convex thorax and

---

[1] *Ann. Soc. ent. France* (4) x. 1870, p. 221. [2] *SB. Ak. Wien*, xci. 1885, p. 392.

large hind legs.   In *Hemerodromia* the front legs are raptorial, the femora being armed with spines on which the tibiae close so as to form a sort of trap.   Many Empidae execute aërial dances, and some of the species of the genus *Hilara* are notorious for carrying veils or nets in the form of silken webs more or less densely woven.   This subject is comparatively new, the fact having been discovered by Baron Osten Sacken in 1877,[1] and it is not at all clear what purpose these peculiar constructions serve ; it appears probable that they are carried by means of the hind legs, and only by the males.   Mik thinks that in *H. sartor* the veil acts as a sort of parachute, and is of use in carrying on the aërial performance, or enhancing its effect ; while in the case of other species, *H. maura* and *H. inter-stincta*, the object appears to be the capture or retention of prey, after the manner of spiders.   The source of the silk is not known, and in fact all the details are insufficiently ascertained. The larvae of Empidae are described as cylindrical maggots, with very small head, and imperfect ventral feet ; the stigmata are amphipneustic, the thoracic pair being, however, excessively small ; beneath the posterior pair there is nearly always a tooth- or spine-like prominence present.

Fam. 27. Dolichopidae.—*Graceful flies of metallic colours, of moderate or small size, and long legs ; usually with bristles on the thorax and legs, the halteres exposed, squamae being quite absent ; antennae of two short stout joints (of which the second is really two, its division being more or less distinct), with a thread-like or hair-like appendage.   Proboscis short, fleshy.   Claws, pulvilli, and empodium small ; wings with a simple system of nervures, those on the posterior part of the wing are but few, there is no anterior basal cross-vein be-tween the discal and second basal cells, which therefore form but one cell.*   This is also a very extensive family of flies, of which we have probably about 200 species in Britain. They are conspicuous on account of their golden, or golden-green colours, only a few being yellow or black.

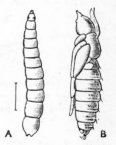

FIG. 235.—**A,** Larva, **B,** pupa of *Mede-terus ambiguus.* France. (After Perris.)

---

[1] *Ent. Mag.* xiv. 1877, p. 226 ; for a discussion of the subject see Mik, *Wien. ent. Zeit.* xiii. 1894, p. 273.

The males are remarkable for the curious special characters they possess on the feet, antennae, face, or wings. These characters are not alike in any two species; they are believed to be of the nature of ornaments, and according to Professor Aldrich and others are used as such in courtship.[1] This family of flies approaches very closely to some of the Acalyptrate Muscidae in its characters. It is united by Brauer with Empidae to form the tribe Orthogenya. Although the species are so numerous and abundant in Europe, little is known as to their metamorphoses. Some of the larvae frequent trees, living under the bark or in the overflowing sap, and are believed to be carnivorous; they are amphipneustic; a cocoon is formed, and the pupa is remarkable on account of the existence of two long horns, bearing the spiracles, on the back of the thorax; the seven pairs of abdominal spiracles being excessively minute.[2]

Series 3. Cyclorrhapha Aschiza

Fam. 28. Phoridae.—*Small flies, with very convex thorax, small head, very small two-jointed antennae, bearing a long seta; femora more or less broad; wings with two dark, thick, approximate veins, meeting on the front margin near its middle, and besides these, three or four very fine veins, that run to the margins in a sub-parallel manner without forming any cells or forks.* This obscure family of flies is of small extent, but its members are ex-

Fig. 236.—Wing of *Trineura aterrima*, one of the Phoridae. Britain.

tremely common in Europe and North America, where they often occur in numbers running on the windows of houses. It is one of the most isolated groups of Diptera, and great difference of opinion prevails as to its classification. The wing-nervuration is peculiar (but varies somewhat in the species), the total absence of any cross-veins even on the basal part of the wing being remarkable. There are bristles on the head and thorax, but they are not arranged in a regular manner. The larvae live in a great variety of animal and vegetable decaying matter,

---

[1] *Amer. Natural.* xxviii. 1894, p. 35.

[2] Perris, *Ann. Soc. ent. France* (4) x. 1870, p. 321, pl. 4; and Laboulbène, *op. cit.* (5) iii. 1873, p. 50, pl. v.

and attack living Insects, and even snails, though probably only when these are in a sickly or diseased condition. The metamorphoses of several species have been described.[1] The larvae are rather slender, but sub-conical in form, with eleven segments and a very small head, amphipneustic, the body behind terminated by some pointed processes. The pupa is remarkable; it is contained in a case formed by the contracted and hardened skin of the larva; though it differs much in form from the larva the segmentation is distinct, and from the fourth segment there project two slender processes. These are breathing organs, attached to the prothorax of the imprisoned pupa; in what manner they effect a passage through the hardened larval skin is by no means clear. Perris supposes that holes for them pre-exist in the larval skin, and that the newly-formed pupa by restless movements succeeds in bringing the processes into such a position that they can pass through the holes. The dehiscence of the puparium seems to occur in a somewhat irregular manner, as in *Microdon;* it is never Cyclorrhaphous, and according to Perris is occasionally Orthorrhaphous; probably there is no ptilinum.

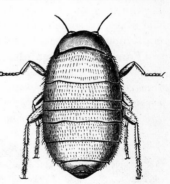

FIG. 237.—*Aenigmatias blattoides.* × 27. Denmark. (After Meinert.)

The Insect recently described by Meinert as *Aenigmatias blattoides*,[2] is so anomalous, and so little is known about it, that it cannot at present be classified. It is completely apterous; the arrangement of the body-segments is unlike that of Diptera, but the antennae and mouth-parts are said to be like those of Phoridae. The Insect was found near Copenhagen under a stone in the runs of *Formica fusca.* Meinert thinks it possible that the discovery of the male may prove *Aenigmatias* to be really allied to Phoridae, and Mik suggests that it may be the same as *Platyphora lubbocki,* Verrall, known to be parasitic on ants. Dahl recently described a wingless Dipteron, found living as a parasite on land-snails in the Bismarck archipelago, under the name of *Puliciphora lucifera,*

---

[1] Perris, *Ann. Soc. ent. France* (4) x. 1870, p. 354.
[2] *Ent. Meddelelser,* ii. 1890, p. 213.

and Wandolleck has recently made for this and some allies the new family Stethopathidae. It seems doubtful whether these forms are more than wingless Phoridae.

Fam. 29. Platypezidae.—*Small flies, with porrect three-jointed antennae, first two joints short, third longer, with a terminal seta; no bristles on the back; hind legs of male, or of both sexes, with peculiar, broad, flat tarsi; the middle tibiae bear spurs; there is no empodium.* Platypezidae is a small family of flies, the classification of which has always been a matter of considerable difficulty, and is still uncertain. The larvae are broad and flat, fringed at the margin with twenty-six spines; they live between the lamellae of Agaric fungi. At pupation the form alters but little; the imago emerges by a horizontal cleft occurring at the margins of segments two and four.[1] We have four genera (*Opetia, Platycnema, Platypeza, Callomyia*), and nearly a score of species of Platypezidae in our British list, but very little seems to be known about them. There is much difference in the eyes of the sexes, in some at any rate of the species, they being large and contiguous in the male, but widely separated in the female.

Fam. 30. Pipunculidae.[2]—*Small flies, with very short antennae bearing a long seta that is not terminal; head almost globular, formed, except at the back, almost entirely by the large conjoined eyes; the head is only slightly smaller in the female, but in the male the eyes are more approximate at the top.* This is

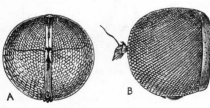

another of the small families of flies, that seems distinct from any other, though possessing no very important characters. In many of the flies that have very large eyes, the head is either flattened (*i.e.* compressed from before backwards, as in Tabanidae,

FIG. 238.—Head of *Pipunculus* sp. **A,** Seen from in front; **B,** side view, showing an antenna magnified. Pyrenees.

Asilidae), or forced beneath the humped thorax (as in Acroceridae), but neither of these conditions exists in *Pipunculus;* in them the head extends far forwards, so that the area of the

---

[1] Frauenfeld, *Verh. Ges. Wien*, xx. p. 37, pl. iii.
[2] For monograph of Pipunculidae, see Becker, *Berlin. ent. Zeitschr.* xlii. 1897, pp. 25-100.

eye compared with the size of the body is perhaps greater than
in any other Diptera.   The general form is somewhat that of
Anthrax, but the venation on the hind part of the wing is much
less complex.   There is a remarkable difference between the facets
on the front and the back of these great eyes.   We have three
genera and about a dozen species of Pipunculidae in Britain but
apparently they are far from common Insects.   What is known
about the life-history is almost confined to an imperfect observation by Boheman, who found the larva of *P. fuscipes* living after
the manner of a Hymenopterous parasite in the body of a small
Homopterous Insect.[1]   The pupa seems to be of the type of that
of Syrphidae.

   Fam. 31. Conopidae.—*Elegant flies of moderate size, of varied
colours, with abdomen slender at the base, at the tip strongly
incurved and thicker; antennae inserted close together. on a
prominence, three-jointed, first joint sometimes very short.   The
upper surface of the body without bristles or with but few.   There
is a slender, elongate proboscis, which is retractile and usually
invisible.*   This rather small family of flies includes some of the
most remarkable forms of Diptera; it includes two divisions,
the Conopinae with long antennae terminated by a very minute
pointed process, and Myopinae with shorter antennae bearing a
hair that is not placed at the end of the third joint.   The
former are the more wasp-like and elegant; the Myopinae being
much more like ordinary flies, though they frequently have
curious, inflated heads, with a white face.   The mode of life of
the larva of *Conops* is peculiar, it being parasitic in the interior
of *Bombus,* or other Hymenoptera.   They have been found to
attack *Bombus, Chalicodoma, Osmia, Vespa, Pompilus,* and other
Aculeates.   Williston says that Orthoptera are also attacked.
Conops has been seen to follow Bumble-bees and alight on them,
and Williston says this act is accompanied by oviposition, the
larva that is hatched boring its way into the body of the bee.
Others have supposed that the flies enter the bees' nests and
place their eggs in the larvae or pupae; but this is uncertain, for
Conops has never been reared from a bee-larva or pupa, though
it has frequently been procured from the imago: cases indeed
having been recorded in which *Conops* has emerged from the body

   [1] *Ofv. Ak. Forh.* xi. 1854, p. 302, pl. v., since confirmed by others, see Giard,
C.R. Ac. Sci. cix. 1889, pp. 79 and 708.

of a *Bombus* several months after the latter had been killed and
placed in an entomologist's collection. The larva is broad, and
when full grown apparently occupies nearly all the space of
the interior of the abdomen of the bee; it has very peculiar
terminal stigmata. The pupa is formed in the larval skin,
which is greatly shortened and indurated for the purpose; this
instar bears, in addition to the posterior stigmata, a pair of
slightly projecting, anterior stigmata. We have several species
of Conopidae in Britain; those belonging to the division
Conopinae are all rare Insects, but the Myopinae are not so
scarce; these latter are believed to be of similar habits with
the Conopinae, though remarkably little is known about them.
This is another of the numerous families, the relations of which
are still a subject for elucidation. Brauer places the Conopidae in
his section Schizophora away from Syrphidae, but we do not comprehend on what grounds; an inspection of the head shows that
there is no frontal lunule as there is in Eumyiidae; both *Myopa* and
Conops agreeing fairly well with *Syrphus* as to this. We therefore
place the family in its old position near *Syrphus* till the relations
with Acalypterate Muscidae shall be better established.

    Fam. 32. Syrphidae (*Hover-flies*).—*Of moderate or rather
large size, frequently spotted or banded with yellow, with a thick
fleshy proboscis capable of being withdrawn into a cleft on the
under side of the head; antennae not placed in definite cavities,
three-jointed (usually very short), and leaving a seta that is not
terminal in position, and may be feathered. Squama variable, never
entirely covering the halteres; the chief (third to fifth) longitudinal
veins of the wings connected near their termination by cross-veins
and usually thus forming a sort of short margin parallel with the
hind edge of the wing; a more or less imperfect false nervure running between the third and fourth longitudinal nervures; no empodium and generally no distinct system of bristles on the back of
the body.* The Syrphidae (Fig. 212) form one of the largest and
best known of all the families of flies; they abound in our gardens
where, in sunny weather, some species may be nearly always
seen hovering over flowers, or beneath trees in places where the
rays of the sun penetrate amidst the shade. There are two or
three thousand species known, so that of course much variety
exists; some are densely covered with hair (certain *Volucella* and
others), many are of elegant form, and some bear a consider-

able resemblance to Hymenoptera of various groups. The peculiar veining of the wings permits of their easy identification, the line of two nervules, approximately parallel with the margin of the distal part of the wing (Fig. 212, D), and followed by a deep bay, being eminently characteristic, though there are some exceptions; there are a few forms in which the antennae are exceptional in having a terminal pointed process. The proboscis, besides the membranous and fleshy lips, consists of a series of pointed slender lancets, the use of which it is difficult to comprehend, as the Insects are not known to pierce either animals or vegetables, their food being chiefly pollen; honey is also doubtless taken by some species, but the lancet-like organs appear equally ill-adapted for dealing with it. The larvae are singularly diversified; first, there are the eaters of Aphidae, or green-fly; some of these may be generally found on our rose-bushes or on thistles, when they are much covered with Aphids; they are soft, maggot-like creatures with a great capacity for changing their shape and with much power of movement, especially of the anterior part of the body, which is stretched out and moved about to obtain and spear their prey : some of them are very transparent, so that the movements of the internal organs and their vivid colours can readily be seen : like so many other carnivorous Insects, their voracity appears to be insatiable. The larvae of many of the ordinary Hover-flies are of this kind. *Eristalis* and its allies are totally different, they live in water saturated with filth, or with decaying vegetable matter (the writer has found many hundreds of the larvae of *Myiatropa florea* in a pool of water standing in a hollow beech-tree). These rat-tailed maggots are of great interest, but as they have been described in almost every work on entomology, and as Professor Miall[1] has recently given an excellent account of their peculiarities, we need not now discuss them. Some of the flies of the genus *Eristalis* are very like honey-bees, and appear in old times to have been confounded with them; indeed, Osten Sacken thinks this resemblance gave rise to the " Bugonia myth," a fable of very ancient origin to the effect that Honey-bees could be procured from filth, or even putrefying carcases, by the aid of certain proceedings that savoured slightly of witchcraft, and may therefore have increased the belief of the operator in the

[1] *Natural History of Aquatic Insects*, 1895, p. 198.

possibility of a favourable result.   It was certainly not bees that were produced from the carcases, but Osten Sacken suggests that *Eristalis*-flies may have been bred therein.

In the genus *Volucella* we meet with a third kind of Syrphid larva.   These larvae are pallid, broad and fleshy, surrounded by numerous angular, somewhat spinose, outgrowths of the body; and have behind a pair of combined stigmata, in the neighbourhood of which the outgrowths are somewhat larger; these larvae live in the nests of Bees and Wasps, in which they are abundant. Some of the *Volucella*, like many other Syrphidae, bear a considerable resemblance to Bees or Wasps, and this has given rise to a modern fable about them that appears to have no more legitimate basis of fact than the ancient Bees-born-of-carcases myth. It was formerly assumed that the *Volucella*-larvae lived on the larvae of the Bees, and that the parent flies were providentially endowed with a bee-like appearance that they might obtain entrance into the Bees' nests without being detected, and then carry out their nefarious intention of laying eggs that would hatch into larvae and subsequently destroy the larvae of the Bees. Some hard-hearted critic remarked that it was easy to understand that providence should display so great a solicitude for the welfare of the *Volucella*, but that it was difficult to comprehend how it could be, at the same time, so totally indifferent to the welfare of the Bees.   More recently the tale has been revived and cited as an instance of the value of deceptive resemblance resulting from the action of natural selection, without reference to providence. There are, however, no facts to support any theory on the subject. Very little indeed is actually known as to the habits of *Volucella* in either the larval or imaginal instars; but the little that is known tends to the view that the presence of the *Volucella* in the nests is advantageous to both Fly and Bee.   Nicolas has seen *Volucella zonaria* enter the nest of a Wasp; it settled at a little distance and walked in without any fuss being made.   Erné has watched the *Volucella*-larvae in the nests, and he thinks that they eat the waste or dejections of the larvae.   The writer kept under observation *Volucella*-larvae and portions of the cells of *Bombus*, containing some larvae and pupae of the Bees and some honey, but the fly-larvae did not during some weeks touch any of the Bees or honey, and ultimately died, presumably of starvation. Subsequently, he experimented with *Volucella*-larvae and a portion of the comb of wasps containing pupae, and again found that the flies did not attack the Hymenoptera; but on breaking a pupa of the Wasp in two, the fly-larvae attacked it immediately and eagerly; so that the evidence goes to show that the *Volucella*-larvae act as scavengers in the nests of the Hymenoptera. Künckel d'Herculais has published an elaborate work on the European *Volucella*; it is remarkable for the beauty of the plates illustrating the structure, anatomy and development, but throws little direct light on the natural history of the Insects. *V. bombylans*, one of the most abundant of our British species, appears in two forms, each of which has a considerable resemblance to a *Bombus*, and it has been supposed that each of the two forms is specially connected with the Bee it resembles, but there is no evidence to support this idea; indeed, there is some little evidence to the contrary. The genus *Merodon* has larvae somewhat similar to those of *Volucella*, but they live in bulbs of *Narcissus; M. equestris* has been the cause of much loss to the growers of Dutch bulbs; this Fly is interesting on account of its great variation in colour; it has been described as a whole series of distinct species.

The most remarkable of the numerous forms of Syrphid larvae are those of the genus *Microdon* (Fig. 239), which live in ants' nests. They have no resemblance to Insect-larvae, and when first discovered were not only supposed to be little Molluscs, but were actually described as such under the generic names of *Parmula* and *Scutelligera*. There is no appearance of segmentation of the body; the upper surface is covered by a sort of network formed by curved setae, which help to retain a coating of dirt; there is no trace externally of any head, but on the under surface there is a minute fold in which such mouth-organs as may be present are probably concealed; the sides of the body project so as to form a complex fringing arrangement; the terminal stigmata are very distinct, the lateral processes connected with them (the "Knospen" of Dr. Meijere), are, however, very irregular and placed at some distance from the stigmatic scar. Pupation occurs by the induration of the external covering and the growth from it, or rather through it, of two short horns in front. Inside this skin there is formed a soft pupa, of the kind usual in Cyclorrhaphous flies; the dehiscence of the external covering is, however, of unusual nature, three little pieces being separated from the anterior part of the upper surface, while the lower face remains intact. The account of the pupation given by Elditt[1] is not complete: the two horns that project are, it would appear, not portions of the larval skin, but belong to the head of the pupa, and according to Elditt are used to effect the dehiscence of the case for the escape of the fly; there does not appear to be any head-vesicle. Nothing is known as to the details of the life of these anomalous larvae. M. Poujade has described two species found in France in the nests of the ant *Lasius niger*.[2] The larva we figure was found by Colonel Yerbury in nests of an *Atta* in Portugal, and an almost identical

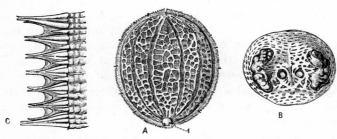

FIG. 239.—Larva of *Microdon* sp. Portugal. **A**, Dorsal view of the larva, × 4; 1, the stigmatic structure; **B**, posterior view of stigmatic structure; **C**, a portion of the marginal fringe of the body.

larva was recently found by Mr. Budgett in Paraguay. The flies themselves are scarce, *Microdon mutabilis* (formerly called *M. apiformis*) being one of the rarest of British flies. They have the antennae longer than is usual in Syrphidae, and the cross-veins at the outside of the wing are irregularly placed, so that the contour is very irregular: the resemblance to bees is very marked, and in some of the South American forms the hind legs are flattened and hairy like those of bees. The oviposition of *Microdon* has been observed by Verhoeff;[3] he noticed that the fly was frequently driven away by the ants—in this case, *Formica sanguinea*—but returned undiscouraged to its task.

A brief résumé of the diverse modes of life of Syrphid larvae has been given by Perris,[4] and he also gives some information as to the curious horns of the pupae, but this latter point much

[1] *Ent. Zeit. Stettin*, vi. 1845, p. 384, pl. i.
[2] *Ann. Soc. ent. France* (6) iii. 1883, p. 23, pl. i.
[3] *Ent. Nachr.* xviii. 1892, p. 13.   [4] *Ann. Soc. ent. France* (4) x. 1870, p. 330.

wants elucidation.   Whether the Syrphidae, or some of them,
possess a ptilinum that helps them to emerge from the pupa is
more than doubtful, though its existence has been affirmed by
several authors of good repute.[1]

Series 4. Cyclorrhapha Schizophora

Fam. 33. Muscidae acalyptratae.—This group of flies has
been the least studied of all the Diptera ; it is generally treated
as composed of twenty or thirty different families distinguished

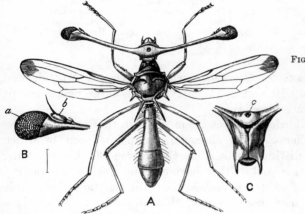

Fig. 240. —*Diopsis
apicalis*.   Natal.
A, The fly ; **B**, extremity of cephalic
protuberance, more
m a g n i f i e d.   *a*,
The eye ; *b*,   the
antenna; **C**, middle
of head, front
view ; *c*, ocelli.

by very slight characters.   It is, however, generally admitted by
systematists that these assemblages have not the value of the
families of the other divisions of Diptera, and some even go so
far as to say that they are altogether only equivalent to a single
family.   We do not therefore think it necessary to define each
one *seriatim ;* we shall merely mention their names, and allude
to certain points of interest connected with them.   Taken collec-
tively they may be defined as very *small flies, with three-jointed
antennae (frequently looking as if only two-jointed), bearing a
bristle that is not terminally placed ; frequently either destitute of
squamae or having these imperfectly developed so as not to cover the
halteres ; and possessing a comparatively simple system of nervuration, the chief nervures being nearly straight, so that consequently
few cells are formed.*   These characters will distinguish the group

[1] See on this difficult subject, Becher, *Wien. ent. Zeit.* i. 1882, p. 49.

from all the other Diptera except from forms of Aschiza, and from certain Anthomyiidae, with both of which the Acalyptratae are really intimately connected. Considerable difference of opinion prevails as to the number of these divisions, but the families usually recognised are :—

1. Doryceridae.
2. Tetanoceridae.
3. Sciomyzidae.
4. Diopsidae.
5. Celyphidae.
6. { Sepsidae
     { incl. Piophilidae.
7. { Chloropidae
     { (= Oscinidae).
8. Ulidiidae.
9. Platystomidae.
10. Ephydridae.
11. Helomyzidae.

12. Dryomyzidae.
13. Borboridae.
14. Phycodromidae.
15. Thyreophoridae.
16. { Scatophagidae.
     { (= Scatomyzidae).
17. { Geomyzidae
     { incl. Opomyzidae.
18. { Drosophilidae ;
     { incl. Asteidae.
19. Psilidae.
20. { Tanypezidae
     { (= Micropezidae).

21. Trypetidae.
22. { Sapromyzidae
     { incl. Lonchaeidae.
23. Rhopalomeridae.
24. Ortalidae.
25. { Agromyzidae
     { incl.   Phytomyzi-
     {   dae.
26. Milichiidae.
27. Octhiphilidae.
28. Heteroneuridae.
29. Cordyluridae.

Brauer associates Conopidae with Acalyptrate Muscids, and calls the Group Holometopa; applying the term Schizometopa to the Calyptrate Muscidae.

No generalisation can yet be made as to the larvae of these divisions, neither can any characters be pointed out by which they can be distinguished from the larvae of the following families. In their habits they have nothing specially distinctive, and may be said to resemble the Anthomyiidae, vegetable matter being more used as food than animal ; many of them mine in the leaves or stems of plants ; in the genus *Dorycera* the larva is aquatic, mining in the leaves of water-plants, and in Ephydridae several kinds of aquatic larvae are found, some of which are said to resemble the rat-tailed larvae of Syrphidae ; certain of these larvae occur in prodigious quantities in lakes, and the Insects in some of their early stages serve the Mexicans as food, the eggs being called Ahuatle, the larvae Pusci, the pupae Koo-chah-bee. Some of the larvae of the Sciomyzidae are also aquatic : that of *Tetanocera ferruginea* is said by Dufour to consist only of eight segments, and to be metapneustic ; Brauer considers the Acalyptrate larvae to be, however, in general, amphipneustic, like those of Calyptratae. The Chloropidae are a very important family owing to their occasional excessive multiplication, and to their living on cereals and other grasses, various parts of which they attack, sometimes causing great losses to the agriculturist. The species of the genus *Chlorops* are

famous for the curious habit of entering human habitations in
great swarms : frequently many millions being found in a single
apartment.   Instances of this habit have been recorded both in
France and England, Cambridge being perhaps the place where the
phenomenon is most persistently exhibited.   In the year 1831 an
enormous swarm of *C. lineata* was found in the Provost's Lodge
at King's College and was recorded by Leonard Jenyns ; in
1870 another swarm occurred in the same house if not in the
same room.[1]   Of late years such swarms have occurred in certain
apartments in the Museums (which are not far from King's
College), and always in the same apartments.   No clue whatever
can be obtained as to their origin ; and the manner in which
these flies are guided to a small area in
numbers that must be seen to be believed, is most mysterious.   These swarms
always occur in the autumn, and it has
been suggested that the individuals are
seeking winter quarters.

Several members of the Acalyptratae
have small wings or are wingless, as in
some of our species of *Borborus*.   The
Diopsidae—none of which are European
—have the sides of the head produced
into long horns, at the extremity of which
are placed the eyes and antennae ; these
curiosities (Fig. 240) are apparently common in both Hindostan and Africa.   In
the horned flies of the genus *Elaphomyia*,
parts of the head are prolonged into
horns of very diverse forms according to
the species, but bearing on the whole a
great resemblance to miniature stag-
horns.   A genus (*Giraffomyia*) with a long
neck, and with partially segmented appendages, instead of horns on the head, has
been recently discovered by Dr. Arthur

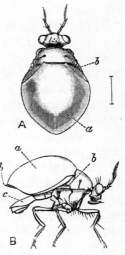

Fig. 241.—*Celyphus* (*Para-
celyphus*) sp. West Africa.
A, The fly seen from
above ; *a*, scutellum ; *b*,
base of wing : **B,** profile,
with tip of abdomen bent
downwards; *a*, scutellum ;
b, b, wing ; *c*, part of
abdomen.

Willey in New Britain. Equally remarkable are the species of
Celyphus ; they do not look like flies at all, owing to the scutellum
being inflated and enlarged so as to cover all the posterior parts

---

[1] *Loudon's Magazine,* v. 1832, p. 302 ; *P. ent. Soc. London,* 1871, p. x.

of the body as in the Scutellerid Hemiptera : the wings are entirely concealed, and the abdomen is reduced to a plate, with its orifice beneath, not terminal; the surface of the body is highly polished and destitute of bristles. Whether this is a mimetic form, occurring in association with similar-looking Bugs is not known. The North American genus *Toxotrypana* is furnished with a long ovipositor; and in this and in the shape of the body resembles the parasitic Hymenoptera. This genus was placed by Gerstaecker in Ortalidae, but is considered by later writers to be a member of the Trypetidae. This latter family is of considerable extent, and is remarkable amongst the Diptera for the way in which the wings of many of its members are ornamented by an elaborate system of spots or marks, varying according to the species.

Fam. 34. Anthomyiidae. — *Flies similar in appearance to the House-fly ; the main vein posterior to the middle of the wing (4th longitudinal) continued straight to the margin, not turned upwards. Eyes of the male frequently large and contiguous, bristle of antenna either feathery or bare.* This very large family of flies is one of the most difficult and unattractive of the Order. Many of its members come close to the Acalyptrate Muscidae from which they are distinguished by the fact that a well-developed squama covers the halteres ; others come quite as close to the Tachinidae, Muscidae and Sarcophagidae, but may readily be separated by the simple, not angulate, main vein of the wing. The larval habits are varied. Many attack vegetables, produce disintegration in them, thus facilitating decomposition. *Anthomyia brassicae* is renowned amongst market gardeners on account of its destructive habits. *A. cana*, on the contrary, is beneficial by destroying the migratory Locust *Schistocerca peregrina;* and in North America, *A. angustifrons* performs a similar office with *Caloptenus spretus.* One or two species have been found living in birds; in one case on the head of a species of *Spermophila*, in another case on a tumour of the wing of a Woodpecker. *Hylemyia strigosa*, a dung-frequenting species, has the peculiar habit of producing living larvae, one at a time ; these larvae are so large that it would be supposed they are full grown, but this is not the case, they are really only in the first stage, an unusual amount of growth being accomplished in this stadium. *Spilogaster angelicae,* on the other hand, according to

Portschinsky, lays a small number of very large eggs, and the resulting larvae pass from the first to the third stage of development,
omitting the second stage that is usual in Eumyiid Muscidae.[1]

Fam. 35. Tachinidae.—*First posterior cell of wing nearly or
quite closed. Squamae large, covering the halteres : antennal arista
bare : upper surface of body usually bristly.* This is an enormous
family of flies, the larvae of which live parasitically in other living
Insects, Lepidopterous larvae being especially haunted. Many
have been reared from the Insects in which they live, but beyond
this little is known of the life-histories, and still less of the structure
of the larvae of the Tachinidae, although these Insects are of the
very first importance in the economy of Nature. The eggs are
usually deposited by the parent-flies near or on the head of the

Fig. 242.—*Ugimyia sericariae.* **A**, The perfect fly, × 6/2 ; **B**, tracheal chamber of a silkworm, with body of a larva of *Ugimyia* projecting ; *a*, front part of the maggot ;
b, stigmatic orifice of the maggot ; *c*, stigma of the silkworm. (After Sasaki.)

victim ; Riley supposed that the fly buzzes about the victim and
deposits an egg with rapidity, but a circumstantial account given
by Weeks[2] discloses a very different process : the fly he watched
sat on a leaf quietly facing a caterpillar of *Datana* engaged in
feeding at a distance of rather less than a quarter of an inch.
" Seizing a moment when the head of the larva was likely
to remain stationary, the fly stealthily and rapidly bent her
abdomen downward and extended from the last segment what
proved to be an ovipositor. This passed forward beneath her
body and between the legs until it projected beyond and nearly
on a level with the head of the fly and came in contact with the
eye of the larva upon which an egg was deposited," making an
addition to five already there. *Ugimyia sericariae* does great

[1] Baron von Osten Sacken informs the writer that this statement has since been
withdrawn by Portschinsky as being erroneous.

[2] *Ent. Amer.* iii. 1887, p. 126.

harm in Japan by attacking the silkworm, and in the case of this
fly the eggs are believed to be introduced into the victim by
being laid on mulberry leaves and swallowed with the food;
several observers agree as to the eggs being laid on the leaves, but
the fact that they are swallowed by the silkworm is not so certain.
Sasaki has given an extremely interesting account of the development of this larva.[1]   According to him, the young larva, after
hatching in the alimentary canal, bores through it, and enters a
nerve-ganglion, feeding there for about a week, after which the
necessity for air becoming greater, as usual with larvae, the
maggot leaves the nervous system and enters the tracheal system,
boring into a tube near a stigmatic orifice of the silkworm, where
it forms a chamber for itself by biting portions of the tissues and
fastening them together with saliva.   In this it completes its

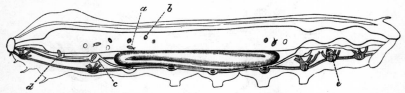

Fig. 243.—Diagrammatic section of silkworm to show the habits of *Ugimyia*. *a*, Young
larva ; *b*, egg of *Ugimyia* in stomach of the silkworm ; *c*, larva in a nerve-ganglion ;
d, larva entering a ganglion ; *e*, larva embedded in tracheal chamber, as shown in
Fig. 242, B. (After Sasaki.)

growth, feeding on the interior of the silkworm with its anterior
part, and breathing through the stigmatic orifice of its host;
after this it makes its exit and buries itself deeply in the ground,
where it pupates.   The work of rupturing the puparium by the
use of the ptilinum is fully described by Sasaki, and also the fact
that the fly mounts to the surface of the earth by the aid of this same
peculiar air-bladder, which is alternately contracted and distended.
Five, or more, of the *Ugimyia*-maggots may be found in one
caterpillar, but only one of them reaches maturity, and emerges
from the body.   The Tachinid flies appear to waste a large proportion of their eggs by injudicious oviposition ; but they make
up for this by the wide circle of their victims, for a single species
has been known to infest Insects of two or three different Orders.
    The species of *Miltogramma*—of which there are many in
Europe and two in England—live at the expense of Fossorial

[1] *J. Coll. Japan*, i. 1886, pp. 1–46, plates i.-vi.

Hymenoptera by a curious sort of indirect parasitism.   They are obscure little flies, somewhat resembling the common House-fly, but they are adepts on the wing and have the art of ovipositing with extreme rapidity ; they follow a Hymenopteron as it is carrying the prey to the nest for its young.   When the wasp alights on the ground at the entrance to the nest, the *Miltogramma* swoops down and rapidly deposits one or more eggs on the prey the wasp designs as food for its own young.   Afterwards the larvae of the fly eat up the food, and in consequence of the greater rapidity of their growth, the young of the Hymenopteron perishes. Some of them are said to deposit living larvae, not eggs.   Fabre has drawn a very interesting picture of the relations that exist between a species of *Miltogramma* and a Fossorial Wasp of the genus *Bembex*.[1]   We may remind the reader that this Hymenopteron has not the art of stinging its victims so as to keep them alive, and that it accordingly feeds its young by returning to the nest at proper intervals with a fresh supply of food, instead of provisioning the nest once and for all and then closing it. This Hymenopteron has a habit of catching the largest and most active flies—especially Tabanidae—for the benefit of its young, and it would therefore be supposed that it would be safe from the parasitism of a small and feeble fly.   On the contrary, the *Miltogramma* adapts its tactics to the special case, and is in fact aided in doing so by the wasp itself.   As if knowing that the wasp will return to the carefully-closed nest, the *Miltogramma* waits near it, and quietly selects the favourable moment, when the wasp is turning round to enter the nest backwards, and deposits eggs on the prey.   It appears from Fabre's account that the *Bembex* is well aware of the presence of the fly, and would seem to entertain a great dread of it, as if conscious that it is a formidable enemy ; nevertheless the wasp never attacks the little fly, but allows it sooner or later to accomplish its purpose, and will, it appears, even continue to feed the fly-larvae, though they are the certain destroyers of its own young, thus repeating the relations between cuckoo and sparrow.   Most of us think the wasp stupid, and find its relations to the fly incredible or contemptible.   Fabre takes a contrary view, and looks on it as a superior Uncle Toby.   We sympathise with the charming French naturalist, without forming an opinion.

[1] *Souvenirs entomologiques*, 1879, pp. 246-254.

Doubtless there are many other interesting features to be found in the life-histories of Tachinidae, for in numbers they are legion. It is probable that we may have 200 species in Britain, and in other parts of the world they are even more abundant, about 1000 species being known in North America.[1] The family Actiidae is at present somewhat doubtful. According to Karsch,[2] it is a sub-family of Tachinidae; but the fourth longitudinal vein, it appears, is straight.

Fam. 36. Dexiidae.—*These Insects are distinguished from Tachinidae by the bristle of the antennae being pubescent, and the legs usually longer.* The larvae, so far as known, are found in various Insects, especially in Coleoptera, and have also been found in snails. There are eleven British genera, and about a score of species.

Fam. 37. Sarcophagidae. — *Distinguished from Muscidae and Tachinidae by little more than that the bristle of the antennae is feathery at the base but hair-like and very fine at the tip.*—Sarcophaga carnaria is one of the commonest British Insects; it is like the Blow-fly, though rather longer, con-spicuously grey and black, with the thorax distinctly striped, and the pulvilli very conspicuous in the live fly. *Cynomyia mortuorum* is a bright blue fly rather larger than the Blow-fly, of which it is a competitor; but in this country an unsuccessful one. The larvae of the two Insects are found together, and are said to be quite indistinguishable. *Cynomyia* is said to lay only about half the number of eggs that the Blow-fly does, but it appears earlier in the year, and to this is attributed the fact that it is not altogether crowded out of existence by the more prolific *Calliphora*. The species of Sarcophagidae are usually viviparous, and one of them, *Sarcophila magnifica* (*wohlfahrti*), has the habit of occasionally depositing its progeny in the nostrils of mammals, and even of human beings, causing horrible sufferings and occasionally death : it is said to be not uncommon in Europe, but does not occur in Britain. The genus *Sarcophaga* is numerous in species, and many of them are beneficial. Sir Sidney Saunders found in the Troad that Locusts were destroyed by the larvae of a *Sarcophaga* living in their bodies; and

---

[1] A list of the Insects known to be attacked by Dipterous parasites has been given by Brauer and Bergenstamm, *Denk. Ak. Wien*, lxi. 1895.

[2] *Berlin. ent. Zeit.* xxx. 1886, p. 135.

Künckel has recently observed that in Algeria several species of this genus attack Locusts and destroy large quantities by depositing living larvae in the Orthoptera. In North America the Army-worm is decimated by species of *Sarcophaga*.

Many of these Insects, when food is scarce, eat their own species with eagerness, and it seems probable that this habit is beneficial to the species. The parent-fly in such cases usually deposits more eggs than there is food for, thus ensuring that every portion of the food will be rapidly consumed, after which the partially-grown larvae complete their development by the aid of cannibalism. It is thus ensured that the food will raise up as many individuals as possible.

Fam. 38. Muscidae.—*Bristle of antennae feathered.* This family contains many of the most abundant flies, including the House-fly, Blue-bottles or Blow-flies, Green-bottles, and other forms which, though very common, are perhaps not discriminated from one another by those who are not entomologists. The larvae live on carrion and decaying or excrementitious matters. The common House-fly, *Musca domestica*, runs through its life-history in a very short time. It lays about 150 very small eggs on dung or any kind of soft damp filth; the larvae hatch in a day or two and feed on the refuse; they may be full-grown in five or six days, and, then pupating, may in another week emerge as perfect flies. Hence it is no wonder that they increase to enormous numbers in favourable climates. They are thought to pass the winter chiefly in the pupal state. The House-fly is now very widely distributed over the world; it sometimes occurs in large numbers away from the dwellings of man. Of Blow-flies there are two common species in this country, *Calliphora erythrocephala* and *C. vomitoria*. The Green-bottle flies, of which there are several species, belonging to the genus *Lucilia*, have the same habits as Blow-flies, though they do not commonly enter houses. The larvae are said to be indistinguishable from those of *Calliphora*.

The larvae of Eumyiid Muscidae are, when first hatched, metapneustic, but subsequently an anterior pair of stigmata appears, so that the larva becomes amphipneustic. They usually go through three stages, distinguished by the condition of the posterior stigmata. In the early instar these have a single heart-shaped fissure, in the second stage two fissures exist, while in the third instar there is a greater diversity in the condition of the breathing apertures.

The various forms of Muscidae show considerable distinctions in the details of their natural history, and these in certain species vary according to the locality. This subject has been chiefly studied by Portschinsky, a Russian naturalist, and a very interesting summary of his results has been given by Osten Sacken,[1] to which the student interested in the subject will do well to refer.

A few years ago a great deal of damage was caused in the Netherlands by *Lucilia sericata*, a Green-bottle-fly, extremely similar to our common *L. caesar*, which deposited its eggs in great quantities on sheep amongst their wool. This epidemic was attributed to the importation of sheep from England ; but, according to Karsch, there is reason to suppose that the fly was really introduced from Southern Europe or Asia Minor.[2]

The larvae of species of the genus *Lucilia* sometimes attack man and animals in South America, but fortunately not in this country. The larva of *Lucilia (Compsomyia) macellaria* is called the screw-worm, and is the best known of the forms that infest man, the larvae living in the nasal fossae and frontal sinuses, and causing great suffering. The fly is common in North America, but is said never to attack man farther north than in Kansas. A little fly (*Stomoxys calcitrans*), very like the common house-fly though rather more distinctly spotted with grey and black, and with a fine, hard, exserted proboscis, frequently enters our houses and inflicts a bite or prick on us. It is commonly mistaken for an ill-natured house-fly that has taken to biting. It is frequently a source of irritation to cattle. A closely allied fly, *Haematobia serrata*, is very injurious to cattle in North America, but the same species causes no serious annoyance in England. We may mention that the various attacks of Dipterous larvae on man have received the general name " myiasis."

The Tse-tse fly (*Glossina morsitans*), another ally of *Stomoxys*, is not very dissimilar in size and shape to the blow-fly.[3]

[1] *Berlin. ent. Zeitschr.* xxxi. 1887, p. 17.

[2] *Biol. Centralbl.* vii. 1887, p. 521.

[3] For an account of the habits of this fly, see Kirk, *J. Linn. Soc.* viii. 1865, pp. 149-156 ; and for a bibliographic list, Wulp, *Tijdschr. Ent.* xxvii. 1884, p. xci. and pp. 143-140.

It bites man and animals in South Africa, and if it have previously bitten an animal whose blood was charged with the Haematozoa that really constitute the disease called Nagana (fly-disease), it inoculates the healthy animal with the disease ; fortunately only some species are susceptible, and man is not amongst them. It has recently been shown by Surgeon Bruce [1] that this fly multiplies by producing, one at a time, a full-grown larva, which imme-

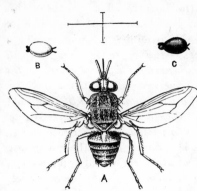

Fig. 244.—The Tse-tse fly (*Glossina morsitans*). **A,** The fly with three divisions of the proboscis projecting ; **B,** adult larva ; **C,** pupa.

diately changes to a pupa, as do the members of the series Pupipara. There are already known other Muscid flies with peculiarities in their modes of reproduction, so that it is far from impossible that the various conditions between ordinary egg-laying and full-grown larva- or pupa-production may be found to exist. Although it has been supposed that the Tse-tse fly is a formidable obstacle to the occupation of Africa by civilised men, there is reason to suppose that this will not ultimately prove to be the case. It only produces disease when this pre-exists in animals in the neighbourhood ; only certain species are liable to it ; and there is some evidence to the effect that even these may in the course of a succession of generations become capable of resisting the disease inoculated by the fly. As long ago as 1878 Dr. Drysdale suggested [2] that this fly only produces disease by inoculating a blood-parasite, and all the evidence that has since been received tends to show that his idea is correct.

Although the facts we have mentioned above would lead to the supposition that Muscidae are unmitigated nuisances, yet it is probable that such an idea is the reverse of the truth, and that on the whole their operations are beneficial. It would be difficult to overestimate their value as scavengers. And in addition to this they destroy injurious creatures. Thus in Algeria *Idia fasciata*, a fly like the House-fly, destroys the

[1] *Preliminary Report on the Tse-tse Fly Disease*, 1895.
[2] *P. Liverpool Soc.* xxxiii. 1878, p. 13, note.

dreaded migratory Locust *Schistocerca peregrina* in great quantities, by the larvae eating the eggs of the Locust. The female of this fly, in order to reach the desired food, penetrates from one to three inches below the surface of the ground.

Fam. 39. Oestridae (*Bot-flies*).—*Rather large or very large flies, with extremely short antennae, bearing a segmented arista, the front of the head prominent, the posterior part of the wings frequently rough, and with but few veins : the mouth usually atrophied, the trophi being represented only by tubercles ; larvae living in Vertebrates, usually Mammals, though it is possible that a few occur in Birds and even in Reptiles.* This is a family of small extent, less than 100 species being known from all the world, yet it is of much interest on account of the habits of its members, which, though of large size, live entirely at the expense of living Vertebrates, to the viscera or other structures of which they have definite relations, varying according to the species. Some (*Gastrophilus*, etc.) live in the alimentary canal; others (*Hypoderma*, etc.) are encysted in or under the skin; while others (*Oestrus*, etc.) occupy the respiratory passages. As many of them attack the animals used by man, and some of them do not spare man himself, they have attracted much attention, and there is an extensive literature connected with them ; nevertheless the life-histories are still very incompletely known. Indeed, the group is from all points of view a most difficult one, it being almost impossible to define the family owing to the great differences that exist in important points. Some think the family will ultimately be dismembered ; and Girschner has recently proposed to treat it as a division of Tachinidae. The chief authority is Brauer, in whose writings the student will find nearly all that is known about Oestridae.[1] Some of them exist in considerable numbers (it is believed that they are now not so common as formerly), and yet the flies are but rarely met with, their habits being in many respects peculiar. Some of them, for purposes of repose, frequent the summits of mountains, or towers, or lofty trees. Some have great powers of humming ; none of them are known to bite their victims, indeed the atrophied mouth of most of the Oestridae forbids such a proceeding. Some deposit their eggs on the hairs of the beasts from

[1] We may specially mention the monograph of Oestridae, published in 1863 by the *K. k. Zool. - Bot. Ges. Wien*, and supplements in *Wien. ent. Zeit.* v. vi. 1886, 1887 ; these include copious bibliographic lists.

which the larvae are to draw their nutriment, but others place
their larvae, already hatched, in the entrances of the nasal
passages.   They do not feed on the blood or tissues of their
victims, but on the secretions, and these are generally altered or
increased by the irritation induced by the presence of the un-
welcome guests.   It would appear, on the whole, that their presence
is less injurious than would be expected, and as they always quit
the bodies of their hosts for the purposes of pupation, a natural
end is put to their attacks.   We have ten species in Britain, the
animals attacked being the ox, the horse, the ass, the sheep, and
the red deer ; others occasionally occur in connexion with animals

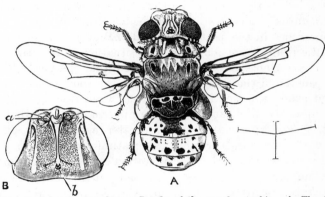

Fig. 245.—*Cephalomyia maculata*, a Bot-fly of the camel.   Arabia.   **A**, The fly with
extended wings ; **B**, under aspect of the head : *a*, antenna ; *b*, the obsolete mouth-parts.

in menageries.   The eggs of *Gastrophilus equi* are placed by the
fly, when on the wing, on the hair of horses near the front parts
of the body, frequently near the knee, and, after hatching, the
young larvae pass into the stomach of the horse either by being
licked off, or by their own locomotion; in the stomach they become hooked to the walls, and after being full grown pass out
with the excreta : the Bots—as these larvae are called—are sometimes very numerous in the stomach, for a fly will lay as many
as four or five hundred eggs on a single horse : in the case of
weakly animals, perforation of the stomach has been known to
occur in consequence of the habit of the Bot of burying itself to
a greater or less extent in the walls of the stomach.   *Hypoderma
bovis* and *H. lineata* attack the ox, and the larvae cause tumours
in the skin along the middle part of the back.   It was formerly

inferred from this that the fly places its eggs in this situation, and as the cattle are known to dread and flee from the fly, it was supposed to be on account of the pain inflicted when the egg was thrust through the skin. Recent observations have shown that these views are erroneous, but much still remains to be ascertained. The details of oviposition are not yet fully known, but it appears that the eggs are laid on the lower parts of the body, especially near the heels, and that they hatch very speedily.[1] As the imago of *Hypoderma* appears for only a very short period in the summer, the time of the oviposition is certain. The newly-disclosed larva is considerably different from the more advanced instar found in the skin of the back; moreover, a long period of many months intervenes between the hatching of the larva and its appearance in the part mentioned. Brauer has shown that when the grub is first found in that situation it is entirely subcutaneous. Hence it would be inferred that the newly-hatched larva penetrated the skin probably near the spot it was deposited on, and passed a period in subcutaneous wandering, on the whole going upwards till it arrived at the uppermost part: that after moulting, and in consequence of greater need for air, it then pierced the skin, and brought its breathing organs into contact with the external air; that the irritation caused by the admission of air induced a purulent secretion, and caused the larva to be enclosed in a capsule. Dr. Cooper Curtice has however found, in the oesophagus of cattle, larvae that he considers to be quite the same as those known to be the young of *Hypoderma;* and if this prove to be correct, his inference that the young larvae are licked up by the cattle and taken into the mouth becomes probable. The larva, according to this view, subsequently pierces the oesophagus and becomes subcutaneous by passing through the intervening tissues. The later history of the grub is briefly, that when full grown it somewhat enlarges the external orifice of its cyst, and by contractions and expansions of the body, passes to the surface, falls to the ground, buries itself and becomes a pupa. If Dr. Curtice be correct, there should, of course, be as many, if not more, larvae found in the oesophagus as in the back of the animal; but, so far as is known, this is not the case, and we shall not be surprised if the normal course of development be found different from what Dr. Curtice supposes it to be. His

[1] Riley, *Insect Life*, iv. 1892, p. 302.

observations relate to *Hypoderma lineata*. Our common British species is usually supposed to be *H. bovis;* but from recent observations it seems probable that most of the "Ox-warbles" of this country are really due to the larvae of *H. lineata.*

The history of *Oestrus ovis*, which attacks the sheep, is also incompletely known, but appears to be much simpler. This fly is viviparous, and deposits its young larvae at the entrance of the nasal passages of the sheep, thereby causing extreme annoyance to the animal. The larvae penetrate to the frontal sinuses to complete their growth. The duration of their lives is unknown, for it is commonly the case that larvae of various sizes are found together. *Cephenomyia rufibarbis* has recently been found in Scotland. It attacks the Red deer, and its life-history is similar to that of *Oestrus ovis*, though the larvae apparently prefer to attain their full growth in the pharynx of the deer.

In reference to the Oestridae that attack man, we may merely mention that the larva of the *Hypoderma* of the ox is occasionally found in Europe infesting human beings, but only as an extremely rare and exceptional event; and that only those engaged in attending on cattle are attacked; from which it is inferred that the flies are deceived by an odour emanating from the garments. In America numerous cases are known of Oestrid larvae being taken from the body of man, but information about them is very scanty. It appears, however, that there are at least four species, one of which, *Dermatobia noxialis*, is known as a fly as well as a larva. Whether any of these are peculiar to man is uncertain.[1] There are several larvae of Muscidae that have similar habits to the Oestridae; hence the statements that exist as to larvae being found in birds and reptiles cannot be considered to apply to members of the latter family until the larvae have been studied by an expert.

The family Ctenostylidae has been established by Bigot for a South American Insect, of which only a single individual exists in collections. It is doubtful whether it can be referred to Oestridae.[2]

Series V. Pupipara

The four families included in this Series are, with the exception of the Hippoboscidae, very little known. Most of

---

[1] See Blanchard, *Ann. Soc. ent. France* (7) ii. 1892, pp. 109, 154.
[2] See Bigot, *Ann. Soc. ent. France* (6) ii. 1882, p. 21, Brauer, *Monograph*, 1863, p. 51, and *Wien. ent. Zeit.* vi. 1887, p. 75.

them live by sucking blood from Mammals and Birds, and sometimes they are wingless parasites. The single member of the family Braulidae lives on bees. The term Pupipara is erroneous, and it would be better to revert to Réaumur's prior appellation Nymphipara. Müggenburg has suggested that the division is not a natural one, the points of resemblance that exist between its members being probably the results of convergence. Recent discoveries as to the modes of bringing forth of Muscidae give additional force to this suggestion. A satisfactory definition of the group in its present extent seems impossible.

Fam. 40. Hippoboscidae.—*Wings very variable, sometimes present and large, then with waved surface and thick nervures confined to the anterior and basal part ; sometimes mere strips, sometimes entirely absent.* Certain members of this family are well known, the Forest-fly, or Horse-fly, and the Sheep-tick belonging to it. The proboscis is of peculiar formation, and not like that of other flies. Seen externally it consists of two elongate, closely adapted, hard flaps ; these are capable of diverging laterally to allow an inner tube to be exserted from the head. The details and morphology of the structure have recently been discussed by Müggenburg.[1] *Melophagus ovinus*, commonly called the Sheep-tick, is formed for creeping about on the skin of the sheep beneath the wool, and may consequently be procured with ease at the period of sheep-shearing : it has no resemblance to a fly, and it is difficult to persuade the uninitiated that it is such. *Hippobosca equina* (called in this country the Forest-fly, perhaps because it is better known in the New Forest than elsewhere), looks like a fly, but will be readily recognised by the two little cavities on the head, one close to each eye, in which the antennae are concealed, only the fine bristle projecting. Very little seems to be known as to the Natural History of this fly. *Lipoptena cervi* lives on the Red deer; the perfect Insect has apparently a long life, and both sexes may be found in a wingless state on the deer all through the winter. When first disclosed in the summer they are however provided with wings, but when they have found a suitable host they bite off, or cast, the wings. The female, it appears, does this more promptly than the male, so that it is difficult to get winged individuals of the former sex.[2] Most of the known

[1] *Arch. Naturgesch.* lviii. i.1892, pp. 287-322, pls. xv. xvi.
[2] Stein, *Deutsche ent. Zeit.* xxi. 1877, p. 297.

Hippoboscidae live on birds, and are apparently specially fond of the Swallow tribe. They are all winged, though in some species the wings are very small. The bird-infesting Hippoboscidae have been very little studied, and will probably form a distinct family; the antennae of *Stenopteryx hirundinis* are quite different from those of *Hippobosca*. The development is remarkable, and has been studied by Leuckart[1] and by Pratt[2] in the case of *Melophagus ovinus*. The ovaries are peculiarly formed, and produce one large egg at a time; this passes into the dilated oviduct, and there goes through its full growth and a certain amount of development; it is then extruded, and undergoing little or no change of form becomes externally hardened by the excretion of chitin, passing thus into the condition of the Eumyiid pupa. Dufour thought that there is no larval stage in this Insect, but it is quite clear from later researches that he was wrong, and that a larval stage of a peculiar kind, but in some respects resembling that of the Eumyiid Muscidae, occurs. The larva has no true head, but the anterior part of the body is invaginated, and the most anterior part again protrudes in the

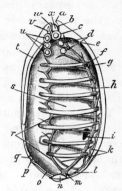

FIG. 246.—Diagrammatic section of the larva of *Melophagus ovinus*. (After Pratt.) *a*, mouth; *b*, suctorial pouch; *c*, imaginal disc for adult head; *d*, meso- and metanotal discs, *e*, anterior tracheal anastomosis; *f*, first muscular belt; *g*, transverse tracheal branch; *h*, the dorsal tracheal tube; *i*, sex-organ; *k*, Malpighian tube; *l*, terminal part of intestine; *m*, terminal chamber of tracheal tube; *n*, stigmatic fossa; *o*, terminal part of intestine; *p*, anus; *q*, anal disc; *r*, ventral tracheal tube; *s*, stomach; *t*, nervous system; *u*, discs for the three pairs of legs of the imago; *v*, ventral pouch; *w*, pharynx; *x*, suctorial lip.

invagination, so that two little passages appear on section (Fig. 246); the upper one leads to the stomach, which is of very large size. The tracheal system is peculiar; it is metapneustic, there being neither anterior nor lateral spiracles. Pratt says that there is at first a single pair of terminal spiracles, and subsequently three pairs, hence he considers that the terminal part of the body corresponds to three segments. This is however probably a mistaken view; it appears more probable that the so-called three pairs of stigmata really correspond with the complex

---

[1] *Abh. Ges. Halle*, iv. 1858, p. 145.   [2] *Arch. Naturgesch.* lix. i. 1893, p. 151.

condition of the stigmata in the later instars of certain other Dipterous larvae. The *Melophagus*-larva is nourished by secretion from certain glands of the mother-fly; this is swallowed and the stomach is greatly distended by this milky fluid. Probably it was this condition that induced Dufour to suppose the larva to be only an embryo.

Some of the Hippoboscidae that live on birds take to the wing with great readiness, and it is probable that these bird-parasites will prove more numerous than is at present suspected.

We may here notice an animal recently described by Dr. Adensamer and called *Ascodipteron*.[1] He treats it as the female imago of a Pupiparous Dipteron. It was found buried in the skin of the wing of a bat of the genus *Phyllorhina*, in the Dutch East Indies, only one individual being known. It is entirely unsegmented, and externally without head. If Dr. Adensamer should prove to be correct in his surmise the creature can scarcely be inferior in interest to the Strepsiptera.

Fam. 41. Braulidae.—This consists only of a minute Insect that lives on bees. The antennae are somewhat like those of

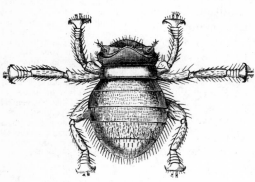

the sheep-tick, though they are not so completely concealed in the cavities in which they are inserted. According to Müggenburg[2] a ptilinum exists, and he is also of opinion that although the parts of the mouth differ very much from those of Hippoboscidae they

Fig. 247.—*Braula coeca.* × $\frac{18}{1}$. (After Meinert.)

are essentially similar. Lucas says that *Braula* specially affects the thorax of the bee: Müggenburg, that it is fond of the queen-bee because of the exposed membranes between the body-segments that exist in that sex. Whether this Insect is truly Pupiparous is unknown, though Boise states that a pupa is deposited in the cell of the bee by the side of the young larva of

---

[1] *SB. Ak. Wien.* cv. 1896, *Abtheil.* i. p. 400.
[2] *Arch. Naturges.* lviii. i. 1892, p. 287.

the bee, and appears as the perfect Insect in about twenty-one days. Müggenburg suggests that *Braula* may be oviparous, as he has never found a larva in the abdomen. Packard says that on the day the larva hatches from the egg it sheds its skin and turns to an oval puparium of a dark brown colour. The Insect is frequently though inappropriately called bee-louse; notwithstanding its name it is not quite blind, though the eyes are very imperfect.

Fam. 42. Streblidae. — *Winged; possessing halteres; the head small, narrow and free.* These very rare Diptera are altogether problematic. According to Kolenati the larvae live in bats' excrement and the perfect Insects on the bats.[1] If the former statement be correct the Insects can scarcely prove to be Pupipara. The wing-nervuration is, in the figures of the Russian author, quite different from that of Hippoboscidae. The Streblidae have been associated by some entomologists with Nycteribiidae, and by Williston with Hippoboscidae.

Family 43. Nycteribiidae.—The species of this family are

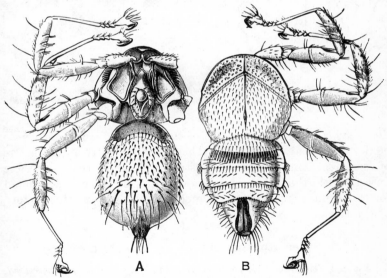

FIG. 248.—*Nycteribia* sp., from *Xantharpyia straminea.* Aden. **A,** Upper surface of female, with head in the position of repose; **B,** under surface of male. × 1½².

found on bats; they are apparently rare, and we have been able to examine only one species. The form is very peculiar, the

[1] *Horae Soc. ent. Ross.* ii. 1863, p. 90.

Insects looking as if the upper were the under surface. They are wingless, with a narrow head, which reposes on the back of the thorax. The prothorax appears to be seated on the dorsum of the mesothorax. According to Müggenburg there is no trace of a ptilinum. A brief note on the metamorphosis [1] by Baron Osten Sacken indicates that the mature larva differs from that of

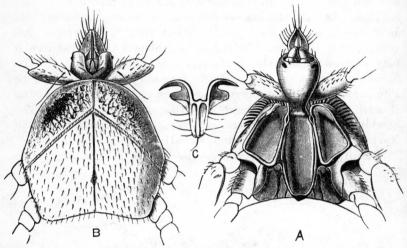

FIG. 249.—Anterior part of the body of *Nycteribia* sp., found on *Xantharpyia straminea* by Colonel Yerbury at Aden. **A**, Upper surface of female, with head extended ; **B**, under surface of male, with head extended ; **C**, claws of a foot.

Melophagus in the arrangement of the stigmata ; they appear to be dorsal instead of terminal. There are apparently no characters of sufficient importance to justify the association of these Insects with the other divisions of Pupipara ; the sole ground for this connection being the supposed nature of the life-history of the larva.

Sub-Order Aphaniptera or Siphonaptera (*Fleas*)

Fam. Pulicidae.—*Wingless, with the body laterally compressed, so that the transverse diameter is small, the vertical one great. The head indistinctly separated from the body, small, with short thick antennae placed in depressions somewhat behind and above the unfaceted eyes. These are always minute, and sometimes wanting.*—

[1] *Tr. ent. Soc. London,* 1881, p. 360.

We all know that the Flea is so flat, or compressed sideways, that it does not mind the most severe squeeze. This condition is almost peculiar to it; a great flattening of the body is common in Insects—as is seen in another annoying Insect, the bed-bug—but the compression, in the flea, is in the reverse direction. In other respects the external anatomy of the flea

FIG. 250.—*Hystrichopsylla talpae.* Britain. (After Ritsema.)

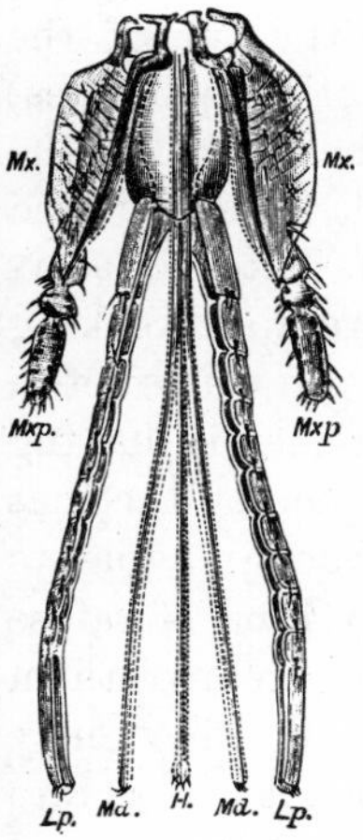

shows several peculiarities, the morphological import of which has not yet been elucidated. The head is of very peculiar shape, small, with the antennae placed in an unusual position; the clypeus is said to be entirely absent, the front legs are articulated in such a manner that they have a large additional basal piece—called by some anatomists the ischium—and in consequence appear to be placed far forwards, looking as if they were attached to the head; the meso- and meta-thorax have certain flaps that have been considered to be homologues of wings; and the maxillary palpi are attached to the head in such a way that they appear to play the part of the antennae of other Insects (Fig. 250), and were actually considered to be the antennae by Linnaeus, as well as others; the mouth-parts themselves are differently constructed from those of any other Insects.[1] The maxillae and labium are considered to be not only present, but well developed, the former possessing palpi moderately well developed, while the labial palps are very large and of highly peculiar form, being imperfectly transversely jointed and acting as sheaths; the mandibles are present in the form of

FIG. 251. — Mouth-parts of a flea, *Vermipsylla alakurt* ♂. *H.* Unpaired pricking organ; *Lp.* labial palp; *Md.* mandible; *Mx.* maxilla; *Mxp.* maxillary palp. (After Wagner.)

---

[1] The best general description of the external anatomy of the flea is to be found in Taschenberg, *Die Flöhe*, 1880. The morphology is better elucidated, though still incompletely, in Wagner's valuable "Aphanipterologische Studien," *Horae Soc. ent. Ross.* xxiii. 1889, pp. 199-260, 5 plates, and *op. cit.* xxxi. 1897, pp. 555-594, 3 plates. Cf. also N. C. Rothschild, *Nov. Zool.* v. 1898, pp. 533-544, 3 plates.

a pair of elongate, slender organs, with serrated edges ; and there is an unpaired, elongate pricking-organ, thought by some to be a hypopharynx, and by others a labrum. The antennae are of unusual form, consisting of two basal joints, and, loosely connected therewith, a terminal mass of diverse form and more or less distinctly, though irregularly, segmented. The full number of ten stigmata exists, Wagner giving three thoracic, with seven

abdominal, placed on segments 2-8 of the abdomen ; but Packard thinks the supposed metathoracic stigma is really the first abdominal. Fleas undergo a very complete metamorphosis ; the larvae are wormlike, resembling those of Mycetophilid Diptera (Fig. 252). The egg of the cat's flea is deposited among the fur of the animal, but (unlike the eggs of other parasites) apparently is not fastened to the hair, for the eggs fall freely to the ground from infested animals ; the young larva when hatched bears on the head a curious structure for breaking the egg-shell. It has the mouth-parts of a mandibulate Insect and is peripneustic, having ten pairs of stigmata. It subsequently becomes of less elongate form. Flea-larvae are able to nourish themselves on almost any kind of refuse animal matter, Laboulbène having reared them on the sweepings of apartments ; they may perhaps sometimes feed on blood ; at any rate the contents of the alimentary canal appear red through the transparent integuments. When

FIG. 252.—Larva of *Pulex serraticeps,* the dog- and cat-flea.   (After Künckel.)

full grown the larva makes a cocoon, and frequently covers it with pieces of dust. The perfect flea appears in a week or two thereafter ; the pupa has the members free. The food of the larvae of fleas has been much discussed and a variety of statements made on the subject. It has been stated that the mother-flea after being gorged with blood carries some of it to the young, but Künckel has shown that there is very little foundation for this tale. Enormous numbers of fleas are sometimes found in uninhabited apartments to which animals have previously had access, and these fleas will attack in numbers and with great eagerness any unfortunate person who may enter the apartment. The cat-flea can pass through its growth and metamorphosis with excessive rapidity, the entire development of a generation in favourable conditions extending but little beyond a fortnight.[1]

About a hundred kinds of fleas are known, all of which live on mammals or birds. *Hystrichopsylla talpae* (Fig. 250) is one of the largest, it occurs on the Mole. It was found by Ritsema in the nests of *Bombus subterraneus* (and was described under the name of *Pulex obtusiceps*). As these nests are known to be harried by Voles, and as this flea has also been found on Field-mice, it is probable that the parasites are carried to the nests by the Voles. The species that chiefly infests man is *Pulex irritans*, an Insect that is nearly cosmopolitan, though arid desert regions are apparently unsuitable to it. *Pulex avium* occurs on a great variety of birds. *P. serraticeps* infests the dog and the cat, as well as a variety of other Mammals. It is a common opinion that each species of Mammal has its own peculiar flea, but this is far from correct. Fleas pass readily from one species of animal to another; the writer formerly possessed a cat that was a most determined and successful hunter of rabbits, and she frequently returned from her excursions swarming with fleas that she had become infested with when in the rabbits' burrows; her ears were on some occasions very sore from the flea-bites. Some of the fleas of other animals undoubtedly bite man. There appears, however, to be much difference in the liability of different individuals of our own species to the bites of fleas. *Sarcopsylla penetrans* differs in habits from other fleas, as the female buries the anterior parts of her body in the flesh of man or other Vertebrates, and the abdomen then becomes enormously enlarged and distended and undergoes a series of changes that are of much interest.[2] While in this position the Insect discharges a number of eggs. This species multiplies sufficiently to become a serious pest in certain regions, the body of one man having been known to be affording hospitality to 300 of these fleas. *Sarcopsylla penetrans* is known as the Sand-flea, or chigger, and by numerous other names. Originally a native of tropical America it has been carried to other parts of the world. Another *Sarcopsylla, S. gallinacea,* attaches itself to the eyelids

[1] Howard, *Bull. Dep. Agric. Ent.* N.S. No. 4, 1896.
[2] Schimkewitsch, *Zool. Anz.* vii. 1884, p. 673.

of the domestic fowl in Ceylon, and an allied form, *Rhynchopsylla pulex*, fastens itself to the eyelids and other parts of the body of birds and bats in South America. In Turkestan *Vermipsylla alakurt* attacks cattle—ox, horse, camel, sheep—fastening itself to the body of the animal after the fashion of a tick. Retaining this position all through the winter, it becomes distended somewhat after the manner of the Sand-flea, though it never forms a spherical body. The parts of the mouth in this Insect (Fig. 251) are unusually long, correlative with the thickness of the skins of the animals on which it lives. Grassi considers that the dog's flea, *Pulex serraticeps*, acts as the intermediate host of Taenia.

Great difference of opinion has for long prevailed as to whether fleas should be treated as a Sub-Order of Diptera or as a separate Order of Insects. Wagner and Künckel, who have recently discussed the question, think they may pass as aberrant Diptera, while Packard,[1] the last writer on the subject, prefers to consider them a separate Order more closely allied to Diptera than to any other Insects. Although widely known as Aphaniptera, several writers call them Siphonaptera, because Latreille proposed that name for them some years before Kirby called them Aphaniptera. Meinert considers them a separate Order and calls it Suctoria, a most unfortunate name.

Order VIII. Thysanoptera.

Small Insects, with a palpigerous mouth placed on the under side of the head and apposed to the sternum so as to be concealed. With four slender wings, fringed with long hairs on one or both margins, or with rudiments of wings, or entirely apterous. Tarsi of one or two joints, terminated by a vesicular structure. The young resemble the adult in general form, but there is a pupal stadium in which the Insect is quiescent and takes no food.

The tiny Insects called Thrips are extremely abundant and may often be found in profusion in flowers. Their size is only from $\frac{1}{50}$ to $\frac{1}{3}$ of an inch in length; those of the latter magnitude are in fact giant species, and so far as we know at present are found only in Australia (Fig. 253). As regards the extent

[1] *P. Boston Soc.* xxvi. 1894, pp. 312-355.

of the Order it would appear that Thysanoptera are insignificant, as less than 150 species are known. Thrips have been, however, very much neglected by entomologists, so it will not be a matter for surprise if there should prove to be several thousand species. These Insects present several points of interest ; their mouth - organs are unique in structure ; besides this, they exhibit so many points of dissimilarity from other Insects that it is impossible to treat them as subdivisions of any other Order. They have, however, been considered by some to be aberrant Pseudoneuroptera (cf. Vol. V.), while others have associated them with Hemiptera. Both Brauer and Packard have treated Thysanoptera as a separate Order, and there can be no doubt that this is correct. Thysano-

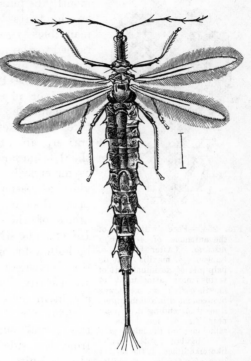

Fig. 253.—*Idolothrips spectrum.*   Australia.

ptera have recently been monographed by Uzel in a work that is, unfortunately for most of us, in the Bohemian language.[1]

The antennae are never very long, and are 6 to 9-jointed. The head varies much, being sometimes elongate and tubular, but sometimes short ; it has, however, always the peculiarity that the antennae are placed quite on its front part, and that the mouth appears to be absent, owing to its parts being thrust against the under side of the thorax and concealed. Their most remarkable peculiarity is that some of them are asymmetrical : Uzel looks on the peculiar structure, the " Mundstachel," *m, m*

[1] *Monographie der Ordnung Thysanoptera*, Königgrätz, 4to, 1895.

(Fig. 254) found on the left side of the body, as probably an enormous development of the epipharynx. Previous to the appearance of Uzel's work, Garman had, however, correctly described the structure of the mouth;[1] he puts à different interpretation on the parts; he points out that the mandibles (*j*), so-called by Uzel, are attached to the maxillae, and he considers that they are really jointed, and that they are lobes thereof; while the Mundstachel or piercer is, he considers, the left mandible; the corresponding structure of the other side being nearly entirely absent. He points out that the labrum and endocranium are also asymmetrical. We think Garman's view a reasonable one, and may remark that dissimilarity of the mandibles of the two sides is usual in Insects, and that the mandibles may be hollow for sucking, as is shown by the larvae of Hemerobiides. There are usually three ocelli, but they are absent in the entirely apterous forms.

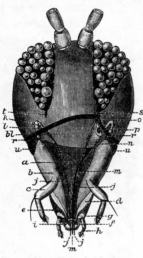

FIG. 254.—Face (with base of the antennae) of *Aeolothrips fasciata*. (After Uzel.) *a*, Labrum ; *b*, maxilla with its palp (*c*); *bl*, terminal part of vertex near attachment of mouth-parts ; *d*, membrane between maxilla and mentum ; *e*, mentum ending in a point near *f* ; *g*, membrane of attachment of the labial palp *h* ; *i*, ligula ; *j, j* the bristle-like mandibles ; *k*, the thicker base of mandible ; *l*, chitinous lever ; *m*, mouth-spine, with its thick basal part *n*, and *o*, its connection with the forehead, *r*, *r* ; *p*, foramen of muscle ; *s* and *t*, points of infolding of vertex ; *u*, a prolongation of the gena.

The wings appear to spring from the dorsal surface of the body, not from the sides; the anterior pair is always quite separated from the posterior ; the wings are always slender, sometimes very slender ; in other respects they exhibit considerable variety ; sometimes the front pair are different in colour and consistence from the other pair. The abdomen has ten segments, the last of which is often tubular in form. The peculiar vesicular structures by which the feet are terminated are, during movement, alternately distended and emptied, and have two hooks or claws on the sides. The stigmata are extremely peculiar, there being four pairs, the first being the mesothoracic, 2nd

---

[1] *Bull. Essex Inst.* xxii. 1890, p. 24 ; also *Amer. Natural.* xxx. 1896, p. 591.

metathoracic, 3rd on the second abdominal segment, 4th on the eighth abdominal segment.[1]   There are four Malpighian tubes, and two or three pairs of salivary glands.   The dorsal vessel is said to be a short sack placed in the 7th and 8th abdominal segments.   The abdominal ganglia of the ventral chain are concentrated in a single mass, placed in, or close to, the thorax ; the thorax has two other approximated ganglia, as well as an anterior one that appears to be the infra-oesophageal.

The metamorphosis is also peculiar ; the larva does not differ greatly in appearance from the adult, and has similar mouth-organs and food-habits.   The wings are developed outside the body at the sides, and appear first, according to Heeger, after the third moult.   The nymph-condition is like that of a pupa inasmuch as no nourishment is taken, and the parts of the body are enclosed in a skin : in some species there is power of movement to a slight degree, but other species are quite motionless.   In some cases the body is entirely bright red, though subsequently there is no trace of this colour.   Jordan distinguishes two nymphal periods, the first of which he calls the pronymphal ; in it the Insect appears to be in a condition intermediate between that of the larva and that of the true nymph ; the old cuticle being retained, though the hypodermis is detached from it and forms a fresh cuticle beneath it.   This condition, as Jordan remarks, seems parallel to that of the male Coccid, and approaches closely to complete metamorphosis ; indeed the only characters by which the two can be distinguished appear to be (1) that the young has not a special form ; (2) that the wings are developed outside the body.

Thrips take their food, it is believed, in the same manner as Aphidae, by suction ; but the details of the process are not by any means certain, and examination of the stomach is said to have resulted in finding pollen therein.   Walsh thought that Thysanoptera pierce and suck Aphidae.   An elaborate inquiry by Osborn[2] failed to elicit satisfactory confirmation of Walsh's idea, though Riley and Pergande support it to some extent ; Osborn concludes that the ordinary food is not drawn directly from sap, but consists of exudation or pollen, the tissues

---

[1] Jordan in an interesting paper, *Zeitschr. wiss. Zool.* xlvii. 1888, p. 573, says that in the division " Terebrantia " there are only three pairs of stigmata.

[2] *Insect Life*, i. 1888, p. 138.

of the plant being pierced only when a supply of food from the usual sources falls short. Members of this family have been reputed as being very injurious to cultivated plants, especially to cereals, and it is said that as a result the harvests in Europe have been seriously diminished. Several species may take part in the attacks. These appear to be directed chiefly against the inflorescence. Lindeman thought that *Limothrips denticornis* (= *Thrips secalina*), and *Anthothrips aculeata* (= *Phloeothrips frumentarius*), were the most destructive species in an attack of Thrips on corn that he investigated in Russia. Uzel suggests that injuries due to other causes are sometimes ascribed to Thrips.[1] In hot-houses these Insects are well known, and sometimes occasion considerable damage to foliage. The German horticulturalists call them black-fly, in distinction from Aphidae or green-fly. Some Thysanoptera live under bark, and even in fungi, and in Australia they form galls on the leaves of trees. This observation is due to Mr Froggatt, and is confirmed by specimens he sent to the writer. Vesicular bodies in the leaves of *Acacia saligna* were traversed on one side by a longitudinal slit, and on a section being made, nothing but Thrips, in various stages of growth, was found inside them. A second kind of gall, forming masses of considerable size on the twigs of *Callistemon*, is said by Mr Froggatt to be also due to Thrips, as is a third kind on *Bursaria spinosa*. It is curious that Thrips' galls have not been observed in other parts of the world.

Thysanoptera are devoured by small bugs of the genus *Triphleps*, as well as by beetles ; a small Acarid attacks them by fixing itself to the body of the Thrips. Nematode worms and their eggs were found by Uzel in the body-cavity. He found no less than 200 Nematodes in one Thrips, and noticed that they had entirely destroyed the ovaries. Woodpeckers, according to him, tear off the bark of trees and eat the Thysanoptera that are concealed thereunder, though one would have surmised that these minute Insects are too small to be game for such birds. They have, it appears, no special protection, except that one species (a larva of *Phloeothrips* sp.) is said to emit a protective fluid.

Parthenogenesis seems to be frequent amongst Thysanoptera,

[1] See Lindemann, *Bull. Soc. Moscou*, lxii. 1886, No. 2, p. 296, and Uzel, *Mon.* 1895, pp. 397, 398.

and is found in concurrence with diversity as to winged and wing-less females of the same species, so as to have given rise to the idea that the phenomena in this respect are parallel with those that are more widely known as occurring in Aphidae.   Under certain circumstances few or no males are produced (one of the cir-cumstances, according to Jordan, being season of the year), and the females continue the species parthenogenetically.   In other cases, though males are produced they are in very small numbers. Some species of Thysanoptera are never winged ; in others the individuals are winged or wingless according to sex.   But there are other cases in which the female is usually wingless, and is exceptionally winged.   The winged specimens in this case are, it is thought, of special use in disseminating the species. Jordan has suggested that these phenomena may be of a regular nature, but Uzel does not take this view.   Another condition may be mentioned, in which the species is usually wing-less, but winged individuals of the male as well as of the female sex occasionally appear.   *Thrips lini* apparently makes regular migrations, feeding at one time underground on the roots of flax, and then changing to a life in the open air on other plants.

Numerous forms of Thysanoptera, belonging to both of the great divisions of the Order, have been found fossil in Europe and North America, but all are confined to deposits of the Tertiary epoch.

Of the 135 species known to Uzel, 117 are European ; they are divided into two Sub-Orders.   1, Terebrantia, in which the females are provided with an external toothed ovipositor, of two valves ; 2, Tubulifera, in which there is no ovipositor, and the extremity of the body is tubular in both sexes.   The British species are about 50 in number, and were described by Haliday about 60 years ago ;[1] of late they have been very little studied.

The name Physopoda or Physapoda is used for this Order, instead of Thysanoptera, by several naturalists.

[1] *Entomological Magazine*, iii. 1836, p. 439, and iv. 1837, p. 144.

CHAPTER VIII

Order IX. Hemiptera.

Mouth consisting of a proboscis or mobile beak (usually concealed by being bent under the body), appearing as a transversly-jointed rod or grooved sheath, in which are enclosed long slender setae (like horse-hairs). Wings (nearly always) four; the anterior frequently more horny than the posterior pair, and folding flat on the back, their apical portions usually more membranous than the base (Heteroptera); or the four wings may cover the abdomen in a roof-like manner, and those of the anterior pair may not have the basal and apical parts of different consistences (Homoptera); sometimes all four of the wings are transparent. The young resembles the adult in general form; the wings are developed outside the body, by growth, at the moults, of the sides of the hinder portions of the meso- and meta-notum; the metanotal prolongations being more or less concealed by the mesonotal.

THE Hemiptera or Bugs are perhaps more widely known as Rhynchota. In deciding whether an Insect belongs to this Order the student will do well to examine in the first place the beak, treating the wings as subordinate in importance, their condition being much more variable than that of the beak. The above definition includes no reference to the degraded Anoplura or Lice. These are separately dealt with on p. 599; they are absolutely wingless, and have an unjointed proboscis not placed beneath the body, the greater part of it being usually withdrawn inside the body of the Insect.

The Hemiptera are without exception sucking Insects, and

the mouth-organs of the individual are of one form throughout its life. In this latter fact, coupled with another, that the young are not definitely different in form from the adult, Bugs differ widely from all other Insects with sucking-mouth. They agree with the Orthoptera in the facts that the mouth does not change its structure during the individual life, and that the development of the individual is gradual, its form, as a rule, changing but little. In respect of the structure of the mouth, Orthoptera and Hemiptera are the most different of all the Orders. Hence, Hemiptera is really the most isolated of all the Orders of Insects. We shall subsequently see that, like Orthoptera,

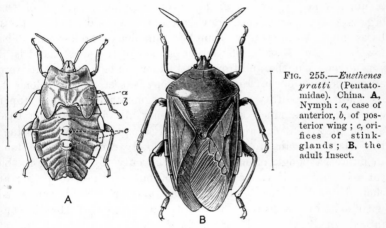

Fig. 255.—*Eusthenes pratti* (Pentatomidae). China. **A**, Nymph : *a*, case of anterior, *b*, of posterior wing ; *c*, orifices of stink-glands ; **B**, the adult Insect.

the Order appeared in the Palaeozoic epoch. Although a very extensive Order, Hemiptera have for some incomprehensible reason never been favourite objects of study. Sixty years ago Dufour pointed out that they were the most neglected of all the great Orders of Insects, and this is still true ; our acquaintance with their life-histories and morphology especially being very limited.

There is probably no Order of Insects that is so directly connected with the welfare of the human race as the Hemiptera ; indeed, if anything were to exterminate the enemies of Hemiptera, we ourselves should probably be starved in the course of a few months. The operations of Hemiptera, however, to a large extent escape observation, as their mouth-setae make merely pricks that do not attract notice in plants ; hence, it is probable that injuries really due to Hemiptera are frequently attributed to other causes.

In the course of the following brief sketch of the anatomy and development of Hemiptera, we shall frequently have to use the terms Heteroptera and Homoptera ; we may therefore here mention that there are two great divisions of Hemiptera having but little connection, and known by the above names : the members of these two Sub-Orders may in most cases be distinguished by the condition of the wings, as mentioned in the definition at the commencement of this chapter.

External structure.—The mouth-parts consist of an anterior or upper and a posterior or lower enwrapping part, and of the organs proper, which are four hair-like bodies, dilated at their bases and resting on a complex chitinous framework. The lower part forms by far the larger portion of the sheath and is of very diverse lengths, and from one to four-jointed : it is as it were an enwrapping organ, and a groove may be seen running along it, in addition to the evident cross - segmentation. The upper covering part is much smaller, and only fills a gap at the base of the sheath ; it can readily be lifted so as to disclose the setae ; these latter organs are fine, flexible, closely connected, rods, four in number, though often seeming to be only three, owing to the intimate union of the components of one of the two pairs ; at their base the setae become broader, and are closely connected with some of the loops of the chitinous ·framework that is contained within the head. Sometimes the setae are much longer than the sheath ; they are capable of protrusion. Although varying considerably in minor points, such as the lengths of the sheath and setae, and the number of cross-joints of the sheath, these structures are so far as is known constant throughout the Order. There are no palpi, and the only additions exceptionally present are a pair of small plates that in certain forms (aquatic family Belostomidae) lie on the front of the proboscis near the tip, overlapping, in fact, the last of the cross-articulations.

Simple as is this system of trophi its morphology is uncertain, and has given rise to much difference of interpretation. It may be granted that the two portions of the sheath are respectively upper lip, and labium ; but as to the other parts wide difference of opinion still prevails. On the whole the view most generally accepted, to the effect that the inner pair of the setae correspond

in a broad sense with maxillae of mandibulate Insects, and the
outer pair with mandibles, is probably correct.   Mecznikow, who
studied the embryology,[1] supports this view for Heteroptera,
but he says (*t.c.* p. 462), that in Homoptera the parts of the
embryo corresponding with rudimentary maxillae and mandibles
disappear, and that the setae are subsequently produced from
peculiar special bodies that are at first of a retort-shaped form ;
the neck of the retort becoming afterwards more elongate to form
the seta ; also that in the Heteropterous genus *Gerris* the
embryology in general resembles that of Homoptera, but the

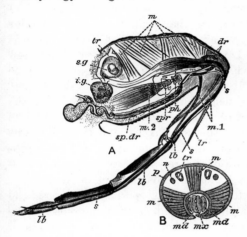

Fig. 256.—Mouth - parts of
Hemiptera.   (After
Wedde.) **A**, Section of
the head and proboscis of
Pyrrhocoris apterus : dr,
gland ; *i.g*, infra - oesophageal ganglion ; *lb*,
labium ; *lr*, labrum ; *m*,
muscles ; m^1, muscle (de-
pressor of labium) ; m^2,
muscle of syringe ; *ph*,
pharynx ; *s*, setae ; *s.g*,
supra - oesophageal gang-
lion ; *sp. dr*, salivary
gland ; *spr*, syringe : **B**,
transverse section of proboscis of *Pentatoma rufipes*, at third joint of
sheath : *m, m*, muscles ;
md, mandibular seta ; *mx*,
maxillary setae ; *n*, nerve ;
p, the sheath or labium ;
tr, trachea.

development of the setae is like that of other Heteroptera (*t.c.* p.
478).   This discontinuity in the development of the Homopterous
mouth has since been refuted by Witlaczil,[2] who found that the
retort-shaped bodies really arise from the primary segmental
appendages after they have sunk into the head.   We are therefore justified in concluding that the mouth-parts are at first
similarly developed in all Hemiptera, and that this development
is of a very peculiar nature.

Smith is convinced that there are no traces of mandibular
structure in any Hemiptera.[3]   On the other hand, numerous
entomologists have supposed they could homologise satisfactorily
various parts of the Hemipterous trophi with special parts of the

[1] *Zeitschr. wiss. Zool.* xvi. 1866, p. 389.   [2] *Arb. Inst. Wien.* iv. 1882, p. 415.
[3] *Tr. Amer. Phil. Soc.* xix. 1896, p. 176.

maxillae and labium of mandibulate Insects. This point has recently been discussed by Marlatt [1] and by Heymons. [2] From the latter we gather that the mode of growth is peculiar by the extension backwards of some of the sclerites, and their becoming confounded with parts of the wall of the head. From all this it appears that at present we cannot correctly go farther than saying that the trophi of Hemiptera are the appendages of three head-segments, like those of other Insects. The views of Savigny, Léon,[3] and others to the effect that labial palpi, and even other parts of the labium of Mandibulata can be satisfactorily identified are not confirmed by Heymons.

Underneath the pharynx, in the head, there is a peculiar structure for which we have as yet no English term. It was apparently discovered by Landois and Paul Mayer,[4] and has been called " Wanzenspritze," which we translate as syringe. It may be briefly described as a chamber, into which the salivary ducts open, prolonged in front to the neighbourhood of the grooves of the setae in the rostrum; behind, it is connected with muscles; it has no direct connection with the pharynx, and though it was formerly supposed to be an organ of suction, it seems more probable that it is of the nature of a force-pump, to propel the products of some of the bug's glands towards the tips of the setae.

The rostrum being extended from its position of repose, the tip of the sheath is brought into contact with the object to be pierced, the surface of which is probably examined by means of sensitive hairs at the extremity of the sheath; these therefore functionally replace to some extent the palpi of other Insects. As a rule the sheath does not penetrate (though there is reason for believing that in various of the animal-feeding bugs it does so), but the setae are brought into action for piercing the skin of the plant; they are extremely sharp, and the outer pair are usually barbed, so that when once introduced a hold is easily maintained. This being established it is thought that the salivary pump comes into play, and that a fluid is injected into the object pierced so as to give rise to irritation or congestion, and thus keep up a supply of fluid at the point operated on: this fluid extends along the grooved setae by capillary attraction, and the

---

[1] *P. ent. soc. Washington*, iii. 1895, p. 241.   [2] *Ent. Nachr.* xxii. 1896, p. 173.
[3] *Zool. Anz.* 1897, No. 527, p. 73.
[4] *Arch. Anat. Physiol.* 1874, p. 313, and 1875, p. 309.

rapidity of the current is increased by a pumping action of the pharynx, and possibly by movements of the setae themselves. Though the setae are often extremely elongate—sometimes several times the length of the body—they are nearly always slender, and there is no reason to suppose that a perfect, or air-tight, tube is formed; hence it is probable that capillary attraction is really the chief agent in the ingestion of the fluid. The slight diversity of structure of the Hemipterous trophi is in very striking contrast with what we find in mandibulate Insects, and in the less purely suctorial Insects, such as Diptera and some divisions of Hymenoptera. Schiödte in com-menting on this has suggested that it is probably due to the small variety of actions the rostrum is put to.[1]

The head exhibits great variety of form; in the Homoptera the front part is deflexed and inflexed, so that it is placed on the under surface, and its anterior margin is directed backwards; it is often peculiarly inflated; in the Lantern-flies or Fulgoridae (Fig. 282) to an incomprehensible extent. In the great Water-bugs, Belostomidae, there is on the under surface a deep pocket for each antenna, beautifully adapted to the shape of the curious.y-formed ap-pendage (Fig. 279). The prothorax is always very distinct, frequently large, and in many of the Heteroptera (Fig. 257), as well as in the Homop-terous family, Membracidae (Fig. 283), assumes the most extraordinary

Fig. 257.—*Saccoderes tuberculatus* Gray. Brazil. (Fam. Reduviidae.) (Antennae absent in the specimen represented.)

shapes. Both meso- and meta-thorax are well developed. The former is remarkable for the great size of the scutellum; in some cases (Plataspides, Scutellerides) this forms a large process,

---

[1] For the structure and development of the Hemipterous trophi, see Mayer, *Arch. Anat. Physiol.* 1874 and 1875 ; Mecznikow, *Zeitschr. wiss. Zool.* xvi. 1866, p. 389 ; Geise, *Arch. Naturgesch.* xlix. 1, 1883, p. 315 ; Wedde, *op. cit.* li. 1, 1885, p. 113 ; Mark, *Arch. mikr. Anat.* xiii. 1877, p. 31 : Smith, *Tr. Amer. Phil. Soc.* xix. 1896, p. 176.

that entirely covers and conceals the alar organs, so that the Insect has all the appearance of being apterous. The exact composition of the abdomen has not been satisfactorily determined, opinions varying as to whether the segments are nine, ten, or eleven in number. The difficulty of determining the point is due to two facts : viz. the extreme modification of the terminal segments in connection with the genital appendages, and the prominence of the extremity of the alimentary canal. If this terminal projection is to be treated as a segment, it would appear that eleven segments exist, at any rate in some cases ; as the writer has counted ten distinct segments in a young Coreid bug, in addition to the terminal tube. This tube in some of the male Heteroptera is very subject to curious modifications, and has been called the rectal cauda. Verhoeff considers that ten segments were invariably present in the females examined by him in various families of Heteroptera and Homoptera.[1] In Aphidae (a division of Homoptera), Balbiani considers there are eleven abdominal segments present ; but he treats as a segment a projection, called the cauda, situate over the anus ; this structure does not appear to be homologous with the rectal cauda we have just mentioned. In Coccidae the number of abdominal segments is apparently reduced. Schiödte states [2] that the older authorities are correct in respect of the stigmata ; there are, he says, in Heteroptera invariably ten pairs ; one for each thoracic segment ; and seven abdominal, placed on the ventral face of the pleural fold of the abdomen. In some cases there are additional orifices on the external surface that have been taken for stigmata, though they are really orifices of odoriferous glands ; these openings may exist on the metasterna or on the dorsal surface of the abdomen. The lateral margins of the abdomen are frequently greatly developed in Heteroptera, and are called " connexivum ; " the upper and lower surfaces of the body meeting together far within the marginal outline. Dr Anton Dohrn many years ago [3] called attention to the extremely remarkable structure of the terminal segments in many male Hemiptera ; and the subject has been subsequently very imperfectly treated by the present writer and other entomologists, but it has never received the attention it deserves.

    Ent. Nachr. xix. 1893, p. 369.

[2] *Naturhist. Tidskr.* (3) vi. 1896 ; translated in *Ann. N. Hist.* (4), vi. 1870, p. 225.   [3] *Ent. Zeit. Stettin,* xxvii. 1866, p. 321.

In the females of numerous Heteroptera and Homoptera (Capsidae, Cicadidae, etc.) there is a well-developed ovipositor, that serves both as a cutting instrument to make slits in the stems of plants, and as a director to introduce the eggs therein. Verhoeff considers that it always consists of two pairs of processes (though one pair may be very small), one from the eighth abdominal segment, the other from the ninth.[1]

The antennae usually have very few joints, often as few as four or five, their maximum number of about twenty-five being attained in the males of some Coccidae, this condition being, however, present in but few of even this family. In *Belostoma* (Fig. 279) they assume extremely curious forms, analogous to what we find in the Coleopterous genus *Hydrophilus*. In addition to the compound eyes, there are usually ocelli, either two or three in number, but wanting in many cases. The usual number of joints of the tarsi is three, but in Coccidae there is only one joint.

The wings (Fig. 258) exhibit much diversity. The anterior pair usually differ greatly from the posterior ; they are called elytra, hemi-elytra or tegmina. This difference in the two pairs is the rule in the first of the great divisions of the Order, and the name Heteroptera is derived from the fact. In this Sub-Order the front wings close over the back, and are more or less horny, the apical part being, however, membranous. Systematists make use of the wings for the purpose of classification in Heteroptera, and distinguish the following parts, " clavus," " corium," " membrane," the corium being the larger horny division, the clavus the part lying next the scutellum and frequently very sharply distinguished from the corium ; the membrane is the apical part. The outer or costal part of the wing is also often

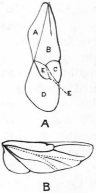

Fig. 258.—Alar organs of a Capsid bug (*Capsus lani-arius*). **A,** Elytron : A, clavus ; B, corium ; C, cuneus ; D, membrane ; E, E, cell of the membrane ; **B,** hind-wing.

sharply delimited, and is called the " embolium ; " in the great family Capsidae and a few others, the outer apical part of the

---

[1] *Ent. Nachr.* xix. 1893, p. 375.

corium is differentiated from the rest of the surface, and is termed the "cuneus." In Plataspides, one of the divisions in which the alar organs are entirely covered by the scutellum, they are modified in a very remarkable manner. In the Homoptera the divisions named above do not exist, and the wings in repose are placed in a different position, as stated in our definition of the Order. It is said to be very difficult to homologise the wing-nervures of Hemiptera, and nothing appears to be known as to the mode of their development.

The alar organs in Hemiptera exhibit a very frequent form of variation within the limits of the same species; this has not yet been elucidated.[1] In some cases in the Heteroptera nearly all the individuals of a generation may have the wings aborted; sometimes this occurs as a local variation. In Aphidae the occurrence of winged and wingless individuals is very common, and has even become an important factor in their extraordinary life cycles. (See *Chermes*, etc., subsequently.)

Internal anatomy.—The alimentary canal presents considerable diversity and some remarkable features. There is a slender tube-like oesophagus and a large crop. It is difficult to assign any of the parts posterior to this to the divisions usual in other Insects, and it is said that the distinction of parts histologically is as vague as it is anatomically. In the Heteroptera the Malpighian tubes open into two (or one) vesicular dilatations seated immediately in front of the short rectum: between this point and the crop there may be a very elongate, slender portion with one or more dilatations, these parts apparently replacing the true or chylific stomach. There is no gizzard. In the Homoptera the relations of the divisions of the alimentary canal are even more puzzling; the canal is elongated and forms coils, and these are connected with tissues and tunics so as to make their dissection extremely difficult. List says that there are great differences in the alimentary canal among the members of the one family Coccidae. There are usually four Malpighian tubes, but in Coccidae there is only one pair, and in Aphidae none. The excretory cells of these tubes are in Hemiptera of remarkably large size. There is a large development of salivary glands, at least two pairs existing. There can be little doubt that some of their products are used for purposes of injection, as

---

[1] On this subject, see Reuter, *Ann. Soc. ent. France* (5) v. 1875, p. 225.

already described, though Künckel came to the conclusion that the saliva when placed in living plants is totally innocuous.[1]

The ganglia of the nervous system are all concentrated in the thorax and head. In some cases (in various Homoptera) the infra-oesophageal ganglion is placed at a distance from the supra-oesophageal ganglion, and may even be united with the thoracic mass of ganglia (*Orthezia*, etc.); in this case the chitinous frame-work of the mouth-parts is interposed between the supra- and the infra-oesophageal ganglia. In *Pentatoma* all the three ganglionic masses are brought into close proximity, but in *Nepa* the thoracic mass of ganglia and the infra-oesophageal ganglion are widely separated.

The ovarian tubes vary greatly in number: according to List in *Orthezia cataphracta* the number differs considerably in different individuals, and even in the two ovaries of the same individual, the number being usually ten. The testes are not placed in a common tunic, though they are frequently approximated or even contiguous.[2]

The smell of bugs is notorious. In many species it is not unpleasant, though as a rule it is decidedly offensive. It is a remarkable fact that the structures connected with the production of this odour are different in many cases in the young and in the adult. The odour emitted by the latter proceeds from a sac seated at the base of the abdomen, and opening exteriorly by means of an orifice on each side of the metasternum; while in the young there are two glands situated more dorsally and a little more backwards, and opening on two of the dorsal plates of the abdomen (Fig. 255, A).[3] In the young the dorsum of the abdomen, where the stink-glands open, is exposed, but this part in the adult is covered by the wings. The odorific apparatus is specially characteristic of Heteroptera, and Künckel states that there is so much variety that generic and even specific characters might be drawn from conditions of the stink-glands. As a rule they are most constantly present in the plant-feeding forms; in some essentially carnivorous forms (Reduviidae, Nepidae, Noto-

[1] *Ann. Soc. ent. France* (4) vii. 1867, p. 45.
[2] The chief work on the internal anatomy of Hemiptera is still Dufour's *Recherches anatomiques et physiologiques sur les Hémiptères, Mem. Savans Étrangers, Paris*, iv. 1833, p. 129.
[3] Künckel, *Ann. Soc. ent. France* (4) vii. 1867, p, 45, and *C.R. Ac. Paris*, cxx. 1895, p. 1002.

nectidae) they are entirely absent.   The offensive matter emitted by *Notonecta* is of a different nature, and is probably anal in origin.

Metamorphosis or postembryonic development.—In the language of the systematists of metamorphosis, Hemiptera are said to be Homomorpha Paurometabola—that is, the young differ but little from the adult.   According to Brauer's generalisations they are Menorhynchous, Oligonephrous, Pterygogenea, *i.e.* they have a sucking mouth that does not change during life, few Malpighian tubes, and are winged in the adult state.   It is generally admitted that the Homoptera do not completely agree with Heteroptera in respect of the metamorphosis, it being more marked in the former, and in Coccidae attaining (as we shall mention when discussing that family) nearly if not quite the condition of complete metamorphosis of a peculiar kind. Unfortunately we are in almost complete ignorance as to the details of the life-histories and development of Heteroptera, so that we can form no generalised opinion as to what the post-embryonic development really is in them, but there are grounds for supposing that considerable changes take place, and that these are chiefly concentrated on the last ecdysis.   The young of some bugs bear but little resemblance to the adult ; the magnificently-coloured species of *Eusthenes* (Fig. 255), before they attain the adult condition are flat, colourless objects, almost as thin as a playing-card ; it is well known that the extraordinary structures that cover and conceal the body in Plataspides, Scutellerides, Membracides, etc., are developed almost entirely at the last moult : it is not so well known that some of these changes occur with much rapidity.   A very interesting account of the processes of colour-change, as occurring in *Poecilocapsus lineatus* at the last ecdysis, has been given by Lintner,[1] and from this it appears that the characteristic coloration of the imago is entirely developed in the course of about two hours, forming a parallel in this respect with Odonata.   When we come to deal with Aphidae we shall describe the most complex examples of cycles of generations that exist in the whole of the animal kingdom.

Fossil Hemiptera.—Hemiptera are believed to have existed in the Palaeozoic epoch, but the fossils are not numerous, and opinions differ concerning them.   *Eugereon hockingi*, a Per-

---

[1] In Slingerland's *Cornell Univ. Bull.* No. 58, 1893, p. 222.

mian fossil, was formerly supposed to be a Homopterous Insect, but it is very anomalous, and its claim to a position in Hemiptera is denied by Brauer,[1] who considers it to be Orthopterous. It is now generally recognised that this fossil requires complete reconsideration. Another Permian fossil, *Fulgorina,* is admitted to be Homopterous by Scudder, Brauer and Brongniart. Scudder thinks the Carboniferous *Phthanocoris* was an Archaic Heteropterous Insect, and if correct this would demonstrate that both of the two great Sub-Orders of Hemiptera existed in Palaeozoic times. Brauer, however, is inclined to refer this fossil to Homoptera, and Brongniart[2] speaks of it as being without doubt a Fulgorid. *Dictyocicada, Rhipidioptera* and *Meganostoma,* from the Carboniferous shales of Commentry, have also been referred to Fulgoridae by Brongniart, but the evidence of their alliance with this group is far from satisfactory. In the Secondary epoch numerous Hemiptera existed, and are referred to several of the existing families. They come chiefly from the Oolite. In the Eocene of the Isle of Wight a fossil has been discovered that is referred to the existing Homopterous genus *Triecphora.*

We are not entitled to conclude more from these facts than that Homoptera probably appeared before Heteroptera, and date back as far as the Carboniferous epoch.

Classification and families.—No complete catalogue of Hemiptera exists, but one by M. Severin is in course of publication. It is probable that there are about 18,000 species at present described, two-thirds of this number being Heteroptera. In Britain we have about 430 species of Heteroptera and 600 of Homoptera. The classification of the Order is not in a very advanced condition. The following table exhibits the views of Schiödte[3] in a modified form :—

Front of head not touching the coxae.   I. HETEROPTERA.
Front of head much inflexed so as to be in contact with the coxae.
                                                         II. HOMOPTERA.

Sub-Order I. HETEROPTERA.

Posterior coxae nearly globose, partly embedded in cavities, and having a rotatory movement. Mostly terrestrial forms.   1. Trochalopoda.
Posterior coxae not globose, larger, and not embedded ; their articulation with sternum almost hinge-like. Posterior aspect of hind femur usually

---

[1] *SB. Ak. Wien.* xci. 1 Abth., 1885, p. 275.
[2] *Les Insectes fossiles, etc.,* 1894, p. 452.   [3] *Ann. Nat. Hist.* (4) vi. 1870, p. 225.

more or less modified for the reception of the tibia when closed on it : mostly aquatic forms.   2. Pagiopoda.

Division 1. TROCHALOPODA.

This division includes the majority of the families of Heteroptera—viz. the whole of the terrestrial families except Saldidae, and it also includes Nepidae, a family of water-bugs.

Division 2. PAGIOPODA.

This includes the six purely aquatic families of Heteroptera, except Nepidae, which appear to have very little connection with the other aquatic bugs. The only terrestrial Insects included in the family are the Saldidae ; in these the femora are not modified as they are in the aquatic forms. Hemiptera that live on the surface of water, not in the water, are classed with the terrestrial species. With these exceptions this arrangement agrees with that of **Gymnocerata** and **Cryptocerata** as usually adopted,[1] and therefore followed in the following pages. Schiödte's characters, moreover, do not divide his two divisions at all sharply.

Sub-Order II. HOMOPTERA.

Tarsi usually three-jointed	.	.	Series Trimera.
„ „ two-jointed	.	.	„ Dimera.
„ „ of one joint	.	.	„ Monomera.

The classification of Homoptera is in a most unsatisfactory state ;[2] no two authors are agreed as to the families to be adopted in the series Trimera. We have recognised only five—viz. Cicadidae, Fulgoridae, Membracidae, Cercopidae, and Jassidae. The Dimera consists of Psyllidae, Aphidae, Aleurodidae ; and the Monomera of Coccidae only. It is usual to associate the Dimera and Monomera together under the name of either Phytophthires or Sternorhyncha, but no satisfactory definition can be given of these larger groups, though it seems probable that the families of which they are composed are natural and distinct.

Sub-Order I. HETEROPTERA.

Series 1. Gymnocerata.

The majority of the terrestrial families of Heteroptera form the series Gymnocerata, in which the antennae are conspicuous, and can be moved about freely in front of the head, while in

---

[1] A table of the families is given by Ashmead, but does not work out quite satisfactorily, *Entom. Americana*, iv. 1888, p. 65 ; a brief table of the characters of the British families is given by Saunders, *Hemiptera-Heteroptera of the British Islands*, 1892, p. 12.

[2] Those who wish to see tables of the families are referred to Ashmead, *loc. cit. ;* to Pascoe, *Ann. Nat. Hist.* (5) ix. 1882, p. 424 ; to Stål's *Hemiptera Africana*, vol. iv. 1866 ; and for the families found in Britain to Edwards, *Hemiptera-Homoptera of the British Islands.* For a discussion in Danish on the value of the characters used, cf. Hansen, *Ent. Tidskr.* xi. 1890, pp. 19-76.

Cryptocerata they are hidden.   The series Gymnocerata includes all the terrestrial Heteroptera, and the two families, Hebridae and Hydrometridae, which live on the surface of the water or in very damp places ; while Cryptocerata includes all the forms that live under water.

Fam. 1. Pentatomidae.—*Scutellum very large, at least half as long as the abdomen, often covering the whole of the after-body and alar appendages.   Antennae often five-jointed.   Proboscis-sheath four-jointed.   Ocelli two.   Each tarsal claw with an appendage.*—This, the largest and most important family of the Heteroptera, includes upwards of 4000 species, and an immense variety of forms.   It is divided into no less than fourteen sub-families.   The species of one of these, Plataspides, are remarkable for their short, broad forms, and the peculiar condition of the alar organs, which are so completely concealed by the great scutellum that it is difficult to believe the Insects are not entirely apterous. The head is usually inconspicuous though broad, but in a few forms it is armed with horns. Though this sub-family includes upwards of 200 species, and is very widely distributed in the Old World, it has no representatives in America.   The Scutel-lerides also have the body covered by the scutellum, but their organs of flight are less peculiar than they are in the Plataspides ; the Insects of this sub-family are highly remarkable on account

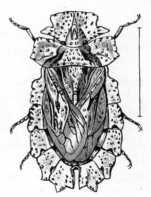

Fig. 259.—*Phloea corticata.* South America.

of their varied and frequently vivid coloration ; some of them are metallic, and the colour of their integuments differs greatly in some cases, according to whether the specimen is wet or dry ; hence the appearance after death is often very different from that of the living specimen.   These Insects are extremely numerous in species.   The sub-family Phloeides (Fig. 259), on the contrary, includes only three or four South American species : they have no resemblance at all to other Pentatomidae ; they are flat, about an inch long, and look like scales of bark, in this respect agreeing with *Ledra* and some other Homoptera. The South American sub-family Cyrtocorides (Fig. 260) is of equally small extent; the species are of strange irregular shapes, for which we can find no reason. The Tessaratomides includes many of the largest Hemiptera-Heteroptera, some of its members attaining two inches in length.

The great family Pentatomidae, containing about 400 species, is represented in Britain by about 36 native species, the most interesting of which are perhaps those of the genus *Acanthosoma*. De Geer noticed long ago that the female of *A. griseum* exhibits great solicitude for its young, and his statement has since been confirmed by Mr. Parfitt and the Rev. J. Hellins, who found that the mother not only protects the eggs but also the young, and that for a considerable time after hatching.[1]

FIG. 260.—*Cyrtocoris monstrosus.* South America. × 3.

Very little is known as to the life-histories of Pentatomidae. In some cases the young are very different in appearance from the adults. The peculiar great scutellum is not developed till the mature condition is reached. But little attention has been given to the habits of Pentatomidae; it is generally considered that they draw their nutriment from plants; the American *Euthyrhynchus floridanus* has, however, been noticed to suck the honey-bee, and we think it probable that a good many Pentatomids will be found to attack Insects.

The term Pentatomidae as applied to this family is of modern origin : in most books the equivalent group is called Scutata, or Scutati, and the term Pentatomidae is restricted in these works to the sub-family called Pentatomides in the system we adopt.

Fam. 2. Coreidae.—*Scutellum not reaching to the middle of the body ; proboscis-sheath four-jointed ; ocelli present ; antennae generally elongate and four-jointed, inserted on the upper parts of the sides of the head ; femora not knobbed at the tip.*—The members of this great family are easily recognised by the above characters; formerly it was called Supericornia in connection with the characteristic position of the antennae. About 1500 species are known, and they are arranged in no less than twenty-nine sub-families. Many of them are Insects of large size, and they

[1] *Ent. Mag.* vii. 1870, p. 53.

frequently have a conspicuous disc, or dilatation, on one of the joints of the antennae. Another very curious and, as yet, inexplicable peculiarity very commonly met with among them, is that the hind legs may be of great size and deformed; either the femora or the tibiae, or both, being very much distorted or armed with projections. Brilliant colour is here comparatively rare, the general tone being indefinite tints of browns, greys, or smoky colours. The South American genus *Holymenia* (*Copius*

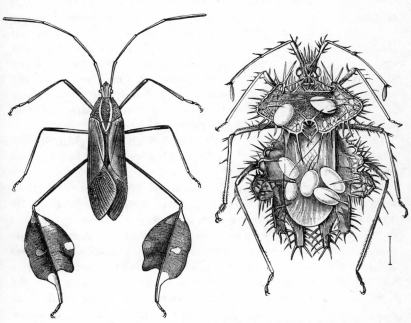

FIG. 261.—*Diactor bilineatus.*
South America. × $\frac{3}{2}$.

FIG. 262.—*Phyllomorpha laciniata,* carrying some of its eggs. Spain.

of older authors) consists of slender forms, having the elytra transparent even on the basal part like Homoptera; this and some other peculiarities give the species of this genus a certain resemblance to Insects of other Orders; Westwood says that *Diateina holymenoides* (Diptera) greatly resembles a bug of the genus *Holymenia.* The tropical American genus *Diactor* consists of a few species of elegant colour having the hind legs very peculiarly shaped, the tibiae being flattened and expanded in a sail-like manner, and ornamented with agreeable colours different

from those on the rest of the body; they are made more conspicuous by the femora being remarkably long and thin; it is
probable that they are used as ornaments. The sub-family
Phyllomorphides consists of about a dozen species, and is found
in several of the western parts of the Eastern hemisphere, one
species, *P. laciniata*, occurring in Southern Europe. This Insect is
of very delicate texture, and the sides of the body are directed
upwards and deeply divided so that a sort of basin is formed, of
which the dorsum of the body is the floor; the Insect is very
spinose, and is thus enabled to carry its eggs, the spines helping
to retain them in position on the back. It is said to be the male
that thus carries the eggs. This species is able to stridulate,
and when doing so vibrates its antennae with excessive rapidity.
We have only about a score of species of Coreidae in Britain,
and none of the remarkable forms of the family are among them.

Fam. 3. Berytidae.—*Very slender Insects with the first
joint of the antennae and the femora thickened at the tips.*—
This small family was not distinguished from Coreidae by the
older authors. It consists of about fifty species, eight of which
are found in Britain.

Fam. 4. Lygaeidae.—*The characters are the same as those
mentioned for Coreidae, except as regards the insertion of the
antennae; the upper surface or face of the head is not so flat, but
is transversely convex, so that seen in profile the antennae appear
to be inserted well down on the sides of the head.*—The name
Infericornia was formerly applied to these Insects. They
are on the average of smaller size than the members of the
Coreidae or Pentatomidae, and are much less conspicuous in colour
and form; a good many of the larger Lygaeids arc, however,
variegate with black, yellow, and red. The family is very numerous
in species, about 1400 being known; they are arranged in
thirteen sub-families; we have about sixty species in Britain,
nearly all small. *Eremocoris* lives, when immature, in the nests
of the wood-ant, according to Wasmann. The family includes
some notorious Insect-pests. The Chinch-bug, *Blissus leuco-
pterus*, commits very serious ravages on corn and grasses in North
America. The Cotton-stainer, *Dysdercus suturellus* is also very
injurious to cotton in certain parts of the New World: its growth
has been described by Riley,[1] who thinks a dye valuable for

[1] *Insect Life*, i. 1889, p. 234.

commercial purposes might be procured from the Insect. This bug has recently developed the habit of sucking oranges, and has thus become injurious in Florida, as the fruit readily decays after it has been punctured by these Insects. The phenomenon of "micropterism" is exhibited by numerous Lygaeids, as well as by Pyrrhocoridae.

Fam. 5. Pyrrhocoridae.—*Distinguished from Lygaeidae only by the absence of ocelli,* and not recognised as a distinct family by all Hemipterists. About 300 species are included. Our only British member is the notorious *Pyrrhocoris apterus;* it is, however, very rare in this country, though it abounds on the Continent, and has been the object of investigation by embryologists and others. It displays in a most marked manner the curious dimorphism as to the alar organs that is so common in certain divisions of Hemiptera ; the elytra and wings being sometimes normally developed, while in other cases the wings are entirely absent, and the horny, basal part of the elytra only is present. In some localities, and in some years, only the micropterous form is found, while on other occasions there may be a large percentage of the macropterous form. The abundance of this Insect has enabled the French chemist Physalix to obtain an amount of its colouring matter sufficient for analysis; as the result he procured a substance, insoluble in water, very closely allied to carotine.[1] The Oriental Insect *Lohita grandis* is one of the most remarkable of Bugs, the male of the Sumatran variety being over two inches in length, having enormously long antennae, and the abdomen extended to about twice the normal length, while the other sex is in the usual condition in these respects. The species is said to be injurious to the cotton-plant in India.

Fam. 6. Tingidae.—*Tarsi two-jointed. Elytra more or less reticulate, consisting of strong, irregular, thick lines forming a framework of cells, the enclosed part of the cell being of different texture and frequently transparent ; antennae with terminal joint more or less knob-like, the preceding joint very long ; ocelli wanting ; pronotum prolonged behind, covering the scutellum ; front coxae placed at the back of the thorax.*—This is the first of a series of families with only two joints to the feet. These little bugs are very remarkable objects, and exhibit much variety in their peculiar

[1] *C.R. Ac. Sci. Paris,* cxviii. 1894, p. 1282.

sculpture, which in numerous forms attains a condition of elegance well worthy of attention. There are nearly 300 species known, and in Britain we have about a score. The characters we have given above do not apply to the genus *Piesma*, though

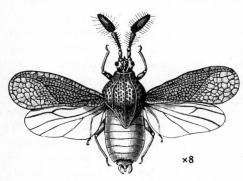

it is usually placed in this family; its scutellum is not covered, and ocelli are present. Although but little is known as to the nature of the lives of Tingidae, yet it was pointed out long ago by Réaumur that a species of the family (probably *C. clavicorne*, Fig. 263), lives in deformations of the flowers of the Labiate

FIG. 263.—*Copium clavicorne.* Europe.
(After Rübsaamen.)

plant now called *Teucrium chamaedrys*; Frauenfeld has more recently confirmed this observation, and shown that the closely allied *C. teucrii* affects the flowers of *T. montanum* in a similar manner.[1]

Fam. 7. Aradidae.—*Very flat, broad; scutellum exposed, large or moderate; abdomen broader than the alar organs, which it frequently encases like a broad frame. Front coxae placed in the middle of the prosternum.*—These very flat Insects, of obscure colour, have frequently very peculiar sculpture. They live under bark, or

on fungi growing from bark, and are supposed to draw their nutriment from the fungi, though but little is actually known as to their natural history. The family is almost cosmopolitan, and includes about 300 species, of which five occur in England. The small sub-family Isoderminae consists of a few species that are placed only provisionally in Aradidae; they

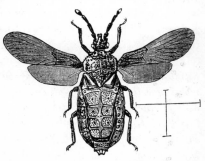

FIG. 264.—*Aradus orientalis.* Siam.

differ from the normal members by there being no groove on the

[1] *Verh. Ges. Wien.* iii. 1858, p. 157.

breast, so that the rostrum is free. Of the five species, three occur in Chili and Patagonia, two in Tasmania, and one in Australia.

Fam. 8. Hebridae.—*Minute bugs, of semiaquatic habits, clothed beneath with a dense, minute, silvery pubescence; antennae five-jointed; legs of not more than average length; elytra in larger part membranous.*—This small family consists altogether of only about a dozen species; we have two species of the genus *Hebrus* in Britain; they are usually found in very wet moss.

Fam. 9. Hydrometridae.—*Form very diverse; antennae four-jointed, tarsi two-jointed. Coxae usually widely separated. Either wingless or with elytra of one texture throughout, having no membranous part. Under surface with a minute velvet-like pubescence. In many forms the legs are of great length.*—Although of comparatively small extent—scarcely 200 species being at present known—this family is of great interest from the habit possessed by its members of living on the surface of water. In the case of the notorious genus *Halobates* (Fig. 265) the Insects can even successfully defy the terrors of Neptune and live on the ocean many hundreds of miles from land. There is great variety of form among Hydrometridae. The European and British genus *Mesovelia* is of short form, and but little dissimilar from ordinary land-bugs, with which, indeed, it is connected by means of the genus *Hebrus*, already noticed. *Mesovelia* represents the sub-family Mesoveliides, which, though consisting of only four species, occurs in both hemispheres, and in the tropics as well as in the temperate regions. Our species, *M. furcata*, walks on the surface of the water, the movements of its legs and the position of its coxae being those of land-bugs.

Fig. 265.—*Halobates sobrinus.* Under surface of a female carrying eggs. Pacific Ocean (Marquesas).

Another British Insect—the highly remarkable *Hydrometra stagnorum*—is of excessively slender form, with long thin legs, by aid of which it walks on the surface-film of water, above which its body is held well separated. It is easily drowned, and if submerged it has great difficulty in escaping from the water. This genus represents the sub-family Hydrometrides, and is apparently almost cosmopolitan. *Velia currens* is another common British Insect ; it loves the eddies and currents of backwaters on burns and streams, and is very abundant in Scotland. An American ally, *Rhagovelia plumbea*, appears to be not uncommon on the surface of the ocean in the Gulf of Mexico, near the shores. The great majority of the family belong to the division Gerrides, of which the curious, long Insects that float so lazily and skim so easily on the surface of quiet streams are typical. The species of the genus now called *Gerris*, but formerly known as *Hydrometra* are apparently distributed all over the world; we have ten in Britain. They have very long legs, and on being alarmed move away with the greatest ease.

The genus *Halobates* includes at present fifteen species. They are found on the ocean, where the surface-water is warm, in various parts of the world. They are destitute of any trace of alar organs, the meso- and meta-thorax are closely united and large, while the abdomen is very small, so that the body is of oval form ; the middle legs are thrown so far back that they are placed immediately over the posterior pair. When the sea is calm these Insects skim over the surface with rapidity, but disappear as soon as it becomes agitated. They are believed to feed on small animals recently deceased ; Witlaczil says on the juices of jelly-fish. The young are frequently met with, and there can be no doubt that the whole life-cycle may be passed through by the Insect far away from land. The Italian ship *Vettor Pisani* met with a bird's feather floating on the ocean off the Galapagos Islands, covered with eggs which proved to be those of *Halobates* in an advanced stage of development. It was formerly believed that the female carries the eggs for some time after their exclusion, and although this has since been denied, it is nevertheless an undoubted fact, for it was observed by Mr. J. J. Walker,[1] to whom we are indebted for a specimen having the eggs still attached to the body, as shown in Fig 265. Mr. Walker believes the bugs shelter themselves when the sea is at all rough by keeping at a sufficient distance

[1] *Ent. Mag.* xxix. 1893, p. 227.

below the surface; they can dive with facility, and are gregarious.
They are frequently found close to the shore, and Mr. Walker
has even met with them on land.   The stink-glands of other

Hemiptera are said
by Nassonoff to be
replaced in *Halobates*
by peculiar ventral
glands.   An allied
genus, *Halobatodes*,
was supposed to be
oceanic, but this is
not the case, some of
the species having
been found recently in
fresh water in India,
and others in estu-
aries at Port Darwin.
A remarkable allied
form, *Hermatobates
haddoni*, was recently
discovered by Pro-
fessor Haddon in
Torres Straits.   Apart
from the oceanic life,
Halobates is by no
means the most ex-
traordinary of the
Hydrometridae.   The
Javanese   *Ptilomera
laticaudata*   repeats
some of its peculi-

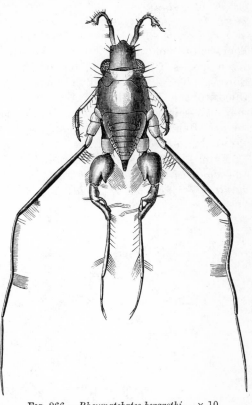

Fig. 266.—*Rheumatobates bergrothi.*   × 10.
West Indies.   (After Meinert.)

arities, and is of larger size, with the sexes very different.   The
most remarkable of the family is perhaps the fresh-water genus
Rheumatobates (Fig. 266), in which the males have peculiar
prehensile antennae that look like legs.   These curious Insects
inhabit North America and the West Indies.

We may here notice an enigmatic Insect called *Hemidiptera
haeckeli* by Léon.   From the single specimen known it is concluded that the Insect has only one pair of wings, and that they
are attached to the metathorax.   It is, however, possible, as

suggested by Bergroth,[1] that the anterior pair have been detached by some accident.

Fam. 10. Henicocephalidae.—*Head swollen behind the eyes so as to form a sort of globe, on the anterior part of which the ocelli are placed. Rostrum extremely short. Elytra rather large, of one consistence throughout ; conspicuously veined.*—There is only one genus; it is very widely distributed, about a dozen species being known ; one of these occurs in the south of Europe. These curious little bugs appear to be most nearly allied to the Reduviidae. According to Westwood and others they are somewhat gregarious; a Tasmanian species dances in the air after the fashion of midges or May-flies, and dispenses an agreeable, musk-like odour.

Fam. 11. Phymatidae.—*Front legs of peculiar structure, short and stout, with long coxae, short thick femora, and tibiae curvate, pointed ; frequently without tarsi.*—The Insects of this family are

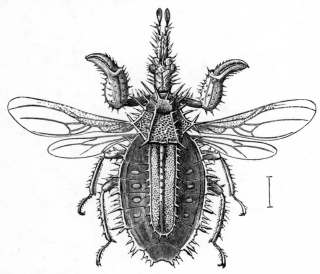

Fig. 267.—*Carcinocoris binghami* (Phymatidae). Burma.

believed to be predaceous, the structure of the legs being such as is called raptorial, and one species, *Phymata erosa*, being known to capture and suck honey-bees in North America. There are only about seventy species of Phymatidae known. We have

[1] *Wien. ent. Zeit.* xi. 1892, p. 169.

none in Britain, though there are a few in Southern Europe; one of these, *P. crassipes,* extends as far north as Paris. The distinction of the family from Reduviidae is doubtful.[1] There are a few very rare forms (Fig. 267) in which the front tibia is articulated to the femur in such a way that a pair of pincers is formed : the tarsus is in this form, as well as in some other Phymatidae, absent.

Fam. 12. Reduviidae.

—Head more or less elongate, very movable, eyes placed much in front of the thorax, ocelli, when present, behind the eyes. Proboscis short, or moderately short, not extending on to the breast, in repose curved under the head so as to form a loop therewith. Elytra, when present, consisting of three divisions. Tarsi three-jointed.—This is one of the largest and most important families of Hemiptera. Upwards of 2000 species are already known; the habits seem to be chiefly of a predaceous nature, the creatures drawing their nutriment from the animal rather than from the vegetable kingdom, and their chief prey being in all probability other kinds of Insects. There is, perhaps, no family of Insects exhibiting a greater variety of form and colour. The Emesids are amongst the most delicate of Insects, equalling in this respect the daddy-

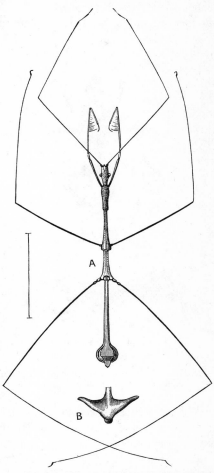

Fig. 268.—*Ghilianella filiventris.* Brazil. **A,** the female Insect. **B,** extremity of the body of the male.

---

[1] *Monograph of Phymatidae:* Handlirsch, *Ann. Hofmus. Wien,* xii. 1897, p. 127.

long-leg flies; they are, however, highly predaceous; their front legs are peculiarly formed for capturing and holding their prey, and have long coxae, like *Mantis*, so that these Insects are commonly mistaken for small or young Mantises, from which their sucking proboscis at once distinguishes them.   This curious starved-looking form of bug reaches its maximum of peculiarity in the South American genus *Ghilianella* (Fig. 268).   According to Pascoe the linear form enables the young larva to be carried about by the mother, the long slender abdomen of the larva being curled around the thorax of the parent. *Ploiaria pallida*, from Woodlark Island, is an Insect of excessive fragility and elegance, with the long thin legs coloured with alternate patches of black on a white ground, giving rise to a very curious appearance remarkably analogous to what we find in some of the equally delicate daddy-long-leg flies.

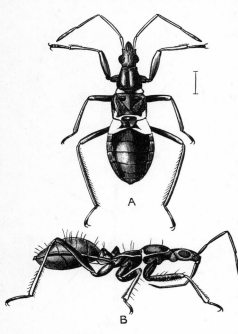

FIG. 269.—*Nabis lativentris*, young. Cambridge.
A, Insect seen from above ; **B**, profile.

We have three species of Emesides in Britain, but most of our Reduviidae belong to the sub-family Nabides.   These approximate to ordinary bugs in appearance and characters more than do any other of the Reduviidae.   One of our indigenous Nabides is of great interest from the curious resemblance it has to an ant (Fig. 269).   The likeness is brought about by the sides of the base of the abdomen being very pallid in colour, except a dark mark in the middle ; this mark is in shape like the pedicel of an ant.   Viewed in profile it is found that on the base of the abdomen there is an elevation like the " scale " in this position in

ants, and that the abdomen is extremely ant-like in form.   This
resemblance is quite parallel with that of an Orthopteron to an
ant (see Vol. V. p. 323); the Insect is by no means uncommon,
and it is strange that this curious case
of resemblance should hitherto have
escaped notice.   The bug runs about on
plants and flowers, and is frequently in
company with ants, but we do not know
whether it preys on them.   Not the

Fig. 270.—*Ptilocnemus sidnicus.*
Australia.   (After Mayr.)

least remarkable of the
facts   connected   with
this Insect is that the
resemblance is confined
to the earlier instars ;
the adult bug not being
like an ant.   We may
here mention that there
are numerous bugs that
closely   resemble   ants,
and that on the whole
there is reason to be-
lieve that the resem-
bling forms are actually
associated   during   life,
though we really know
very little as to this last
point.

The little sub-family
Holoptilides,   with
twenty-five species, but
widely   distributed   in

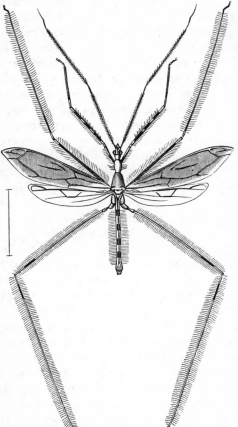

Fig. 271.—*Myiodocha tipulina.*   China.

the Eastern hemisphere, is remarkable on account of the feathered

antennae and legs of its .members (Fig. 270). Altogether fourteen sub-families are recognised, the most extensive one being
Harpactorides, including a great variety of remarkable forms ; in
the South American genus *Notocyrtus* (better known as *Saccoderes,*
Fig. 257), the prothorax is swollen and covers the body to a
greater or less extent in the fashion of a hood.   In *Yolinus*
and *Eulyes* the coloration is the most conspicuous system that
could be devised, the sides of the abdomen (connexivum) being
expanded into bright-red lobes on which are placed patches
of polished-black.   The most remarkable form of Reduviid
is, perhaps, one from China (Fig. 271) of considerable size,
of great fragility, and greatly resembling, like some Emesides,
a daddy-long-legs fly, though it does not belong to the Emesides.   It is an altogether anomalous form.   According to
Seitz there is found on the Corcovado in Brazil a Reduviid

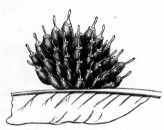

Fig. 272.—Eggs of *Endochus cinga-
lensis.* "The eggs are attached
to a leaf and to each other by a
viscid substance ; eggs red, the
cover pale yellow, with the club
white at the tip."—MS. note of
E. E. Green.

that exactly resembles one of the
dark stinging-wasps of the genus
Pepsis, and the bug makes the same
sort of movements as the wasp does,
though these are of a kind quite
different from those of ordinary bugs.[1]

Although the attacks of Reduviidae on animals are usually confined to the smaller and more
defenceless kinds, yet this is by no
means invariably the case ; there
are in fact numerous species that do
not hesitate to attack man himself.

Several species of *Reduvius* do this
in Southern Europe, and are frequently met with in houses.   *R.
personatus* is the only species of the genus in England ; though
far from common anywhere, it is sometimes found in houses, and
is said to destroy the common bed-bug ; it is able to pass its
whole existence in our habitations, for the young are found as
frequently as the adult, and are usually concealed by a quantity
of dusty matter, or refuse, adhering to the body.   This habit of
covering the body with some foreign substance is natural to the
Insect, the young that are found on trees being covered with
matter derived therefrom.   Darwin has given us an account of

---

[1] *Ent. Zeit. Stettin,* li. 1890, p. 281.

the Benchucha,[1] a bug an inch long, which in South America attacks human beings after the fashion of the common bed-bug. In this case no ill-effects follow the attack, but in the case of *Conorhinus sanguisuga* in Arizona, great pain and inflammation ensue and may end in the gathering and discharge of pus.

Not the least remarkable of characters of *Reduviidae* is the form of the eggs of some of the species (Fig. 272, and Vol. V. Fig. 78, C); the egg bearing a peculiar operculum, the purpose of which is at present quite mysterious.

Fam. 13. Aëpophilidae.—A single species forms this family. It is of considerable interest, as it is incapable of flight, passing a large part of its life covered by the sea. *Aëpophilus bonnairei is a small Insect with quite short head, without ocelli, and with the organs of flight represented by a pair of very short elytra, with rounded hind-margins.* It is found on the shores of Western France, and, as a great rarity, on our own south coast. It no doubt sucks small soft animals. In the Channel Islands it occurs in spots where it is nearly always covered by a considerable depth of water.

Fam. 14. Ceratocombidae.—*Minute bugs with ocelli and elytra. Rostrum free. Head not broad, somewhat prolonged in front; eyes close to the thorax. Elytra usually without a distinctly separated membrane. Tarsi three-jointed.*—This family includes at present only a few, minute, fragile bugs, that have often been classified with Cimicidae or Anthocoridae. We have only two British species, one of which, *Dipsocoris alienus*, is common amongst the damp shingle at the margins of the burns and waters of Scotland.

Fam. 15. Cimicidae.—*Ocelli absent; elytra very short and broad, so that the broad abdomen is left uncovered. Head short and broad. Rostrum received in a groove beneath the head. Tarsi three-jointed.*—Although this family consists of only a dozen species, it is the most notorious of all the Order, as it includes the detestable *Cimex lectularius* or common Bed-bug. This Insect is now peculiar to the habitations of man, and is said not to trouble savage races; or rather it is supposed to be present only when the habitations have a certain degree of comfort and permanence. It has no fixed period of the year for its development, but the generations succeed one another so long as the temperature

---

[1] *Naturalist's Voyage*, ed. 1884, p. 330 ; chap. xv.

is sufficiently elevated; during too cold weather the Insects merely become stupefied, their lives being as it were interrupted till warmth returns.   It is a favourite food with other Insects, and is destroyed by cockroaches and ants as well as by *Reduvius*; the small black ant *Monomorium* will, it is said, clear a house of the bed-bug in a few days.   Nothing is really known as to the origin of this Insect; it is now very widely distributed.   The other species of the family frequent birds and bats, and are very similar to the common bug.   The genus to which the bed-bug belongs is in many works called *Acanthia* instead of *Cimex*. Other authors apply the term *Acanthia* to *Salda*, but it is better to allow the name *Acanthia* to fall into disuse.

Fam. 16. Anthocoridae.—*Minute bugs, usually with ocelli and with elytra; the latter occasionally abbreviated, but usually fully developed, with membranous tip.   Head prolonged in the middle in front much beyond the insertion of the antennae; eyes not far from the thorax.   Rostrum free.*—These small and obscure Insects appear to be rather numerous in species, and to be chiefly connected with woods and forests.   Some of the species live in ants' nests.   We have 27 British species belonging to 11 genera.   About 200 species of the family are known.   The members of the sub-family Microphysides are remarkable from the great dissimilarity of the sexes, for which it is not possible to assign any reason.

Fam. 17. Polyctenidae. —*Proboscis-sheath three-jointed, tarsi four-jointed, antennae four-jointed.   Tegmina quite short, of one consistence.*—The four or five anomalous species forming this family are parasites on

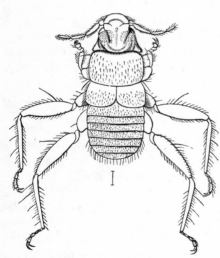

Fig. 273.—*Polyctenes fumarius.*
(After Westwood.)

bats of the genus *Molossus,* and have been found in both the Eastern and Western hemispheres.   Westwood, who first described

them,[1] treated them as aberrant Anoplura or Lice, but there do
not appear to be any sufficient grounds for removing these parasites from Hemiptera-Heteroptera.   The condition of their alar
organs reminds one of what exists in *Cimex* and *Aëpophilus,* and
the mouth is not known to possess any very peculiar structure.
We have had no opportunity of making a thorough examination
of *Polyctenes,* and therefore speak with some diffidence.

   Fam. 18. Capsidae.—*Moderate-sized or small bugs, of delicate
consistence, without ocelli ; the elytra and wings usually large in
proportion to the body, the former with two cells (occasionally*

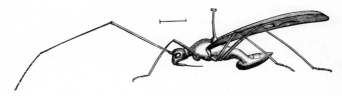

FIG. 274.—*Helopeltis* sp.   East India.

*only one) in the membrane.   Antennae four-jointed, the second joint
usually very long, the terminal two more slender than the others.
The proboscis not received in a groove.   Scutellum exposed, moderately large.   Tarsi three-jointed.   Female with an ovipositor
capable of exsertion.*—This family is one of the most extensive of
the Hemiptera ; we have about 170 species in Britain, where
they are most abundant in the south.   The exotic species have
been but little collected.   Their colours
are usually delicate rather than vivid,
and are never metallic.   They frequent
plants of all kinds, and many of them
skip by the aid of their wings with great
agility in the sunshine.   The majority
probably suck the juices of the plants, but
some are known to prey on other Insects.
The species of the Indian genus *Helopeltis* (Fig. 274) are remarkable by
possessing a knobbed spine projecting
straight up from the scutellum, making
the individual look as if it were a specimen with a pin through

FIG. 275.—Section of a stem with
egg of a Capsid bug allied
to *Helopeltis* (Moesa-blight).
× 58.   (After Dudgeon.)

---

[1] *Thesaurus ent. Oxoniensis,* 1874, p. 197.

it : they attack the tea-plant and do considerable damage.   They
are known as Mosquito-blight.   The egg is of comparatively large
size, and is placed by the bug in the stems of the tea-plant,
but attached to one end of the egg are two long slender threads
that project externally.   A similar egg (Fig. 275) and method
of oviposition have been described by Mr. Dudgeon as occurring
in another species of Capsidae, called Moesa-blight, in India.[1]

   Fam. 19. Saldidae.—*Head short and broad, with large, prominent eyes.   Ocelli present.   Proboscis not applied to under surface
of head or breast in repose.   Scutellum large, not covered.   Elytra
covering the upper surface of the abdomen, formed of three distinct
parts.   Tarsi three-jointed.*—These little bugs run with velocity
over mud in damp places, or live in wet moss ; some of them can
jump ; they are all of dark or obscure colour.   There are only
three genera : *Salda*, of which we have numerous British species,
being the principal one.

Series 2. Cryptocerata.

   The remaining families of Heteroptera are of aquatic habits,
and form in nearly all works a separate division called Hemiptera
Cryptocerata (or Hydrocorisae, or Hydrocores), distinguished by
the antennae being apparently absent ; they are, however, really
present, being situate on the under side of the head, to which
they are closely pressed, or in some cases placed in a pocket in
front of each eye.   There are six of these families.   Schiödte
is doubtless correct in treating this division as an unnatural one ;
it is, however, generally adopted, and is convenient for the purposes of nomenclature and arrangement.

   Fam. 20. Galgulidae or **Pelogonidae.**—*Form short and
broad ; head very broad, with prominent eyes, ocelli present.   Hind
legs thin, formed for running.*—The Insects of this family are
but little known ; they are only sub-aquatic in habits, frequenting damp places at the margins of streams and waters.   The
presence of ocelli distinguishes them from other water-bugs, with
which indeed the Galgulidae appear to be but little related.
There are only about twenty species of the family known.   We
possess none in Britain ; but one, *Pelogonus marginatus*, occurs

---

[1] *Ind. Mus. Notes*, iii. No. 5, 1894, p. 53.

in South Europe.   The other members of the family are very widely scattered over the surface of the earth.

Fam. 21. Nepidae.——*Abdomen furnished behind with a long slender siphon; front legs more or less elongate for capturing prey, placed quite at the front edge of the prothorax.*——This family consists of two interesting but very dissimilar genera, *Nepa* and *Ranatra*.   Both are widely distributed over the earth, and are rather numerous in species.[1]   We have one species of each genus in Britain. *Nepa cinerea*, the common "water-scorpion," is one of the commonest of Insects in Southern Britain, living concealed in shallow waters when nearly or quite stagnant. *Ranatra linearis* (Fig. 276) is much less common, and appears to be getting rarer; it is not recorded from farther north than Cambridge.

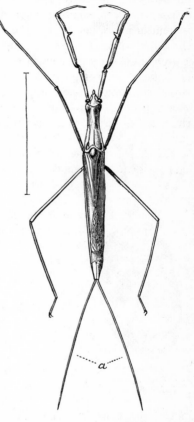

The nature of the respiratory arrangements in these Insects is of considerable interest; the long tube at the extremity of the body consists of two parts (as shown in Fig. 276) brought together in the middle, one from each side. Lacaze-Duthiers states that the processes are elongated pleurae, but in the young it is far from clear that this is the case.

Fig. 276—*Ranatra linearis*, with the two portions, *a*, of the respiratory siphon separated.   Cambridge.

However that may be, they seem to convey air to the true breathing organs, situate inside the cleft on the apical part of the abdomen itself; but details as to the way in which transfer of air is effected along this

[1] Ferrari, Monograph of *Nepa, Ann. Hofmus. Wien*, iii. 1888, p. 171.

very protracted passage are not forthcoming. The development in *Nepa* has been studied to a certain extent. The
apical stigmata are the only pair of the abdominal stigmata
that exist in the imago of *Nepa*, the other six pairs being
obliterated ; the third, fourth, and fifth, according to Schiödte, in
a very peculiar manner : hence, as Martin says,[1] the respiratory
system is metapneustic. In an earlier stage of the life, however,
these six pairs of stigmata exist in functional activity placed in
a groove on the under surface of the body ; so that the condition
is that termed peripneustic, and remains so till the final moult,
when the long siphon appears. In the early life there is a
short prolongation from the end of the body in connection with
the pair of grooves alluded to, but it is a single unpaired organ,

and does little therefore to explain the appearance of the siphon, which must, at present, be
considered as being suddenly developed at the
last moult.

The eggs of Nepidae are remarkable objects ;
that of the common water-scorpion bears seven
filaments at one end (Fig. 277); while that of
Ranatra is more elongate, and bears only two,
very elongate, threads. These eggs are deposited
in the stems of water-plants, being introduced
therein, so that the body of the egg is concealed
while the threads project : those of *Ranatra* are
placed in stems floating on the water, and in
consequence of the threads the stems look as if
they were infested by some fungus. The structure and formation of the eggs have been
investigated with considerable detail by Korschelt.[2] He looks on the filaments as pneu-

Fig. 277. — Egg of
Nepa cinerea.
(After Korschelt.)

matic, and considers that they supply a coating of air to the
body of the egg ; they consist of a spongy mass encircled by two
layers of egg-shell, both of these latter being peculiar in structure ; the spongy mass is continuous with a layer of the same
kind of substance placed on the interior of the shell of the body

---

[1] *Bull. Soc. Philomat.* (8) v. 1893, p. 57. There is some diversity of opinion
as to the respiratory orifices, and some authorities say that thoracic stigmata exist
even in the imago.

[2] *Acta Ac. German.* li. 1887, p. 224, and *Zeitschr. wiss. Zool.* xliii. 1886, p. 537.

of the egg.   It will be recollected that we have described (p. 562) an egg, apparently of the same nature, deposited by Capsids in the stems of land plants, so that it is very doubtful whether the threads are really connected with the aquatic development of the embryo in Nepidae.   But the most interesting feature connected with these eggs is, according to Korschelt, the mode of development of the filaments, which is *sui generis;* the shell of the egg is developed in the ordinary manner as an exudation or excretion from epithelial cells; but the shell of the filament is formed as an intracellular product; a mode of chitin-formation that appears to be peculiar to this structure.   Korschelt remarks that " it is in the highest degree worthy of attention how by any process of development through a large number of successive generations so complex a condition could be established as the result of adaptation to external conditions; and this becomes even more interesting when we remember that highly peculiar special processes and departures from the usual modes of tissue-formation are necessary to permit the development of this apparatus." [1]

Fam. 22. Naucoridae.——*No ocelli, and no terminal process to the body; front legs inserted on or near the front of the prosternum.   Anterior femora usually broad and flat.*——The members of this family are truly aquatic, and swim readily in the water.   The family is small, including about nine genera and thirty species, but, like many water-Insects, the genera are widely distributed.   We have two in Britain——one of them, *Naucoris,* common; the other, *Aphelocheirus,* rare.

Fam. 23. Belostomidae.——*No ocelli, and no long terminal tube to the body; front legs inserted near the front of the pro-sternum.   Posterior tibiae not spiny; flattened and provided with swimming hairs.*——Although these Insects have been classified with Nepidae they have but little relation therewith; on the other hand, the distinctions from Naucoridae are far less important.   The family includes some of the largest Insects.   The South American *Belostoma grande* attains a length of four or four and a half inches.   Notwithstanding their considerable size Belostomidae exist in very large numbers in some localities, and frequently destroy young fish by aid of the powerful though

---

[1] Korschelt, *Acta. t.c.* p. 245.   Compare the remarks we have made on p. 559 as to the peculiarities of eggs of many other Hemiptera.

short rostrum.   They appear to be unable to resist the attraction of artificial light, and are consequently sometimes destroyed in large numbers.   It has long been known that species of the genera *Diplonychus* and *Zaitha* carry their eggs on their backs.   There is no special receptacle for the purpose, but the eggs are kept in their peculiar position by means of a cement insoluble in water. It has been stated by Dimmock that they are placed in position by means of a long, flexible ovipositor.   Schmidt, however, found that a specimen of *Diplonychus*, bearing eggs and examined by him, was a male, and he subsequently found that this was the case with other egg-bearing individuals of other species, so that the mode in which the eggs are placed in this position and the object of

Fig.   278. — *Zaitha anura*, carrying eggs on its back. West Indies.

so curious a habit, remain uncertain.   The species of *Belostoma* are highly remarkable on account of the curious and complex structure of their antennae, in respect of which the nearest analogy is to be found in the large Coleoptera of the genus *Hydrophilus*.   A very deep, ear-like pocket, exactly suited to the form of the antennae, exists on the under side of the head ; hence in repose no sign of the peculiar shape of the antennae exists.   When the antennae are placed in this ear-like pocket only the one side of the basal joints is exposed, the long processes being received into the deep pocket. In *Hydrophilus* the antenna is used as an accessory organ of respiration, and it will be interesting to learn whether this

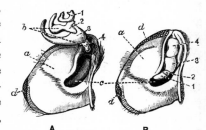

A   B

Fig. 279.—Antenna of *Belostoma* sp. **A,** One side of the under surface of the head, with antenna, *b*, extended ; **B,** with the antenna retracted. *a*, Side of head ; *c*, pocket for antenna ; *d*, position of the eyes. The corresponding joints of the antenna are numbered 1, 2, 3, 4 in each figure.

is also the case in *Belostoma*.   Belostomidae have patches of air-carrying pubescence, analogous with those of *Hydrophilus*, on the under sides of the body, elytra and wings, but we do not know how they are charged. Another extremely interesting analogy is found in the manner in which the elytra are locked to the body; a projection from the thoracic side-pieces, forming a long pouch, into which a fold on the inner side of the elytra fits, the two being subsequently locked by the action of some special projections. This arrangement is similar to that which exists in the anomalous family of water-beetles Pelobiidae. In order to make this mechanism more perfect the side-pieces in *Belostoma* form free processes. Martin has informed us that the young have the metasternal episternum prolonged to form a lamella that he thinks may be for respiratory purposes.[1] About twelve genera and upwards of fifty species of Belostomidae are known. None exist in our isles, but several species extend their range to Southern Europe. In the waters of the warm regions of the continents of both the Old and New Worlds they are common Insects, but as yet they have not been found in Australia.

Fam. 24. Notonectidae.—*Prosternum short, so that the legs are placed near the back part of it as well as near the front; back of the head overlapped by the front of the pronotum.*—The water-boatmen are extremely common in our ponds, where they may be seen rising to the surface and raising the posterior extremity of the body for breathing. They swim on their backs instead of in the usual position, and have an elaborate arrangement of long hairs on the body to assist them to carry about an air-supply. They are said to be lighter than the water, and to have some difficulty in keeping away from the surface. *Notonecta glauca* is the only British species, but we have a second minute Insect, *Plea minutissima*, belonging to the family. It lies in the mud at the bottom of shallow waters, and may sometimes be fished up in great numbers. It is considered by some authors to form a distinct family. The oviposition of *Notonecta* has been observed by Regimbart; the eggs are inserted into the stems of aquatic plants.

Fam. 25. Corixidae.—*Prosternum short, as in Notonectidae; summit of the head free from the thorax.*—We have numerous species of the genus *Corixa* in Britain; and others extremely similar in appearance occur in various parts of the world. The head is remarkably free, and capable of great rotation. On dissection it is found to be attached to the thorax only by a

[1] *Bull. Mus. Paris*, 1896, p. 238.

narrow area; in this respect it differs widely from *Notonecta*, which possesses an extremely large occipital foramen, and the head of which possesses but little freedom of movement. The extremely short proboscis is more or less retractile, and therefore frequently appears absent. A second British genus consists of a single species, *Sigara minutissima*. These Insects, unlike *Notonecta*, are quite at home beneath the water, where they scurry about with extreme rapidity, and occur sometimes in enormous numbers. In Mexico the eggs of *Corixa americana* and of *C. femorata* are used as food, and are said to be very nice. The Insects themselves are used as food in both Mexico and Egypt. The species of this family can make a noise beneath the water by rubbing the front feet against the proboscis.[1] The males have a very complex asymmetry of the terminal segments, and in some species possess on one side of the dorsal surface a curious asymmetrical organ consisting of rows of very closely-packed, intensely black, comb-like plates, called by Buchanan White a strigil. This organ seems to be similar to the peculiar structures found on the terminal segments of certain species of Scutellerides.

Sub-Order II. Homoptera.[2]

Fam. 1. Cicadidae.—*Head with three ocelli, placed triangularly on the summit between the compound eyes; antennae consisting of a short basal joint, surmounted by a hair-like process divided into about five segments. Front femora more or less thick, armed with teeth. Peduncle (or basal joints) of antennae without sensitive organs.*—This important family consists chiefly of large Insects, few being as small as one inch across the expanded wings, while in some the expanse is as much as seven inches. As a rule the four wings are transparent and shining, with the nervures remarkably distinct and dark coloured; but there are numerous forms where the whole creature, including the wings, is highly pigmented in a showy manner; frequently in black and yellow. Cicadas are said to be without any special protection, and to be destroyed in considerable numbers by birds and other animals. The body is broad and robust, and is never shaped into the extravagant forms we meet with in some of the other families of Homoptera. Cicadidae are almost confined to the warmer regions

---

[1] See Carpenter, *Irish Naturalist*, iv. 1895, p. 59.
[2] See remarks on pp. 543, 544.

of the earth, but we have one species, a great rarity, in the extreme south of England ; altogether there are about 800 species
known.   These Insects are seen above ground—so far as the
life-histories are at present known—only in the perfect condition, the creatures in their earlier stages being subterranean and
living on roots.   As soon as the individual comes out of the
ground it splits open the nymph-skin, and the perfect Cicada
emerges.   One species—the North American *Cicada septendecim*
—is a most notorious Insect owing to its life-cycle of seventeen

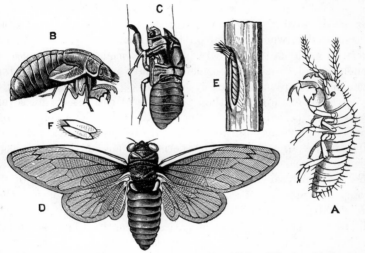

Fig. 280.—*Cicada septendecim.*   North America.   (After Riley.)   **A,** Larva ; **B,**
    nymph ; **C,** nymph skin after emergence of the imago, **D ; E,** section of twig with
    series of eggs ; **F,** two eggs magnified.

years.   It is considered that the individual, after nearly seventeen years of underground existence, comes to the surface and
lives for a brief period the life of a noisy Insect.   This is the
only Insect at present known having so considerable a longevity.
This fact, and several other peculiarities, have attracted much
attention, so that there is an extensive literature connected with
the seventeen-year Cicada.   It has a wide distribution over the
United States, but does not confine its appearance to every
seventeenth year, being found somewhere or other—frequently
in numerous localities—almost every year.   The evidence as to
its periodicity has been obtained by taking the locality and other
points into consideration as well as the year of appearance.

By so doing it has been found possible to establish the existence of twenty-two broods which are distinguished by consecutive numeration. This being done, the evidence as to the years during which Cicadas have appeared in any given locality is examined, and the result is believed to bear out the view that the life-cycle of the individual Insect is really one of seventeen years. According to this view there are, underground, in certain localities individuals of different ages that will appear on the surface as mature individuals in different years. Thus in 1885 it was understood that there were underground in Alabama two broods, viz. brood xviii. that would appear on the surface in 1894, and brood iv. that would appear on the surface in 1896. The predictions made as to the years in which Cicadas would appear in some given locality are considered to have proved correct. Moreever, particular entomologists have in certain localities verified by personal examination the appearance of the Insects for several consecutive periods of seventeen years. These facts appear fairly conclusive, but they are much complicated by another point, viz. that in certain localities the period is one of thirteen, not of seventeen, years. This is to some extent a question of climate, the thirteen-year interval being chiefly characteristic of the Southern States. It is not, however, entirely so, for there are localities in which the broods have an interval of either thirteen years or seventeen years. Another fact should be remembered, viz. that it is admitted that not quite all the individuals of a particular brood are true to their proper time of appearance; in other words, a few specimens may appear precociously a year or two before their comrades, while some may lag behind to a considerable extent. It is therefore a matter for great surprise that, under these circumstances, the broods should keep distinct at all, for one would suppose that time-variation of this kind would lead to completely obscuring the distinctness of the broods. We must also call attention to the fact that both the seventeen-year and the thirteen-year broods have a dimorphic form, or sub-species, called *C. cassinii* which accompanies the ordinary form, with which it is apparently as a rule not connected by intermediates.[1]

---

[1] We must refer those who may wish for further information as to this complex and difficult question to the writings of the late Professor Riley, especially to Bulletin No. 8, 1885, U.S. Department of Agriculture, division of entomology; and to the more recent report by Marlatt, *Bull. Dep. Agric. Ent.*, N.S. No. 14, 1898.

Cicadidae are provided with powerful ovipositors. The eggs of *C. septendecim* are deposited in the woody stems of bushes; after remaining there a few weeks the young hatch out, drop to the ground, and, as previously stated, disappear for nearly seventeen years, nearly the whole of which time is passed in the larval state, the nymph-condition existing for only a few days. They feed on the roots of various trees; it has been said that they are injurious in this way, but other authorities maintain that they suck only a moist exudation from the roots. It is very difficult to obtain information as to their strange, prolonged, subterranean life; it said that the Insects sometimes penetrate to a great depth—ten feet, even twenty feet are mentioned;—and as great changes may take place on the surface during their long lives, these Insect Rip Van Winkles sometimes emerge in very strange conditions, and may appear even in deep cellars. When the pupa comes to the surface it hooks itself on to the stem of some plant or other object, the skin of the back splits, and the Cicada emerges. Among the inexplicable peculiarities of this Insect must be mentioned the fact that when emerging it sometimes constructs chimneys, or flues, extending several inches above the surface of the ground. The reason for this is much disputed; it was said that they are for refuge against inundations, but this appears to be very doubtful. Certain of the broods consist of an almost incalculable number of individuals, and it is very strange to hear woods, or other localities, that have been for many years free from these Insects, all at once resounding with their noisy song. The seventeen-year Cicada is considered to be doomed to a speedy extinction; the extension of cultivation and building, and the introduction to America of the English sparrow, are likely to prove too much for the Insect.

Although Hemiptera are classified by many among the Ametabola or Insects without metamorphosis, it is impossible to deny that the Cicadidae exhibit a considerable amount of metamorphosis, and they are usually mentioned as exceptional. The young (Fig. 280, A) is totally unlike the adult in form and colour, and maintains, to a certain extent, its existence by the aid of a different set of implements. The larva of the Cicada is colourless, with an integument of very feeble consistence, rather large antennae, and a remarkable pair of fossorial legs;

the wings are totally wanting.   The mode of passage from the
larval to the pupal state has not been recorded.   The pupa, or nymph,
differs from the larva by its much shorter, compressed form; by
being encased in a remarkably hard shell; and by the antennae
approximating in form to those of the adult.   It has short wing-
pads at the sides of the body; the front legs are remarkably
powerful, and the creature is capable of moving about; the imago
escapes from the pupa by the splitting dorsally of the middle of
the thoracic segments.   The empty pupa-skin does not shrivel,
but retains its form, and in countries where Cicadas occur, frequently attracts attention by the strange form it presents, being
often placed in a conspicuous position.

Song.—Cicadas are the most noisy of the Insect world; the
shrilling of grasshoppers and even of crickets being insignificant
in comparison with the voice of Cicada.   Darwin heard them
in South America when the *Beagle* was anchored a quarter
of a mile from the shore; and *Tympanoterpes gigas*, from the
same region, is said to make a noise equal to the whistle of a
locomotive.[1]   A curious difference of opinion prevails as to
whether their song is agreeable or not; in some countries they
are kept in cages, while in others they are considered a nuisance.
The Greeks are said to have decided in favour of their performances, the Latins against them.   Only the males sing, the
females being completely dumb; this has given rise to a saying
by a Greek poet (so often repeated that it bids fair to become
immortal) "Happy the Cicadas' lives, for they all have voiceless wives." [2]   The writer considers the songs of the European
species he has heard far from unpleasant, but he is an entomologist,
and therefore favourably prepossessed; and he admits that
Riley's description of the performances of the seventeen-year
Cicada is far from a satisfactory testimonial to the good taste of
that Insect; Riley says, "The general noise, on approaching the
infested woods, is a combination of that of a distant threshing-
machine and a distant frog-pond.   That which they make when
disturbed, mimics a nest of young snakes or young birds under
similar circumstances—a sort of scream.   They can also produce

---

[1] Some entomologists consider that this "railway-whistle" note is the result
of the combined efforts of several individuals.   Cf. Mathew, *Ent. Mag.* xi. 1875,
p. 175.

[2] It is unnecessary to say that the poet was not Sappho, but one of the baser sex,
named Xenarchus.

a chirp somewhat like that of a cricket and a very loud, shrill screech prolonged for fifteen or twenty seconds, and gradually increasing in force and then decreasing." The object, or use of the noise is very doubtful; it is said that it attracts the females to the males. " De gustibus non est disputandum ! " perhaps, however, there may be some tender notes that we fail to perceive; and it may be that the absence of any definite organs of hearing reduces the result of a steam-engine whistle to the equivalent of an agreeable whisper. No special auditory organs have been detected [1] as we have already intimated; and certain naturalists, amongst whom we may mention Giard, think that the Insects do not hear in our sense of the word, but feel rhythmical vibrations; it is also recorded that though very shy the Insects may be induced to approach any one who will stand still and clap his hands—in good measure—within the range of their sensibilities. There is a good deal of support to the idea that the males sing in rivalry.

Vocal structures.——Although we may not be able to pronounce a final opinion as to the value to the Insect of the sounds, yet we cannot withhold our admiration from the structures from which they proceed. These are indeed so complex that they must be ranked as amongst the most remarkable voice-organs in the animal kingdom. They are totally different from the stridulating organs that are found in many other Insects, and are indeed quite peculiar to the Cicadidae. Some difference of opinion has existed as to the manner in which the structures act, but the account given by Carlet, some of whose figures we reproduce, will, we believe, be found to be essentially correct. The structures are partly thoracic and partly abdominal. On examining a male *Cicada* there will be seen on the under surface two plates—the opercula—usually meeting in the middle line of the body and overlapping the base of the abdomen to a greater or less extent according to the species, sometimes nearly covering this part of the body; these are enlargements of the metathoracic epimera; they can be slightly moved away from the abdomen, and, as the latter part is capable of a still greater extent of movement, a wide fissure may be produced, displaying the complex

---

[1] Swinton claims that one of the membranes in the vocal apparatus is an auditory organ ; if so, the male would be deafened by his own noise, while the females, not possessing the organ, should not hear the song.

structures. In order to see the parts it is better to cut away an operculum; underneath it three membranes can be seen, an external, the timbal; an anterior, the folded or soft membrane; and a posterior, the mirror. This last is a most beautiful object, tensely stretched and pellucid, yet reflecting light so as to be of varied colours; there are also three stigmata, and some chambers connected with the apparatus. The sound is primarily produced by the vibrations of the timbal, to which a muscle is attached; the other membranes are probably also thrown into a condition of vibration, and the whole skeleton of the Insect helps to increase or modify the sound, which is probably also influenced

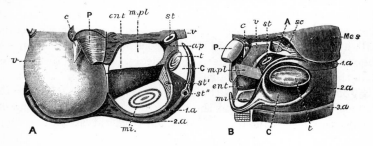

FIG. 281.—Musical apparatus of *Cicada plebeia*. (After Carlet.) **A**, Ventral view (Operculum on right side is removed); *ap*, apophysis; c, cavern; *c*, trochantin (cheville of Réaumur); *ent*, part of internal skeleton of abdomen; *mi*, specular membrane; *m.pl*, soft or folded membrane; P, base of leg; *st, st', st''*, stigmata; *t*, drum "timbale"; *v*, operculum; 1*a*, first, 2*a*, second abdominal segment: **B**, same seen laterally, portion of abdominal wall as well as operculum removed; A, point of insertion of hind wing; *Mes*, mesothorax; *sc*, scutum of metathorax; 3*a*, third abdominal segment; rest as in **A**.

by the position of the opercula. The stigmata probably play an important part by regulating the tension of the air in the chambers. In the female some of the structures are present in a rudimentary form, but there are no muscles, and this sex appears to be really quite voiceless.

Fam. 2. Fulgoridae.—*Ocelli two (rarely three, or entirely obsolete), placed beneath the eyes or near the eyes, usually in cavities of the cheeks, antennae placed beneath the eyes, very variable in form; usually of two joints terminated by a very fine hair, the second joint with a peculiar texture of the surface, owing to the existence of sensitive structures* (Hansen). *Form of head very diverse; vertex and face forming either a continuous curve, or the planes of the vertex and face forming an acute angle, or both pro-*

*longed so as to form a projection or growth that may be monstrous.
Prothorax neither armed nor unusually developed.*

This family is of large extent, and includes at present so great a variety of forms that it is really almost impossible to frame a definition that will apply to all. The unusual situation of the ocelli and the peculiar second joint of the antennae must at present be taken as the best diagnostic characters : occasionally a third ocellus is present. Some of the Fulgoridae are amongst the largest Insects, others are quite small. The family includes the so-called Lantern-flies, in which the front of the head forms a huge misshapen proboscis that was formerly believed to be luminous.

Fig. 282.—*Fulgora candelaria.*   × 1.   China.

Many of the species are of brilliant or beautiful coloration. A great many—and of very different kinds—have the curious power of excreting large quantities of a white, flocculent wax. This is exhibited by our little British Insects of the genus *Cixius,* and in some of the exotic forms is carried to an extent that becomes a biological puzzle. The Tropical American genus *Phenax* may be cited as an example ; being about an inch long it flies about with a large mass of this waxy substance twice as long as itself ; indeed, in the Mexican *P. auricoma,* the waxy processes are four or five inches long. This wax forms a favourite food of certain kinds of Lepidoptera, and two or three larvae of a maggot-like nature may frequently be found concealed in the wax of the live Fulgorids ; this has been recorded by Westwood as occurring in India ; and Champion has observed it in the New World.[1]

[1] *P. ent. Soc. London,* 1883, p. 20.

The wax of Fulgorids is used by the Chinese for candles and other purposes; and this white Insect-wax is said to be much esteemed in India.   Very curious chemical substances have been obtained from it, but its importance in the economy of the Insects that produce it is quite obscure.   We have about seventy species of Fulgoridae in Britain.   They belong to the sub-families Tettigometrides, Issides, Cixiides, and Delphacides, which by many authors are treated as separate families.   The exotic sub-family Flatides is highly peculiar.   In some of its members the head is very different from that of the ordinary forms, being narrow, and the vertex and front forming a continuous curve. Some of these Insects are remarkably like butterflies or moths (*e.g.* the African *Ityraea nigrocincta* and the species of the genus *Pochazia*), but the young are totally unlike the old, the posterior part of the body bearing a large bush of curled, waxy projections, several times the size of the rest of the body.

Fam. 3. Membracidae.—*Prothorax prolonged backwards into a hood or processes of diverse forms; antennae inserted in front of the eyes; ocelli two, placed between the two eyes.*—This family is of

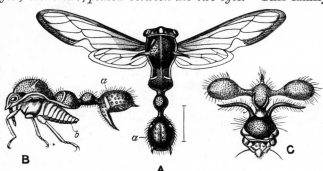

Fig. 283.—**A, B,** *Heteronotus trinodosus.* **A,** Male seen from above ; **B,** profile of female ; *a,* terminal part of pronotum ; *b,* terminal part of abdomen : **C,** front view of head and pronotum of *Cyphonia clavata.* Both species from Central America. (From *Biol. Centr. Amer. Rhynch. Homopt.* II.)

large extent but its members are chiefly tropical, and are specially abundant in America.   Although not of large size the Membracidae are unsurpassed for the variety and grotesqueness of their shapes, due to the unusual development of the pronotum.   We figure two of these forms (Fig. 283).[1]   Very little is known about their

---

[1] A considerable variety of these extraordinary creatures are figured in *Biol. Centr. Amer. Rhynch. Homopt.* ii.

habits and life-histories.   We have only two species of the family
in Britain, and these do not afford any ground for supposing that
there are any peculiarities in their lives at all commensurate
with the oddness of the Insect's structures.   Belt has recorded
the fact that in Nicaragua the larvae of certain Homoptera were
assiduously attended by ants for the sake of a sweet juice
excreted by the bugs, but it is by no means clear that these larvae
were really those of Membracidae.   In North America *Ceresa
bubalus* and *C. taurina* place their eggs in an extremely neat
manner in the woody twigs of trees.   The young have but little
resemblance to the adults, the great thoracic hood being absent,
while on the back there is on each segment a pair of long, sub-
erect processes having fringed, or minutely spiny, margins.[1]

Fam. 4. Cercopidae.—*Ocelli two (occasionally absent) placed
on the vertex ; antennae placed between the eyes.   Thorax not
peculiarly formed.*—In the characteristic forms of this family
the front of the vertex bears a suture, touched on each side
by one at right angles to it, or converging to it so as to form a
triangle or a sort of embrasure ; the hind tibiae have only one to
three strong spines.   The Cercopidae are much less extraordinary
than many of the previously considered families.   But some of
them have the habit of secreting a large quantity of fluid ; and
when in the immature stages, certain of them have the art of
emitting the liquid in the form of bubbles which accumulate
round the Insect and conceal it.   These accumulations of fluid
are called cuckoo-spits or frog-spits ; and the perfect Insects are
known as frog-hoppers, their power of leaping being very great.
The most abundant of the frog-hoppers in our gardens is
Philaenus spumarius, a little Insect of about a quarter of an inch
long, obscurely coloured, with more or less definite pale spots ;
it is so variable in colour that it has received scores of names.
Some of the Insects do not use their fluid in this manner, but
eject it in the form of drops, and sometimes cast them to a considerable distance.   The phenomena known as weeping-trees are
due to Cercopidae ; some of the species make such copious exuda-
tions of this kind that the drops have been compared to a shower
of rain.   In Madagascar it is said that *Ptyelus goudoti* exudes
so much fluid that five or six dozen larvae would about fill a

---

[1] Riley, *P. ent. Soc. Washington*, iii. 1895, p. 88.   For the younger stages of
Membracis foliata, see *Tijdschr. Ent.* (2) iv. 1869, pl. viii.

quart vessel in an hour and a half. The frog-spit is considered
by some naturalists to be a protective device ; the larvae are,
however, a favourite food with certain Hymenoptera, which pick
out the larvae from the spits and carry them off to be used as
stores of provision for their larvae. In Ceylon the larva of
Machaerota guttigera constructs tubes fixed to the twigs of the
tulip-tree, and from the tube water is exuded drop by drop.
According to Westwood, this Insect is intermediate between
Cercopidae and Membracidae.[1]

Fam. 5. Jassidae.—*Ocelli two, placed just on the front
margin of the head (almost in a line with the front of the eyes
or more to the front) or on the deflexed frons. Hind tibiae
usually with many spines.* This vaguely limited family includes
a very large number of small or minute Insects, usually of narrow,
parallel form, and frequently excessively delicate and fragile.
They are often mentioned under the name of Cicadellinae.
Ashmead distinguishes two families, Bythoscopidae, in which the
ocelli are clearly on the frons or front, and Jassidae, in which
they are on the upper edge thereof. *Ulopa, Ledra,* and a few
other exceptional forms, are also by many distinguished as
representatives of distinct families. Very little is actually known
as to the life-histories of these small and fragile Insects, but it is
believed that the eggs are usually deposited in the leaves or
stems of plants, and more particularly of grasses. In North
America the development of *Deltocephalus inimicus,* from hatching
to assumption of the adult form, has been observed by Webster
to occupy about six weeks. As Jassidae are numerous both in
species and individuals it is believed that they consume a considerable part of the vegetation of pastures. Osborn has
calculated that on an acre of pasture there exist, as a rule, about
one million of these hoppers, and he considers they obtain quite
as large a share of the food as the Vertebrates feeding with
them.

Fam. 6. Psyllidae. — *Minute Insects with wings usually
transparent, placed in a roof-like manner over the body ; with three
ocelli, and rather long, thin antennae of eight to ten joints. Tarsi
two-jointed.*—These small Insects have been studied chiefly in
Europe and North America, very little information having yet
been obtained as to the exotic forms. They are about the

---

[1] *Tr. ent. Soc. London,* 1886, p. 329.

size of Aphidae, but in form and general appearance remind
one rather of Cica-
didae.   The wings
are in many cases
even more perfectly
transparent   than
they are in many
Cicadidae. They are
sometimes called
springing plant-lice,
as their habit of
jumping distin-
guishes them from
the Aphidae. Löw
has called attention
to the remarkable
variation in colour
they present in con-
formity with either
the age of the indi-
vidual, the food-
plant, the climate,
and, more particu-
larly, the season of
the year.[1]   Réaumur long since pointed out that at their ecdyses
these Insects go through a remarkable series of changes of colour,
and Löw found that this did not take place in the normal
manner in the winter generation that hibernates.   This has
been confirmed by Slingerland in North America in the case
of *Psylla pyricola*,[2] which has been introduced there.   He finds
that there are several generations in the year, and that the
hibernating adults differ from the summer adults in size, being
nearly one-third larger; in their much darker colouring; and
especially in the coloration of the front wings.

In the earlier stages, Psyllidae differ greatly in appearance from
the adult forms; the legs and antennae in the newly hatched larvae
are short, and have a less number of joints.   In the nymph the
shape is very peculiar, the large wing-pads standing out horizontally

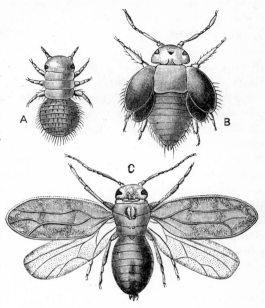

Fig. 284.—*Psylla succincta*.   × 15. Europe. (After
Heeger.) **A**, larva before first moult. **B**, larva after
third moult. **C**, adult.

[1] *Verh. z.-b. Ges. Wien*, xxvi. 1876, p. 167.
[2] *Cornell Univ. Agric. exp. station Bulletin*, 44, 1892, and *Bull.* 108, 1896.

from the sides of the body, so that the width of the creature is about as great as the length. The period occupied by the development apparently varies according to season. Witlaczil, who has given an account of many details of the anatomy and histology of various Psyllidae,[1] considers that there are four larval stages; Heeger's account of *Psylla succincta* is not quite clear on this point, and Slingerland indicates a stage more than this, the perfect Insect being disclosed as the result of a fifth moult; it is probable that he is correct. In these earlier stages the body bears long hairs called wax-hairs; according to Witlaczil in the young larvae of certain species—*Trioza rhamni*, e.g.—these are broad and flat, so as to make the body appear studded with oval processes; he states that these hairs change their form during the growth of the individual. Nothing is more remarkable in Psyllidae than the amount of matter they secrete or exude from their bodies; in some species the substance is a "honey-dew," and the nymph may keep itself covered with a drop of it: in other cases it is solid, as shown in Réaumur's figures of *P. buxi,* where this exudation forms a string several times longer than the body, and attached to it. Another form of exudation is a light downy or waxy matter. Slingerland says that honey-dew was exuded by *P. pyricola* in such quantities that it "literally rained from the trees upon the vegetation beneath; in cultivating the orchard the back of the horse and the harness often became covered with the sticky substance dropping from the trees. It attracts thousands of ants, bees, and wasps, which feed upon it." The writer last year observed in the New Forest a stunted sloe-bush, about which a large number of Bombi were busily occupied; and examination showed that they were thrusting their proboscides into the curled and deformed leaves, in which were secreted nymphs of a *Psylla* exuding honey-dew. It must not be assumed that this honey-dew is the excrement of the Insect; this also is known, and is a different substance. Those who have tasted it say that the honey-dew has a clean, good flavour. The source of the honey-dew is not quite certain, but it seems probable that it comes, like the solid matter figured by Réaumur, directly from the alimentary canal, and not from hairs or pores on the body. Psyllidae give rise to definite formations or galls on certain plants; sometimes these Psyllid galls are mere changes in form of a limited part, or

---

[1] *Zeitschr. wiss. Zool.* xlii. 1885, pp. 569-638.

parts, of a leaf, giving rise either to crumpling or to growth of a portion in one direction only, so that on one surface of the leaf a swelling is formed, and on the opposite side a more or less deep cavity in which the Insect dwells. A formation of this kind on the leaves of *Aegopodium podagraria* is described by Thomas [1] who states that the growth is due to the deposition of an egg of the *Psylla*, and is independent of the after life of the Insect ; a fungus —*Puccinia aegopodii*—forms similar structures on the leaves. Structures much more definite than this may be the result of the attacks of Psyllidae ; for an example the reader may refer to Réaumur's account of *Psylla buxi*.[2] In Australia and Tasmania there are Psyllidae known as Laap or Lerp Insects, the products of which are called leaf-manna or Lerp, and are used as food. This manna is a scale produced by the young Insect on the leaves of *Eucalyptus* as a covering or protection. The scale is fastened to the leaf by a hinge, and is somewhat like the shell of a cockle. Although the scales are said to be in some cases objects of great beauty, very little is known about these Australian Psyllidae, one of which has, however, been referred by Schwarz to the genus *Spondyliaspis*, Signoret.[3] About 160 species of Psyllidae are known to occur in the Palaearctic region, and about fifty of them have been found in Britain.[4]

Fam. 7. Aphidae (*Plant-lice or Green-fly.*)—*Minute Insects ; as usually met with destitute of wings, though many individuals have two pairs of transparent wings. Antennae long, or moderately long, three- to seven-jointed ; abdomen frequently with a pair of tubes (siphons), or short processes on the upper side of the fifth abdominal segment. Tarsi two-jointed, first joint sometimes excessively short.*—These soft-skinned Insects are frequently called blight, and are so abundant in temperate climates that a garden, however small, is sure to afford abundance of specimens during the warm months of the year. This great abundance is due to peculiarities in the physiological processes that render these obscure little animals highly important creatures ; the individual life for several generations is restricted to constant, or at any rate copious, imbibition of food, accompanied by an almost uninterrupted

---

[1] *Zeitschr. Naturw.* (2) xii. 1875, p. 438.
[2] Réaumur, *Mém.* iii. 1737, *Dixième Mémoire.*
[3] *P. ent. soc. Washington*, iv. 1897, p. 66.
[4] For list see Scott, *Ent. Mag.* xviii. 1882, p. 253.

production of young by parthenogenetic females, the young so produced becoming rapidly (sometimes in the course of eight or ten days, but more usually in about twenty days) themselves devoted to a similar process; so that in the comparatively short period of a few months the progeny resulting from a single individual is almost innumerable. This remarkable state of affairs is accompanied by other peculiarities of physiology, with the result that the life-histories of successive generations become very diverse, and complex cycles of series of generations differing more or less from one another are passed through, the species finally returning to bi-sexual reproduction, and thus inaugurating another cycle of generations. The surprising nature of these facts has in the last 150 years caused an immense amount of discussion, but no satisfactory light has yet been thrown on the conditions that really give rise to the exceptional phenomena. These phenomena are (1) parthenogenesis; (2) oviparous and viviparous reproduction; (3) the production of generations of individuals in which the sexes are very unequally represented, males being frequently entirely absent; (4) the production of individuals differing as to the acquirement of wings, some remaining entirely apterous, while others go on to the winged form; (5) the production of individuals of the same sex with different sexual organs, and distinctions in the very early (but not the earliest) stages of the formation of the individual; (6) differences in the life-habits of successive generations; (7) differences in the habits of individuals of one generation, giving rise to the phenomenon of parallel series. All these phenomena may occur in the case of a single species, though in a very variable extent.

The simple form of Aphid life may be described as follows:— eggs are laid in the autumn, and hatch in the spring, giving rise to females of an imperfect character having no wings; these produce living young parthenogenetically, and this process may be repeated for a few or for many generations, and there may be in these generations a greater or less number of winged individuals, and perhaps a few males.[1] After a time when temperature falls,

---

[1] There is some doubt on this point, as the earlier observers seem to have supposed that a winged individual appearing in a generation chiefly apterous was *ipso facto*, a male; it seems, however, to be certain that perfect winged males appear in some species in generations producing no perfect sexual females. Speaking generally,

or when the supply of food is less in quantity, or after a period of deliberate abstention from food, sexual individuals are produced and fertilised eggs are laid which hatch in the spring, and the phenomena are repeated. In other cases these phenomena are added to or rendered more complicated by the intercalated parthenogenetic generations exhibiting well-marked metamorphosis, of kinds such as occur in apterous or in winged Insects; while again the habits of successive generations may differ greatly, the individuals of some generations dwelling in galls, while those of other generations live underground on roots.

Parthenogenesis. — Returning to the various kinds of peculiarities we have enumerated on the preceding page, we may remark that the phenomena of parthenogenesis have been thoroughly established as occurring in Aphidae since Bonnet discovered the fact 150 years ago; and though they have not been investigated in much detail it is known that the parthenogenesis is usually accompanied by the production of young all of the female sex. In other cases males are parthenogenetically produced; but whether these males come from a female that produces only that sex is not yet, so far as the writer knows, established. A note by Lichtenstein [1] suggests that usually only one sex is produced by a parthenogenetic female, but that both sexes are sometimes so produced. There is not at present any species of Aphid known to be perpetuated by an uninterrupted series of parthenogenetic generations. It was formerly supposed that there are no males at all in *Chermes*, but, as we shall subsequently show, this was erroneous. It has, however, been observed that a series of such generations may be continued without interruption for a period of four years, and we have no reason to suppose that even this could not be much exceeded under favourable conditions. The parthenogenetic young may be produced either viviparously or oviparously, according to species.

Oviparous and viviparous reproduction.—The distinction between these two processes has been extensively discussed, some naturalists maintaining that they are thoroughly distinct *ab initio*. This view, however, cannot be sustained. The best

the course of events seems to be that in summer there exist only wingless and winged parthenogenetic females, and that the sexually perfect forms appear for the first time in autumn.

[1] *Mitt. Schweiz. ent. Ges.* iv. 1876, p. 529.

authorities are agreed that in the earliest processes of individual-
isation the ovum, and the pseudovum [1] giving rise to a viviparous
individual, are indistinguishable.   Leydig, Huxley, Balbiani, and
Lemoine are agreed as to this.   Nevertheless, differences in the
development occur extremely early.   The nature of these differences may be briefly described by saying that in the viviparous
forms the embryonic development sets in before the formation of
the egg is properly completed.   Balbiani says, " In fact at this
moment [when the viviparous development is commencing] the
germ [pseudovum] is far from having obtained the development
it is capable of, and from having accumulated all the matter
necessary for the increase of the embryo, so that the evolution
of the former coincides, so to speak, with that of the latter.   On
the other hand, in the true ovum the two processes are chrono-
logically separate, for the rudiment of the new individual never
appears before the egg has completed the growth of its constituent
parts." [2]   As regards the difference in structure of the organs of
viviparously and oviparously producing individuals, it is sufficient
to remark that they are not of great importance, being apparently
confined to certain parts remaining rudimentary in the former.
Leydig, indeed, found an *Aphis* in which certain of the egg-tubes
contained eggs in various stages of development, and others
embryos in all stages.[3]

As regards the physiology of production of winged and wingless individuals there has been but little exact inquiry.   Vast
numbers of individuals may be produced without any winged
forms occurring, while on the other hand these latter are occasionally so abundant as to float about in swarms that darken
the air ; the two forms are probably, however, determined by the
supply of food.   The winged forms are less prolific than the
apterous forms ; and Forbes has noticed in *Aphis maidi-radicis*,
where the generations consist partly of apterous and partly of
winged individuals, that when the corn begins to flag in consequence of the attacks of the *Aphis*, then the proportion of

[1] The term pseudovum is applied, as a matter of convenience, to the earlier condition of the viviparously-produced form, and the term pseudovarium to the ovary
producing it.

[2] Balbiani, *Ann. Sci. Nat. Zool.* (5) xi. 1869, p. 29.   For concise recent remarks on the early embryonic states, see Lemoine, *Bull. Soc. ent. France*, 1893,
p. lxxxix.

[3] *Acta Ac. German.* xxxiii. 1869, No. 2, p. 81.

winged individuals becomes large.[1]   The appearance of winged individuals is frequently accompanied by a peculiar change of habit ; the winged individuals migrating to another plant, which in many cases is of a totally different botanical nature from that on which the apterous broods were reared : for instance *Aphis mali*, after producing several apterous generations on apple, gives rise to winged individuals that migrate to the stems of corn or grass, and feeding thereon commence another cycle of generations. The study of this sort of Aphis-migration is chiefly modern, but many very curious facts have already been brought to light ; thus *Drepanosiphum platanoides*, after producing a certain number of viviparous generations on maple (*Acer*), quits this food-plant for another, but after two or three months returns again to the maple, and produces sexual young that lay eggs.[2]   Histories such as this are rather common.   Even more interesting are the cases of those species that, after some weeks of physiological activity on a plant, pass into a state of repose on the same plant, and then after some weeks produce sexual young.   On the whole, it would appear that the appearance of winged forms is a con-comitant of decreasing nutrition.   It is a very remarkable fact that the sexually perfect females are invariably apterous, and this is frequently also the case with the males.   It is also highly remarkable that the sexually perfect individuals are of com-paratively small size.   There are at least three kinds of males in Aphidae—1, winged males ; 2, wingless males with mouth well developed ; 3, wingless small males with mouth absent. As regards some of these points the conditions usual in Insect life are reversed.[3]   Huxley inclined to treat all these products of a fertilised egg, that are antecedent to another process of gamo-genesis (*i.e.* production with fertilisation), as one zoological indi-vidual : in that case the Aphis zoological individual is winged before attaining the mature state, and is wingless and smaller when mature.   Some species may have as a rule two, others three, winged generations in a year.

Parallel series.—In certain cases individuals of one genera-tion assume different habits, and so set up the phenomenon

---

[1] *Seventeenth Rep. Insects Illinois*, 1891, p. 66.

[2] Kessler, *Acta Ac. German.* li. 1887, pp. 152, 153.

[3] In connection with this the absence of a functional mouth in the imago state of numerous Lepidoptera, and of Oestrid Diptera, should not be forgotten.

known as parallel series.   This has been recently investigated in
the genus *Chermes* by Blochmann, Dreyfus, and Cholodkovsky.
This latter savant informs us [1] that a wingless parthenogenetic
female of *Chermes* hibernates on a fir-tree—*Picea excelsa*—and
in the spring lays numerous eggs ; these hatch, and by the effects
of suction of the *Chermes* on the young shoots, galls are formed

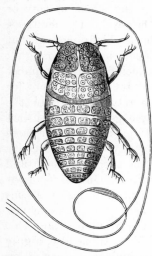

(Fig. 286), in which the Insects are
found in large numbers ; when they
have grown the galls open, and allow-
ing the Insects to escape these moult
and become winged females.   They
now take on different habits ; some of
them remain on the *Picea*, lay their
eggs thereon, and out of these there
are produced young that grow into
hibernating females, which next spring
produce galls as their grandmothers
did ; but another portion migrates to
the Larch (*Larix*) ; here eggs are laid,
from which proceed wingless parthenogenetic females, that hibernate on their
new or secondary plant, and in the
following spring lay their eggs and
give rise to a dimorphic generation,
part of them becoming nymphs and
going on to the winged condition,

Fig. 285.—*Chermes abietis ;* hibernating female or "winter-
mother." Europe. Much magnified. (After Cholodkovsky.)

while the other part remain wingless and lay eggs, that give rise
to yet another wingless generation ; in fact, a second pair of parallel
series is formed on the new plant, of which one is wingless, and
exclusively parthenogenetic, and continues to live in this fashion
for an indefinite period on the secondary plant, while the other
part becomes winged ; these latter are called sexuparous, and go
back to the *Picea*, and there lay eggs, that give rise to the
sexual forms.   If we would summarise these facts with a view
to remembering them, we may say that a migration of a part of
a generation from the *Picea* was made with a view of producing
a sexual generation, but that only a portion of the migrants succeeded in effecting the object of the migration, and this only in
their third generation.   Thus portions remained on the *Picea*,

[1] *Horae Soc. ent. Ross.* xxiv. 1890. p. 386.

producing unisexual (female) individuals, and a portion of those that emigrated to the *Larix* remained thereon, producing also unisexual (female) individuals, while the others returned to the *Picea* and produced a sexual generation. How long the production of the unisexual generations may continue has not been determined.

Phylloxera.—The *Phylloxera*, that has caused such an enormous amount of damage in the Old World during the last thirty years, is a small Aphid that was introduced from North America into Europe. In North America it is not so injurious as it is in Europe, owing, no doubt, to slight distinctions in the conditions of life in the two hemispheres, as one of which may be mentioned that in Europe a larger proportion of the individuals produced appear to confine themselves to feeding on the roots, *P. vastatrix* being one of the species that lives both in galls on leaves, and underground on the roots. The species is one that exhibits in their most complex form the peculiar phenomena of Aphid life we have already mentioned. It has probably only one congener, *Phylloxera quercus,* and of this Lichtenstein says that in its cycle, from the starting-point of the winter-egg to the assumption of the sexual condition, it exhibits a series of no less than twenty-one forms.[1] The life of *Phylloxera vastatrix* apparently differs essentially from what we have described in *Chermes*, inasmuch as the migrations are only between leaf and root of the same plant—the vine—and not from one species of plant to another. Some authorities treat *Phylloxera* and *Chermes* as a separate family under the name of Phylloxeridae.

FIG. 286.—Gall, or false cone of *Chermes abietis*. Cambridge. The small figure, to the left, is a section made at the level indicated by the pointing line *a*, and shows the chambers containing young.

Galls.—Like *Phylloxera*, many species of Aphidae live partially, others wholly, in galls that are produced by plants as the result of one or more Aphids interfering with a delicate part of the plant when it is in a young and growing state. The usual position of Aphid galls is on a leaf or leaf-stalk. But in the case of the genus *Chermes*,

[1] *Ent. Zeit. Stettin*, xxxvi. 1875, p. 368.

a bud or some growing part of the spruce-fir is affected in such a way that it gives rise to an object having externally the appearance of a little fir-cone, while inside it consists of chambers in which the Aphids reside. The forms of Aphid-galls are very diverse, but this is probably due to the plant rather than to the Insect, for the same species of Aphis may give rise to different forms of galls. Réaumur thought that each Aphid-gall was due to a single individual that irritated the tissue of the plant, so that the latter grew up at the point of irritation and enclosed the Insect.

A few points as to the anatomy of Aphids should be noticed. It is doubtful whether the antennae have ever really more than six joints, the apparent seventh joint being actually a sort of appendage of the sixth. The rostrum is externally three-jointed, and is remarkable for the great diversity in its length, sometimes it is quite short, at others several times longer than the body (Fig. 285); the setae are often very much longer than the sheath; in cases where this great length of rostrum exists, the individual may often be found with the tip firmly fixed in the bark, and, as it were, tethered by means of the rostrum, the length of which allows, nevertheless, considerable locomotion. Suction is performed by contractions of the pharynx. There has been much difference of opinion as to whether there is a salivary syringe, and Witlaczil failed to find it. Krassilstschik is, however, positive that it exists,[1] and that it is analogous to that described by Mayer in *Pyrrhocoris*, but there are great differences of structure between the two. It is very difficult to determine the number of segments at the extremity of the body; this is terminated dorsally by a median organ placed above the anus, and known as the cauda. Balbiani apparently considers that there are ten abdominal segments and the cauda. The alimentary canal has a small stomach, and an elongate intestine, the terminal division of which is capacious and remarkably long. There are no Malpighian tubes; according to Kowalevsky, their function is discharged by the posterior part of the alimentary canal. There exists, however, a peculiar structure, the pseudo-vitellus, a sort of cellular, double string; and Witlaczil, in his valuable paper [2] on the anatomy of Aphidae, suggests that this

---

[1] *Zool. Anz.* xv. 1892, p. 220.
[2] *Arb. Inst. Wien*, iv. 1882, Heft iii. p. 397 ; see on this organ also Mordwilko, *Zool. Anz.* xviii. 1895, p. 357.

organ may in some way replace the missing Malpighian tubes. Another highly peculiar structure is the siphons, frequently called nectaries, honey-tubes, or siphuncles. They are situated on the dorsal aspect of the fifth abdominal segment, but exist only in certain of the sub-families; they are of very different lengths according to the species, and are capable of movement; they open directly into the body cavity, though exceptional openings into the body cavity are extremely rare in Insects. They excrete a waxy matter, which first appears as oil-like globules. It was formerly supposed that they were the means of secreting the sugary matter, called honey-dew, so much prized by ants and some other Insects; but this is now ascertained to be erroneous. This matter comes from the alimentary canal, and is secreted in large quantities by some species, Büsgen having observed that forty-eight drops, each about 1 mm. in diameter, were emitted by a single individual in twenty-four hours.[1] Certain gall-dwelling Aphidae—*Pemphigus, Chermes* (Fig. 285), *Schizoneura*—possess numerous wax glands; these seem to replace the siphons, and excrete the peculiar, whitish flocculent matter that is so conspicuous in some of these Aphids.

Earlier anatomists failed to find any dorsal vessel, and it is consequently reported in books to be absent. It has been, however, recently detected by Witlaczil, and Mordwilko states that it does not differ from that of other Insects.

We have already alluded to the fact that the mode of reproduction of Aphids leads to an unrivalled increase. This, however, is not due to the prolificness of the individual, which, in point of fact, appears to be considerably below the average in Insects, but rather to the rapidity with which the young begin to reproduce. This has been discussed by Huxley, Buckton, and others. The first-named naturalist calculated that the produce of a single *Aphis* would, in the course of ten generations, supposing all the individuals to survive, "contain more ponderable substance than five hundred millions of stout men; that is, more than the whole population of China." [2] It has since been contended that Professor Huxley's calculation was much below the mark. Although it is somewhat difficult to make a calculation dealing adequately with the actual facts, yet it is clear that the increase

<hr>

[1] *Biol. Centralbl.* xi. 1891, p. 193.
[2] See, *inter alia*, Webster, *J New York ent. Soc.* i. 1893, p. 119.

of Aphids is such that, drawing as they do their nutriment directly from the plant in its growing state, in the course of two or three years there would be no nutriment available for other animals, except such as might be derived from plants not attacked by Aphids. The numbers of Aphidae would be so great that they could not be expressed by ordinary numerical methods, and their increase would be actually limited only by the relations existing between different kinds of plants, and between plants and Aphids. This result is avoided by the fact that Aphids are themselves the victims of a whole army of Insect enemies. They have the numerous members of a special group (Braconidae, Aphidiides) of minute Hymenoptera to live inside their bodies, and many Aculeate Hymenoptera depend entirely on the Aphidae as the source of food for their own progeny. The Lady-birds— Coccinellidae—live on Aphids and Coccids, and themselves increase to such an extent as to be in many years a conspicuous part of the Insect world. Crowds of the larvae of Hemerobiids and Syrphids are constantly engaged in spearing and sucking the Aphides. Hence the old naturalist Bonnet said that, just as we sow grain for our benefit, Nature has sown Aphids for the benefit of multitudes of different Insects. He might have added that these different Insects are for the benefit of man, it being clear that without them the population of the world must rapidly decrease.

Ants treat Aphidae more intelligently than most other Insects do, for they do not destroy the helpless creatures, but utilise their products in the way man does those of the cows he keeps. The relations between ants and Aphids is itself an extensive chapter in Natural History ; many facts have been brought to light showing that the ants manage the Aphids in a prudent or intelligent manner, distributing them when too numerous in one place, keeping guard over them, even building shelters for them, and in some cases keeping them in direct association, by retaining the Aphids in their own dwellings. The further investigation of these points goes, the more it tends to raise the actions of the ants to the level we call in ourselves intelligent. It would even appear that the ants are acquainted with the migrations of the Aphids from one species of plant to another, Webster informing us that as the Aphis-population on an apple tree multiplied the ants in attendance anticipated their migration to wheat and grass by carrying them to those plants.[1]   We have nearly 200 species of Aphidae in Britain,[2] and there may perhaps be 800 known altogether.   To what extent they may occur in the tropics is undetermined.   There are said to be no native species in New Zealand.

Fam. 8. Aleurodidae.—*Minute Insects, with four mealy wings, seven-jointed antennae, two-jointed feet, terminated by two claws and a third process.*   These minute Insects are at present a source of considerable perplexity, owing to the curious nature of their metamorphosis, and the contradictory accounts given of them. In the earlier stages they are scale-like and quiescent, being fixed to the under side of a leaf. The French authors Signoret and Girard state that the young are hatched having visible appendages and segmentation, but that after they are attached to the leaf the organs gradually suffer atrophy. Maskell states the opposite, saying that the organs in the

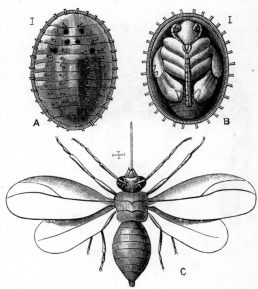

Fig. 287.—Instars of *Aleurodes immaculata.*   Europe. (After Heeger.)   **A,** Nymph, from above ; **B,** nymph, under surface ; **C,** imago.

earliest stages are not usually recognisable, but become faintly visible with the growth of the Insect.   Heeger states that the larva undergoes three ecdyses, and he gives the figures we reproduce ; if he be correct it would appear that the nymph undergoes a great development.   Réaumur, on account apparently of their great metamorphosis, treated the species

---

[1] *J. New York Ent. Soc.* i. 1893, p. 120.   See also as to knowledge on the part of ants, Forbes, *Eighteenth Rep. Insects Illinois*, 1894, pp. 66, etc.

[2] Monograph by Buckton, *Ray Society*, 4 vols. 1879-1883.

known to him as being Lepidopterous, though he correctly pointed out their distinctions.   At present we can only conclude that the Aleurodidae undergo a metamorphosis of a kind peculiar to themselves, and requiring renewed investigation.   The family has been monographed by Signoret, and more recently by Maskell, who has increased the number of species to about sixty.[1] We have three or four in Britain, one of which, *A. brassicae*, is extremely abundant on various kinds of cabbage in certain years.

Fam. 9. Coccidae (*Scale - Insects, Mealy - bugs*). — *Insects, usually minute, with only a single claw to the foot; the male with one pair of wings, but without mouth-parts; the female wingless and usually so degraded in form that most of the external organs and appendages cannot be distinguished.*   The form in which these

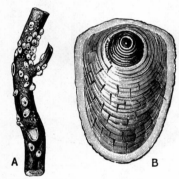

Insects are most generally known is that of a small scale or shell-like body closely adhering to leaves, fruits, or bark.   The scales are of the most varied form, so that no general description can be given of them.   The scale may be defined as an accumulation of excreted matter, combined with the cast skin or skins of the Insect, covering the body either totally or partially, and thus acting as a shield under which the subsequent development takes place.   All Coccidae do not form scales; but the habit of

FIG. 288.—Scale-Insect, **A**, *Aspidiotus camelliae*, on the stem of a plant; **B**, a female scale magnified. (After Green.)

excreting a large quantity of peculiar matters to the outside of the body is universal; this excreted substance is frequently white, and of a powdery nature, and Coccids of this kind are known as mealy-bugs.   In other cases the exudation is like shell or glass, and the creature may become quite encysted therein.   In this way the forms of Cocidae known as "ground-pearls" are formed.   When first hatched from the egg Coccidae are mite-like creatures, and it is only subsequently that the females lose the power of locomotion.   The females of numerous forms of Coccidae—more particularly the mealy-bugs—do not lose the antennae and legs. There is also a group (Brachyscelides) of Coccids that live in

[1] *Tr. New Zealand Inst.* xxviii. 1895.

galls. This highly aberrant group is, however, peculiar to Australia; elsewhere very few gall-making Coccids have been discovered.

There are upwards of 800 species of Coccidae at present known.[1] The family was monographed by Signoret about twenty-five years ago, and since then there has been very much matter concerning them published in a scattered manner.[2] No general work has been published on the British species, but Mr. Newstead is preparing one. The classification of Insects so minute as Coccidae, and with such extreme difference in the sexes, is, of course, a matter of great difficulty; the best divisions are those given by Green in his *Coccidae of Ceylon*.[3]

The fact that there is only one pair of wings in the perfect male Coccid would appear to ally these Insects with the Diptera; these Coccidae have, too, like the Diptera, a small appendage on each side of the metathorax. Witlaczil shows that these little processes may really represent a pair of wings, inasmuch as they are developed from imperfect folds of hypodermis, *i.e.* imaginal discs. Beyond these facts and the occurrence in certain females (Margarodes) of a great histolysis during the

FIG. 289. — *Dactylopius longispinus.* Female on portion of a fig-leaf. (After Berlese.)

post-embryonic development, there is nothing to indicate any relationship between Coccidae and Diptera. It has been shown by Riley that these little processes, in some forms, serve as hooks to attach or control the true wings, and this function is never assumed by the halteres of Diptera. Although Coccidae are placed next Aphidae, yet the two families appear to be really very different. The modes of reproduction so peculiar in Aphidae reappear to a certain extent in Coccidae, but are associated with profound

---

[1] A catalogue of Coccidae has recently been published by Mr. T. D. A. Cockerell in *Bull. Illinois Lab.* iv. 1896, pp. 318-339.

[2] Signoret's papers are to be found in eighteen parts in *Ann. Soc. ent. France*, 1868 to 1876: the most considerable subsequent systematic papers are those by Maskell in the *Transactions of the New Zealand Institute* from 1878 to the present time.

[3] *Coccidae of Ceylon*, pt. 1, 1896, p. 16.

distinctions.   Though   the viviparous method of reproduction
and parthenogenesis occur in Coccidae, yet they are only exceptional, and they are not put to the same uses by the species
that exhibit the phenomena.   Thus we have seen that in Aphidae
generations of imperfect individuals are produced with rapidity,
while the individual is not directly very prolific.   In Coccidae
the reverse is the case—the generations are usually similar to
one another; they do not, as a rule, follow with rapidity, and the
female is usually very prolific, thousands of young being sometimes produced by a single individual.   The extraordinary polymorphism of the species of Aphidae is not exhibited by Coccidae,
though, contrary to what we find in Aphidae, the males and
females are usually excessively different.   The two families apparently also differ in that Coccidae are specially characteristic
of warm climates, Aphidae of the temperate regions.

    Parthenogenesis.—Owing to the fact that the males are very
minute creatures, totally different from the females, and living
but a very short time, they were but little known to the earlier
observers.   It was therefore only natural to suppose that parthenogenesis was very common.   Of late years the males of a great
many species have become known, so that ordinary sexual reproduction must be considered as the normal method in Coccidae,
although, in the great majority of cases, the male is still unknown.
It has, however, been shown in numerous cases that parthenogenesis
may occur even when males exist ; and there are some abundant
species of which it has not been possible to find a male.   In
1887 Moniez[1] announced that he had discovered the male of
Lecanium hesperidum (one of the notoriously parthenogenetic
species) in an ovarian cul-de-sac in the body of the female, and
he therefore considers that sexual reproduction occurs.   He does
not say how pairing takes place, and we are not aware that his
observation has been confirmed.   If correct it will be necessary
to reconsider the whole question as to parthenogenesis in
Coccidae.   Apterous males are known in two or three species.

    The post-embryonic development of Coccidae is of the most
unusual character.   It is quite different in the two sexes, and in
each of them it presents features not found elsewhere.   It has,
however, as yet been studied in only a few forms, and even in
them is incompletely known.   When hatched from the egg

---

[1] *C. R. Ac. Sci. Paris*, civ. 1887, p. 449.

the young Coccids are all similar, male and female being indistin-
guishable. A difference soon appears, with the result that the male, after passing through more than one pupal condition, appears as a winged Insect. The female never becomes winged, but, if we may judge from the incomplete accounts we at present possess, her development varies much according to species. In some she retains the legs, antennae, and mouth-organs; in others she loses these parts, though retaining the original form in a general manner; while in a third (*Margarodes*) she becomes en-cysted, and apparently suffers an almost com-

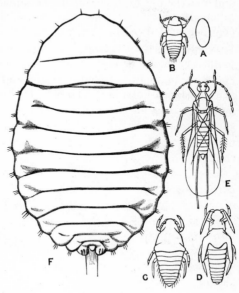

FIG. 290.—Instars of *Dactylopius citri*. (After Berlese.) **A**, Egg; **B**, young larva; **C**, first male nymph; **D**, second male nymph; **E**, adult male; **F**, adult female. All equally magnified. × 20.

plete histolysis, reappearing after a very long period (it is said it may be as much as seven years) in a considerably altered form. The post-embryonic development of *Aspidiotus nerii* has been studied by Schmidt[1] and Witlaczil,[2] whose accounts agree except as to some points, such as the number of ecdyses. The young, or larva, is hatched with fairly well-developed legs, antennae, and rostrum; there is no external difference between the sexes. The larva selects some spot on the plant and drives its rostrum therein, thus becoming fixed; moults occur, and the body excretes waxy matter from its sides in processes that fell together and form the shield; the female becomes much larger than the male. The legs and antennae of both sexes disappear, so that the power of movement is completely lost. The mouth-parts also atrophy. The female after this undergoes no further change, except that of growth in connection with ovarian development. The male,

[1] *Arch. Naturgesch.* li. i. 1885, p. 169.   [2] *Zeitschr. wiss. Zool.* xliii. 1886, p. 156.

however, continues development; notwithstanding the impossibility of taking food, owing to the absence of a mouth, it increases much in size, and the organs of the future perfect Insect commence to develop from imaginal discs in a manner similar to that which occurs in the Dipterous genus *Corethra*; no mouthparts are however developed, these being merely represented by spots of pigment, or rudimentary additional eyes.   The wings are developed outside the body.   Difference of opinion prevails as to the nature of the instars between the young larva and the imago.   It is clear, however, that Fig. 291, D, corresponds fairly

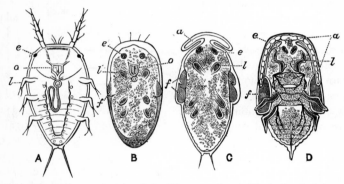

Fig. 291.—Development of male of *Aspidiotus nerii*. **A**, Newly hatched larva; **B**, prae-pupal instar; **C**, pupa before ecdysis; **D**, pupa shortly before the emergence of the imago: *a*, antenna; *e*, eye; *f*, wing-rudiment; *l*, leg; *o*, basal part of mouth-organs. (After Schmidt.)   Magnification not definitely stated.

with the pupa of Insects, with complete metamorphosis, and the instars shown in Fig. 291, B, C, may therefore be looked on as equivalents of the resting-larva stage of ordinary Insects with complete metamorphosis.   Witlaczil considers this development to be a condition of incomplete, approaching very nearly to complete, metamorphosis.   The condition is perhaps more precisely estimated if we recollect that winged Insects are divided into two series, in one of which the wings are developed outside the body; in the other, inside the body.   The Insects with very complete metamorphosis all belong to the second of these two series, while in the male Coccid we have the highest form of metamorphosis attained by any of the first series.   As regards the development of the female encysted nymph or pupa, previously alluded to as being found in the "ground-pearls" of the genus *Margarodes,* we can at present offer the reader no satisfactory account.[1]

Products of Coccidae.—Honey-dew is secreted by Coccidae, but as a rule not so extensively as by Aphidae and some other Homoptera; nevertheless, it is often sufficient to make the plants frequented by Coccids very sticky and unclean. Some species make a really extensive exudation of such matter. Réaumur records that a Coccid, which is doubtless *Lecanium persicae,* excretes a supply of honey-dew that drips to the ground; he says it tastes sweet and nice. The manna mentioned in the book of Exodus is pretty certainly the honey-dew secreted by *Coccus* (now *Gossyparia*) *mannifera,* which lives on *Tamarix* in many places in the Mediterranean basin. This substance is still called by the Arabs " Man," and is used as food; in its natural state it is a substance very like honey; it is doubtless excreted by the *Coccus,* and is not produced directly by the *Tamarix* as some have supposed. Waxy matters are produced by several Coccidae. *Ceroplastes ceriferus,* a Lecaniid, produces white wax in India. *Ceroplastes* is a widely distributed genus, and various species of it have been used for the purpose of producing wax in other parts of the world. The white wax of China is understood to be produced by another Lecaniid, *Ericerus pela;* but little is known as to this Insect; it is said that the wax is produced by the winged males. The substance was formerly greatly prized in China, but is falling into disuse on account of the introduction of Kerosene. Lac is produced by *Carteria lacca,* a Lecaniid living in India on *Anona squamosa,* as well as on species of *Ficus, Rhamnus* and other trees; the lac is the shelly scale produced by the Insect as a covering; it is composed in larger part of resinous matter, with which there is mixed a comparatively small quantity of wax and other substances. The body of this Insect also affords the red substance called lake. Various species of *Kermes* formerly afforded a red dye well known to the Greeks and Romans. These Insects live on *Quercus coccifera* in the Mediterranean region. A medicinal syrup is also obtained from them. *Porphyrophora polonica* was used in North and Central Europe for the same purposes as *Kermes;* it is a Coccid living on the roots of *Polygonum cocciferum.* These European Insects were replaced commercially

---

[1] For summary as to our present knowledge of this curious condition of Insect life, see Mayet, *Ann. Soc. ent. France,* 1896, p. 419.

after the discovery of America by the cochineal Insect, *Coccus cacti*, a Mexican Coccid feeding on a Cactus called Nopal (*Opuntia coccinellifera*). This Insect was subsequently introduced to the Eastern hemisphere, and was established with more or less success in a few spots on the borders of the Mediterranean. In the Canary Islands it flourished on other species of *Cactus*, became acclimatised, and was the object of an extensive commerce. The colour in the case of all these Coccid dyes was obtained from the bodies of the Insects, in the tissues of which it is contained. The dyes have now been largely displaced in commerce by the derivatives of Aniline. Axin is produced by the Mexican Coccid *Llaveia axinus;* this substance appears to be of a very peculiar nature ; it is apparently chiefly fatty, and contains a peculiar acid, axinic acid. Axin is used as an external medicinal application in various affections; and it is also employed as a varnish; it dries and hardens on exposure to the air, and is said to be of considerable value.[1] In our British genus *Orthezia* the body of the female is completely covered with a symmetrical snow-white armour, from which project the pink legs and antennae. This is one of the forms in which the female preserves the legs to the end of her life. The objects called ground-pearls, already alluded to, have long been known in various parts of the world, and in the island of St. Vincent they are sufficiently large to be collected and strung for necklaces. These bodies are the encysted pupae of Coccids of the genus *Margarodes;* the cyst is said to be of chitin. *M. vitis* commits serious ravages on the vines in Chili by sucking their roots, and it is probable that all the species are of subterranean habits; this would partially explain the fact that very little is known about the history of these pearls, though naturalists have been acquainted with them for many years.

The gall-making Coccids of the group Brachyscelides have only recently been at all investigated; the galls they give rise to are sometimes about a foot in length, and there appear to be numerous species and several genera in Australia; they are especially abundant on *Eucalyptus* and Acacias. The females are highly remarkable from the variable conditions the legs assume, so that in some cases they may be described as biped Insects, the

---

[1] For additional information as to useful Coccidae, see Blanchard, *Bull. Soc. Zool. France*, viii. 1883, p. 217.

hind legs remaining, though the others have atrophied.[1]   Very
little indeed is known as to these Insects.   One of the most
peculiar points of their economy appears to be that the galls
giving rise to males are different from those producing females.

Anoplura or Lice.

*Small Insects with thin integument; entirely wingless, the
three thoracic segments indistinctly separated; the head
bearing in front a short tube furnished with hooks; from which
tube there can be protruded another very delicate sucking-
tube.   Feet terminated by a single long claw.*   The Anoplura,
Pediculidae, or lice are disgusting Insects about which but little
is known.   The most contrary opinions have been expressed as
to their mode of taking their nourishment, which is, without
exception, the blood of Mammals; on the bodies of which they
pass the whole of their life.   It is a most
difficult matter to examine their mouth;
the best information on this point is given
by Schiödte and Graber, but though these
two authorities agree, their results are very
incomplete, and do not warrant us in expressing a confident opinion as to the nature
of the relationship between Hemiptera and
Anoplura—a question that has been for
long a moot one.   The short tube furnished
with hooks in front (Fig. 293, *d*) is considered to be the lower lip, and the tube
inside is, it is suggested, a combination of
the homologues of maxillae and mandibles; there is also what may be a labrum

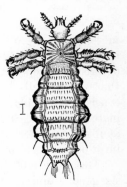

Fig. 292.—*Pediculus capitis*, ♀.   Human head.
(After Piaget.)

(*g*); and inside the head a framework, at any rate analogous to
if not homologous with, the parts of this kind we have described
as existing in Hemiptera.   All the parts, with the exception of
the basal tube or head of the beak, are of the most minute and
delicate nature, so that it is difficult to see their form or comprehend their relations.   It is evident that they are very different
anatomically from the mouth-parts of Hemiptera; still there is

---

[1] Rubsaamen's paper on these Insects gives references to most of the previous
literature, *Berlin. ent. Zeitschr.* xxxix. 1894, p. 199.

sufficient general resemblance to warrant the belief that the parts
in the two may ultimately be shown to be also morphologically

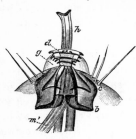

FIG. 293. — Mouth - organs of
louse. (After Graber.) *b*, *c*,
Chitinous   envelope   into
which the beak can be withdrawn ; *d*, head of the beak,
with crown of spines ; *g*,
labrum ; *h*, delicate tube
protruded (very rarely seen
in this state) ; *m'*, unpaired
muscle.

similar.   If Meinert be correct, this
view will, however, not prove to have
any foundation.   He considers that
morphologically the mouth of the louse
has no similarity to that of the bug ;
the protrusible parts in the former he
considers to be modifications of epipharynx and hypopharynx ; and the
rod-like structures to be hypopharyngeal
lamellae ; and that they are thus totally
different from the setae of bugs.[1]   He
considers Lice to be a distinct Order of
Insects for which he proposes the name
Siphunculata.

The alimentary canal and nervous
system resemble those of Mallophaga
more than they do those of Hemiptera.   The oesophagus leads
into a large stomach bilobed in front ; at the posterior extremity
of this there open the four Malpighian tubes, and behind these
there is a well-marked small intestine.   The nervous system
consists of a cephalic ganglion and of three other closely approximated ganglia, the posterior one the larger.   It remains
doubtful whether or not the first of these three ganglia is the
infra-oesophageal one.[2]

The species of lice, so far as known, are not numerous, some
six genera and about forty species being all that are recorded ;
they occur on various kinds of mammals, including some that live
in water.   Seals have a genus, *Echinophthirius*, peculiar to them.
Monkeys are specially liable to be affected by lice ; the genus
that chiefly occurs on them is *Pedicinus*, a very distinct one, in
which there are only three instead of five joints to the antennae.
Perhaps the most remarkable louse is *Haematomyzus elephantis*,
that of the elephant ; it has a long proboscis in front of the head.
As a rule each species of louse is confined to one species of Mam-
malia, or to very closely allied forms.   Man is said to be infested

[1] *Ent. Meddel.* iii. 1891, p. 82.
[2] Cf. Graber, *Zeitschr. wiss. Zool.* xxii. 1872, p. 165, and Landois in the same
Journal, xiv. 1864, p. 24.

by three species, *Pediculus capitis, P. vestimenti* and *Phthirius inguinalis ;* Meinert is of opinion that *P. capitis* and *P. vestimenti* are only one species, and Schiödte appears also to have thought this probable.   Andrew Murray was of opinion that the heads of different varieties of men are infested by distinct varieties of *P. capitis.*   His conclusion was chiefly based on examination of specimens preserved by Charles Darwin ; it requires confirmation. Very little is known as to the life-history of the louse.   Leeuwenhoek made himself the *corpus vile* for an experiment, from which he concluded that the *Pediculus vestimenti* is very prolific.   That scientific men did not know whether the louse bites or sucks was formerly made the ground for a taunt.   Schiödte has given an almost pleasing account of the way in which he settled this,[1] showing that the sucking action is beyond all doubt.   Accounts of disease called Phthiriasis, attributed to lice, are to be found in many old books, but the evidence does not warrant us in believing anything more than that persons suffering from some disease, and in a neglected and filthy condition, were horribly infested with these disgusting Insects.

It is usual to say that Pediculidae are Hemiptera degraded by a long exclusive persistence in parasitic habits.   At present, however, this must be looked on as a pious opinion, rather than as an induction from our knowledge of their morphology and embryology ; for this is at present too imperfect to warrant any final conclusion.

[1] *Ann. Nat. History* (3), xvii. 1866, p. 213.

NOTE.

Since the remarks on the classification of Hymenoptera were written Mr. W. H. Ashmead has published several important papers proposing a classification to a considerable extent new. He adopts 10 superfamilies and 94 families. His views are summarised in *P. U. S. Mus.* xxiii. No. 1206, 1900. Pastor Konow has also discussed this subject in *Ent. Nachr.* xxiii. 1897, pp. 148-156.

INDEX

Every reference is to the page : words in italics are names of genera or species ; figures in italics indicate that the reference relates to systematic position ; figures in thick type refer to an illustration ; f. = and in following page or pages ; n. = note.

A CATALOGUE OF SELECTED DOVER BOOKS
IN ALL FIELDS OF INTEREST

A CATALOGUE OF SELECTED DOVER BOOKS
IN ALL FIELDS OF INTEREST

WHAT IS SCIENCE?, *N. Campbell*
The role of experiment and measurement, the function of mathematics, the nature of scientific laws, the difference between laws and theories, the limitations of science, and many similarly provocative topics are treated clearly and without technicalities by an eminent scientist. "Still an excellent introduction to scientific philosophy," H. Margenau in *Physics Today*. "A first-rate primer . . . deserves a wide audience," *Scientific American*. 192pp. 5⅜ x 8.
60043-2 Paperbound $1.25

THE NATURE OF LIGHT AND COLOUR IN THE OPEN AIR, *M. Minnaert*
Why are shadows sometimes blue, sometimes green, or other colors depending on the light and surroundings? What causes mirages? Why do multiple suns and moons appear in the sky? Professor Minnaert explains these unusual phenomena and hundreds of others in simple, easy-to-understand terms based on optical laws and the properties of light and color. No mathematics is required but artists, scientists, students, and everyone fascinated by these "tricks" of nature will find thousands of useful and amazing pieces of information. Hundreds of observational experiments are suggested which require no special equipment. 200 illustrations; 42 photos. xvi + 362pp. 5⅜ x 8.
20196-1 Paperbound $2.75

THE STRANGE STORY OF THE QUANTUM, AN ACCOUNT FOR THE GENERAL READER OF THE GROWTH OF IDEAS UNDERLYING OUR PRESENT ATOMIC KNOWLEDGE, *B. Hoffmann*
Presents lucidly and expertly, with barest amount of mathematics, the problems and theories which led to modern quantum physics. Dr. Hoffmann begins with the closing years of the 19th century, when certain trifling discrepancies were noticed, and with illuminating analogies and examples takes you through the brilliant concepts of Planck, Einstein, Pauli, Broglie, Bohr, Schroedinger, Heisenberg, Dirac, Sommerfeld, Feynman, etc. This edition includes a new, long postscript carrying the story through 1958. "Of the books attempting an account of the history and contents of our modern atomic physics which have come to my attention, this is the best," H. Margenau, Yale University, in *American Journal of Physics*. 32 tables and line illustrations. Index. 275pp. 5⅜ x 8.
20518-5 Paperbound $2.00

GREAT IDEAS OF MODERN MATHEMATICS: THEIR NATURE AND USE, *Jagjit Singh*
Reader with only high school math will understand main mathematical ideas of modern physics, astronomy, genetics, psychology, evolution, etc. better than many who use them as tools, but comprehend little of their basic structure. Author uses his wide knowledge of non-mathematical fields in brilliant exposition of differential equations, matrices, group theory, logic, statistics, problems of mathematical foundations, imaginary numbers, vectors, etc. Original publication. 2 appendixes. 2 indexes. 65 ills. 322pp. 5⅜ x 8.
20587-8 Paperbound $2.50

THE MUSIC OF THE SPHERES: THE MATERIAL UNIVERSE — FROM ATOM TO QUASAR, SIMPLY EXPLAINED, *Guy Murchie*
Vast compendium of fact, modern concept and theory, observed and calculated data, historical background guides intelligent layman through the material universe. Brilliant exposition of earth's construction, explanations for moon's craters, atmospheric components of Venus and Mars (with data from recent fly-by's), sun spots, sequences of star birth and death, neighboring galaxies, contributions of Galileo, Tycho Brahe, Kepler, etc.; and (Vol. 2) construction of the atom (describing newly discovered sigma and xi subatomic particles), theories of sound, color and light, space and time, including relativity theory, quantum theory, wave theory, probability theory, work of Newton, Maxwell, Faraday, Einstein, de Broglie, etc. "Best presentation yet offered to the intelligent general reader," *Saturday Review*. Revised (1967). Index. 319 illustrations by the author. Total of xx + 644pp. 5⅜ x 8½.
21809-0, 21810-4 Two volume set, paperbound $5.00

FOUR LECTURES ON RELATIVITY AND SPACE, *Charles Proteus Steinmetz*
Lecture series, given by great mathematician and electrical engineer, generally considered one of the best popular-level expositions of special and general relativity theories and related questions. Steinmetz translates complex mathematical reasoning into language accessible to laymen through analogy, example and comparison. Among topics covered are relativity of motion, location, time; of mass; acceleration; 4-dimensional time-space; geometry of the gravitational field; curvature and bending of space; non-Euclidean geometry. Index. 40 illustrations. x + 142pp. 5⅜ x 8½.   61771-8 Paperbound $1.50

HOW TO KNOW THE WILD FLOWERS, *Mrs. William Starr Dana*
Classic nature book that has introduced thousands to wonders of American wild flowers. Color-season principle of organization is easy to use, even by those with no botanical training, and the genial, refreshing discussions of history, folklore, uses of over 1,000 native and escape flowers, foliage plants are informative as well as fun to read. Over 170 full-page plates, collected from several editions, may be colored in to make permanent records of finds. Revised to conform with 1950 edition of Gray's Manual of Botany. xlii + 438pp. 5⅜ x 8½.   20332-8 Paperbound $2.50

MANUAL OF THE TREES OF NORTH AMERICA, *Charles Sprague Sargent*
Still unsurpassed as most comprehensive, reliable study of North American tree characteristics, precise locations and distribution. By dean of American dendrologists. Every tree native to U.S., Canada, Alaska; 185 genera, 717 species, described in detail—leaves, flowers, fruit, winterbuds, bark, wood, growth habits, etc. plus discussion of varieties and local variants, immaturity variations. Over 100 keys, including unusual 11-page analytical key to genera, aid in identification. 783 clear illustrations of flowers, fruit, leaves. An unmatched permanent reference work for all nature lovers. Second enlarged (1926) edition. Synopsis of families. Analytical key to genera. Glossary of technical terms. Index. 783 illustrations, 1 map. Total of 982pp. 5⅜ x 8.
20277-1, 20278-X Two volume set, paperbound $6.00

IT'S FUN TO MAKE THINGS FROM SCRAP MATERIALS,
Evelyn Glantz Hershoff
What use are empty spools, tin cans, bottle tops? What can be made from
rubber bands, clothes pins, paper clips, and buttons? This book provides
simply worded instructions and large diagrams showing you how to make
cookie cutters, toy trucks, paper turkeys, Halloween masks, telephone sets,
aprons, linoleum block- and spatter prints — in all 399 projects! Many are easy
enough for young children to figure out for themselves; some challenging
enough to entertain adults; all are remarkably ingenious ways to make things
from materials that cost pennies or less! Formerly "Scrap Fun for Everyone."
Index. 214 illustrations. 373pp. 5⅜ x 8½.   21251-3 Paperbound $2.00

SYMBOLIC LOGIC and THE GAME OF LOGIC, *Lewis Carroll*
"Symbolic Logic" is not concerned with modern symbolic logic, but is instead
a collection of over 380 problems posed with charm and imagination, using
the syllogism and a fascinating diagrammatic method of drawing conclusions.
In "The Game of Logic" Carroll's whimsical imagination devises a logical game
played with 2 diagrams and counters (included) to manipulate hundreds of
tricky syllogisms. The final section, "Hit or Miss" is a lagniappe of 101 additional puzzles in the delightful Carroll manner. Until this reprint edition,
both of these books were rarities costing up to $15 each. Symbolic Logic:
Index. xxxi + 199pp. The Game of Logic: 96pp. 2 vols. bound as one. 5⅜ x 8.
                                                        20492-8 Paperbound $2.50

MATHEMATICAL PUZZLES OF SAM LOYD, PART I
selected and edited by M. Gardner
Choice puzzles by the greatest American puzzle creator and innovator. Selected
from his famous collection, "Cyclopedia of Puzzles," they retain the unique
style and historical flavor of the originals. There are posers based on arithmetic,
algebra, probability, game theory, route tracing, topology, counter and sliding
block, operations research, geometrical dissection. Includes the famous "14-15"
puzzle which was a national craze, and his "Horse of a Different Color" which
sold millions of copies. 117 of his most ingenious puzzles in all. 120 line
drawings and diagrams. Solutions. Selected references. xx + 167pp. 5⅜ x 8.
                                                        20498-7 Paperbound $1.35

STRING FIGURES AND HOW TO MAKE THEM, *Caroline Furness Jayne*
107 string figures plus variations selected from the best primitive and modern
examples developed by Navajo, Apache, pygmies of Africa, Eskimo, in Europe,
Australia, China, etc. The most readily understandable, easy-to-follow book in
English on perennially popular recreation. Crystal-clear exposition; step-by-
step diagrams. Everyone from kindergarten children to adults looking for
unusual diversion will be endlessly amused. Index. Bibliography. Introduction
by A. C. Haddon. 17 full-page plates, 960 illustrations. xxiii + 401pp. 5⅜ x 8½.
                                                        20152-X Paperbound $2.50

PAPER FOLDING FOR BEGINNERS, *W. D. Murray and F. J. Rigney*
A delightful introduction to the varied and entertaining Japanese art of
origami (paper folding), with a full, crystal-clear text that anticipates every
difficulty; over 275 clearly labeled diagrams of all important stages in creation.
You get results at each stage, since complex figures are logically developed
from simpler ones. 43 different pieces are explained: sailboats, frogs, roosters,
etc. 6 photographic plates. 279 diagrams. 95pp. 5⅝ x 8⅜.
                                                        20713-7 Paperbound $1.00

PRINCIPLES OF ART HISTORY,
H. Wölfflin
Analyzing such terms as "baroque," "classic," "neoclassic," "primitive," "picturesque," and 164 different works by artists like Botticelli, van Cleve, Dürer, Hobbema, Holbein, Hals, Rembrandt, Titian, Brueghel, Vermeer, and many others, the author establishes the classifications of art history and style on a firm, concrete basis. This classic of art criticism shows what really occurred between the 14th-century primitives and the sophistication of the 18th century in terms of basic attitudes and philosophies. "A remarkable lesson in the art of seeing," *Sat. Rev. of Literature.* Translated from the 7th German edition. 150 illustrations. 254pp. 6⅛ x 9¼. 20276-3 Paperbound $2.50

PRIMITIVE ART,
Franz Boas
This authoritative and exhaustive work by a great American anthropologist covers the entire gamut of primitive art. Pottery, leatherwork, metal work, stone work, wood, basketry, are treated in detail. Theories of primitive art, historical depth in art history, technical virtuosity, unconscious levels of patterning, symbolism, styles, literature, music, dance, etc. A must book for the interested layman, the anthropologist, artist, handicrafter (hundreds of unusual motifs), and the historian. Over 900 illustrations (50 ceramic vessels, 12 totem poles, etc.). 376pp. 5⅜ x 8. 20025-6 Paperbound $2.50

THE GENTLEMAN AND CABINET MAKER'S DIRECTOR,
Thomas Chippendale
A reprint of the 1762 catalogue of furniture designs that went on to influence generations of English and Colonial and Early Republic American furniture makers. The 200 plates, most of them full-page sized, show Chippendale's designs for French (Louis XV), Gothic, and Chinese-manner chairs, sofas, canopy and dome beds, cornices, chamber organs, cabinets, shaving tables, commodes, picture frames, frets, candle stands, chimney pieces, decorations, etc. The drawings are all elegant and highly detailed; many include construction diagrams and elevations. A supplement of 24 photographs shows surviving pieces of original and Chippendale-style pieces of furniture. Brief biography of Chippendale by N. I. Bienenstock, editor of *Furniture World.* Reproduced from the 1762 edition. 200 plates, plus 19 photographic plates. vi + 249pp. 9⅛ x 12¼. 21601-2 Paperbound $4.00

AMERICAN ANTIQUE FURNITURE: A BOOK FOR AMATEURS,
Edgar G. Miller, Jr.
Standard introduction and practical guide to identification of valuable American antique furniture. 2115 illustrations, mostly photographs taken by the author in 148 private homes, are arranged in chronological order in extensive chapters on chairs, sofas, chests, desks, bedsteads, mirrors, tables, clocks, and other articles. Focus is on furniture accessible to the collector, including simpler pieces and a larger than usual coverage of Empire style. Introductory chapters identify structural elements, characteristics of various styles, how to avoid fakes, etc. "We are frequently asked to name some book on American furniture that will meet the requirements of the novice collector, the beginning dealer, and . . . the general public. . . . We believe Mr. Miller's two volumes more completely satisfy this specification than any other work," *Antiques.* Appendix. Index. Total of vi + 1106pp. 7⅞ x 10¾. 21599-7, 21600-4 Two volume set, paperbound $10.00

THE BAD CHILD'S BOOK OF BEASTS, MORE BEASTS FOR WORSE CHILDREN, and A MORAL ALPHABET, *H. Belloc*
Hardly and anthology of humorous verse has appeared in the last 50 years without at least a couple of these famous nonsense verses. But one must see the entire volumes — with all the delightful original illustrations by Sir Basil Blackwood — to appreciate fully Belloc's charming and witty verses that play so subacidly on the platitudes of life and morals that beset his day — and ours. A great humor classic. Three books in one. Total of 157pp. 5⅜ x 8.
20749-8 Paperbound $1.25

THE DEVIL'S DICTIONARY, *Ambrose Bierce*
Sardonic and irreverent barbs puncturing the pomposities and absurdities of American politics, business, religion, literature, and arts, by the country's greatest satirist in the classic tradition. Epigrammatic as Shaw, piercing as Swift, American as Mark Twain, Will Rogers, and Fred Allen, Bierce will always remain the favorite of a small coterie of enthusiasts, and of writers and speakers whom he supplies with "some of the most gorgeous witticisms of the English language" (H. L. Mencken). Over 1000 entries in alphabetical order. 144pp. 5⅜ x 8.
20487-1 Paperbound $1.25

THE COMPLETE NONSENSE OF EDWARD LEAR.
This is the only complete edition of this master of gentle madness available at a popular price. *A Book of Nonsense, Nonsense Songs, More Nonsense Songs and Stories* in their entirety with all the old favorites that have delighted children and adults for years. The Dong With A Luminous Nose, The Jumblies, The Owl and the Pussycat, and hundreds of other bits of wonderful nonsense. 214 limericks, 3 sets of Nonsense Botany, 5 Nonsense Alphabets, 546 drawings by Lear himself, and much more. 320pp. 5⅜ x 8.   20167-8 Paperbound $1.75

THE WIT AND HUMOR OF OSCAR WILDE, *ed. by Alvin Redman*
Wilde at his most brilliant, in 1000 epigrams exposing weaknesses and hypocrisies of "civilized" society. Divided into 49 categories—sin, wealth, women, America, etc.—to aid writers, speakers. Includes excerpts from his trials, books, plays, criticism. Formerly "The Epigrams of Oscar Wilde." Introduction by Vyvyan Holland, Wilde's only living son. Introductory essay by editor. 260pp. 5⅜ x 8.
20602-5 Paperbound $1.50

A CHILD'S PRIMER OF NATURAL HISTORY, *Oliver Herford*
Scarcely an anthology of whimsy and humor has appeared in the last 50 years without a contribution from Oliver Herford. Yet the works from which these examples are drawn have been almost impossible to obtain! Here at last are Herford's improbable definitions of a menagerie of familiar and weird animals, each verse illustrated by the author's own drawings. 24 drawings in 2 colors; 24 additional drawings. vii + 95pp. 6½ x 6.   21647-0 Paperbound $1.00

THE BROWNIES: THEIR BOOK, *Palmer Cox*
The book that made the Brownies a household word. Generations of readers have enjoyed the antics, predicaments and adventures of these jovial sprites, who emerge from the forest at night to play or to come to the aid of a deserving human. Delightful illustrations by the author decorate nearly every page. 24 short verse tales with 266 illustrations. 155pp. 6⅝ x 9¼.
21265-3 Paperbound $1.50

THE PRINCIPLES OF PSYCHOLOGY,
William James

The full long-course, unabridged, of one of the great classics of Western literature and science. Wonderfully lucid descriptions of human mental activity, the stream of thought, consciousness, time perception, memory, imagination, emotions, reason, abnormal phenomena, and similar topics. Original contributions are integrated with the work of such men as Berkeley, Binet, Mills, Darwin, Hume, Kant, Royce, Schopenhauer, Spinoza, Locke, Descartes, Galton, Wundt, Lotze, Herbart, Fechner, and scores of others. All contrasting interpretations of mental phenomena are examined in detail—introspective analysis, philosophical interpretation, and experimental research. "A classic," *Journal of Consulting Psychology*. "The main lines are as valid as ever," *Psychoanalytical Quarterly*. "Standard reading . . . a classic of interpretation," *Psychiatric Quarterly*. 94 illustrations. 1408pp. 5⅜ x 8.
20381-6, 20382-4 Two volume set, paperbound $6.00

VISUAL ILLUSIONS: THEIR CAUSES, CHARACTERISTICS AND APPLICATIONS,
M. Luckiesh

"Seeing is deceiving," asserts the author of this introduction to virtually every type of optical illusion known. The text both describes and explains the principles involved in color illusions, figure-ground, distance illusions, etc. 100 photographs, drawings and diagrams prove how easy it is to fool the sense: circles that aren't round, parallel lines that seem to bend, stationary figures that seem to move as you stare at them — illustration after illustration strains our credulity at what we see. Fascinating book from many points of view, from applications for artists, in camouflage, etc. to the psychology of vision. New introduction by William Ittleson, Dept. of Psychology, Queens College. Index. Bibliography. xxi + 252pp. 5⅜ x 8½.   21530-X Paperbound $1.75

FADS AND FALLACIES IN THE NAME OF SCIENCE,
Martin Gardner

This is the standard account of various cults, quack systems, and delusions which have masqueraded as science: hollow earth fanatics. Reich and orgone sex energy, dianetics, Atlantis, multiple moons, Forteanism, flying saucers, medical fallacies like iridiagnosis, zone therapy, etc. A new chapter has been added on Bridey Murphy, psionics, and other recent manifestations in this field. This is a fair, reasoned appraisal of eccentric theory which provides excellent inoculation against cleverly masked nonsense. "Should be read by everyone, scientist and non-scientist alike," R. T. Birge, Prof. Emeritus of Physics, Univ. of California; Former President, American Physical Society. Index. x + 365pp. 5⅜ x 8.   20394-8 Paperbound $2.00

ILLUSIONS AND DELUSIONS OF THE SUPERNATURAL AND THE OCCULT,
D. H. Rawcliffe

Holds up to rational examination hundreds of persistent delusions including crystal gazing, automatic writing, table turning, mediumistic trances, mental healing, stigmata, lycanthropy, live burial, the Indian Rope Trick, spiritualism, dowsing, telepathy, clairvoyance, ghosts, ESP, etc. The author explains and exposes the mental and physical deceptions involved, making this not only an exposé of supernatural phenomena, but a valuable exposition of characteristic types of abnormal psychology. Originally titled "The Psychology of the Occult." 14 illustrations. Index. 551pp. 5⅜ x 8. 20503-7 Paperbound $3.50

FAIRY TALE COLLECTIONS, *edited by Andrew Lang*
Andrew Lang's fairy tale collections make up the richest shelf-full of traditional children's stories anywhere available. Lang supervised the translation of stories from all over the world—familiar European tales collected by Grimm, animal stories from Negro Africa, myths of primitive Australia, stories from Russia, Hungary, Iceland, Japan, and many other countries. Lang's selection of translations are unusually high; many authorities consider that the most familiar tales find their best versions in these volumes. All collections are richly decorated and illustrated by H. J. Ford and other artists.

THE BLUE FAIRY BOOK. 37 stories. 138 illustrations. ix + 390pp. 5⅜ x 8½.
21437-0 Paperbound $1.95

THE GREEN FAIRY BOOK. 42 stories. 100 illustrations. xiii + 366pp. 5⅜ x 8½.
21439-7 Paperbound $2.00

THE BROWN FAIRY BOOK. 32 stories. 50 illustrations, 8 in color. xii + 350pp. 5⅜ x 8½.
21438-9 Paperbound $1.95

THE BEST TALES OF HOFFMANN, *edited by E. F. Bleiler*
10 stories by E. T. A. Hoffmann, one of the greatest of all writers of fantasy. The tales include "The Golden Flower Pot," "Automata," "A New Year's Eve Adventure," "Nutcracker and the King of Mice," "Sand-Man," and others. Vigorous characterizations of highly eccentric personalities, remarkably imaginative situations, and intensely fast pacing has made these tales popular all over the world for 150 years. Editor's introduction. 7 drawings by Hoffmann. xxxiii + 419pp. 5⅜ x 8½.
21793-0 Paperbound $2.25

GHOST AND HORROR STORIES OF AMBROSE BIERCE,
edited by E. F. Bleiler
Morbid, eerie, horrifying tales of possessed poets, shabby aristocrats, revived corpses, and haunted malefactors. Widely acknowledged as the best of their kind between Poe and the moderns, reflecting their author's inner torment and bitter view of life. Includes "Damned Thing," "The Middle Toe of the Right Foot," "The Eyes of the Panther," "Visions of the Night," "Moxon's Master," and over a dozen others. Editor's introduction. xxii + 199pp. 5⅜ x 8½.
20767-6 Paperbound $1.50

THREE GOTHIC NOVELS, *edited by E. F. Bleiler*
Originators of the still popular Gothic novel form, influential in ushering in early 19th-century Romanticism. Horace Walpole's *Castle of Otranto*, William Beckford's *Vathek*, John Polidori's *The Vampyre*, and a *Fragment* by Lord Byron are enjoyable as exciting reading or as documents in the history of English literature. Editor's introduction. xi + 291pp. 5⅜ x 8½.
21232-7 Paperbound $2.00

BEST GHOST STORIES OF LEFANU, *edited by E. F. Bleiler*
Though admired by such critics as V. S. Pritchett, Charles Dickens and Henry James, ghost stories by the Irish novelist Joseph Sheridan LeFanu have never become as widely known as his detective fiction. About half of the 16 stories in this collection have never before been available in America. Collection includes "Carmilla" (perhaps the best vampire story ever written), "The Haunted Baronet," "The Fortunes of Sir Robert Ardagh," and the classic "Green Tea." Editor's introduction. 7 contemporary illustrations. Portrait of LeFanu. xii + 467pp. 5⅜ x 8.
20415-4 Paperbound $2.50

EASY-TO-DO ENTERTAINMENTS AND DIVERSIONS WITH COINS, CARDS, STRING, PAPER AND MATCHES, *R. M. Abraham*
Over 300 tricks, games and puzzles will provide young readers with absorbing fun. Sections on card games; paper-folding; tricks with coins, matches and pieces of string; games for the agile; toy-making from common household objects; mathematical recreations; and 50 miscellaneous pastimes. Anyone in charge of groups of youngsters, including hard-pressed parents, and in need of suggestions on how to keep children sensibly amused and quietly content will find this book indispensable. Clear, simple text, copious number of delightful line drawings and illustrative diagrams. Originally titled "Winter Nights' Entertainments." Introduction by Lord Baden Powell. 329 illustrations. v + 186pp. 5⅜ x 8½.   20921-0 Paperbound $1.25

AN INTRODUCTION TO CHESS MOVES AND TACTICS SIMPLY EXPLAINED, *Leonard Barden*
Beginner's introduction to the royal game. Names, possible moves of the pieces, definitions of essential terms, how games are won, etc. explained in 30-odd pages. With this background you'll be able to sit right down and play. Balance of book teaches strategy — openings, middle game, typical endgame play, and suggestions for improving your game. A sample game is fully analyzed. True middle-level introduction, teaching you all the essentials without oversimplifying or losing you in a maze of detail. 58 figures. 102pp. 5⅜ x 8½.   21210-6 Paperbound $1.25

LASKER'S MANUAL OF CHESS, *Dr. Emanuel Lasker*
Probably the greatest chess player of modern times, Dr. Emanuel Lasker held the world championship 28 years, independent of passing schools or fashions. This unmatched study of the game, chiefly for intermediate to skilled players, analyzes basic methods, combinations, position play, the aesthetics of chess, dozens of different openings, etc., with constant reference to great modern games. Contains a brilliant exposition of Steinitz's important theories. Introduction by Fred Reinfeld. Tables of Lasker's tournament record. 3 indices. 308 diagrams. 1 photograph. xxx + 349pp. 5⅜ x 8. 20640-8 Paperbound $2.50

COMBINATIONS: THE HEART OF CHESS, *Irving Chernev*
Step-by-step from simple combinations to complex, this book, by a well-known chess writer, shows you the intricacies of pins, counter-pins, knight forks, and smothered mates. Other chapters show alternate lines of play to those taken in actual championship games; boomerang combinations; classic examples of brilliant combination play by Nimzovich, Rubinstein, Tarrasch, Botvinnik, Alekhine and Capablanca. Index. 356 diagrams. ix + 245pp. 5⅜ x 8½.   21744-2 Paperbound $2.00

HOW TO SOLVE CHESS PROBLEMS, *K. S. Howard*
Full of practical suggestions for the fan or the beginner — who knows only the moves of the chessmen. Contains preliminary section and 58 two-move, 46 three-move, and 8 four-move problems composed by 27 outstanding American problem creators in the last 30 years. Explanation of all terms and exhaustive index. "Just what is wanted for the student," Brian Harley. 112 problems, solutions. vi + 171pp. 5⅜ x 8.   20748-X Paperbound $1.50

SOCIAL THOUGHT FROM LORE TO SCIENCE,
H. E. Barnes and H. Becker
An immense survey of sociological thought and ways of viewing, studying, planning, and reforming society from earliest times to the present. Includes thought on society of preliterate peoples, ancient non-Western cultures, and every great movement in Europe, America, and modern Japan. Analyzes hundreds of great thinkers: Plato, Augustine, Bodin, Vico, Montesquieu, Herder, Comte, Marx, etc. Weighs the contributions of utopians, sophists, fascists and communists; economists, jurists, philosophers, ecclesiastics, and every 19th and 20th century school of scientific sociology, anthropology, and social psychology throughout the world. Combines topical, chronological, and regional approaches, treating the evolution of social thought as a process rather than as a series of mere topics. "Impressive accuracy, competence, and discrimination . . . easily the best single survey," *Nation.* Thoroughly revised, with new material up to 1960. 2 indexes. Over 2200 bibliographical notes. Three volume set. Total of 1586pp. 5⅜ x 8.
20901-6, 20902-4, 20903-2 Three volume set, paperbound $10.50

A HISTORY OF HISTORICAL WRITING, *Harry Elmer Barnes*
Virtually the only adequate survey of the whole course of historical writing in a single volume. Surveys developments from the beginnings of historiography in the ancient Near East and the Classical World, up through the Cold War. Covers major historians in detail, shows interrelationship with cultural background, makes clear individual contributions, evaluates and estimates importance; also enormously rich upon minor authors and thinkers who are usually passed over. Packed with scholarship and learning, clear, easily written. Indispensable to every student of history. Revised and enlarged up to 1961. Index and bibliography. xv + 442pp. 5⅜ x 8½.
20104-X Paperbound $3.00

JOHANN SEBASTIAN BACH, *Philipp Spitta*
The complete and unabridged text of the definitive study of Bach. Written some 70 years ago, it is still unsurpassed for its coverage of nearly all aspects of Bach's life and work. There could hardly be a finer non-technical introduction to Bach's music than the detailed, lucid analyses which Spitta provides for hundreds of individual pieces. 26 solid pages are devoted to the B minor mass, for example, and 30 pages to the glorious St. Matthew Passion. This monumental set also includes a major analysis of the music of the 18th century: Buxtehude, Pachelbel, etc. "Unchallenged as the last word on one of the supreme geniuses of music," John Barkham, *Saturday Review Syndicate.* Total of 1819pp. Heavy cloth binding. 5⅜ x 8.
22278-0, 22279-9 Two volume set, clothbound $15.00

BEETHOVEN AND HIS NINE SYMPHONIES, *George Grove*
In this modern middle-level classic of musicology Grove not only analyzes all nine of Beethoven's symphonies very thoroughly in terms of their musical structure, but also discusses the circumstances under which they were written, Beethoven's stylistic development, and much other background material. This is an extremely rich book, yet very easily followed; it is highly recommended to anyone seriously interested in music. Over 250 musical passages. Index. viii + 407pp. 5⅜ x 8.
20334-4 Paperbound $2.50

THE TIME STREAM
John Taine
Acknowledged by many as the best SF writer of the 1920's, Taine (under the name Eric Temple Bell) was also a Professor of Mathematics of considerable renown. Reprinted here are *The Time Stream*, generally considered Taine's best, *The Greatest Game*, a biological-fiction novel, and *The Purple Sapphire*, involving a supercivilization of the past. Taine's stories tie fantastic narratives to frameworks of original and logical scientific concepts. Speculation is often profound on such questions as the nature of time, concept of entropy, cyclical universes, etc. 4 contemporary illustrations. v + 532pp. 5⅜ x 8⅜.
21180-0 Paperbound $3.00

SEVEN SCIENCE FICTION NOVELS,
H. G. Wells
Full unabridged texts of 7 science-fiction novels of the master. Ranging from biology, physics, chemistry, astronomy, to sociology and other studies, Mr. Wells extrapolates whole worlds of strange and intriguing character. "One will have to go far to match this for entertainment, excitement, and sheer pleasure . . ."*New York Times.* Contents: The Time Machine, The Island of Dr. Moreau, The First Men in the Moon, The Invisible Man, The War of the Worlds, The Food of the Gods, In The Days of the Comet. 1015pp. 5⅜ x 8.
20264-X Clothbound $5.00

28 SCIENCE FICTION STORIES OF H. G. WELLS.
Two full, unabridged novels, *Men Like Gods* and *Star Begotten,* plus 26 short stories by the master science-fiction writer of all time! Stories of space, time, invention, exploration, futuristic adventure. Partial contents: *The Country of the Blind, In the Abyss, The Crystal Egg, The Man Who Could Work Miracles, A Story of Days to Come, The Empire of the Ants, The Magic Shop, The Valley of the Spiders, A Story of the Stone Age, Under the Knife, Sea Raiders,* etc. An indispensable collection for the library of anyone interested in science fiction adventure. 928pp. 5⅜ x 8.
20265-8 Clothbound $5.00

THREE MARTIAN NOVELS,
Edgar Rice Burroughs
Complete, unabridged reprinting, in one volume, of Thuvia, Maid of Mars; Chessmen of Mars; The Master Mind of Mars. Hours of science-fiction adventure by a modern master storyteller. Reset in large clear type for easy reading. 16 illustrations by J. Allen St. John. vi + 490pp. 5⅜ x 8½.
20039-6 Paperbound $2.50

AN INTELLECTUAL AND CULTURAL HISTORY OF THE WESTERN WORLD,
Harry Elmer Barnes
Monumental 3-volume survey of intellectual development of Europe from primitive cultures to the present day. Every significant product of human intellect traced through history: art, literature, mathematics, physical sciences, medicine, music, technology, social sciences, religions, jurisprudence, education, etc. Presentation is lucid and specific, analyzing in detail specific discoveries, theories, literary works, and so on. Revised (1965) by recognized scholars in specialized fields under the direction of Prof. Barnes. Revised bibliography. Indexes. 24 illustrations. Total of xxix + 1318pp.
21275-0, 21276-9, 21277-7 Three volume set, paperbound $7.75

HEAR ME TALKIN' TO YA, *edited by Nat Shapiro and Nat Hentoff*
In their own words, Louis Armstrong, King Oliver, Fletcher Henderson, Bunk
Johnson, Bix Beiderbecke, Billy Holiday, Fats Waller, Jelly Roll Morton,
Duke Ellington, and many others comment on the origins of jazz in New
Orleans and its growth in Chicago's South Side, Kansas City's jam sessions,
Depression Harlem, and the modernism of the West Coast schools. Taken
from taped conversations, letters, magazine articles, other first-hand sources.
Editors' introduction. xvi + 429pp. 5⅜ x 8½.   21726-4 Paperbound $2.50

THE JOURNAL OF HENRY D. THOREAU
A 25-year record by the great American observer and critic, as complete a
record of a great man's inner life as is anywhere available. Thoreau's Journals
served him as raw material for his formal pieces, as a place where he could
develop his ideas, as an outlet for his interests in wild life and plants, in
writing as an art, in classics of literature, Walt Whitman and other contemporaries, in politics, slavery, individual's relation to the State, etc. The
Journals present a portrait of a remarkable man, and are an observant social
history. Unabridged republication of 1906 edition, Bradford Torrey and
Francis H. Allen, editors. Illustrations. Total of 1888pp. 8⅜ x 12¼.
                    20312-3, 20313-1 Two volume set, clothbound $30.00

A SHAKESPEARIAN GRAMMAR, *E. A. Abbott*
Basic reference to Shakespeare and his contemporaries, explaining through
thousands of quotations from Shakespeare, Jonson, Beaumont and Fletcher,
North's *Plutarch* and other sources the grammatical usage differing from the
modern. First published in 1870 and written by a scholar who spent much of
his life isolating principles of Elizabethan language, the book is unlikely ever
to be superseded. Indexes. xxiv + 511pp. 5⅜ x 8½. 21582-2 Paperbound $3.00

FOLK-LORE OF SHAKESPEARE, *T. F. Thistelton Dyer*
Classic study, drawing from Shakespeare a large body of references to supernatural beliefs, terminology of falconry and hunting, games and sports, good
luck charms, marriage customs, folk medicines, superstitions about plants,
animals, birds, argot of the underworld, sexual slang of London, proverbs,
drinking customs, weather lore, and much else. From full compilation comes
a mirror of the 17th-century popular mind. Index. ix + 526pp. 5⅜ x 8½.
                                          21614-4 Paperbound $3.25

THE NEW VARIORUM SHAKESPEARE, *edited by H. H. Furness*
By far the richest editions of the plays ever produced in any country or
language. Each volume contains complete text (usually First Folio) of the
play, all variants in Quarto and other Folio texts, editorial changes by every
major editor to Furness's own time (1900), footnotes to obscure references or
language, extensive quotes from literature of Shakespearian criticism, essays
on plot sources (often reprinting sources in full), and much more.

HAMLET, *edited by H. H. Furness*
Total of xxvi + 905pp. 5⅜ x 8½.
                    21004-9, 21005-7 Two volume set, paperbound $5.50
TWELFTH NIGHT, *edited by H. H. Furness*
Index. xxii + 434pp. 5⅜ x 8½.   21189-4 Paperbound $2.75

CATALOGUE OF DOVER BOOKS

La Boheme by Giacomo Puccini,
translated and introduced by Ellen H. Bleiler
Complete handbook for the operagoer, with everything needed for full enjoyment except the musical score itself. Complete Italian libretto, with new,
modern English line-by-line translation—the only libretto printing all repeats;
biography of Puccini; the librettists; background to the opera, Murger's La
Boheme, etc.; circumstances of composition and performances; plot summary;
and pictorial section of 73 illustrations showing Puccini, famous singers and
performances, etc. Large clear type for easy reading. 124pp. 5⅜ x 8½.
20404-9 Paperbound $1.50

Antonio Stradivari: His Life and Work (1644-1737),
W. Henry Hill, Arthur F. Hill, and Alfred E. Hill
Still the only book that really delves into life and art of the incomparable
Italian craftsman, maker of the finest musical instruments in the world today.
The authors, expert violin-makers themselves, discuss Stradivari's ancestry, his
construction and finishing techniques, distinguished characteristics of many
of his instruments and their locations. Included, too, is story of introduction
of his instruments into France, England, first revelation of their supreme
merit, and information on his labels, number of instruments made, prices,
mystery of ingredients of his varnish, tone of pre-1684 Stradivari violin and
changes between 1684 and 1690. An extremely interesting, informative account
for all music lovers, from craftsman to concert-goer. Republication of original
(1902) edition. New introduction by Sydney Beck, Head of Rare Book and
Manuscript Collections, Music Division, New York Public Library. Analytical
index by Rembert Wurlitzer. Appendixes. 68 illustrations. 30 full-page plates.
4 in color. xxvi + 315pp. 5⅜ x 8½. 20425-1 Paperbound $3.00

Musical Autographs from Monteverdi to Hindemith,
Emanuel Winternitz
For beauty, for intrinsic interest, for perspective on the composer's personality,
for subtleties of phrasing, shading, emphasis indicated in the autograph but
suppressed in the printed score, the mss. of musical composition are fascinating
documents which repay close study in many different ways. This 2-volume
work reprints facsimiles of mss. by virtually every major composer, and many
minor figures—196 examples in all. A full text points out what can be learned
from mss., analyzes each sample. Index. Bibliography. 18 figures. 196 plates.
Total of 170pp. of text. 7⅞ x 10¾.
21312-9, 21313-7 Two volume set, paperbound $5.00

J. S. Bach,
Albert Schweitzer
One of the few great full-length studies of Bach's life and work, and the
study upon which Schweitzer's renown as a musicologist rests. On first appearance (1911), revolutionized Bach performance. The only writer on Bach to
be musicologist, performing musician, and student of history, theology and
philosophy, Schweitzer contributes particularly full sections on history of German Protestant church music, theories on motivic pictorial representations
in vocal music, and practical suggestions for performance. Translated by
Ernest Newman. Indexes. 5 illustrations. 650 musical examples. Total of xix
+ 928pp. 5⅜ x 8½. 21631-4, 21632-2 Two volume set, paperbound $5.00

THE METHODS OF ETHICS, *Henry Sidgwick*
Propounding no organized system of its own, study subjects every major methodological approach to ethics to rigorous, objective analysis. Study discusses and relates ethical thought of Plato, Aristotle, Bentham, Clarke, Butler, Hobbes, Hume, Mill, Spencer, Kant, and dozens of others. Sidgwick retains conclusions from each system which follow from ethical premises, rejecting the faulty. Considered by many in the field to be among the most important treatises on ethical philosophy. Appendix. Index. xlvii + 528pp. 5⅜ x 8½.
21608-X Paperbound $3.00

TEUTONIC MYTHOLOGY, *Jakob Grimm*
A milestone in Western culture; the work which established on a modern basis the study of history of religions and comparative religions. 4-volume work assembles and interprets everything available on religious and folkloristic beliefs of Germanic people (including Scandinavians, Anglo-Saxons, etc.). Assembling material from such sources as Tacitus, surviving Old Norse and Icelandic texts, archeological remains, folktales, surviving superstitions, comparative traditions, linguistic analysis, etc. Grimm explores pagan deities, heroes, folklore of nature, religious practices, and every other area of pagan German belief. To this day, the unrivaled, definitive, exhaustive study. Translated by J. S. Stallybrass from 4th (1883) German edition. Indexes. Total of lxxvii + 1887pp. 5⅜ x 8½.
21602-0, 21603-9, 21604-7, 21605-5 Four volume set, paperbound $12.00

THE I CHING, *translated by James Legge*
Called "The Book of Changes" in English, this is one of the Five Classics edited by Confucius, basic and central to Chinese thought. Explains perhaps the most complex system of divination known, founded on the theory that all things happening at any one time have characteristic features which can be isolated and related. Significant in Oriental studies, in history of religions and philosophy, and also to Jungian psychoanalysis and other areas of modern European thought. Index. Appendixes. 6 plates. xxi + 448pp. 5⅜ x 8½.
21062-6 Paperbound $2.75

HISTORY OF ANCIENT PHILOSOPHY, *W. Windelband*
One of the clearest, most accurate comprehensive surveys of Greek and Roman philosophy. Discusses ancient philosophy in general, intellectual life in Greece in the 7th and 6th centuries B.C., Thales, Anaximander, Anaximenes, Heraclitus, the Eleatics, Empedocles, Anaxagoras, Leucippus, the Pythagoreans, the Sophists, Socrates, Democritus (20 pages), Plato (50 pages), Aristotle (70 pages), the Peripatetics, Stoics, Epicureans, Sceptics, Neo-platonists, Christian Apologists, etc. 2nd German edition translated by H. E. Cushman. xv + 393pp. 5⅜ x 8.
20357-3 Paperbound $3.00

THE PALACE OF PLEASURE, *William Painter*
Elizabethan versions of Italian and French novels from *The Decameron*, Cinthio, Straparola, Queen Margaret of Navarre, and other continental sources — the very work that provided Shakespeare and dozens of his contemporaries with many of their plots and sub-plots and, therefore, justly considered one of the most influential books in all English literature. It is also a book that any reader will still enjoy. Total of cviii + 1,224pp.
21691-8, 21692-6, 21693-4 Three volume set, paperbound $8.25

THE WONDERFUL WIZARD OF OZ, *L. F. Baum*
All the original W. W. Denslow illustrations in full color—as much a part of
"The Wizard" as Tenniel's drawings are of "Alice in Wonderland." "The
Wizard" is still America's best-loved fairy tale, in which, as the author expresses
it, "The wonderment and joy are retained and the heartaches and nightmares
left out." Now today's young readers can enjoy every word and wonderful picture of the original book. New introduction by Martin Gardner. A Baum
bibliography. 23 full-page color plates. viii + 268pp. 5⅜ x 8.
20691-2 Paperbound $1.95

THE MARVELOUS LAND OF OZ, *L. F. Baum*
This is the equally enchanting sequel to the "Wizard," continuing the adventures of the Scarecrow and the Tin Woodman. The hero this time is a little
boy named Tip, and all the delightful Oz magic is still present. This is the
Oz book with the Animated Saw-Horse, the Woggle-Bug, and Jack Pumpkin-
head. All the original John R. Neill illustrations, 10 in full color. 287pp.
5⅜ x 8.
20692-0 Paperbound $1.75

ALICE'S ADVENTURES UNDER GROUND, *Lewis Carroll*
The original *Alice in Wonderland*, hand-lettered and illustrated by Carroll
himself, and originally presented as a Christmas gift to a child-friend. Adults
as well as children will enjoy this charming volume, reproduced faithfully
in this Dover edition. While the story is essentially the same, there are slight
changes, and Carroll's spritely drawings present an intriguing alternative to
the famous Tenniel illustrations. One of the most popular books in Dover's
catalogue. Introduction by Martin Gardner. 38 illustrations. 128pp. 5⅜ x 8½.
21482-6 Paperbound $1.00

THE NURSERY "ALICE," *Lewis Carroll*
While most of us consider *Alice in Wonderland* a story for children of all
ages, Carroll himself felt it was beyond younger children. He therefore provided this simplified version, illustrated with the famous Tenniel drawings
enlarged and colored in delicate tints, for children aged "from Nought to
Five." Dover's edition of this now rare classic is a faithful copy of the 1889
printing, including 20 illustrations by Tenniel, and front and back covers
reproduced in full color. Introduction by Martin Gardner. xxiii + 67pp.
6⅛ x 9¼.
21610-1 Paperbound $1.75

THE STORY OF KING ARTHUR AND HIS KNIGHTS, *Howard Pyle*
A fast-paced, exciting retelling of the best known Arthurian legends for young
readers by one of America's best story tellers and illustrators. The sword
Excalibur, wooing of Guinevere, Merlin and his downfall, adventures of Sir
Pellias and Gawaine, and others. The pen and ink illustrations are vividly
imagined and wonderfully drawn. 41 illustrations. xviii + 313pp. 6⅛ x 9¼.
21445-1 Paperbound $2.00

Prices subject to change without notice.

Available at your book dealer or write for free catalogue to Dept. Adsci,
Dover Publications, Inc., 180 Varick St., N.Y., N.Y. 10014. Dover publishes more
than 150 books each year on science, elementary and advanced mathematics,
biology, music, art, literary history, social sciences and other areas.